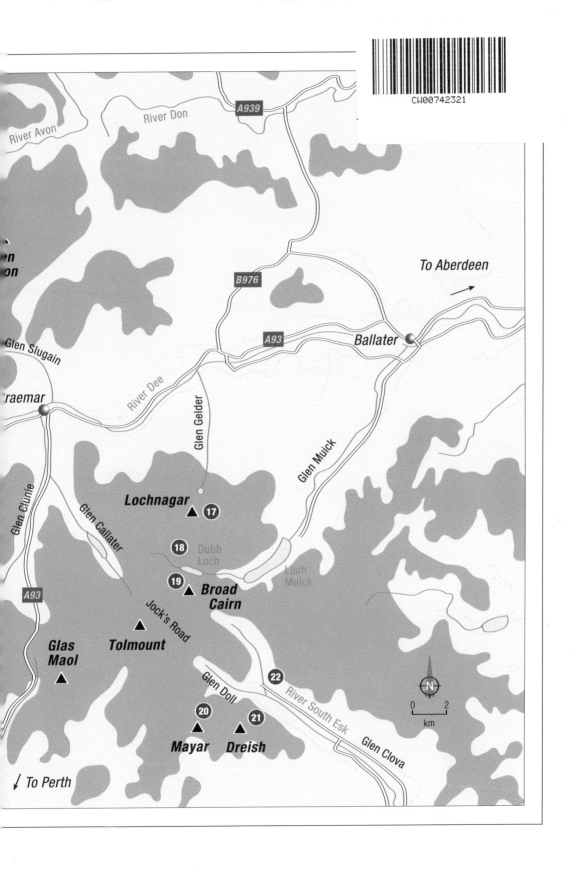

THE
CAIRNGORMS

100 Years of Mountaineering

G<small>REG</small> S<small>TRANGE</small>

SCOTTISH MOUNTAINEERING TRUST

First published in Great Britain by the Scottish Mountaineering Trust, 2010

ISBN 978-1-907233-11-1
A catalogue record for this book is available from the British Library

This book is published by the Scottish Mountaineering Trust, a charitable trust registered in Scotland. Revenue from books published by the Trust is used for the continuation of its publishing programme and for charitable purposes associated with Scottish mountains and mountaineering. Visit <www.smc.org.uk/trust/trust.htm> for more information

Front cover:
Main picture, Càrn Etchachan and the Shelter Stone Crag from Loch Avon *Andy Nisbet*.
Below from left, Sandy Wedderburn on the first ascent of Mitre Ridge, Beinn a' Bhùird, 1933 *Stephen Cumming*; Tom Patey at Luibeg, February 1957 *Gordon Leslie*; John Cunningham front-pointing in Coire an Lochain, Northern Corries, 1973 *Allen Fyffe*; Bob Barton on the first ascent of The Devil's Alternative, Hell's Lum Crag, August 1981 *Allen Fyffe*

Produced and co-designed by Tom Prentice for Scottish Mountaineering Trust (Publications) Ltd
Typesetting and co-design: Derek Pyper
Printed and bound in Thailand by Kyodo Printing Co

Distributed by Cordee Ltd, Leicester, United Kingdom
(t) 0116 254 3579, (w) www.cordee.co.uk

Contents

Introduction

AT FIRST the allure of the Cairngorms may be difficult to fathom. Only when viewed from the north does our premier mountain range show its true splendour, where the distinctive facade of Braeriach and Cairn Gorm rises majestically above the forests of Glenmore and Rothiemurchus. From other directions, distant panoramas tend to be dominated by intervening ridges which obscure all but the highest slopes and summit tors. There are no dramatic sharp peaks to draw attention, but once among them their huge scale becomes apparent and you are struck by the great expanse and feeling of remoteness. Vast plateaux of shattered granite, spectacular rocky corries, dark lochs and deep glens all combine in a scene which will cast a spell and have you returning again and again.

These hills were once the roots of an alpine mountain range which eroded down to expose the underlying granite in the form of a high plateau with gently-sloping sides. During the ice ages, glaciers cut great troughs into the plateau leaving features like Loch Avon and the Làirig Ghrù. They also carved out the numerous corries which are an integral part of the landscape today.

As well as the huge scale, it is the climate of the Cairngorms that sets them apart from other mountain areas in Scotland. Being situated near the centre of the country the weather follows an East Coast pattern with substantially lower average rainfall than mountains farther west. In winter they are influenced more directly by snow-bearing winds from the north and east which can deposit great depths of snow. This combination of snow build-up, altitude, and distance from the sea accounts for a winter season which often extends over seven months of the year.

The Cairngorms are the granite hills lying between the straths of the River Spey in the north and the River Dee in the south. They include the mountains of Ben Avon and Beinn a' Bhùird in the east, the 'Four Thousanders', Ben Macdui, Cairn Toul, Braeriach and Cairn Gorm in the centre and Sgòr Gaoith in the west. To the south, across the Dee, lies a closely associated smaller granite range containing Lochnagar and Creag an Dubh-loch, and south again, the heads of the Angus Glens. In keeping with local mountaineering tradition, 'The Cairngorms' have been taken to include all these areas.

With four of the five highest mountains and the largest tract of land above 3000ft in Britain it is not surprising that this region has attracted many visitors in the past. Most of the larger natural features were named by the original Highlanders who as farmers and hunters crossed the high passes and probably reached some of the summits. By the 18th and 19th centuries, map-makers, landscape painters, gem-hunters, sportsmen, naturalists and travellers were all being challenged by these big hills. Occasionally, they ventured on to steep ground, and in July 1810, two men from Aberdeen, Dr George Skene Keith and Mr Warren climbed the Dee waterfall on Braeriach where it cascades 500ft down broken rock from the rim of the plateau. This early scramble occurred at a time when alpinism in Europe had already been established. Later, it became fashionable for well-to-do people from Britain to visit and climb in the Alps. Increasing interest in mountaineering led British alpinists to look more closely at their own hills. Initially, they were seeking convenient places to hone their skills but it was soon discovered that the gullies, ridges and rock faces of our mountains could provide challenging and rewarding climbs in their own right.

It was at this stage, in the late 1800s, that mountaineering began in the Cairngorms, starting with the earliest roped ascents then progressing through the great classic, rock snow and ice climbs to the fearsome test-pieces of today.

Here is a tale of human endeavour played on and among the remote crags of the Cairngorms. It recounts the activities of ordinary people from differing walks of life who were drawn to these high hills. The kind of folk who relished a long walk to a lonely bothy, who were intrigued by the challenging granite cliffs and found excitement and adventure in exploring them at all times of the year. This is their story.

Greg Strange
Aberdeen 2010

Acknowledgments

PARTICULAR thanks go to Pete Hodgkiss for initiating the project all those years ago, Allen Fyffe for early research work, writing Chapter 1, giving advice and commenting on the first draft, Malcolm (Mac) Smith for encouragement, help and advice on historical accuracy, Bill Brooker for keeping a diary and checking the first six chapters, Derek Pyper for help throughout, editing, typesetting and co-designing the book, Douglas Dinwoodie for information, advice and checking the text, Andy Nisbet for much help with the later chapters, Ken Crocket for critical comment on the first draft, Hugh Spencer and Rob Archbold who kindly read the final script with fresh pairs of eyes and Tom Prentice who not only planned, co-designed and produced the book but gave much appreciated advice on photographic content and general guidance in the final run in.

Many others have given their time to correspond, advise and inform – Davie Agnew, Rab Anderson, Dick Barclay, Tony Barley, Dave Bathgate, James Bolton, John Bower, Martin Burrows-Smith, Martin Boysen, Rick Campbell, Robin Campbell, Rab Carrington, Bill Christie, Geoff Cohen, Jeff Connor, Jim Cosgrove, Alastair Cram, Adrian Crofton, Dave Cuthbertson, Brian Davison, Graeme Ettle, Innes Ewen, Brian Findlay, Mike Forbes, Louise Forsyth, Richard Frere, Affleck Gray, Murray Hamilton, John Hay, Archie Hendry, Bill Hendry, Alison Higham, Graeme Hunter, Steve Kennedy, Doug Lang, Graeme Livingston, Gordon H Leslie, Gary Latter, Brian Lawrie, Charlie Ludwig, John Lyall, Freddy Malcolm, Jimmy Marshall, Rob Milne, Neil Morrison, Norrie Muir, Bill Murray, Malcolm McArthur, Bill McKerrow, George McLeod, Dave Nichols, Graeme Nicol, Ian Nicolson, Malcolm Nicolson, Rebecca Ogilvie, Mike O'Hara, Simon Richardson, Ronnie Rob, Mungo Ross, Sandy Russell, Syd Scroggie, George Shields, Raymond Simpson, Ernie Smith, Ken Spence, Colin Stewart, Dave Stuart, Elizabeth Symmers, Mike Taylor, Sandy Tewnion, Alec Thom, John Vigrow, Adam Watson, Drennan Watson, Mike Watson, Pete Whillance, Allan Will, Paul Williams, Ken Wilson and Ted Wrangham.

John H. Gibson at Dalwhinnie, May 1891. Gibson died of TB seven years later while in his mid-30s

SMC Archives

1: The First Mountaineers (1893 – 1915)

IN THE EARLY afternoon of March 12, 1893, two men reached the summit plateau of Lochnagar, and in so doing ushered in a new era of exploration in the Cairngorms. Unlike the many who had passed that way before, they had arrived, not by the usual well-trodden path, but by climbing up the cliffs of Lochnagar's great North-east corrie. They had made the first ascent, in winter conditions, of the Black Spout by its steep Left-Hand branch. These two gentlemen, clad in their tweeds and hobnailed boots with their long ice axes and short length of hemp rope were of a new breed. They were mountaineers and members of the infant Scottish Mountaineering Club which had been formed in Glasgow in 1889 as a result of growing interest and enthusiasm for the outdoors. Mountaineering in the Alps was in its golden age, and in Scotland there were those who saw the Scottish peaks in winter as ideal training for the greater ranges, or as an enjoyable and rewarding pursuit in its own right.

Lochnagar was already established as the most popular peak in the area due to its dominant position overlooking Deeside, its Royal connections and its fame in verse. The North-east corrie was an obvious challenge and had been spoken about among SMC members in the months previous. Access from the Central Belt was difficult. However, this problem and the subsequent one of climbing the cliffs, was solved by two Edinburgh climbers, William Douglas and John Henry Gibson.

In 1893, both men were in their early 30s and – like most of the original SMC members – they were professional gentlemen, Douglas a publisher, Gibson a lawyer and Writer to the Signet. Gibson was one of the most experienced climbers in the Club, having had five alpine seasons before joining in 1891. He had made guideless ascents of peaks such as the Aiguille de Talèfre and the Grépon and was experienced on snow and ice as well as being a fine rock climber.

The two men overcame the problem of reaching Lochnagar with help from fellow SMC member, Hugh Munro, who lived at his family estate at Lindertis, near Kirriemuir. (It was Munro who first compiled a list of all Scottish mountains higher than 3000ft, these mountains now being referred to as Munros) After meeting them off the train at Kirriemuir, Munro drove Douglas and Gibson to the inn in Glen Clova on the afternoon of March 10, and spent the night there. The next day was windy, but fine, and shouldering their rucksacks, they set off to the north on the 10 miles or so across the Capel Mounth to Glen Muick. However, near the top of the pass Munro was troubled by his rheumatism and had to turn back. The others pressed on past Loch Muick and by afternoon were surveying the cliffs of Lochnagar for possible routes.

The North-east corrie of Lochnagar is one of the finest in the Cairngorms, possibly in Britain. It consists of two sectors of differing aspect. The southern part is mostly scree with a rim of small buttresses at the plateau edge. These increase in size rightwards to eventually merge

North-east corrie of Lochnagar, March 1893, taken at the time of Gibson and Douglas's ascent of Black Spout Left-Hand Branch

Photo: W.Lamond Howie

with the northern sector. This is the pride of Cairngorm corries, a great amphitheatre of grey granite lying above the inky waters of the loch which has given its name to the whole mountain.

The huge arc of rock is made up of a series of distinct buttresses separated by gullies which likewise have shape and form of their own. Only one of these features was named, the Black Spout, the largest of the gullies lying in the western corner of the corrie. This big scree-filled fault gives scrambling access from the corrie floor to the summit plateau and as such was fairly popular when free of snow. It had probably been named by the quartz-diggers who operated throughout this area in the 1800s, searching for Cairngorm stones among the scree.

When the two Edinburgh men looked at this great line of cliffs, winter snow filled the gullies in unbroken white lines, while the buttresses were, for the most part, dark and bare, except for snow on the larger ledges. Mist hung persistently round the summits preventing them from seeing the top portion of the gullies.[1] So, still unsure of the feasibility of any of the routes, they returned to Glen Muick where they found a bed for the night in a small cottage.

The next day they returned by way of the col between Cuidhe Crom and Meikle Pap and traversed in below the cliffs. The mist still hung about concealing the top. The previous day they had seen in the eastern corner of the corrie a long straight snow-filled gully. Although its finish was obscured they decided to attempt it and at 10 o'clock tied onto the rope and began their climb.

At first the snow was soft enough to kick steps, but as they gained height it became harder and steeper, forcing the leader, Gibson, to cut steps. They estimated the angle to be about 50 degrees with steeper sections of rotten ice replacing the snow. After two and a half hours they reached the previously hidden upper section of the gully. "We were

William Brown,
SMC Yacht Meet,
Easter 1897

SMC Archives

now, we estimated, about from 80 to 100ft below the top, and were faced by a quite impossible vertical wall of smooth black rock. On our left lay a sloping slab of rock some 10ft high, thickly coated with rotten ice, but placed at such an awkward angle that, with only two men on the rope, it was not considered advisable to try it. Beyond we could see all the way to the top, which was apparently about 70ft above, and although difficult we thought it would have 'gone' had these first 10ft been overcome. On our right was an equally nasty corner, round which we could not see, and we decided that it was best to defer a further attempt to another day."[2]

With Gibson now bringing up the rear they made their way down the line of steps and reached the foot an hour later. Although their time was now limited, they were reluctant to leave empty-handed so they turned their attention to the Black Spout. Climbing quickly up the easy snow they soon reached the point where this huge gully forked. Here they went left into the steeper Left-Hand branch and 35 minutes after leaving the foot of the gully they emerged on the summit plateau. Quickly now, because of the force of the wind, they made their way along the corrie edge, still looking for possible routes. They descended by the usual 'ladder path' to Glen Muick where they were pleasantly surprised to be offered afternoon tea at Allt-na-giubhsaich Lodge. At 4.30pm they started back to Glen Clova arriving at 8pm to meet Munro, who sufficiently recovered, drove them back to Lindertis. They caught an early train to Edinburgh the next morning.

Their ascent of the Black Spout they found easy, and they hoped to return to their original attempted climb. The 'East Snow Gully', as they dubbed it, became variously known as the Gibson Gully or, more usually, the Douglas Gully, until they eventually shared the honour with Douglas-Gibson Gully. Despite regular attention, this famous gully was not successfully climbed in winter for more than half a century. As it turned out, neither climber did any more pioneering work in the area. Gibson died in 1898, but Douglas continued his mountaineering activities, mostly in the West, in Glen Coe, Arran, Torridon and, of course, on the eponymous 700ft high Douglas Boulder at the foot of Tower Ridge on Ben Nevis.

Although Douglas did not return to Lochnagar to climb, a friend of his, William Brown, did. Brown, a young lawyer working in Edinburgh, came originally from Aberdeen and both he and Douglas, like several other early SMC men, were also members of the more senior Cairngorm Club, based in Aberdeen. Brown was having a very good season in 1895. In May he made the second ascent of the great North-East Buttress on Ben Nevis with his climbing partner and fellow SMC member, William Tough. (They believed the buttress to be virgin but heard later that it had been climbed three years earlier by the Hopkinsons from Manchester.) In July, the two friends visited Glen Coe, where among other climbs they made the first ascent of North Buttress on Buachaille Etive Mòr with James Rose. While staying at the Clachaig Inn Brown noted: "You simply rise from the table and step on to the rocks, a blessing which only those can properly appreciate who have walked 15 miles to climb 200ft of granite in the Cairngorms."[3]

Both Tough and Brown were regular visitors to the Cairngorms. That

April, Brown (with Lionel Hinxman) had ascended the Fiacaill a' Coire an t-Sneachda, the prominent rocky spur dividing Coire an t-Sneachda from Coire an Lochain on Cairn Gorm. Although little more than a scramble, it looks impressive from some angles and this, he felt, was probably the first ascent.[4] Brown and Tough had also made previous inspections of Lochnagar "to ascertain, from the climber's point of view, the possibilities of 'the crags that are wild and majestic'."

They noted that the Black Spout looked straightforward, but several of the other "shoots" would be suitable for the "cracks" of the club and decided that "there is room for much interesting work".[5] The opportunity to sample this interesting work came on August 1, 1895, after their week in Glen Coe. They travelled from Aberdeen to Ballater by train, then cycled to Inchnabobart in Glen Muick. Leaving there about midday, they walked up to the cliff and despite the top being once again hidden by mist, a reconnaissance some weeks earlier by Brown enabled them to make straight for the intended route. This lay in the middle of the corrie, right of the Douglas-Gibson Gully where the cliffs are highest. Here are three unequal buttresses separated by two parallel gullies, the right-most and largest buttress having a steep slabby lower face tapering to a defined ridge at the top. The upper left hand flank of this buttress is scored by a series of discontinuous diagonal turf ledges and ramps which angle up right towards the ridge.

For these first rock climbers, with their primitive equipment and absence of meaningful belaying techniques, these vegetated ramps offered access to the ridge, the feature that first attracted them. Gaining the ridge from below was obviously out of the question and they spent no more of their single day here on its investigation but started on the left-hand buttress. Making good progress at first, they soon noted that it was more difficult than expected. The rock was slabby and lacking in projections over which to run the rope for some feeling of security, also every crack held soil and vegetation.

Soon they crossed the first gully and gained the central buttress. Here they tried to climb straight up to where they thought they would cross the next fault and gain a hopeful-looking ledge system. This line was soon blocked by smooth rock and a descent was made to cross the second gully lower down. They were now on the Great Terrace which ran part of the way across the third buttress above its steep base. At its end Tough and Brown were denied access to the ridge by mossy slabs so they returned some way along the terrace to where a rock shelf ran back up left and offered their only hope of progress. They followed this to a small grass patch above which a rock step barred their way to the terrace above.

"As it was impossible to climb the place without aid, Brown came to my help, and it was certainly due to his efficient backing that the place was conquered. With considerable difficulty, for I was in front and Brown close up to me, there being barely standing room for two, I managed to scramble from his knee to his shoulder. But, even when mounted on this lofty pedestal, I failed to reach the necessary hold by a good couple of feet. For a minute or two I remained helplessly spread-eagled on the face of the cliff, almost despairing of getting up, and not at all clear as to how I should ever get down from my awkward perch, when suddenly the thing was done. How he managed it, considering the position he was in, I don't know, but with a supreme effort Brown shot me upwards the required distance by a sudden powerful jerk. My outstretched fingers caught the welcome crack, and mounting rapidly I found safe anchorage about 40ft above one of the most awkward places it has ever been my fortune to tackle successfully."[6]

Now totally committed by these desperate combined tactics they, fortunately, found these higher terraces did offer a means of precarious progress. They were covered with grass or moss which slid off below them but Tough and Brown soon discovered their best means of progress was to run up them on all fours, going up faster than the vegetation went down. However, these diagonal ramps at last led to the ridge they were seeking. Things now changed for the better with the broken and shattered rocks forming a staircase to the plateau, which was reached three hours after the start. Almost predictably they arrived on the summit plateau in strong wind and cloud.

"For a minute or two I remained helplessly spread-eagled on the face of the cliff, almost despairing of getting up."
– William Tough

Their route, the Tough-Brown Traverse, was the first rock climb on the mountain, but not one which created much enthusiasm for these cliffs. Although long and exposed in places, it had provided many of the problems associated with Cairngorm climbing – lack of protection on the deceptive slabby rocks, cracks filled with vegetation, difficult route finding and the unhelpful nature of the granite. They had also encountered a particular Lochnagar hazard. Walkers on the plateau enjoyed trundling boulders down into the corrie, an obvious source of danger to those at work on the rocks below. On this occasion it was only stopped with much shouting. Tough and Brown's pioneering climb never gained popularity as a summer route and was not repeated until 1932. Nevertheless, it had been a bold undertaking when most climbers preferred the seemingly safer confines of the gullies. It was one of these gullies that attracted the next climbing visitor to Lochnagar. In August 1896, William Inglis Clark was staying at a farmhouse in Strath Girnock, near Ballater. He also hoped to explore the cliffs, but lack of a partner and bad weather limited his opportunities to one day on the crags. Had things worked out differently, more might have been achieved as Inglis Clark was a keen and able mountaineer (as were his wife, son and daughter).

He was a wealthy Edinburgh chemist who owned the city's first motor car. On that one good day he was joined by a young climber named Shannon. They traversed below the cliffs until they reached the gully immediately right of the buttress ascended by Tough and Brown. Their first sight of the forbidding cliffs no doubt reminded them of the warning they had received from the shepherd at Allt-na-giubhsaich: "Only yin man, ca'ad Brown, ever gaed up thae awfu' rocks, and wha can say if even he did it? Man, I wadna gang yonder for a thousan' pun'. Turn, man, and dinna commit suicide." [7]

But they went on, past recent rock-fall scars and debris, noting that the rock was very different from the gabbro of Skye: "The holds were few and water-rounded, affording a delightful feeling of insecurity, even on short pitches." [8]

The wind was bitterly cold, the gully streamed with water and the holds were covered with moss, but they met no special difficulty until fairly near the top where the gully was blocked by a huge boulder.

Although they could get below the block, it projected too far above them to be surmounted so they tried the left wall. Here a few holds enabled Clark to climb to a point above the obstruction but the traverse of 10ft or so to regain the gully was judged impossible. A retreat was called but Shannon thought he saw a way farther left.

Lochnagar, Creag nam Bàn and the River Dee from above Coilacriech in May

Photo: Greg Strange

Despite Clark's misgivings he gave in to his companion and they traversed along a narrow, wet, mossy ledge then worked upwards until well above the offending boulder. Here they were stopped again and a dangerous descent made back to the block before they could continue their escape. After "several involuntary spread-eagle glissades" they reached the scree. They christened the gully Tantalus.[9]

During the following winter, in February 1897, another attempt was made on the Douglas-Gibson Gully, this time by Brown and George Duncan. They got no higher than the pioneers of 1893.[10] Sadly, this was Brown's last climbing excursion to Lochnagar for he contracted a wasting illness from which he died in September 1901, aged 33.

As well as being an excellent climber, William Brown distinguished himself at both Aberdeen and Edinburgh Universities. At the former he graduated in Arts, winning the Bain Gold Medal and taking a first class honours in mental philosophy. At Edinburgh he gained his LLB, then eight years later returned after being appointed lecturer in civil and criminal law

These unfinished gullies were an obvious attraction to other SMC members who were driven by the urge for new climbs and the next to take on Lochnagar's 'steep frowning glories' was one of Britain's finest mountaineers.

Harold Raeburn was a brilliant, all-round mountaineer whose ascents, both at home and abroad, marked him out as one of the greats. A climber both talented and innovative who had the strength of will and determination to forge many fine climbs in his native Scotland as well as in the greater ranges.

Raeburn was born in Edinburgh in 1865 and lived there for most of his life. Unlike most of his contemporaries in the SMC he was not a professional man but began his early years as a brewer. Even before joining the SMC in the autumn of 1896, his name appeared with those of Brown, Hinxman and Douglas on the first ascent of the Direct Route on the Douglas Boulder of Ben Nevis. Although Brown led on that occasion, it was not long before Raeburn took over the dominant role, and on Nevis, of the 30 new climbs done between 1896 and 1921, Raeburn was involved in half of them. Elsewhere in Scotland he made new climbs in Glencoe, Arrochar, Arran, the North-west Highlands and Skye.

Many of these routes seem not to have been named at the time and now take their title from their pioneer. Hence we have several Raeburn's Gullies, Buttresses and the like to remind us of this prolific climber. Not only were his first ascents numerous but they were also of a high standard for the day. Many are still graded Very Difficult, some are Severe.

No doubt, Raeburn had heard of the unclimbed gully 'Tantalus' from his friend, Inglis Clark, and on November 12, 1898, with fellow SMC members Henry Lawson and John Rennie, he paid a visit to Lochnagar. From the start things did not go as planned as they were prevented from getting from Aberdeen to Ballater on the early train by Queen Victoria's unexpected departure from Balmoral that Friday. This lost them four and a half hours to start with. Then there was trouble with their bicycles and the weather was poor with persistent mist all day. On the hill they were forced to navigate, none too accurately, by map and compass and then entered the corrie high up in the Southern Sector. This necessitated a tedious descent over rough ground into the main corrie where they still had to locate their proposed route. To do this they had to descend to near the loch then climb again to find the Black Spout. The gully was then 100 yards or so to the east.

At first they encountered old, but soft snow leading to the first pitch where they roped up and put on gloves because of the cold, icy rocks. It was now 3.15pm and the light was failing, but they made good progress up to the huge chokestone.[11] The line to the left, tried by Inglis Clark and Shannon, was attempted, but the return to the gully above the block was judged impossible. A kind of belay round a loose block was found for the second man and combined tactics tried. The upper edge of the block remained an elusive two feet away, so unorthodox tactics were deemed necessary.

"The ice axe was now employed, first to clear away the earth and stones from the upper edge of the block, then the pick was hung upon the edge, the right hand of the leader found a crevice which admitted of its being inserted and half clenched, then pushing down with the right arm and pulling hard with the left, the body was raised high enough to allow of the left hand being thrown up to catch the edge of the jammed block; instantly the right hand joined it, then a pull, and the right knee was thrown up on the slope of the overhanging chockstone, the body thrust for a second against the slope of the left wall, while the hands were transferred to an upper block; it proved firm, and a hitch was found about 10ft higher up the gully. The ice axe, the moment the steady pull was relaxed, slipped off, and bounded away down the gully and was lost."[12]

Combined tactics and a tight rope saw the others join Raeburn above the block, now below a series of gigantic boulders crowned by a projecting mass. It looked unclimbable, but fortunately, a through-route led behind the boulders and after a weary plod up soft snow, they reached the top.

It was 4.45pm and nearly dark when they set off down but, unable to face the slight rise to cross the shoulder of Cuidhe Crom, they started descending to the south east. After struggling with the wind and wet, Rennie's lamp was lit at 5.15pm and in its feeble light they toiled over scree and boulders until they came to the Glas Allt. This was followed until eventually it disappeared in a waterfall whose height they could only guess at from the roar drifting up. Keeping to one side they descended by candlelight and eventually reached Loch Muick. All that remained was the walk down the loch then the cycle to Ballater where they arrived at 10.45pm after another hazardous journey through the rain and the pitch black.

After this episode, Raeburn was keen to try some of the other gullies on Lochnagar. In April 1901, with William Garden, George Duncan and Peter Crombie, he made the third winter attempt on the Douglas-Gibson Gully, again being defeated below the top wall. In July, he was back with Garden and Duncan to try it in summer conditions.[13] This time, no doubt because of Raeburn's last late-night epic, they had an early start from Inchnabobart in Glen Muick and by 9.45am were making their way up the lower snows and onto the rock. Soon they came to a huge boulder blocking the gully and forming a cave. There was another chokestone above this and both were turned on the left wall. The main gully continued up pitches of steep, wet rock, until they were below the upper wall.

Here Raeburn went left across the gully and worked up below this headwall to a belay where Duncan joined him. The chimney above was dismissed and Raeburn continued his traverse left over disintegrating rock and vegetation to another chimney. The way was still not obvious and, after consultation, they began to descend. This was not easy, and they had to abandon part of the rope after it jammed at the abseil past the double cave pitch. Although tired, hungry and wet from the eight hours they had been in the gully they went up the Black Spout to inspect the top of the climb. As far as they could see the final chimney looked easy but thick mist had descended and made even this inspection less than satisfactory.

Lochnagar was not the only mountain in the Cairngorms to attract these early climbers. Braeriach with its massive bulk and 13 named and unnamed cirques is pre-eminently the mountain of corries. Of these the most inviting is Coire Bhrochain, the big open corrie facing south down the Làirig Ghrù, the great pass which cuts the main mass of the Cairngorms from north to south. The summit of Braeriach stands on the very edge of these cliffs and its height and remoteness make it particularly appealing. The cliff itself is divided into three main rock masses by two very pronounced breaks, West Gully and East Gully and it was the former which was climbed on September 10, 1898 by Arthur Russell

Harold Raeburn, Salisbury Crags, Edinburgh, February 1920

Photo: Robert Moyes Adams. Courtesy of St. Andrews University Library

SMC Easter Meet to Aviemore, 1902: Frank Goggs, standing second left; William Douglas, sitting left; John Rennie, standing sixth right and James Parker, standing seventh right

Photo: SMC Archives

After this episode, Raeburn was keen to try some of the other gullies on Lochnagar

and Alex Fraser. The gully was found to consist of scree and slabs with steeper rocks of no great difficulty at the top. Russell returned to Coire Bhrochain three years later in April 1901 to climb the East Gully with Tom Gibson and James Drummond. The whole ascent was over easy snow. Up to this point climbing exploration in the Cairngorms had been limited to small parties, usually SMC members on short diversions from their main areas of activity in the West. The situation changed in 1902 when the SMC visited the Cairngorms *en masse*. Since its first official meet in 1891, the Club had traditionally held two meets each year, one at New Year and one at Easter, reflecting a preference for winter mountaineering. Most of the meets had taken place in the West with Tyndrum, Dalmally. Inveroran, Loch Awe and Fort William being favoured locations. Although Aviemore was an obvious base for climbing in the Northern Cairngorms it was not until June 1901 that a hotel opened in the village. Now that there was a suitable venue the first SMC meet to the Cairngorms was arranged for Easter 1902.

On March 8, before the official meet, Raeburn and Lawson went to Aviemore to investigate the line of crags on Sgoran Dubh and Sgòr Gaoith which dominate the west side of upper Glen Einich. Although the situation is very dramatic with steep slopes running down on three sides to the dark waters of Loch Einich, the floor of the glen is flat and opens out towards Aviemore and the north giving easy access. Only nine miles from the railway, much of it passable by bicycle, it was then the most accessible climbing area in the Cairngorms.

The cliffs form a rampart nearly two miles long consisting of five broad buttresses. These are composed of complicated discontinuous ribs, aretes, slabs and pillars and the whole mass was described thus: "It is as though four gigantic funnels or wine-fillers had been let into the rock, the splayed-out portion being a high upper corrie, often fringed by rock, and the stroop a very steep water-slide. The five rock-masses thus

*Buttresses 1 and 2 on
Sgoran Dubh Mòr,
Glen Einich in May*

Photo: Derek Pyper

separated take much the same form reversed, a broad and steep buttress narrowing towards the top and breaking away into a spectacular ridge of low angle and no difficulty. Each mass is cut by gullies and chimneys into several aretes more or less continuous."[14] These buttresses are not of great angle and lack the monolithic and uncompromising appearance of many of the granite crags in the Cairngorms. This, along with defined ridges at the top of the buttress, made them attractive to the climbers of the day. They do, however, take on a very alpine appearance in winter.

Raeburn's objective, the ridge with the prominent pinnacle known as A' Chailleach, lay on No. 5 Buttress. This was the farthest south rock mass lying above the head of the loch. The buttresses are numbered from north to south, and although there are six buttresses, the first two are treated as one. The weather was dull and wet, the area surprisingly free of snow and, after walking along the road and the excellent track on the west of the loch, they roped up at one o'clock. Their chosen route went up the right-hand side of the buttress and was mostly a scramble until the pinnacle was reached. Here the direct line looked uninviting so they traversed the north side to reach the neck behind, from where a 30ft knife-edge led to the summit. This edge was only about a foot wide and was climbed *à cheval*.

The top proved too small to stand on in the conditions of wind and sleet. They descended, traversed the south side looking for traces of previous ascents and, deciding that there was none, hurried to complete their route by the ridge leading to the summit cornice. Their 1200ft route (Pinnacle Ridge) gave a fair indication of what could be expected on the other buttresses and their verdict was that given moderate luck regarding the weather, the Aviemore meet would be highly successful.

As it turned out moderate luck was all they did have, with only one good day out of the four. In spite of this, the rocks of Sgoran Dubh attracted members on every day. No doubt, one of the reasons for this was the convenient transport organised by Dr Inglis Clark. He had arranged for "several large machines"[15] to ferry parties each day to the lower bothy in Glen Einich (The lower bothy, and the upper bothy by the loch, were convenient sheltering spots which were destroyed in the mid 1940s).

On the first day, Friday, March 28, two parties arrived below the crags. George Glover with guests R.W.Worsdell and Mr Leathart turned their attention to the big gully known as the Willow Spout or Sput Seilich which divides No. 1 Buttress into its Northern and Southern Sections. It provided a straightforward snow climb through attractive scenery. The other party consisting of Raeburn, Herbert Boyd, Stair Gillon and Alexander Mackay made its way farther up the glen to No. 3 Buttress. Here the lower slabs were covered in good snow enabling steps to be kicked up the first third as they headed for a defined arete formed by the buttress edge. Despite a determined effort they were forced to the right of the direct line and regained the ridge by a small gully. The easy upper ridge finished close under the summit of Sgoran Dubh Mòr. Unfortunately, the exact line of their route has never been successfully traced.

There was heavy snow on the Saturday, but the next day had perfect weather and Raeburn was back in Glen Einich to take advantage of it. This time in the company of Herbert Kynaston and Wilfred Mounsey he climbed the Southern Sector of No. 1 Buttress avoiding the imposing smooth wall known as the Northern Rampart by a steep open chimney on its left. The large amounts of snow that had fallen the previous day helped the ascent, but it still took six hours. The descent was very much faster. The Willow Spout, ascended three days earlier, gave the party a good glissade to the bottom.

On Monday, the weather had again reverted to blizzards, but with major buttresses still to be explored two parties braved the elements and returned to the crags. Both teams made their way to the unclimbed No. 2 Buttress. William Wickham King, Ernest Maylard and Godfrey Solly, whose names are more noted for their exploration in Skye and the West, took a short, but steep, ridge to the north of the main mass. Their route, Married Men's Buttress, is another climb whose exact location has never been discovered, lost under the Easter snows and the vague descriptions of the day. The other climb hereabouts, Bachelor's Chimney, proved the best and hardest route done on the meet. This was the work of the talented and active team of single men, Raeburn, William Naismith, Mackay and Frances Conradi Squance. They started at the foot of the main ridge just right of the great gully which divides No. 2 and No. 3 buttresses and were soon forced by smooth slabs into a well defined chimney on its right. This provided two interesting pitches before the angle eased off.

This very successful first SMC meet to the Cairngorms engendered for a few years a limited enthusiasm for these huge granite hills and their untouched cliffs. Perhaps, in a way, this was not all to the good, for these crags in Glen Einich, although intriguing in their complexity, are by no means the most attractive of the major Cairngorm cliffs.

Compared with the rock climbing of the time being done on Ben Nevis, in Glen Coe and particularly in Skye, they were of poor quality, but this meet started a trend within the SMC which continued for a few years. Of more than 30 separate crags throughout the Cairngorms the cliffs of Sgoran Dubh Mòr and Sgòr Gaoith were the main draw, perhaps limiting exploration of other cliffs.

In the autumn of 1902, Raeburn returned to Lochnagar. During the summer he had produced several good hard routes on Ben Nevis, including Raeburn's Arete (Severe), and made guideless climbs in Norway. In October, he was again lured back into the Cairngorms with the unclimbed Douglas-Gibson Gully as the main objective. This time his companions were Mackay and Frank Goggs, forming a strangely mixed team as Goggs claimed to be a Salvationist while the other two were firmly placed in the Ultramontane camp. Like most clubs, the SMC had members representing all facets of mountaineering, but in this case the climbing and walking elements were humorously separated into groups whose origins came from an article by Hely Almond in 1893.

"Members of the Mountaineering Club may be divided into two classes. There are those whose ambition it is to scale the inaccessible side of peaks with unpronounceable names...I admire these people; I like to dine with them, and hear them talk; for the sake of a name I call them Ultramontanes.

"But let me confess, with all due humility and shame, that I have permanently enlisted in the Salvation Army, which is the name I give to the second class of mountaineers. As our name implies, we like to know that we are safe – absolutely safe. We don't like contusions; we would rather go home to dinner than lie on the ground till people come to set our bones, or carry us off on a stretcher; we have no desire to be the conscious element of an avalanche or a land-slip. And yet, like Mark Twain on his celebrated ascent of the Riffelberg, we like something of the pomp and circumstance of war – an alpenstock, a bit of rope, blue spectacles – a good deal of noise and fuss about it when we come home again."[16]

So, with Raeburn and Mackay as the climbing members and Goggs supposedly along for the experience, they left Ballater at 10.30pm on October 18 and went by horse-power to Inchnabobart then by foot to the corrie. The cliffs were lightly powdered with snow and time was short so they made their way up the Black Spout to Lochnagar's summit (to satisfy Goggs's Salvationist principle) then traversed round to the top of Douglas-Gibson Gully. Here Raeburn tied onto their two 60ft ropes and, with Mackay and Goggs serving as his anchor, climbed down the top section of the gully. On his return after descending the 120ft, Raeburn reported that he had got to within 30ft of his previous high point and that he could see a route.[17] This technique of inspection was not a new one and had been used by various teams previously, notably by Raeburn on Church Door Buttress in Glen Coe. With the limited techniques and equipment then available it appears to have raised no ethical questions at that time.

The next day, they assembled at the foot of the gully. The walls glistened with ice and a stream tumbled over the first cave pitch. Raeburn felt they had little chance of success so they switched objectives to the

Looking up Douglas-Gibson Gully in mid summer conditions. This formidable rift between Shadow Buttress B (left) and Eagle Ridge (right) was the main attraction on Lochnagar for early pioneers, particularly Raeburn

Photo: Scott Muir

They made their way up the Black Spout to Lochnagar's summit (to satisfy Goggs's Salvationist principle)

ridge on the left (Shadow Buttress B) where they started up the obvious groove just left of the buttress edge.

Climbing up disintegrating turf and rotten rock with Raeburn in the lead, sending down quantities of unstable material, they at length reached a point about 250ft up the buttress. Here they were stopped by a typically blank section of rock which forced them to abandon the route. Back at the bottom Raeburn unleashed his next suggestion, much to Goggs's horror, to cut a new route through the traverse on the Tough-Brown Ridge. Since this climb had a desperate reputation one can understand Goggs's dismay.

This too failed, the attempt being on the rocks right of the second parallel gully where Raeburn reached a point about 40ft up on the edge of the main sweep of boiler-plate slabs before being forced down again. So they turned west again towards the area of cliff right of the Black Spout. Here the rocks are more broken and are cut near their right side by West Gully which is deep in its upper portion. Lower down it is less well defined but the more broken nature of the ground offered a choice of starts.

Taking the left-hand alternative they climbed over wet rock and vegetation to enter the gully at the midway terrace. Once in the gully proper they reached a cave pitch 20ft high, eventually overcome by the use of the rope thrown over a spike as a handhold. Scrambling then took them to the final pitch, again a cave pitch of about 20ft. The sides looked unpromising but investigation revealed a small hole at its back and at his second attempt with his coat off, Raeburn squeezed through to find easy ground leading to the plateau. Next Mackay just managed to wriggle through then Goggs passed up their coats on the end of the ice axe. Unfortunately, while repeating this manoeuvre with the rucksack, it slipped off and fell to the corrie floor, thus adding to the axe, cap and jammed rope that had been lost on Raeburn's previous trips to Lochnagar. It was by then nearly dark so they hurried back down to Inchnabobart, leaving the fallen rucksack.

Bill Ewen leading an ascent of Black Spout Pinnacle from the col in 1929

Photo: Innes Ewen

The following day a search for the rucksack was unsuccessful, so at Raeburn's suggestion they made an attempt on the Black Spout Pinnacle from near the branch in the Black Spout. The route followed was up a green recess and, being steeper than the previous route, a fair amount of time was spent on the turf ledges. Time enough to contemplate what could happen if Raeburn fell, there being little or nothing in the way of security for the party. At last they assembled on a large grass ledge about 150ft from the start. Above and to the left was a narrow chimney which Raeburn managed to enter but could not overcome, having to be helped back on to the ledge by Mackay. Lunch then followed and Raeburn surveyed the chimney again, coming to the conclusion that its overhanging top would stop them anyway. So it was down again. With 10 minutes to spare before having to leave to catch the last train from Ballater they attacked the Pinnacle by the ridge leading from the plateau, finding it little more than a scramble – but at least one to an untouched summit, where they built the usual cairn.

Of the routes that were attempted during these two days, all would eventually be climbed. Douglas-Gibson Gully in 1933 at Severe, the route on Shadow Buttress B in 1986 as a hard winter climb called Raeburn's

*The two main
northern corries of
Cairn Gorm, Coire an
t-Sneachda and Coire
an Lochain, in late
winter conditions*

Photo: Dave Morris

Groove. The route on the Tough-Brown Face is less easy to locate but appears to have been on a line right of Parallel Gully B, and on the Pinnacle, Twin Chimneys Route, a Very Difficult, was climbed in 1952. With four failures and more lost gear it is surprising that Raeburn returned to this corrie, but as others have found, granite climbing can be addictive, especially when there are new climbs to be discovered.

The SMC were back in Aviemore for their Easter meet of 1904 which was again dogged by stormy weather. On April 1, two climbing teams headed into Coire an t-Sneachda of Cairn Gorm where, unknown to each other, they made for the same objective. Archie Robertson, Tom Goodeve and Arthur Russell climbed up an open gully round the foot of the first steep rock mass. They were heading for a fine pinnacle they could see on their left but "when cutting across a gully just beside it Raeburn's party were seen below us coming up. It was not judged sportsman-like to pass in front of them, so traversing back to our original line, we gained the ridge. The small cornice was easily surmounted. Goodeve and I, after lunch, still hankering after that pinnacle, retraced our steps for 150ft and climbed it".[18]

The route this party climbed was probably Central Gully, a simple snow climb. Raeburn, who was with William Garden, George Almond and A. Roth, ascended a steep rightward slanting snowline heading to the foot of a defined rib. This approach was possibly up the start of Aladdin's Mirror, which leads to the foot of the upper rocks. The rib itself, now called Pygmy Ridge, gave an excellent little climb. The rock is sound and clean, the climbing interesting and the situations pleasant. Ironically, they did not describe this route in any detail or apparently even name it, although it is certainly, by modern standards, a better climb than anything done in the Cairngorms up to that point. Perhaps, another irony is that Raeburn carried his skis up to the snow at about 3000ft and used them up and down to the foot of the climb. However, they were of limited use due to the patchy snow cover.

In some ways, it is surprising that so little attention was paid to Coire an t-Sneachda at this time. The corrie, the central of the three north-facing corries of Cairn Gorm, would seem to possess many of the features desirable for early exploration. It is large and sprawling with fairly

*Time enough to
contemplate what
could happen if
Raeburn fell, there
being little or noth-
ing in the way of
security for the
party*

*William Morrison
and William
Newbigging en route
to Glen Einich to
climb Rose Ridge,
April 1904*

Photo: A.E.Robertson

defined, but not deeply, incised gullies which hold few secrets when viewed from below. The rocks themselves are not particularly steep and offer scope for wandering about with several towers and pinnacles providing interest, all in a superb setting looking out over Loch Morlich and Glen More.

Three days after the climbs in Coire an t-Sneachda, Solly, Robertson, Sandy Moncrieff and James Rose attempted another ridge on No. 2 Buttress of Sgoran Dubh, right of the Married Men's Buttress. The whole face was covered with new snow but the climbing was straightforward to begin with until after a col it became more difficult and eventually they stopped below a 40ft wall cut by a vertical crack. Although they thought it would go, the late hour forced a retreat by way of the gully south of the ridge. Solly, who had been the leader, named the ridge after James Rose and felt keen enough about the climb to write in the next journal.

"Comparing this with other climbs that I know, it lacks the interest of the scenery such as there is on some of the Ben Nevis routes, but as a gymnastic climb I know nothing in Great Britain to equal it for long and continuous interest."[19]

With such a write-up it was hardly surprising the climb was re-visited in next to no time. On April 29, Robertson returned to Glen Einich with William Newbigging and William Morrison. The ridge was now completely clear of snow and commenced with low-angled rock which higher up narrowed to an arete. In places they climbed *à cheval*, the last man carrying three ice axes and finding the assistance of the rope more than just moral. The main difficulties of the previous visit came next, a 40ft slab with crumbly holds which led to the gap. Finally, the steep wall with the vertical slit proved to be an interesting pitch over piled blocks. Rose Ridge was the hardest route on Sgoran Dubh at the time, (Very Difficult). It retained its reputation for quality a bit longer than most of the routes here.

The next year, 1907, Raeburn was back in the Cairngorms, this time in June, his first visit when summer conditions could realistically be expected. His companion was again Goggs, no doubt still proclaiming himself a Salvationist. Goggs, who was in the insurance business, was working at that time in Kingussie and asked Raeburn to come and join him for a climb. As Raeburn had only a day available they left Kingussie by bike the evening he arrived and travelled to a bothy beside the path leading to the Làirig Ghrù (probably the old shieling of Altdrue near the confluence of the Allt Druidh and Am Beanaidh). Leaving at 2.40am they walked over Creag an Leth-choin, Cairn Lochain and across the plateau to the top of the Shelter Stone Crag.

Here they decided to descend and taking a line overlooking the wide fault of Castlegates Gully they worked down ground which was at first ill-defined, but lower developed into a more definite arete. This took them 55 minutes for a 600ft Difficult route, Castle Wall. 'Lunch' was then eaten down at the Shelter Stone followed by a sleep in the sun before roping up at 9.15am at the foot of the rocks.

Their chosen line lay just right of their descent route where a large pillar of rock stands proud from the crag. On its left a gully separates this from the arete of Castle Wall. On its right an ill-defined slabby gully

*Coire an t-
Sneachda, the
central of the three
north facing corries
of Cairngorm,
would seem to
possess many
of the features
desirable for early
exploration*

Loch Avon, Hell's
Lum Crag and the
Shelter Stone Crag
June 1906.
Castlegates Gully is
the snow-filled gully
on the left. In June,
1907, Raeburn and
Goggs descended the
rocks on the immedi-
ate right of the gully,
Castle Wall, then
climbed back to the
top by the vague
buttress right of the
two snow patches;
Raeburn's Buttress

Photo: A.W.Russell

forms the dividing line between the edge of the pillar and the mono-lithic Central Slabs at the heart of the very impressive Shelter Stone Crag. The first two thirds of the pillar was very steep and, although they thought the rock good, much was obscured by moss and vegetation.

"After ascending about 60ft, the direct route became so steep and slabby that it was thought better to make a slight traverse to the left, almost into the gully cutting us off from the 'Snow Couloir Ridge'. A very neat little chimney, with overhanging ledge at the bottom, and somewhat difficult and exposed exit at the top, then allowed of the arete being gained. Then followed 40ft of slabby rockwork, which Goggs wishes me to label as dangerous. Possibly, that label is no libel. Certainly, it is no place for the exhibition of the chamois-like agility mountaineers are credited with displaying. Rather it is a place for a combination of the walk of a certain character who was said to 'walk delicately', and the adhesive crawl of a remarkably sluggish lizard."[20]

More zig-zagging back and forth connecting the lines and ledges of vegetation eventually took them to the obvious level shoulder atop the pillar proper. The ground above was less steep and by 10.55am they were sitting down to another breakfast, or lunch, on the plateau. The route, now called Raeburn's Buttress, was one with a degree of boldness not seen before in the Cairngorms. Dangerous rather than technically diffi-cult it was eventually given a grade of Severe.

There was another influx of SMC men to the Cairngorms in 1908, but this time the venue for the Easter meet was Braemar. Awkward to get to from the Central Belt, it necessitated a train journey to Ballater via Aberdeen then some other form of transport to the village itself. In spite of this it was a large meet with some 36 members and 15 guests. The weather was again mixed with the usual blizzards and periods of bright sun. On Good Friday, several parties made their way from Ballater to Braemar via Lochnagar.[21] Raeburn, Goodeve and William Ling made another attempt on Douglas-Gibson Gully. This time they were defeated by a sudden thaw and consequent avalanching so they turned their attention to the rock ridge immediately right of the Black Spout. The resulting route, Black Spout Buttress, gave a pleasant Moderate climb.

James Parker

Photo: Cairngorm Club Archives

The next day the same party plus William Garden and Henry Watson made two climbs in Coire an Dubh Lochain of Beinn a' Bhùird, one of which was probably the ridge later named Slab and Arete. Two days later Raeburn and Ling visited Coire Brochain of Braeriach where they climbed Central Buttress Gully. This was a straightforward climb but the nature of the cover, soft snow on hard, made step-cutting difficult and the risk of avalanches considerable. It followed a twisting course up the central mass of rock ending close to the summit of Braeriach.[22]

The meet of 1908 marked the end of the SMC's early interest in climbing in the Cairngorms. The climbs so far achieved, apart from a few exceptions such as Tough-Brown Traverse and Raeburn's Buttress, followed gully-lines which tended to be wet and in places rotten. Most had long sections of unpleasant scrambling over gravel, scree and boulders and the cruxes were predominantly cave pitches. The moves on to the open faces were even more frightening, insecure and unlikely to tempt those who enjoy clean rock with good holds. Another fact may be that many of the climbs were done at times of the year when good weather and dry rock are unlikely to be found. A number of the early ascents, such as those on the first Aviemore meet, would now be considered as winter climbs. This, of course, makes some of these early achievements much more impressive than would appear from merely looking at their present rock climbing grades.

After the Easter meet at Braemar in 1908, it was almost two years before further exploration took place in the Cairngorms. In fact, all over Scotland the pace of mountaineering exploration had tailed off, the exception being in Skye which continued to attract keen and capable English ropes such as Steeple and Barlow. However, when things did begin to move again in the Cairngorms it was not on the crags so far explored, nor was it by the pioneers of before. Previously, the climbers who visited the area were primarily SMC members from the Central Belt who went there as a change from their usual West Coast haunts. For many, once was enough and few became granite devotees.

The new group interested in the area's mountaineering potential was based in Aberdeen, home city of the Cairngorm Club. It clearly irked some members of the SMC that their club had been forestalled by one year from becoming the first, and therefore the oldest climbing club in Scotland. That accolade belongs to the Cairngorm Club, which had its birth on the shores of Loch Avon in June 1887.

Aberdeen's link with the Cairngorms goes back for centuries. Its position at the mouth of the River Dee had provided it with easy and natural access up the valley to Ballater and Braemar lying at the centre of the massif. The railway to Ballater, completed in 1866, gave Aberdonians convenient access to the mountains and helped them form a relationship with the area and Lochnagar in particular. However, this was not the way in which the next phase of exploration began. On the southeast edge of the Cairngorms overlooking the wide fertile farmlands of Strath More are the Braes of Angus. This plateau area of rounded hills is cut by several long roughly parallel glens whose rivers flow southeast into Strathmore then into the North Sea. Perhaps the finest of these is Glen Clova, the upper part of the valley of the South Esk.

Here is a deep cut, steep-sided trench at the bottom of which the river meanders through flat green fields. Higher up the glen where the sides begin to close in, is a series of fine hanging corries and at Braedownie, three miles above the inn at Milton of Clova, the glen divides. Continuing to the north is the main glen while the more rugged Glen Doll runs westwards. The appearance, due to its geology, is more reminiscent of the Lake District or parts of Argyll. Here the granite gives way to schist, gneiss, diorite and epidiorite, heather gives way to grass, and the vegetation is rich and more varied than that found elsewhere in the region. In fact, the variety of rare arctic-alpine plants found on the steep vegetated crags had long attracted plant hunters to this glen. But for the climbers, the main draw was not the plants, but the unclimbed rock which was so accessible from the east.

The attractions of Glen Clova had previously been mentioned in the SMC guide to this area which appeared in the May Journal of 1904.[23] It specifically mentioned Glen Doll as a place worth trying and singled out Craig Rennet as a suitable objective. Although Clova was in Dundee's hinterland, it was the Aberdonians, James Parker and Howard Drummond, who arrived in the glen on Hogmanay 1909. The next day, the two Cairngorm Club men walked up Glen Doll to Craig Rennet. In the dull winter light the crag looked steep and held little snow, but an ill-defined gully ran part way up its east face and Parker and Drummond followed a line to the left of this. The rock was mica schist and consisted of steep steps separated by easier angled vegetation which, on this occasion, was frozen solid. No difficulties were encountered and although the buttress had a fine appearance, standing as a bold headland, it was open to many variations.

The next day, Parker and Drummond were joined by J.Bruce Miller for an attempt on the Scorrie, the large buttress overlooking Braedownie. However, lack of snow and excess of vegetation made them turn their attention further left to the cliffs at the back of the Winter Corrie. The Aberdonians skirted the steep lower rocks on the left and found an easy gully cutting up right to reach a big vegetated basin. They tried to climb out of this directly but were forced by the difficulties and lack of daylight to escape farther right. Their opening climb in the Winter Corrie became known as Backdoor Gully.

These early excursions must have had some appeal for climbers in the Cairngorm Club as they returned to Glen Clova the following New Year. Their objective this time was Craig Maud, the best defined buttress on The Dounalt, the steep south wall of Glen Doll lying to the west of Craig Rennet.

Drummond, Miller and Henry Alexander climbed the buttress from the left on January 3, 1911. They made their way up rightwards on to the crest of the buttress and finished over the prominent pinnacles. Although this Pinnacle Ridge is little more than a scramble in summer, it provided a more demanding outing under snow and ice.

Late September that year, saw two other Cairngorm Club members, James McCoss and George Merchant, visit the great amphitheatre of Braeriach and Cairn Toul. They were not heading for any of the three main corries but to the north-facing rocks of Sgòr an Lochain Uaine, some distance west of its north-east ridge. Here they found a well defined bay or corrie, high up below the plateau with a dark twisting gash

Sir Henry Alexander
Photo: SMC Archives

The south facing cliffs of Braeriach's Coire Bhrochain taken in July from the foot of West Gully. The Black Pinnacle is the highest piece of rock on the left

Photo: Greg Strange

Mabel Inglis Clark, June 1914

Photo: LSCC Archives

cutting the steepest rocks. The gash gave a rather grimy route up a series of boulder pitches which led to a final great chokestone evaded on the right. They named the climb Chokestone Gully and through usage the whole basin later became known as the Corrie of The Chokestone Gully.

Across An Garbh Choire from the Chokestone Gully lies the high Coire Bhrochain. It was here in October that Parker, Alexander, Miller and Walter Reid came to investigate an unclimbed pinnacle on the crags below the summit of Braeriach. Due to its appearance from several vantage points it had become known as the Black Pinnacle. Earlier in the month Parker had descended from the plateau to reach the neck separating the pinnacle from the summit slabs. Unfortunately, without some safeguard, the first few moves seemed too tricky and having no rope his companions could not join him and they were forced to return empty-handed. This unclimbed little summit became such a priority that they returned a few weeks later for a conventional approach from below where the Black Pinnacle could be distinguished by the shadow it cast on the cliff face. The route to the neck was obvious. First up an easy-angled big slab slanting left (Slab Terrace), and then easy ground and snow to the foot of a small loose chimney where they roped up. Above this they followed a gully (Central Buttress Gully) to a fork then by its left branch they reached the saddle. (All this to the fork climbed by Ling and Raeburn under snow conditions 1908.) Ten feet of Moderate climbing on the east face of the pinnacle lead to the top of the highest central tooth, where the obligatory 'stone man' was built. The other teeth looked too unstable to visit.[24]

It was on Lochnagar in December 1913, that the last new route was recorded before the outbreak of the First World War. This was the short wide chimney cutting the right wall of the Black Spout's Left-Hand Branch. It was as steep as any winter gully yet climbed in the area, although the main difficulty was, as usual, the cornice. More significantly, it was the first female ascent in the Cairngorms, being climbed by Mabel Inglis Clark (daughter of W.Inglis Clark) and Mrs W.Hunter.

In Henry Alexander's *The Cairngorms*, they were to be accompanied by "a friend" who in later guides turns out to be Alexander himself.[25] The chimney was named Crumbling Cranny by the party who made the first summer ascent in 1926.

During the bleak years of the Great War very little exploration took place in the Scottish hills. Raeburn, too old for active service at 49, contributed to the war effort by working in an aeroplane factory. Although there was little or no time for climbing, he did manage to make his last new routes in the Cairngorms at the end of May 1915. With Reid and William Galbraith he visited Corrie Fee, the big cirque on the north-east flank of Mayer, one of the finest features of the Glen Clova area. On the main south wall they climbed the best defined gully (B Gully) and the buttress on its left which ended at a pinnacle (B Gully Buttress).[26]

After the war, Raeburn published his instructional book *Mountaineering Art* and went on expeditions to Kanchenjunga and Everest. Unfortunately, he fell ill on the Everest trip and suffered continuous poor health thereafter and died in Edinburgh on December 21, 1926 at the age of 61. His legacy of climbs in Scotland, including the Cairngorms, was inspirational. It is generally agreed that the technical standards of winter climbing which he achieved on Ben Nevis (Observatory Ridge and Green Gully) were not surpassed until after the Second World War. When one considers the speed at which technical advances are made nowadays, Raeburn's accomplishments were quite remarkable.

Exit from Crumbling Cranny in February 1934

Photo: Bill Aitken

1.　Scottish Mountaineering Club Journal (SMCJ) Vol. 2, No. 5, p247. Photo of NE corrie taken the same day by W.Lamond Howie.
2.　SMCJ Vol. 2, No. 5, p247.
3.　SMCJ Vol. 4, No. 19, p48.
4.　SMCJ Vol. 3, No. 17, p305.
5.　SMCJ Vol. 2, No. 5, p275 – 276. (Tough's note of visit on January 2, 1893).
6.　SMCJ Vol. 4, No. 19, p40.
7.　SMCJ Vol. 4, No. 22, p218.
8.　SMCJ Vol. 4, No. 22, p219.
9.　SMCJ Vol. 4, No. 19, p220.
10.　SMCJ Vol. 8, No. 43, p66.
11.　Chokestone for chock-stone is the traditional spelling in the Cairngorms.
12.　SMCJ Vol. 5, No. 28, p178.
13.　SMCJ Vol. 6, No. 36, p231 – 234.
14.　SMCJ Vol. 7, No. 39, p118.
15.　SMCJ Vol. 7, No. 38, p81.
16.　SMCJ Vol. 2, No. 5, p253.
17.　SMCJ Vol. 7, No. 40, p186.
18.　SMCJ Vol. 8, No. 44, p115.
19.　SMCJ Vol. 8, No. 44, p120.
20.　SMCJ Vol. 10, No. 55, p10.
21.　SMCJ Vol. 10, No. 57, p146.
22.　SMCJ Vol. 10, No. 57, p151.
23.　SMCJ Vol. 8, No. 44, p 1.
24.　SMCJ Vol. 12, No. 68, p84 – 88.
25.　SMC *The Cairngorms*, Sir Henry Alexander (1928), p90.
26.　SMCJ Vol. 13, No. 78, p338.

2: Recovery (1918 – 1929)

East Face of Mitre Ridge, Beinn a' Bhùird, in March

Photo: Greg Strange

THE GREAT WAR reaped a heavy toll of Britain's young men and mountain exploration was slow to revive. During and immediately after the war, members of the Cairngorm Club continued to hold regular walking excursions both to the high tops as well as to many minor peaks within easy reach of Aberdeen. There seemed to be little incentive among local climbers to follow in the steps of Tough, Brown and Raeburn.

There were a few active rock climbers in the Cairngorm Club and during the early 1920s they continued to climb on the Kincardineshire sea cliffs just south of Aberdeen where 100 climbs had been recorded.

The old guard of James Parker, William Garden, Henry Alexander, Howard Drummond and James McCoss were all now quite long in the tooth, the first four being more than 40 years of age. Despite the enthusiasm and encouragement of these experienced men it was to be five or six years before the gulf left by the Great War would be filled and local young men and women would be seeking their own new climbs in the corries of the Cairngorms

Meanwhile, in July 1921, Parker and Drummond were investigating the climbing possibilities in the Eastern Cairngorms. They were particularly intrigued by the mysteries held on the remote northern slopes of Beinn a' Bhùird which remain hidden from view on all the usual southern approaches to the mountain from Deeside. Between Ben Avon and the northern outlier of Beinn a' Bhùird, Stob an-t Sluichd, lies a deep glen running north towards the River Avon known as the Slochd Mòr. At its head, tucked high under the plateau below Cnap a' Chlèirich, are the wild crags of the lonely Garbh Choire. It was here, nine miles from the nearest public road that Parker and Drummond came upon a spectacular rocky ridge. They were very excited with their find and decided to explore its upper part by descending to it from the plateau. After an awkward traverse to a col they climbed along a narrow knife-edge to its outer limit where their venture ended abruptly. A small stone man was built on top of the highest tooth of rock before returning to the plateau assisted by a top rope from Henry Kellas at the awkward traverse.

The following year, in June, Parker was back in the Garbh Choire with Alexander. This time they approached the foot of the ridge from the high pass between Ben Avon and Beinn a' Bhùird, the Sneck, and took some photographs. They prospected a start at the foot of the west face which seemed to offer a chance of attaining a platform on the crest about halfway up, but above this, things looked pretty hopeless. Nevertheless, Parker was still very enthusiastic about his ridge and despite not having climbed it he gave it the name of Mitre Ridge: "Because, as seen from the corrie floor it shows two peaks of nearly equal height. The name also seems appropriate, as the hill is called the Priest's Hill. Why should he not have a mitre?" (Cnap a' Chlèirich translates as Knoll of the Clergyman).

Parker wrote a lengthy article in the SMC Journal, 1923, in which he virtually challenges someone to attempt the ridge. Three photographs accompanied the article and these, coupled with Parker's

James Parker and Howard Drummond were particularly intrigued by the mysteries held on the remote northern slopes of Beinn a' Bhùird

statement: "It will be a magnificent climb if ever accomplished,"[1] ensured that further expeditions would be heading for the remote Garbh Choire of Beinn a' Bhùird in the future.

The summer of 1924 had been very cool and it may well have been for this reason that Parker and Alexander decided to take ice axes when they visited the Garbh Choire Mòr of Braeriach on the July 20.

"This inner corrie is a very secluded place, a holy of holies and it is seldom visited. It is girt all round with steep slopes and precipitous rocks and on the occasion of our visit with many big patches of snow, one of which is believed to be permanent. Of these the largest was in the north-west corner of the corrie and it consisted of a big slope of snow probably about 500ft high set at a steep angle and sending many tongues of snow up into the gullies in the rock. To the right of the east-most tongue of snow a momentary bit of mist revealed the existence of two respectable pinnacles and their attractive appearance at once determined us to climb the big snow slope to the foot of the pinnacles and to climb them, or, failing that, chance getting up the gully which was certain to run up to the top of the hill behind them."

Garbh Choire Mòr of Braeriach "is a very secluded place, a holy of holies and it is seldom visited"

Once across the bergschrund they attempted the lower pinnacle but abandoned this for the easy gully. Thus they made the first known climb out of the Garbh Choire Mòr via Pinnacle Gully and named and attempted Pinnacles Buttress.[2]

The remote corries of Braeriach were visited again in the summer of 1925 this time by two SMC men, Sandy Harrison and Louis Bartholomew. They explored Coire Bhrochain and like Parker and Alexander the previous year were attracted to an apparent pinnacle which seemed to be the highest point above the 700ft West Buttress. They climbed up easy rocks diagonally left to reach an open chimney to the west of the buttress. This they followed, sometimes in the chimney and sometimes on the east side of it. The going was good and the only difficult pitch, about 150ft from the top, was turned on the east.[3] This first recorded ascent of the West Buttress was later named Pioneer's Recess Route by Malcolm Smith.

On August 1, 1926, a 20-year-old Aberdeen University student, Godfrey Roy Symmers, made his first exploratory probe on Lochnagar when with a friend, F.King he recorded the first snow-free ascent of the Left Hand Branch of the Black Spout. This he achieved using a threaded rope and combined tactics at the great chokestone. (Its time-honoured through-route was discovered four years later by Nesta Bruce.) Above 'the pitch' in the branch, Symmers gained the plateau by Crumbling Cranny, the disintegrating chimney on the right wall, previously climbed under winter conditions by Inglis Clark's party. Symmers was the son of a merchant sea captain and it was while on holidays in Ballater during his last school years that he became interested in the hills. He was introduced to climbing by Parker and Bill Malcolm who both encouraged him to join the Cairngorm Club. This he did in 1926, later becoming a life member.

Symmers returned to Lochnagar the following July, accompanied by M.Sturm and attempted a snow-free ascent of Raeburn's Gully. After failing at the double cave pitch they took to the left wall and gained the crest of Tough-Brown Ridge by a loose chimney, thus completing the

*Roy Symmers and
Nesta Bruce at the
CIC Hut, Ben Nevis,
August 1932*

Photo: Bill Ewen

Roy Symmers and Nesta Bruce at the CIC Hut, Ben Nevis, August 1932

Photo: Bill Ewen

variation tried by Inglis Clark and Shannon in 1896. In August, this time with J.Silver, he again intended climbing Raeburn's Gully but "the appearance of a crack slanting upwards at 60° excited our curiosity".[4] The pair then proceeded to climb the Black Spout Pinnacle from the foot of Raeburn's Gully by a route later named Pinnacle Gully 1. This was Symmers's first completely new route on Lochnagar. He was back again in September to climb the Black Spout Buttress, unaware of Raeburn's ascent. On this occasion he was climbing with Bill Ewen, a red-haired lad from Ballater. Ewen left Ballater intermediate school at 14 and continued his education in Aberdeen, staying in lodgings and only going home at weekends and holidays. He first met Symmers at a cricket match in Ballater – Monaltrie CC v Visitors (Ewen played for Monaltrie) but he could not remember how they discovered a mutual interest in climbing. They had other things in common however, notably both were of the same age and fellow graduates of Aberdeen University. Ewen read English and Latin for his MA. Symmers graduated BSc in Engineering.

At New Year 1928, an incident took place in the Western Cairngorms that had a profound and lasting impact on all those who lived, worked or took recreation in the Scottish hills. On December 29, 1927, two young men from Glasgow University, Thomas Baird, a junior staff member of the Geology Department, and Hugh Barrie, a medical student, left Whitewell Croft, in Rothiemurchus to walk through the Làirig Ghrù to Corrour Bothy. It was their intention to spend a few days walking and exploring from the bothy before returning on January 1. Nothing further is certainly known of their movements until on the morning of Monday, January 2, when two Perth men, Alastair Cram and Edward McConnachie found Baird alive but unconscious near the lower bothy in Glen Einich. He expired in a few minutes. Despite considerable effort by many volunteers, searches from both Speyside and Deeside failed to find Hugh Barrie. His body was eventually found when the snows receded on March 25, lying in a peat hag about 400 yards above the upper bothy beside Loch Einich. It is known that the two friends reached Corrour, and it is generally assumed that they were overtaken on the return journey by the short but very severe snow storm which swept over the hills on the afternoon of January 1.

That two very strong, fit young men could perish in such dramatic circumstances is widely understood today, but in the 1920s comparatively few people walked and climbed in the hills for pleasure, particularly in winter. It may be that Baird and Barrie were the first recreational hill walkers from outwith the North-east to die in the Cairngorms, so it is hardly surprising that the tragedy caused something of a sensation and evoked widespread sympathy throughout Scotland. One of the strange features of the incident is that Hugh Barrie contributed to the *Glasgow University Magazine* a remarkably prophetic poem anticipating his own fate in which he requests that after his death he did not wish to be buried but:

> "Find me a windswept boulder for a bier
> And on it lay me down,
> Where far beneath drops sheer the rocky ridge
> Down to the gloomy valley, and the streams
> Fall foaming white against black beetling rocks,
> Where the sun's kindly radiance seldom gleams;
> Where some tall peak, defiant, steadfast, mocks
> The passing Gods: and all the ways of men forgotten."

Hugh Barrie was laid to rest in Rothiemurchus about 300 yards from Whitewell, at a place facing Braeriach. Thomas Baird is buried at Baldernock Parish Church near Milngavie.

Sir Henry Alexander's comprehensive guidebook to the Cairngorms was published in 1928 by the Scottish Mountaineering Club. It contained more than 200 pages of detailed information on the Cairngorms and other hill areas of North-east Scotland. Alexander, came from Aberdeen. He was a very public figure in his home city and was aged 53 when the guide was published. His invaluable contribution to the literature of the Cairngorms did much to broaden people's knowledge of the area and the guide quickly became one of the SMC's best sellers.

In August of this year Symmers was back in action on Lochnagar, this time with Aberdonian, Nesta Bruce. A degree of rivalry had developed among local climbers to repeat the earlier routes and the second 'summer' ascent of Raeburn's Gully became the main objective. On August 5, after a period of prolonged settled weather Symmers and Bruce succeeded. This was Symmers's third attempt, and in Bruce, whose previous climbing experience had been limited to the tors of Clachnaben and Ben Rinnes, he had found an ideal companion. At the second cave of the double cave pitch, the crux (where Raeburn had used his ice axe) was overcome with a stirrup made from a length of thin rope doubled and threaded behind the chokestone. In the upper gully they saw no sign of the through-route used by the pioneers.[5] This ascent, 30 years after that of Raeburn's party, seems to have opened the flood gates, for within a month the Ballater team of Ewen and A.Paterson had also climbed the route.

In later years, Malcolm Smith said of Raeburn's Gully: "A sporting route often used as a yardstick with which one measured his capabilities. The highlight lay in the ascent of a great, double-tiered cave pitch. This, although a large part of it was living rock, collapsed under a rock

A degree of rivalry had developed among local climbers to repeat the earlier routes and the second 'summer' ascent of Raeburn's Gully became the main objective

A.Patterson following the cave pitch in Raeburn's Gully September 1928

Photo: Bill Ewen

*Nesta Bruce on
Central Buttress,
Lochnagar, August
1928*

Photo: Roy Symmers

*Somewhat
crestfallen by their
defeat Symmers
suggested a
wander up the
Black Spout, but
a mettlesome Bruce
would have
none of this and
promptly proceeded
to lead off up the
rocks to the left*

fall in 1940 and not a vestige of it remains." [6] The gully's present grade
is Hard Severe.

One week after their success in Raeburn's Gully, Symmers and Bruce
made the second ascent of West Gully on Lochnagar in very wet conditions with Bruce leading the 30ft cave pitch. Having completed all the
existing climbs on Lochnagar except for Tough and Brown's route,
Symmers was now looking for something new. The project he and Bruce
had in mind was to try and force a route up a shallow gully on the right
face of the big central buttress whose rocks may be traced right down
to the lochside. The gully, lying below and well to the left of Douglas-
Gibson Gully, appeared to run almost straight up to the skyline, giving
out on the crest of the buttress more than halfway up. This choice of
Shallow Gully seems odd when you consider that most of the buttresses
and five of the major gullies were still unscaled. Nevertheless, on August
26, they climbed Shallow Gully for 200ft until stopped by a smooth slab
barring access to the easy upper depression. Despite its appearance from
below, the main difficulties were of loose and rotten rock, and a fairly
harrowing descent was accomplished. Somewhat crestfallen by their
defeat Symmers suggested a wander up the Black Spout, but a mettlesome Bruce would have none of this and promptly proceeded to lead
off up the rocks to the left. Thus they quickly made the first ascent of
Central Buttress.[7] (Bruce completed Shallow Gully four years later, leading all the pitches with H.A.Macrae.)

The summer was not quite over and on a beautiful late September
day the intrepid pair set off from Glas-allt-Shiel on the shore of Loch
Muick, bound for Creag an Dubh-loch, that massive precipice a few miles
south of Lochnagar.

"What a vision of grandeur! What heavenly blue, merging to a deep
purple where the shadow of the overhanging crags fell upon the surface
of the tarn."[8]

I well recall my first visit to Creag an Dubh-loch as a schoolboy and
confess that although I vividly remember our scramble up the Central
Gully my recollections of the size and magnificence of the cliff as a whole
did not register as anything particularly significant. It is tempting to
wonder if our two explorers could possibly have imagined that in the
future, climbers would make their different ways over all parts of these
'overhanging crags'. Probably, they only had eyes for the lines which
seemed to offer a chance to them and knowing that the South-east Gully
had already been attempted this was an obvious choice for the first rock
climb on Creag an Dubh-loch. It gave them two hours of strenuous, but
rather unpleasant, climbing under and over chokestones, and at one
point lying sideways in the stream of water.

In July 1929 Symmers and Bruce climbed No. 5 Buttress Gully on Sgòr
Gaoith. This is the prominent gully which cuts into the right flank of
No. 5 Buttress. They had been spending a few days in Glen Einich based
at the stable of the upper bothy. Nesta Bruce continued to climb in the
Cairngorms until 1932 when she and her new husband, H.A.Macrae,
left for Tokyo, Mr Macrae taking up a post as Trade Attaché. In the early
1970s, now widowed and retired from teaching, she was again living
in Aberdeen.

Looking back we see that the 1920s were notable mainly for the very few people climbing and walking in the Scottish hills. What little exploration there was in the Cairngorms seems to have been undertaken solely by members or associates of the Cairngorm or Scottish Mountaineering Clubs. There is no record of visiting climbers from England where rock climbing had revived quickly after the war and the standards of their best activists were already impressively high. Most climbers from south of the Border went to Skye or Ben Nevis.

By 1929, no real technical advance had been made in the Cairngorms beyond that achieved by Raeburn before the war and climbing was still almost exclusively restricted to gullies and chimneys which are notoriously loose and damp. However, in Roy Symmers we see the first home grown Cairngorm climbing devotee. Already his knowledge of the great cliffs of the North-east corrie of Lochnagar was second to none, and he and his companions were beginning to lay the foundations for future generations of Aberdeen climbers. Apart from the ascents of easy gullies like the Black Spout on Lochnagar, winter climbing had virtually ceased for the time being.

Creag an Dubh-loch from the east, pre-1908

Photo: George Washington Wilson / Aberdeen University

1.   SMCJ Vol. 16, No.95, 1923.
2.   Cairngorm Club Journal (CCJ) No. 63, p143.
3.   SMCJ Vol. 17, No. 100, p200.
4.   SMCJ Vol. 18, No. 104, p119.
5.   CCJ Vol. 11, No. 67, p6.
6.   SMC *Climber's Guide to the Cairngorms Area Vol. 2* (1962), p43.
7.   CCJ Vol. 11, No. 67, p10 – 12.
8.   CCJ Vol. 11, No. 67, p31.

3: The Formative Years (1930 – 1939)

THE MAIN THRUST of climbing in the early 1930s was centred on Lochnagar. That is with one notable exception – Mitre Ridge on Beinn a' Bhùird. Seven years had passed since Parker wrote his article and there is no record of any attempt to climb the ridge in that period. However, such a challenge was unlikely to go unheeded for long.

Two founder members of the Glasgow Junior Mountaineering Club of Scotland (JMCS), Archie Hutchison and Arthur Rusk, inspired by Parker's enthusiasm paid a visit to the Mitre Ridge on June 23, 1930. Although intimidated by its forbidding appearance they made an

West Face of Mitre Ridge, Beinn a' Bhùird, June 1930

Photo: Arthur Rusk

attempt from the foot of the west wall close to where Parker had tried. They made a little progress but were put off by the rounded granite and the loose moss which seemed to crown the exits to many of the cracks.

"It is not inconceivable that detailed investigation by means of a roped descent might enable a possible, though excessively severe, route to be worked out, but to tackle the climb in a straightforward way would be almost certainly impossible, owing to the great improbability of finding resting places throughout the climb and the extreme difficulty involved in making any progress."[1]

This observation by Hutchison seemed to confirm Parker's view that finding a route up the ridge was pretty hopeless. Nevertheless, Hutchison's note in the SMCJ was accompanied by a superb photograph of the west face of the Mitre Ridge taken by Rusk in the late afternoon of a mid-summer day with much of the wall bathed in sunlight. This same photograph appeared in the second edition of Alexander's District Guide and must have evoked a quickening of the heart of many a climber at the prospect of tackling such a compelling piece of rock.

The great granite bastions which encircle the head of Loch Avon were once just as remote and inaccessible as the cliffs of Beinn a' Bhùird. The well-known Glaswegian climber Jock Nimlin was in the area during the summer of 1930 and climbed the spur of rock forming the left wall of the diagonal scree-filled gully on the cliff opposite the Shelter Stone. Although Nimlin was a regular visitor to the Cairngorms this was his only recorded first ascent. A description first appeared in Bill Ewen's 1950 edition of *The Cairngorms* where it was named Serrated Rib and given the first ascent date of July 1930. A party of three was indicated but only Nimlin's name was given.[2] This was the first new ascent in the Loch Avon basin since Raeburn's climb on the Shelter Stone Crag 23 years previously. It was also the first rock climb on these south facing cliffs of Cairn Gorm, collectively known as the Stag Rocks.

During 1930 Roy Symmers left Aberdeen and took up a post as engineer with the LNER at York. His association with the Cairngorm Club practically ceased but he did continue to climb with Bill Ewen and others when he came north on holiday. Symmers and Ewen struck up a good climbing partnership about which Ewen later said: "We found we suited each other – Symmers was tall with a long reach, but disliked operating in narrow chimneys etc., where long legs could be something of a handicap, they suited me. We did not set out to become expert rock climbers; our practice was to avoid difficulty where possible, our aim first to be able to tackle any Scottish mountain e.g. The Inaccessible Pinnacle. I felt more confident with Symmers than with anyone else – why I don't know."

In 1987 Symmers's wife, Elizabeth, herself an able rock climber, recalled that "Bill was a small bunch of muscle and beautiful balance, Roy was long and strong. He (Roy) said they supplied each others deficiencies but there was more to it than that – you could trust Bill with your life on a rope".

Whether Symmers had by now departed for York is not clear, but nevertheless on August 10 and 17 he and Ewen made two significant new climbs on Lochnagar. Immediately to the right of the Shallow Gully attempted in 1928 lie two distinct buttresses which, on account of this

The great granite bastions which encircle the head of Loch Avon were once just as remote and inaccessible as the cliffs of Beinn a' Bhùird

section of the cliff remaining for the greater part of the day in shade, had been named by Symmers as the Shadow Buttresses A and B. (It was Shadow Buttress B that Raeburn attempted in 1902.) Skirting the base of the larger Buttress A there comes into view a couloir on its right flank into which converge three defined gullies or chimneys. It was the central one of these they climbed on August 10.

The chimney is a well-defined cleft for 200ft up to an overhang, above which it reappears as a crack in steep slabby rock leading directly up to the crest of Shadow Buttress A. They climbed the lower cleft in four short pitches – the hardest moves being at a large chokestone where combined tactics were used. At the overhang they contemplated traversing left across the line of the chimney, but the lack of any belay persuaded them to seek an easier alternative out to the right where a wide vegetated depression runs up to the skyline.

Symmers's account reads: "About 80ft of rope was run out by the leader before a suitable stance became available. The rock on this section is most unreliable, and a good deal of excavation may be necessary. A very perfect profile of a man's head can be noticed on the rib of rock which forms the left wall of the gully near this point, and it is on account of this feature that the gully gets its name." [3] Several hundred feet of easier climbing took them to the top of the Giant's Head Chimney. This, their first major new climb on Lochnagar, was probably the most important route on the mountain for more than 20 years, since Raeburn climbed Black Spout Buttress.

Clearly not put off by loose or vegetated rock the pair returned to the corrie the following week this time to try the easier looking of the two gullies crossed by Tough and Brown. At this time Symmers had named several of the features on this central section of the cliff. He referred to the steep buttress immediately right of 'the Douglas Gully' as the Eagle's Buttress and the two great gullies and the slender buttress between this and 'Tough-Brown Ridge' as Parallel Gullies A and B and Parallel Buttress.[4] It was the Parallel Gully A that he went to look at with Ewen on August 17.

It was the first time that tennis shoes had been worn in the Cairngorms to help overcome difficult rock

Like Tough and Brown before them they were forced to commence their climb on Eagle Buttress where a rising traverse soon brought them to the bed of the gully above its steep initial pitch. From here, easy, but wet, climbing took them to a bifurcation. They had hoped to gain and climb the right branch but this appeared too difficult so they moved on to the dividing ridge between the forks. After 100ft of sustained climbing they arrived at a mossy cup below an overhang. Here Symmers led part way up a steep slab on the right until forced to cross back left into a small groove before reaching easy ground. The climbing on this upper rib, which is Severe, was probably the most difficult yet achieved on the mountain. Certainly, it was the first time that tennis shoes had been worn in the Cairngorms to help overcome difficult rock. Symmers had carried them specifically to use if the going became hard and at some stage on the climb he had changed from his nailed boots.[5]

The use of bothies has long been a tradition with visitors to the Cairngorms. This is due in no small measure to the long distances involved in walking and climbing in the more remote parts of the area. Climbers found it practical to have a reliable base close to the cliffs or

Roy Symmers climbing the upper rib of Parallel Gully A, Lochnagar, August 1930

Photo: Bill Ewen

at least somewhere between the public road and the high tops. Of the original bothies perhaps the best known is the old deer watchers' house in Glen Dee known as Corrour. Situated in a wild and magnificent setting beneath the sweeping outline of the Devil's Point, it has served as a haven for travellers passing through the Làirig Ghrù since it ceased to be used by the estate in 1914. Constructed in 1877, the stone building was originally wood lined and had partitions but the timber was gradually torn out to use as fuel.

Corrour is an ideal base from which to explore the Central and Western Cairngorms, and for this reason Pat Baird and Ramsay Traquair spent a week at the bothy in late March 1931. At this time of the year snow conditions can be alpine with warm daytime temperatures and hard frost at night. During their week at Corrour they experienced a mixture of cold snow-laden south-east winds as well as good settled days. On one of the better days they visited Coire Bhrochain. Their intention had been to climb the Black Pinnacle but tiring of very wet snow in the approach gully they abandoned this plan and took to the dry rock on the Braeriach Pinnacle and made its first ascent.[6]

In 1925 when Harrison and Bartholomew were climbing in Coire Bhrochain they stayed at a cottage at Coylum Bridge where the old keeper had told them an intriguing story. He said that looking down the cliffs of Coire an Lochain of Cairn Gorm one saw the waters of a

The cliffs of Coire an Lochain, Cairn Gorm, showing the line of Central Crack Route, July 1931

Photo: Louis St C. Bartholomew

small lochan glistening with more than usual brilliance. This, he explained, was due to Cairngorms which had fallen from the unscalable cliffs above and glistened in the depths of the water. While scarcely giving the story full credence it tickled their fancy sufficiently that on a return visit to Speyside in July 1931 they decided to investigate this, the most impressive corrie on the north side of the Cairngorms.

When they reached the inner and larger of the two lochans that lie below the cliffs they found debris from a recent avalanche which appeared to have been carried across ice on the lochan and deposited on the far side. The avalanche had swept down a great inclined slab of red granite about 350ft high on which they noticed a crack running the full height from top to bottom. They spent a little time searching for crystals then set off to climb the crack, which proved no more than a wet scramble. At the top they discovered that the line of the crack continued up the face of the cliff above as a shallow chimney.

"We found the first pitch in the chimney difficult, and turned it by going to the right and traversing back and upwards. The second pitch was narrow and unpleasantly loose, but once it was negotiated the route opened out and presented no undue difficulty, although the rocks were not all too secure." [7] Their climb on the upper buttress was about 350ft and they built a cairn at the point of their exit – still in the line of the crack.

From the plateau edge they observed that further climbs were possible on these spectacular crags which resembled titanic masonry. In particular, they thought the nearest buttress to the west should give an interesting route but that the most westerly appeared impractical. Although Central Crack Route, as it became known, had not provided rock climbing of either great difficulty or quality it was nevertheless the first climb in this prominent high corrie and led the two pioneers to speculate that climbing in Coire an Lochain may prove to be as good as any other corrie in the Cairngorms. It is interesting to note they were possibly the first visitors to record finding evidence of sizeable avalanches in the vicinity of the Great Slab – something for which in recent times the corrie has become notorious in winter.

Six members of the Perth JMCS, held a weekend meet to Glen Einich in May 1932, using the stable of the upper bothy as a base. On the Sunday, a party of three comprising James Bell, Colin Allen and David Myles climbed the diamond-shaped buttress in the hanging Coire Olc (named Fan Corrie by Bell) between No. 2 and 3 Buttresses. [8]

Jim Bell was already one of Scotland's foremost mountaineers. He was born in Auchtermuchty, the son of a Scottish minister and a German mother. He started hill-walking in his teens, often alone and with the aid of a bicycle to cover the long distances out of Fife. He said that in his earliest climbing days the Cairngorms exercised a great fascination over him. His first venture was a cycle trip over the Cairnwell Pass on the way to Braemar and a breakfast by the Linn of Dee. The southern aspect of the Devil's Point and the higher hills behind made a deep impression and gave birth to a resolve to explore them fully. The Diamond Buttress of Sgoran Dubh (Very Difficult) was Bell's first new climb in the Cairngorms. It was one of the few recommended rock climbs in Glen Einich at that time.

Late September 1932 saw Symmers and Ewen climb the big Shadow Buttress A, immediately right of the Shallow Gully on Lochnagar. The climbing proved to be only moderately difficult despite the steep and forbidding appearance of its central area. The key to the ascent was the prominent grassy spiral terrace which curves up below large overhangs and leads to a high balcony overlooking the Shadow Couloir. Here they followed a rock rib alongside the left-hand Shadow Chimney which gave access to the easy upper crest. Although quite vegetated, this original climb on Shadow A provided a good mountaineering route and became a popular rock climb.

In 1932 there was a revival of interest in winter climbing. On Lochnagar, several attempts were made to climb Raeburn's Gully. W.Brockie, E.Gordon and R.Yunnie spent a whole day trying to cut a way up, but were stopped by a wall of ice above the first cave. Later that year, on Christmas Day, Yunnie, Gordon and J.Gove turned their attention to West Gully and succeeded in making an ascent in three hours. Unfortunately for them, they reported a scarcity of snow for the time of year and their winter ascent was discounted as not being in condition.

Surprisingly, only two days after the disallowed West Gully climb, Symmers, Ewen and Sandy Clark made the prized first winter ascent of Raeburn's Gully, described by Ewen as a very fine snow climb. Such are the vagaries of Scottish winter climbing conditions! The lower pitches were masked in ice, but, above the cave pitch, the snowfield extended unbroken to the cornice. The climb occupied three hours and the leader, Symmers, stated that there was perhaps just not enough snow to make conditions perfect.[9]

The next day Clark and Ewen climbed the short gully which enters the Left-Hand Branch of the Black Spout almost opposite the Crumbling Cranny. Ewen had already climbed this in July, naming it Pinnacle Gully 2, a counterpart to Symmers's Pinnacle Gully 1. As on the previous day the snow conditions were excellent. The crux chokestone was

Colin Allan, Jim Bell and David Myles on Sgoran Dubh Mòr. May 1932

Photo: David Myles

Sandy Clark, Roy Symmers and Bill Ewen – the first winter ascent team of Raeburn's Gully, Lochnagar, in December 1932

Photo: Innes Ewen

not snowed over, but a passage was found on the left wall, from which the snow above the block was gained with difficulty. It would be16 years before another new winter route was made on Lochnagar.

At Easter 1933 five men were staying in Maggie Gruer's house at Thistle Cottage, Inverey. In the party were John Menlove Edwards and his friend Alec Keith from Turriff. They had met at Fettes College in Edinburgh. Edwards was 23-years-old and already established as a formidable rock climber, having made many very difficult first ascents, mainly in North Wales. Apparently, he was a rock climber pure and simple, not a mountaineer, and he hated walking.

A visit to the Cairngorms would seem an unexpected choice for such a person, yet on their first day Edwards and Keith walked from the Derry Gates to Loch Avon and back, a round trip of 20 miles. They took with them one ice axe and a rope and climbed Castle Wall on the Shelter Stone Crag which was still snowed up. Next day, they went to Lochnagar and climbed part way up the Black Spout on hard snow then moved on to the Black Spout Buttress and continued to the top.

According to Keith: "There was a good deal of snow to be cleared off the holds and a good deal of poorish rock too and I was frightened most of the way up, but Menlove enjoyed this part of the day and put up with my fear and ineptitude without complaint."

Clearly, these two unrecorded climbs would qualify as winter ascents nowadays. It was during this stay at Inverey that Edwards undertook one of his better known escapades. After a close inspection of the foaming peaty water in its narrow rock channel Edwards swam down the Linn of Dee tied to a climbing rope with the other end attached to a birch tree. Afterwards, he and his friends went to look at the Linn of Quoich, but Edwards pointed out that this was a much more dangerous affair with a long vertical fall at one place.[10]

Towards the end of April, conditions in the Cairngorms are often

Apparently, John Menlove Edwards was a rock climber pure and simple, not a mountaineer, and he hated walking

still very wintry, especially in high north-facing corries like Coire an Lochain of Cairn Gorm. On April 23, snow lying on the great slab was in splendid condition when John Ewen, Edwin Davidson and Fred Davidson climbed up from the lochan to the foot of the cliffs. Their objective was the ridge-like buttress observed by Harrison and Bartholomew lying immediately west of the Central Crack Route. Ewen led the whole climb over several short pitches up the left edge overlooking a snow-filled couloir. All three men were members of the Elgin-based Moray Mountaineering Club (MMC) which had been founded in November 1931. Ewen, from Lonmay in Aberdeenshire, was a principal teacher of mathematics at Elgin Academy. Two years after this ascent he was killed by a small rock avalanche while leading a climb on Le Brévent above Chamonix. After his death this commanding No. 3 buttress in Coire an Lochain was named Ewen Buttress in his memory.[11]

A lean winter in 1932-33 was followed by an exceptionally dry summer which lasted into the autumn and brought about the first disappearance in living memory of all the snow beds in the Cairngorms including those of the Garbh Choire Mòr of Braeriach. This very dry summer saw some particularly significant events in the development of rock climbing in the Cairngorms.

In 1932, at a place far removed from the wild corries of the Cairngorms, a group of Cambridge undergraduates were plotting an ascent of Mitre Ridge. Alexander's Guide stated that: "The finest cliffs on Beinn a' Bhùird are those of the Garbh Choire, beyond the Sneck. Rocks 400 to 600ft high form the south wall of this corrie, the boldest feature being a great ridge of sheer rock. This ridge has not been climbed." This statement together with Rusk's photograph in the SMCJ, so encouraged this small band of exiled Scots that they resolved to attempt the ridge as soon as possible. Plans were laid in the Michaelmas term to try the ridge the following summer. At Easter 1933, JMCS members Jock Leslie and Dufftown man Stephen Cumming, reconnoitred the ridge in thick mist and on returning to Cambridge it was decided to make the attempt after the Cambridge University Mountaineering Club (CUMC) summer meet to Skye.

So it was that a party of five very fit young men fresh from a week's climbing in the Cuillin set out from Tomintoul heading for the Garbh Coire on the evening of July 3, 1933. The party comprised Leslie, Cumming, Sandy Wedderburn, Pat Baird and John Crofton. At about 10 o'clock the next morning they left their campsite at the head of the Slochd Mòr and scrambled up tumbled blocks into the upper corrie to the foot of the Mitre. The weather was glorious with bright sunshine and a slight cooling breeze. Half an hour was spent prospecting through glasses, and it was decided to attack in two parties, Wedderburn, Baird and Leslie to attempt the 'direct' ascent as straight as possible from the lowest point of the rocks; Cumming and Crofton an interesting alternative on the north-west side of the main arete.

The 'direct' route commenced a few yards to the west of the lowest rocks and followed a deep groove for more than 100ft. It turned out to be the hardest part of the climb up smooth slabs at an angle of 55 degrees with an overhanging wall on the left. In places it was necessary to progress by backing up the holdless slabs, using the scanty holds on

At a place far removed from the wild corries of the Cairngorms, a group of Cambridge under-graduates were plotting an ascent of Mitre Ridge

Sandy Wedderburn giving his all in an unsuccessful attempt to climb the left-hand crack up the crest of the first tower on Mitre Ridge in July 1933

Photo: Stephen Cumming

the wall for boots and fingers. The slabs were topped by a seven foot wall, which overhung slightly, above which a stance with a poor belay was found on a mossy ledge. Having accomplished a pitch which was more difficult and sustained than anything hitherto achieved in the Cairngorms (Hard Severe), they temporarily found themselves on easy ground. They continued up and round onto the West face and in so doing arrived at the probable high point of previous attempts reached by easier climbing on the right. The deep chimney which had halted previous attempts surprisingly did not merit description and soon they reached the first step on the ridge itself. From here 90ft of exposed moderate climbing right on the crest brought the three men to a narrow ledge below a formidable obstacle – the first tower.

"Two slender cracks filled with detached stones, moss, etc., led straight up the tower, which bulged out into a slight overhang straight in front. The leader (Wedderburn) made a gallant attempt to make one of these go, but was forced to give up when he had climbed up 10ft and had been out of balance for at least a quarter of an hour. The second also tried, but with no more success. Either might go in rubbers, but it would be very severe indeed."[12]

Eventually, an easier line was found out left onto a broad grass platform then the top of the tower gained in 50ft. Across a small gap lay the second tower and once again this was attempted direct by Wedderburn. By now Crofton and Cumming had completed their climb and Crofton described how they watched Wedderburn on the second tower "edging his way slowly up a steadily increasing overhang which looked to us utterly impossible – as indeed it proved. Suddenly, with 15 or 20ft out, he fell directly on to the rope, 30 or 40ft; but the imperturbable Pat, firmly ensconced and well belayed, calmly held him, miraculously unhurt. We later picked up his hat 600ft below." [13] After this excitement the easier left side was taken to reach Parker's Cairn at the top of the second tower and the plateau was gained at 2.45pm.

The 'interesting alternative' line taken by Cumming and Crofton produced a tremendous direct climb of sustained difficulty and exposure although nowhere quite as technical as the first pitch of the Direct. A subsidiary triangular buttress projects out from the west wall and forms two prominent corners running up to an apex level with the main ridge. The longer left-hand corner was the line of their climb. Sharing the leads they started up a difficult chimney with an awkward bulging chokestone which led to a comfortable recess not far right of the deep chimney on the Direct. Their next pitch went right by a smooth groove until stopped by a vertical wall. Here a traverse back left gave access to a sloping ledge directly below the corner.

By now they had climbed two severe pitches and the feeling of commitment must have been very real indeed. Starting up that big pitch in the corner must have been quite daunting not knowing if it could be climbed or even if a ledge could be reached before the rope ran out. Some 15ft of hard climbing just right of the corner took the leader to a point where he could step left and follow the crack directly to a welcome ledge at 80ft. Unfortunately, this good stance was not provided with a belay, but the main difficulty appeared to have been passed so there was no thought of retreat. They continued up a 20ft crack and eventually followed a loose gully to gain the main ridge below the second tower. Here they also attempted the central crack but abandoned it in favour of the easier alternative on the left. The ascent was completed in the fast time of two hours, and although Cumming and Crofton left the recording of their climb to Jock Leslie, hence the use of the eponyms, their comments to him indicated they thought the difficulties were mainly due to perched blocks on ledges and the long lead-outs.

So it happened, despite suggestions of impossibility by earlier suitors, that Mitre Ridge was climbed by two separate routes simultaneously in the remarkably dry summer of 1933. The secret of this success was due to the combination of careful planning and the rare occurrence in the Cairngorms at that time of a very strong party finding perfect rock climbing conditions.

After leaving Cambridge, Sandy Wedderburn continued to climb in Scotland and abroad. During the war he played a major role in the training of troops in mountain warfare, later becoming second in command of the Lovat Scouts. He died in tragic circumstances on Christmas Eve 1944 in Italy. He slipped while descending the marble staircase of a hotel at Aquila and fell over a low banister to the well beneath.

Pat Baird graduated as a geologist in 1933 and went on to lead a long and distinguished career as a mountaineer, Arctic explorer and

Campsite below Mitre Ridge, Beinn a' Bhùird, July 1933. Left to right, John Crofton, Stephen Cumming and Sandy Wedderburn

Photo: Stephen Cumming

George Taylor,
Charlie Ludwig and
Donald Dawson at
the top of Mitre Ridge
in September 1933

Photo: Charlie Ludwig
collection

glaciologist – Baird Peninsula on the West Coast of Baffin is named after him. After the war he became director of the Arctic Institute of North America in Montreal and led the first major expedition to explore the mountains of the Cumberland Peninsula of Baffin Island. In all, he took part in almost a dozen expeditions to this area and made several important first ascents. He died in Ottawa on January 1, 1984.

Stephen Cumming went to the Far East to work and during the war took part in an epic retreat from upper Burma to Assam across a high mountain pass. Later, he was awarded an OBE for sabotage work behind Japanese lines. Despite suffering long-term ill health from his wartime activities he returned to Hong Kong and became a company director until retirement. He died at Nairn, aged 62.

Jock Leslie died in the 1950s while serving in the Colonial Service in Kenya. Of that band of five, John Crofton survived them all by 25 years. He became an eminent professor and head of the Medical Faculty at Edinburgh University and was knighted for his work on respiratory illnesses. He died in 2009, aged 97.

The events of that hot July day do not quite conclude the year's activity on Mitre Ridge. Two months later, Charlie Ludwig and Donald Dawson from Aberdeen, unaware of the Cambridge party's achievement, made what they believed to be a first ascent on September 9. Ludwig, climbing in stocking soles, led the whole climb and took a line similar to the Direct. He repeated the climb with three other companions on October 1, again leading the whole route in socks.

Ludwig was an exceptional climber. He took the opportunity to climb whenever and wherever possible, sometimes using the external granite walls of the family home in Rubislaw Den South. After leaving Aberdeen Grammar School he went to Aberdeen University. It was there in 1931 that he scaled the Mitchell Tower of Marischal College in the dark and attached a top-hatted skeleton to the pinnacle. He was also the first person to cross the 'Blondin' transporter cables above the 450ft deep Rubislaw Quarry.

Three days after his September ascent of Mitre Ridge, Ludwig accomplished a most impressive feat of cragsmanship. Climbing in gym shoes and with no prior knowledge of the difficulties he set off alone up the notorious Douglas-Gibson Gully on Lochnagar. One hour and 15 minutes later he emerged triumphant on the plateau. His brief note given to Parker for publication in the SMCJ said: "There were no very serious technical difficulties but the rock throughout was so rotten that the climb may be considered as quite unjustifiable."[14] He graded the climb Severe. Normally, the gully is wet as well as unstable and modern climbers consider the climb to be Very Severe. Anyone who has viewed the Douglas-Gibson headwall from the security of Eagle Ridge could not fail to be impressed by this bold adventure.

Ludwig graduated from Aberdeen University in 1934 and after a spell of research work at Cambridge he became a lecturer in physiology at Leeds University. He continued to climb both in Britain and abroad, and then in early 1941 he gave up a brilliant medical career and volunteered for service with the RAF. In January 1942, a few months after gaining his commission, his Hampden bomber crashed near Aylesbury after a raid on a French port and he and the three other crew members were killed.

Two other new climbs were made in the North-east corrie of Lochnagar in the summer of 1933, both by Symmers and Ewen. In August, they climbed Gargoyle Chimney, the prominent deep fault above the midway terrace on the West Buttress between the Black Spout Buttress and West Gully. It proved to be something of an impostor, being less formidable than its appearance suggested – Difficult. The gargoyle, after which the chimney was named, is the very striking toad-like feature jutting out from the plateau rim not far to the right of the upper amphitheatre.

Their other climb was the right-hand gully of the Shadow Couloir trio which they named Polyphemus Gully. It branches off Giant's Head Chimney about 50ft above the scree and forms the true dividing line between Shadow Buttress A and Shadow Buttress B. On their first attempt they reached a point 150ft up where farther progress would have required the use of an apparently unstable tooth of rock on the left wall. Their remedy for the problem was to return on a later occasion and descend from the top to test the offending tooth. Thus having convinced themselves that it would support the weight of a climber they made their successful ascent on September 16 – Very Difficult.

Climbers today consider the northern corries of Cairn Gorm very accessible, but prior to construction of the ski road, Loch Morlich was the closest point of access from the north. This meant at least an hour of additional effort was required to reach the corries. It also meant that the day commenced with a walk through the magnificent pines of the Glenmore Forest.

In April 1934, a party from the MMC found themselves lunching below the steep right-hand buttress in Coire an Lochain prior to making an ascent of the prominent Y Gully lying to the right of Ewen Buttress. The party comprised Tom Stobart, his father, Miss Harbinson and

The sunlit crests of Shadow Buttress B (left) and Eagle Ridge (right) rise above the early morning mist in the North-east corrie of Lochnagar. The Tough-Brown Face is in the right foreground

Photo: Greg Strange

E. Thompstone. They followed the right branch up steep soft snow, noting an interesting frozen waterfall in the left fork. The main difficulty of their climb was the cornice which was composed of frozen névé filled in with deep fresh snow from a recent storm. Faced with possible benightment the situation called for a special effort. Eventually, Tom Stobart led the cornice using combined tactics from a small cave below the lip. This ascent of the right branch of Y Gully was the first of the now classic winter climbs in Coire an Lochain.[15]

Summer 1934 saw the last appearance on Lochnagar of the Symmers and Ewen partnership. Their final project was to be the conquest of the imposing Shadow Buttress B. On several occasions they had investigated the buttress to determine where the line of least resistance lay. They had tried the groove on the left and fared no better than Raeburn. Twice they climbed down from the top without much difficulty to reach a large vegetated platform above the steep 300ft lower rocks. Eventually, they decided to try the slabby wall just inside the Douglas-Gibson Gully where they hoped a hanging chimney would take them past the overhang at 250ft which had stopped Raeburn.

On August 30, Symmers was back in Ballater bent on making the ascent. According to Ewen, he had been training at Almscliff and on railway bridges.

With Symmers in the lead they followed a rising line rightwards up slabs, ledges, grooves and short walls until they reached the hanging chimney, which although steep and loose, yielded with care. The crux occurred lower down where a thin traverse had to be made using small finger holds and an "intermediate minute scratch"[16] for one nail. They celebrated gaining easy ground by constructing a small cairn on the vegetated platform. The remainder of the climb was already known to them and they completed it in very little time.

Their climb on Shadow B (Severe) was the most difficult buttress route on Lochnagar for a number of years. It never became popular due to its reputation for loose rock. However, it was the easiest line on a major buttress and as such, like many of their other summer ascents, it was destined to become a classic winter route. After Symmers's mother died he never came back to the North-east. His last mountain was the Aonach Eagach which he climbed with his two eldest children in 1946. He died in 1967, aged 61.

Further winter exploration took place in the northern corries of Cairn Gorm during 1935. On March 24, Alexander Henderson and Edwin Davidson climbed the dog-leg gully bounding the left side of the central buttress in Coire an t-Sneachda. Following a narrow initial section they found a fine corridor opening out to the right. Although straightforward, this felt quite alpine as it led to the plateau via a col behind a 30ft pinnacle. Their unusual choice of name, Aladdin's Couloir, well reflects the character of this now very popular snow climb. Once on the plateau they continued westwards to Cairn Lochain and descended into Coire an Lochain by The Couloir, the prominent slanting gully left of Ewen Buttress.

A few weeks' later, on April 13, another MMC party climbed The Vent, the much steeper gully in the left corner of Coire an Lochain. The team comprised John Geddes, Stobart snr, Ed Davidson, Helen Harrison and

Mae MacBain. The cliffs were in very snowy condition but once the fresh snow had been swept aside good ice was revealed below. It took the leader about four hours to cut his way up a 70ft two-tiered ice pitch before arriving at the easy upper gully.[17]

By the mid 1930s the most appealing unclimbed rock in Glen Einich was on the Northern Section of No. 1 Buttress. Perth climber, Alastair Cram claimed he had attempted this Northern Section on no fewer than 14 occasions – each time being thwarted by wintry conditions! The main buttress is split into two ridges by a vegetated central chimney. On one of his attempts Cram climbed on small ledges up the wall left of this central chimney but did not continue. Finally, on July 21, 1935 with Eva Bailey, who was later killed on Scafell Pinnacle leading another girl, he managed to climb the narrow right-hand ridge starting at the foot of the central chimney. His 450ft climb, with a Very Difficult corner low down and airy slabs leading to the buttress crest, took two hours. There was a sting in the tail because an exposed 8ft drop had to be nego-tiated onto a knife edge before easy ground was reached.

Cram was a distinguished advocate as well as an all-round moun-taineer, being a member of the Perth JMCS, the SMC and the Alpine Club. During the war he was captured in the Western Desert and from 1942 he used all his considerable resources on numerous escape bids from POW camps in Italy and Czechoslovakia. Eventually in 1945 he made it to the American lines and was awarded the Military Cross. After the war he became a judge in Kenya and then Malawi before retiring in Scotland.

When Henderson and Davidson made their winter ascent of Aladdin's Couloir they noted the possibility of climbing the left edge of the imposing dome-shaped lower buttress right of the Couloir. This, Aladdin Buttress, is the most prominent feature in Coire an t-Sneachda when viewed from Glenmore. A year after the Couloir ascent they were back on a cold snowy day in April 1936 accompanied by John Geddes and Affleck Gray. Commencing at the foot of the Couloir, Henderson led all the way, starting up a slabby rib and finishing on a steep edge where combined effort was required. (Very Difficult). Once they had all assembled above the last difficulties an easy scramble led to the 30ft pinnacle which they named Aladdin's Seat.[18]

In July 1936, Jim Bell, David Myles, and the New Zealander W.G.McClymont, went to Lochnagar with no particular objective in mind "but in the hope that something good had been overlooked by former visitors. A great buttress of rock with grand, sweeping lines caught the rays of the sun. It rose just beyond the steep rift known as the Douglas Gully".[19] It seems that Bell was unaware of Symmers's 1931 article on Lochnagar in which he named this impressive feature the Eagle's Buttress.[20] He was however, correct in assuming that it was still unclimbed and resolved to attempt it there and then.

Starting just inside the gully they climbed a chimney, then a crack and easier ground, to gain the crest about 90ft up. From there they could see the true crest of the buttress sweeping upwards in an enticing series of walls and interconnected ridges. Immediately above them was an almost vertical, smooth wall. The Douglas-Gibson Gully side looked impossible so they climbed a little gully and another chimney on the west side of the edge hoping to return to the crest as soon as practicable. Bell did reach this at a narrow notch overlooking the Gully, but the ridge above looked "steep, exposed and holdless".

In view of their limited time they decided to abandon the attempt on the crest to pursue a natural, upward traverse on the west face which led to an unavoidable barrier of steeper rock overlooking Parallel Gully A. Here they enjoyed the best climbing of the day up a series of corners and cracks – the outcome in doubt right up to the top. In Bell's own words, the first ascent of Eagle Buttress had taken "a sort of flank attack".[21] The obvious challenge of a more direct ascent of the main ridge still remained.

The late 1930s revival of winter climbing in the West of Scotland led to a re-think about equipment. Ropes 120ft long were introduced and ice axe shafts were shortened to make it easier to wield the axe on steep ice. In 1937, which was one of the great snow years, one weekend in March, Edinburgh climber Archie Hendry made the first winter ascent of Chokestone Gully on Sgòr an Lochain Uaine. The hardest part of the weekend for Hendry was crossing the Devil's Elbow on his bicycle! Quite by chance he met a Glaswegian called Andy in Corrour Bothy and they teamed up for the climb. It was the most difficult winter gully in the Cairngorms at the time, now graded at III.

For almost 50 years the Cairngorm Club had been the only climbing club based in Aberdeen, yet for some time a few enthusiasts had felt that there was both scope and demand for another. The type of club envisaged was one which would be inexpensive and which would provide transport as near to the hills as roads permitted. Nothing came of these dreams until George Beck-Slinn, William Lawson, Garth Lorimer and others learned of the Lomond Mountaineering Club. This club had started by running lorries to climbing centres accessible from Glasgow. Members found their own accommodation and they were completely free to climb when and where they wished. This was the type of club they wanted and after a successful trial meet to Auchallater an inaugural meeting was held in Aberdeen on March 17, 1938. According to Beck-Slinn: "The Lomond Club had so caught our fancy that we resolved to name our club in similar fashion. We would make the name a link with the Cairngorms, those grand hills so near our door. Many suggestions were made. However, Loch Etchachan seemed to have the greater appeal, and a vote left the matter in no doubt. Henceforth we were 'the Etchachan Club'."[22]

A month after the formation of the Etchachan Club (EC), Jim Bell with Ernest Roberts and Denis Howe climbed the left-hand ridge on the Northern Section of No. 1 Buttress in Glen Einich. April 24, was a day of perfect weather for rock climbing and they were able to keep close to the edge overlooking the Willow Spout. They climbed a steep lower wall by a difficult chimney then moderate rock led to an upper wall climbed by a long crack, the highlight of the route. At the top they joined Cram's Route before the 8ft drop to reach the easy upper slopes. They named their climb Robert's Ridge in honour of their friend's 64th birthday. It was graded Severe and for many years it was considered the best and most popular rock climb in Glen Einich.

Bell was back in the Cairngorms in mid-June. After a night at Thistle

Jack Scott belayed by Jack Scroggie on Three J Chimney in July 1938, the first climb on the Red Craigs in Glen Clova

Photo: John Ferguson

Cottage, Inverey, he had a long day alone on Braeriach and Cairn Toul where he climbed the Black Pinnacle by a more direct route following a 40ft crack. On his return to Deeside he made a promised call back at Inverey to see Maggie Gruer. Her home, Thistle Cottage, was the best known hostelry in the area and the grand lady herself was the friend to generations of walkers and climbers in the Cairngorms. She welcomed them at all hours of the day and night, and somehow there was always room for everyone. This was the last time Bell saw her for she died at her home the following March at the age of 77.

In July 1938, Jack Scroggie, Jack Scott and John Ferguson climbed a 40ft Very Difficult chimney on the south-east buttress of the Red Craig in Glen Clova. Their climb, Three J Chimney, was the first recorded on these very accessible south-facing crags above the road just before Braedownie. The three Js were all members of the Corrie Club of Dundee,

The right flank of Tough-Brown Ridge in summer showing the terrain down which Bell and Murray descended in May 1939. Their descent later became known as Backdoor Route, now a popular winter climb following the obvious black central groove

Photo: Greg Strange

formed in 1936 by Scott and Kenny McLaren. According to Jim Cosgrove the club was a small informal group of climbers which disbanded during the Second World War. Syd Scroggie, (Jack's brother), said: "The Corrie Club I think of as having had a kind of phantom existence, no funds, no equipment, no transport, a few members, but they had the odd meet." Jack Scott was an engineer in the Caledon Yard and Kenny McLaren was a commercial artist. Other members included Jim Nisbet, Gordon and Doug Beedie, Jim Cosgrove, twins Jack and Syd Scroggie and John Ferguson.

It was while travelling north over the Devil's Elbow in late May 1939 that Jim Bell made his now famous statement: "Any fool can climb good rock but it takes craft and cunning to get up vegetatious schist and granite." His companion, Bill Murray, was disinclined to argue since in his own words "they were bound for Lochnagar the greatest citadel of vegetatious granite".[23] The weather was glorious and at Bell's suggestion they planned to go straight to the summit, make a new route down the cliffs of the Tough-Brown ridge, and then if all went well, make an ascent of the unclimbed Parallel Buttress. The programme was ambitious enough, but nothing seemed impossible that morning.

After sleeping out in Glen Callater they approached the plateau via Cairn Taggart and by midday were starting the descent of Tough-Brown Ridge. The easy upper section was followed for several hundred feet, passing the point where the original line came up from the right. The ridge soon broadened to a buttress and the climbing became more difficult. Finding the easiest line was tricky but generally trended towards the Raeburn's Gully side. Some 200ft from the scree they were eventually faced with steep convex granite devoid of holds and belays and were forced to turn sharply left towards Raeburn's Gully. They managed to descend steep, difficult rock immediately right of a prominent mossy scoop. This led to a point just below the bend in Raeburn's Gully – 150ft above its foot.

By its nature this climb later became known as Backdoor Route. The main challenge of the ridge direct and of the formidable wall of slabs to its left would have to wait for a more conventional attack from below. In 1993, when Murray was asked if they had carried out any investigation prior to their descent, he said they did not. This is surprising when you consider that even today an attempted direct descent without abseiling seems very ambitious. When asked about this Murray said: "We did not expect to be forced into Raeburn's Gully, in the sense that we gave our prospects no thought other than to try to get down, for we were both confident in ourselves and in each other, that we would be able to extricate ourselves if we ran into rock we couldn't climb. And so it turned out."

After the excitement of the descent they spent some time swimming in the loch and sunbathing before turning their attention back to the cliffs. Parallel Buttress is the attractive flat-faced piece of rock tapering to a narrow ridge about 150ft below the plateau. It lies centrally at the back of the corrie sandwiched between Parallel Gully A and B. At about one-third height the buttress is crossed by the easy traverse used by Tough and Brown to reach the upper section of their ridge. Climbing unroped, Bell and Murray attempted the steep rocks at the base of the buttress but were unsuccessful. They were forced to move left and climb by rocks just left of the waterfall issuing from Gully A. They then ascended obliquely up to the right, crossing Gully A above its lower basin. This oblique ascent continued until they reached the formidable middle band of slabs which girdle Parallel Buttress. There was no way through on the left or centrally, but there was a weakness on the Gully B face.

"Our only hope was to turn them by a right-hand traverse along a thin and vegetatious ledge to the extreme edge of the gully. There, on the actual brink, we found a breach in the defences and climbed for a moment with our heels projecting over the gloomy depths. A short upward scramble, a slanting traverse up a long scoop in the gully wall and the crest was ours once more."[24]

Progress continued reasonably well until the buttress finally narrowed to a ridge below a very difficult looking 30ft tower with vertical drops on either side. At this point they roped up. The only route lay up the frontal convex slab which was holdless except for one finger-wide crack on the left. Murray tried first but after eight feet had to retreat there being no holds. On Bell's attempt he came to the same conclusion and it looked as if the tower was going to see them off.

"However, we still had one last card to play. Bell dug into his rucksack and produced – I wish that I could write in a whisper – two pitons. Their use is frowned upon by many British mountaineers. Like the Queen of Spain's legs, a piton not only ought never to be seen, but must not be supposed even to exist. Its use, in fact, should be sparing and reserved for exceptional circumstances. Bell and I solemnly declared that this was an exceptional circumstance."[25] Bell climbed back up and with a small hammer drove a ring piton into the thin crack. He then contrived to stand on its head and placed another piton in a horizontal crack to the left. This he only used as a handhold to swarm up to a spike in a recess below the final overhang. Here he discovered a hidden ledge on the left with a good belay. Murray then followed removing the two pitons and managing to pass the position of the first without aid from the rope. He then attempted to cross right below the overhang but once again found no purchase for his nails and had to return to the ledge. At this point Bell decided to remove his boots and succeeded in crossing this severe traverse in stocking soles. A short, steep chimney gave access to the top of the tower. To save time Murray kept his boots on and, as he expected from his first attempt, he required a constant tight rope for the traverse. After the tower there were no more difficulties. An easy scramble and a beautiful knife-edge of snow led them directly to the top which they reached at 5pm.

Two hours was a very fast time for this 700ft climb. Perfect dry conditions had enabled them to solo all but the tower. The use of pitons was unprecedented at that time in the Cairngorms and when asked abut this somewhat controversial action Murray said in 1993: "Bell was always more ruthless than me in the use of pitons. Left to myself, I'd have turned away from the tower and left it to a better climber or else used rubbers. I carried no pitons (except in winter) and did not know Bell had any until he fetched them out and drove them in."

With more than 50 years of hindsight he felt that the tower could have been done in one run-out without nailing the rock, but at the time they had not known this.

"Had we gone to do it again we'd have used no pitons. My own view now is that we should have left the climb to bolder climbers, or else, changed into rubbers before starting up the tower in which event I'd have climbed it, although finding it Very Severe. We had behaved like lazy climbers, taking the easy way out. But we did have a great day!"(The tower is graded Severe. It is doubtful if it was ever led in nails without the use of one piton)

At about the time of the Parallel Buttress ascent, possibly a little later in the summer of 1939, another important climb was made on the north side of the Cairngorms. The largest and most westerly buttress in Coire an Lochain sports a fair area of clean steep rock with no obvious easy lines of weakness. A closer inspection reveals that the aspect facing Ewen Buttress is riven by several corners which cut straight up through the striking horizontally jointed granite. In the back of the largest corner and hidden from the normal approach from Glenmore is a very impressive crack. It was this crack that had become the focus of attention for two young climbers from Inverness, Richard Frere and Kenneth Robertson. They had first been told about 'the long crack in the buttress above the Red Slab' by either John Geddes or Ed Davidson, and it was while climbing in Coire an Lochain during the previous winter that they had seen it for themselves, as a long narrow slit full of snow, and blocked by a chokestone near the top.

Their first opportunity to try the crack was blessed with fine sunny weather. Nevertheless, despite these favourable conditions they were both quite taken aback by its forbidding appearance when seen at close quarters. They rested a while after the walk up from Glenmore Lodge and took some refreshment. Then leaving the sacks behind and wearing plimsolls Frere climbed the steep moderate rock to gain the base of the fissure. Here he was surprised to find how narrow the initial section of the crack was and only after spending some time freeing his foot, which had become jammed, did he manage to climb this awkward 20ft passage to gain a small, jammed stone and a stance from which to bring up Robertson.

The true nature of the crack was now apparent. According to Frere it was a fantastic place. "The stone over which we had clambered was but one of hundreds that lay along the floor of the fissure. The crack was, in reality, a vertical slit in the buttress and from our present position it would have been possible to penetrate horizontally into the mountain for as much as 15 yards." [26]

For the next 15ft they were able to scramble up the bed of the fault to reach another jammed stone. Above this, the slit was wide enough to climb by back and foot technique. It rose vertically for 40ft to where it was roofed in by the very large square-cut chokestone which they had noted the previous winter. The angle seemed to lie back beyond that.

They decided that since Frere was the taller he should continue in the lead. So, while Robertson scuttled into the mountain to belay, Frere began to work his way upwards within the slit, utilising good holds near the outside edge. After 10 minutes, he was below the chokestone and wondering how best to surmount the obstacle. He was reluctant to quit the apparent security of the enclosing walls and went for the inside route, spending some anxious moments struggling behind the huge block before eventually sliding out onto its top. With great feelings of elation he called for Robertson to follow and soon they were both standing on the chokestone. "We felt the full sense of exposure: for it was as though we stood upon a bridge over the tremendous drop." [27]

The final 60 or 70ft of the crack was straightforward. At the top they built a cairn on the square pinnacle of rock which is separated from the plateau by the narrow fault up whose eastern side they had just climbed. They gave their climb the appropriate name of the Savage Slit, and although only 180ft long it is a route of great character following an impeccable line – one of the best climbs in the country – Severe.

During 1939, members of the Corrie Club continued to explore in Glen Clova. In August, Ferguson met Bill Ward of the Climber's Club in the Clova Youth Hostel – he was in the area while attending a meeting of the British Association in Dundee. They got talking, and Ferguson suggested that he might like to try some of the unclimbed lines on the Red Craig. As a result, on August 27, Ward led the classic Severe routes Hanging Lum and Flake Route, the latter still considered one of the best climbs in the glen with its delightfully exposed and delicate crux moves above the celebrated flake. According to Syd Scroggie the climb was known for a while as Ward's Wall.

Just a few weeks' later the Nation was once again at war with Germany. There had been just 21 years of peace and now young men were again being called to fight for our allies in Europe, against the Nazi tyranny.

Syd Scroggie, belayed by John Ferguson, making the second ascent of Flake Route on the Red Craig in Glen Clova, March 1940

Photo: Jack Scroggie

1. SMCJ Vol. 19, No 110, p135.
2. SMC *The Cairngorms* Third Edition 1950, p184.
3. CCJ No. 70, Jan 1931, p191.
4. CCJ No. 70, Jan 1931, p193.
5. CCJ No. 70, Jan 1931, p195.
6. SMCJ Vol. 19, No. 113, p253.
7. SMCJ Vol. 19, No. 113, p244.
8. SMCJ Vol. 20, No. 115, p9.
9. CCJ Vol. 13, No. 75, p192.
10. Information from Menlove. *The Life of John Menlove Edwards*. (Jim Perrin. 1984).
11. SMCJ Vol. 20, No 120, p412.
12. SMCJ Vol. 20, No. 117, p186.
13. SMCJ Vol. 33, No. 175, p91.
14. SMCJ Vol. 20, No. 116, p154.
15. Moray Mountaineering Club Journal (MMCJ) No. 1, p36.
16. CCJ Vol. 14, No. 76, p17.
17. MMCJ No. 1, p45.
18. MMCJ No. 2, p40.
19. *A Progress in Mountaineering*, p256 (J.H.B.Bell).
20. CCJ Vol. 12, No. 70, p186.
21. *A Progress in Mountaineering*, p259.
22. Etchachan Club Journal No. 1, p1.
23. *Mountaineering in Scotland*, p122 (W.H.Murray).
24. *Mountaineering in Scotland*, p126 – 127.
25. *Mountaineering in Scotland*, p126 – 127.
26. *Thoughts of a Mountaineer*, p89 – 100 (R.B.Frere).
27. *Thoughts of a Mountaineer*, p89 – 100.

4: The Second World War (1940 – 1945)

IN AUGUST 1940, Corrie Club members, Syd Scroggie and John Ferguson had ambitious plans when they set out for a few days climbing on Lochnagar. They had recently made the second ascent of Flake Route in Glen Clova and were in good form for attempting a new route. Ferguson had enlarged a photograph of the cliff and had worked out a possible line up the crest of Eagle Buttress. On August 9, undaunted by wet and windy weather, they started on their attempt to straighten out Bell's climb. Scroggie says that they were well up the new line by midday: "Wet through, we sat snugly belayed on a little ledge, Douglas Gully on one side, Parallel Gully on the other, and above our heads, dimly visible in the mist, bulging rock challenging us to find a way, if we could summon up enough nerve."[1]

"Dimly visible in the mist, bulging rock challenging us to find a way, if we could summon up enough nerve"
– Syd Scroggie

The exact location of their little ledge is uncertain, but Ferguson's description confirmed that the climbing above the point where the pioneers abandoned the crest was Severe and on excellent rock. It appears that they climbed what is now known as the tower, starting with a swing up right into a scoop, then by steep, exposed climbing to reach the crest just below a holdless slab. Some way above this they also had to give best to the true line and a traverse was made to the right before a crack led back to the crest. Easy slabs on the left soon took them to the top. This was an impressive achievement by young Scroggie who led the whole route. Climbing wet Lochnagar granite can be most precarious even in stocking soles and it was hardly surprising that he used four pitons. Given better weather, he believed they would have been able to follow the crest all the way.

Unfortunately, Syd was never able to return to what is now Eagle Ridge. He was called up for the war effort and became a lieutenant in the Lovat Scouts. Just before the war ended he was blown up by a land mine in Italy and lost a leg as well as his sight. He spent many years after the war convalescing then rehabilitating, and eventually, with that same spirit and athletic frame which enabled him to succeed on Eagle Buttress in the rain, he learned to walk again and once more became a regular hill man, tramping the braes and glens that he so loved.

By the summer of 1940, interest in the buttresses of Sgoran Dubh was waning. There was, however, still no direct climb on the 150ft high Northern Rampart of No. 1 Buttress. This, the steepest piece of rock in the glen was still inviolate – a fact that had not escaped the notice of one of Scotland's most promising young climbers – Henry Ian Ogilvy.

Ogilvy had recently graduated from Cambridge University and was waiting to be called up to the Seaforth Highlanders. In the space of less than a year he had made first ascents of three very bold and difficult climbs on the Rannoch Wall of Buachaille Etive Mòr with his fiancée, Esme Speakman (Satan's Slit, Red Slab and January Jigsaw) and four new routes on Ben Nevis with Cambridge companions. Although most of his school and college days were spent in England his family home was in Aviemore.

He had been to the No. 1 Buttress on Sgoran Dubh at Easter 1940 with the Dundee climber, Graham Ritchie, and had taken the opportunity to observe the Northern Rampart at close quarters. Two months later after a successful traverse of Rannoch Wall on the Buachaille, Ogilvy asked Richard Frere if he knew about the steep face to the left of the gully on the first buttress of Sgoran Dubh. Frere said that he did and referred to it as "a vile spot".[2] Ogilvy agreed, but said that he thought it would go on a fine day in plimsolls. The two friends made plans to attempt the Northern Rampart as soon as practicable. That was the last time Frere was to see Ogilvy.

Apparently, on August 18, 1940, Ogilvy and a companion, Charity Lucy Scott-Robson, went to Sgoran Dubh and made a completely new climb up the full height of the Northern Rampart. The only information about the climb was taken from Ogilvy's notes and recorded in the 1940 CUMCJ.[3] A month later, the two climbers returned to Sgoran Dubh, and as they did not return that night a search party was organised. Their bodies were found the next day in the deep cleft of the Willow Spout.

Since both climbers were killed in this tragedy nothing is known of how, or from, where they fell, but it was thought at the time that they were attempting another new route on the ridge to the left of the Willow Spout which leads to the very steep right-hand prow of the Northern Rampart. Ogilvy's route in August was the first recorded Very Severe rock climb in the Cairngorms. As such, one would have expected it to be well known, yet this is not the case and the climb itself may never have been repeated. Richard Frere made several visits to Sgoran Dubh in an attempt to trace the line on the Northern Rampart. Apart from a rusty piton low down on the cliff he was not successful. He found no natural route on what was partly grass with steep rocky outcrops. In the mid-1950s Tom Patey, climbing alone while checking for a new guidebook, attempted the first depression left of the steepest section of the Rampart and had to abandon the line at the second of two overhangs, describing the rock as treacherous.

Little is known about Lucy Scott-Robson. Frere had never met her although she was known to his parents. She was laid to rest at New Hadden. Ian Ogilvy's love of the mountains probably originated at Eton, then while at Cambridge he joined the University Mountaineering Club becoming secretary in October 1939, and president in January 1940. Ian was the adopted son of Sir Herbert Ogilvy Bart of Inverquerity. He is buried alongside his father in a small family enclosure on the North side of Loch Pityoulish, looking out to Glen Einich and Sgoran Dubh.

In the second full year of the war very little exploration took place in the Cairngorms, except during a short period at the end of July 1941 when Jim Bell and Nancy Forsyth accounted for at least six separate climbs in the North-east corrie of Lochnagar and a major new route on Creag an Dubh-loch. Commencing on Lochnagar they ascended both Shadow Buttresses, making a direct start to Buttress A and a completely new line on the steep lower half of Buttress B. Bell must then have felt ready to tackle what was probably the main objective of their visit – a completely direct ascent of Eagle Ridge. He had clearly been impressed by Scroggie and Ferguson's achievement in wet conditions the previous year, yet despite his claim that he "had little hope of doing better"[4]

Nancy Forsyth, Suilven at Easter, 1939

Photo: Ilse Bell, LSCC Archives

he must really have been quietly optimistic in view of the fine weather and very dry rock.

On July 24, he and Forsyth set off following the same initial pitches that he had taken in 1936. Quite low down they picked up a piton lying loose on a ledge and some way higher they came across a little cairn left by the Corrie Club men at the point where they had reached the crest. Above the cairn a narrow ridgeway swept up to vertical rocks at the start of the tower and here Bell found it necessary to pull up into a smooth groove.

"Here we found another piton, securely fixed in a crack of the rock. I was unable to move it. In the prevailing conditions, with dry rocks, I was able to climb the pitch without touching the piton. The former party, of course, had vile conditions of rain and wet rocks, and the piton was well placed for securing the leader's rope over the next 40ft of severe climbing."[5] The tower provided a steep, exhilarating pitch which finished with a hard pull up into a secure niche. After the tower the crest became temporarily less steep. A smooth knife-edge and a whaleback formation led them on to the next steep wall where a difficult crack on the left could be climbed back up to the sharp crest. Bell went up the crack and found himself in a dramatically exposed position.

"On my left was a sheer drop, slightly undercut, into the depths of Douglas Gully. The knife-edge crest on which I was sitting astride was neatly fitted to the middle of a triangle of blank, vertical cliff in front."[6] Bell was now contemplating the crux of Eagle Ridge, a route which by then he must have realised was destined to become one of the country's great classic climbs. The wall ahead was only 10ft high, yet apart from the crack it appeared holdless.

At the top of the wall, and slightly to the left, was a sloping scoop with a raised edge on its left side. If that edge provided a sharp, incut handhold it could be used for pulling up. He wrestled with his conscience for a moment then took of his boots, lowered them in a rucksack to his second, drove the piton which they had found into the crack with a handy lump of granite, and clipped in his rope with a snaplink.

"My right foot had a good hold, but not a high one. The hold for the left foot sloped badly. By raising my right hand to a higher crack on the face it was possible to get my left foot up to a small toecrack. Here the balance was extremely delicate, as I reached up with my left hand and grabbed the edge of the coping above the scoop. It was a perfect hold. My right foot used the piton as a steady while I heaved myself up, pulling now with both hands side by side on the coping and hunching up my knees on to the scoop. There is no pausing in such a situation, for the scoop had only press and friction holds. Persistent effort, friction and wriggling put me in reach of another perfect handhold and I was safe."[7]

After the boots and sack had been hauled up Forsyth managed to knock out the piton and follow the crux moves without being pulled. The ridge continued to provide interesting sustained climbing above the crux with another short section being climbed in stocking soles. Eventually, they reached easy slabs leading up right to the plateau.

"We had enjoyed three and a half hours of the very best of rock climbing, without any halt, for about 700ft of ascent. We felt a luxurious and contented fatigue settle down upon us. The strain of the climbing, unheeded at the time, had left its mark. We had not come upon any further traces of the passage of the Dundee men, so we could not tell where they had left or regained the crest of the ridge, but we felt certain that everything above and including the crucial pitch was virgin ground."[8]

Bell had another score to settle on Lochnagar which had resulted from his attempt with Murray to descend directly down the Tough-Brown Ridge. He must have seen enough on that occasion to convince himself that a possible line lay on the extreme right edge of the very imposing lower slabs.

Climbing without sacks he and Forsyth started just inside Raeburn's Gully and followed a line of slabs and vegetated grooves to reach a prominent narrow raking terrace. The only apparent line of weakness lay a few feet up to the right where exceedingly steep slabs rose in three ill-defined steps. From the top of a perched block Bell moved onto the slabs.

Eagle Ridge, Lochnagar

Photo: Scott Muir

"Persistent effort, friction and wriggling put me in reach of another perfect handhold and I was safe." – Jim Bell

Jim and Pat Bell
on the crux pitch
of Eagle Ridge,
May 1948

Photo: William Thompson

An ascent of the
impressive frontal
face of the Black
Spout Pinnacle was
becoming the 'last
great problem'
of Lochnagar

"After the second step one is standing in a smooth, shallow scoop and all handholds have vanished. The leader here discarded boots. On the right was an edge above a vertical wall. It was necessary to lean across this and drive a piton into a crack in the wall. A stone was used for this purpose. Even in stockings the balance was most delicate and the friction doubtful. The problem is to stand on the piton and reach up to a rounded, flat ledge in order to swarm up on to it. There is a good pulling-edge beyond, but it is a very severe pitch."[9] This very hard pitch brought them out from the steep lower slabs onto the easy ground from where they descended the Backdoor Route.

Bell thought that the crux pitch of this, the Tough-Brown Ridge Direct, was the hardest that they had done on Lochnagar. Later ascents of both this and Eagle Ridge confirmed his assessment. In May 1948 he climbed Eagle Ridge again, this time with his wife, Pat. On this ascent he managed to lead the crux without using the piton for aid. A year later two young Aberdeen climbers, Doug Sutherland and Bill Brooker climbed both Eagle Ridge and Tough-Brown Direct. They also found the piton unnecessary on Eagle Ridge but had a hard struggle on the crux of Tough-Brown even using the in-situ piton for aid. Brooker, who seconded the pitch, said that at the time he could not imagine how Bell had managed to put the piton in! Tough-Brown Direct retains its Very Severe rating to this day where it is considered technically 4c in modern rock boots.

An ascent of the impressive frontal face of the Black Spout Pinnacle was becoming the 'last great problem' of Lochnagar. So far no-one had had any success and now even Bell concluded: "There was no feasible start below the entrance of the left branch."[10] On a day marred by a thick, wet mist he and Forsyth spent some time searching for a chink in the armour. It was not until they turned up into the left branch that they noticed a possibility in the form of a long, narrow chimney between an expanse of smooth, steep slab on the left and a vertical wall on the right, well left of the chimney-line attempted by Raeburn. Bell succeeded in climbing the chimney.

"It is nearly 100ft long, and has an awkward entry from below and a narrow, difficult section more than halfway up. At the top one is on a little ridge projecting outwards from the upper, vertical cliff. I prospected beyond, along the face and downwards, hoping to turn a corner to the right and so effect an ascent, but the exposure was severe and the project abandoned."[11] They returned to the Left-hand Branch and from a point just above its pitch finally managed to climb to the Pinnacle summit by a long shallow, vegetated gully, left of Pinnacle Gully 2. This rather loose climb later became known as Slab Gully.

The keeper at the Spittal of Glen Muick had told Bell and Forsyth that he had heard climbers praising the rock climbing possibilities on Creag an Dubh-loch. Apparently, the quality of the rock there was much sounder than on Lochnagar. Bell had gone to Creag an Dubh-loch to investigate but found the huge main face of the crag most intimidating and he held little hope of finding a route there. Nevertheless, on what was probably the last day of their visit, July 27, he and Forsyth walked to the Dubh Loch and discussed matters. According to Bell: "The first glint of faith I owe to my partner, who thought there was a sort

Sandy Tewnion at Corrour Bothy in July 1950

Photo: A. Tewnion

of a break in the cliff wall just short of the big expanse of lower slabs, beyond which was the scree shoot emanating from Central Gully. The intuition proved brilliantly right, and the result was a splendid rock climb of continuous difficulty."[12]

The break which Forsyth had noted was a long, slightly curving groove which ended in a formidable cul-de-sac some 200ft below the plateau. To the left of the cul-de-sac lay a huge amphitheatre like a small hanging corrie. They managed to climb the lower groove more or less directly with at least two Severe sections. When they neared the grassy slope of the amphitheatre the only way seemed to lie up steep ribs and grooves between the back wall of the amphitheatre and the vertical left wall of the cul-de-sac. This proved to be the case with a series of pitches, some Severe, following "a tortuous route through an inner amphitheatre of the crags" with the issue in doubt almost to the end. "The rock proved to be excellent, the rock scenery magnificent with gradually extending vistas over the Dubh Loch and Loch Muick."[13]

Their climb which they named The Labyrinth was 900ft long and ended on the plateau close to the summit of Creag an Dubh-loch. It was a fitting climax to their foray in the North-east. The Labyrinth was the first major rock climb on Creag an Dubh-loch and a tribute to Bell's route-finding skills.

While exploring the Garbh Choire Mòr of Braeriach in September 1941, Sandy and Sydney Tewnion, with Sandy McArthur, succeeded in climbing the Pinnacles Buttress, attempted by Parker and Alexander in 1924. As youngsters, the Tewnions often visited their grandfather's farm at Blackhills, Longhaven, on the Aberdeenshire coast. Later, after they had started rock climbing they made the first climbs on the Longhaven sea cliffs between 1939 and 1941, including the feature known as Scimitar Ridge.

As well as the Tewnions, another young Aberdeen climber was fascinated by the great amphitheatre of An Garbh Choire. Bill Hendry, a medical student at Aberdeen University had been introduced to the hills by his parents. It was the reference in Alexander's guide to two miles

Slugain Bothy in 1942. It was burned down by Invercauld Estate in 1944

Photo: Malcolm Smith

Sandy Tewnion became 'famous' as the man who fired his service revolver at the Grey Man while fleeing from the apparition on the Macdui plateau during wartime leave in October 1943

of cliffs with very few climbs that inspired Hendry and George Lumsden to plan a 10 day expedition to Braeriach in August 1942. On their way they spent a couple of nights beside Derry Lodge at the summer camp of the recently constituted Aberdeen University Lairig Club. This, the third climbing club in the city, had been formed in 1940 from a previous university organisation called the Open Air Club.

By the end of their stay in the Garbh Choire they had climbed seven unrecorded gullies and chimneys, including the first rock climb on the steep slabby wall of Garbh Choire Dhaidh to the right of the Dee waterfall (The Chimney Pot). At some stage during the 10 days they were lucky to meet in with Sandy Tewnion with whom they joined forces on several climbs. It was on the Braeriach Pinnacle that they made their best discovery. All previous ascents of the Pinnacle had been on the south face, but they were attracted by the steep, left edge overlooking Central Buttress Gully.

From just below the gully's bifurcation they moved up right to a platform on the edge. Here they were confronted by a steep, exposed wall which appeared holdless at the start. After some discussion it was decided that since Tewnion was the tallest and strongest he should provide the ladder for the others.

Sandy recalled: "Bill climbed first on my shoulders, then my head (I put on a balaclava) and finally onto my up stretched hands, and then he reached a secure stance. Geordie climbed over me similarly, held on the rope above by Bill. Finally, I climbed up the rope to join the other two."

Above this, Tewnion led up the exposed edge more or less directly until a left traverse on the gully face gave access to horizontal ledges and the final easy crest to the summit. The steep main section of the climb provided 250ft of sustained climbing and was by far the best rock climb on Braeriach at that time. West Wall Route, as it became known, is graded Severe and is still considered one of the classics of the western Cairngorms.

The following day, Sandy Tewnion had to return to Aberdeen and report back to the Army. Unfortunately, he never had the opportunity to climb with anyone again. In the summer of 1944 he was so badly wounded in action that real climbing was no longer an option. He did, however, continue his passion for the high tops of the Cairngorms, studying and photographing birds of the Alpine zone, in particular the snow bunting and dotterel. He also became 'famous' as the man who fired his service revolver at the Grey Man while fleeing from the apparition on the Macdui plateau during wartime leave in October 1943. Sandy was Principal Teacher of Biology at Dollar Academy for many years until his retirement.

In late 1942, the commander of the Special Services Brigade invited Frank Smythe to form a school where Commandos could receive training in mountain and winter warfare. Smythe chose the Cairngorms and set up a base in the Fife Arms Hotel in Braemar. In June 1943, several visits were made to the Garbh Coire of Beinn a' Bhùird where half a dozen separate ascents were made of Mitre Ridge. One notable climb was that by Sergeant-Major Langlands, who soloed the Direct

Route via Ludwig's start, under the impression that it had not been done before. On another occasion, Langlands and David Cox descended the North-West Gully alongside the vertical west wall of Mitre Ridge and made a new climb up the corner to the right of Cumming-Crofton Route. This, the second climb on the West Face of Mitre Ridge was later named Commando Route by Malcolm Smith. Also climbed was the South-East Gully which defines the south side of Mitre Ridge. This was the work of John Hunt (of Everest) and A.Y.Greenhalgh. They found it quite straightforward except that there were few ledges or belays.[14] Later in 1943, the Arctic and Winter Warfare unit moved from Braemar to St Ives in Cornwall and became known as the Commando Cliff Assault Centre.

Towards the end of the war several well-frequented Cairngorm both-ies were destroyed. A particular favourite with local climbers was the timber-slatted Slugain Bothy which stood 100 yards beyond the ruined Slugain Lodge at the head of the Fairy Glen. It was an excellent base from which to climb and walk on Ben A'an and Beinn a' Bhùird. Unfortunately, the estate factor found Farquharson plaids in the bothy in 1944 and had the place burned down. The plaids had been stolen from Alltdourie cottage near Invercauld House. The original Slugain Lodge was built in 1845 and stood higher up, facing Beinn a' Bhùird.[15] The existing ruin, built as a replacement in 1875, had already been abandoned by the time Alexander wrote his guide in 1928.[16]

It was at about this time that both Upper and Lower Einich bothies also met their demise, the lower being burned in mysterious circumstances and the upper blown down in a storm.

After the departure of the commandos in 1943 there was to be no further exploratory climbing in the Cairngorms for almost three years. Excepting perhaps in the imaginations of those deprived of their hill-going by the duties and privations of wartime.

Bill Malcolm ensconced in Slugain Bothy, December 1931

Photo: Roy Symmers

1. *The Cairngorms Scene and Unseen,* p115.
2. *Thoughts of a Mountaineer,* p146 (R.B.Frere).
3. Cambridge Mountaineering 1940, p50
4. *A Progress in Mountaineering – The Eagle Ridge of Lochnagar.* Now included in *Bell's Scottish Climbs* (1988).
5. *A Progress in Mountaineering – The Eagle Ridge of Lochnagar.* Now included in *Bell's Scottish Climbs* (1988).
6. *A Progress in Mountaineering – The Eagle Ridge of Lochnagar.* Now included in *Bell's Scottish Climbs* (1988).
7. *A Progress in Mountaineering – The Eagle Ridge of Lochnagar.* Now included in *Bell's Scottish Climbs* (1988).
8. *A Progress in Mountaineering – The Eagle Ridge of Lochnagar.* Now included in *Bell's Scottish Climbs* (1988).
9. SMCJ Vol. 23, No 133, p28 – 34.
10. SMCJ Vol. 23, No 133, p28 – 34.
11. SMCJ Vol. 23, No 133, p28 – 34.
12. SMCJ Vol. 23, No 133, p28 – 34.
13. SMCJ Vol. 23, No 133, p28 – 34.
14. Climber's Club Journal Vol. 7, No. 2, p166 – 167.
15. CCJ Vol. 1, p249.
16. *The Cairngorms* (1928), p163.

5: The New Found Playground (1945 – 1949)

IT TOOK SOME time for the nation to re-adjust to peace after six years of disruption by war. For some of the newly demobilised walkers and climbers in Aberdeen the New Year of 1945 – 46 was the first opportunity to get away from the city and spend a few days in the hills. Robertson's Bothy in Glen Muick and Luibeg Bothy near Derry Lodge were both frequented at this time.

At Easter 1946, members of the EUMC made several snow climbs in Coire an t-Sneachda, including the now popular gully known as The Runnel. In May, two of that club's best climbers, Derek Haworth and George Ritchie spent a few days in Glen Muick. At Creag an Dubh-loch they made a rather disappointing climb on the North-West Buttress, well right of the main face. The following day, despite fresh snow, they went to Lochnagar and climbed the West Buttress by a route approximating to the rib on the left of West Gully. Their climb, Gargoyle Direct, was for many years one of the more popular rock climbs on Lochnagar, being open, sunny and on fairly clean rock. Unfortunately, a rockfall in the 1970s spoiled the original crux pitch.

It was while returning home to Edinburgh from Lochnagar on Haworth's motorbike that an amusing incident occurred. In the gloaming, anxious to catch the ferry, Haworth misjudged a bend somewhere in Glen Shee and went through a hedge into someone's garden. The lights in the house were switching on as they manhandled the bike back through the hedge and roared off down the road. Ritchie had to keep wiping stuff off his head but did not give it much thought, until they were on the last ferry over the Forth when Haworth expressed concern at Ritchie's blood covered face, only to discover that the blood was his own. He had torn his scalp back on breaching the hedge and the slipstream delivered the gore across Ritchie.[1]

By 1947 quite a number of hill folk from Aberdeen were regularly weekending in the Cairngorms. It was not uncommon for those with the time, to cycle to Ballater or Braemar, stay a night or two in a bothy, and have a day on the hill, then cycle back to Aberdeen, hopefully, in time for work on Monday morning. Those who worked in the building trade or the shipyards were not free until Saturday lunchtime. The Deeside bus company, Strachan's of Ballater, recognised this particular demand and laid on a special service to Braemar which left Bon-Accord Square at 3.15pm.

On occasions such as holiday weekends, when demand was high, the bus would continue to the Derry Gates, near the Linn o' Dee. Sometimes two buses were used, one for the passengers, the other for rucksacks. Aberdeen climber, Alan Will, remembers a time when the bus was grounded on the hump-back bridge at Inverey and everyone had to alight via the bridge parapet before the vehicle could move off.

Another mode of transport occasionally used by climbers and walkers was the taxi. It could be hired in Braemar to cover the journey to the Derry Gates. A pick-up time for Sunday could be arranged in order to be back in Braemar at 7pm for the last bus to Aberdeen.

After the war, ex-WD clothing and equipment became readily available in the shops enabling the increasing number of climbers to kit-out inexpensively. Normal equipment included a pair of leather-soled army ammunition boots nailed with tricounis, 120ft of three-quarter weight Italian hemp or hawser-laid British Viking nylon rope (after 1947), ex-army snaplinks (some of the lads who worked in the shipyards made their own), and ex-army ice axes. A very few of the latter which found their way into the shops were German army Aschenbrenners and these were considered a great prize.

Other items of equipment included US reversible parkas, Arnhem jumping jackets, German reversible padded jackets from the Russian Front, camouflaged trousers, puttees, gas capes, (indispensable as groundsheets and as rainproof outer wear), thirty-bob (£1.10/-) skis, US bivies in two halves, US tricounis whose teeth, instead of being brazed, were riveted to their plates, cut down raincoats and even lounge suit waistcoats worn as handy outer jackets in summer. The latter were brought into fashion by Doug Sutherland. Followers of his natty wear were known as the 'Weskit Boys'.

In January 1947, two Etchachan Club members, Sandy Russell and Malcolm (Mac) Smith, together with Bill Stephen were staying at Robertson's Bothy at the Spittal of Glen Muick. Smith, the older and more experienced of the three had started walking and scrambling in the late 1930s before joining the Army, where he served for the duration of the war. On the 26th the three men walked to Creag an Dubh-loch where they hoped to make the first winter ascent of South-East Gully. They found the climb in good winter condition with an ice pitch at the big chokestone where a previous attempt had failed at Easter 1918. Above this, progress was straightforward and after three and a half hours they reached the plateau, avoiding the cornice on the left by a knife edge of snow.[2]

During the summer of this year a new rock climb was made on the 800ft high, flat-topped, Shelter Stone Crag, the single most impressive rock feature in the Cairngorms. For a climber standing boggle-eyed below its concave central prow the upper rocks appear to tilt over the vertical, an illusion which compounds the impression of impregnability. More than 30 years elapsed after Raeburn and Goggs climbed the left-hand pillar before another attempt was made on this formidable bastion. By moving away to the right of the steepest part of the crag it will be seen that the rocks flanking Pinnacle Gully lie at a more amenable angle. Here the main feature of the lower part of the crag is a conspicuous fault known as Clach Dhian Chimney.

In the early 1940s attempts to climb here resulted in two accidents. In 1941 a leader dislodged a loose boulder, injuring the second man. Then in October 1942, James Mitchell, a Glasgow University student, fell a considerable distance and was killed. The Fort William climber, William Thompson, visited the Shelter Stone Crag in August 1947 with a party of students. According to his note in the Shelter Stone visitors' book they succeeded in climbing a line similar to that attempted by Mitchell, finding a broken climbing rope some way up the rocks on the

Mac Smith

Photo: Mac Smith Collection

left of the initial chimney. Above this they moved right and after a fine traverse landed on the buttress on the right of the crag. They then climbed to the summit 'by an indeterminate route'. Thompson reported that the climb, West Wall Route, was of no great difficulty, but that the rock was very shattered.[3]

Just after the war the standard of winter climbing in the Cairngorms was not as advanced as it was in the West. The hard climbs on Ben Nevis and in Glen Coe had not been matched by either local or visiting climbers. This may have been partly due to the belief that ice did not form in the Cairngorms. This, of course, was untrue for although the West, with its significantly higher average rainfall, does have more regularly forming ice features, prolonged freeze-thaw cycles do produce ice in quantity on the buttresses and faces of cliffs in the Cairngorms.

In January 1948, Sydney Tewnion and his younger brother, John, climbed Central Buttress on Lochnagar in winter conditions. Two months later, in March, two Aberdeen University students Peter McIntyre and Anthony Nash made the accepted first winter ascent of West Gully, omitting the large initial icefall by approaching from the midway terrace. A week later, George Ross and Bob Still made a breakthrough when they succeeded in climbing Parallel Gully A, using the Eagle Buttress start and finishing by a hidden left fork.

This awakening of interest in snow and ice climbing was not just seen on Lochnagar. The magnificent eastern corries of Beinn a' Bhùird had long been known for their snow-holding qualities. Coire na Cìche, with its distinctive cup shape and prominent tor, has a steep rocky wall hidden from view on the approach from Invercauld. In the middle of this south wall, just left of an hourglass-shaped buttress, a shallow, curving gully ascends to the plateau. This is Twisting Gully which was climbed on February 28, 1948 by Kenny Milne and two companions, Jimmy Reid and J.Davidson. Kenny worked in the shipyards and was well known among the hill folk, although he did not belong to any particular club or group. His winter ascent of Twisting Gully was the first recorded climb in Coire na Cìche, the most accessible corrie on Beinn a' Bhùird.

Jim Bell made a return visit to Creag an Dubh-loch in May of this year accompanied by his wife, Pat, and William Thompson. On his Labyrinth ascent seven years earlier Bell had noticed a possible climb on the back wall of the high amphitheatre left of upper Labyrinth, a feature which he had named the Hanging Garden. They reached the amphitheatre by exposed scrambling in from the left, passing below a formidable 400ft upper wall. From the top left hand corner of the sloping grassy floor they followed a natural gully and chimney-line up rightwards to finish at the top of Labyrinth.

Hanging Garden Route provided a pleasant climb with good situations and a relatively easy way out of that high mini-corrie. As it turned out, it was Bell's last new climb in the Cairngorms. The next generation of North-east climbers had good cause to be grateful to him. He had pioneered some of the best and most difficult climbs on 'their' crags and spoke and wrote enthusiastically about the Cairngorms, extolling the virtues of climbing on granite. Although Bell made no further new climbs in the Cairngorms he continued to influence future developments as editor of the SMCJ, a position he held for an unprecedented 24 years from 1936 to 1959.

In 1950 his book *A Progress in Mountaineering* was published. He had been commissioned to write a book for young mountaineers to help them technically and inspire them to go from the Scottish mountains to the greater ranges of the world. This concept of progression was something Bell felt very strongly about, for he believed, quite rightly, that the hills of home were an excellent arena in which to learn skills in

Pat Bell

Photo: LSCC Archives

Aberdeen hill folk beside the Black Bridge, Glen Lui 1947. Back, from left: Ada Adams, Kenny. Milne, Isobel Noble and Mac Smith. Front, from left: Mac Graham, Joan Davie, Sandy Russell and Ronnie Repper

Photo: Mac Smith Collection

Luibeg Bothy, May 1948. From left: Sydney Tewnion, Ronny Corbet and John Tewnion

Photo: Sandy Russell

snow, ice and rock-craft as well as route-finding that would stand the test in any climbing area abroad. This outstanding book was essential reading for aspiring Scottish climbers in the 1950s. It included two chapters on the Cairngorms and a full account of the first direct ascent of Eagle Ridge on Lochnagar.

Bell was an industrial chemist by profession and as such his leisure time was relatively limited. According to his wife "his climbing was the most important thing in his life, great refreshment from his working life". He continued to walk and climb well into his 70s starting to count his Munros from his 60th birthday. He died in 1975, aged 79.

The year 1948 saw the opening climbs in Coire Sputan Dearg of Ben Macdui. The footpath to the summit of Macdui via Coire Etchachan and Loch Etchachan skirts the top of Coire Sputan Dearg, the beautiful southeast facing corrie at the head of Glen Luibeg. Why it took so long before exploration started in Sputan Dearg remains a mystery, but a contributory factor may have been a statement in Alexander's guide that the rock of Coire Sputan Dearg "is not suited for climbing, being rounded and devoid of holds", a comment which proved to be completely untrue. There are close on a dozen definable buttresses or ridges of clean, rough granite, separated by the eponymous red scree-filled 'spoots'.

The third buttress from the left is by far the largest in the corrie. Its front presents a series of attractive groove and crack-lines running up the full 500ft height. In the summer of 1941, on their way back from the Garbh Choire of Braeriach, Sydney and Sandy Tewnion, together with Peter Marr, went to Coire Sputan Dearg for a look. They were so inspired by what they found that they decided to try the most prominent groove just left of centre on the big buttress. It slanted slightly left to reach a grass bay at half-height, and then a dark chimney appeared to lead directly to the top. They found the first 100ft of the groove quite easy to a chokestone, but above this a short, steep corner proved too difficult. Sandy fell back on to the rope three times in his attempt to climb the bulge at the top. They retreated, vowing to return.

As previously mentioned, Sandy was seriously injured during the war and was unable to climb again. Sydney, who was the middle of the three climbing Tewnion brothers, was injured twice in action as a bombardier but made a full recovery. After the war he moved to Glasgow and only made occasional trips back to the Cairngorms. On one of these, in May 1948, he, his brother John, and Sandy Russell went back to Coire Sputan Dearg and climbed the extreme left-hand buttress, naming it Pinnacle Buttress. Although only of moderate difficulty the climbing was very enjoyable on clean, sound granite and they must have then realised that a similar quality of climbing was going to be found on all the buttresses in the corrie.

Bob Scott in Glen Derry 1949

Photo: Etchachan Club Archives

The news about 'Sputan' was out. On September 1, Bob Still and Elizabeth Lawrence climbed the attractive crest of the large slab that angles into the left side of the big buttress. They named their route Crystal Ridge and its highlight was a 100ft slab pitch climbed directly on the crest overlooking the steep left wall. It became an instant classic, often climbed as an introductory route for novices. Even today, it still ranks as one of the few good quality easier rock climbs in the Cairngorms.

Hogmanay is traditionally a popular time to visit a favourite bothy and by all accounts there were upwards of 40 people in or around Luibeg to see in the New Year of 1949. This was Bob Scott's second year in Luibeg Cottage as he had taken over the Derry beat from the previous keeper, Aal Beattie, in 1947. Bob was born at Linn Cottage, Linn o' Dee and being a local man he quickly established a good rapport with local climbers. This New Year was bitterly cold, particularly so for those well down the Luibeg pecking order. They had to make the best of the extremely draughty stick shed as opposed to the kennels or the bothy itself with its roaring fire. Among the usual crowd were a number of youngsters, including a group of kilted Robert Gordon's College schoolboys referred to by Bob as the 'Horrible Heelanders'.

By January 4, many of the revellers had left. However, Mac Smith was still keen to climb and fortunately, so was an enthusiastic 17-year-old Bill Brooker whose companions had returned to Aberdeen. Despite his modest age Brooker had had a good grounding in hill-walking and climbing. He was a pupil at Aberdeen Grammar School and from the age of 14 had spent holidays in Skye. In 1946, while staying at the Glen Brittle hostel, he had innocently asked the warden if the Inaccessible Pinnacle was really inaccessible. The curt reply: "It is for the likes of you," was good enough to inspire the young Brooker to go out and climb it solo the next day.

On January 5, Smith and Brooker walked the five miles to Sputan.

It had been thawing but all was now frozen and they both thought the recently climbed Crystal Ridge looked inviting. Once embarked on the climb they discovered good conditions with hard snow on the ledges and the rock generally bare, apart from ice covering some of the holds. With Brooker in the lead they took three hours to complete the first winter ascent of Crystal Ridge, just three months after its first summer ascent.

A few days later, on January 9, a party comprising John Tewnion, Charlie Hutcheon, Doug Sutherland and Kenny Winram made a complete winter ascent of the Black Spout Buttress on Lochnagar. According to Tewnion: "The upper buttress afforded some fine climbing on snow-covered rock, the only real difficult section being situated about 100ft above the arete where a 15ft wall was climbed direct. In summer, the holds on this pitch are large, but now they were obscured by hard snow and were difficult to find."[4]

Later that winter two CUMC members, Alan Parker and John Young completed an Easter tour of the Cairngorms in which they made a total of six first ascents. Whether by intuition or pure chance they started their programme virtually where Brooker and Smith had left off in Coire Sputan Dearg. On March 17, they climbed the short, but impressive, gully which cuts up behind the big buttress immediately right of Crystal Ridge. They encountered two steep sections, the first an ice pitch, which occupied two hours, the second, similar to the first, was climbed on the right on account of powder snow cascading down the gully. They named their climb Slab Chimney. The weather became milder during the second week and their last climbs were made entirely on rock.

In his 1961 Climbers Guide, Mac Smith, when introducing Creagan a' Choire Etchachan wrote: "Many rock climbers in the past must have used the path to Ben Macdui and the Shelter Stone which climbs through the defile of Coire Etchachan, yet the grand crag flanking the left side of the corrie remained untouched until 1949 – last but one of the great Cairngorm faces to be explored. The most accessible of cliffs; steep, defined buttresses; forbidding overhangs and slabs – the neglect could not have been due to a contempt occasioned by familiarity, the more

The cliffs of Coire Sputan Dearg in June

Photo: Greg Strange

Creagan a' Choire Etchachan in July

Photo: Greg Strange

likely cause was the dismissal of the rocks in an earlier guide as being 'rather fragmentary'. There is no Cairngorm cliff with less talus!"[5]

This straight face of granite, 400ft high must have caught the eye of Parker and Young. They were not put off by Alexander's comments about the rock. In fact, they were clearly inspired by its appearance, likening it to a miniature Grandes Jorasses.

The right-hand side of the face is dominated by an impressive sweep of high-angled pink slabs defined on their left by a prominent chimney. From the top of the chimney a line of overhangs descends leftwards almost reaching the foot of the cliff near the centre of the crag. It was here, just left of the lowest overhangs, that the Cambridge men mounted their attack, on an ill-defined triangular buttress. Once across a bergschrund they discovered the rock to be far less accommodating than they had expected and after some 60ft were forced to make a long traverse leftwards to gain the easy left edge of the buttress. The climbing up to this point had been sustained with two moves of Severe. Above this they followed the left edge over broken rocks which merged into a rib higher up and eventually led to the top.

Parker and Young wanted to name this first climb on Creagan a' Choire Etchachan, Grandes Jorasses, but they were dissuaded from this by Bill Ewen who was preparing a new edition of the SMC's Cairngorm District Guide and thought the name too radical for the rather staid local nomenclature of the time. They settled for Pioneer Route. Later their climb became known as Cambridge Route and the whole buttress named Pioneer Buttress.

Two days after their tussle on Creagan a' Choire Etchachan they returned to Coire Sputan Dearg to climb the big buttress right of Crystal

New Year at Luibeg 1948 – 49. From left, standing: Bob Porter, Bill Brooker, Unknown, John Tewnion. Front, from left: Johnny Morgan, Doug Sutherland and Kenny Winram

Photo: Bill Brooker

Ridge. The weather was fair and the rock predominantly dry so they took the unusual decision, for late March in the Cairngorms, to climb in gym shoes. They noticed, towards the right side of the frontal face (well right of the groove attempted by the Tewnions), a 15ft wide slab with parallel cracks slanted up left to the foot of a corner which higher up developed into a chimney. This was the line they chose to follow.

The slab was quite easy at first with good holds, then slightly harder to the start of the corner. Here they followed a geological dyke which formed the steep left rib of the corner. This 60ft pitch on small holds was the crux of the climb. Just as the rib became untenable, the corner on the right, now a chimney, eased back sharply and they were able to cross right to a large block belay. A farther 100ft of easier climbing led to the top of the buttress.

Their route on 'No. 2 Buttress' (named Grey Man's Crag by Mac Smith) was a good one, the crux rib being exposed, delicate and technically Very Difficult. In June of the same year the climb was repeated by an Aberdeen party who were unaware of the Cambridge ascent. By that time there was little snow covering the lower rocks and the second party followed the geological dyke all the way from the bottom. Later it became clear that they were in fact the same climb, but contrary to tradition, the name given by the second ascent party, Hanging Dyke, was the one adopted.

Parker and Young's Easter visit to the Cairngorms in 1949 had been well planned. They had stolen a march on the locals by opening up the cliff of Creagan a' Choire Etchachan and by making the first climb on the Grey Man's Crag. It may be pure coincidence, but during the following summer 1949, an unprecedented number of new rock climbs (30) were made throughout the Cairngorms and all but one of these were by Aberdeen based climbers. Pioneering activity on this scale had never been seen before. Although a similar increase was occurring in Glen Coe at this time, through the activity of Glasgow and Edinburgh climbers, it is worth considering why it came about in the Cairngorms.

By 1949, a loose-knit group of keen young climbers had formed in Aberdeen with the slightly older Mac Smith as their mentor and link with the pre-war years. Smith believes that a major contributing factor to this upsurge of interest was the fact that most climbers travelled to the hills by bus for the weekend and it was on this journey and after it in the various bothies that friendships were kindled and aspirations discussed. A certain amount of friendly rivalry naturally developed but, with most of the Cairngorm corries virtually unexplored, this new-found playground offered rich pickings for all. There were any number of buttresses and ridges to be climbed.

On May 1, Kenny Winram joined Doug Sutherland and Bill Brooker to climb the rocks forming the right edge of West Gully on Lochnagar. (West Rib). This was potentially a very strong climbing partnership. Winram had started climbing just after the war. He was a plater in the shipyards and was described by his friend, Mac Smith, as endearingly 'hally racket' – the local vernacular for, among other things, good-natured boisterousness. Doug Sutherland was a small, powerful man who worked as an engineer. He had been two years ahead of Brooker at Aberdeen Grammar School, although they had only met recently while climbing on the sea cliffs at Souter Head, south of Aberdeen.

That same day, across the Dee on Beinn a' Bhùird, John Tewnion, Sandy Russell, Mac and Ernie Smith were climbing in the beautiful, secluded Coire an Dubh Lochain. To the right of the long scree shoot known as the Main Rake lies a 300ft sweep of smooth, pale green slabs. The climbers were tempted to try a challenging corner on the left of these slabs but chose instead on this first visit to ascend the ridge of rock bounding the Main Rake on its right. (May Day Route).

Sutherland and Brooker had been honing their climbing technique on the Aberdeen sea cliffs and by the end of May felt ready to tackle some of Bell's climbs on Lochnagar. During the weekend of May 29, they climbed Eagle Ridge, Parallel Buttress and Tough-Brown Ridge Direct. These were the first known repeats of Parallel Buttress and Tough-Brown Direct. This impressive weekend of climbing earned the pair guarded praise. On the bus going home Mac Smith said to Brooker: "You'll be deid afore you're 21 if you cairrie on like this!"

Once Winram heard about the Lochnagar climbs he resolved to try Eagle Ridge himself and with John Tewnion and Ernie Smith made the fourth ascent on June 4. A week later Winram was back on Lochnagar with Bob Porter. On Saturday 11, June, they went to the Southern Sector of the corrie and climbed Jacob's Slabs, a small isolated buttress high under the plateau rim. As the day was still young they decided to try the triangular-shaped buttress left of Central Buttress. (Later named Sinister Buttress for its associations and its lichenous and vegetated rock). Starting near the centre, Winram led out most of his single three-quar-ter-weight nylon rope, placing a piton at one point, and then he fell. The piton pulled out, the rope snapped and he plummeted 100ft to the scree. He was severely injured and unconscious.

The accident happened at three o'clock in the afternoon. Porter left almost immediately and ran the four miles to the Spittal of Glen Muick where he was able to contact the police. Fortunately, the Kinloss Mountain Rescue Team was at Ballater that weekend and set off quickly

Doug Sutherland climbing Multiple Chimneys on the left wall of Polyphemus Gully, Lochnagar. August 1949

Photo: Bill Brooker

Kenny Winram returns in triumph from Eagle Ridge

Photo: Mac Smith

Ernie Smith and John Tewnion looking towards the lower slabs of Glaucous Buttress, Coire an Dubh Lochain, Beinn a' Bhùird, August 1949

Photo: Mac Smith

for Lochnagar via Gelder Shiel. At Gelder, the team met Mac and Ernie Smith, John Tewnion and Sandy Russell and they all went up to help evacuate Winram. It was a long, difficult carry back to Gelder before the injured climber was safely on his way to hospital in Aberdeen, the ambulance leaving the bothy just after midnight.

Kenny had a fractured skull and a punctured lung and it was two weeks before he began to regain his memory. A long period of recuperation followed. The accident came as a big jolt to the regular Aberdeen

*John Tewnion
leading Polypody
Groove, Glaucous
Buttress, Coire an
Dubh Lochain,
August 1949*

Photo: Mac Smith
Collection

climbers, especially to Kenny's close friends who saw him immediately after the fall. He had been fortunate to survive and they all knew that.

As soon as Winram was on the mend thoughts once again turned to the hills. For Sutherland and Brooker it was time to return to Lochnagar for a close look at the corrie face of the Black Spout Pinnacle. They had been attracted by the Pinnacle for over a year and now felt sufficiently experienced to give it a go. Bell's account of his attempts did not sound too promising and his surprising comment in *A Progress in*

Hourglass Buttress with the three fault-lines of Sickle (left), Jason's Chimney (centre) and Sandy Crack (right)

Photo: Greg Strange

"*Sutherland decided that life was too sweet to throw away on an attempt to traverse beneath the overhang, and descended to the platform.*"
– Bill Brooker

Mountaineering that: "For those who hanker after the impossible there is always the challenge of the terrifying wall of Black Spout Pinnacle"[6] was positively off-putting. Nevertheless, the younger men were hopeful of finding a line of weakness near the foot of the Black Spout.

"The Pinnacle presents a very steep, slabby face of about 600ft to the corrie. The right half of this face plunges in a sheer wall to the Black Spout. The left is rather more broken and less steep. The lower 200ft consists of a smooth wall of slabs, at the top of which is a prominent green ledge. We dubbed this ledge the 'Springboard', as it was obviously the jumping-off place for any attempts on the upper face."[7] On August 13, they stood below the Pinnacle trying to pick out the easiest way to the Springboard. About 150ft up from the entrance to the Black Spout, beyond a vertical groove in a steep smooth wall, they found a ramp slanting up left to a shallow cave below an overhang. Sutherland climbed 50ft to the cave where he discovered that the holds above the overhang were wet. He made several attempts to pull onto the slab above before resorting to direct aid from a piton. The way to the Springboard was now open. A grooved slab and a short wall at the top of a column of blocks soon led Brooker to the untrodden grass ledges of the Springboard.

Three fault-lines leading up the pinnacle originate from the Springboard. The right-hand one is less obvious and goes right onto the sheer wall directly above the Black Spout. The central and left-hand faults form chimneys which run slightly leftwards up the face. Of these, the central fault leads more directly to the Pinnacle summit but after 200ft it is blocked by a great overhang. The two men decided to try the more sporting central line and Brooker led out 100ft of rope before belaying at the start of the difficulties.

Sutherland took over and climbed much steeper rock, using a piton at one point, until he reached a stance below a big overhanging crack. "Slightly to the right a vertical crack petered out in a smooth, convex slab which swept up to the great jutting overhang, 50ft above our platform. I could make nothing of the pitch, but, with a shoulder, Sutherland gained a footing in the right-hand crack and, using a piton, climbed it until it merged with the pitiless slab. He decided that life was too sweet to throw away on an attempt to traverse beneath the overhang, and descended to the platform. I was of the same mind, and so we left a sling, roping down for 60ft to a point about 100ft from the Springboard."[8]

Feeling deflated to be almost back on the Springboard after all that effort and excitement they quickly resolved to find an alternative route to the summit. They traversed into the left-hand fault and managed to climb this with combined tactics at one point. They were now on to easier ground above and to the left of the great roof. After 200ft of fairly straightforward climbing (including further use of combined effort) they reached the plateau six and a half hours after leaving the Black Spout.

The last of Lochnagar's major buttresses had now been climbed. Reaching the Springboard had been the key passage and although a piton was used for aid it was later found unnecessary in dry conditions. Route 1 was too vegetated to become a classic rock climb; nevertheless it took the easiest line on this impressive buttress and opened the way to further possibilities in the future. Sutherland's attempt to force the central fault out right below the great roof was a bold piece of climbing and 27 years were to elapse before that particular problem was resolved – Hood Route HVS 5a.

August was a busy month for the new Aberdeen school. During the third weekend, two parties headed for Beinn a' Bhùird. Sutherland and Brooker went to Coire na Cìche to look at some attractive lines on the south wall. They started by climbing Slugain Buttress on the left of Twisting Gully, and then tried the much steeper hourglass-shaped buttress to the right. On this they turned back at the neck below the upper buttress. The next day they climbed the obvious sickle-shaped crack right of the hourglass and made an indirect ascent of the chimney to its right. These opening rock climbs on the South Wall of Coire na Cìche were enjoyable and not too difficult. The granite, however, though generally clean, was much coarser-grained than that found on Lochnagar.

Perhaps the greatest attraction for climbing on Beinn a' Bhùird lies in the mountain's splendid remote environment. No doubt, this was the sentiment felt by the other party at large in the area that weekend. Mac Smith and his companions were heading for Coire nan Clach, the expansive boulder-strewn cirque separated from Coire an Dubh Lochain by the peninsula of Dividing Buttress. They had two objectives on this visit. One was to climb in Coire an Dubh Lochain; the other, to complete work on a howff which had been occupying their thoughts and efforts for some time.

It had all started when Smith and Winram read Jock Nimlin's article on mountain howffs which extolled the virtues and advantages of sleeping in caves and natural shelters. The essay had so fired their imagination they vowed to start looking for a suitable cave or natural recess in the Cairngorms to adopt as their own howff. The Shelter Stone at Loch Avon and the Warren under the Red Craig in Glen Clova were the only natural shelters that they knew of in the area. There had to be others!

For many weekends they kept a howff-eye open for a suitable boulder but with very little success. Then came a visit to Beinn a' Bhùird – their old friend and favourite mountain. On this occasion poor weather dissuaded them from rock climbing so they decided to explore Coire an Dubh Lochain and Coire nan Clach. Surely, they would find their grail in one of these rocky amphitheatres?

After hours of scrambling and squirming over the whole floor of Coire nan Clach, Smith thought he could see a dark shadow of a crevice under a pyramidal block below the Dividing Buttress.

"I shouted to Winram, intent on searching his own allotted area. He dashed across and together we advanced expectantly. It was it! Our spiritual home! Our Howff! In the damp, dark atmosphere of the mist-laden corrie I must admit it did not look a prepossessing place at first glance. On closer inspection it improved. A large block lay on a smaller slab forming one straight wall, and a semi-circle of rubble and small blocks provided the other walls and further support. Much work would be needed to make it windproof. The ceiling was flat, a quartz-encrusted slab of pink unweathered granite standing about five feet

"I shouted to Winram, intent on searching his own allotted area. He dashed across and together we advanced expectantly. It was it! Our spiritual home! Our Howff!."
– Mac Smith

Ernie Smith

Photo: Mac Smith

above the floor. From the middle of the floor rose a stony stalagmite, a veritable Aiguille, fully three feet in height. Its removal would be difficult."[9]

The discovery of the Smith-Winram Bivouac had taken place in 1948 and now they hoped to remove the offending stalagmite with the help of a stonemason – John Tewnion. Charlie Petrie, Tewnion, Mac and Ernie Smith worked through the night with a drill and 4lb. hammer and by morning it was done. Well satisfied with their labours and their new home they were now able to turn attention back to climbing. Next day, they walked the short distance up beneath the left edge of Dividing Buttress to the foot of the slabby face right of May Day Route. Tewnion wanted to try the prominent corner marking the junction between smooth slabs on the right and an area of pillared rock on the left. From the corrie floor it appeared as a dark, slanting shadow with two zigzag overhangs high up. With Ernie Smith as his second, he set off up the groove. For 100ft the climbing was easy, then 80ft of more delicate friction work took him beyond the first overhang. Some way above this the corner steepened and became less accommodating. Here they moved left and continued up the edge, passing the upper overhang by a Severe move before reaching a terrace. It was now possible to work out left to join the upper rocks of May Day Route. This they did, mainly to save time as it was becoming clear that they were about to be caught in a storm.

Meanwhile, Petrie and Mac Smith had climbed a line right of the smooth slab which they named Crow-Step Route. Eventually, they all made it back to their howff in what Smith described as a fitting climax to the weekend – as fine a thunder storm as any of them had seen in all their climbing days. The big groove climbed by Tewnion and Ernie Smith had given an excellent route on clean rock up to the terrace. Near its foot a fern species of the Polypodiaceal family was growing in plenty, hence the name Polypody Groove was chosen for this Beinn a' Bhùird classic.

During 1949, two new rock climbs were made in Coire an Lochain of Cairn Gorm. In May, a Moray Mountaineering Club party comprising C.Ross, Dr John Brewster and President D.Banks climbed No. 4 Buttress to the right of Savage Slit. Starting well to the left of the north-facing rocks they followed a crack and ledge system diagonally up right to a platform below a short blank wall. The wall proved to be most stubborn and was eventually overcome by combined tactics, still Severe. (Western Route) The other route was an indirect ascent of the rib right of the Vent climbed by EC members Harry Watt and Sandy Russell. (Vent Rib and Traverse).

Exploration in Coire Sputan Dearg continued throughout the summer. It was Brooker, Sutherland and Charlie Hutcheon who repeated the Cambridge route naming it Hanging Dyke. On that same day in June the trio climbed a long ridge right of the Grey Man's Crag. The climbing was enjoyable and quite straightforward except for the crux pitch about halfway up. Here a short overhang barred access to a smooth eight foot groove above which the climbing appeared to become easier. Brooker recalls watching Sutherland go over the bulge then hearing terrible scrabbling sounds as he failed to find any purchase for his nails in the groove. Somehow he managed to scart his way back down to safety. After a rest he went back up and succeeded in overcoming the groove. They thought the pitch was quite hard. Even today it is considered Hard Severe in rock boots. They named the climb Snake Ridge on account of its "fancied resemblance as seen from the top, to a snake head down". A further four routes were climbed elsewhere in the corrie, Janus, Cherub's, Flake and Terminal Buttresses. All were the work of John Tewnion accompanied by Mac and Ernie Smith with Winram on Janus and Sandy Alexander on Cherub's Buttress. (The youthful Alexander was the Cherub).

The final new route of the summer was also climbed in Coire Sputan Dearg. It had always been the intention of Sandy and Sydney Tewnion to return for another attempt at the unclimbed groove on Grey Man's Crag. Sandy was no longer able to climb, but the next best thing to taking part in the action was to see where the action was taking place. By now, Sydney had been living in Glasgow for a number of years. He had maintained his interest in the hills and had become an accomplished rock climber. During that summer he had led his brother John, with Ernie Smith up Raven's Gully on Buachaille Etive Mòr, one of the most difficult climbs in Glen Coe at that time.

On September 18, the three brothers together with Ernie Smith and Sydney's girlfriend, Anne Williamson, went to Sputan to have another go at the groove. While Sandy and Anne watched from a good vantage point the other three started up the easy lower section. At the place where the 1941 attempt failed, Sydney managed to use a small knob of rock almost out of reach at the top of the short corner and pull up to easier ground. This movement was probably the technical crux, but the upper chimney above the grass bay was very wet and gave much more of a struggle. It rose for 60ft in four steps, each progressively more difficult. At the top the angle fell back and Sydney was thankful to find a belay at the back of a shallow cave. No further problems were encountered in the next 200ft to the top.

Pilgrim's Groove (named after the three early pilgrims) was given a grade of VS and was the most difficult of the eight new rock climbs made in Coire Sputan Dearg in 1949. At about this time Sydney enrolled at Jordanhill College of Education to train as a technical teacher. Two years later he died of exposure along with three fellow male members of the Glen Coe Mountaineering Club when they were caught in a bad storm while walking from Corrour Lodge to Benalder Cottage at New Year 1951 – 52. Anne Williamson, who had married Sydney four months before the tragedy, was the only survivor from the party of five.

Charlie Petrie

Photo: Mac Smith

1. SMCJ Vol. 36, No. 188, p427.

2. CCJ Vol. 16, p86.

3. *The Cairngorms* 1950 Edition, p182 – 183.

4. ECJ No. 1, p5.

5. SMC *Climber's Guide to the Cairngorms Area Vol. 1* (1961), p61.

6. *A Progress in Mountaineering* p211 and Bell's Scottish Climbs, p151.

7. SMCJ Vol. 24, No. 141, p202.

8. SMCJ Vol. 24, No. 141, p203.

9. CCJ Vol. 16, p172.

Bill Brooker at Corrour Bothy, April 1950

Photo: Mac Smith

6: The Golden Years (1950 – 1960)

AT THE BEGINNING of the new decade almost all exploratory climbing in the Cairngorms was being undertaken by folk from the North-east. Private transport for the masses was still over the horizon, so most people took the bus, hitch-hiked, cycled and occasionally shared the cost of a taxi from Braemar to the Derry Gates. All the bothies were well frequented, with Corrour, Luibeg, Gelder, Lochend and Robertson's being popular with climbers. Influences from outwith the area were minimal and it was still considered a matter of honour to climb in nailed boots, even in dry weather. There was, however, a growing recognition that pitons could provide better security on granite, particularly in winter when it was often impossible to find adequate anchors. Wooden-shafted axe belays only gave psychological security. Loading from a big fall usually snapped the shaft or pulled the axe through the snow.

Bill Ewen's revision of Alexander's District Guide to the Cairngorms was published in 1950. It contained a record of all known climbs in the area as well as many excellent new photographs. As both writer and photographer, Ewen was an ideal choice for editor of the Cairngorm Club Journal, a position he held from 1934 to 1953. He was headmaster at the Aberdeen Demonstration School until retirement.

At the start of the 1949 – 50 winter, expectations were high among the newly recruited snow and ice devotees. The period marked a significant shift in the concept of what the locals believed would make worthwhile winter climbs. Building on the previous winter's experience and following a summer of wide ranging exploration throughout the Cairngorms, the Aberdeen school realised that given favourable conditions many of the buttresses could provide better and more rewarding climbs in winter than they did in summer.

After Christmas, Brooker and Johnny Morgan made the first winter ascent of one of Lochnagar's classic routes, Shadow Buttress A. They followed the original line across a snowy spiral terrace, at the end of which continuous difficulties were encountered all the way to the crest of the upper buttress. The exhilaration of this climb carried them through to the New Year when they were once again based at Luibeg. On January 2, 1950, they were joined by Sutherland for a climb on Creagan a'Choire Etchachan. Believing the whole cliff to be virgin they started up a gully in the centre of the face. For 100ft it was easy angled, and then it reared up into a tremendous vertical pillar of ice before continuing as bare slabs to the top. At the point where the gully steepened they moved right and followed the line of least resistance up onto the crest of the buttress climbed by Parker and Young (Pioneer Buttress). They then reached the top via a 50ft ice pitch. Their climb, Winter Route, was not, as they thought, the first route on the face, but it was the first winter climb.

By the end of January at least one freeze/thaw cycle had taken place and climbing conditions were now excellent. On January 27, Brooker and Morgan joined a Cairngorm Club bus meet bound for Lochnagar. The club has an enviable record for maintaining regular bus meets throughout its long history. These are well attended though climbers are usually very much in the minority. This is mainly due to the club's strict rules on punctuality, which makes no allowance for the unpredictable nature of mountaineering. The two young men were fully aware of the retribution likely to be taken should they be responsible for delaying high tea in one of the hotels in Ballater. They dashed up to the corrie already having decided which route they would attempt.

Conditions were indeed near perfect with hard snow, ice, frozen turf and no spindrift. They made for the Shadow Couloir and roped up below the Giant's Head Chimney. Although not a great deal of snow lay on the cliff the lower chimney held a reasonable build-up, allowing the chokestone to be surmounted without too much difficulty. Once out of the enclosing walls of the chimney the climbing became exposed and felt very committing. The shallow trough of the 'Escape Route' was icy and ascending the first 80ft of it from the end of the terrace provided the crux. It took a steady nerve to cut a ladder of small holds up the ice, knowing all the while that a single slip would almost certainly send them both crashing to the foot of Polyphemus Gully.

There was no time for celebration, just another mad rush back to the bus

The tension began to ease as they gained height and, eventually, when the trough became a snow slope they took a more direct line to the plateau by slanting right to finish up a slender feathered arete. The climb had taken a little more than five hours. There was no time for celebration, just another mad rush back to the bus.

Giant's Head Chimney was a whole grade harder than any winter climb so far made in the Cairngorms. Brooker described it as a 'dry mouth climb', on account of its poor belays and protection rather than for its technical difficulties. He regards it as one of his most rewarding climbs.

On March 17, Sutherland, Brooker and Morgan had another exciting day on Lochnagar, this time in different circumstances. They had endured a stormy night camping at the entrance to the North-east corrie and in the morning they found everything plastered with fresh snow. Despite these unfavourable conditions they decided to try an ascent of Polyphemus Gully, the most formidable of the Shadow Couloir climbs, which to their knowledge had never been attempted before in winter.

At the top of the couloir, just right of Giant's Head Chimney, the gully commenced with a long double-tiered pitch which formed a gutter of ice in the steep wall of Shadow Buttress B. This impressive pitch appeared to be the main difficulty, although what awaited them in the upper gully was hidden from view. Sutherland attacked the first section of ice which, after 15ft, gave way to a shelf leading to a shallow cave in the gully bed. This took an hour as the powder snow had to be cleared to a depth of three feet before steps could be cut in the hard surface beneath. While Morgan waited at the foot of the gully, Brooker contemplated the next tier of ice, the summer crux. Above the cave a very steep groove curved left below the impending right wall. The 50ft left wall hung in bulging folds of ice buried beneath wind-packed snow.

"Close to the cave a rib of ice, distorted by bulges and cavities, had been formed by the dripping from an overhang at the top of the wall.

I chose this rib and very slowly began to cut my way upwards. The ice was tough and wet and all the time I was a target for the stream of drips from the overhang. The first 20ft occupied an hour and then I made swifter progress after the welcome appearance of a solid flake of névé on the right. Using this as a handhold I made contact with the overhang sooner than I expected. The overhang presented a knotty problem until I saw that the top of the rib had formed a stalagmite with a delicate crowning spire of new snow. I swept aside the decoration and cut across a bulge to the lip of the wall. A moment later and I moved on to the easy snow of the gully bed, and 20ft up in a corner below a vertical wall I drove my axe in to the head and summoned Sutherland."[1]

By the time Morgan was leading the next pitch they had been on the climb for more than four hours. However, they made good progress up the easy middle section of the gully and were beginning to feel quite optimistic, when they came to a partially iced overhang barring the way. Just below this, a thin shallow groove led out on to the easier-angled left wall, but they could not climb it. Both Morgan and Sutherland tried the overhang with no success. It was now 5.30pm and almost dark so they decided to retreat. By reversing the first 200ft of snow they only required two abseils to get down the steep lower section. Despite their long day and being very wet, the descent in the dark went without a hitch until Sutherland, on the last 20ft of the final abseil, lost his grip on the icy rope and fell, thankfully unharmed, into soft snow at the top of the Shadow Couloir.

This tour-de-force had again pushed the standard of winter climbing on the mountain up another notch

This *tour-de-force* had again pushed the standard of winter climbing on the mountain up another notch. Although not succeeding on Polyphemus Gully they did manage to climb its major pitch. Had they known that the summer line quit the gully below their high point and taken to the left wall they may well have reached the top. As it was, they had had to give best to the mountain on this occasion.

In early April, Brooker spent a week based at Luibeg, climbing at first with a school friend, Steve McPherson, then at the weekend with Sutherland and Morgan. On April 15, this trio were joined by Winram and Mac Smith to make a winter ascent of Chokestone Gully. (They did not know about Hendry's ascent). All five set off up the gully in two ropes, Brooker and Morgan in front followed by the other three. No difficulties were encountered up to the final ice pitch which forms over the great chokestone. Here Morgan took an axe belay while Brooker set about cutting his way up the steep ice. There were waves of spindrift pouring down the gully so he kept to the left initially until he reached some exposed rock where he was unable to find a runner. At this point Smith recalls hearing Brooker shout: "This stuff's numbing my brain." (Anyone who has climbed on steep ice while being bombarded by spindrift avalanches will know exactly what he meant!).

Despite his state of mind he set off again, cutting up right towards the final bulge. In a slight lull he went for it, climbing over the steepening but forgetting to cut handholds above. When the spindrift restarted he was thoroughly committed. Standing precariously with no handholds he struggled for a while to remain in place until finally he shouted that he was coming off.

"It was quite a relief to be falling and I wasn't worried. I landed in soft snow and just kept going. It was like riding the Cresta Run." Brooker thought that the rope must have broken and was surprised when it caught him violently around the neck causing some discomfort. He came to rest well below the base of the cliff having fallen 500ft. He stood up expecting to have to trudge all the way back up to the others, then he saw movement in the snow beside him. It was Morgan. Slowly Winram, Smith and Sutherland all surfaced in various states of disarray. The rope which had caught Brooker's neck was the second party's rope and all five of them had been swept down after the ice axe belays had snapped or pulled out under the strain.

Corrour Bothy 1939

Photo: Etchachan Club Archives

Smith appeared to be the worst injured, for although he had no broken limbs he was coughing up blood. Morgan, Winram and Brooker were unhurt but Sutherland had damaged his ankle and could not walk. After some soul-searching and discussion they made a rope stretcher and set off for Derry carrying Sutherland, no easy task under the circumstances. At some stage on the journey they met another party who agreed to go on ahead to get help and collect the emergency stretcher kept at Derry Lodge. The five climbers eventually met the rescue party with the stretcher coming round the shoulder of Càrn a' Mhaim.

The accident in Chokestone Gully brought the winter season to an abrupt end. It also marked the last appearance of Sutherland on the Aberdeen climbing scene. He was now preparing to leave for India where he had secured a post near Sikkim. He left Aberdeen in August 1950 then returned briefly two years later to get married. Sadly, he died of pneumonia in North-east India in 1960. For two years he had been one of the North-east's most influential climbers and the loss of his good company and outstanding climbing ability was keenly felt by his friends.

After the war it became increasingly apparent that the roof of Corrour Bothy would not survive many more winters. With this in mind, the Cairngorm Club gained permission from the Fife Estates to refurbish the building, on the understanding that it would remain the property of the estate, and that it would be left as an open shelter. The deterioration of one of the country's best known mountain shelters was of concern to many hill-goers so it was not surprising when an appeal was published in several daily papers the necessary sum for reconstruction was quickly over-subscribed.

Construction work took place in July 1950, supervised by George Taylor of the Cairngorm Club, ably assisted by many volunteers. The roof was removed and replaced with the now familiar aluminium sheeting. The door, window, lintels and fireplace were renewed, walls re-pointed and a large buttress built against the north gable in an attempt to prevent further outward movement. All the masonry work was carried out by John Tewnion.

Dr Taylor said in his article in the CCJ in 1951: "Let us hope that the many, who will avail themselves of the bothy's shelter may be imbued with the same constructive spirit as all the helpers who gave their time and effort on behalf of the wider fraternity of climbers and hill-walkers."[2]

In late June, Brooker and Morgan investigated the West Wall Route on the Shelter Stone Crag, finding Mitchell's rope still lying on the cliff. They followed the chimney throughout before zig-zagging to reach the

Allan Will
Photo: John Hay

lower step on the skyline. The final wall was ascended via parallel cracks and an overhang, which provided the hardest move of the whole climb. Unaware of Thompson's ascent, they named the 600ft route Clach Dhian Chimney, the name by which it is known today.

When looking towards Cairn Lochain from the top of Shelter Stone Crag a steep granite cliff is seen lying between the Feith Buidhe and the Allt Coire Domhain. At its left end there is a dark gully known as Hell's Lum. In September, Ian Brooker (Bill Brooker's older brother) and Marie Newbigging, visited this crag and climbed the impressive vertical chimney which separates the distinctly grey buttress right of Hell's Lum from the pink water-washed slabs of the frontal face. They found the lower chimney vegetated, but with walls close enough to back and foot and thus avoid greenery. As they gained height so the slit went deeper into the rock until near the top the outlet was blocked by jammed chokestones. Here the scenery was remarkable as the chimney was almost a tunnel through the cliff. They escaped onto the right wall by an exposed mantelshelf. The ascent of Deep-Cut Chimney was the first recorded climb on the cliff now known as Hell's Lum Crag, one of the last major faces in the Cairngorms to be explored.

Douglas-Gibson Gully had attracted many winter suitors since March 1893. The lower part fills quickly under normal conditions leaving the top 200ft plus the cornice as the main area of difficulty. In December 1950, at the start of what Mac Smith described as "an exceptionally severe winter in the hills", accumulations of snow in the corrie were already deep.

Around Christmas, three Aberdeen climbers, Alan Will, George McLeod and Jim Hardie walked to the corrie from Gelder Bothy for an attempt on Gibson's. There was much unconsolidated snow lying and Will was avalanched in the narrows when snow was released from below the cornice. He was swept down onto McLeod's head. In spite of this incident and the potentially dangerous conditions they continued up to the final wall, where most previous attempts had failed. Here Will moved left and followed a steep, snowy groove passing to the right of the summer crux to reach a rock recess with a built-up snow-ice floor forming a cave. A home-made piton driven straight into the crumbling rock served as a belay. With McLeod now at the cave Will set off to try and reach the cornice, but he was unhappy about the stability of the snow as there was water running over the rock beneath. He eventually gave up 20ft from the cornice and successfully reversed back to the cave.

An abseil was contemplated, but the piton seemed so poor they decided to untie from the rope and down climb using the doubled rope through the peg as a handrail. As McLeod started his descent he lost his footing. Unable to hold on to the doubled rope he fell, almost to the loch, a distance of 1000ft. Miraculously, he survived this spectacular fall with only a broken thumb and a gashed cheek. He made his way back up through the mist into the lower gully where he shouted to his companions, who, thinking he was dead, were now affecting their own much slower descent. To round off this eventful day, Will fell through the ice on the loch while making his way back to Gelder.

This sterling effort indicated that the top wall could probably be climbed provided the snow was sufficiently firm. Some time after this latest attempt (three days according to McLeod), another party of Aberdeen climbers entered the foot of Douglas-Gibson Gully bent on making its first winter ascent. They were Gordon (Goggs) Leslie and Tom Patey, both second-year medical students at Aberdeen University. Two hours of steady step-cutting took them to below the upper wall which they discovered was plated in well frozen snow-ice. From this point onwards they had to cut both hand and footholds. Like Will and McLeod they passed the summer crux groove on the right, where a run-out of 90ft brought them to the rock cave where the previous party had left the piton.

After an abortive attempt on the chimney above the cave they moved left and climbed beside a rib until only 15ft of near vertical snow barred access to a large snow cave at the cornice. Here they formed a stance in deeper snow in order that the leader could be safeguarded. This short section up into the cave proved to be one of the hardest parts of the climb and Patey had to use an ice axe driven horizontally into the snow as a foothold. From the back of the cave the cornice projected over the void for some 25ft, presenting one last formidable obstacle. By now, totally committed, "the second belayed at the back of the cave while the leader, after much hard work, fashioned a tunnel three to four feet in depth in the roof of the cave, through which the party climbed to the welcome security of the summit plateau".[3]

Tom Patey and Mike Taylor on Garbh Bheinn, March 1952

Photo: Bill Brooker

Despite the excellent conditions, the 200ft terminal wall had required nearly seven hours of continuously difficult and exposed climbing. Patey later wrote in his Cairngorm Commentary that the principal factor in their surprise coup was that having climbed well beyond the point where they could have safely withdrawn and finding no belays for an abseil they had little option but to continue climbing.[4] This assertion that they had climbed past the point of no return was probably true but this does not detract from what was a very determined effort by a relatively inexperienced party. Douglas-Gibson Gully is generally considered to have been the most difficult winter climb in Scotland at that time.

Patey was 19-years-old when he made this ascent. He was born in Ellon, Aberdeenshire where his Irish father was the local Episcopalian minister. His mother was from Derbyshire. He went to Ellon Academy and then to Robert Gordon's College in Aberdeen for his final year at school. From an early age he had been encouraged in outdoor interests, and like many other climbers his lifelong love of the hills started while in the Boy Scouts. He was one of those 'Horrible Heelanders' bagging Munros at Bob Scott's bothy at New Year 1949. It was while travelling home by bus during the first month at Aberdeen University that Patey discovered that a fellow medical student, another Buchan lad, from Peterhead, Mike Taylor, was also interested in climbing. Between them they bought a full weight nylon rope and together with Patey's friends from Ellon, Morrice Coutts and Charlie Morrison (nicknamed Goudie), they started exploring the Buchan sea cliffs, beginning at Collieston then moving to Longhaven. Morrison was an apprentice engineer and was able to provide a good supply of home-made pitons.

Patey (like Symmers and Ewen before him), initially wished only to be able to climb to a standard which would enable him to ascend any peak in Scotland with competence. However, this Salvationist approach

Tom Patey at Luibeg February, 1957

Photo: Gordon Leslie

was soon abandoned once the group began to acquire new skills. During the winter of 1949 – 50 Patey with Taylor and Goggs Leslie climbed Raeburn's Gully as well as a few easier snow gullies with the Lairig Club. At Easter, he had the good fortune to spend a few days on Ben Nevis with the experienced Ayrshire climber, Jock Pirrit, who was studying at Glasgow University. While on the Ben they climbed several classics including Tower Ridge in a very fast time, much to the surprise of the resident experts in the CIC hut. According to Mike Taylor, this would have been the full extent of Patey's winter experience at the time of the Douglas-Gibson ascent. He also says that the climb was not just a spur of the moment decision; it was something that Patey had been thinking and talking about for some time.

During 1951, Patey continued his explorations on the Longhaven sea cliffs, where among other climbs he ascended the well known Diagonal Crack with Coutts and then the infamous Hallelujah Staircase with Morrison, barefoot in a snowstorm! It was not until August 8, that he made his first new rock climb away from the North-east coast. For this he chose the rather loose left-hand fault on the Shadow Couloir face of Lochnagar – Shadow Chimney. He was accompanied on this Severe climb by Coutts.

The following month, Brooker and Leslie made a rare visit to that most intimidating of crags, Creag an Dubh-loch. A year earlier Brooker, with Morgan, had made the third ascent of Labyrinth Route. On that occasion he had studied the left flank of the great 1000ft sweep of slabs lying between the Labyrinth and Central Gully Buttress. The lower third of this left edge is broken and vegetated, but higher up it forms a distinct ridge overlooking the unclimbed cul-de-sac of the Labyrinth. The only obvious barrier to an ascent of the edge lay at half-height where a sea of very smooth boiler-plate slabs extended to the very brink of the Labyrinth. However, from below, there appeared to be a thin vertical crack running almost to the top.

About 400ft of straightforward, vegetated climbing brought them to a terrace below the sea of slabs. The vertical crack did indeed appear to be the only feasible way up this barrier. It was more than 100ft long, continuously grass-choked and ideally suited to Brooker's tricounis. Near the top the crack ran out but he was able to gain the sanctuary of a large spike jammed in a line of overhangs. From this he jumped down left and gained a platform back on the edge. They ascended the upper section of this Labyrinth Edge via three big steps, the last climbed on the right by a hidden chimney. Brooker later jokingly referred to Labyrinth Edge as "the great grass climb".

During 1952 the development of Lochnagar's winter potential continued apace. On a day of perfect conditions in January, Brooker and Taylor climbed Gargoyle Chimney in six hours. The chimney itself was full of ice and gave them 80ft of sustained cutting, with the hardest moves going over the chokestone at the top. On the same day Patey and Donald Aitken succeeded on Tough-Brown Traverse, taking five hours for this 1000ft climb. All the ledges and terraces were banked with hard snow and some of the rocks were iced. The crux of the climb was escaping from the Great Terrace where they had to use combined tactics.

Towards the end of this winter, in April, Ian Brooker and Newbigging returned to Hell's Lum Crag to make an ascent of the Lum. The gully was in semi-winter condition with snow masking a major rock pitch halfway up. They encountered steep snow, ice, and 'Very Difficult' rock climbing on this atmospheric route. Two days later, Patey, Leslie and Taylor bagged the last unclimbed buttress in Coire Sputan Dearg – the central of the trio of buttresses lying between Snake Ridge and the Main Spout. "The form of the buttress changes when seen from different angles. From the corrie floor it is squat and compact; its finer and truer form is best seen from Cherub's Buttress from where it appears as a tapering, twisted spire having a curious, square summital block reminiscent of the greater Aiguilles."[5] This marvellous description written by Smith in his 1961 guide certainly gives a flavour for the climb and more than a hint as to why the first ascent party named it Aiguille Noire or the Black Tower. Although short, the climb, which they made up the left edge, was similar in standard and quality to Eagle Ridge.

Goggs Leslie
Photo: Bill Brooker

The university lads were out again on May 10. This time, Patey and Taylor were joined by Bill Brooker, for an ascent of the last major gully on Creag an Dubh-loch. Bill Ewen had already referred to the intermittent terraces which slant leftwards onto the great face of slabs forming the right wall of Central Gully as the False Gully, a name this party thought most appropriate since the situations bore no resemblance to any gully they had climbed before. It commenced as a gentle grass rake then steepened with indefinite pitches leading up below an impressive, smooth wall. Near the top a barrier of rock lay between the climbers and more broken ground to the left. Here they moved left on a ledge and climbed a short distance up into a steep chimney. A rope thrown over a projection enabled the leader to pendulum across the bed of the chimney and climb the left edge to a stance. Once they were all safely across they continued straight up before moving left on to the broken ground and so gained the plateau.

With the successful, if somewhat unconventional ascent of False Gully, attention turned back to Lochnagar and its remaining unclimbed gully, Parallel Gully B. This major feature is divided into an upper and lower section by the grassy scoop crossed by Tough and Brown. The lower half took the form of a 250ft chimney cutting vertically through the steep slabs of lower Tough-Brown Buttress. The upper section funnels out and contains several big pitches.

On May 26, Ian Brooker and Sandy Lyall, having been forced to retreat from the lower section without reaching the main chimney, decided to attempt the upper gully, approaching via Tough-Brown Traverse. Above the scoop the gully is blocked at 50ft by a large jammed chokestone so they started up the rocks on the right until they came to a 30ft crack which seemed holdless. After much effort in foot-jamming and wriggling, Brooker managed to climb the crack and reach a sloping ledge on the left, about 12ft up. Here he hammered in a piton for a running belay and continued up left to below a large rectangular block. After trying to climb directly over this Lyall was forced left before making a hard move over a small overhang to reach a big bay below a steep final wall. This whole passage, starting with the holdless crack, had proved very hard in nailed boots and contained at least two VS moves.

After this excitement they took the easiest way up right avoiding the

Tom Patey, Mike Taylor, Adam Watson and Gordon H. Leslie at the Bruachdryne Tearoom, Braemar 1954

Photo: Mac Smith

steep, loose-looking final wall by a shallow gully leading to the top of Tough-Brown Ridge.

Once word of Lyall and Brooker's breakthrough filtered back to Aberdeen the race was on to see who would be the first to bag the whole gully. Two weeks later, glorious weather coincided with a meet of the Aberdeen University Lairig Club to Lochnagar on June 8. According to Patey: "Interest in the route was now so general that no fewer than eight assembled at the foot of the crags.[6] The party comprised four ropes of two with Patey and Taylor in front, followed by Bill Brooker, Mike Dixon, Donald Aitken, Mike Philip, John Henderson (who carried a cine camera) and Charlie Morrison."

Climbing in tricounis on dry rock the leading pair soon passed the short overhang which had stopped Brooker and Lyall. The chimney itself proved relatively straightforward except at the exit where the side walls became too wide to bridge and the back wall had to be climbed on small holds. By now all eight climbers were strung out on the lower part of the climb, their various conversations lending an unusually light-hearted atmosphere to the ascent of the mountain's last great problem. By the time the whole party was gathered on the terrace some were content to continue to the plateau via Tough-Brown Traverse. However, Patey, Taylor, Brooker and Dixon were anxious to complete the climb by the line opened two weeks previously. At the holdless crack they nearly turned back but spotted the new piton up the wall on the left. "The challenge was accepted, and progress made up the groove by vigorous contortion – entertaining to watch but painful to perform. The ensuing traverse leftwards to the top of the second pitch was severe all the way and ended in a remarkable hand traverse which almost exacted the last reserves of energy from everyone concerned."[7]

The first complete ascent of Parallel Gully B had been made. It had lived up to expectations by providing many interesting and varied pitches on good clean rock, quite atypical of a Lochnagar gully. It was one of the most difficult rock climbs yet achieved in the Cairngorms and probably as hard as anything in the area to be led in nails. The crux contortion groove is VS 4c.

It will be seen that two fairly distinct groups of North-east climbers were now exploring in the Cairngorms. On the one hand, there was the established hill folk loosely based around the Etchachan Club with Mac Smith as its mentor. Then there were 'The Students', the newly emerging group from Aberdeen University with Tom Patey as its driving force. As is common in these situations some of the older crew regarded the newcomers as upstarts, while they in turn, were determined to out-climb their experienced counterparts. As the years went by these groups tended to merge and lasting friendships were formed between climbers of differing backgrounds.

By 1952, Braeriach was becoming the Mecca for the Etchachan group. They found its remoteness and alpine atmosphere very rewarding. The area was also unknown to most other climbers so they had the place to themselves. Although Corrour was the nearest bothy for exploring An Garbh Choire, climbers often preferred to camp closer to the crags, either below the Angel's Peak or at a delectable site just inside the Garbh Choire Dhaidh. In September 1951 George Dey and Mac Smith built up a cave-like recess below a large boulder close to the 'Dhaidh' campsite. The Dey-Smith Bivouac, as it is known, holds two comfortably.

In May 1952, Winram, Dey, Smith and Bill Kelly climbed the shapely Sphinx Ridge in Garbh Choire Mòr. Situated centrally at the innermost point of the corrie the accumulation of snow at its base can be very deep, estimated as up to 80ft at times. On this occasion the 'rimaye' was 20ft deep and quite wide, but there was a convenient snow-bridge giving access to the left edge of the near vertical triangular front face of the buttress.

With Winram in the lead they climbed a fine pitch of 90ft up the chamfered left edge of the frontal face on a steep slab with good holds. Once on the undercut crest, the ridge gave easier climbing up round the left side of the Sphinx to a narrow col, the point reached by Hendry and Lumsden from the plateau in 1941. (Hendry had named the rock obelisk, the Sphinx). For many years it was thought the ridge was inaccessible in later months of the year because a smooth nose of rock became uncovered as the old snow receded. However, ascents have now been made at all times of the year and the climb is considered Very Difficult.

On August 12, Patey and Charlie Morrison went to Creag an Dubhloch to investigate the right wall of Central Gully. This tremendous face of very steep granite curving round for one-third of a mile from the foot of False Gully to the top of Central Gully appeared to Patey as completely inaccessible. However, despite appearances they did discover that a little more than halfway up Central Gully the wall was broken by a steep mossy chute, beyond which the wall reared up again in a series of vertical aretes. Although the first arete left of the chute was completely undercut at half-height, they could see a huge detached flake abutting the bulging section and thought this offered a chance of success.

Steep, worrying climbing on slightly loose rock took them to the base

*The central cliffs of
the North-east corrie
of Lochnagar in late
April. The large
almost snow-filled
gully on the left is
Douglas-Gibson
Gully. The thin
central fault linked by
snow patches is
Parallel Gully B*

Photo: Greg Strange

of the flake which Patey referred to as the needle. By backing up within
the crevasse between this 20ft pinnacle and the parent rock he gained
the tiny summit. The problem now was to lunge across the gap and climb
a slight bulge before moving round left to a comfortable recess. This
was achieved by Patey standing on Morrison's shoulders, a manoeuvre
which proved to be the crux of the climb (Severe). Once they had both
reached the big recess they were able to thread the final steep walls by
traversing out to the arete and passing the overhang on the right.
Although only 250ft long Sabre Edge gave three hours of continuous
exposed climbing with the outcome always in doubt until the last
move. This was the first climb to breach the Central Gully Wall and apart
from the mossy chute itself (Sabre Cut) it remains the easiest line
on the whole face.

The steep, squat buttress lying in the angle between the branches of
the Black Spout on Lochnagar is known as the Stack. In October, Patey,
Taylor and Bill Brooker climbed it by a slanting line of chimneys on
the face overlooking the left branch. This Hard Severe climb became
second only to Eagle Ridge in popularity in the 1950s and 1960s on
account of its excellent series of pitches on relatively clean rock.

Winter 1952 – 53 turned out to be one of the most significant in the
history of climbing in the Cairngorms. Cold conditions came early that
season and by early November ice was already forming in the higher
corries. On November 16, the Lairig Club organised a bus meet to
Glenmore and a number of students headed up into Coire an Lochain.
Graeme Nicol, a first-year medic, recalls that although he had never
before met the person out in front he knew it was Tom Patey. By the
time they reached the cliffs only three of them were left, Patey, Nicol

and Andy Wedderburn. They climbed the Left Branch of Y Gully finding the 20ft icicle at the crux "quite hard". (This was the icefall Stobart's party had seen when climbing the Right Branch, in 1934).

The following weekend Freddy Malcolm and Dave Ritchie from Aberdeen had a difficult struggle making the first winter ascent of Shadow Chimney on Lochnagar. This Severe rock climb which had only received its first summer ascent the previous year was not in favourable condition. The lower pitches were iced and everything was covered in fresh snow. The upper chimney proved especially difficult. Here Malcolm fell, but thanks to the rope being threaded through a chokestone he was held by Ritchie. The whole route to the top of Shadow Buttress A took seven hours.

Climbing conditions were virtually unchanged a week later when Mike Taylor, Goggs Leslie and fellow medic Leslie Fallowfield found themselves plodding up the Black Spout. It was a glorious cold day, with still only a little ice in the main gullies – a fact which persuaded them that for a first winter ascent they would have to turn to the buttresses. "The Stack with a golden crown of sunlight appeared most desirable and so it was decided".[8] They would attempt The Stack.

For Taylor, the decision to try this intimidating climb had been strongly influenced by his detailed recall of the summer ascent made less than two months previously. Nevertheless, he must have nurtured some doubts, especially knowing that he would have to lead the whole climb. They started at midday, cutting up right on a steep slope of green ice. This was the only time they climbed entirely on ice. Generally, the rocks were coated in deep wind-blown snow which had to be laboriously cleared to reveal holds below. Verglas added to the difficulty.

They followed the first two pitches of the summer line using combined tactics at a short wall low down. Farther on they had to make a very exposed left traverse where a difficult move was solved when Taylor managed to push the pick of his axe into a thin crack in the rock. This provided a good handrail where no holds existed. By the time the sun had been replaced by the rising moon, Taylor had reached the upper crux where the chimney is abandoned by stepping off a bollard on to a sloping shelf. Leslie was belayed beside him, and Fallowfield, out of sight in an alcove below could only speculate as to how things were going: "An increasing urgency in the voices above gave me an impression of difficulty encountered. From the top of the block a delicate balance move is made to the outward sloping ledge. I had gathered from the conversation that the vital holds were buried deep in ice, when the clatter of ironmongery and an apologetic shout indicated that the move had been solved by a piton. There were slow scraping sounds and a tense silence. Mike's voice, a tone higher than usual, announced the possibility of his imminent take-off. The rest was silence, but after several centuries my strained ears could detect no further movements. Then a shower of snow and ice made me look up to see Mike clinging to a wall directly above me. He moved out of sight, called down, and it was my turn."[9] At the moment when Taylor committed himself to the soft snow above the bollard, it gave way under his weight and he was left clutching the verglased rock. Fortunately, he kept cool and teetered round to easier ground, success now virtually guaranteed.

Graeme Nicol in 1954 at the time of his first Alpine trip to Chamonix

Photo: Graeme Nicol Collection

The first winter ascent of The Stack had been observed by Bill Murray who was climbing Black Spout Buttress at the time. It is said that he could not believe what he was seeing! There is no doubt it was an impressive achievement which pointed the way to further winter possibilities on steep mixed ground. The tricuoni-nailed boots were ideally suited to climbing on snow-covered or verglased rock and the local climbers were gaining more and more experience on this type of terrain. Taylor remembers the thin traverse as being the technical crux on The Stack and clearly recalls the satisfaction of solving the hard balance move by wedging his axe pick into the deep, thin crack. In those days it was very unusual to use the axe for direct aid.

After The Stack we might have expected a lull in the winter activities, if only temporarily. Not at all! With continued good, cold weather, the action shifted from Lochnagar to Ben Macdui and its Northern ramparts.

The big crag of Càrn Etchachan, above and to the left of the Shelter Stone Crag, was still completely unexplored. The cliff has two facets, a main north facing wall, split horizontally by a prominent terrace (The Great Terrace), and a gully face forming the left wall of Castlegates Gully. It is surprising that a crag of this size had escaped attention for so long but observations taken from Castlegates indicated that the gully face, at least, was vegetated and had poor quality rock. Patey had discussed the cliff with Mac Smith and his quick confirmation that the rock was indeed bad with nothing there worth climbing immediately heightened his resolve to go and have a closer look.

Not long after the Y Gully ascent Patey had arranged for Nicol and some of his friends to join him for a day rock climbing at Longhaven. Apparently, he had been none too impressed with Nicol's safety and thought he could do with some tuition! Nicol was a founder member of the Corrour Climbing Club, a small band of Aberdeen Grammar School pupils better known as the Boor Boys. Other founder members included David Grieve and Gordon Lillie. Together, with 'the likeable rogue' Ken Grassick who was an academic year behind the others, they had all progressed from hill-walking to climbing in their later years at school. The trip to Longhaven must have been successful for only a few days later Patey invited Nicol and Grassick to join Taylor and himself for an attempt on Càrn Etchachan.

On December 6, they made the four hour walk from Derry Lodge to the col overlooking Loch Avon. By the time they reached their objective "the mists had cleared revealing a magnificent pointed crag split by a multitude of cracks and chimneys all plastered with snow and ice. We had never seen the cliff at close quarters before and estimated that there were at least 20 routes for the taking. So much for Smith".[10] At the apex of the east and north faces, where The Great Terrace peters out, the upper cliff is split by a deep twisting fault. They decided to start near the foot of Castlegates Gully and take the easiest line up a vague rib which led to the start of the upper fault.

After several false starts Nicol and Grassick had managed to get themselves stuck, but the two senior members of the party, with Patey in the lead, had reached a snow-covered shelf 80ft up. "The others were still well out of our reach to the right, and the way ahead was barred by a

The 'Boor Boys' en route to Gelder Shiel 1950 – 51. From left: Ewen Gregor, Gordon Lillie, Ken Grassick, Graeme Nicol and Ronnie Wood

Photo: David Grieve

blank wall, or so we thought, for I had only advanced a few feet when the thin drapery of snow collapsed in front of me revealing a deep crack going straight into the rock. It was very dark inside but there appeared to be an opening at the top, blocked by snow. I squirmed up inside the rock for 20ft, feeling like one of the little chimney-sweeps who were sent up chimneys in Victorian days to clean out the soot. Any elbow movement was severely restricted, so I had to break an exit through the snow crust with my head. From the short ledge above the end of the tunnel we could look down on Graeme's white mop of hair, and before long both he and Grassick had been drawn up to safety."[11]

Several sustained pitches followed before they gained broken ground beyond the end of The Great Terrace. Here, below a steep rampart they moved up rightwards into the upper gully. "With only an hour of daylight remaining we stared dumbfounded at the termination of our gully. Two tiers of overhangs, smooth and shining with verglas blocked the gully, and there was no way to right or left."[12] They were really up against it now with failure, a bivouac, or both looking likely.

Patey's lead of the first overhang was definitely the hardest of the day. With insufficient ice to cut steps and everything glazed progress up to the bulge was extremely tenuous. Here, crouched under a frieze of small icicles he was forced to make a wild swing out right before pulling up on frozen turf to the foot of a long, smooth groove. Nicol came up next using a nylon cord which Patey had fixed, then the two of them pressed on up the groove to the final overhang where "at the last minute a horizontal, foot-wide ledge appeared, traversing the vertical right-hand wall of the gully. Our escape was assured".[13] At this moment of apparent salvation Grassick fell while leading up the fixed rope. Fortunately, he landed in deep soft snow and Taylor managed to field him without injury to either. To his credit, Grassick went straight back up and completed the pitch. They all reached the top at 5.30pm, seven hours after leaving the screes.

Tom Patey and Alan Will climbing Route 2 on the Black Spout Pinnacle, Lochnagar during the first crossing of the girdle traverse in May 1955

Photo: John Hay

Several days after this tremendous climb, rated at Very Severe, Patey met Nicol at college and explained enthusiastically that he thought they should name the route Scorpion on account of the 'sting in the tail'. He also maintained that he could trace the outline of a scorpion on a photograph which he had of the cliff, the upper gully being the tail!

This small group of activists were now on a winter roll. Each time they went out they bagged another first ascent. On December 29, Patey, Taylor, Brooker and Morgan climbed North West Gully on Creag an Dubh-loch in good conditions, then there was a respite during the first part of January when changeable weather brought thawing conditions which stripped away all the unstable snow leaving only névé and ice. All that was now required was a change to cold calm weather and this occurred over the weekend January 24 and 25.

On the Saturday, Grassick and Hamish Bates, another Boor Boy, went for Polyphemus Gully and found it in excellent condition. There was plenty of ice, hard snow, and no spindrift. The big pitch at the bottom was climbed entirely on snow-ice, making it somewhat easier than when Sutherland and Brooker climbed it. The crux occurred in the upper gully. They were unable to ascend directly above the cave but managed to force the groove a bit lower on the left which had been attempted by Sutherland. This proved very hard due to thin ice. Only one further ice pitch was encountered and the plateau gained after six hours of superb climbing.

The next day conditions were again perfect. Starting from the Danzig Bridge on Deeside, Patey, Taylor and Brooker walked up to Lochnagar and climbed Eagle Ridge in the very impressive time of four and a half hours. Iron-hard old snow covered the slabs and ledges, while the chimneys and grooves had ice. Patey led most of the way using combined tactics on the tower and at the summer crux, the former pitch being the most difficult due to brittle ice in the groove above the old piton. This outstanding ascent demonstrated just how far mixed winter climbing had advanced. It was one of those rare occasions with the right team in the right place at the right time!

The accessible north-facing corries of Mayar and Driesh overlooking Glen Doll and Glen Clova had seen very little winter exploration beyond that of the easy gullies. Tom Train's excellent sketch of Corrie Fee in the District Guide showed four gullies on the main face. Three of these were clearly straightforward, A, B, and D gullies, but a narrow fault marked 'C' appeared to be unclimbed and this became the objective for two Edinburgh JMCS members on a weekend meet to Glen Clova in February 1953.

It was Charles Donaldson's suggestion that he and Jimmy Marshall go and see if the ice in Gully C had survived the mild weather. According to Marshall it was very warm with hardly any snow, but the great ice groove he had been told about was filled with white ice. After a mixed section Marshall came to the first steep ice: "Water gurgled merrily down behind the ice, would it hold? A few blows with the axe proved the ice was magnificently tough and sound." They had to go on.

There were five ice pitches in all, the most substantial being that first steep wall where the ice did, in fact, collapse and they had to climb the rocks on the right; and then 100ft higher the 'great ice curtain' which Marshall led by an exposed upward right traverse. Look C Gully, as they named it, later became the classic ice route of Glen Clova.

At the end of February the mild weather had completely stripped snow and ice from the buttresses on Lochnagar. On the last day of the month Patey and Taylor made the second major route on the Black Spout Pinnacle using the line investigated by Bell. At the top of the 100ft

Mike Taylor, North-West Gully, Creag an Dubh-loch, December 1952

Photo: Tom Patey

Members of the Kincorth Club at Glen Derry, June 1955. From left: George (Dod) Adams, Dickie Barclay, Alex Thom, George and Freddy Malcolm

Photo: Mac Smith

chimney climbed by Bell, they descended from the little projecting ridge before making a very exposed traverse across the steep Black Spout wall to reach easy ground at the top of Route 1. Although rock climbing conditions were reported to be excellent, boots were discarded for the traverse as the crux moves were on ice-glazed rock. This exciting rock climb was named Route 2 and graded Severe.

On Sunday, April 12, just before this eventful winter gave way to spring, Brooker and Patey snatched an ascent of the Direct Route on the Mitre Ridge, approaching by Glen Slugain on Brooker's BSA 'Sloper' vintage motorbike. Conditions on the ridge were good with a plastering of recent snow varying from a few inches to two feet in depth. They avoided the long summer crux groove by using the much easier 'Ludwig' start farther right. Where the two starts join, just before the deep chimney, a hold broke and Patey took a short fall. "The key to a fairly straightforward move was a rounded ear of rock about the size of a big ashet. I watched from about 10ft away as Tom reached out, tested it carefully and swung on it. There was a crack as it snapped off and I braced the rope round my waist as he fell downward. I crouched awaiting the shock but it came merely as a gentle tug. He had plunged into the soft snow packing the little gully beneath and had only fallen about 15ft. Remarkably, he still had his ice axe."[14] Although uninjured he was sufficiently shaken to decline the lead (very unusual for Patey). Brooker rose to the occasion, took the sharp end and kept it, all bar one pitch, for the remainder of the climb.

At the shoulder, they were unable to make the delicate right traverse but managed to climb the wall directly by combined effort: Patey, being the shorter going first. Passing the first tower involved the most difficult climbing of the day. Brooker traversed left over slabs then climbed the hard 20ft splintered chimney before easier but sustained work took them to the little col at the top of Cumming-Crofton Route. The second tower was also passed on the left beyond which an impressive, snow-mantled final arete led them to the top.

The Mitre had provided yet another magnificent mixed winter climb to add to those of The Stack, Scorpion and Eagle Ridge. These four climbs had set a quality and standard of technical difficulty for mixed winter climbing not to be surpassed for more than a decade in the Cairngorms.

The summer of 1953 saw the emergence of another small group of climbers, The Kincorth Mountaineering Club, named after the residential area of Aberdeen, south of the Dee, where they lived. According to Freddy Malcolm, the club was formed in 1952 and included himself, his brother George and Alex (Sticker) Thom. The nickname Sticker did not refer to his adhesive qualities on rock, superb though they were, but to a time in the shipyards when an injured leg forced him to walk in such a way it appeared that his foot was stuck to the ground!

Freddy and Sticker first met and started climbing together in 1949. After a chance meeting with Winram they began to think more about exploring new ground and this led them to the local library where they discovered in the District Guide that Hourglass Buttress in Coire na Cìche of Beinn a' Bhùird was unclimbed! This was just the information they were looking for.

By 1953, some of the younger climbers from the North-east were wearing Itshide soled boots for rock climbing. These moulded rubber soles were copies of the Vibram invented by Vitale Bramine in 1935, but the name Itshide never ousted the original and for long all cleated soles were known as Vibrams. They were lighter, warmer and gave better friction on dry rock than nails. However, they were much more of a liability in wet weather or on snow and ice. Malcolm and Thom's first opportunity to use their Vibrams on the Hourglass Buttress came on May 10. Unaware of Sutherland and Brooker's previous attempt they used the long easy groove on the left to reach the neck below the steep upper 'glass' of the buttress. Direct ascent from here looked impossible but a line of steep cracks out on the right edge took them to a small, exposed rock shelf overlooking the recess of Sickle. The problem was now to overcome a short convex wall where they could see a good hold high on the left, but just out of reach. After several attempts they resorted to combined tactics, finding the moves positive but very strenuous. They were now on a substantial platform below the final rocks.

In order to progress from here they used a piton to climb a slightly overhanging crack, then a left traverse and a wide, easy groove took them to the top. This success on Hourglass Buttress was the start of a long affair between the Kincorth Club and Coire na Cìche. Their climb on the upper buttress was exposed and on excellent steep granite. The route became a classic and remained the hardest on Beinn a' Bhùird until the 1960s – VS 4c.

After the destruction of Slugain Bothy there were no open shelters or huts on the normal south-east approach to Beinn a' Bhùird. There was, of course, the Smith/Winram bivouac but this required a long walk from the bus on a Friday night and only provided limited accommodation. After much discussion the Kincorth Club resolved to build their

Freddy and Sticker's Howff, October 1955. Back, from left: Bill Chalmers, Freddy and George Malcolm. Front, from left: Tom Patey, John Hay and Joan Allan

Photo: Freddy Malcolm Collection

own 'bothy' at a secret location roughly halfway between Invercauld and Coire na Cìche. Work started in 1952, making good use of naturally occurring flat slabs of schist as well as material from the ruined Slugain Lodge. The shelter was partly subterranean with a small wooden door, fireplace and telescopic chimney. Freddy and Sticker's Howff, as it became known had further improvements made in 1954, the year when it was officially inaugurated. Two further howffs were built nearby, one by Raymond Ellis and Dave Gaffron, the other, in 1953, by Charlie Smith, Jim Robertson, Doug Mollison, Ashie Brebner, Jim Doverty and Jack Innes. Of the three Slugain Howffs only the latter, Charlie's Howff, is still in use today. The other two ceased to be visited on a regular basis in the late 1950s and fell into disrepair.

On the same day that Hourglass Buttress was climbed Hamish Bates and Tom Shaw made a snow-free ascent of Scorpion on Càrn Etchachan. A fortnight later Bates was back, this time with Grassick and Nicol on a return visit to the scene of their December triumph. Their objective now was the big ridge some way up Castlegates Gully, but their attempt was abandoned in preference for the slabby Castle Gully on its right. Grassick and Bates were still not done with this gully wall of Càrn Etchachan for they returned yet again in August with Alexander Quentin Gardiner and Al Farquharson to climb the horribly loose depression above the Sentinel leading into the upper gully of Scorpion. Neither Bates nor Grassick recorded this climb and it was not until later that Patey named it False Scorpion.

Few would have argued that the biggest rock climbing challenge in the central Cairngorms was a direct ascent of the Shelter Stone Crag. An uncompromising appearance coupled with a relatively remote setting and tales of poor rock had all combined to keep the number of interested parties to a minimum. As might be expected the big crag was now high on Patey's hit list. He and Taylor decided that time was right for a serious attempt and approached on Taylor's motorbike via Glen Derry on May 14.

The north face of the Shelter Stone Crag (An Sticil) is dominated by a magnificent shield of smooth granite slab lying between Raeburn's Buttress on the left and a prominent chimney system near the central prow. From the foot of Raeburn's Buttress a series of grass ledges slant across to the right below this slab.

"At first we followed the ledges well across to the right till they petered out high on the face, with further upward progress extremely problematical. Accordingly, we returned to the point where a steep slabby gully ascends between the middle tier of slabs and Raeburn's Buttress."[15] Their climb, Sticil Face, followed the general line of this slabby gully, mainly on its left. The crux occurred 200ft up, where Taylor led a steep edge alongside the smooth wet gully bed. Higher up they traversed away right on a higher ledge system above the central slabs to reach the plateau by an intriguing 100ft chimney left of the central prow of the crag. The climb was very much an exploratory route being circuitous and extremely vegetated. If nothing else the initial foray across the low ledges gave the Aberdonians a taste of what climbing on the main bastion would be like. As for Sticil Face, its day would come, but not as a summer climb!

If their climb on the Shelter Stone Crag was a little disappointing, they certainly made up for it in July, with the ascent of a real gem in the Garbh Choire of Beinn a' Bhùird. From the Sneck between Ben Avon and Beinn a' Bhùird the cliffs of the Garbh Choire run westwards and form a near vertical, blank wall of granite high under the plateau rim. This imposing wall, about 300ft high, ends where a narrow gully, rising from a high bay, cuts back into the hillside. The left wall of the gully is an impressive rectangular face of high angled slabs, facing west. Mac Smith, Roy Greig and Winram were the first to explore this area when they climbed the narrow gully in August 1952. Smith named it Back Bay Gully after a jazz number by Artie Shaw called Back Bay Shuffle. Smith also named the rectangular face, Squareface. He later explained:

Squareface with climbers on the second pitch

Photo: Greg Strange

"The face is squarish and this might lead one to think the name was at one and the same time factual and a play on Scarface, but the clincher was Squareface, another well-loved 78 classic on which, with a superb backing including Berigan, a self-disgusted Wingy Manone intones this drunken soliloquy to a gin bottle."[16] Unfortunately, for Smith, he had made the mistake of going into print earlier about the "magnificent Squareface Buttress",[17] before he had time to attempt it himself. He arrived just in time to watch Patey and Taylor climb the final pitches.

When viewed across the High Bay the west face of Squareface does look desperate – an apparently holdless, perpendicular wall with few features except for one prominent vertical crack cleaving the last 30ft to its flat top. If it could be climbed it would surely be one of the hardest routes in the area. In fact, the wall is really a steep slab, 300ft high, sharply defined on its left edge by an arete which drops from the apex of the North and West faces. Patey and Taylor climbed 100ft up to the easy-angled lower section of the arete then ascended the face in two exposed pitches, using an intermediate belay perched on the edge at a prominent step 60ft from the top. Although both these pitches gave excellent climbing on near-perfect rock, the last pitch, involving foot-jamming in its final crack, was undoubtedly the highlight. When they reached the top they could hardly believe that they had climbed the wall so quickly. But the reality was that, despite the climbing being very continuous, it was never harder than Very Difficult. In the years that followed many parties were equally surprised that such an impressive piece of rock could be climbed with such relative ease. Some were simply defeated by its appearance. There is no doubt that Squareface possesses the quintessential qualities of a great rock climb.

The summer of 1953 was marred by several rock climbing accidents, one of which ended in tragedy. In early August, Graeme Nicol fell from below the main chimney section of Parallel Gully B and was held on the fully extended rope by his second, Dave Smith, just as he hit the scree. He was badly shaken, bruised and had four broken ribs. Fortunately, there were others nearby, including Mac Smith and Roy Greig. When they reached Nicol his first immortal words were: "Turn me round and let me see where I fell."

When they reached Nicol his first immortal words were: "Turn me round and let me see where I fell"

That same day another Aberdeen rope was climbing higher up the gully. Twenty-one-year old Bill Stewart and James Bruce (Chesty) abandoned the climb after the accident but returned the following weekend with two female companions, intending to complete the upper pitches. It was when Stewart was making the difficult traverse left above the contortion groove that he slipped. Although the initial fall was very short, the rope severed at the point where he had placed it behind a spike as a running belay. He fell to the terrace, rolled and continued to the corrie floor, receiving fatal injuries. Bruce and the two girls managed to descend by Tough-Brown Traverse.

On a Lairig Club meet to Glen Clova a large party was ascending the rock climb known as The Comb, in Corrie Fee. At the start of the second pitch, Grassick pulled off the block to which his second, Bates, was belayed. Grassick fell, dragging the unfortunate Bates behind him. They passed over another pair of climbers and crashed onto the steep slope below. The club organised and performed a successful rescue and

Constructing the Hutchison Memorial Hut, Coire Etchachan, July 1954

Photo: Innes Ewen Collection

both climbers lived to climb another day. Grassick quickly recovered from a fractured skull, but Bates spent several weeks in hospital with a cracked pelvis.

Bill Stewart was one of a number of young hill folk from the Kaimhill area of Aberdeen. He was a very good natural climber, just beginning to make his mark on the local scene. His death was a great shock to all those who knew him, in particular the younger crowd who travelled on the bus each weekend. For a while, climbing completely lost its appeal and those who continued to go away contented themselves with walking or skiing. Graeme Nicol believes that Bill Stewart's death, and the accidents to Bates, Grassick and himself greatly affected their attitude to climbing and set the Boor Boys back several years.

Winter activity during the 1953 – 54 season was relatively quiet. On December 5, Patey and Tom Bourdillon made a second winter ascent of Eagle Ridge. The rocks were well plastered with new powder snow and presented conditions that were much more exacting than those of the previous January. Bourdillon seconded the climb in vibrams without crampons. He was unprepared for winter climbing being in the North-east to give a lecture on the 1953 British Everest Expedition where with Charles Evans he had pioneered the route to the South Summit, prior to the successful ascent by Hillary and Tensing.

The east-facing gullies and slabby corners of Creagan a' Choire Etchachan are natural ice traps in winter. A wide couloir tucked into the vertical gable of the Bastion is often very wet in summer, an observation which had been noted by Freddy Malcolm and Alex Thom. They were certain this steep fault would make a good winter climb. During thawing conditions in March the Kincorth men reached a cave below the final ice wall before abseiling off. Conditions were much better the following weekend with everything frozen solid, including their steps of the previous weekend. The wall above the cave was 30ft of bulging ice which still looked very hard. They decided to traverse right from the cave, then, cutting hand and foot holds they climbed back up and left, fixing two home-made ice pitons as very dubious running belays. To help maintain balance while cutting the leader used a third piton as an ice-claw for his left hand. Although the overall length of the climb was only 300ft, the final steep pitch was as hard as anything yet climbed on ice in the Cairngorms. The Corridor was indeed an excellent climb.

On the last day of March, Patey, Taylor, Nicol and Goggs Leslie went to the Garbh Choire of Beinn a' Bhùird. Taylor and Leslie climbed The Flume, the icefall formed where the Allt an t-Sluichd tumbles down the cliffs between Squareface and the Mitre Ridge. The other pair attempted South-East Gully, the beautiful couloir bounding the Mitre Ridge on its left. Unfortunately, the gully's aspect makes it prone to rapid thaw in sunny weather and on this occasion they were forced to abandon it after 200ft. They moved on to the east wall of the Mitre Ridge where they climbed a sustained ice-couloir with a difficult exit and eventually joined the normal ridge route just below the second tower. Afterwards, Patey described this East Wall Route as a fine winter climb. To round off a good day they all climbed Back Bay Gully via the Approach Gully to the High Bay. These were the last new routes Leslie took part in. After leaving university he joined the Royal Medical Corps and later became an eye specialist. He was a real character, an eccentric among eccentrics.

Over the years, climbers and walkers in the North-east had considered the possibility of building another shelter similar to Corrour Bothy. The consensus seemed to be that one additional bothy in the heart of the Cairngorms would have minimal effect on the area's quality of wildness and remoteness. At about this time it became known that friends of the late Dr Arthur G. Hutchison had decided a fitting tribute to his memory would be a hut situated in the midst of the hills, where climbers and hill-walkers could find refuge or spend the night. Dr Hutchison, an Aberdonian geologist, who graduated from Aberdeen and Cambridge Universities, had been killed in a cliff accident in Pembrokeshire in 1949.

Early in 1954, the Fife Estates gave permission for such a hut to be built in Coire Etchachan, near the path on the approach to Ben Macdui. Work commenced at the end of June and was completed within the scheduled time of three weeks. Despite its earth floor the Hutchison Hut quickly became popular, providing an ideal base for climbing in Coire Etchachan, Coire Sputan Dearg and the Loch Avon basin. Stewardship was bestowed on the Etchachan Club who installed a small stove in 1956, then removed it in the 1960s. Up until the 1980s the Club organised occasional work parties to maintain the fabric of the hut and also to carry out rubbish. Both the Hutchison Hut and Corrour Bothy are now maintained by the Mountain Bothies Association.

Completion of the Hutchison Memorial Hut coincided with an

important event for the Cairngorms. On July 9, the Nature Conservancy formally declared the establishment of the Cairngorms Nature Reserve, covering 62 square miles of the southern and western core area. It had taken 18 months of discussion involving Aberdeenshire and Inverness-shire County Councils, The Nature Conservancy, the Forestry Commission and the proprietors of Mar, Rothiemurchus and Inshriach Estates, on whose land the greater part of the Reserve is located. The purpose of establishing the Reserve was to safeguard plant and animal life against exploitation, and against the destruction of species particularly characteristic of the region. In so doing it was also hoped that the wild unspoiled character of the Cairngorms would be preserved as a permanent inheritance for future generations.

During the summer of 1954, Patey began explorations on the upper cliff of Càrn Etchachan. This is the steep wall above the Great Terrace which had looked so splendid on the day of the Scorpion ascent. According to Mac Smith it "is riven by a bewildering array of vertical ribs, chimneys and cracks, 300ft in height".[18] Patey persuaded Bill Brooker to accompany him to Càrn Etchachan on August 10. "Tom was keen to show someone around his cliff." They traversed along the Great Terrace, noting all the possible lines on the wall above. Where the terrace faded and the upper cliff lay back at an easier angle, ledges led naturally upwards to a large V groove. This they climbed by a ladder of holds on the right wall, then 200 feet of scrambling took them to the summit cairn. This Moderate climb, taking the easiest line above the terrace, was named the Battlements.

A month later, on the first day of the Aberdeen September Holiday weekend, a group of local climbers were staying in Bob Scott's Bothy. Although the weather was poor, Patey, Thom and Malcolm went to Càrn Etchachan to try one of the steeper lines on the Upper Cliff. Neither Freddy nor Sticker had been to the crag before but soon found themselves soloing up Scorpion, desperately trying to keep up with Patey. Once they reached the top they descended the Battlements and moved back along the terrace to below a shallow amphitheatre near the centre of the Upper Cliff. On the vertical left wall of this amphitheatre they could see a magnificent hanging crack resembling the Crack of Doom on Sròn na Cìche of Skye. Patey led and named the crack Boa, which turned out to be Severe and on excellent rock.

On their return to Luibeg, Patey suggested they should all go to Lochnagar, where he had spied a fantastic unclimbed chimney. According to Freddy, the disclosure of this climb was part of a trade-off between Patey and himself. It all started earlier in the month when he, Sticker and Mac Smith had climbed the prominent chimney on the steep slabby face left of the Chimney Pot in Garbh Choire Dhaidh. Although this fine climb had been Mac's discovery, Freddy thought that The Clam would be an appropriate name. When Patey heard this, he said they would have to think of something else because he had already used The Clam for the name of a climb on Lochnagar. The fact that he had not even climbed his Clam yet was of no consideration! It was agreed that the Lochnagar climb would take preference, provided Freddy and Sticker were involved with its first ascent. Smith later named the chimney in Garbh Choire Dhaidh, The Great Rift.

Mac Smith in the Clam, Lochnagar, September 1954. Tom Patey belaying and Freddy Malcolm looking on

Photo: Gordon Leslie

Alex Thom (Sticker)
and Freddy Malcolm
in Braemar, 1953

Photo: Mac Smith

On the holiday Monday, the Boa team plus Mike Taylor, Mac Smith, Gordon H. Leslie and Adam Watson raced to the top of Lochnagar via the Ballochbuie. Patey's chimney was an impressive narrow slit on the right wall of Raeburn's Gully. Leaving Watson on the plateau, the six men descended the gully to a point just above the jammed blocks of the winter crux. Here, just as they were established at the foot of the slit, a huge boulder, over which they had just climbed, came hurtling down the gully, providing a sobering reminder of their mortality. The Clam gave a strenuous 250ft climb calling for all the tricks in the repertoire of the chimney specialist. Mac Smith's description of the last pitch was as follows: "From the flake return directly into the narrow upper chimney (crux). Exhausting work threading the chokestones on the inside, with an exit akin to that of a cork from a bottle."[19]

It was now well into autumn of 1954, yet conditions for rock climbing on the higher hills were still good. Patey knew of another potential climb on Central Gully Wall of Creag an Dubh-loch, a huge open corner about 150ft down from Sabre Edge. October 10 was a sunny day and a number of Aberdeen climbers were in residence at Lochend Bothy at the north-east corner of Loch Muick. Freddy and Sticker had been asked by Patey to join him for an attempt on the big line and unknown to the Kincorth men he had also invited Will and McLeod. Not surprisingly, when a rather large gathering assembled in Central Gully there was some confusion as to who was going to climb with whom. The situation resolved itself when, without any discussion, Patey suddenly set off up the first pitch and McLeod stepped forward and tied on to the free end of the rope. Freddy and Sticker, somewhat piqued by these manoeuvrings, left Will with McLeod and moved up the gully to try something else.

The line on which Patey had embarked looked most improbable, especially high up where the final wall appeared impending and without ledges. A key feature, at half-height, was a dark chimney running with water. However, this apart, and despite the lateness of the season, the rock was mainly dry, affording good friction for the vibrams all three climbers were wearing. To reach the chimney the easiest line took several lengthy traverses both to left and to the right, and at one point a short, steep crack required two pitons for aid. As expected the chimney was streaming with icy-cold water and gave an unpleasant struggle before yielding with a further two pitons.

The climb now became much more exposed. The line above the chimney was blocked by overhangs so Patey made another 30ft traverse right then regained the line above the overhangs at a large recess. From here a direct ascent looked impossible but a horizontal ledge ran out onto the great wall on the right, now bathed in warm sunlight. After 30ft, an alarming loose flake had to be passed before a steep little corner could be climbed and a poor piton placed as a running belay. Further delicate traversing right, above the void, reached a point where the ledge dwindled, and here, unexpected good holds allowed a final pull up to easy ground.

According to McLeod, Patey had already decided to name the climb Vertigo Wall before he and Will had even been brought up to the top. It certainly was appropriate, for although the climb was technically easier than they expected (VS), it had a high grip factor on account of the difficult route finding and the tremendous exposure. The large recess and part of the final traverse fell away from the cliff three years later and the final pitch now starts up a steep slab and joins the original traverse just before the alarming flake. Freddy and Sticker's consolation prize was the second ascent of Sabre Edge.

During 1954, work commenced on a climber's guide to the Cairngorms under the joint editorship of Mac Smith and Patey, assisted initially, by Taylor. It was to be a further addition to the Scottish Mountaineering Club's series of pocket-guides which already covered Glen Coe, Ben Nevis and Arrochar. Patey was the driving force behind the guide at first until in 1956 he had to drop out of the venture, leaving the writing to Smith.

The quest to make winter ascents of all the gullies and buttresses on Lochnagar continued. Before Christmas Ronnie Sellers and George Annand started the season with Gargoyle Direct, then in January 1955, Patey and Alan Will accounted for Bell's Route on Shadow Buttress B, using a piton for aid at the summer crux. Conditions were perfect, with rock-hard snow enabling an amazing time of one and a half hours. In March, the same pair, together with McLeod and Thom climbed Tough-Brown Ridge via the Backdoor Route. This excellent winter line was buried deep in snow and ice after a blizzard and no rock was visible. During this period of heavy snow cover, Patey and Will made an attempt on the direct line of Labyrinth on Creag an Dubh-loch. They climbed the lower couloir but were defeated by the great unclimbed pitch in the cul-de-sac. They escaped from the Hanging Garden by traversing left along a narrow ledge which soon widened and eventually led them down to the foot of South-East Gully. This exposed narrow ledge leading into the Hanging Garden was named by Patey as the Broad Terrace.

By all accounts the summer of 1955 was blessed with brilliant, dry weather. Many new climbs were discovered and there was plenty of activity on established routes.

Since their ascent of Hourglass Buttress, Freddie and Sticker had continued their exploration of Coire na Cìche, putting up half a dozen climbs, including Trident, on the extreme left, with Elma Gordon and Sheila Anderson. Between Trident and Slugain Buttress lies an impressive slab poised above steep lower walls. Direct entry to this is problematical, the only weakness being a right-trending series of slabs and corners which form the three steps of a giant staircase. The Kincorth men reached no farther than the first corner on this line and soon came to the conclusion that the great slab, which they had named The Carpet, would have to be gained from the left.

By 1955, the Kincorth MC had grown in number to seven with the addition of Dick Barclay, George (Dod) Adams, Dave Henderson and Bill Chalmers. Freddy and Sticker were about to be called up for National Service and felt that if they did not climb The Carpet soon someone would steal it while they were away. Freddie took the unusual action of making an abseil inspection to determine the best line of attack. Forearmed with this knowledge he led Sticker, Adams, Barclay and his brother George up The Carpet in August.

They started in a grassy bay above and left of the lowest rocks and

The corrie face of the Black Spout Pinnacle in June. Pinnacle Face starts close to the bottom left corner of the snow patch

Photo: Greg Strange

followed a vegetated depression up right to a piton belay below the great slab. This commenced with a thin crack slanting rightwards. Freddy climbed the crack for 50ft. Here the easiest way trended left and up to the sanctuary of a grass shelf with a belay below an overhanging cleft. This fine sustained pitch had required some gardening and a number of pitons were used both as runners and for aid.

To complete the climb they took the overhanging cleft by combined tactics, then further slab climbing led to the top. Soon after this, they repeated The Carpet, using two pitons only as running belays, and the climb became a popular companion route to the Hourglass Buttress – VS 4c.

In July and August three more climbs were added to the upper tier of Càrn Etchachan, including the delightful Crevasse Route by Patey, Mac Smith and Bert Duguid. Across Loch Avon, Patey, climbing solo, managed to breach the overhang at half-height on the right section of the Stag Rocks. He thus completed the 600ft Relay Climb up the left edge of Longbow Crag. This was an impressive solo by Patey on a pitch which had defied several roped parties, including one led by himself. The key passage involved moving right below a large overhang in order to make committing moves into an upper groove. At the time he thought it one of the hardest pitches he had done and graded it Very Severe.

During these hectic years of Cairngorm exploration it was unusual for people from furth of the North-east to become involved. Jerry Smith was a notable exception. A talented and experienced rock climber, he came to live in Aberdeen in the early 1950s as a soil scientist at the Macaulay Institute. At first he had little contact with local climbers, but when it became known that he was working his way through the harder Lochnagar climbs, like Parallel Gully B, often solo, they naturally became intrigued by this shy, unassuming Englishman. He was eventually welcomed into the fold and became a regular on the Aberdeen scene.

On his return from Chamonix in early September, Smith and J. Dennis made ascents of Vertigo Wall and Sabre Edge on the same day. Dennis led the move off the Needle on Sabre Edge without combined tactics and Smith led the wet chimney on Vertigo with only one piton for aid. The following day, September 4, they went to Lochnagar where Smith had worked out a possible line on the corrie face of Black Spout Pinnacle, well left of Route 1. Viewed from below no obvious way was evident, just a number of discontinuous cracks and grooves leading to bulges or blank-looking slabs. Friction was going to play an important role in this type of climbing and Smith's secret weapon was a pair of espadrille, (rope-soled shoes) giving better friction than rubbers on greasy rock and more comfortable than stocking soles.

About 30ft up from the lowest rocks, near the corner of the Black Spout, two grooves slant leftwards onto the face. They chose the shallower left-hand groove to start the climb which, after an awkward initial wall, led up left in two pitches to an exposed little ledge below a bulge. Just above this Smith placed a piton in a short corner to protect himself for the next few moves. It was necessary to make a thin step up right on a steep slab to reach easier vegetated slabs leading left to a big grass stance. This VS friction move turned out to be the crux of the climb.

Up to this point they had been gradually moving left across the face

This was an impressive solo by Patey on a pitch which had defied several roped parties

but now the objective was to head back right on steeper rock towards the upper Pinnacle. Although the climbing in the next 100ft never reached the difficulty of the friction move, it was continuously interesting and sustained, following cracks, flakes and an overhanging corner to reach a grass ledge leading into the fault of Route 1, 100ft above the Springboard. Three hours after starting they stood triumphant at the summit cairn.

Although it was not realised at the time, Pinnacle Face was a breakthrough in Cairngorm climbing. It was the first major climb to venture onto open faces away from easier, more obvious lines of weakness. The climb was fairly vegetated and no move was more difficult than those in Parallel Gully B, but it was a forerunner of the modern face route which now represents much that is best in Cairngorm rock climbing.

On that same day, an equally important route was established on the spectacular pink-streaked slabs that terminate the right flank of Creagan a'Choire Etchachan. Continuity of the slabs is broken vertically by two prominent left-facing corners and it was the right-hand of these that Patey and John Hay selected for their climb. Unlike its counterpart, the right-hand corner does not commence until 80ft up. They avoided a direct ascent by scrambling up broken ground on the right then traversing back left to a good ledge at the foot of the corner.

The way ahead was obvious. A shallow, 70ft corner went straight up for more than 100ft, uninterrupted by overlaps or ledges, to culminate in a forbidding overhang. The rock was damp and in places the crack in the corner was full of vegetation. Opting to climb in stocking soles Patey set off up the first 20ft where the slab is less steep, but the rock smooth. As the slab steepened the corner became grass-choked. Here he discovered that despite the smoothness of the slabs the rock did, in fact, run to small incut holds, and by making best use of these while laybacking in the corner, progress could be made without having to rely entirely on friction. At 40ft the crack was clean and would admit only fingers and toes. Here he placed two pitons on the right wall and used them to pass this, the hardest section. The remainder of the pitch continued unrelenting until right at the overhang he found a perfect rock spike on which to belay and rest. Once Hay had seconded the corner, also in stocking soles, it became apparent that the overhang was an impostor. By stepping left they passed the main bulge using one piton for aid. The whole character of the climb then changed, surprisingly easy grassy grooves led quickly to a large platform below a final tier of slabs. This was climbed by a mossy crack slanting right using a further piton, then good holds led to the top.

After the big pitch, which Patey described as "an inch-by-inch struggle throughout", the climbing had been disappointing. As for the corner itself, it was certainly the most sustained VS climbing yet accomplished in the area. They named their climb Crimson Slabs, but a few years later, when the new guidebook was nearing completion, it was decided to change the name to The Dagger as the whole area of slabs right of the Red Chimney were now known as the Crimson Slabs. The Dagger has remained one of the great classic Cairngorm pitches giving 120ft of sustained 4c climbing.

As each new winter set in, so the aspirations of the local climbers

Stag Rocks Right-Hand Section. The 600ft Longbow Crag is the tallest part of the cliff on the right. Relay Climb follows its left edge overlooking the prominent central feature of Amphitheatre Gully

Photo: Greg Strange

Although it was not realised at the time, Pinnacle Face was a breakthrough in Cairngorm climbing

*Tom Patey and Jerry
Smith, Parallel
Buttress Lochnagar,
March 1956*

Photo: Bill Brooker

widened. Any new climb achieved in summer was now considered a potential winter target. The possibilities were legion. At Hogmanay 1956 Sellers and Jim White saw in the New Year at one of the Slugain howffs. The round trip to the Garbh Choire and back in early January leaves very little time for climbing, yet they made a determined effort to conquer the Cumming-Crofton route on the west face of the Mitre Ridge. With everything iced up they had to give best to the cliff, but not before reaching the main corner pitch. This was a bold venture by Sellers on a hard and very remote climb.

January and February 1956 were not blessed with good weather for climbing. The wind rarely moved from an easterly quarter and much fresh snow was dumped on the Cairngorms. For some time many minds had centred round the winter ascent of Parallel Buttress, and according to Mac Smith "rivalry, though not quite on a par with that for the Croz, was fairly evident – but friendly".[20] Brooker and Adams were the first to try that year, but time-consuming, icy conditions forced them to give up before leaving Tough-Brown Traverse. Patey and Will were next. At the end of February they reached the first major pitch above the terrace before abseiling off.

The following weekend Patey was back to Glen Muick with Jerry Smith and Brooker. They joined five other climbers in Lochend Bothy, having arrived in the small hours from Aberdeen via bus, a local dance in Ballater, a taxi, and a four mile walk through drifted snow from the Bailey bridge. It was still windy the next morning but Patey at least, was optimistic. So despite the late hour they headed for Lochnagar. When they reached the corrie they found it "so plastered with new snow and hoar frost that scarcely any rocks were visible".[21]

As usual, Patey set off at a terrific rate soloing the unclimbed lower pitch of Parallel Gully A. By the time that Smith and Brooker, with the ropes, had caught up with him he was waiting impatiently at a belay just left of the scoop on Parallel Gully B. There was some discussion about who was going to lead but despite an initial agreement that they should all share this responsibility Patey went first and managed to keep this position for most of the climb.

Tying directly onto one of the full weight nylon ropes, he took a few slings and pitons and quickly climbed 30ft of ice-glazed rock to another stance where he brought up Smith. According to Brooker, both Patey and Smith were 'slingless wonders' in that they chose not to attach their ice axe to themselves either by a wrist loop or sling, although Smith would clip his axe to a carabiner on his waist-line when rock climbing. There was much debate at the time as to the pros and cons of being slingless but the majority of climbers chose to put up with the hassle of a sling in preference to running the risk of dropping the axe.

A little way above Smith's stance Patey reached the ring piton from which he and Will had retreated the previous weekend. Using this for tension he made a difficult right traverse in to the slabby corner over-looking Gully B. This was well iced and gave sustained cutting up to easier ground on the edge of the gully. After a quick look at the next pitch he decided that since there was now only three and a half hours of daylight left they would move into Gully B, then traverse back onto the buttress at the upper scoop, thus avoiding 100ft of the crest.

By the time all three had reached the ledge below the tower Patey appeared to be all-in. He was inadequately clad for climbing in these conditions, being dressed mostly in borrowed clothing. Smith, described him as "looking cold, his hair matted with snow. His face, where visible, shades of mauve and green". The tower was to be Smith's pitch. "The sepulchral walls of rock suppurating verglas looked uncompromising."[22] A few feet above the ledge he found an old piton, but even by pulling on this he could find no further holds above. He retreated, and almost like Bell 17 years previously, he produced two secret weapons from inside his sack. This time, however, it was not pitons but a set of etrier (short rope step ladders). By standing on the top rung of one of the etriers hung from the piton he was able to drive a 12 inch ice piton into the ice-filled crack above, and using this he pulled up to a small ledge. After clearing away more powder snow he placed a rock piton in the same horizontal crack Bell had used, but still could not reach any holds standing on the top rung of his second etrier. "With my right limbs pressed across the groove, I stooped down and mantelshelved onto the piton, a movement of such ghastly delicacy that at once I wanted to reverse it. But now the steps of the etrier were flat against the wall and I could not go back. I called to Bill asking him where to look for holds, but had to wait while he photographed Tom, a shot that he hoped would rival Rebuffat's Après le second bivouac in convey-ing the atmosphere of the climb. Apparently, there was a good flake under the overhang above me, but first I had to remove several cubic yards of compact snow, my left toe quivering unsteadily on the peg all this while. At last, jamming my axe behind the flake, I swung over to a bank of snow on the left."[23]

The transition from steep, intimidating, ice-glazed rock to gently-angled snow was as dramatic as it was unexpected. Smooth slabs on the

Patey appeared to be all-in. He was inadequately clad for climbing in these conditions, being dressed mostly in borrowed clothing

*Jerry Smith climbing
the first pitch of
Route 1, Lochnagar*

Photo: Bill Brooker

Gully A side of the ridge were now covered in firm snow allowing an easy traverse to regain the crest beyond the apparent summit of the tower. With daylight rapidly fading they dashed up a beautiful snow arete and reached the plateau after seven and a half hours of climbing.

Given the unfavourable snow conditions and the strong winds this was a most commendable climb by a very strong party. It could hardly be described as a true ascent of Parallel Buttress since the lower third and 100ft of the mid-section had been avoided. The use of four pitons and etriers was seen by a few as rather unsatisfactory.

With Parallel Buttress now in the bag the only major buttress on Lochnagar still unclimbed in winter was the Black Spout Pinnacle. This situation lasted precisely one week, for the following Sunday, Jerry Smith and Brooker returned to the North-east corrie to climb the Pinnacle by way of Route 1. Conditions had changed radically during the week.

"The large quantities of powder snow had shrunk to crisp frozen sheets lying on the ledges and holds. Steep rock surfaces were bare and dry; ice gleamed cold and grey in cracks and was smeared here and there like black varnish."[24]

Indeed conditions were nigh perfect. Smith led the first pitch out of the gully, and as expected it proved to be the crux. It needed delicate work on steep thinly iced slabs up to the bulge, where he used a piton for aid while cutting hand holds in the ice on the upper slab prior to making the big pull up. Brooker continued up to the Springboard, where the nervous tension eased, for they knew that although there was still 400ft of sustained climbing to follow, none of it would be as difficult, nor as intimidating, as that they had already overcome. Revelling in the superb conditions and the magnificent situations on the Pinnacle they followed the original line throughout, except that the central fault above the Springboard was entered from the right to avoid an awkward little chimney.

At this time discussions were taking place among Aberdeen climbers concerning the introduction of a separate grading system for winter climbs. For a while they had felt the adjectival system in use for rock climbing "was inappropriate and could be misleading – the climber's snow technique often varying greatly from his performance on rock".[25] After much debate a numerical system was proposed starting with Grade 1 for the easiest snow gullies and rising to Grade V for the hardest climbs. The classifications were to be explained and used in the forthcoming guide, but meantime it was hoped that all new winter ascents would be recorded with an appropriate numerical winter grade. Using the new system Smith and Brooker gave Route 1 a Grade V rating on account of its length and technical standard, which even in the very favourable conditions was still VS.[26] The new system was intended to give an overall assessment of the whole climb, similar to the method of grading Alpine climbs. (Other climbs considered Grade V at this time were Polyphemus Gully, Douglas-Gibson Gully, Eagle Ridge, Parallel Buttress and Scorpion.)

On March 31, Brooker climbed his third new winter route on Lochnagar that month, this time accompanied by Mike Taylor. They followed the line of least resistance on the broad face of Eagle Buttress between Eagle Ridge and Parallel Gully A. Starting just left of Gully A they climbed 400ft of hard snow and ice until steeper rocks forced a traverse right to below three parallel grooves overlooking Gully A. The central of these was full of ice and provided the hardest climbing of the day. They finished up the left edge of the winter finish to Gully A.

Also at the end of March, George McLeod and Ian Brown made the first 'true' winter ascent of Hell's Lum which they found high angled but straightforward. Both men were working at Glenmore Lodge, the Scottish Centre of Outdoor Training. McLeod, having started in 1954 as a handyman, went on to become a full-time instructor. He was employed at the Lodge until 1963, during which time he made two trips to Antarctica. After this, he went to Denver, Colorado to work in Outward Bound.

John Hay was three years junior to the Boor Boys at Aberdeen Grammar School. He developed an interest in the hills through his parents who were both members of the Cairngorm Club. In his early days he enjoyed solo climbing within his capabilities, and had made several first ascents in this way. It was when he went to Aberdeen University to study law that he met Patey and other local climbers.

After the ascent of The Dagger, Hay was keen to return to the Crimson Slabs to try the left-hand corner. He investigated the line with Will and Adams on a number of occasions in 1956. On April 10, when the rock was still very wet, they started directly below the corner and followed an easy diagonal crack up left to a large platform overlooking the Red Chimney. From here they worked their way back up right into the main corner via a small groove set in the middle of the slab. At this point, halfway up the cliff, they found an old abseil piton. Their own attempt was abandoned a little higher. It was on this same visit that the three men attempted the impressive crack running straight up the slabs, midway between the two main corners. They climbed the crack for 40ft to a curious round hole where to their amazement they found another old peg. They replaced this with a new ring piton then retreated naming the crack-line Willpower.

Jerry Smith high on Route 1, Black Spout Pinnacle, Lochnagar, March 1956

Photo: Bill Brooker

Two days later they were joined by two friends to climb the left-hand flying ridge of Janus in Coire Sputan Dearg. At the crux, Hay laybacked a vertical crack then used several pitons to traverse right on to the easy crest. When Mac Smith got to hear about this use of pitons on such a short climb, a 200ft variation to one of his own climbs no less, he was not amused. Sensing Smith's disapproval they named the climb Hackingbush's Horror in his honour. Hackingbush, a Marx Brothers character, was a name used by both Smith and Gordon Leslie for each other, in times of mild frustration or annoyance. Hay thought it quite appropriate as both men were heavy smokers. When Smith's Guide appeared in 1961 he included the climb, but under the name of Janus Left Face!

Two months' later, Barclay and Brooker repeated Hackingbush, hoping to eliminate all the aid, but were forced to use one piton on the traverse. On this same day in early June they made a first ascent on the Grey Man's Crag. Between Slab Chimney and Pilgrim's Groove lies a prominent steep buttress with a dark slanting crack low down on its left. They climbed this easy crack then moved back right onto the buttress and followed its crest until it became impending. Here they moved up left and with assistance from Brooker, Barclay succeeded in swinging up right

*"I am always
astounded by
Grassick on
a rock climb,"
– Bill Brooker*

over the overhang to grasp a flake. This hard move gave access to a 30ft vertical crack which led to the top. Although not a particularly good route, Amethyst Wall became the test-piece of Sputan for many years. Climbed without combined tactics at the crux it is HVS.

Inspired by this success, Brooker's thoughts turned to one of his favourite haunts, the Black Spout Pinnacle. Six days later he and Grassick arrived in the corrie of Lochnagar to be greeted by mist and damp rock. It would have been easy to abandon their plans for a second ascent of Pinnacle Face (unknown to them Jimmy Marshall and Archie Hendry had made the second ascent a few weeks earlier) but Grassick's enthusiasm was not going to be quashed by greasy slabs and he launched up the first pitch in his Vibrams with great determination. As they climbed, a strong wind developed which cleared the mist and dried the rock. By the time they had finished the route both the climbers and the rock were in good shape.

As they descended ledges on Route 1 Brooker suggested attempting a steep line going up the Black Spout face, starting in the right hand fault above the Springboard and heading up across the traverse of Route 2 towards a projecting nose, seen high on the skyline. He had been aware of this line ever since he and Sutherland climbed Route 1, but had never given it serious consideration until now. The right-hand fault formed a shallow trough which rose for 100ft to a triangular overhang. Passing this overhang to gain an upper crack descending from the start of the Route 2 traverse looked like being the major obstacle to success.

Brooker led up the trough and took a belay on the right edge where a small ledge blocked the fault. "From our stance a shallow rib rose steeply and discouragingly to form the edge of the trough. At its steepest, the crest was fissured by a kind of incipient flake which proved to be the key to the problem. I am always astounded by Grassick on a rock climb; that a man of his gross and ungainly shape could ever move gracefully would seem incredible, and yet he can, and does. Here today was gone the shambling gait he keeps for terra firma and in its place was a kind of tip-toe alertness. Smoothly, he laybacked the flake then with reptilian grace glided up the slabby trough beyond to a belay hard under the big overhang we had noted earlier."[27]

By moving right round a large, pointed block Brooker found himself in a tiny alcove, still below the overhang. He made a piton belay and offered Grassick the lead. The situation was very exposed but Grassick succeeded on his second attempt, luckily finding a good crack above the bulge, allowing him to pull strenuously through to gain a comfortable stance beside another huge block. Above them a big vegetated groove slanted left to the finish of the Route 2 traverse but Brooker ignored this in preference for a steeper and cleaner 100ft crack leading to one of Patey's giant pitons at the belay before the crux of Route 2.

They were now only about 30ft from the jutting nose. Grassick climbed a good crack to reach a peculiar wedged flake which pivoted alarmingly through an arc of six inches. He carefully threaded a sling round its axis and pulled up right to a small ledge just right of the nose. A mere 20ft now separated them from easy ground, but ahead was another overhang split by twin cracks which looked most unfriendly (the Direct Finish climbed by Guy Muhlemann in 1974). At this point Brooker noticed a horizontal break in the left wall. "I heaved myself into the cleft, wormed along on my stomach for a few feet, stood up, and made a final stride across the extreme tip of the Nose, with almost the entire Pinnacle plunging beneath my heels."[28]

This unexpected finish rounded off a great day. Both men agreed that the combination of Pinnacle Face with their new climb, which they called The Link, had given them the best and most continuous rock climbing they had ever enjoyed on Lochnagar. Brooker thought the over-hanging corner on Pinnacle Face was harder than anything on the Link, but that the latter was steeper and had more sustained difficulty. Despite Brooker's immediate impression after the climb, the general consensus is that The Link held the status of being the hardest rock climb on Lochnagar for 10 years (VS 4c), while in the 1970s and 1980s it became the main thoroughfare on the upper Pinnacle.

The Grassick-Brooker team was in action again before the end of June to produce one of the best known rock climbs in the Cairngorms. On June 24, while staying in the Hutchison Hut, they went to try The Dagger. However, when they reached the Crimson Slabs their attention was drawn away left by the striking profile of the Corridor edge of the Bastion. Perhaps they could find a way onto this clean cut edge and follow it throughout?

The Corridor side of the crest is dominated by a great slab, 200ft high which abuts a near vertical top wall. The first 80ft of the crest is steep and apparently holdless. They decided to start on the great slab, and then traverse back to the crest where it became more amenable. Commencing between two huge blocks, 20ft up the Corridor, they climbed a wide crack up right, then ascended the slab with little diffi-culty for 40ft and made a piton belay. The 50ft left traverse from here to the edge was exposed and delicate but only mildly Severe. So far so good! Directly above, the crest overhung slightly. They passed this section on the left then continued to below an overhanging corner which seemed to offer the only way ahead. By fixing a piton belay they were able to use combined effort to start the corner, then, an awkward thrutchy exit onto the right edge led to an excellent stance. They thought this short pitch to be the crux and graded it Hard Severe. The crest was now much easier-angled and could have been avoided by a groove on the left, but they continued right on the edge all the way for a farther 120ft of sustained climbing, sometimes using holds on the sheer right wall. They named the climb Talisman, which with its steep, clean rock and grand situations is considered by many to be the best route on the crag. According to Brooker the actual Talisman was a piece of aluminium alloy angle which he was lugging around as a belay for turf or wide cracks at that time. It provided the belay piton at the crux and it seemed like a good name.

Another contender for best route on the crag must go to the climb made by Hay in July. On a warm day with dry rock he completed the left-hand corner on the Crimson Slabs. Unfortunately, Adams and Will were unavailable on this occasion but he was joined by fellow Etchachan Club member Ronnie Wiseman (Esposito) and Allan Cowie. He followed the main corner directly using two pitons for aid, one at the

The steep Black Spout Wall of the Pinnacle. The Link commences from the Springboard (obvious grass ledges low down) and follows the right-hand fault-line heading more or less straight up to the summit

Photo: Douglas Dinwoodie

The Link, had given them the best and most continuous rock climbing they had ever enjoyed on Lochnagar

prominent overlap and the other at a smooth section higher up. This excellent 120ft pitch was comparable to the Dagger in quality, but not quite so difficult. (VS 4c). The name Djibangi was suggested by Adams early in the campaign, and to a man, all who had been involved agreed it had an intriguing ring to it. (Will thinks the name referred to an empty oil drum which Adams carried to the foot of the climb – Hay says it is a type of Australian duck!)

Hay and Adams were involved with two further projects at the end of summer 1956. On the Crimson Slabs they climbed a good independent start to The Dagger, but it was over on the Shelter Stone Crag that they investigated a much more ambitious line near the centre of the main bastion. At the base of the crag a girdling apron of lower slabs tapers down to a point just a few hundred feet above the Shelter Stone itself and almost directly below the apparent summit of the crag. From these lowest rocks a series of right-facing corners, one above the other, but not in line, lead up to the western end of the ledge system which Patey and Taylor had crossed in 1953.

Starting just right of the first corner Hay and Adams scrambled up a vegetated gully until a steep wall at 80ft forced a traverse left to a belay below an upper corner. This they climbed for a short distance before moving left again to a larger, smooth-floored parallel corner. Utilising two pitons in cracks on the left wall Hay climbed this 40ft corner and exited back right to broken ground and the terrace. Here they abandoned their attempt and escaped left across the ledge system leaving the main part of the bastion untouched.

There was a fair cover of snow lying on upper Deeside in early January 1957. On January 13, Patey completed his trilogy of climbs on Central Gully Wall when with Freddy and Sticker he forced the 'steep mossy chute' just right of Sabre Edge, naming it Sabre Cut. The crux was a two-tiered ice pitch, climbed initially close into the left wall, then a right traverse below an overhang of icicles to a trough and further steep ice. They used icicle belays more than once! Although only 250ft this was the first difficult winter climb made on Creag an Dubh-loch, a cliff with enormous winter potential – Grade IV.

The following month, Patey made a return visit to Càrn Etchachan. He had noted a possible winter line following ramps and grooves starting just left of Scorpion and linking with the Battlements on the upper tier. This combination he believed would give one of the longest natural climbs in the area. February 10 dawned clear and cold. Patey and Mac Smith left early from Derry and made quick work of the seven mile walk to the foot of Castle Gates Gully. Conditions were ideal with hard snow, ice and bare rock. Starting to the right of the lowest rocks they took a zig-zag course for 250ft to reach a snow bay with a deep tapering chimney on its left margin. The ascent and exit of this chimney proved to be the crux of the lower part of the climb. For the next three or four pitches they first trended left, then back right to eventually gain the Battlements Groove, unseen from below. This gave 50ft of steep ice, the hardest climbing on the upper cliff. Further steep climbing up left for 120ft and a short rock wall led to the summit slopes and the top of Càrn Etchachan. This very fine mountaineering climb, which they appropriately named Route Major, ran out at just more than

George Adams following the main corner pitch on the second ascent of Djibangi, August 1956

Photo: John Hay

900ft and took three and a half hours: "The axe required for every step." [29] – Grade IV.

This had been a winter of less than average snowfall, and by the end of March most steep rock and all south-facing corries were virtually clear of snow. However, during the Aberdeen Spring Holiday, Dod Adams, Jim White and Fraser Henderson found a late cold spell had deposited a fresh fall of snow on all the rocks in Coire an Lochain of Cairn Gorm. This presented an opportunity for a winter ascent of Savage Slit. With Adams in the lead they set about this Cairngorm classic. "The slit itself between chokestones was blocked out partially with old ice, partially with packed powder. The upper chokestones provided the hardest moves. These were heavily iced and the walls of the Slit sheathed in verglas. One rock piton used at each; at the first for a runner, at the second (crux) for direct aid on an extremely hard move out of the crack." [30] This was quite a coup for the easy-going Adams, for although the climb was given a rating of Grade IV at the time it was probably as technically hard as any snowed-up rock climb accomplished in the Cairngorms by then – Grade V.

With the approach of longer days, thoughts naturally turned to climbing on warm dry rock; rare though these occasions are in the high corries of the Cairngorms. For those with pioneering ambitions, solutions to several 'last great problems' were high on the agenda, in particular a direct ascent of the Shelter Stone Crag and further climbs on Creag an Dubh-loch. By the summer of 1957 several parties had begun probing the more obvious lines of weakness on the latter's Central Gully Wall, but no-one had made any significant progress. The technical and psychological step-up required for these bold ventures had still not been attained by the locals. Surprisingly, at this time, even the most accomplished rock climbers from south of the Border and from the Creagh Dhu and JMCS Clubs in Scotland continued to concentrate their efforts in Glen Coe, on Ben Nevis and in the Cuillin, still unaware of the great potential in the Cairngorms.

June saw a partial success on the Shelter Stone Crag when Grassick, Nicol and Gordon Lillie continued the line started by Hay and Adams the previous September and managed to find a way to the top of the crag. On the lower slabs they climbed a right-facing corner parallel to, and right of the one taken by Hay but it still required two pitons for aid. The lower slabs end at a narrow grass terrace, named the Gallery, which leads right from the conspicuous chimney system near the centre of the crag. Above the Gallery the rock steepens considerably and here the Boor Boys moved right and followed a well-defined slanting crack leading up to the lower step on the right skyline. At the point where Clach Dhian Chimney joins this slanting crack they climbed a deep 30ft chimney in the left wall. Further climbing up and left, then back right brought them to the upper step on the right skyline. They did not attempt the final vertical wall, but escaped right to join the last pitch of Clach Dhian Chimney. The climbing above the Gallery was no more difficult than the lower slabs, and the route, now Postern, graded Hard Severe.

The straight face of Hell's Lum Crag presents an attractive wall of slabby granite, smooth and glaciated in the lower reaches, but more

Hell's Lum Crag Frontal Face. Devil's Delight follows a line just right of centre, passing through the grass ledge of the Haven to finish up the dark overlapping top wall. Deep Cut Chimney is the prominent long black slit towards the left

Photo: Andy Nisbet

fissured and steeper towards the top. The cliff is prone to seepage but the open south-easterly aspect and the clean rock are adequate compensations, especially in periods of dry weather.

Ronnie Sellers recognised the potential of this splendid crag and visited it several times towards the end of 1956. (The two excellent little climbs on Stag Rocks made by Sellers and Smith, Afterthought Arête and Final Selection, resulted from attempts on Hell's Lum Crag being thwarted by unfavourable conditions.) On August 4, 1957 Sellers with Annand finally succeeded in climbing the frontal face by a line near the centre. Above the Haven, a prominent green ledge at half-height, three good pitches up cracks through bulges led to the top. They named this Hard Severe climb Devil's Delight, thus starting a trend for a 'Hellish' nomenclature on this cliff.

During the summer of 1957, Edinburgh University officer cadets constructed the Sinclair Hut, a small stone shelter at the north end of the Làirig Ghrù, 100 yards above the Allt Mhòr at the junction of the Lairig path and the path from the Chalamain Gap. The shelter was erected in memory of their former CO, Colonel Angus Sinclair who died during a training exercise in the Cairngorms in 1954. It provided accommodation for about four people in two small rooms. Despite the presence of a bench and two iron beds the 'Sinky' hut was always an austere place, likened by many to a pillbox. The main drawback was the concrete floor which became awash with condensation in winter. Its one redeeming feature was its grand location at the entrance to the narrowing pass with a wide panorama out over Glen More. At the time of its construction, local climbers doubted its value and quite a number were opposed to it on environmental grounds.

Grassick and Nicol's summer visit to the Shelter Stone Crag had given them a chance to become better acquainted with the massive cliff. It occurred to them that a winter ascent would be a terrific challenge and wondered why no-one had yet attempted it. Delicate questioning among the Aberdeen climbers seemed to suggest that no-one had yet contemplated such an undertaking. They decided that Sticil Face was the best line and vowed to give it a try at the first opportunity. The previous winter Nicol had been with Patey and Hamish MacInnes on the first winter ascent of Zero Gully on Nevis and both he and Grassick were uneasy about how Patey would react when he discovered that they planned to 'steal' a winter ascent of one of his routes. The situation was really a *fait accompli* since Patey was by then away from Aberdeen doing his National Service with the Royal Navy attached to 42 Royal Marine Commando. They could not ask him to join them for an attempt anyway.

Winter conditions looked promising over Christmas 1957, so Boxing Day found the pair back at the Hutchison Hut. The next day was cold and clear with only a little wind. Within an hour they were roping-up below Raeburn's Buttress pondering the climb ahead. This was going to be the first major winter climb using their new 10-point French crampons. Also, remembering their anxiety about lack of daylight five years earlier on Scorpion, they had brought home-made head torches.

Looking up the face they could see the slabby gully alongside the summer line, filled with ice leading unbroken to the High Ledge – a most impressive sight. They reached the gully up easy snow-covered slabs round the base of Raeburn's Buttress then Nicol led the first difficult pitch up snow-covered blocks and vegetation left of the ice to a big ledge below the summer crux. At this point the gully formed a steep, narrow column of ice which looked too desperate to climb so Grassick tackled the rocks on the left. Whether he followed the exact summer line or climbed farther left is uncertain, but his pitch ended with a hard V-groove before snow led back on to the ice.

"Here the gully becomes more defined as the walls close in and a direct assault on a 90ft ice wall was the only way. The danger, in those days, was lack of security; rock and piton belays were not always possible. It was, therefore, with great relief that we hammered in two reasonable pitons on this pitch, for it turned out to be the crux of the climb. Graeme led it in his usual fearless fashion, leavened by the occasional blasphemous aside. He ended with his most famous retort of all: "We die together."[31]

Passage of the High Ledge was accomplished in two exposed 120ft run-outs, and then a short ice pitch took them to below the final 100ft chimney. In the gathering gloom, Grassick gave this a go but had to give up. They remembered Scorpion and a feeling of deja vu inspired

Angus Sinclair Hut.

Photo: Gordon Leslie

them to try elsewhere. Following the beam of his torch Grassick traversed right beneath an overhang and found a stance below a 12ft wall.

"There appeared to be sky above and our spirits rose. Aberdonians have long been known to be experts in combined tactics when finesse and style have failed. Standing on Graeme's shoulders, I scrambled desperately for handholds (I don't think I drew blood). A push, a lunge, a heave, a knee, two knees and I was there. A short snow arete led up onto the plateau."[32] Tired, wet, yet elated the two young men made their way back to the cold comfort of the Hutchison Hut knowing their nine hours on Shelter Stone Crag had produced an outstanding winter climb comparable to Scorpion but even more difficult – Grade V.

The fact that Patey was no longer based in the North-east did little to prevent him from pursuing his great passion for winter climbing. During January and early February 1958, while in Aviemore ski-training with the Marines, he managed to pack in several days climbing in the Northern Corries and on Hell's Lum Crag. On January 17, he went to Coire an t-Sneachda and soloed Fiacaill Couloir, the curving gully tucked high under the east wall of the Fiacaill Ridge. A more taxing climb was the winter ascent of Deep Cut Chimney on Hell's Lum Crag which he made with D. Holroyd two days later. "A fine ice route climbed under exceptionally unfavourable conditions. Two feet of recent powder snow overlying ice. Blizzard and much spindrift."[33] Just how bad conditions really were can only be imagined, but he found the hardest climbing getting to the recessed part of the chimney and made no mention of the exit at the top which most climbers find to be the crux. He likened the climb to Comb Gully on Ben Nevis, but with more sustained difficulties – Grade IV.

A fortnight later, again climbing solo, he made the first winter ascent of Central Crack Route in Coire an Lochain, another excellent winter climb – Grade IV.

This reawakening of interest in the winter potential of the Northern Corries of Cairngorm and the Loch Avon Basin, accessed from Speyside, coincided with an influential incursion by an outside party into the heartland of North-east climbing. For nearly 10 years mountaineering in the Cairngorms had been completely dominated by Aberdeen-based climbers. They had enjoyed a prolonged period of isolation with no competition from elsewhere, a situation which was inevitably going to change.

A nucleus of talented climbers had emerged from Edinburgh with the 'Old Man' Jimmy Marshall as their unofficial leader. Twenty-nine-year-old Marshall and his associates in the Edinburgh JMCS had served long apprenticeships, climbing many of the hardest winter routes in Glen Coe and on Ben Nevis. The previous April, Marshall had given a slide show to the Etchachan Club, after which he spent a great day with Patey on Lochnagar.

"I had Pierre Allain kletterschuhe thinking we'd be on warm rock but we ended up on Lochnagar. The cliff was pretty well cleared of snow but for the gullies so Tom insisted we climb Polyphemus Gully, which we did unroped at great pace. Then we went up Route 2 and finally made the first ascent of Shylock's Chimney. Of course, Patey led everything; he could be a real hog." This conducted tour in the corrie of Lochnagar

A nucleus of talented climbers had emerged from Edinburgh with the 'Old Man' Jimmy Marshall as their unofficial leader

Jimmy Marshall,
Parallel Gully B,
February 1958

Photo: Graham Tiso, SMC
Collection

reminded Marshall that ever since reading Patey's article in the 1953 SMCJ about the first ascent of Parallel Gully B what a great joke it would be to make that route in winter!

And so it came about that in the evening of February 23, a party comprising Marshall, his brother Ronnie, Graham Tiso and Jim Stenhouse just made it over the Devil's Elbow on their way to Allt-na-giubhsaich bothy in Glen Muick. The next day winter conditions in the North-east corrie were excellent and Marshall and Tiso made a bee-line for the Parallel Gullies. Gully B looked magnificent. Its lower chimney was lean with bare side walls and only the back plated in ice. There appeared to be two steep ice bulges, one just below the main chimney and the other at its exit onto the Tough-Brown crossing.

Marshall started by climbing directly in the line of the gully passing two awkward sections of iced rock before taking a piton belay 40ft up. From here, Tiso, who according to Marshall was a novice on ice, led the next pitch which commenced with the first steep ice wall and took them into the main chimney. Ninety feet below the exit they encountered another fierce ice bulge: "The next 30ft were the most difficult, left leg in the chimney, right leg extended to the full and only just making contact with the walls by the points of the crampons, and cutting vertical slots in the ice on the left wall; where the chimney went into

the ice. I got a piton in under a flake at the back of the gully and stood in a sling while cutting holds above the bulge. This whole section was extremely severe."[34]

Fortunately, the final ice overhang went relatively easily by bridging and they reached the scoop after four and a half hours climbing. The first pitch in the upper gully was climbed directly on good steep ice and this led into the bay below the final steep wall which was bare. Here they followed a groove up right to reach easy snow slopes at the top of Tough-Brown Ridge.

At the time of this ascent, Marshall thought it was the finest and most difficult winter climb he had done anywhere in Scotland. (Grade V). It is doubtful if any of the local climbers had seriously thought about a winter ascent of what was still considered to be a hard rock climb. All, that is, except Patey who, when learning of Marshall's success while in southern England, wrote to Nicol asking why they had allowed this Edinburgh raiding party to get away with stealing his route!

That same day, Robin Smith and Doug Dingwall, coincidentally from a separate Edinburgh party based in Lochend Bothy, had a hard tussle on Eagle Ridge before turning back from below the summer crux. They had no working torch and the retreat down the ridge in darkness took a long time. Their EUMC friends back at the bothy were greatly relieved when the pair walked in around midnight still linked by the frozen rope. This attempt would have been the first by a party from outwith the North-east and although, according to Jimmy Marshall, Smith "was a bit shame-faced about his failure", it was a good effort under the circumstances with no prior knowledge of the route in summer.

There were a number of important rock climbs pioneered during the summer of 1958. July saw renewed activity on Creag an Dubh-loch, with attention focusing on two specific areas of this huge crag, namely the very steep Central Gully Wall just below Vertigo Wall and the big frontal face farther down at the gully entrance. A prominent feature on the gully wall is a vast, seemingly precarious wedged block, 50ft above the scree and about the same distance below a series of slabby shelves which slant across the face from the start of Vertigo. Below and right of the wedged block a sloping ramp goes up to the base of a tremendous vertical groove system which cuts its way straight up the full height of the cliff. Several parties had attempted to climb the groove system from the bottom.

In 1957, Grassick and Nicol had started up above the ramp but retreated after a short distance, leaving at least one piton. Jerry Smith and Dick Barclay had also investigated the rock hereabouts.

Earlier, Patey had traversed the slabby shelves out right from below Vertigo Wall using rope tension from a piton. He managed to reach a ledge 60ft directly above the wedged block. From this point a straight line of weakness rose steeply for a 100ft to the base of an upper system of slabs. He did not climb beyond the ledge but proposed to ascend to the upper slabs, then to work out right, crossing the big groove attempted by Grassick and Nicol to reach easy ground through a notch on the right skyline. This projected climb became known as Patey's Giant.

Grassick and Nicol had also tried a line on the frontal face starting from the lowest rocks well down below the entrance to Central Gully. One of the many crack systems hereabouts springs from a large recess and crosses a prominent jutting roof 150ft up. They started at the right side of the recess and climbed a fault up right until it steepened 50ft below the level of the jutting roof. Here the climbing became markedly harder so they retreated.

In early July 1958, Barclay re-entered the scene with Brooker. Could they fare any better than their fellow Aberdonians? On the far right side of the frontal face an obvious left slanting crack runs up below False Gully to reach the right end of a sloping grass terrace, known as the Caterpillar. It runs left for 100ft, rising slightly to peter out below a prominent steep Red Wall, 300ft above Grassick and Nicol's recess. Barclay and Brooker climbed this Caterpillar Crack to the terrace then continued up to join the lower shelf of False Gully. Most of the climbing was heavily vegetated except for 60ft of the Crack which they found very awkward and used two pitons for aid.

While making this ascent, the two men scrambled across the Caterpillar to check on the possibility of climbing the face above. Brooker accidentally dropped his sack from just below the Red Wall. It smashed into the scree 300ft below, having only touched rock once. If they were going to make a direct ascent of the cliff their line would be that taken by the falling rucksack – a daunting thought. Some time later they did investigate the line attempted by Grassick and Nicol but both climbers failed to make any progress beyond 60ft The steep slabs and vertical walls were too difficult for them to climb without resorting to excessive aid. They decided their best chance was to start on the Caterpillar and follow ledges out left below the Red Wall. They then hoped to find a way up through the final steep section to reach the easier-angled upper slabs and perhaps climb the obvious crack which continues directly up above the Red Wall.

They made their bid on August 26, just four days after their successful

The great Central Gully Wall of Creag an Dubh-loch. Caterpillar Crack is the left-slanting crack (bottom right) leading via the grass Caterpillar to below the prominent Red Wall. Waterkelpie Wall approximates to the crack line rising from the Red Wall. The smooth face above and right of Caterpillar Crack is False Gully Wall

Photo: Andy Nisbet

ascent of Dawn Grooves on Sgùrr Mhic Choinnich in Skye. Brooker was wearing soft suede kletterschuhe while Barclay sported his usual pair of 'magic slippers' (baseball boots). They gained the Caterpillar by descending and traversing from the lower shelf of False Gully and soon found themselves at a good rock ledge close under the Red Wall, looking straight up its twin vertical cracks. A pitch for the future maybe! Twenty feet round left they came across an obvious fault which led up and right to near the top of the Red Wall. Barclay gave this a try then retreated, leaving a piton, and continued the left traverse across smooth granite until he was able to ascend a slab to reach a small ledge.

They were now in the middle of the face with nothing but rock in all directions. Above and slightly to the left was a 10ft wet, leaning corner. This provided the first VS climbing and took them to a point where they could start back up right to a ledge below the final bulge. By utilising a good piton belay Brooker was able to give Barclay assistance to gain a narrow shelf above the left end of the ledge. He was then level with the bulge, but he still could not pull over. Just to the left he found a crack into which he hammered a piton. Using this he succeeded in swinging up onto the slabs above – a scary and very exposed move. He now had to traverse right on unprotected slabs before gaining a poor belay almost in the line of the crack running directly up from the Red Wall. Elated with their good progress they could now look up and see a line which they could follow all the way to the top. After a 15ft wall the crack continued as a chimney through slabs and walls, and although wet in places the rock was so clean it was never very greasy. Some 250ft above the Red Wall the continuous climbing began to ease and here they were able to slant up left on grassy ledges and short walls which eventually led to the top.

This was the first climb on the frontal face of Central Gully Wall and according to Brooker it "provided an exciting, continuously hard route on steep, clean rock".[35] It was certainly a climb on a scale not previously seen in the Cairngorms. The addition of a direct start up the 300ft lower wall would give a very sustained climb of more than 800ft. They named their route Waterkelpie Wall – VS.

A few days later Barclay was back at Creag an Dubh-loch on a glorious late August day. The Etchachan Club ran a bus meet to Glen Muick on the 31st and although most of the climbers had gone to Lochnagar a small group visited the Dubh Loch. Despite the limited time Alex Thom, Barclay, John Vigrow and Bill Christie all set off up the line of Patey's Giant. Once across the traverse it became obvious that a party of four would be far too slow so Christie and Vigrow offered to go back, leaving the two Kincorth men to continue.

It is thought that they followed Patey's proposed line and climbed the steep 30ft twin corners directly above the belay to reach a shelf on the right. From there the easiest way appeared to follow a slabby ramp up rightward, but it led to overhangs higher up. After several hours the two men were in a recessed area approximately 100ft below the top. A shouted discussion took place between the climbers and their companions, the outcome of which was that an attempt be made to get a rope down to them. The rescue operation was directed by Mac Smith and Derek Pyper who had placed themselves opposite the cliff near the top of Central Gully Buttress. Bill Christie descended the vegetated slopes above the gully wall in an attempt to pin-point the climbers. Unfortunately, he disturbed a boulder which sailed out over the edge.

When recalling this incident in 1997, Alex Thom said: "Dick and I were together, I think on a small platform. About 10ft above us was a sloping ledge and we were stuck. This I remember like it was yesterday because Bill (Christie) dislodged a boulder about two feet long and one foot wide. We couldn't move and the stone smashed on the sloping ledge and riddled us with splinters, one of my ears was bleeding and I think Dick's scalp. I remember saying to Dick: 'The bastards are trying to kill us not save us'."

Three ropes were tied together, weighted with a peg hammer and eventually dropped to the stranded pair. They were then hauled up one at a time by six rescuers, Barclay being the first to reach the plateau. Both climbers were convinced that they had completed the hardest part of the climb and that given more time they could have found a way to the top. Unfortunately, neither Thom, Barclay nor any of their companions are able to recall precise details of the line taken or the nature of the climbing. One thing is certain; it was a bold attempt to climb an intimidating section of the cliff. Had they succeeded, even with the use of some aid, the climb would have been in a league of its own in the Cairngorms, in terms of commitment.

The August activity on Creag an Dubh-loch was matched by a major breakthrough on the Shelter Stone Crag by Sellers and Annand. Although Sellers was well known for his secrecy when it came to new climbs, it was common knowledge that he had attempted the big chimney-line immediately right of the Central Slabs. Earlier that summer, he and Barclay had climbed the lower chimneys until forced out left by big overhangs. They discovered that by moving up left over grass ledges they

Dick Barclay beyond the Red Wall on Waterkelpie Wall, Creag an Dubh-loch, August 1958

Photo: Bill Brooker

could traverse back right to reach a short corner beside the overhangs. They both succeeded in laybacking up this but neither could make the exit out right above the bulge.

In July, Sellers and Annand had spent a fortnight of poor weather in Chamonix. On their return they took the first opportunity in August to go back to the Shelter Stone Crag, much to Dick Barclay's annoyance. At the bulge above the corner Sellers still could not free-climb so he used two pitons to move up right and gain a hold on the lip of the over-hang. An easy slab then took him to the end of the lower difficulties. Looking up from this point they could now clearly see the upper crag looming menacingly 250ft above. It was dominated by a smooth impending wall split by a single slanting crack.

Not far above, ledges and terraces led easily up left above the central slabs to join the High Ledge of Sticil Face. This was an obvious escape route, but their aim was to climb as directly as possible to the top. They moved right and found relatively easy climbing up a corner, a chim-ney then a 60ft ridge on the crest which brought them close to the final rampart. By traversing left over a nose they reached a good stance beside a large flake which leaned against the impressive overhanging wall. The only way on from here was by what Sellers described as a "beautiful hand traverse". A 15ft horizontal flake handrail was crossed leftwards to just beyond the edge of the big wall where he discovered a crack system going straight up. The situation was breathtaking with a clear drop of more than 600ft to the scree.

After mantelshelfing onto a block, Sellers used a wooden wedge to overcome a wide crack, and then he climbed a thinner crack on a smooth wall "with an etrier". At the top a delicate step right into a chimney led to a stance near the edge of the overhanging wall, 50ft above the hand traverse. The situation still felt impressive and the outcome uncer-tain, although the rock was now more of slab angle. Another 60ft pitch up right, following the rim of another steep wall, proved to be straight-forward; then a fault and a short chimney led abruptly to the plateau.

The Shelter Stone Crag had at last been climbed by a direct line. A major psychological barrier had been breached and Sellers and Annand had much to be pleased about. Their 800ft climb had its fair share of vegetation but the situation and the climbing on the upper bastion were magnificent – VS. A year earlier, Grassick and Nicol had named their climb up the west side of the bastion The Citadel, but after consulta-tion, the Sellers-Annand line became The Citadel and the former route re-named Postern. The two big routes of Waterkelpie Wall and The Citadel marked a high point in Cairngorm rock exploration by the Aberdonians in the 1950s. They had come a long way in the 12 years since the war and seemed poised to open further climbs on the great cliffs of the Shelter Stone Crag, Creag an Dubh-loch and Lochnagar.

New Year's Day 1959 dawned wet and blustery. In Braemar a party of five hill walkers from the Glasgow Universal Hiking Club left the Youth Hostel, attended morning mass at St Andrew's Roman Catholic Church, called in to the bar of the Invercauld Arms then set off on the 14 mile walk over the Tolmounth from Glen Callater to Glen Doll Youth Hostel at the head of Glen Clova. By early afternoon the intermittent showers became more continuous and although the freezing level was

The Shelter Stone Crag had at last been climbed by a direct line

The mighty Shelter Stone Crag in June with Càrn Etchachan on the left and the Forefinger Pinnacle on the right

Photo: Greg Strange

still around 3000ft sleet was falling at lower levels. When daylight began to fade a full blizzard was raging over the whole region and temperatures began to plummet. Friends and relatives waiting at the Hostel were becoming increasingly worried as the hours went by with no sign of the five men. The blizzard lasted for two days and was considered by some locals to have been the worst for many years. The severe winds blew down telegraph wires and many upland roads were blocked by drifts, including the road up Glen Clova.

It was not until Saturday January 3, that the weather abated and contact was made between Glen Doll and Braemar, confirming that the men had definitely set off and had not returned. On that Saturday afternoon a party of local men and some hostellers from Glen Doll searched the first four miles of the route westwards up Jock's Road as far as Jock's Bothy beside the Lunkard, but found no trace of the missing men.

The next day a very large search operation got under way, made particularly arduous due to renewed gale force winds. A party from Braemar followed the route up Glen Callater and found footsteps in old snow believed to be those of the missing men. On the high ground these tracks deviated away from the Mounth path and crossed the Aberdeenshire – Angus County boundary just south of Tolmount, apparently heading directly down towards the White Water and Glen Doll. Around midday on January 4, another search party found the body of the youngest man, 17-year-old James Boyle, not far from Jock's Bothy in a gully just above the waterfall of the White Water. He was laying face down where he had apparently collapsed with exhaustion. Despite intense

searching both on the ground and from the air none of the other men could be found and the search was abandoned on January 6, to wait for a significant thaw.

The effect of this as yet unresolved tragedy cast a sombre veil over the Scottish hills. The cold, sometimes stormy weather in the Cairngorms continued well into January, by which time there was a good build up of hard snow and ice on the high mountain cliffs. As is often the case, a spell of inhospitable weather in winter, precedes a period of calm, when walking and climbing conditions become near perfect. The weekend of January 31, marked the beginning of a fortnight of just such weather when all the higher Scottish hills were in superb winter condition.

As might have been expected, Patey managed to be based in the Highlands for the whole of the first two weeks in February, ostensibly ski-training with the Marines while staying at the Norwegian Huts at Glenmore. Fresh from a weekend on Ben Nevis with Jimmy Marshall, where they had made winter ascents of Hadrian's Wall and the Girdle Traverse (the former also with Bill Brooker), he turned his attention back to Coire an Lochain and Coire an t-Sneachda of Cairngorm where the winter potential on the buttresses was virtually untapped. In the space of three days he made four first winter ascents.

On February 3, he and Vivian Stevenson climbed Ewen Buttress in excellent snow-ice condition. The next day Coire an t-Sneachda was the venue. Here he soloed Spiral Gully which twists up rightward through the upper columns of the large fluted buttress well to the right of Aladdin's Buttress.

Having now seen the climbing potential in both corries he went out on the third day with a most ambitious plan to solo a major buttress in each. On the right flank of Aladdin's Buttress he had noted a narrow chimney cutting straight up the lower rocks from near the foot of Aladdin's Mirror. This was full of snow and ice and gave him a hard climb. There were two short vertical ice bulges which he climbed almost directly with slight deviations on to slabs on the left. He felt that both these sections were VS and gave the climb a Grade IV rating (Patey's Route). In Coire an Lochain he climbed Western Route on No. 4 Buttress in the amazing time of three-quarters of an hour. Snow and ice conditions were exceptional with the whole route "climbed almost entirely on ice; apart from the summer crux, which was simplified by a snow take-off".[36] It should be remembered that the summer crux is a 20ft wall, Severe in standard. Apparently, there was sufficient snow banking to climb the wall directly and it was the chimney above which he found as hard as anything on the route. Nowadays, Western Route is a hard Grade IV and modern winter climbers will consider Patey's original grade of III a joke.

All the while Patey was dashing about making the most of these perfect conditions, his friends back in Aberdeen had to wait until the weekend before they could put their ice axes to good use. Not surprisingly, many parties were out on Sunday, February 8, which resulted in several important winter ascents being made. Sellers, Jerry Smith and George Annand took a chance that Creag an Dubh-loch would be in favourable winter condition and went to look at The Labyrinth.

Luck was with them, for although the cliff was quite bare, especially in the lower reaches, they found excellent ice and névé as well as dry rock. The lower Labyrinth up to the level of the Hanging Garden was continuous snow with only one ice pitch near the bottom. Above this, the unclimbed direct continuation appeared completely snow-free. It was obvious that they would have to enter the Hanging Garden basin and find a way up its back wall.

Climbing in nails with Sellers and Smith alternating leads they avoided the steep ice pitch in the lower groove on the right and made quick progress to the basin. From here to the top their route is uncertain but it most likely went close to Bell's original line, probably overlapping with a much later climb known as Labyrinth Buttress. At the top of the snow slope in the Hanging Garden an icefall had formed over the line of Hanging Garden Route. Farther right two shallow vegetated faults led up onto the ill-defined buttress lying between Hanging Garden Route and the cul-de-sac of Labyrinth Direct. In all probability they used one of these to commence the upper section of their climb. According to Sellers they ascended an open chimney for 200ft to reach an overhang. Then a 100ft ice pitch led to a point where they could move left on to a snow-filled groove, which they followed, trending right at the top to reach the plateau.[37] The whole route took just five hours, a fast time for this impressive Grade V climb.

On Lochnagar, the last major gully received its first winter ascent when Duncan Macrae and Fraser Henderson climbed Shallow Gully. Difficulties were concentrated in the first 150ft, thereafter, continuous step-cutting on hard snow led to a rock arete and the plateau – Grade IV.

The third new route that day was on the cliffs of Creagan a' Choire Etchachan. John Hay had previously been defeated high up in the Red Chimney at New Year 1958. This time he found conditions more favourable although the ice was thin in places. With Ross Ibbotson, he started up twin grooves on the right to reach an ice sheet flowing over smooth slabs. A very delicate left traverse from the top of the iced slabs proved to be the crux of the climb. Once in the chimney a difficult ice bulge and a move on to the left rib led to easier climbing and a snow bay below the impressive final icefall.

*Douglas Duncan
taking stock of
Labyrinth, Creag an
Dubh-loch, February
1959*

Photo: Bill Brooker

Here, as in summer, he moved right and finished up the rib on the right. The upper icefall was climbed direct by Ian Paterson and Stuart Hepburn in January 1967 – Grade V.

The conditions looked set to last for at least a few more days, but Brooker was not prepared to miss his chance. For several years he had thought that his climb, Labyrinth Edge, would make an excellent winter route, so when he heard that Sellers had climbed The Labyrinth in good condition he just had to get up to the Dubh Loch. Douglas Duncan, a friend from teacher training college, had done little climbing but was strong, fit and knew how to belay. After a little persuasion he agreed to go with Brooker two days after the Labyrinth ascent. The rocks up to the Midway Terrace were rather bare of snow, but climbing on the Sea of Slabs was superb "its lower part a snowy ribbon of frozen turf and the upper part coated in grey ice and hard snow".[38] Good snow allowed the first tower to be climbed on the right but the exit from the chimney in the upper buttress proved very tricky in the dark – the crux of the route. As Brooker predicted, this was a magnificent climb under perfect hard snow and ice conditions – Grade IV.

Towards the end of his second week at Glenmore, Patey visited Hell's Lum Crag with Stevenson and climbed the summer route Kiwi Slabs, the ascent being made almost entirely on thin ice ribbons. Their final contribution, snatched just as the thaw arrived, was a semi-winter ascent of The Slash, the prominent gully in the lower slabs of No. 5 Buttress of Sgòr Gaoith. Climbing in crampons they found no fewer than eight pitches, including one which involved climbing on the right wall for 50ft then regaining the gully by abseil. (The gully was climbed direct in good winter conditions by John Lyall and Jim Grosset in March 1987 – Grade V.)

The thawing conditions experienced by Patey and Stevenson in the relatively low-lying Glen Einich were not apparent in the remote Garbh Choire of Beinn a' Bhùird. For on that same day it was to that corrie that Sellers and Annand made the long walk from Invercauld to be rewarded with an ascent of South-East Gully, the beautiful couloir left of the Mitre Ridge. Just as with their Labyrinth climb the previous weekend this was a highly-prized first winter ascent which had been on the tick list of most local winter activists since Patey and Nicol had had to abandon their attempt in 1954. From the point where the East Wall Route went right, the gully steepened and from here to the summit there was a succession of fine ice pitches providing magnificent climbing which Sellers rated as Grade V.

This excellent climb brought to a close this period of a frantic winter activity in February 1959. By early March the snow lying at all levels had diminished and the search for the missing men on Jock's Road resumed. On March 2, a party led by Davie Glen found the body of Harry Duffin not far from the spot where Boyle had died. Robert McFaul and Joseph Devlin were found during March and finally on April 15, the last member of that ill-fated party, Frank Daly, was discovered on the south side of Craw Craigies. All five had died of hypothermia at separate locations along a two mile stretch of the White Water. The whole episode was a salutary reminder to all hill-goers of just how fierce the Scottish winter weather can be.

Jock's Bothy collapsed not long after this incident and was replaced by an earth-roofed shelter farther up Jock's Road, below some outcrops on the south side of Cairn Luncard. Davie Glen was the prime mover in the construction of this howff which later became known as Davie's Bourach.

There were no further substantial snowfalls during the winter of 1959 which meant that mountain crags were well clear by the end of April. In fact, this absence of late snowfall coupled with a dry summer brought about the complete disappearance of all the Cairngorms snow beds for the first time since 1933. With this early occurrence of summer climbing conditions, folk were eager to get back on the rocks.

The Etchachan Club was blessed with glorious weather for its bus meet to Lochnagar on May 10. A good show of climbers was out on the cliffs with parties on Eagle Ridge, Parallel Buttress, Black Spout Pinnacle and The Stack. Sellers had teamed up with Jerry Smith to climb The Link. Whether or not they had completed the climb is uncertain, but during the afternoon, while abseiling from the Springboard, a huge block, to which the rope was attached came away under Sellers's weight. He fell to the foot of the Pinnacle and was killed instantly. A very sombre group of six club members, including Sellers's close friend, George Annand, carried his body on a rope stretcher down to meet an ambulance at Gelder Shiel.

What had promised to be a great day had ended in tragedy. It was a terrible blow for the club, losing one of its most popular members as well as its secretary. Ronnie was a key figure in the development of climbing in the Cairngorms during the mid to late 1950s. At 26 years of age he was in his prime. He had recently joined the SMC and would undoubtedly have gone on to greater things. His list of rock and ice climbs throughout the Cairngorms is a fitting testament to his skill and determination as an outstanding mountaineer. Sellers's death touched everyone within the small circle of Aberdeen climbers. As one of its leading lights his loss was keenly felt and his companions had little enthusiasm for rock climbing during the remainder of 1959. Just as North-east climbers were coming to terms with the death of Sellers, news came from the Alps that Jerry Smith had been killed while abseiling on the Aiguille Noire de Peuterey. It was a terrible irony that he should have died in exactly the same manner as his friend. It was difficult to believe that this time Smith, the passionate explorer, would not be returning to Aberdeen as he had always done in the past from trips to the Alps and far away places like Spitzbergen, the Ruwenzori, South Georgia and Graham Land. The loss of these two fine climbers during the summer of 1959 cast a long shadow over the Aberdeen school.

Whereas the activities of North-east climbers had been very low key during the summer of 1959 this certainly could not be said of the Edinburgh group. Robin Smith, the Marshall brothers, Dougal Haston and co. had kept up high standards set in 1958 with climbs like Smith's Shibboleth on the Slime Wall of Buachaille Etive Mòr. They put up further hard climbs in Glen Coe and on Ben Nevis, culminating in the very impressive line of The Bat on Càrn Dearg Buttress.

Descriptions of Waterkelpie Wall and Caterpillar Crack published that year in the SMCJ had caught Jimmy Marshall's eye. He and his brother

Ronnie Sellers climbing Brimstone Groove, Hell's Lum Crag, October 1958

Photo: Bill Brooker collection

Jimmy Marshall on Stob Coire nan Lochain

Photo: Jimmy Marshall Collection

felt that there could not be a buttress in existence which required so many of its climbs to be overcome with the use of pitons. They decided to visit Creag an Dubh-loch to see for themselves.

In the unlikely month of November the two brothers, with Ronnie Anderson, drove north to Glen Clova. At one point on the journey, during a heavy downpour they spotted a field mouse trapped between the headlights darting through the deluge from beam to beam. Happily, for the mouse they managed to slow down and it was able to run off into the night.

The next day, on descending Central Gully to its foot they noticed a grassy fault above them on the huge face of lower Central Gully Wall. This fault was up and left of the recess where the Aberdonians had been trying. Reaching it looked problematical since it was guarded at its base by completely smooth slabs. However, just to the left of the recess an easy-looking groove curved up left across the slabs to reach a line of steep cracks. These started right of the grass fault and led into it higher up. Marshall thought the lower cracks looked definitely climbable. That would then only leave 300ft in the upper crack system, which cut its way up through smooth, overlapping slabs from the top of the fault to the plateau. The climb was as good as made!

Before starting they replaced their walking boots with PAs, a specialist high friction lightweight climbing boot developed in France by Pierre Allain. This was not a deliberate ploy to steal a march on the Aberdonians, for PAs were now the standard footwear for leading rock climbers throughout Britain, their adoption playing an important part in the advances in technical standards from the late 1950s onwards. However, this was certainly the first occasion that PAs had been worn on a pioneering ascent in the Cairngorms.

The Edinburgh men climbed the easy groove, traversed the slab and took a belay below the cracks. At first these were well furnished with holds, but higher, where the rock steepened, a particularly wide crack had to be negotiated and Jimmy found this short section as hard as anything on the whole climb. A little higher the angle eased and he entered and followed the grassy fault for 70ft to where it ended below a steep wall. This vegetated section was the only place where they came across wet rock – very unusual for November. They now appeared to be in a cul-de-sac just 60ft left of Waterkelpie Wall. Climbing directly ahead looked very hard, but the Gods seemed to be with them that day for they discovered that by taking a short corner on the left they could gain a large flake and step back into the line of cracks above the steep wall. This pitch provided the key to the remainder of the climb. From there on they followed the upper crack system in three pitches until a final 60ft slab gave way to broken ground below the plateau. These final pitches were not too difficult, but the climbing was sustained and at times quite delicate. The friction and precision afforded by the PAs was certainly helpful in overcoming the smooth granite.

Marshall was at pains to point out that they had only used pitons at belay stances, a comment which prompted one local climber to muse that it was probably untrue and that it was an attempt to kill off a few Aberdonians when they went to repeat the route. When asked about the climb in 1996 Marshall said: "On coming down Central Gully, we were more or less delivered right to the start of the climb. The route was extremely enjoyable, the more so as we made our point."

They named the climb The Mousetrap for reasons alluded to previously. At the time of its ascent Mac Smith was preparing the final draft of the new guide and was able to include a description of The Mousetrap. As a footnote he added: "This would appear to be one of the hardest and most outstanding routes of recent years on granite. For sustained difficulty and exposure it is perhaps unique amongst Cairngorm face climbs." With hindsight, this generous comment can be seen to have been very close to the mark. Only Waterkelpie and Citadel could compare and their hardest sections involved the use of pitons for aid. Nowadays The Mousetrap is the trade route on the frontal face of Central Gully Wall. It is graded VS with several sections of 4c climbing. No easier climb has subsequently been discovered that takes the full height of the cliff. Surely the mark of a great line!

Winter 1959 – 60 was very quiet compared to the previous one. In February Patey and John (Zeke) Deacon explored and named The Mess of Pottage, the obvious slabby crag left of Jacob's Ladder in Coire an t-Sneachda. The name would suggest that they were none too inspired with this 250ft high cliff yet they did make two climbs, one taking an obvious snowy line on the broken right flank, and the other, following a steep right to left diagonal staircase in the middle of the crag. On this second climb, over iced rock, they were unable to make a direct finish and were forced to traverse 100ft away to the left in order to escape. Apart from another winter climb made by Haston in 1965 it was to be another 26 years before climbers began to show interest in the winter potential of The Mess of Pottage. Patey and Deacon's second climb was probably the opening pitches of a line which later became known as The Hybrid.

It would not have escaped the notice of visitors to Cairngorm that a new road was under construction, taking public vehicular access to a car park in lower Coire Cas at an elevation of 2100ft. Pressure from downhill skiing enthusiasts and hoteliers on Speyside had eventually prevailed and the new Cairngorm road was started in 1959. For several years the vision of a 'ski resort' in the Cairngorms had fuelled much behind the scenes work by a group of businessmen, including the local laird, who in time formed themselves into the Cairngorm Winter Sports Development Board.

Coire Cas was the favoured site for the initial development, therefore the main priority was to build an access road along the route of the existing private road from Coylumbridge to Glenmore, then on up via a series of hairpin bends to the foot of Coire Cas. Surprisingly, the CWSDB had little trouble persuading the Scottish Secretary and Inverness District Council that the road should be publicly funded. The Forestry Commission, whose land included the hillside above Glenmore where the ski development was envisaged, gave their backing and the new road was finished and open to the public by July 1960. Then on August 4, a flash flood washed out two sections beside the Allt Mòr and the road was closed again for repair until the following winter.

Reaction to the road among hill folk was of general acceptance. At a stroke the Northern Corries of Cairngorm had become the most

"For sustained difficulty and exposure it is perhaps unique amongst Cairngorm face climbs,"
– Mac Smith

accessible high mountain terrain in the country. It was now only an hour's walk from the new car park to the summit of Cairngorm or up to the foot of the cliffs in Coire an t-Sneachda. Access to the Loch Avon basin was now markedly easier from the north than it was by approaching from the Braemar side.

The fact that the road had been built and would be maintained by the local authority, principally for the benefit of skiers, did not seem to rankle that much since most skiers up to that time had, by necessity, been hill-walkers and climbers anyway. The Etchachan Club, for example, was a skiing and mountaineering club and most of its members had done both at one time or another. A number of more discerning walkers and climbers viewed the road as a mixed blessing. It did make it easier to approach from the north, but at what cost to the Cairngorms?

There would be an inevitable loss of solitude, and most worrying, where else did the downhill ski industry intend to develop? Tom Patey summed up these thoughts in his Cairngorm Commentary when he wrote that "the danger in the Coire Cas scheme is that it may be the forerunner of others which would threaten the finer and more remote fastnesses of the Cairngorms".[39]

"The danger in the Coire Cas scheme is that it may be the forerunner of others which would threaten the finer and more remote fastnesses of the Cairngorms,"
– Tom Patey

While there was a little concern in the North-east for the future of the northern Cairngorms two of the new generation of Aberdeen climbers, Derek Pyper and Davie Reid were combining a local tradition of marathon hill walks with classic rock climbs, in what, by the 1990s would have been called an 'enchainment.' In one 16 and a half hour day in August they walked from Gelder Bothy on the Balmoral Estate to Derry Lodge, climbing en route Lochnagar by Eagle Ridge, Beinn a' Bhùird by The Mitre Ridge and Ben Macdui via Snake Ridge. This combination of the Three Ridges involving 40 miles of walking and 2000ft of climbing, was undertaken carrying a full weekend sack!

There is no doubt that linking climbs in different corries on different mountains is a most satisfying way of appreciating the finest aspects of the Cairngorms. Perhaps the best known long hill walk in the area is the traverse of 'The Six Tops' of the Cairngorms, namely, Ben Avon, Beinn a' Bhùird, Cairngorm, Ben Macdui, Braeriach and Cairn Toul. This was first recorded in 1908 by five men from Aberdeen, Henry Butchart, L.J.Davidson, Howard Drummond, Henry Kellas and Ian McLaren. Over the years, the time for the crossing (Loch Builig to Corrour Bothy) was gradually whittled down until in September 1968, Professor Wynne-Edwards of Aberdeen University completed it in 9 hours 34 minutes.[40]

The first point-to-point traverse of the 'Six Tops' was made by David Duncan in the early 1960s, starting and finishing at Derry Lodge.

Volume 1 of the SMC's Climbers Guide to the Cairngorms Area was published in 1961. It covered the district north of the Dee, namely the Cairngorms proper. The slimmer, Volume 2, which appeared a year later, included Lochnagar, Creag an Dubh-loch and Glen Clova. Mac Smith devoted six years of his life to this project, a labour of love for which he received no financial remuneration. The effort was well worthwhile for the guide set a very high standard and became a classic. There was no doubting Smith's knowledge of the subject, or his enthusiasm for the area. These two little red books were an inspiration to the next generation of climbers.

During the years of preparation the prospect of a new guide had served as a catalyst for exploration. A great number of summer and winter climbs had been recorded and whole corries and cliffs opened up for the first time. With all this virgin rock around, local climbers tended to stick very much to their own patch. The Aberdeen school rarely climbed from the Aviemore side, preferring the easier approach up Deeside. Being rather introspective by nature, they enjoyed their mountaineering in remote, quiet settings. The long walks, the camping and bothying, only served to enhance their appreciation. A number found their way to the Alps in summer, particularly to the Chamonix area where the style and character of the climbing was similar to the Cairngorms, but on a much grander scale. Despite their trips abroad few had experience of climbing on very steep rock such as that found in Glen Coe, the Lake District and North Wales. There were no specialist rock climbers who trained regularly on accessible outcrops or man-made walls. Not surprisingly, the upper limit of technical difficulty on rock lagged behind that of the best climbers from the Central Belt of Scotland. By 1959, Robin Smith had led climbs which are now graded E2 5c, whereas the hardest climbs in the Cairngorms were only VS 4c.

Technical difficulty was of no great concern to North-east climbers at that time for they could point out that most of the major buttresses and gullies in the Cairngorms had been climbed, many under winter conditions. The most important developments during the 1950s had been the opening up of Central Gully Wall, the Black Spout Pinnacle, the Crimson Slabs, the main bastion of Shelter Stone Crag and the face of Hell's Lum Crag. In winter, standards were as high as anywhere in Britain. Moreover, for several years in the 1950s, Cairngorms winter climbing led the way, particularly on mixed ground. Lochnagar was quite rightly described as the crucible of Scottish winter climbing.

By the time the new guide was published a number of 1950s activists had either moved on or left the scene. Johnny Morgan was the first to go. He was a friend of Winram before meeting and climbing with Brooker. An architectural draftsman he went to Canada in the mid-1950s then returned in 1959. A few years later, in June 1962, Johnny, his wife Sandra and Jock Pirrit died in a boating accident in the Firth of Clyde. All three were drowned when Pirrit's small boat was driven ashore at Wemyss Bay in a severe storm. Freddy Malcolm, a welder to trade, moved to Sheffield after finishing his National Service in 1958. He returned to Aberdeen in 1972 and continues his interest in walking and climbing. He worked as an offshore rope access engineer until retirement.

The employment situation in Aberdeen in the late 1950s was not good. Traditional industries like shipbuilding, engineering and paper making took on young apprentices then made many of them redundant just as they finished their training. In this way employers could maintain a constant semi-skilled workforce to whom they only had to pay minimum wages. Dod Adams worked in the shipyards and imigrated to Australia in 1960. In that same year Fraser Henderson, another draftsman, left for New Zealand. Alex Thom had trained as an electrical engineer. He imigrated to Canada in 1961 and found employment in one of the Ford factories. He continued to pursue his love of mountaineering and is now retired and living in Canmore, near Calgary.

Fraser Henderson

Photo: Etchachan Club Archives

Roy Greig

Photo: Malcolm Smith

Of the remaining Kincorth Club members, Dick Barclay had always indicated a preference for socialising rather than hill-walking so when he gave up climbing in the early 1960s his contact with the hills virtually ceased except for downhill skiing.

George Annand and his younger brother Charlie were both painters to trade. They went to Australia at the same time that Thom left for Canada. Before emigrating, George was a back-drop painter at His Majesty's Theatre in Aberdeen.

Most of Mac Smith's cronies, Kenny Winram, Ernie Smith, George Dey, Gordon Leslie, Roy Greig, Charlie Petrie and Sandy Russell maintained their interest in the Cairngorms and all continued to live in the North-east. Mac himself worked as a joiner while writing his guide. He had been a keen entomologist-botanist since late childhood and obtained a post with the RSPB for its first successful Osprey Watch in 1959. From 1961 he was an officer with the Nature Conservancy, firstly working six summer months for three years on St Kilda, mainly on the Soay Sheep Study, and wintering in Braemar and Fife. Then followed 11 and four years respectively at Tentsmuir Point and Sands of Forvie NNRs, and finally two years on survey work from the Aberdeen Headquarters.

On retirement he was delighted to be retained on contract for three years to survey the broadleaf woodlands of North-east Region with the result that many new SSSIs were added to the list. "Heaven, I was in heaven," he said, "and no longing for the hills."

For 16 years Smith had been the orchestrator of Cairngorms exploration. A good, neat climber, he rarely led, mainly because he was usually a good deal older than his companions and, as he said, he did enjoy his generalship from the rear. A very self-contained man, he was as responsible as anyone for championing the Cairngorms as one of Scotland's outstanding areas for climbing.

Bill Brooker and Mike Taylor continued to climb. Brooker's last Cairngorms first ascent was the short, but difficult, Twin Chimneys Route on Lochnagar which he climbed with Patey and Dixon in April 1961. An enthusiasm for all aspects of mountaineering coupled with an outgoing personality made Brooker a natural ambassador for climbing in Scotland. In 1972 he became one of the youngest Presidents of the Scottish Mountaineering Club and served as its Journal Editor from 1975 to 1986. After working as a teacher he moved to Extra Mural Studies at Aberdeen University, where he later became Head of Department.

Mike Taylor channelled his considerable energies into general practice in his home town of Peterhead. In the early 1960s he did a number of climbs but after an accident with Sidney Wilkinson, while attempting a winter ascent of Scarface, he concentrated his winter activities on ski mountaineering. In the winter of 1978 he completed the first crossing of the Scottish Haute Route from Crathie to Fort William with David Grieve. A modest man, Taylor's early contribution to Cairngorm climbing was somewhat overshadowed by his companion, Patey, but he was a very talented climber in his own right.

After leaving university John Hay became a solicitor in Aberdeen. Although he stopped serious climbing in 1960 he is still a very keen hill man, lately becoming involved in Arctic travel and exploration. His friend, Alan Will, became a journalist in Aberdeen.

Tom Patey's stint in the marines ended in 1960. He returned briefly to the North-east where he worked as a locum, first in Braemar then in Aberdeen. In 1962 he set up in general practice at Ullapool, the ideal base for exploring the North-West Highlands. His visits back to the Cairngorms in future years were infrequent as he set about discovering new climbs across the length and breadth of the Highlands, with the same undiminished enthusiasm he had shown during the 1950s.

The departure or retirement of many of these personalities, the deaths of Sellers and Smith, and publication of the guide, all combined to mark the end of an era. The 1950s had passed and the Cairngorms would no longer be a climbing backwater. With improved communication, greater availability of private transport and the new road up Cairn Gorm, the period of isolation was finally over.

1. CCJ Vol. 16, No. 87, p197.
2. CCJ Vol. 16, No. 87, p192.
3. CCJ Vol. 16, No. 87, p226.
4. SMCJ Vol. 27, No. 153, p209 and *One Man's Mountains*, p69.
5. SMC *Climber's Guide to the Cairngorms Area Vol. 1* (1961), p57.
6. SMCJ Vol. 25, No. 144, p115 and *One Man's Mountains*, p17.
7. SMCJ Vol. 25, No. 144, p119 and *One Man's Mountains*, p21.
8. CCJ Vol. 17, No. 89, p9.
9. CCJ Vol. 17, No. 89, p11.
10. ECJ Vol. 2, No. 4, p146 and *One Man's Mountains*, p23.
11. ECJ Vol. 2, No. 4, p145 and *One Man's Mountains*, p26.
12. ECJ Vol. 2, No. 4, p145 and *One Man's Mountains*, p26.
13. ECJ Vol. 2, No. 4, p145 and *One Man's Mountains*, p26.
14. SMCJ Vol. 37, No. 192, p557.
15. CCJ Vol. 16, p291.
16. ECJ (On the Veg) 1996 *What's in a Name?* p9.
17. CCJ Vol. 16, No. 88, p288.
18. SMC *Climber's Guide to the Cairngorms Area Vol. 1* (1961), p83.
19. SMC *Climber's Guide to the Cairngorms Area Vol. 2* (1962), p46
20. ECJ Vol. 2, No. 4, p158.
21. Climber's Club Journal 1957, p52 (*Sestogradists in Scotland*).
22. Climber's Club Journal 1957, p56 (*Sestogradists in Scotland*).
23. Climber's Club Journal 1957, p57 (*Sestogradists in Scotland*).
24. SMCJ Vol. 26, No 149, p231.
25. SMC *Climber's Guide to the Cairngorms Area Vol. 1* (1961), pXV1.
26. SMCJ Vol. 26, No. 147, p42.
27. CCJ Vol. 17, p178.
28. CCJ Vol. 17, p179.
29. SMC *Climber's Guide to the Cairngorms Area Vol. 1* (1961), p91.
30. SMC *Climber's Guide to the Cairngorms Area Vol. 1* (1961), p136.
31. *Cold Climbs*. Diadem (1983), p161.
32. *Cold Climbs*. Diadem (1983), p161.
33. SMCJ Vol. 26, No. 149, p264.
34. Notes sent to Mac Smith from Jimmy Marshall in 1958.
35. SMCJ Vol. 26, No. 150, p378.
36. SMCJ Vol. 27, No. 151, p56.
37. SMCJ Vol. 26, No. 150, p378.
38. SMCJ Vol. 26, No. 150, p378.
39. SMCJ Vol. 27, No. 153, p220 and *One Man's Mountains*, p26.
40. CCJ Vol. 17, No. 93, p273.

7: The Early Sixties (1961 – 1966)

THE NORTH-EAST climbing scene was relatively quiet in the early 1960s. A new ginger group had evolved going by the name of the Clach Dhian Club. It included Davie Reid, Derek Pyper, Ronnie Kerr, Sandy Kane, Mike Main, Sandy Sands and briefly Jim McArtney. According to Pyper they had become disenchanted with the Etchachan Club and wished to organise their own weekend meets. It was the usual conflict of interest between the up-and-coming climbers and the older members, many of whom were now more interested in hill-walking. Reid, Pyper and McArtney all worked at the Aberdeen University Press where they were three of many apprentices, who, over the years had become interested in the hills, mainly through the influence of Stan Long. Kerr was an apprentice engineer at Hendersons, while his friend, Kane, worked at Stoneywood Paper Mills.

Despite good accumulations of snow the number of people winter climbing was not on the same scale as in the late Fifties. There had been a break in the continuity of active local climbers and the new group had to find its own way without the benefit of older more experienced hands. Although some Scottish climbers were now using crampons, most Aberdonians still wore nailed boots for winter climbing, often walking up to the bothy in vibrams then donning their nailed boots for the day's climbing – adding considerably to the weight of the winter weekend sack. Nailed boots were put to good use on two short, difficult winter climbs in 1961, Terminal Buttress in Coire Sputan Dearg by Pyper and Reid, and Twin Chimneys Route on Lochnagar by Patey, Brooker and Dixon.

On rock, vibrams and Klettershuhe were still the most widely used footwear for climbing in the mountains, PAs being thought to be necessary only for the very hardest technical routes. September 1961 saw independent visits to Hell's Lum Crag by three of Scotland's foremost exploratory climbers. Following the lead of Sellers, Patey and Taylor went to the Loch Avon Basin on the 3rd and climbed the Wee Devil, a left-facing corner system between Devil's Delight and Kiwi Slabs. This Hard Severe route was subsequently marred by rockfall although Patey reported at the time that it was on firm rock. At the southern end of the crag, the grey buttress defined by Hell's Lum on the left and Deep-Cut Chimney on the right was climbed by Jimmy Marshall and Stenhouse. Their climb, Hell's Lump, was also Hard Severe and had a particularly good second pitch.

The third party to take a look at 'The Lum' that month was another Edinburgh team comprising Robin Smith and Graham Tiso. Twenty-three-year old Smith was by now one of Scotland's most outstanding climbers, with a string of impressive first ascents, both in summer and in winter. Fresh from his climb of The Big Top in Glen Coe, he no doubt had much larger projects in mind, perhaps on the Shelter Stone Crag, but these would have to wait. Meanwhile, he and Tiso made a direct

Clach Dhian Club in Glen Coe 1960. From left, (back): Derek Pyper, Sandy Sands, Sandy Smith, Sandy Kane, Mike Main and Ronnie Kerr. Front: Davie Reid and Bill Gault

Photo: Derek Pyper Collection

start to Hellfire Corner, the prominent central corner on the frontal face, climbed by Sellers and George Annand in September 1958. (Sellers had planned to do this start as he believed it would much improve the overall climb). While on this route they spotted an enticing pink leaning groove just right of, and overlooking Hellfire's main corner and this was the objective of their next climb.

They started up a whale-backed buttress and continued up slabs to a huge block belay directly below the pink groove. This gave a superb pitch on beautiful, clean rock, similar in difficulty and quality to Djibangi on the Crimson Slabs. A steep, juggy edge of grey rock concluded The Clean Sweep, which Smith mischievously graded Severe. Nowadays, it is considered VS 4c and still one of the best routes in the area.

Before the winter set in, another climb was made on the Crimson Slabs by Ronnie Kerr and Sandy Kane. On November 15, they climbed

*Robin Smith and
Davie Agnew, 1961*

Photo: Jimmy Marshall

the dark red slab right of The Dagger. Kerr led the route in vibrams and although it did not match the two main corners for purity of line The Sheath had a hard crux, involving HVS 5a climbing, probably the first on-sight lead at this grade in the area.

Two days before Christmas 1961, a double-seater chairlift was opened for public use on Cairn Gorm. It ran from a little above Jean's Hut in Coire Cas (a private wooden hut run by Glenmore Lodge, located on the east bank of the Allt a' Choire Chais) and terminated on the broad north shoulder of Cairn Gorm, 500ft below the summit. The lift was intended for both winter and summer use, thus providing all year round access. Barring a short stroll from the new car park to the bottom station, soon to be linked by a further chairlift, mechanised access could now take climbers to a point within two miles of Loch Avon. For those who appreciated the isolation of this unique area a road and chairlift up Cairn Gorm was not good news. There is no doubt that this significant intrusion into the wilderness devalued Cairn Gorm and the Loch Avon Basin for many walkers and climbers.

Cairn Gorm was not the only place to see changes in the early 1960s. In 1962 part of the Mar Estate, including the lodge itself was sold to the Panchaud brothers from Switzerland. They bought all the land north of the River Dee and west of the Bynack Burn, while Captain Ramsay retained the area south of Dee. Initially, there was a degree of friction between the new owners and local hill folk. Adam Watson, writing as Editor of the Etchachan Club Journal 1962, said: "We began to realise, perhaps for the first time, how fortunate we had been in having so much freedom in the past, and how over-critical we sometimes were about the old Mar Estate. For a time, feelings ran high, several local hotheads threatened dire action to the estate during the coming stalking season, and some hard words against climbers were given to reporters. The situation was clearly getting out of hand. It was time for some behind the scenes work. The participants must remain anonymous but happily this smoothed out the trouble to everybody's satisfaction in the end".[1]

During February and March 1962, three first winter ascents of existing summer rock climbs were made. On February 15, Pyper and Bill Gault climbed Pikestaff, the rib to the right of the Corridor on Creagan a' Choire Etchachan. The following weekend, Pyper, this time with Reid, made the long walk from Braemar to Garbh Choire Dhaidh to try the Great Rift. Unfortunately, the sun was shining directly into the gully so they moved right and climbed Boomerang which was in the shade and full of ice.

Later, in March, Jimmy Marshall and Stenhouse were staying at Lochend Bothy with big ideas to shock the 'Lochnagarians' once again. This time they planned to make a winter girdle traverse, starting on Route 2 and finishing up either Eagle Ridge or Douglas Gibson Gully. It was a glorious day when they climbed the ice-filled chimney of Route 2. It led to a magnificent blade of snow at the little ridge projecting from The Pinnacle's gable wall. The next pitch is Severe in summer and takes a very exposed traverse across the face with the difficulty increasing as one proceeds. "One becomes aware of the abyss at one's heels."[2] Marshall found this very hard in crampons and was forced to use a piton for aid halfway across. This 50ft traverse occupied two and a half hours and effectively scuppered their plans for the girdle. Marshall later calculated that they would have needed a week for the conceived route, based on their progress on Route 2.

By the end of winter 1961 – 62 there was an unusually large accumulation of snow in the Cairngorms. In April, the combination of good continuous snow cover and beautiful weather enabled Adam Watson to ski the six tops of the Cairngorms in 16 hours. Using langlauf ski, he commenced his mammoth journey in Glen Slugain and took in the summits of Ben A'an, Beinn a' Bhùird, Ben Macdui, Cairn Gorm, Braeriach and Cairn Toul, before finishing at Derry Lodge, a distance of 36 miles, with 8700ft of climbing. "I'd had a good 24 hours' worth of seeing the whole Cairngorm range and other parts of the North-east from innumerable viewpoints. Time had passed so slowly that it seemed more like a week – a good indication of a day lived to the full."[3]

New route activity in the summer of 1962 was concentrated around the head of Loch Avon. This may have been due to easier access from the north but more likely it was the new guidebook that had stimulated the interest.

The lofty Shelter Stone Crag was an eye-catching target for ambitious climbers. Both the Central Slabs and much of the rock forming the main bastion had been described as 'manifestly impossible', unless mechanised techniques were employed to excess on the bastion. In the late 1950s Patey had been up close to the big corner in the centre of the upper bastion and this had prompted Mac Smith to write in the guide: "There may yet be other lines of attack on the vertical bastion between Citadel and Postern but all is problematical and intimidating. Undoubtedly, a great challenge is a direct finish by the stupendous 100ft

Greg Strange starting The Needle in 1972. The twin zigzag cracks commence just above and left of the climber. The 'f' formation is at two thirds height and the Needle crack can be seen as a black vertical line below the big skyline notch

Photo: John Ingram

hanging crack cleaving the perpendicular rocks midway between the Citadel and the right skyline. From surveys on very hard sorties from Postern it appears that it will just admit a climber and a chink of light seen from directly below seems to indicate a through-route near the plateau".[4] The gauntlet had been thrown down.

At first sight the main bastion appears to be a tower of uninterrupted granite, commencing with slabs at its base and ending in perpendicular rock at the summit. However, a closer inspection reveals one or two ledge systems which partially cross the face, the lowest one, the Gallery, separating the 200ft basal slabs from a middle band of much steeper rock. Two further, less pronounced, systems cross above this before the final 150ft rampart. The tremendous hanging crack to which the guidebook referred is the right-hand and larger of two huge right-facing corners in the final rampart, the top of which forms a distinctive notch on the skyline. As Patey had discovered, it is possible to reach the corner from Postern using ledges. Similarly, it could be reached from upper Citadel, but the real challenge was a direct ascent of the whole face, finishing by the hanging crack.

Edinburgh climbers, Robin Smith, Jimmy and Ronnie Marshall, Stenhouse and Ritchie were all interested in making this ascent. They made quite a few trips to the Shelter Stone Crag, both as a group and individually, but these were largely thwarted by poor weather. On one occasion, in 1961, the Marshalls climbed the prominent right-facing groove system immediately left of Postern's starting gully, using the Hay and Adams smooth-floored corner for their second pitch. Above the Gallery they drifted too far left and ended up on a large grass patch, invoking Ronnie's wrath and the memorable declaration "I'm not making a climb with a f—ing field on it!" They had a good laugh at themselves, then roped off, but saw in the process how to make the link up to the final crack.

Between the starts of Postern and Clach Dhian Chimney the lower slabs are clean and continuous. Here at a point directly below the hanging crack Robin Smith had been making little sorties on to the rock trying to determine the best line of attack. Using these investigations and by studying photographs of the cliff he strung together a possible route all the way to the crack. He would have to act quickly for he knew that competition for the climb was hotting up. He was desperate to get it done before leaving for Russia with the British-Soviet Pamirs Expedition.

When the dry weather arrived at the beginning of June, he still had the problem of finding someone to climb with. None of his usual Edinburgh partners were available, so on Thursday, June 7, he travelled to Glasgow and went, unannounced, to the Clydebank home of Creagh Dhu climber, Davie Agnew. "I was cleaning up in the kitchen having just completed another day in the yards when I heard my younger brothers and sister yelling, 'Davie, Davie, there's a man oot here tae see ye.' Drying my face, I headed for the door thinking proviman, polisman, tickman. It was with great relief and surprise that I opened the door to find Robin Walker Wheech man!"[5] The opportunity to be on the first ascent of "this great line in the Gorms" was too good to miss. Agnew agreed to go with Smith there and then despite just finishing a full day as an apprentice in the shipyard. They travelled to Perth by bus, hitch-hiked to Aviemore and eventually bivouacked behind a dyke on the road to Loch Morlich. It was dry and clear next day and they were on the road by seven. A chance lift from a friend working on the chairlift saw them quickly over Cairn Gorm and down to the Shelter Stone by 10am.

Looking straight up from his chosen spot Smith could see a ragged line of weakness which appeared to be a downward continuation of the slanting crack on Postern. If they could gain and follow this it would take them directly to the Gallery. Their combined pile of hardware was typical for a big rock climb at that time – about 12 rope slings and kara-biners, 10 assorted soft metal pitons, two hammers and a rope. Donning PAs they climbed a pleasant slab up over a bulge to a grass ledge below the line of weakness. They could now see that this comprised twin zig-zag cracks which started with a double overlap and finished just below the terrace, at a little wall with a pronounced beak of rock. Steeper, balance climbing took Smith over the opening laps; then sustained slabs in the line of the cracks led directly to the short wall. He tackled this head-on and was forced to move right on to the beak of rock before finding reasonable holds to make the pull-up onto ledges.

They were now on the Gallery, close to the point where the slant-ing crack of Postern leads away up rightwards. The first steep band lay directly above and in its centre was a scooped wall containing a verti-cal crack which cut through a narrow black overhang in the form of a near perfect 'f'. To reach the crack would be easy enough, but contin-uing straight up through the 'f' formation looked most improbable. They climbed a slab and a flake to reach a comfortable stance on top of a huge block. Here, at last, the climbing became much steeper. Good holds led up left for 20ft before a step back right gained the crack. This turned out to be the edge of a big flake, providing delightful climbing up to the black overhang. Here Smith discovered a very narrow ledge running out horizontally across the left wall. Tiptoeing close to the point of over-balancing he crossed this to its end below a short bulging crack. The situation was very exposed, but sensing that easy ground lay only 15ft above, and knowing also that the granite had been more accommodat-ing than expected, he launched up the crack with confidence. Unfortunately, once committed, he found the little recess above disap-pointingly lacking in good handholds and was quite relieved when he eventually pulled through into balance and moved easily up to a ledge.

At this point, halfway up the face, they were somewhat left of the direct line to the hanging crack. There were a number of possible ways up the next section. Directly above was a groove which appeared to lead towards the big corner left of the crack. They eschewed this, opting instead, to move round rightwards on a shelf to below a shallow left-facing corner 20ft up the wall. This looked very hard with no apparent holds except for a narrow crack where the two faces of the corner met. Smith tried to get Agnew to have a go, but the canny Glaswegian said they should stick with their prior agreement to lead alternate pitches, which had resulted in Smith getting all the hard bits so far. "So, away the Bauchle went, mumbling and grumbling, thrutching and pedalling. 'Tight rope. Slack rope.' Assorted cursing and then loud chortling and screaming, I'm up. A piece of cake. You'll love it!"[6]

"I was cleaning up in the kitchen having just completed another day in the yards when I heard my younger brothers and sister yelling... Drying my face, I headed for the door thinking proviman, polis-man, tickman. It was with great relief and surprise that I opened the door to find Robin Walker Wheech man!"
– Davy Agnew

Agnew did not exactly love it. In fact, he thought it was the hardest pitch he had ever done. After moving up into the corner he had to hunch into an awkward layback position. Then using what Smith described as a 'crack for thin fingers' for his left hand he managed to make a long reach out right and swing round into a much larger, easier groove. The way was now clear right through to the base of the hanging crack, which they quickly reached over broken ground and some left-trending grooves.

Thirty feet away was the very impressive left-hand corner which they were tempted to try, but thought it should be left to become the finish of a more direct line. While Agnew belayed on an exposed ledge Smith surveyed the prospects ahead. The crack was really a deep, narrow chimney somewhat like a grand, but slimmer, version of Savage Slit. This was the finale of eight hours concentrated effort. There was no doubting the way to go, yet even Smith must have been feeling the effects of all that climbing. Gradually, he gained height, bridging, wedging, and fixing runners round little chokestones and into cracks on the side walls. Sometimes the rock was loose, requiring careful handling, and occasionally, he was forced to remove pieces of granite, tossing them way out of the corner in a great arc to bounce on the lower rocks before exploding into the scree 800ft below. Just below the top, he could feel cool air wafting from deep within the mountain and here where the crack widened to a blocky recess, he took his last belay. All that remained of this tremendous climb was an easy scramble under a pile of chokestones to reach the plateau.

According to Agnew they named the climb The Needle after the striking top crack with its eye of daylight. The fact that it could also be interpreted as a dig at the Aberdonians was a little bonus. It was undoubtedly a big leap forward for the Cairngorms, both in terms of technical difficulty and in its concept. Four of the nine pitches were harder than anything hitherto climbed in the area, with the bulging crack at the top of the fourth pitch meriting 5b. It is a testament to Smith's skill and determination that the whole route was led on sight, using pitons only as running belays. It was the most outstanding achievement on granite at that time – E1 5b.

The Needle was the earliest extreme rock climb in the Cairngorms and it ranks high among Smith's other great classics. It was also his last new climb in Scotland, for just a few weeks later he was killed with his companion, Wilfred Noyce, in a fall on Peak Garmo in the Pamirs. He was just 23-years-old. Davie Agnew heard of Smith's death on BBC radio and later that same day he received a postcard from Smith. It said: "The Hills are mighty big here. Keep climbing. Robin."[7]

Across from An Sticil, the less imposing Longbow Crag on Cairn Gorm also sported a big expanse of unclimbed rock. A glance in the guide at the diagram of Stag Rocks indicated a large blank space to the right of the Relay Climb. This 600ft high, south-facing cliff had obvious appeal to sun-worshippers, but unfortunately it lacked striking lines. Derek Pyper was interested in making a route near the centre of this cliff and had already been up close to the Longbow roof. In August, he went for another look, this time accompanied by Jim McArtney, a strong outgoing lad with a confident air about him. He was a few years younger than Pyper and still a relatively inexperienced climber, but what he lacked

John Ingram hunched up below the Crack for Thin Fingers, on The Needle, 1972

Photo: Greg Strange

in technique he made up for in enthusiasm. After two pitches of slabby climbing they belayed at the foot of a red wall. Previously, Pyper had avoided this on the left but McArtney went straight up, following a line of unlikely holds to the top. On the next pitch Pyper soon reached his earlier high point beneath the Longbow roof and traversed gingerly rightwards below it for 20ft. He discovered that he could swing round an arete to reach a good stance below a crack, thus successfully outflanking the major obstacle. Another run-out of good climbing saw them on to broken ground, leaving 200ft of scrambling to the plateau. They both

The Longbow Crag viewed from the top of Shelter Stone Crag. Longbow Direct starts at the pink area of rock low down and goes more or less straight up. The Sand-Pyper lies to its right but left of the discontinuous patches of vegetation

Photo: Derek Pyper

thought the climb, Longbow Direct, to be one of the cleanest and best routes they had done in the Cairngorms – VS 5a.

Back down at the Shelter Stone the Aberdonians met the Marshall Brothers. There was an exchange of pleasantries during which neither party gave much away about the day's activities. Jimmy Marshall later revealed that they had spent most of the day on the Shelter Stone Crag trying unsuccessfully to link the lower corners climbed the previous year with the big upper corner left of the Needle Crack.

After his success on Longbow Direct, Pyper was keen to try a line to its right. An opportunity arose in October when the Etchachan Club ran a bus meet to the Linn o' Dee. Although the weather was damp on the walk in, by the time he and his companion, Sandy Sands, had reached Loch Avon it had turned warm and sunny. They commenced climbing midway between Longbow Direct and a series of vegetated depressions on the right. Two pitches of clean slab climbing took them to a ledge below a large cracked overlap. This proved troublesome and forced a detour up right to near its right end. Here Pyper had to stand in a short sling, hung from a piton, before he was able to pull over using a slightly suspect hold. A traverse back left gained a stance in the line of a prominent diagonal fault. This they followed up rightwards for two pitches to an area of more vegetated rock, where cracks and a final steep chimney finished the climb.

It had been a very satisfying day pioneering a 600ft rock climb above Loch Avon during an autumn bus meet to upper Deeside. The eponymous name, The Sand-Pyper, raised a few eyebrows at the time, but it did not prevent the route becoming popular. In 1972, Mike Geddes and John Higham found a more direct finish breaking out from the diagonal fault and taking corners and cracks to the top. The combination of the original line and the direct finish, now known as The Sand-Pyper Direct, is considered to be the best climb on Longbow Crag – HVS 5a.

The winter 1962 – 63 was notable for its prolonged spell of continuous cold weather which lasted from Christmas until early March. For much of the first half of this period the wind blew from the east resulting in heavy snowfall in the Cairngorms, while in the far west there was drought and the hills there were almost snow-free. At the start of the big freeze, on December 29, Dundee climbers Davie Crabb and Doug Lang made the first winter ascent of B Gully Chimney in Coire Fee of Glen Doll. The ascent of this now popular Grade III ice route did not herald an avalanche of winter climbs. On the contrary, very little climbing took place on account of the huge amounts of snow. Week after week it piled up in enormous drifts so that when settled weather developed in February many features were buried and approaches deep and heavy going.

Pyper recalls skiing from Derry Lodge to Coire Etchachan four weekends out of six, each time following the same set of tracks left on the first visit. He also remembers a substantial igloo built at the start of the Derry flats which could still support a man's weight more than a month after construction. It had been constructed by members of the Gritstone Club who had been staying at Derry Lodge during the previous week. During one of his trips on February 23, Pyper and McArtney climbed Bastion Wall, a route towards the left side of the

Bastion on Creagan a' Choire Etchachan. The main features of this sustained winter climb were long, iced grooves and a 100ft chimney near the top – Grade IV.

In the summer of 1963 the comfortable, stone-built, Lochend Bothy was bulldozed by the Glen Muick Estate. It stood a short distance from the north-east shore of Loch Muick, close to a small wood, just over half a mile south of Spittal of Glen Muick. Close proximity to the public road was the main cause of its demise for although the bothy was well looked after by its regular visitors; less responsible people had been caught using the internal timber for firewood.

The loss of Lochend coincided with the construction of two small metal huts on the plateau of Cairn Gorm. Engineers from the 51st Highland Division TA had erected these shelters the previous year for the emergency use of people caught out in bad weather. The tiny storm refuge of El Alamein was situated one mile north-east of Cairn Gorm summit in such an obscure location that Glenmore Lodge parties used it as a difficult point to reach in navigation training! The St Valery Refuge

From left: Derek Pyper, Davie Reid and Jim McArtney, Lochnagar, 1962

Photo: Mike Smith

From left: Mitch Higgins, Derek Pyper and Jim Innes, 1964

Photo: Lesley Pyper

stood beside a small tor close to the plateau edge at the top of the Stag Rocks. The latter provided overnight accommodation for up to four people and was used frequently by climbers visiting the Loch Avon area.

September saw the discovery of two excellent rock climbs in Coire Sputan Dearg which had been missed during the first wave of exploration. The right-hand side of Terminal Buttress is dominated by a steep wall with a series of cracks running up its left edge. These cracks provided the line of Terminal Wall for Brian Lawrie and McArtney. It was a short, exposed climb on good holds and Lawrie's first lead on virgin rock. A week later, Lawrie was back at Scott's Bothy to make up a trio with Mitch Higgins and Jim Innes to climb a route on the Grey Man's Crag.

The line which they had in mind was the prominent corner between Pilgrim's Groove and Hanging Dyke, which slants leftwards up the centre of the crag. The opening groove looked hard so Lawrie avoided this, regaining the line 40ft up. Higgins then took over and led three pitches following the corner until the natural line went left below an area of steep smooth slabs. Here they joined an existing climb, Lucifer Route, for its crux step left into the final easy section of Pilgrim's Groove. Despite most of the climb being in a corner they named this excellent route Grey Slab on account of the large slab bordering the left side of the middle pitches. Both Terminal Wall and Grey Slab are Hard Severe.

The first ascentionists on Grey Slab were part of a new influx of young Aberdeen climbers. Brian Lawrie was 14-years-old when he joined the Etchachan Club in 1960. He was a couple of years younger than McArtney with whom he struck up a good climbing relationship. Mitch Higgins was a member of the Cairngorm Club. He and his partner, Jim Innes, together with McArtney and Lawrie climbed regularly as a group for several years during which time they made many early repeat ascents of the harder Cairngorms routes of the 1950s.

Another Severe rock climb was made on Halloween by Patey and Don Whillans. While investigating the rock climbing potential of No. 4 Buttress in Coire an Lochain they found a number of steep, inviting corner and groove-lines, the best being an impressive corner right of Savage Slit. Unfortunately, it was raining so they turned their attention to a line of discontinuous grooves a few feet left of Savage Slit and climbed these – Gaffer's Groove.

After the big freeze of 1963 the following winter proved to be almost tropical by comparison. In early January rock climbing was the order of the day on the buttresses of Coire Sputan Dearg and Creagan a' Choire Etchachan while only high, north and east facing gullies contained any snow. These lean conditions continued for the remainder of the season.

Not surprisingly, the high crags came into summer condition early and Patey was quick to return to the big corner right of Savage Slit. With Mary Stewart and Aberdeen University student, Robin Ford, he succeeded in climbing Fall-out Corner on May 17. It gave an exciting climb which like its near neighbour proved to be technically easier than its forbidding appearance had suggested. Entry to the corner was blocked by a wet overhang which he passed on the right using a piton for aid. Thereafter, the corner gave two pitches of sustained climbing on clean horizontally jointed granite – VS 4b.

A week later, Ford and fellow Aberdeen University student, Alan

*St Valery Refuge.
Ed Grindley, Tony
Gowland and John
Ingram looking out*

Photo: Greg Strange

North, upstaged the Beinn a' Bhùird regulars by climbing Three Step in Coire na Cìche. This line of slabs and overhanging walls between The Carpet and Slugain Buttress had been eyed and attempted on a number of occasions in the 10 years since Malcolm and Thom had been turned back. So far no one had managed to exit from an overhanging crack on the second pitch to reach the second 'step'. In the early 60s a large wooden wedge used for propping open the bar door of the Fife Arms in Braemar was reputed to have been specially made to fit this crack.

Ford and North climbed the crack using an undisclosed number of pitons, then crossed diagonally up right on the slab forming the second

*Brian Lawrie
preparing to do battle
on Lochnagar*

Photo: *Greg Strange*

step to a belay below the next steep wall. Here a crack with good holds at its start ran up the wall, but the rounded, slabby nature of the rock above offered little hope of an easy passage out to the right. A piton was used to initiate a swing up right on to a narrow ledge, from which it was possible to continue farther right round a corner to reach easier ground. Ledges and a short wet corner took them to a grass terrace at the third 'step'. At this point it would have been easy to walk off but they climbed the big slab above in three pitches, finishing up the right edge. The students did not record details of their climb at the time and rumours of excessive aid being used on a 'last great problem' were heard among some of the locals. It was not until a repeat ascent was made in

August 1969 by Mike Rennie and John Bower that the good quality and difficulty of Three Step was confirmed. Rennie used two pitons in the overhanging crack and also required the piton on the upper crux wall. The whole route was eventually led free by Colin MacLean in 1982 – E1 5c.

A good spell of weather in July coincided with a lengthy working visit to Aberdeen by Jim Stenhouse. He was quickly in contact with local climbers and on his first weekend away made the second ascent of Amethyst Wall with McArtney. On the upper buttress McArtney led a steep crack directly up the crest to join the original line near the top. This gritstone-like crack provides one of the best pitches in Coire Sputan Dearg – HVS 5b.

Stenhouse was aware of the potential for high quality rock climbs on Creag an Dubh-loch, so a week after Amethyst Wall he went to the big cliff with Brian Lawrie. They were immediately struck by the tremendous sweep of slabs right of Labyrinth Edge and decided there and then to try and climb them as directly as possible. These Central Slabs are best viewed face-on from the shore of the loch where their full 1100ft length may be seen with less foreshortening. Continuity is interrupted at a little over half-height by a rightward trending ledge system, effectively creating an upper and lower tier, with the most continuous rock on the upper tier being slightly offset towards Labyrinth Edge in relation to the main area on the lower tier. The initial problem was to choose one of the dozen or so vertical cracks with which to start their climb. They could see a very hard-looking barrier of overhangs girdling the cliff 300ft up. These appeared to ease towards the left so they decided to follow a central crack system slightly rightwards through a lower overlap and so reach the big overhangs left of a huge open-mouth formation. If they could not pierce these overhangs directly they would still have options farther left.

Stenhouse was already familiar with the type of friction climbing they expected to encounter having been on previous skirmishes with Jimmy Marshall while making first ascents of climbs like Jaywalk on the Etive Slabs. As for the young Lawrie, he had only recently acquired a pair of PAs and was keyed-up at the prospect of making a new route on one of the country's biggest crags.

Once they got going they soon found that the slabs were generally just too steep to climb entirely on friction. Clearly, it would be the cracks and grooves that would provide the holds and piton protection to make progress up these bald slabs. After 130ft of sustained climbing Lawrie reached a small ledge and made a piton belay below the first overlap. This first overlap went easily, and then a tricky second bulge brought Stenhouse on to the slabs immediately below the main overhangs. All looked hopeless for a direct ascent but he could see 30ft away to his left a shallow corner running up to a recessed area left of the main overhangs. By placing a high piton runner he was able to protect himself initially as he made his way delicately leftwards and slightly downwards to a little ledge near the base of the corner. This crucial traverse opened the way via the shallow corner up over slabs into the base of a disappointingly easy gully. This they followed by its left fork for two full pitches until they came to the terrace directly below the large area of smooth slabs which Brooker had referred to as "a sea of polished slabs".

Douglas Dinwoodie climbing McArtney's Crack on Amethyst Wall, Coire Sputan Dearg, in 1975

Photo: Greg Strange

*The Central Slabs of
Creag an Dubh-loch
in July. Broad Terrace
Wall is the steep area
of rock top left*

Photo: Greg Strange

By now it was getting late so they escaped across the terrace onto Central Gully Buttress.

They were back below the sea of slabs the following Saturday, fortunate to find the cliff still dry. A shallow corner defines the right side of the slabs and to its left a crack runs up towards a big overlap 150ft above. Stenhouse led the 90ft crack then Lawrie continued directly to a small slanting bulge. Hard moves along this to the right eventually took him to a belay below the big overlap which Stenhouse climbed with a piton for aid. Lawrie's difficult pitch on the sea of slabs had taken a long time and light was fading as they climbed a short corner onto grass ledges below the final overhangs. Here they estimated at least a full rope length of climbing remained to reach easier ground and everything looked hard. They descended left on grass and traversed to Labyrinth Edge, where they groped their way up its final pitch in the dark. At 1200ft this was the longest rock climb in the Cairngorms. A big route required a big name so they settled for Dinosaur. Although the first three pitches gave excellent climbing the route as a whole was a little disappointing due to the easy Dinosaur Gully and the vegetated finish. Early repeats in the 60s moved left onto Labyrinth Edge after the first pitch on the sea of slabs and it is doubtful if Lawrie's hard pitch has been repeated in its entirety. In the 70s Dinwoodie climbed a variation to this pitch and freed the aid point. He also made an independent finish, climbing left of the final overhangs – HVS 5a.

The dry weather held through to the next weekend when Lawrie returned once more to the Dubh Loch, this time with fellow Aberdeen climbers, McArtney, Higgins, Innes, William Barclay (Winky) and Dave Mercer. Sunday found them lounging at the tents gazing up at the great frontal face of Central Gully Wall. They traced the lines of Mousetrap and Waterkelpie Wall, the only climbs on this section of cliff, and both unrepeated. McArtney and Lawrie wanted to try the big crack-line between Mousetrap and Waterkelpie which cut through a large roof 150ft up. However, they could not agree where to start and in the end McArtney teamed up with Mercer to try a direct start to Waterkelpie Wall. The other four went off to climb Vertigo Wall.

Mercer climbed the open groove previously attempted by Grassick, Barclay and others, passing an old karabiner at 60ft where the groove steepened. He belayed at a stance below a shallow vertical corner in the first steep band. McArtney found a loose flake in the corner which he carefully removed to reveal a thin crack for a piton. Using this as a handhold he could peer over the top and explore for finishing holds on the steep slab above. After a short rest he climbed the corner without using the piton and continued upwards, now on perfect rock, to reach a stance with several belays below a second steep band. This band was the rightward continuation of the roof through which the big unclimbed crack-line passed, 30ft to their left.

It was Mercer's turn again. This time there was only one real option for progress, a right-angled corner 15ft high – the sort of thing that would be simple with good holds. He attacked the corner, but found nothing to pull on. He tried several times and took a short fall before succeeding with a piton for aid. A few feet higher he reached a stance with an enormous block belay and brought up McArtney. By now the rain that had been threatening all day set in and quickly made the rock very greasy. They still had more than 100ft of steep slabs and walls to climb before reaching the relative sanctuary of The Caterpillar. Being most unwilling to retreat after all the hard work they put socks over their PAs and carried on, following a line slightly right of the cracks which led directly to the foot of the Red Wall. The elation on completing the direct start was somewhat tempered by the thought of getting back down in the pouring rain. Two long abseils and some rope manoeuvres near the bottom saw them safely back at their packs.

Mac Smith had predicted that the addition of a direct start to Waterkelpie Wall would make the whole "one of the finest climbs of its kind in the country". Although a complete ascent was still awaited there was no doubt that this long, intricate route was in the same league as The Needle for difficulty and length. The first complete ascent was made by Dinwoodie and Dave Innes in 1973 when they freed Barclay's upper bulge. In 1984, Mercer's little corner was freed by Andy Nisbet at E1 5c.

The ascents of Dinosaur and Waterkelpie Wall Direct were significant events in the development of Creag an Dubh-loch. The former opened a large area of hitherto virgin cliff, while the latter broke new ground in terms of difficulty on a line which had defeated the previous generation. The adoption of PAs and the availability of a wider range of pitons played a role in this advance but it still required a determined approach to overcome the psychological barrier presented by these smooth-looking granite walls. After the summer of 1964 it was clear to local climbers like Lawrie, McArtney and Mercer that there were many more exciting days in prospect on Creag an Dubh-loch, provided it stopped raining long enough.

During 1964, a public bar opened in the west wing of Mar Lodge. It was part of an ambitious plan by the Panchaud brothers to create an Alpine ski resort based at the Lodge and utilising the nearby slopes of Creag Bhalg for its pistes. It was hard to credit that anyone with knowledge of the area would have considered such a relatively low-lying, south-facing site for commercial skiing. Not surprisingly, even with the use of Europe's largest artificial snow-making plant, the project was abandoned after a few short seasons.

Fortunately, the demise of the ski centre did not bring about closure of the bar, nor did it stop the occasional dance being held in the nearby Stag ballroom. The Mar Lodge bar, with its central open fire as a focal point, became a favourite watering-hole for climbers and walkers throughout the 1960s and 1970s. Prior to its opening, the Fife Arms in Braemar was the last licensed premises on the Deeside approach to the high Cairngorms. Traditionally, climbers arriving in Braemar on the Saturday 3.15pm bus from Aberdeen went first to the Bruachdryne for high tea, and then adjourned to the Fife for stronger refreshment before making the long walk to Derry Lodge or Scott's bothy. With Mar Lodge being three miles closer to the hills it provided a further stop-off and an opportunity to mingle with the locals. There was always the chance that Bob Scott would be there and might be persuaded to make room in his Land-Rover when he eventually drove back up the Derry road to Luibeg.

In November, the removal of Jean's Hut to its new location at the entrance to Coire an Lochain was completed. It had been two years since it was dismantled at its original site in Coire Cas. The hut was built in 1952 in memory of 21-year-old Jean McIntyre Smith who died as a result of head injuries sustained on a mountain craft course at Easter 1948. She had slipped on snow while descending the Fiacaill a' Choire Chais.

For 10 years the hut was run by Glenmore Lodge as a base from which students could ski or walk. It could sleep up to 18 people but was usually locked and therefore not available to the public. In fact, apart from Ryvoan, two miles north-east of Glenmore Lodge, the only open shelter on the north side of Cairn Gorm had been the tiny, but splendid, wooden hut known as Clach Bharraig Bothy situated on the west bank

of the Alt Mhòr beside the path from Glenmore to the Chalamain Gap. It was demolished in the late 1950s.

With the advent of a new road and ski development Glenmore Lodge no longer required accommodation like Jean's hut in Coire Cas. Besides, the hut was now being regularly vandalised and had become a liability. In 1962, a decision was made to dismantle the hut and re-erect it in Coire an Lochain where it would serve as an open bothy for climbers. It would also continue as an advanced base for the Cairngorm Mountain Rescue Team who used it to store emergency equipment.

Creag an Dubh-loch continued to be the focus of attention among local climbers into the winter months. Grassick, Taylor, and Bill James made a difficult six hour ascent of False Gully on December 19. Cold, stormy weather in the period leading up to the day of the climb had deposited a good cover of fresh snow over both the rock and the ice. They followed the summer line throughout using rope tension from a piton at the crux. Grassick led the climb in crampons and although he gave it a Grade IV rating, Taylor later admitted that it felt harder – VI.

A few days of slight thaw preceded further stormy weather with severe drifting on Christmas and Boxing days. On the evening of December 27, 1964 four young men were staying in Bob Scott's Bothy at Luibeg. Alexander Mackenzie, Alistair Murray, Robert Burnett and Alexander McLeod had motored up that afternoon from Cowdenbeath. The next day they planned to walk up Beinn a' Bhùird then descend and spend

Jean's Hut at the entrance to Coire an Lochain. The hut stood at this location for 22 years until it was removed in 1986

Photo: Hamish MacInnes

*Coire an Dubh
Lochain (left) and
Dividing Buttress,
Beinn a' Bhùird*

Photo: Greg Strange

the second night under canvas beside the Allt na Beinne, a tributary of the Quoich.

On Monday, December 28 they reached the South top of Beinn a' Bhùird in deteriorating weather. A strong north-westerly wind was driving snow and there was poor visibility. They opted to descend the south-west slopes in the line of a snow-filled gully, the Allt Tarsuinn, a feeder stream running into the Allt na Beinne. At about 2.30pm they were walking down the north bank of the burn, on what Burnett later described as firm snow, when Murray slipped and fell unhurt into the gully. As he started back up to join his companions Burnett advised him to cross to the south bank, which was almost denuded of snow, and meet them at the bottom. Moments later, while Burnett and the others continued down the north side, a huge slab avalanche broke away under their feet. Murray watched in horror as his friends disappeared under the mass of snow. When all was still he made a desperate search of the debris hoping to find them, but after half an hour without any success he gave up and went for help.

Murray ran the five miles down the Quoich to the nearest habitation beside Mar Lodge. Once the police had been informed a rescue party was quickly raised. The local police were joined by climbers, skiers, hostellers and estate workers. Although they were able to get a long way up the Quoich by tractor and Land-Rover, time was not on the side of the buried men. Few of the rescuers were hopeful of finding anyone alive. Searching by torchlight they discovered McLeod's body just before giving up for the night at 4am.

Next morning, December 29, reinforcements arrived from Aberdeen, but hours of searching still failed to discover the two remaining men. Then at 12.30pm one of the rescuers found a small hole in the debris, yellowed around the edges. Peering down this, he was amazed to see

Burnett, alive and calling for help. He was buried between one and two feet deep and apart from some frostbite he was uninjured. Unfortunately, Mackenzie, like McLeod, had not been so lucky – his body was found a few hours later.

Burnett's extraordinary survival of 22 hours buried within the avalanche debris is the longest recorded in Scotland and one of the longest in full contact with the snow on record anywhere. A number of factors may explain his good fortune, not least his obvious great will to live. Although he passed into unconsciousness immediately after burial he was not physically injured. When he came round he was laying on his back with his arms stretched above his head. Quite often in slab avalanches the snow breaks up into angular blocks which may leave air passages penetrating some distance into the debris. Despite being completely trapped he was able to move his arms and this allowed him to clear a gap in front of his face. This coincided with a small air passage which saved his life.

There had been previous recorded avalanches in the Cairngorms which had resulted in the deaths of mountaineers. These had been on steep snow in the gullies of Coire an Lochain and Coire an t- Sneachda. However, the significance of the Beinn a' Bhùird accident was that it had occurred on an open hillside, on a slope of no more than 30 degrees. It sent a message to all winter visitors that they would not only have to be avalanche aware while climbing in steep gullies, but that they should also consider approaches and descents from the plateau, partic- ularly in periods of prolonged cold, windy weather, when firm but weakly anchored wind slab could be lying ready to trap the unwary trav- eller. This type of slab avalanche, triggered by the victims, became more common as the number of winter visitors to the Cairngorms increased.[8] This accident on Beinn a' Bhùird helped bring about the formation of the Braemar Mountain Rescue Association in May 1965.

Weather and climbing conditions were mixed throughout the first month of 1965, then on the very last day of January a period of settled weather set in. For several weeks the crags were in perfect condition and the approaches easy. Early on January 31, McArtney and Barclay crept out of Derry Lodge and made their way up onto the frozen Derry Flats and onwards to Coire Etchachan. "The first glimpse as one rounds the last bend into Coire Etchachan is, for me, always an exciting one, but today the sight which confronted us was even more so, for the entire corrie was bathed in a delicate rose-pink colour of the morning sun, and the cliff was heavily plastered. Looking at it, one got the feeling which one rarely gets in winter, that, today, anything would go."[9] Their enthusiasm was unbounded, and despite waist-deep powder on the slopes below the cliff they resolved to have a go at Djibangi as it appeared to be covered in continuous snow and ice. McArtney led the climb taking a natural line of ice which flowed down from the base of the main corner. The first two pitches involved delicate ice work, cutting small holds in the half-inch thick ice below a superficial covering of powder, and balancing up on the front points of his crampons. The long corner of the summer crux was well banked with snow and turned out to be one of the easiest sections of the climb. Instead of taking the easy ramp up right to join the final pitch of The Dagger they continued more directly.

Garbh Choire Dhaidh, Braeriach. The Great Rift follows the almost snow-filled depression near the centre of the picture

Photo: Greg Strange

A final verglased slab covered in powder snow proved to be the most exacting pitch of the day. The tension eased only when McArtney managed to place a piton after running out 100ft of rope. The cornice was dispatched with little trouble and after six and a half hours they reached the plateau having accomplished a most outstanding climb, one that would not be repeated for another 18 years – Grade V.

Conditions were still good three weeks later when Graeme Nicol and Jerry Light went to the Garbh Choire Dhaidh to attempt The Great Rift, which had taken on the mantle of Braeriach's last great winter problem but was seldom in condition. After a night in Corrour they entered the corrie just as the sun rose. "The spirit of competition was so strong that we imagined a steel-shod McArtney, lurking in tent or snow-hole, and bounding out to forestall us. But we were alone with the mountain, probably no living soul within 10 miles."[10] The sun had not yet stripped the winter cover and the cliff was really plastered. The Rift, a chimney set in the corner of a big diedre, looked hard but climbable.

Two pitches took them to below a big cave where continuing directly looked very hard. Here Nicol moved left on a shelf, surmounted an overlap, then worked up and back right on iced slabs to regain the gully above. This proved to be the hardest pitch on the climb and they were glad to have brought along some of the new Salewa tubular ice screws. Nicol fixed one of these on the overlap and used tension while cutting steps above. It was 2pm before they were both back in the line of the gully.

By now the weather had changed and they were in cloud with spindrift blowing down the cliff. They had expected things to get easier above the great cave but the climb was far from beaten yet. Another pitch with a little cave led to a point where the gully cut back right as a steep chimney. Nicol attempted this before taking to the rocks on the left. A run-out of 100ft brought him to a snow slope, and then Light led an easy pitch up to and through a small cornice. It had taken 10 hours – Grade V.

Light was involved in another impressive winter ascent on March 14, this time in the company of Nicol's old sparring partner Grassick. On a poor day of rain and wet snow they climbed Grassick's own Talisman on Creagan A' Choire Etchachan in six and a half hours. They followed the summer line to reach the final crest where they moved left to finish up a difficult icy groove. The hardest pitch was the 50ft traverse to gain the left Corridor edge. At the overhanging groove of the summer crux they used a piton high in the corner for aid. This was a technically very difficult winter climb following a line previously considered solely the preserve of the rock climber. It bore few characteristics of a traditional winter climb in that it was on steep, exposed rock with little or no vegetation. It did not follow a water course and was unlikely ever to have a build-up of snow. It was, in fact, an early example of the modern 'mixed' winter climb – Grade VI.

During 1965 a number of new faces were seen on the bus to Braemar. In August, 16-year-old Mike Rennie with fellow Aberdonians Raymond Stirton and John Bower climbed a new route on Slab Buttress in Coire na Cìche. Their line, Lamina, gave 300ft of sustained friction climbing on the clean slabs right of South Corner Gully. (VS). Also on Beinn a' Bhùird, in Coire an Dubh Lochain, Aberdeen University students, Allen Fyffe and Malcolm Mowat (Mouse), climbed the shallow corner system immediately right of Polypody Groove to give the enjoyable VS – Tearaway. Fyffe, from Longforgan near Dundee, first became interested in the outdoors while at Harris Academy where he walked and camped in the Cairngorms and made his first rock climbs on the Red Craig in Glen Clova.

Tearaway, climbed in October, was followed two days later by another excellent discovery on Hell's Lum Crag by Perth JMCS members Ian Small and George Brown. With Ian Houston they climbed Auld Nick on the attractive overlapping slabs just left of the watercourse of The Escalator. Auld Nick is now thought to be the best Severe in the Loch Avon Basin. Sadly, Small and Houston died later that year in Coire an t-Sneachda. Houston's body was found on Boxing Day near the entrance to the corrie where he had collapsed after making a valiant attempt to go for help. Despite much searching by rescue teams Small was not found for another 12 days when his body was located beneath a large boulder by a search dog. The two companions had planned to climb in Coire an Lochain and it is thought that while returning across the plateau in

Allen Fyffe in Glen Coe, 1968

Photo: Robin Turner

thick weather they fell over the edge in the vicinity of Fiacaill Couloir.

Most of October 1965 had been very dry and even by the end of the month conditions were still good for rock climbing. On Saturday, October 23, three heavily laden climbers entered Central Gully on Creag an Dubh-loch and stopped directly below the tremendous vertical groove system right of Vertigo Wall. They had come to climb the Giant.

Dave Bathgate, Arthur Ewing and Jim Brumfitt were members of the Squirrels Climbing Club which now boasted among its ranks some of Scotland's finest climbers. The year so far had been a busy one for Bathgate and Ewing. In the spring they had been involved in early developments on Creag Dubh, the big roadside crag near Newtonmore. Then, during July and August, accompanied by other Squirrels, they had had a successful trip to the Alps accounting for many difficult aid routes in the Dolomites, as well as climbs at Chamonix including the West Face of the Petit Dru. They were obviously in good form and unlikely to be intimidated by a 500ft wall on Creag an Dubh-loch.

Their equipment included some of the latest American hardware. Graham Tiso had recently opened a climbing shop in Edinburgh and was importing the full range of chrome-alloy steel pitons being manufactured by Chouinard and Leeper. These hard steel pitons, developed by some of the world's leading aid-climbers, had been designed specially for use in granite. They could be driven into more marginal cracks than the soft metal pitons from Europe which tended to bend to the shape of the rock

It was Ronnie Marshall who had encouraged Bathgate to try the big corner on Central Gully Wall which he had seen in 1959 while descending to do Mousetrap. Bathgate had already been to look at the line but unfavourable weather precluded an attempt. This time, despite the lateness of the season, the weather was calm, sunny, and most important of all, the rock was dry.

The opening section of the climb appeared to follow a series of discontinuous, very steep, leaning grooves which cut through the bulging lower part of the great wall. Beyond this the groove looked easier and more recessed, but it soon reared up again in an overhang before the impressive, 100ft final corner.

With Brumfitt belaying at the top of the introductory ramp Bathgate launched out onto the first major pitch, soon passing the rusty piton left by Grassick. Although the wall was very steep, the holds were good and after fixing a runner he reached an awkward resting position beside two parallel grooves. Choosing the one on the left, he used a piton to pull over a bulge, then a further two pitons to reach a good belay ledge below two similar grooves. As the day was rapidly drawing to a close, Brumfitt lowered Bathgate back to the top of the ramp, and leaving all the gear and the rope in place, they descended to a comfortable bivouac down by the loch.

Sunday was cloudy and cool and it was a while before they re-established their high-point. This time Ewing took the lead with Brumfitt belayed on the comfortable ledge and Bathgate still on the ramp. The twin overhanging grooves looked really mean. Bathgate had thought the shorter left hand one appeared easier so Ewing gave this a try. Climbing in etrier, he placed a small piton and moved up. Above this

*Arthur Ewing belayed
by Jim Brumfit on the
Giant, Creag an
Dubh-loch October
1965*

Photo: Dave Bathgate

he found no suitable cracks or hand holds. Optimistically, he
hammered another very small piton into a blind crack and eased up
cautiously. Whang! The piton came out and he was back down level
with Brumfitt, held by the first piton. After this he tried the right-hand
groove which, although longer and more impending did have a better
crack for pitons. He was near the top of the crack when he found he
could not free-climb from his position in etriers, despite having found
some hand holds above.

Ken Grassick, Jerry Light and Graeme Nicol, Pinnacle Face, Lochnagar, January 1966

Photo: Gordon Leslie

At this point, Ewing handed over the lead to Bathgate. "In no time at all I was attached to the peg at the top of the diedre with my hands on the hold but my body in the most contorted position I'd ever used in etriers. It was just impossible to make a free move from there."[11] By fixing another piton slightly higher he was able to use this to move out left onto a slab and back into balance. Another short, steep crack followed which he climbed with the aid of a jammed nut and two pitons to reach a good ledge above the lower difficulties.

Ewing followed quickly but Brumfitt had to remove all the pitons which took up time. Unfortunately, he was unable to retrieve his etriers after making the move out of the overhanging crack and they were left hanging forlornly from the top piton. Bathgate pressed on over blocks in the groove and was amazed to find two old pitons left by Dick Barclay. Higher up he used a piton in a smooth slab before moving right onto an overhanging nose. Soon he was belayed on a platform below the final corner and bringing up his companions.

After 15ft of wide bridging in the corner Bathgate hammered a wooden wedge into the crack and continued. Two more wedges and he was reduced to using etrier. While attempting to clip his rope into the top wedge the one which was supporting his weight suddenly came out. "I didn't notice any jerk as the second wedge came out. The only thing I was conscious of was the rim of the belay ledge coming up to meet me and then I was scraping past it to twang to a halt just beside the groove above the block overhang. I dangled upside down for a second or two watching a sling and krab that had been round my neck ping-pong their way down the gully and thought bloody hell that could have been me."[12]

He had taken a spectacular 70ft fall, held by one wooden wedge and Brumfitt's solid belaying. Fortunately, he was not badly hurt, just shaken and missing some skin. Brumfitt offered to take over the lead but Bathgate insisted that he was perfectly all right and said that he would use pitons all the way as there was no time left for fancy free. In the gathering gloom he aided his way up the corner using "about 14 pegs etc" until he was able to cross a slab and take a belay at a grass ledge which would be their home for the night. Once again, Brumfitt was the last man up. He was able to remove the belay piton, but while climbing in complete darkness all he could manage was to unclip the karabiners and progress up the corner, even with the others pulling hard on both ropes. All the pitons were left in the corner.

They spent a miserable 10 hours, huddled together on the ledge before sufficient daylight allowed them to make their way up the last 200ft of broken ground to the plateau, thus completing this epic climb. Some weeks later they returned and retrieved most of their pitons and other bits of equipment on abseil. The Giant had almost returned to its pristine condition.

Bathgate later wrote in his article *Explanation Giant*: "Classic lines deserve to be ascended with style and grace," so he expected criticism from some quarters for using so much aid. North-east climbers, who knew this part of the cliff, were not surprised to hear that the big corner weighed in at a hefty VS A2. They did, however, wonder why the Squirrels chose this line for the first all-out aid-climb in the Cairngorms. Other climbers thought it a travesty, believing that when it became apparent that they could not climb without pitons and etrier they should have retreated and left it for someone who could.

Pioneering climbs with more than a few pitons for aid was not new in Scotland. The Creagh Dhu had been doing it throughout the '50s, in Glen Coe (Engineer's Crack 1951), on the Etive Slabs (Agony 1957), in the Cuillin (Vulcan Wall 1957) and on Ben Nevis (Titan's Wall 1959). Only the previous summer, fellow Squirrel, Brian Robertson, had used pitons when he climbed King Kong on Ben Nevis. The acceptance by some of this type of climbing probably resulted from developments in the Alps and America, where big walls were being ascended by artificial means. In the '50s and '60s British climbers regularly visited the Dolomites and some became very proficient in the use of aid-climbing techniques. The ethical issue at the time was whether or not big wall tactics were appropriate on our relatively small Scottish crags. Some thought it was acceptable up to a point, while others were totally

Ken Grassick,
Lochnagar 1964

Photo: Bill Brooker

opposed to the use of more than one or two pitons for aid on any climb.

It was five years before The Giant received a repeat ascent. In 1970 it was climbed by Wilf Tauber and Bill Sproul (another Squirrel) who reduced some of the aid on the lower half but could not free the final corner which was very wet. Between 1970 and 1977 there were no more than half a dozen ascents, one of which, in 1974 by Paul Braithwaite and Nick Estcourt was reported to have been free. On the overhanging grooves, Braithwaite started to aid the right-hand crack, and then thought he might be able to free-climb the left one. He retreated to the belay leaving his ropes through the karabiners, and then led the left-hand groove protected by the pitons in the right. In July 1997 another free ascent was made by Dave Cuthbertson and Murray Hamilton. Cuthbertson led the very hard twin grooves reporting the grade to be 6a. The climb was repeated free again the next day by Mick Fowler and Phil Thomas. The current grade of The Giant is E3 6a and the seriousness of its 6a crux is still dependent on the existence and condition of an in-situ piton in the right-hand crack.

A wide cover of deep snow blanketed the Cairngorms over the Christmas holiday period 1965 – 66. The snow gradually consolidated after several thaws and freeze so that by the second weekend of the New Year winter climbing conditions were good, if somewhat thin. Grassick had long held an ambition to make a winter ascent of Pinnacle Face on Lochnagar. On no less than six occasions since 1962 he had set out to make this ascent. He had been on the lower section twice in winter and had climbed the route three times in summer. Despite all his foreknowledge he still knew that the climb would require a strong team and favourable weather.

A good forecast and a phone call from Jerry Light set the seal for an attempt on Sunday January 16. Graeme Nicol was persuaded to join them to make up a threesome. They arrived by car at Gelder Shiel on the Balmoral Estate, at 6.30am, Light having unlocked the gate using his own key (He was undertaking research work in the area). As dawn broke they were already at the foot of the cliffs, contemplating the steep slabs guarding the lower Black Spout Pinnacle. It was cold and settled with barely any wind.

Although the face was covered in a thin layer of fresh snow they found ice and névé overlying the ledges and filling the cracks, but there was little in the way of a build-up to ease the difficulties. The first 120ft up to the stance below the summer crux occupied most of the morning. The climbing was continuously difficult and time consuming, hand holds having to be cut in the ice or the rock cleared to expose holds below. They split this first section into three pitches with Light and Grassick alternating leads.

By early afternoon, Grassick was engaged on the summer crux. It will be remembered that this involves a VS step-up from a smooth slab to a rounded ledge – a movement heavily dependant on friction and made especially difficult in crampons. After several attempts he succeeded in making the moves using a poor piton for aid, protected by the original piton in the corner 10 feet above the belay ledge. The pitch now went left following a slabby fault. After a few feet he brought up Light to an intermediate belay. With direct assistance from his companion,

Grassick continued precariously upwards, scraping for handholds, until another hard move over a bulge brought him to a large ledge. It was 3.30pm when Light commenced the next pitch. He followed the summer line exactly. A layback crack, an icy groove then a horizontal flake traverse took him to the little ledge below the final steep corner.This was a particularly good lead by Light under the pressing circumstances. At 75ft it was the longest pitch of the day and involved continuous Severe rock climbing in the fading daylight. By the time they were all gathered on the ledge it was well and truly dark. They had already given up thoughts of continuing to the top of the Pinnacle. It was now a question of surmounting this final corner to complete the climb then finding their way back down Route 1.

After an hour of struggling in the impending corner Grassick returned to the ledge and swapped over with Light. It was at this point that they discovered that only one of their head torches was working. A serious situation called for serious tactics! Light faired no better than Grassick at the bulge so he called for his partner to climb up a few feet to a much smaller ledge.

With Nicol belaying them both, a supreme combined effort brought Light in reach of a good hold and he pulled through onto the ledge above. The first winter ascent of Pinnacle Face had been achieved. They now had to get down. "A spine-chilling traverse in darkness on narrow ledges which looked straight down the face into the black abyss was the most frightening part of the day."[13]

As it happened this was both Grassick and Nicol's last new winter route in the Cairngorms. It was a most impressive climb with which to bow out from the forefront of Scottish winter climbing. They both continued their interest in mountaineering (more so Grassick) but demanding medical careers meant that their climbing activity lessened. In the 14 years since the early days of the Boor Boys they had played important roles in the development of Cairngorms climbing, particularly in winter. After a short period in the RAF, Grassick left Scotland and settled as a GP in Newcastle. He was still a relatively young man when he died of acute leukaemia in 1989. With his passing North-east climbing lost one of its more colourful and sociable characters. He was a bold and very determined climber in his day. At the time of its ascent, Pinnacle Face was a close contender for the most technically difficult winter climb in Scotland – Grade VI.

Jerry Light leading the second pitch of Pinnacle Face, Lochnagar, belayed by Ken Grassick

Photo: Graeme Nicol

1.   ECJ Vol. 3, No. 4, p177.
2.   SMC *Climber's Guide to the Cairngorms Area Vol. 2* (1962), p54.
3.   SMCJ Vol. 27, No. 154, p352.
4.   SMC *Climber's Guide to the Cairngorms Vol. 1* (1961), p95.
5.   *High Endeavours*, p226.
6.   *High Endeavours*, p226.
7.   *High Endeavours*, p228.
8.   *A Chance in a Million*, Second Ed. 2000, p12 – 14.
9.   ECJ Vol. 4, No. 1, p18.
10. Aberdeen University Lairig Club Journal 1966, p3.
11. SMCJ Vol. 28, No. 157, p190 – 196.
12. SMCJ Vol. 28, No. 157, p190 – 196.
13. AULCJ 1966, p24.

8: On To The Big Blank Spaces (1966 – 1969)

FROM THE MID-1960s onwards, exploratory climbing in the Cairngorms was never dominated by one particular group. Gone were the days when North-east climbers ruled the roost. That is not to say the influence of the Aberdeen School had declined, it was just that more and more climbers from other parts were becoming interested in the area.

At the end of the 1966 winter, two prominent ice features received first ascents by recent newcomers to winter climbing. Mike Forbes burst onto the scene in 1965 when he completed more than 100 rock climbs in one year on numerous mountain crags throughout the Highlands. In March, accompanied by Mike Lowe, Forbes climbed the impressive ice pillar on Creagan a' Choire Etchachan which forms the direct continuation of Winter Route. The ascent was made in thawing conditions and gave two major pitches. The first at the vertical pillar where he used tension from two ice screws in order to cut hand and foot holds, and the second, a steep slab covered in deep fresh snow which required a piton for aid. This difficult climb, already named Square-Cut Gully, was given Grade IV by Forbes, but 19 years later on the second ascent, it was led free by Des Rubens using front-point technique and found to be Grade V.

The second ice route to fall was the previously attempted direct start to West Gully on Lochnagar. This was climbed by Fyffe and Mowat. Unlike Square-Cut Gully it became very popular and the accepted normal way to climb West Gully at Grade IV. It was McArtney who had previously retreated from near the top of the direct ice pitch when he dropped his axe.

Lairig Club member, Jerry Light, continued his explorations in An Garbh Choire of Braeriach. From a snow-hole below Great Gully, he and John Vigrow climbed Sphinx Ridge and the right fork of Buntings Gully in March. A snow plastered Sphinx Ridge gave them a relatively straightforward climb amid impressive scenery, at one point progressing *à chéval* up a knife-edge of snow. A big problem with many winter climbs here, particularly late in the season, is surmounting or circumventing the enormous cornice. On Sphinx Ridge it was at its lowest, presenting only 10ft of vertical snow, but at the top of Buntings Gully it was a monster. They were lucky, however, because 20ft to the right a big flake of snow had split from the cornice proper and the resulting chimney was used to gain the plateau. The day after the Sphinx ascent Graeme Nicol arrived with three Aberdeen Grammar School boys. He had agreed to take them winter climbing and thought a first winter ascent of Sphinx Ridge would be a good experience! Disappointed at being pipped at the post by one day, they nevertheless made a second ascent and the ridge became an instant Braeriach classic.

It was in April of this year that another informal climbing club was founded at a gathering in Aberdeen's Blue Lamp bar. The club had no constitution and ran no organised meets, but its members carried a card and were entitled to wear a cloth badge depicting the club logo – a black

Jerry Light taking samples from Lochain Uaine in March 1967 at the time of the winter ascent of Phoenix Gully

Photo: Malcolm McArthur

In fine fettle, (from left) are Brian Abernethy, Mike Rennie, Graeme Millar and Mike Forbes celebrating Forbes's 21st birthday in the Fife Arms Hotel, Braemar

Photo: Mike Forbes Collection

spider. The Aberdeen Spiders, named after their more illustrious Italian counterparts from Lecco, was the concept of Mike Forbes who envisaged a club to rival the Edinburgh Squirrels. The six founder members were Brian Abernethy (Biscuits), John Bower, Ian Cameron, Mike Forbes, Mark McLennan and Mike Rennie. Forbes was the most experienced climber among them. He had become interested in hill-walking and climbing through the local Adventure Club. As a trainee psychiatric nurse he often had time off when others were working, and for this reason he did a lot of soloing. Rennie was three years younger than Forbes. He was an apprentice engineering draughtsman at the Mugiemoss Paper Mill where Ian Cameron also worked as a trainee manager. McLennan and Bower had been at Aberdeen Academy together. Bower worked at a fisheries research station near his home in Torry. He had heard about climbing while at school and had started visiting his local sea cliffs just south of Nigg Bay at a place known by the locals as 'The Bonnie Shores'. Biscuits also worked in the fishing industry. Both he and Cameron had their own transport which meant that these Spiders had wheels.

During the summer of 1966, Light was the prime mover among members of the Lairig Club who constructed a small shelter on the left bank of the Allt a' Garbh-Choire directly below Lochain Uaine. The Garbh Choire Hut was designed on similar lines to St Valery Refuge, but had the major addition of a wooden floor. For those intent on climbing within the great amphitheatre of An Garbh Choire this was a most welcome addition to the Cairngorm bothies. Not being situated on an established through-route the hut was rarely over-visited and never vandalised. The Lairig Club was also involved in the official opening of its Club Hut beside the Royal Lodge of Allt-na-giubhsaich at the start of the path to Lochnagar in Glen Muick. This well-appointed bunkhouse, converted from the servants' quarters, and leased from the Balmoral Estate, is run by the University's department of Physical Education.

In July, Graeme Hunter and Graeme Millar (Mesh) from Dundee,

Creagan a' Choire Etchachan in January. The ice pillar of Square-Cut Gully is just right of the dark Corridor Wall of the Bastion on the extreme left

Photo: Greg Strange

visited the Central Slabs at Creag an Dubh-loch intent on making a climb straight up the middle. They knew nothing about the ascent of Dinosaur and believed the slabs were still virgin. They started at the lowest rocks and climbed two long pitches either on Dinosaur or possibly farther right, to arrive below the big open-mouth formation. Here, unlike their predecessors, they avoided the largest overlaps by moving right. They traversed on sloping ledges at first then used rope tension to cross a smooth slab before climbing up to the right of the biggest overhang. A farther 150ft of continuous slab climbing brought them on to broken ground at the right-hand end of the terrace.

Hunter recalled in 1998 that they found the climbing sustained and hard all the way up to the terrace. At the time they were heavily into 'The Goons', hence the bizarre name Yakaboo. When the climb was recorded the description stated that 10 pitons had been used in all for belays and assurance – thus leaving doubt as to the actual number employed for direct aid. Although the route covered a lot of new ground it was thought to have relied too heavily on aid. Over the years more direct lines were established which resulted in this early climb being largely, and perhaps unfairly, ignored – VS 5a.

The summer of 1966 saw a number of interesting second ascents. In the same month that Yakaboo was climbed, Forbes and Cameron repeated Mousetrap on Creag an Dubh-loch. Also around this time McArtney and Lawrie succeeded on Citadel after a previous attempt two years earlier with Mercer and Pyper had been thwarted by rain. They managed to free both the upper and lower cruxes. The big event on the Shelter Stone Crag, however, was Forbes and Rennie's ascent of The Needle in August. This was a real test for the two Spiders and Forbes had to pull out all the stops to lead the hard pitches with only a handful of pitons and a few slings to use as runners. In Aberdeen, at least, their repeat of Robin Smith's great climb did much to enhance their growing reputation as a climbing force to be reckoned with.

As a prelude to the Needle, Forbes and Rennie had climbed the crack-line of 'Willpower' on the Crimson Slabs. They reached this via the Direct Start to The Dagger then Rennie continued up to the niche and took a belay in slings at the old ring piton. Above this the slabs became steeper. Forbes placed a good piton, tried to climb on, but found it too diffi-cult. He decided to use the piton to gain height, and, having achieved this, he was forced to use another to reach better holds. It was a splendid situation isolated in the middle of that great sweep of gran-ite. He continued upwards on small but adequate holds finding short, difficult sections always followed by reasonable rests. At 70ft there was another thin section where he used a third piton before trending right to join The Dagger.

This impressive pitch gave Forbes his first new route on rock. Even with the pitons it was substantially harder than The Dagger and repre-sented a definite technical advance for the Crimson Slabs. Willpower was a good name, but being the first ascentionists, they opted to change it to Stiletto as follow-on to The Dagger. A number of repeat ascents of Stiletto were made using all, or some, of the pitons, but it was not until the long dry summer of 1976 that Dougie Dinwoodie led it free, using the pitons as runners only, at E2 5c.

The Crimson Slabs had a particular appeal to the Aberdonians and Rennie and Forbes made another visit in September. This time they had their eye on a series of cracks which ran up the prominent rib of The Dagger. In its own way this line looked just as imposing as Stiletto, but once Forbes had started up the initial single fissure he found a succes-sion of deep, friendly cracks, ideal for jamming and bridging. These provided exhilarating climbing all the way up the edge overlooking The Dagger. The climb, Scabbard, was considerably easier than Stiletto and quickly became popular – VS 4c.

Yet another climb was made here in October by Fyffe, who with Willy Forbes, Mowat and Ray Burnett, led a good two pitch direct start to Djibangi following the downward continuation of the main corner. Apparently, Forbes and Rennie were after this line and this was why Fyffe's party were determined to make the climb despite wet conditions.

The Severe rock climb known as Trident in Coire na Cìche of Beinn a' Bhùird was popular in the 1950s and 1960s, despite being a little vege-tated. It had become the winter target for several Aberdeen teams and already one attempt in the previous year had ended abruptly when Alec Rae took a flier off the layback crack on the slabs above the summer crux. Much fresh snow fell in the Cairngorms during the first weeks of January 1967. Bower and McLennan made a mid-week attempt on Trident, but were defeated at the crux by loose snow and lack of time. A substantial thaw then set in for several days, stripping away all the fresh powder but leaving traces of their steps visible on the first pitch. The following Saturday, a rival party, seeing these steps, assumed the climb had been done and diverted their attention elsewhere.

The next day, Sunday, January 15, there was a hard frost and the two Spiders quickly reached their high point after a night spent in the Howff. This time the problem was not one of too much snow, more the lack of it. According to Bower conditions were perfect with lots of verglas on the crux wall and the layback crack above, making these sections

Mike Forbes in the Gelder Shiel

Photo: Mike Forbes Collection

John Bower at Allt-na-giubhsaich, March 1970

Photo: Raymond Simpson

both precarious and strenuous. Bower removed his crampons to lead the wall of the summer crux, but was forced to use a piton and sling for aid. McLennan followed this pitch in crampons then continued straight up the layback also using a piton for aid.

After Trident, Bower began to consider other possible objectives for first winter ascents. He had arranged a holiday during the last week in January and planned to spend it climbing in the Cairngorms with Peter Kale. (Pedro). The weather had become unsettled, with plenty of fresh snow on high ground. They made abortive forays in bad weather on climbs in Coire Etchachan and Garbh Choire Dhaidh and by the Wednesday they were testing the storm-proof qualities of the new Garbh Choire Hut, wondering where to try next. On the 26th they reached the foot of Crown Buttress in Garbh Coire Mòr. Here they encountered deep powder overlying ice. It was on the opening pitch that Kale, who has a slight speech impediment, came out with the often quoted expression "Sh-shite. It's ice!" To which Bower replied: "Of course it's bloody ice. That's what we've come here for!" The penultimate pitch of Crown Buttress gave them excellent climbing up a long, ice-filled chimney.

The plateau was particularly inhospitable that evening with poor visibility and continuous spindrift. They tried to get down a gully, possibly Great Gully, but the cornices were huge. In the style of these times neither climber had a map or compass, although Kale did have a torch with a weak battery. In the faint light of its beam they attempted to find somewhere to fix an abseil anchor but with such deep snow they concluded it was not on and set off following the cornice rim in the direction of the Angel's Peak. Not surprisingly, they soon lost sight of the edge and after an indeterminate period of wandering came across what they assumed to be their own tracks. Bower recalled: "I'll never forget my feelings at that point. We were forced to snow-hole and 12 hours of hell followed. At first light visibility was nil as the blizzard raged. At this point it transpired that Pedro did, in fact, have a compass, but he had been leaving everything to me! We did not know how to take a bearing and anyway we still did not have a map. We thought about Glen Einich and headed west through deep powder until we were in a U-shaped valley which swung east towards the Lairig Ghru. We had descended into Glen Geusachan."

The two men finally reached Corrour Bothy where they dumped all their climbing gear, then continued round the foot of Cairn Toul and back up to their sleeping bags in the Garbh Coire hut. The result of their enforced bivouac was mild frostbite from which Bower suffered painful feet for several months, and Kale, less fortunate, for several years.

During a period of settled weather in February, McArtney and Fyffe made the second winter ascent of Parallel Gully B on Lochnagar. It had a huge reputation at the time and it was McArtney who wanted to do it. He had the push and the drive and was not overawed by reputation and stories such as Nicol falling out of it. The climb was in excellent condition and they were up it in a fast time of less than six hours, through leading. A few days' later the route was climbed again by the strong southern team of Martin Boysen and Jud Jordan, both parties confirming the high quality of Lochnagar's hardest gully.

Good winter conditions continued in the Cairngorms right through into April. On March 19, Light led a Lairig Club party including Malcolm McArthur, Dave Halliday and Alan McGregor up the 300ft Phoenix Gully to the right of Pinnacles Buttress in the Garbh Choire Mòr of Braeriach. The ascent was dominated by a huge 40ft high cornice which protruded 20ft out above its base. Such an obstacle would normally preclude any thoughts of attempting an ascent, but Light was a man of faith, or vision, for when they reached the cornice they discovered a crescent-shaped slit which led into a beautiful 15ft high ice cavern. From inside this they were able to make an exposed traverse left to a gap behind a detached snow flake, and using this they reached the plateau.

By the summer of 1967, a whole decade had passed since a new rock climb had been made on Lochnagar. This is surprising when you consider how accessible the magnificent North-east corrie is to Aberdeen. A glance around the 'steep frowning glories' would have shown the potential for difficult new routes, particularly on the major buttresses. The forbidding frontal wall of the Tough-Brown Ridge was by far the largest area of unclimbed rock on the mountain. A great triangular face of steep boiler-plate slabs, 400ft wide and up to 500ft high, stretching from the chimney of Parallel Gully B on the left to the edge followed by Tough-Brown Direct. Immediately to the right of Parallel B there was a sheaf of corners and grooves running up to the grassy scoop crossed by Tough-Brown Traverse. The most prominent feature on this section was a pair of corners, slightly offset and one above the other. This was attempted by Patey in the late 1950s and known as Parallel C. Farther right from these corners, near the centre of the face, an impressive crack-line slants rightwards in a direct line to merge with the upper crest of the buttress. This challenging line had caught the eye of Mike Rennie.

During a dry spell of weather in early June, Rennie and Forbes went to Gelder Bothy for the weekend to try the big line. Sunday 11, was a scorcher, and sitting below the face they could see that the crack started from a terrace 100ft up and they reached this in one pitch of VS climbing up a vegetated corner. Then from a belay halfway along the terrace they could look up to the first obvious difficulty, a big downward pointing tooth of rock where the crack cut through a prominent roof 30ft above.

With a good selection of pitons Forbes set off up the steep, cracked groove heading towards the roof. Although the rock on the face was generally sound and clean, the cracks were often earth-filled and difficult to use for free-climbing. A certain amount of cleaning by pulling off divots and grass sods, and scraping with the piton hammer was normal on a first ascent, but this activity is limited by the steepness and difficulty of the actual climbing. It was also time-consuming and energy-sapping. Forbes was always a man in a hurry. His attitude to the use of aid on first ascents was to use as little as possible, but he admitted to not having the patience to persevere in looking for a free way if he could not climb a particular section on the first few attempts. He was focused on getting to the top and if he needed artificial aid, so be it.

He did require a piton to get to the roof, then a further two to surmount it using twin cracks in a recess just right of the tooth. He then found himself poised on a smooth slab, right of the right-hand crack,

and facing some thin moves to reach a small rock ledge. With only a moment's hesitation he laybacked the crack and made a difficult mantelshelf onto the ledge. At this point the twin cracks were separated by a narrow rib of rock. It was now necessary to move across this rib and continue in the line of the left-hand crack before gaining a belay on an upper raking grass terrace. The last section of this 100ft pitch required a further four pitons for aid.

Direct ascent of the continuation groove looked uninviting, so when Rennie arrived, he went farther up the terrace to a grassy niche. Here, he pulled on to the wall and traversed back left into the groove using four aid pitons. The climbing now became gradually easier until they were on the upper buttress and able to remove the rope and scramble to the plateau. They gave the climb the name Mort, a macabre warning to anyone contemplating a repeat ascent. Although it appeared to be a long climb, the difficulties were confined to two main pitches, the roof pitch being the most sustained, meriting the aid climbing grade of A2. There was no doubt that Mort was a significant advance for Lochnagar in terms of technical difficulty.

The excellent weather that weekend had encouraged many parties to various corries and crags throughout the Cairngorms. At Creag an Dubh-loch, McArtney and Lawrie put in a good effort on the line of Patey's Giant. From the old ring piton belay at the end of the tension traverse McArtney led the steep twin corners above to gain the sloping shelf. He then continued up right following the slabby ramp and a steeper continuation to below overhangs. A narrow ledge took him back left to a grassy bay where he took a piton belay. When Lawrie arrived they convinced themselves that they had insufficient pitons to continue. They retreated in two abseils, vowing to return as soon as possible. This hard pitch (HVS 5a) is the line which Alex Thom believes he and Barclay took in 1958.

In the summer of 1967 Fyffe spent much of his time based at Allt-na-giubhsaich carrying out field work for his thesis on the 'geomorphology of the Lochnagar area'. It was during this period that he and McArtney made two attempts on the great crack-line left of Waterkelpie Wall. Starting in the bay directly below the big roof they climbed steep rock for 70ft to some flakes, and then traversed left to emerge on to the open frontal slabs. A turfy crack continued to a big grass ledge 30ft down and left of the widest part of the roof. Unfortunately, it was too windy to continue so they abseiled off.

On the next attempt, McArtney got to grips with the roof. By traversing out right from the ledge he was able to climb cracked slabs to a shallow cave-like recess in the overhang 30ft left of Mercer's corner on Waterkelpie Wall. It was a very intimidating place with the roof jutting out beyond his head. The rock was none too inspiring as it appeared blocky and loose in places. He tried several times to free-climb up the left side of the recess but found it too strenuous. Leaving two pitons in the roof he retreated back to the ledge. Fyffe then set off for a look, but while removing a piton on the slab for possible use higher up, a big block fell from the lip of the roof and hit the rock just six inches below his heels. "This spooked us out and since it was a nice day we went to lie in the sun on the beach!"

The weather became unsettled at the end of June when two Yorkshire climbers, Robin and Tony Barley, spent a holiday in Scotland. The brothers were already a forceful climbing partnership and had made many difficult new routes on their native gritstone and limestone crags. At the end of the week they decided to take a look at Creag an Dubh-loch. En route they drove below the crags in the Pass of Ballater and stopped to make a few climbs. (It was this early visit that inspired Tony to return 10 years later with Jerry Peel to climb a number of new routes, including the well-known test-piece, Peel's Wall.)

On July 5, they walked from Glen Clova to the foot of Creag an Dubh-loch. They had planned to climb on the Central Slabs or on Central Gully Wall but the rock was damp and streaked with water. Convinced that friction would play a crucial part in climbing these smooth-looking faces, they gave themselves little chance of success in the wet. However, high on the left they noticed an impressive dark wall with several prominent crack-lines. On consulting the Guide they found this to be "the exceedingly steep face nearly 400ft in height" above the Broad Terrace. It was apparently unclimbed. Could this be their salvation from an otherwise disappointing holiday? Okay, it did look very steep, but surely, if they tried one of those cracks there were bound to be holds. Anyway, the wall was only half the height of the main face. Having talked themselves into making an attempt, they set off up the 400ft of hanging meadow that led to the base of one of the most intimidating unclimbed walls in the area. They had been climbing well that year and felt reasonably confident that they could make progress in spite of the damp rock.

Near the centre of the face was a very smooth wall topped by two prominent overhangs. From here to the right edge, the cliff was seamed by crack and groove systems slanting slightly rightwards. They decided to attempt the first line right of the smooth wall, noting an obvious dark groove at half-height. Just below the highest point on Broad Terrace

Tony Barley. Cwm Silin, Snowdonia, 1965

Photo: Robin Barley

they moved easily up left to a large grass platform at the start of the difficulties. Once they got going they found the rock quite accommodating. In fact, they began to feel at home as the nature of the climbing reminded them of Guisecliff, a north-facing gritstone outcrop which they had been developing in Yorkshire. Two pitches up cracks, grooves and a juggy wall brought them to a belay ledge out right on top of what they described as a monster flake.

They were now directly below the dark V-shaped groove, but separated from it by a barrier of bulging rock. Tony tried to climb an overhanging crack above the belay. It was mossy and too hard so he moved to the left end of the flake and found a shallow left-facing corner. Strenuous laybacking up this took him to a resting place level with the bottom of the V-groove, still tantalisingly out of reach across a steep, smooth slab. Reluctantly, he found it necessary to use a piton to gain the slab, then another to tension into the groove. Although the exposure was now tremendous, a deep crack in the back of the flaring groove offered security. Removing handfuls of moss and earth from the crack he made progress by wide bridging and hand jamming until, suddenly, he was on a commodious ledge with good piton belays.

The general angle now appeared to lie back, a prospect that should have filled them with confidence after the hard pitch below. Unfortunately, much of the rock above was wet. They contemplated climbing in socks, but continued in their rock boots up shallow grooves to a difficult bulge 40ft higher. This proved troublesome and was finally climbed with two pitons to reach a small perch. Then more greasy climbing up grooves and small walls took them triumphantly to the top.

This was an influential, if somewhat unexpected coup for the Barley brothers. Rumours of their visit to Creag an Dubh-loch reached the North-east and it was generally assumed that they had completed the line of Patey's Giant. It was only when the SMC Journal was published in July 1968 that the truth was known. It is doubtful if anyone had seriously contemplated climbing on this forbidding wall prior to July 1967, particularly since there were easier and less daunting pickings to be had elsewhere at the Dubh Loch. Needless to say, the locals were impressed by this opening route on Broad Terrace Wall, if somewhat irked by the name Culloden. To rub salt into the wounds, the second ascent was also made by a southern party. In June 1975, the Lakeland pioneers, Jeff Lamb and Pete Whillance, managed to free the whole route in dry conditions. Lamb forced the short overhanging crack attempted by Tony Barley, thus gaining direct entry into the V-groove. He found it very hard work cleaning off just enough black moss with his fingers to make it climbable. Whillance eliminated the two pitons on the top pitch. Nowadays, the climb is given the grade of E2 with the overhanging crack providing a 5c crux.

In mid-September, another major climb was made on Creag an Dubh-loch. Brian Robertson of the Squirrels had gained a reputation as a very able technical climber both on rock and ice in Scotland as well as in the greater ranges. During the summer he had been climbing in the Alps with an American client, Bill Wilkins, who later set up the mountaineering business, Ultimate Equipment. Robertson had promised Wilkins that he would take him up a 'new route', and with this in mind the two men made their way to Creag an Dubh-loch. Co-incidentally, McArtney and Fyffe had a tentative arrangement to climb together on the weekend September 16 – 17, but despite the likelihood of further glory on the rocks, McArtney's priorities lay very much with a young female friend and he called off. He did, nevertheless, introduce Fyffe to Robertson as some-one who could show him where the blank spaces were on the Central Slabs. McArtney knew several of the Squirrels and had made an early repeat ascent of Hee-Haw in Glen Coe with Alistair (Bugs) McKeith.

As might have been expected, Robertson wanted to make the most direct climb on the Central Slabs. About 15ft right of Dinosaur, he started up a crack system which led directly up into the big open-mouth forma-tion in the largest overlap. He quit this 15ft above a small overlap, crossed farther right, and followed another system to small ledges 40ft below the main overlap. Immediately to the right lay the smooth slab which Hunter and Millar had crossed using tension. Robertson dispensed with the rope move and padded across the slab to the foot of a shallow groove. This offered a convenient break in the big over-lap 30ft right of the open-mouth. By climbing the groove until it closed, it was possible to traverse right on a short, steep wall and pull through onto slabs above, and 20ft up take a piton belay hanging in etriers.

Up to this point the climbing had been excellent with the smooth slab giving the hardest moves. The obvious way to go from here was to continue straight up the crack system above, but, to quote Fyffe: "Robertson was into difficulty over logic." The configuration of the rock had forced a right-ward drift to avoid the biggest overlap and now Robertson was keen to get back onto his projected direct line. A second overlap crossed the slabs 20ft above the belay, and, wedged directly below this, some 25ft to the left was a huge triangular-shaped block. Robertson jammed up the right side of this, moved left to its apex then made a tricky mantelshelf over the overlap to a small ledge. He was now at the foot of a right-facing groove which was blocked a few feet above by a bulge. At this point he produced one of Chouinard's tiny pitons called a Rurp. (Realised Ultimate Reality Piton). It looked like a thick razor blade with a little loop by which to attach a karabiner. He hammered this into a thin crack in the side of the groove, attached a sling, and lent out on this, searching for holds on the left rib. He could see what looked like a small spike, and after several attempts managed to lasso this with another sling. All he had to do then was to pull up on the sling and hope it remained in place long enough to run his feet up the rock and stand on the spike. Once committed he discovered that his little spike was no more than a flat protuberance. But all went well as he moved up and found a large ledge. Much easier climbing followed up cracks and slabs to reach the raking grass terrace below the upper tier.

Well to the right of the Sea of Slabs several big grooves lie beyond the right edge. By scrambling up right they reached a flat platform below one of these grooves, where a 20ft corner was tucked round an edge, unseen from below. Robertson climbed this corner, moved left, and then followed the left-hand of twin, smooth grooves to emerge onto the upper slabs. A series of cracks then led to a grass ledge below a promi-nent nose. This was as far as he got on the Saturday. He rigged one of the ropes and abseiled down to his two companions. All three then escaped via the terrace and spent a pleasant night under boulders at the foot of the slabs.

The next day was wet with cloud down to the base of the cliff. Wilkins declined to join the party so Robertson and Fyffe went back up without him. From the start of the climb Robertson had led every pitch despite requests from Fyffe to be allowed to take his turn. When they reached the terrace Robertson climbed the fixed rope using mechanical ascenders. Fyffe then followed hand-over-hand up the fixed rope protected by the second rope held by Robertson. According to Fyffe, Robertson would not allow him to use the ascenders in case he broke them! From the high point they had 200ft of climbing to reach the plateau. Despite the deteriorating weather Robertson still wanted to push on. Forty feet directly above was a left-facing corner which appeared to offer the easiest line. By climbing out right and returning left he reached the corner, but was unable to climb it free in the rain. After 10ft of straightforward aid-climbing with pitons he managed to pull out on to the right edge and continue up the rib to a small stance and piton belay. Vegetated grooves led more easily to the top. Although the change to inclement weather had been disappointing, Robertson did get his new route and his client half of one. At 1200ft it was the same length as Dinosaur, only more direct and with much more sustained climbing. Robertson rewarded himself by naming the climb The Blue Max, one of the highest honours for bravery in the German Air force.

The contrived, but excellent crux pitch was repeated at least twice in the early 1970s by parties using the lasso technique. In 1971, Ian Nicolson attempted to climb straight up the groove from the point where Robertson had used the Rurp. As luck would have it, the rock was wet, his PA slipped and he fell back down over the overlap, pulling off a block around which he had attached a sling as a runner. Unfortunately, he was unable to avoid the falling missile and it hit him full on the head. He staunched the resultant scalp wound by wrapping his waist belt around his head, and in this battle-scarred state he, and his companion, Rab Carrington, met Princess Margaret on their way out to Ballater. After a night at Casualty in Aberdeen, Nicolson was declared fit to go on his way. Not long after this it was discovered that the best way to complete the pitch was not to go directly up the groove, as Nicolson had tried, but to surmount the initial bulge on the right using a cleaned out crack. Nowadays, the pitch is graded 5b and the whole route is E1.

Yet another shelter appeared on the plateau of Cairn Gorm in the summer of 1967. The Curran bothy, situated just south of Lochan Buidhe on the normal walking route from Cairn Gorm to Ben Macdui, was built by naval apprentices from HMS Caledonia at the request of the Cairngorm Mountain Rescue Association. Many local hill folk thought this latest shelter was unnecessary, and several voiced the opinion that it was dangerous because of the likelihood of it being buried in winter by snow. It did quite often get buried and as the door opened outwards it was possible to be trapped. Allen Fyffe remembers an occasion when he could get out only by removing the Perspex pane and crawling through the window. Construction of the three high-level emergency bothies, Curran, St Valery, and El Alamein, had resulted from the concerns of certain mountain rescue organisations for the safety of the

Bulldozed road in Glen Quoich looking towards the south west slopes of Beinn a' Bhùird

Photo: Greg Strange

substantially increased numbers of people taking recreation on or near the Cairn Gorm plateau, most of whom were approaching from the north via the ski road.

The potential for the Cairngorms to provide all types of outdoor recreation, both summer and winter, was the subject investigated by a technical working group set up by the Scottish Development Department in 1964. Its report, published in 1967,[1] recognised the Cairngorms as one of the rapidly shrinking remote areas of Europe and highlighted the dilemma between conservation and development. From a mountaineering point of view, it is interesting to note that even in the late 1960s, this report maintained that the granite of the Cairngorms was poor for climbing compared with the volcanic rocks of Glen Coe, Ben Nevis and the Cuillin, and that the rock climbs of the Cairngorms could not compete with those of the West Coast areas for length, exposure and variety. It did concede, however, that the Cairngorms were equal to the best for snow and ice climbing.

Whereas informed Scottish mountaineers may have been amused at this West Coast bias with regard to rock climbing in the Cairngorms, few would have been amused by the number of new and improved access roads proposed in the report. These included major through-roads in Glen Feshie and Glen Tilt linking Upper Deeside with Speyside and Atholl, a road from Tomintoul to Crathie via Loch Builg and another from Nethy Bridge to Glenmore via Ryvoan. Clearly, the members of the Technical Group had no intention of recommending measures to slow or halt the reduction of remote areas in the Cairngorms.

Meanwhile, the very process of shrinking the wild country was taking place on Mar Lodge Estate, where, during spring of 1967, a rough, bulldozed track was pushed through Glen Quoich up onto the south-west spur of Beinn a' Bhùird to within a few hundred yards of the plateau edge. This was one of the first of many hundreds of miles of poorly constructed bulldozed roads created by estates in the Cairngorms during the 1960s and 1970s. Their purpose was to provide quick access by four-wheel drive vehicles for deer-stalking and grouse-shooting. They were (and still are) a major cause of reduction in the wilderness areas of the Cairngorms, not only because they provide easier access but also because they are unsightly and artificial against the natural landscape. Unfortunately, a loophole in planning law meant that permission was not required because these roads were interpreted as being for agricultural use.

At Easter 1968, John Bower, Raymond Simpson and I made a winter ascent of the 700ft Direct Route on the West Buttress in Coire Bhrochain of Braeriach. Raymond and I had been at Aberdeen Grammar School but actually met for the first time on the summit of the Angel's Peak during an all night tramp with the school hill-walking club. We got talking and I was struck by his knowledge of the hills and his enthusiasm for mountaineering. His father, Gordon, was a letterpress printer at Aberdeen University Press and through this connection Raymond knew people in the Etchachan Club like Jim McArtney and Alec Rae. We began climbing together with another friend, Doug Cameron, at New Year 1966. By the end of that winter we had done half a dozen routes up to Grade 3, although I had still not made a proper rock climb.

We first got the notion to make a winter ascent of West Buttress Direct in April 1967 when we climbed two rock routes on the East Buttress in blazing sunshine with cornices collapsing all around. Looking across to the West Buttress we noticed several long icy runnels which appeared to be unclimbed. We had arranged to meet Bower and Mick McKie (Mickey Boo) in the Garbh Coire Hut to do some winter climbing, but despite clear skies and hard frosts at night, by the time we were up and about everything was melting in the warm sunshine. We realised, too late on this occasion, that with very early starts, excellent winter climbing could still be experienced in the corries of Braeriach as late as mid-April.

On Good Friday 1968, with Bower, we climbed the atmospheric Pinnacles Buttress in Garbh Coire Mòr. Then the next day, the three of us rose at 3.30am and were starting up the opening snow ramp on the West Buttress well before the sun appeared. Taking turns to lead we followed the general line of the summer route, up the long ramp, back left to gain a shallow depression, then on directly to the prominent tower. Raymond led the last pitch up the right-hand of twin chimneys on the right flank of the tower. Although relatively straightforward (Grade IV), the climbing was immensely enjoyable on perfect névé and water-ice with the occasional section on rock. By 9am we were on the plateau, contemplating another day of glorious Braeriach weather.

Enjoying all this good weather in April there was a real buzz of anticipation among the various climbing groups in Scotland. A number of impressive rock faces in the mountains were still awaiting the tread of PAs, several of which were in the Cairngorms. Among the Aberdonians Mike Rennie was the first to make a move. He had his sights set firmly on the big blank spaces, in particular, the Central Slabs on Shelter Stone Crag which he and Forbes always referred to as The Shield; the West Face of the Mitre Ridge, and the complex mass of smooth slabs and overlaps between Mousetrap and The Giant on Central Gully Wall of Creag an Dubh-loch. It was to this last spectacular arena that Rennie went in early May with Yorkshireman Paul Williams, one of several very active members of the Lairig Club at that time. Williams was an experienced limestone climber who included the aid-climbing test-piece of Main Overhang on Kilnsey Crag in Yorkshire among his previous ascents.

Just to the left of Mousetrap there are two distinct, almost parallel fault-lines. The one on the right starts 150ft up at a point level with the top of the Mousetrap recess, whereas the left-hand one, a big left-facing, left-slanting groove ascends from the bottom of the cliff for more than 300ft before petering out among the upper slabs. From the foot of this groove, all the way round to the base of The Giant, there is only one continuous vertical line of weakness on the whole of this seemingly impossible wall – a futuristic soaring crack system a little to the right of The Giant.

For Rennie and Williams, though, the obvious line to try was the left-facing groove. It looked amenable until blocked by a big overhang 100ft up. Here there were two possibilities: either to climb the overhang on the right or, to avoid it altogether by taking steep cracks going out left on a line which led up to a huge hanging slab in the middle of the face. Despite the early month and the cliff's reputation for dampness this steep section of Central Gully Wall was mostly dry.

A short section at the start was wet and required a piton before Rennie took a belay on top of a block 30ft up on the right of the opening corner. Williams continued in the corner, moved out left, then went back up and right to a good ledge below the big overhang. So far the climbing had been steady VS and very pleasant. They now had to decide between the overhanging crack on the right or the apparently easier option of going out left. From their restricted viewpoint going left seemed logical, so Rennie climbed up over a bulge to below a steep, hidden corner. This proved very awkward with the cracks choked with grass. He used four pitons on this pitch before stopping at a small stance 30ft below the rim of the hanging slab. Williams followed, removing the pitons, then continued through to a belay at the right-hand end of the hanging slab. The situation was impressive. The slab was approximately 70ft long by 25ft wide and held a single crack which ran its full length. The rocks above looked impregnable. Perhaps the way to go would be to follow the crack in the slab and hope that a route could be found through the overhangs at the far left end.

For the time being the solution would have to wait. They hammered in a home-made ring piton and abseiled off, leaving Rennie's beautiful new 300ft Perlon rope hanging on the cliff, tied into boulders at the bottom. They returned the next weekend but it was too cold to climb. Rennie prusiked back up to the slab swapped his new rope for an old single 9mm laid rope and abseiled back down. His projected climb was now clearly marked for all to see!

A month later, in early June, Fyffe teamed up with Bower to climb The Watchtower, a small flying buttress on the left of the Hourglass in Coire na Cìche of Beinn a' Bhùird. This obscure climb was a preamble for much bigger things the following weekend. Despite Bower's claim not to have been performing well due to an over-indulgence of alcohol the previous evening, the pair arranged to go to Creag an Dubh-loch the following Sunday. McArtney was leaving for the Alps, but generous

Mike Rennie following the second pitch of Cougar, Central Gully Wall, Creag an Dubh-loch, early May 1968

Photo: Paul Williams

*Allen Fyffe and John
Bower on the roof
pitch of King Rat,
June 1968*

Photo: Malcolm McArthur

as ever, he had given Fyffe his blessing to go ahead and finish the big crack-line just left of Waterkelpie Wall on Creag an Dubh-loch. His only concern was that it should be climbed by a party from Aberdeen.

Although it had rained overnight, Sunday, June 9, was fair and the cliff mostly dry. Fyffe led all the previously climbed pitches up to and including the big roof. He tried initially to free this but tired himself out in the process. In the end, he went up left from the cave across the side of the roof using four pitons for aid until he could pull up onto the prow using big holds. He found this pitch as hard and as gripping as expected, so gripping that he used three ropes to improve his chances should there be rock fall. By contrast, the rest of the climb was surprisingly straightforward. Switching leads, they went more or less straight up in cracks and grooves until they reached Waterkelpie Wall coming in from the right. They followed this up its leaning corner to below a final barrier with a prominent block overhang just a short distance left of Waterkelpie's upper crux. Bower led the steep wall left of the overhang using a piton. He was then able to move right above the bulge and back left to a good ledge. Two pitches of easier, but continuous climbing soon brought them to broken ground below the plateau. The 750ft plum line of King Rat had been climbed at last.

Apart from the roof, which merited the artificial grade of A2, the climb was no more difficult than Mousetrap. Fyffe repeated the climb a year later with John Grieve. Thereafter, it became the norm to climb the route with two pitons and slings for aid at the roof. The future popularity of King Rat was ensured when the climb was included in *Hard Rock*, Ken Wilson's book of great British rock climbs published in 1975. In 1977, Mick Fowler and Phil Thomas freed the roof at 5c, thus nudging this great VS rock climb into the E1 category.

When the King Rat team returned to Aberdeen they were able to inform Rennie that his rope was still suspended on Central Gully Wall. They also took the opportunity to wind him up about the poor condition it was likely to be in. He and Williams knew that they would have to move quickly, so with the promise of fine weather at last, they went back to the Dubh Loch the very next weekend. Sunday, June 16, was a beautiful warm day, just perfect for testing one's nerve on a 150ft prusik up an old rope that had been hanging on the cliff, blasted by the wind, for six weeks. With some considerable relief the two men re-established themselves at the right-hand end of the hanging slab. While Williams sat down for a bout of sunbathing Rennie made his way leftwards along the crack to the far end of the slab. Everything above was leaning the wrong way. By stepping down and round an edge he found himself below a short impending corner with a good clean crack. Straightforward, but overhanging aid-climbing on pitons took him up this and onto a little recessed triangular slab. Now the way went up leftwards over huge hollow blocks and flakes to a stance below a short wall – an exciting pitch.

When Williams arrived he was happy to let Rennie continue. It was difficult to work out the best line. Beyond the short wall easier climbing led to an overhang which he climbed with a piton. Then round a corner on the right he came to a shallow crack with a stone protruding from it. The ascent of this proved to be the crux of the climb. Although not excessively steep, the crack would not accept ironmongery easily. He eventually got up using seven, mainly tied-off pitons, some of which Williams removed by hand when he seconded this scary pitch. Beyond the crack a slab led to a terrace at the end of all difficulties. They named their 450ft climb, Cougar. It had been a serious, committing route on a very impressive piece of rock – HVS and A2.

During the weekend Cougar was climbed, the Etchachan Club ran a mini-bus meet to Aviemore. The quiet Speyside community, with its railway station, Cairngorm Hotel, and guest houses was going through the initial stages of metamorphosis from Highland village to international ski resort. A new building complex known as the Aviemore Centre was being developed just west of the village. It already contained three hotels, restaurant, cinema, dance hall, and chalet accommodation. Despite the completely out of character appearance of its whitewashed concrete structures, it was fast becoming a magnet for the younger generation. It was not long before the Wolf Bar in the Badenoch Hotel acquired a status similar to the Fife Arms in Braemar, or the Jacobite in Fort William, as the local meeting place for climbers and walkers.

On the Saturday night four of us bivouacked on the plateau beside the St Valery Refuge. Next morning, we were lying in the first warm rays of the mid-summer sun, looking across to the Shelter Stone Crag, when Bower quietly proclaimed: "It could be as easy as Squareface!" He was referring, very optimistically, to the thin, straight crack on the right side of its Central Slabs, a tremendous line crying out to be climbed. Later, Bower and I made our way to the foot of the Slabs while our companions, Brian Findlay and Norman Keir, went off to The Clean Sweep on Hell's Lum Crag.

Apart from the straight crack there were other possible lines on the Central Slabs. In the centre was a great right-trending diedre, its lower end finishing in a large overlap which ran left into the slabby gully of Sticil Face 100ft above the Low Ledge. In its upper section the diedre dwindled, until it appeared to blank out just before reaching the top of the straight crack. About halfway up the great diedre, a short subsidiary S-shaped groove branched off left and led straight up into an area of smooth, featureless rock near the upper apex of the slabs. The finishes to both the great diedre and the S-shaped groove looked very problematical. Another possible line was a continuous crack or seam on the left side of the slabs which started at a large overhang at the base of the diedre and trended left towards the top of Raeburn's Buttress.

We roped up and went directly over easy slabs and vegetation, crossing the Low Ledge, until after 300ft we stood on the last grass ledge below the straight crack. It was immediately obvious that Bower's optimism was way off the mark. The first 60ft of slab was almost a wall and the narrow crack looked shallow and very unfriendly. We both made a few half-hearted attempts before retreating, leaving a channel piton and an old karabiner. On reflection, we thought it could be climbed free, although not by us at that time.

Over on Deeside, the old granite stable at Gelder Shiel on the Balmoral Estate had been a favourite haunt of North-east climbers for many years. Its location, midway between the Deeside Road and the corrie of Lochnagar, made it one of the easiest bothies to reach from the bus on

Norman Keir
Photo: Greg Strange

The Gelder Shiel,
Balmoral Estate.
North-east corrie of
Lochnagar in the
distance

Photo: Greg Strange

a Friday night. Although the building had long ceased to be used by hill ponies, the cobbled floor, six stalls and associated mangers still provided the accommodation. In wet weather a small stream ran along a central channel to collect in a large puddle just inside the threshold of the door. Close proximity of the stable to the shiel may well have influenced the Estate's decision to keep the bothy unlocked all year round. Like other remote houses in the area, at Glas Allt, Corndavon and Callater, the presence of an open room or outhouse could dissuade people from forcing entry into the main part of the building.

During the previous summer, Forbes and Rennie had spent a weekend at Gelder. As they were about to leave, a Royal party, including the young princes, Andrew and Edward, arrived for a picnic. During a conversation with the climbers, the Queen inquired as to what conditions were like in the stable and heard first-hand about sleeping on the cobbled floor and the problems with ground water. In the early summer of 1968 the bothy floor was screeded level and four sturdy sets of box bunks installed, courtesy of Her Majesty. Gelder is currently maintained by the Mountain Bothies Association.

Coire an Lochain of Cairn Gorm saw an unprecedented level of exploration during July and August of 1968. In the space of just two months the number of rock climbs almost doubled with the addition of seven new routes by George Shields with various partners.

Thirty-eight-year-old Shields from Dunfermline became a member of the Creagh Dhu climbing club after meeting a few of them on Ben A'n and The Cobbler. He soon gained a reputation as a strong, bold climber. One of his early claims to fame was the second ascent of Kipling Groove on Langdale's Gimmer Crag, which he climbed with Mick Noon in 1950. He was a cobbler to trade but moved to Aviemore in 1962 to work as a ski instructor. According to Shields, 1968 was to be one of his "come back years", for although he had been living in Aviemore for some time he had done little or no climbing in that period, at least not in the Cairngorms.

It was at around this time that another well-known Creagh Dhu climber became established on Speyside. John Cunningham joined the staff at Glenmore Lodge in December 1967 as a full-time climbing instructor, having returned in 1965 from a third spell working and exploring in Antarctica. Cunningham's exploits on rock are legendary. He started pioneering new routes in 1946 in Glen Coe, and in 1947 climbed Gallows Route, now graded E2 5b, the hardest rock climb in Scotland for a long time. He continued to produce high quality routes throughout the 1950s and 1960s. Like Shields, two years his junior, he had done very little climbing in the Cairngorms but aimed to rectify this in the near future.

In early July, the two Creagh Dhu men went to Coire an Lochain and climbed Procrastination on No. 4 Buttress, a pleasant Severe following the central of three shallow corners between Fall-out Corner and Western Route. They then moved across to the Vent to investigate its steep left wall. Here they found two good crack and groove-lines and climbed the left one naming it Ventricle. This 300ft route started with an overhanging crack which they climbed with the aid of jammed nuts on slings. The technique of inserting small chockstones or pebbles into cracks then threading a thin line behind had been used by rock climbers for many years. The process is fiddly and time-consuming but is much improved by pre-threading drilled-out machine nuts of various sizes onto a short sling. This eliminates the threading of the nuts once placed and at the same time gives a range of different shapes. In the late 1960s purpose-made wedge-shaped threaded chockstones were starting to be manufactured and more climbers were using these, wherever possible, instead of hammering in pitons. The use of these chockstones or nuts was considered better practice because no damage was caused to the rock.

Some time after climbing Ventricle, Cunningham introduced Shields to Sydney Wilkinson, an experienced mountaineer who had climbed with various North-east folk including Patey, Taylor, Brooker and Pyper. What Cunningham did not mention was that Wilkinson was the chaplain at Peterhead prison. On July 25, Shields and Wilkinson climbed The Vicar, an impressive, steep line taking the right edge of a prominent overhanging recess on the right wall of Ewen Buttress. Shields led the 220ft climb in five pitches using a number of pitons for aid. Shortly after this, he led another very steep climb just to the left of The Vicar, going up the right wall of the recess, again using some aid from pitons and jammed nuts. On this occasion his partner was unable to follow, hence the name Nocando Crack – a play on the name of the Speyside village, Knockando.

In early August, attention switched to the Shelter Stone Crag with the arrival there of four climbers from Glen Coe – Edinburgh Squirrels, Kenny Spence and Mike Watson and Creagh Dhu members Jimmy Gardner and Rab Carrington.

Carrington and Watson had recently returned from a trip to the Alps which sadly ended in tragedy when their companion, John Jackson, fell to his death on the Aiguille Noire de Peuterey. Jackson was one of a small group of very talented climbers from Glasgow known as the Dumbarton Boys who, along with Carrington, were currently advancing

Rab Carrington in the Alps, 1968

Photo: Mike Watson

The Main Bastion of the Shelter Stone Crag. The Needle Crack finishes at the obvious notch in the summit crest. The Steeple Corner lies on its immediate left

Photo: Greg Strange

Kenny Spence 1971

Photo: Allen Fyffe

the upper limits of free-climbing in Scotland. Earlier in the year, prior to the Alpine visit, Carrington and Jackson had broken new ground by climbing The Pinch, an extremely thin route on the Etive Slabs, and later, in June, succeeding on the oft-attempted Carnmore Corner on Beinn a' Chaisgein Mòr. Spence was also gaining a reputation as a forceful climber as his bold lead of The Hill on Creag Dubh near Newtonmore had recently demonstrated.

On Tuesday, August 6, both the Edinburgh and the Glasgow teams headed for the Central Slabs – the scene of our own explorations in June. For Carrington, 'the line' on the slabs had to be the vertical crack just left of the Citadel chimney: "There it was, obvious once the large slabs could be forgotten, a long straight wire of a crack on the right of the slab." [2] He and Gardner quickly reached the ledge where Bower and I had left a piton and karabiner in June and drawn similiar conclusions.

"The first pitch looked magnificent, steep and a holdless crack. The toss put me in the lead and the first step from the homely ledge showed me the steepness to be expected; very small holds and sparse, with protection frighteningly lacking. Halfway up and a resting place. Which way now, right or left? Neither promising – well, only way – straight up. A few funny moves and I was up to a ledge and my first breath for five feet."[3]

This 60ft pitch was a brilliant lead by Carrington and must have filled him with confidence to complete the climb. Gardner's pitch looked straightforward by comparison, lying as it did at a much easier angle. He climbed steadily on up the crack until stopped by an innocuous little overlap. After several attempts he offered his companion the lead, suggesting that he was off form. They swapped ends and soon Carrington could see the problem – no holds. "He definitely is not off form, and I humbly batter in a Leeper and keep going."[4] Gardner tackled the next overlap which was very wet and only succumbed with the aid of a nut. "A little while later the rope stops and he brings me up. The slabs are deceptive and once again the easy isn't." That was as far as they got on the first day. They abseiled back down the line of the crack having spent more than five hours climbing 150ft.

During halts on their climb they had been able to view the Edinburgh team, Spence and Watson, engrossed in the intricacies of their chosen central line on the slabs 100ft to the left of their own climb. They had started more or less directly below the S-shaped groove which branches off the great diedre. Difficult slab climbing had brought them to the mid-section of the diedre where Spence gained the foot of the S groove. Their situation appeared very dramatic and hopes of further progress slender. Spence did make some progress in the groove, but found it difficult to place pitons. After attempting one tension move out left he gave up and he and Watson went down leaving all their gear on the cliff.

The next day was dull after rain overnight. It was too wet for serious climbing, but in the afternoon, Spence and Watson climbed Raeburn's Buttress to the shoulder, traversed down to the High Ledge and roped down the line of their attempted climb, retrieving all their equipment. At the same time Carrington and Gardner undertook a similar ploy except that they made a long roped traverse round Raeburn's Buttress and across to the exit of their crack. Carrington then abseiled to just above the high point of the previous day, attempting to clean out the crack as he went. (This may have been the first instance of pre-cleaning a new route in the Cairngorms.) As he prusiked back up, safeguarded by a top rope from Gardner, he saw enough to convince him that although it looked hard with very strange holds and little choice, it would be possible. They re-crossed to the shoulder and scrambled up over the top before returning to the Shelter Stone.

It rained again on the Thursday, but Friday was dry. Carrington and Gardner re-climbed the crack up to their last belay, and then Gardner made a farther 15ft, leaving a nut before handing over to his companion. "I moved up and, semi-laybacking from three fingers, I grabbed the nut and out it popped. Sticking my fingers in the now vacant pocket I explored the next pocket – no joy. My strength flew out through the soles of my PAs. The only way out now is to swing on to the wall and rely on friction once there. A quick move and I'm over, but mud does not help the friction and as I take one foot off to clean it the other slips; like trying to stay in the same place on an escalator. No time to stop;

Rab Carrington and Jimmy Gardner at the Shelter Stone, August 1968

Photo: Mike Watson

just keep going and hope the Almighty is smiling. Many awkward moves later and I reach the belay at the top."[5]

The Pin, 230ft, had been climbed with only two points of aid. It had been a remarkable achievement on a piece of rock which only recently was thought to be impossible. As they abseiled down the crack for the last time they wondered how Spence and Watson were getting on with their climb. The Edinburgh men had abandoned the attempt on the Central Slabs and had gone for the big line on the main bastion between The Citadel and The Needle.

Just left of the starting gully to Postern lies the lower of the two prominent right-facing corners which lead up to The Gallery. Watson led this 100ft pitch using a jammed nut for aid at the first of two short overlaps. The corner took three hours to climb, mainly because the cracks needed a lot of cleaning. Spence led through, free-climbing the smooth-floored diedre taken by Hay and Adams in 1956, then a long easy pitch took them to The Gallery, at a point immediately right of the lower chimney of The Citadel.

Directly above was a very steep crack going straight up through a slight break in the bulging wall. Spence climbed the crack on good holds for 25ft until it steepened noticeably. He then moved out right and up a smooth groove using a nut for aid and took a piton belay in a cramped recess below an overhang, just left of a narrow ramp. When Watson arrived he took the gear and made an awkward traverse right to gain a short corner at the start of the ramp. This was tricky at first, but soon the difficulties eased as he gained height. After 60ft of climbing he reached a good stance and belay at the top of the fourth pitch of The Needle. They had cracked the link between the lower corners and the upper bastion.

A long easier pitch now led up and right following the obvious line of layback cracks avoided by Smith and Agnew. These brought them to a grass ledge with big detached blocks directly below the great corner splitting the upper crag left of The Needle. By this time it was getting late and it was obvious that even if they could make progress up the lower, very hard-looking section of the corner, they would not reach the top before darkness. They both had a quick look at the strenuous opening moves, in the process of which they discovered a surprisingly helpful hidden crack inside the main corner crack. They then traversed right across The Needle and escaped back down to the Shelter Stone. They all returned to Glen Coe that night.

Spence and Watson had to wait a whole week before they could get back. On Friday, August 16 they made a spectacular abseil down the Needle crack and re-gained the ledge below the big corner. This time they were accompanied by Spence's regular climbing partner and fellow Squirrel, John Porteous. Spence made a determined attempt on the corner, making progress by very strenuous laybacking. He was aiming for a small niche 50ft up, the only feature that broke the smooth continuity of the corner. After much effort he succeeded in fitting a number of good nut runners before being lowered back to the ledge. Watson took over, leaving his camera with Porteous to capture the action. Being fresh and with encouraging pre-placed runners he soon passed the high point and pressed on until he was able to make an awkward belay in

Mike Watson leading the Steeple Corner, August 1968

Photo: Mike Watson Collection

he niche, less than halfway up the 130ft corner. Spence continued up
he corner finding the crack becoming wider and the rock more blocky
nd loose with height. One particularly worrying section held him up
or a while, but he finally hauled out onto a big ledge on the left just
s it started to rain. Suddenly, there was a real sense of urgency. Surely,
hey were not going to be robbed of their victory by the weather. The
orner was so steep that it remained dry for most of its length but the
inal wall was already greasy by the time Watson was leading it. The
vall started with a deceptively difficult crack in a wildly exposed posi-
ion directly above the corner. It felt as hard as anything on the whole
oute, but was mercifully short-lived. Easier walls and cracks then took
nim without further incident to the flat top of the crag. They had
ompleted the 840ft Steeple just in time. It was a very happy trio that
eturned to the Cairn Gorm car park that night.

John Porteous
Photo: Mike Watson

For a climb of such stature, Steeple had only a week or so to wait for
a second ascent. It was that man Shields again, climbing with Robert
Doig, a young lad keeping company with the Creagh Dubh. Unaware
hat Steeple had been climbed, they used its top corner as a finish to
an ascent of The Needle. They returned to the crag a few days later to
climb the lower pitches of Steeple, finishing by the Needle crack.

On August 21, Shields and Doig climbed Bulgy, the fifth new route
n Coire an Lochain. This Hard Severe took the bulging crack in the arete
between Savage Slit and Gaffer's Groove. The following Sunday, Shields
vas back in the corrie with Brian Hall, a ski instructor at Glenmore
Lodge. The day was fine and dry and already several parties were climb-
ng on No. 4 Buttress. According to Shields it was the threat of
competition posed by these climbers that influenced his decision to try
he unclimbed line right of Ventricle, even though he had already agreed
o attempt the route with Cunningham. The 210ft route, named Daddy
Longlegs, was climbed in five short pitches using twelve points of aid
from both pitons and jammed nuts. To say that Cunningham was disappointed on hearing about the climb would be an understatement. When
Shields returned to The Lodge, Cunningham's comment concerning the
broken pact was very much to the point – "even Big McLean wouldn't
do a thing like that and he's a real bastard!" (Big McLean was their
mutual friend and fellow Creagh Dhu member – John McLean, The
White Hope)

Shields's final new route for the summer was climbed with Willie
Gorman on the last day of August. The line of War and Peace went up
he steep blocky wall just right of Fallout Corner. It required some aid,
and the name reflects the continuous banter that took place between
he two climbers as they made the ascent – rather too slowly for Shields's
iking. None of these new rock climbs in Coire an Lochain became very
popular despite the fact that they all followed good, steep, natural lines.
Early repeats reduced much of the aid and by 1986 they had all been
freed, with The Vicar, Nocando Crack and Ventricle proving to be the
most difficult at E1. In 1999, when asked about the use of aid on these
first ascents, Shields said simply that he found the climbing in cracks
and grooves, difficult. The granite was not wet or particularly dirty, it
was just different from what he had been used to in the West. There
were not so many holds to pull on.

*Mike Rennie below
the Central Slabs of
the Shelter Stone
Crag, September 1968*

Photo: Greg Strange

During August, Hunter and Lang made an interesting discovery on the Eagle's Rock, the south-facing cliff opposite Creag an Dubh-loch. McArtney and Dave Duncan had opened these scattered slabby crags two years' earlier with three climbs on the most continuous section of cliff beside the prominent waterfall. Well to the right of these climbs and not far above the head of the Dubh Loch lies a disc of clean slab 300ft high. It is traversed by two overlaps, and just right of centre in the upper one, a smooth crescent-shaped corner curves up right to a notch. The Dundee men started on the right and made lengthy traverses to reach the little corner which they climbed with five pitons. Above this, a zig-zag course was followed before gaining the top. Afterwards when they pointed out to Mike Main that they had made a 520ft climb on that wee bit of slab above the Dubh Loch, his comment, not unexpectedly, was: "A likely story!" And so it was named. Two years later they made a direct start, while Fyffe and John Grieve freed the crux and found a direct finish. Although other routes have been made on the Likely Story slab, the direct version of the original is still the most popular climb on Eagle's Rock – HVS 5a.

It was while we were in Chamonix during August that Rennie suggested going to look at the great diedre on the Shield. He knew that Bower and I had been up to the start of the right-hand crack, yet despite my unwitting view that this was still the most feasible line for a first ascent on the slabs he was only interested in that beautiful curving diedre.

We had no trouble getting a lift to the Derry Gates on the Friday night as many folk from Aberdeen were heading up Deeside to attend the first Braemar Gathering held on a Saturday. Games Day, September 7, was dry and sunny, although the shadow of Raeburn's Buttress was already moving across the water-streaked Central Slabs as we arrived from the Hutchison Hut. Mike started on an easy-angled slab directly below the commencement of the great diedre and followed a left-facing corner to a wet overlap. Using tension from a piton, he moved left, then, removing a sodden divot he found a good hold with which to pull over the bulge. Soon, with two further pitons, he reached a belay with a tiny ledge at the base of the diedre proper, 100ft up from the Low Ledge.

When I arrived he took most of the pitons and karabiners and left me with our token selection of nuts saying: "They'd be nae eese on a climb like this, and oniewye, I dinna trust 'em!" Initially, the diedre was rather constricted with a wide crack, then the angle eased for a while and the crack became thinner. When he was out 60ft there was an outburst of cursing. He had found what he thought were piton marks in the corner and was convinced the climb had already been done. Higher up he settled down when he found no further marks – so we put it down to his imagination. (He was quite correct of course. These were the piton scars left by Spence and Watson from their attempt on the S crack.) For some way the crack in the back of the diedre had been of a constant width, with the result that Rennie had now run out of small channel pitons. He asked to be lowered in order to retrieve some of these. This he did, leaving a big gap between pitons, where he said I ought to be able to layback with a tight rope. By the time most of the rope had been run out, he had reached a point where the diedre was becoming more of an overlap. He informed me that he was unhappy about belaying on two poor pitons and that he was going to drill a small hole and fix a bolt. I acknowledged his decision, probably not fully appreciating the significance of this action. As far as we knew, no climber had drilled a hole for a bolt in Cairngorms granite before.

Once I got going, I found climbing on the steep slab using etriers very enjoyable. I removed all the pitons and even managed to free-climb the gap without a tight rope. The situation at the belay was fantastic. I had only seen pictures of climbing like this. We seemed to be surrounded by completely blank granite. There were no ledges, cracks, or vegetation, just the diedre continuing away up and right. I sensed that Mike was uneasy. He felt guilty about the bolt from which I was now suspended. Apparently, the drill bit had been slightly too small, and when he hammered in the Stubai Golo, the stem only went part way in before it bent over.

A few feet beyond the belay he was able to place a large angle piton in a hollow flake below the overlap, then followed a section of difficult pegging, using knifeblades and Rurps to reach a solitary grass tuft marking the end of the diedre, 30ft short of the vertical crack-line taken by what we later knew was called The Pin. Without too much trouble he surmounted the overlap and was able to stand comfortably and contemplate his next moves. Somehow he had to climb diagonally up right. The angle was reasonable and he thought it should go. He tried for ages, but could not bring himself to launch out into the unknown, with no immediate prospect of a runner. In the end he tensioned down right from a piton above the overlap to gain a steep fold running up right. By this time the rope drag was terrible and pulling in handfuls of rope was almost as difficult as the climbing. Slowly, he pegged his way via shallow cracks, up right until he reached the crack-line.

Now he could no longer pull in the rope, so I tied it off at my end, leaving a 40ft loop hanging from my waist. Once again, following the pitch was okay as none of the pitons came out under my weight. I removed all the gear except the Rurps and the piton above the overlap. At the belay I found Mike exhausted, but very pleased with himself. He said that he had done his bit and that it was up to me to get us out. Still standing in etriers after six hours, I used two pitons before realising that they were no longer required. It was a relief to move freely up the last part of the crack, and there, at the top, much to my surprise, I found the piton and karabiner that Bower and I had left at the bottom three months earlier. Someone had climbed the crack-line.

Rennie liked the name Thor, which seemed appropriate considering all the hammering we did. The 390ft climb had followed a tremendous natural feature, and despite the controversial use of much artificial aid it proved to be an excellent route of its kind. HVS A2. With hindsight we both agreed that the bolt was unnecessary and regretted having used it. The climb was repeated a year later by John Cunningham and Malcolm McArthur who climbed free from the end of the tension traverse into The Pin.

The ascent of Thor marked the end of exploratory climbing in the Cairngorms for the summer of 1968. Many new climbs had been found at the Dubh Loch, on the Shelter Stone Crag and in Coire an Lochain, but pride of place went to The Pin and Steeple for their high quality free-climbing, with only two points of aid being used on each. They both merited the modern grade of E2.

A novel aspect to winter climbing in 1969 was the introduction of 'New British Time', the equivalent to all year British summer time without moving the clocks back or forward. This meant that even on the shortest winter day the sun did not set until after 5pm, a factor much appreciated by mountaineers in Scotland. The experiment only lasted a couple of years before the Government was forced by public pressure to revert back to the old system.

Early in the season a number of new winter climbs were made, most of which were in the northern Cairngorms. In mid-January John Dempster and Ian Wallace made an ascent of Fingers Ridge, the prominent spur topped by several pinnacles, on the right side of Fluted Buttress in Coire an t' Sneachda. It gave a good Grade IV. This ascent had a sad sequel, for just a fortnight later, these two Edinburgh University students died while climbing Eagle Buttress on Lochnagar. The morning of Saturday, February 1, was fair when they left Gelder Bothy, but the weather deteriorated quickly with gale force winds and snowfall by afternoon. It is believed that somewhere in the vicinity of the crux grooves, Wallace sustained injuries from a fall and could not continue. Dempster made his companion safe, unroped, and then climbed alone up the final 200ft to the plateau where he eventually succumbed to the weather. His body was found two days' later by Aberdeen Mountain Rescue Team 200 yards south of the rocky summit of Cac Càrn Mòr. The body of Wallace was recovered from Eagle Buttress the following day.

Edinburgh climbers were to the fore again on two occasions during March. On the 9th, Ian Rowe and Peter MacDonald made the long journey to the Garbh Coire of Beinn a' Bhùird to climb Commando Route on the West Face of the Mitre Ridge. They found the climbing time

Mike Rennie leading the second pitch of Thor, September 1968

Photo: Greg Strange

consuming as much powder snow had to be cleared from the holds. The crux involved using rope tension from a piton placed high in the introductory gully in order to make an exposed move round a rib to gain access to the main fault which they climbed by its long right fork. They took six and a half hours on this excellent route. Grade IV. It was at this time that Porteous and Spence made an ambitious attempt to climb The Citadel in full winter conditions. According to Spence it was cold and clear with lots of snow. They made good progress in the opening chimneys up to the lower crux. Here they found the climbing very tricky and were forced to use two pitons for aid. A short distance beyond this they decided to retreat.

In mid-April the Aberdonians made their annual winter visit to the Garbh Coire Hut and accomplished several first winter ascents on Braeriach. Their best route was She-Devil's Buttress in Garbh Choire Mòr, climbed by Simpson, Findlay, Graham Boyd and myself. Instead of following the summer line throughout we took the shaded left-hand twin groove tucked into the right flank of the upper buttress. It was another blue sky day. At the start of the difficulties, Brian, Graham and I were belayed at a big flake in the full glare of the sun, while Raymond, unseen above, cut his way up the groove. There was absolute silence in the corrie except for the steady chopping of his axe and the tinkle of ice particles as they cascaded down the face. The groove gave a very fine pitch on névé and water-ice, with some thin climbing in places. When I came to follow I was surprised how quickly he had been moving as it seemed as hard as any ice pitch we had done up until then.

Favourable rock climbing weather was slow to establish in the summer of 1969. May was particularly wet in the Cairngorms and it was not until the first week in June that things began to improve. After graduating in 1968, Fyffe spent the winter in Glen Coe working as a climbing instructor with McArtney on Hamish MacInnes's winter courses, and was about to start at the Glen Coe School of Mountaineering, run by

Exit from She-Devil's Buttress, Garbh Choire Mòr Braeriach, April 1969. Raymond Simpson on top, Brian Findlay climbing

Photo: Greg Strange

Ian Clough. Meanwhile, the enterprising MacInnes had been commissioned by publishers, Constable, to produce a two volume pictorial climbing guide to the whole of Scotland. With a deadline looming he was anxious to get some climbing photographs of Creag an Dubh-loch. To this end he organised a trip to the East and enlisted the help of other Glen Coe based climbers – Fyffe, Clough, John Hardie and John Grieve.

Hunter was assisting MacInnes with the maps and photographic art work for the book and he and Lang arranged to meet the Glen Coe team at the Dubh Loch on the Friday night. Fyffe and Grieve were intent on plundering as many new routes as possible and had brought food for a week. Everyone else had to return on the Sunday evening.

Saturday, June 7, was as fine a day as anyone could have wished for. At the top of Fyffe's list was the unfinished line of Patey's Giant. According to Grieve, who had never seen the cliffs of Creag an Dubh-loch until that morning, "Fyffe's eyes had waxed large as he lovingly spoke of The Dwarfie (self-identification?), that half-finished McArtney line a little uphill from The Giant. Now he's off up Central Gully to guard the approach slab, for others are about. Then an awesome cry echoes down the walls, followed by a stream of invective I never thought the little man was capable of. Halfway up 'our' route hang Rennie and Findlay from Aberdeen, posing for a MacInnes who needs good photies for his book. A pathetic figure returns, trailing his rope, muttering about a line on the big slabs alongside Blue Max, twice as long as, and much better than, The Dwarfie anyway."[6] It was quite by chance that Rennie and Findlay had chosen that weekend to go for the unfinished line. They had arrived early on the Friday evening to find the howff below the Central Slabs unoccupied. In the morning they made a bee-line to the foot of Vertigo Wall, where Findlay led the slab traverse out right towards The Giant using tension from a sling hung on Patey's old piton. They found another piton in the steep corner above the belay and Rennie used this and a wooden wedge to gain the foot of McArtney's shelf. Instead of going up the shelf he stepped left and followed the obvious fault straight up over a slight bulge and belayed on the right, at the abseil piton left by McArtney and Lawrie two years earlier.

Rennie then crossed a slab on the left using a piton and continued with little trouble up the continuation of the lower fault until a ledge led left to below a big slab on the right of the huge diagonal corner. In the middle of the slab he climbed a delightful thin crack for 30ft, then moved right to the edge and followed this to a belay about halfway up the diagonal corner. He could hardly believe how pleasantly straightforward the climbing had been.

Direct ascent of the final corner suggested climbing of a much more testing nature, so when Findlay took over the lead he decided to try out right where he could see some inviting deep cracks in the slab. This proved to be the best way and after 100ft of exhilarating climbing he emerged onto a big ledge, with only scrambling left to reach the plateau. Patey's Giant had been vanquished some 13 years after the man himself first launched out across the opening traverse. They named this excellent 500ft climb Goliath.

Once Fyffe had cooled down, he and Grieve went round to the foot of the Central Slabs where he had further unfinished business to deal with. To the right of the Blue Max, cracks in a smooth slab ran straight up to join a pronounced right-facing corner leading to the big overlap. Fyffe had already climbed the opening slab and had been halfway up the corner with Williams and John Haigh, but they had turned back at what appeared to be loose blocks. If he could get up the corner, there appeared to be a continuation groove through the big overlap a few feet right of Blue Max, then further cracks went straight on up towards the terrace, probably on the line taken by Yakaboo.

While Fyffe and Grieve started up their proposed direct route on the slabs, the other Glen Coe pair, Hardie and Clough, were already making progress on the rocks between Cougar and Mousetrap on Central Gully

*Raymond Simpson
and Brian Findlay,
1969*

Photo: Greg Strange

Wall. They were attempting to follow the big corner up which Cougar starts, but had already been forced out right towards Mousetrap.

The fourth party in action that day was the Dundee rope of Hunter and Lang. They were round on North-west Buttress attempting the very steep unclimbed wall rising above the introductory section of False Gully. A distinctive feature of this wall is a very smooth horizontal band of near vertical granite. Low down, close to the centre of the wall and bounding the smooth band on the right, a short, dark corner leads to cracks and grooves going straight up to the top of the cliff. Hunter had spotted this fine line, and with Lang, had already been up to the foot of the corner during the previous summer. On that occasion he had discovered that the distinctly leaning corner was much more difficult than it looked from below. This time he did manage to climb it, but only after employing six pitons for aid. He belayed at the right-hand end of a long sloping ledge running leftwards into False Gully immediately below the smooth band.

After Lang had seconded the corner he stepped up onto the wall above, moved right and found a hidden chimney which provided a surprisingly easy passage to a little ledge below an overlapping wall. At this point the way ahead was none too obvious. Hunter used two pitons to surmount an overlap and gain a smooth slab. He tried to cross this rightwards below another overlap, but only succeeded after taking tension from a tied-off piton in the lip of the overlap.

Aware of the great drop below and sensing that he had passed the point of no return, he grasped the welcome holds at the far end and climbed steadily up and left to find a big rock ledge which had been out of sight from below.

The pleasure of discovering the ledge was tempered by its lack of a good natural belay. However, the problem was solved using a number of poor pitons fixed at the back of the ledge near its right-hand end. Directly above, the wall overhung before the angle eased and a choice of several possible exits led to the crest of the buttress. Lang tried first, tackling the black, mossy wall at the left side of the ledge. He placed one shaky piton, but even when standing in a sling hanging from this he was unable to reach into the groove above. Hunter took over and with his superior reach was able to aid his way over the bulge to gain a grass ledge on the left using four tied-off pitons. Lang then completed the 450ft Falseface by climbing a corner to a block, before trending right to the skyline.

By this time, Fyffe and Grieve were well up their new climb on the slabs. The loose blocks pitch proved to be an impostor and they quickly gained a stance on the rib at the top of the corner. Here they were virtually on Blue Max, just below and right of its pitch through the main overlap. The groove which they had spotted from the cliff base gave a delightfully straightforward way past the big overhangs on the right and led to ledges. Another pitch zig-zagged up cracked slabs and then they made their way easily up left to reach the terrace below the right edge of the upper slabs.

So far, the climbing had been excellent with, perhaps, the first pitch being the most difficult. Fyffe now wanted to find a line taking the full height of the upper slabs. Just left of the opening corner of Blue Max

*Doug Lang and
Graeme Hunter, 1968*

Photo: Graeme Hunter

was a prominent crescent-shaped groove. Starting below this, they went up leftwards on a slab below little bulges until they reached a pink slabby rib. The easiest way now went back right and up to join the crack-line of Blue Max. Fyffe was now on familiar ground and with the climb almost in the bag they raced on up to the plateau taking much pleasure in free-climbing the quartz corner on which Robertson had been forced to use aid in the rain.

On the way down Central Gully they shouted encouragement to Hardie and Clough who were still on the frontal face of Central Gully Wall. They had spent the day working their way up difficult rock, first in the line of the big groove, then on the overlapping slabs to its right. They were now in the black crack system immediately left of Mousetrap. They announced their intention to retreat, but after one abseil they reached a block-strewn ledge and decided to sit it out until first light.

Fyffe and Grieve later named their 1000ft new route Black Mamba, and, like the other two climbs made that memorable June day, it became a Dubh Loch classic – VS 4c.

Goliath received a number of early repeats and was freed by Ian Nicolson the following summer at its current grade of HVS 5a. Like King Rat, it too was included in Hard Rock on account of its high quality and varied climbing. Falseface took a little longer to catch on. It received a second ascent in 1976 by Dave Wright and myself. We dispensed with all the aid except for four nuts on the leaning corner. Wright completed the route by climbing the modern top pitch, which goes up a big black corner immediately left of Hunter and Lang's finish. A year later the whole route was freed by Dougie Dinwoodie and Bob Smith – E2 5c.

On Sunday, Clough and Hardie returned early to terra firma, then later, Grieve and Fyffe made the second ascent of King Rat to provide pictures for MacInnes's book. By evening, everyone had departed leaving the King Rat team with Creag an Dubh-loch to themselves for six

days of perfect weather. Looking back 30 years later Fyffe recalled: "Tha
week was great and it only ended when we were completely out of food
There was just so much to do and we were realising that it was not neces
sarily hard. Although we were keen, it was not too frantic. We had late
starts, lazed about and generally had a good time. I really regret no
having had a camera."

On the Monday, they started in the afternoon and went up to the
highest section of the Eagle's Rock where they climbed Gibber, a route
whose main feature is a prominent inverted L-shaped corner in pink
water-washed rock – VS 5a.

The next day it was too hot to climb! However, the lassitude passed
and Wednesday found them on the crack system immediately right o:
Mousetrap, which they named The Kraken. Although the climbing was
very good the line went disappointingly close to Mousetrap in its middle
section. They started up the first pitch of Mousetrap and continued
directly following steep cracks to pass near the Mousetrap recess before
veering away right via a grass moustache. A series of sustained pitches
midway between King Rat and Mousetrap then took them on to the top

On Thursday, they crossed The Catwalk, a 1350ft rising traverse o:
Central Gully Wall: "A girdle of the big crag had screamed at us all week
Unable to stomach the Caterpillar Crack so early in the afternoon, we
abseil from False Gully and join Waterkelpie Wall, which takes us to
King Rat, and from there yesterday's moustache deposits us ir
Mousetrap. Tremendous climbing and we sit under the final corner o:
The Giant, reflecting that Dave Bathgate must have got one hell of a
fright when he flew out of it; impressive hereabouts. Down a groove,
along a slab, to Rennie's Goliath, which takes us by a desperate Fyffe
variation to the top of the crag. A great route."[7]

For the final two days they returned to the Central Slabs to make a
route finishing by the prominent pink groove left of the final pitches
of The Blue Max. This groove, and the crack system leading to it, is a
natural water course and one of the last areas of the cliff to dry. They
wanted to find a way up the lower slabs independent from Dinosaur.
But to achieve this they took a rather contrived route, starting up pink
slabs on the left, crossing Dinosaur below its easy gully then rejoining
it before the Sea of Slabs. Following another late start they reached the
terrace on Friday evening, descended Labyrinth Edge, and then climbed
the whole route the next day.

From the terrace they took the shallow left-facing corner right of
Dinosaur, then continued straight up a wet crack, through a slot to reach
the right end of the big grass ledge on Dinosaur. The pink groove now
lay round to the right and had to be attained by an interesting traverse.
This involved climbing up right on a steep slab to a short, horizontal
knife edge of rock, then lowering down off the edge into the base of
the groove. It was Fyffe who led this traverse, so Grieve got the
groove, which he could now see was still wet in places despite the days
of dry weather. Fortunately, the climbing proved reasonable except
for a bulging section where he took to the left wall before continuing
back in the groove to the top. It was a fitting end to a marvellous week
of exploration.

They called this last climb The Pink Elephant, and it brought their

Graeme Hunter climbing the leaning corner of Falseface, June 1969

Photo: Doug Lang

tally of first ascents to six. They had covered around 5000ft of quality new rock climbing without using a single piton for aid. This was a very fine achievement which, along with other recent discoveries, greatly enhanced the growing reputation of Creag an Dubh-loch as one of the country's foremost mountain crags.

June and July saw the initial development of Stac an Fharaidh, the last sizeable cliff in the Cairngorms to be explored. It lies on the south side of Cairn Gorm overlooking the narrows of Loch Avon. The crag comprises an area of glaciated slabs divided into two flanks by a

*Stac an Fharaidh –
East Flank. The open-
ing pitch of Pushover
follows the single
straight crack on
the right*

Photo: Greg Strange

*Stac an Fharaidh –
East Flank. The open-
ing pitch of Pushover
follows the single
straight crack on
the right*

Photo: Greg Strange

shallow grassy gully. An easy-angled spur bordering the left edge of the western flank was climbed in 1952 by J.Hansbury and W.Rae. They recorded the ascent in the Shelter Stone visitors' book and acting on this, Mac Smith repeated the climb, naming it Rectangular Rib.

Smith's guidebook described the slabs as 'holdless', which may well explain why they invoked little interest among climbers until John Cunningham chanced upon them while out with a party from Glenmore Lodge. He immediately saw the potential for climbing of a type similar to that on the Etive Slabs. He made his first visit in June, with a Glenmore Lodge 'voluntary instructor'. The eastern flank, although slightly less steep than the western, appears smoother and more attractive. Near its centre a clean crack ascends directly for 150ft to a large overlap. This was clearly the major line on this flank and an obvious target for someone with Cunningham's ability. He climbed the VS crack to reach the overlap below a crescent-shaped overhang. The ascent of this, up on to the upper slab, provided the crux of the climb and the hardest pitch on Stac an Fharaidh that year. Using underclings, he swung up over the initial bulge to grab a handrail, and then worked up left to a pocket hold. A committing mantelshelf then led to a ledge and piton belay. HVS 5a. A further 300ft of climbing trending slightly left, up slabs and short walls completed the route which he called Pushover.

Cunningham and Shields must have patched up their differences over the Daddy Longlegs affair, for the two Creagh Dhu men went to Stac an Fharaidh on July 1, and made a route on the western flank. This face is crossed at half-height by a prominent slanting vertical wall which increases in size and rises slightly from right to left, before merging into a pillar formation at the far left edge. They could see that crossing this wall would probably constitute the crux of any direct ascent, so they opted to out-flank it near the right edge. Their climb, Après Moi, gave a pleasant VS route of 500ft.

They next turned their attention back to the eastern flank. On the left at the top of the crag, a steep, grey prow leaned out over the dividing gully. They chose to attempt an obvious crack running straight up close to the left edge, thus avoiding the main overlap, but heading directly for a steep wall right of the grey prow. The crack was vegetated at first then became cleaner with height. Two 150ft pitches then led to the steep wall where they belayed at the top of a huge detached flake. Going straight up looked improbable. Fortunately, they were able to trend up right and break through a bulge going rightwards to gain slabs above the steep wall. Delicate climbing back left then straight up completed the route.

Cunningham named this second climb on the eastern flank, Whispers, an indication of his desire not to publicise his discovery until he had climbed all the best lines! Two further routes were made before the end of July, both by Shields and Wilkinson on the steeper tower formation at the left end of the west flank. Mack's Dilemma, a reference to an earlier foray here by Malcolm McArthur and Eric Beard, followed the left edge of the west flank, while Sermon took a direct line of parallel cracks 40ft to its right. Both climbs are VS.

The innermost recess of Braeriach's Garbh Choire Mòr is, without doubt, one of the most fascinating places in the Cairngorms. During the last few summers Jerry Light had been working away at the remaining unclimbed lines in this, his favourite corrie. He was now ready to try the compact central buttress of the Pinnacle trio which looked as if it would give a difficult and worthwhile rock climb.

On a showery day in July, Light and McGregor scrambled up the 100ft of broken ground from the top of the old snow bed to the start of the buttress proper. They opted to try an inviting line of cracks and corners on the south-east face which angled into an unclimbed fault on the right. An initial 70ft pitch took them up cracks through an overlap and then left to a stance near the edge. From here, Light climbed a good crack over a bulge and continued up a thin slab before moving right to a corner which completed a fine 100ft pitch. An awkward overhanging crack and its continuation then led to easier ground on the right. By following a deep diagonal crack back left they found more continuous climbing up the crest, including a little corner which required a piton for aid. The 400ft Tower of Babel was an excellent rock climb – the most difficult on Braeriach at the time – HVS 5a.

Shortly after this, Light left the North-east. He made at least one trip to the Antarctic before taking a post in Wales at a centre for alternative science. Later, he moved to France and set up home south of Grenoble. A strong, determined climber, he revelled in the challenge of remote unexplored terrain, particularly in winter conditions. He had been the driving force behind the building of the Garbh Choire Hut and the establishment of Allt-na-giubhsaich as the University hut in Glen Muick.

As one enthusiastic character was about to leave the Cairngorm scene so another arrived in the shape of 28-year-old Bill March who had just been appointed Deputy Principal of Glenmore Lodge. Originally from

John Cunningham, 1970

Photo: Ken Wilson Archives

George Shields, 1972

Photo: George Shields Collection

Garbh Choire Mòr,
Braeriach – The
Pinnacles Buttress
trio with the Tower of
Babel in the centre

Photo: Greg Strange

London, he was a member of the Rock and Ice Climbing Club and came to Glenmore via the Benmore Adventure Centre in Argyll and Loughborough College. He was a tall, athletic man who lived his life to the full. I remember first meeting him at the Biolet Campsite in Chamonix on the occasion when he and McArtney entertained the gathering of climbers by taking turns to walk across the blazing embers of a large camp fire. On his way to take up the post at Glenmore, March met Fyffe in Glen Coe. He was so desperate to climb that despite terrible weather they went to Glen Etive and made a new route on the Upper Slabs with March climbing in stiff-soled mountain boots. According to Fyffe: "The whole ascent and subsequent descent in lashing rain was an epic and although not a great route, the climb, Monsoon, was an example of March's drive and enthusiasm."

Big Bill soon got in tow with Cunningham, but only after J.C. had tested the newcomer's climbing ability by delegating him the soaking wet overhanging crack on their direct ascent of Hell's Lum. Apart from the bonding process of this initiation, the ascent of the Lum gave March the opportunity to study the rocks on either side. At the end of June 1969, Boyd, Kale, Bower and Simpson had climbed three new routes on the slabs well left of Hell's Lum. This area of the Crag is very slow to dry and appears to require a drought for all the springs and weeps to vanish. On July 27, with Dave Marden, March climbed the 350ft Styx, a fine VS route on the steeper overlapping slabs between the Lum and the right-hand of the fault-lines climbed by the Aberdonians.

On another visit to the Crag in September, with McArthur, he put up two further new routes on the grey buttress to the right of Hell's Lum. A prominent raking fault cuts up the overhanging right wall of the Lum and this provided a difficult, strenuous climb with loose rock in places. The fault starts as an overhanging ramp and finishes as a crack, which required a piton and a nut for aid. The climb, Drop Out, is now rated

E2 5b when climbed free. The other climb, Good Intentions, ascended the front face of the grey buttress near its left edge. The crux involved a steep little groove of excellent rock which succumbed with a nut for aid. 'The road to Hell is paved with good intentions!'

The weekend following the ascent of Styx, March and Cunningham had planned to visit the Shelter Stone Crag to attempt the crack on the Central Slabs left of Thor. Unfortunately, for the two Lodge staff, others had similar ideas. Scottish ski instructors tend to have plenty of free time during the summer months, which explains why Shields always managed to climb whenever conditions were favourable. Friday, August 1, promised to be a good day, so he arranged with Carrington to go to the Shelter Stone Crag.

A major obstacle to climbing the crack is the big overlap guarding access from the top of the first pitch of Thor. Although this is at its maximum height here, it has only a short overhanging cap through which the crack forms a little groove. While Carrington belayed beside a loose flake on Thor, Shields moved up onto the lap. He could see that the crack in the back of the little groove would take a thin piton, but even with gymnastic wide bridging he could not reach high enough to place it. He was forced to use a low intermediate piton to support his weight while he hammered in a Hiten. These highly prized, ultra-thin pitons were made in the late 1960s by John Hartley from a very strong lightweight metal, reportedly from a scrapped missile project. Once Shields had clipped into this he was able to pull up, stand in a sling, and observe what lay ahead. It all looked very smooth and holdless so he came back down.

When it came to thin slab climbing Carrington was the man for the job. Stepping out of the sling to stand on the slab was both difficult and committing. Thankfully, he soon found a place for a piton runner before continuing up the crack to reach an awkward stance and piton belay in a little niche. From this point the crack rose upwards, over a tricky bulge, then on through more smooth slabs, gradually easing towards the High Ledge. Shields climbed this 130ft section in one long runout with virtually no protection – a very scary lead.

According to Shields the climb was named Snipers for no particular reason other than that he liked the name. Whether or not this was said with tongue in cheek is open to speculation. Nevertheless, on August 2, Cunningham and March worked off their frustration by climbing the groove system up the crest of Raeburn's Buttress, naming it Consolation Groove. The long third pitch required three pitons for aid due to dampness. These were later dispensed with and the climb graded HVS 5a. Snipers was Carrington's second route on the Central Slabs. Although perhaps not so sustained as The Pin, the climbing felt more serious on account of the sparse protection. Even with the two aid pitons at the overlap the climb is still rated E2 5b.

A number of interesting routes were discovered in the northern corries of Cairn Gorm this summer by locally based climbers. In early July, G. Bradshaw and Bob Taplin ascended the fine arete between Savage Slit and Fall-out Corner giving it the nautical name of Prore – VS. In the same corrie, Cunningham and March, still smarting from the Snipers incident, climbed the steep pillar between the two branches of Y Gully

Bill March
Photo: Ken Wilson Archives

The beetling right-hand section of the West Face of the Mitre Ridge. Slochd Wall follows the prominent central stepped corner system

Photo: Guy Robertson

to create Never Mind. It followed cracks and corners on the front of the pillar until near the top, where a piton was used to make a tension traverse to the right, followed by a controlled slide down the edge to gain a foot hold on the lip of an overhang. Further difficult climbing up right, involving a piton, led to the top – HVS.

In Coire an t-Sneachda, Dave Sharp and Taplin explored the slabby face of Aladdin's Buttress between the left edge and the chimney on the right climbed by Patey in winter. Starting left of the chimney they went up cracked slabs then climbed the right-hand of three prominent corners to finish on broken ground below The Lamp. The corner itself gave a good pitch requiring a piton for aid. They called their climb Damnation. HVS 5a. Farther round into this expansive corrie Shields made a direct ascent of Fiacaill Buttress using two pitons for aid.

Apart from the good spell in mid-June weather conditions in the Cairngorms had been mixed throughout the summer of 1969. In August, Rennie had still to make a trip to the Garbh Choire of Beinn a' Bhùird to try the west face of the Mitre Ridge. He had been warned by older Aberdeen climbers that the rock on the face was loose and it was generally believed that no one had attempted a new route there for more than 25 years. He knew that I had climbed both the original routes on the Mitre Ridge and mindful of this, asked if I would join him for a look at the face that next weekend.

On August 31, we left our companions, John Ingram and Dave Stuart, in the Howff, made our way through thick mist to the top of the Mitre Ridge and peered down its west face into a white abyss. By mid-morning the weather was improving and we were able to get our first clear view of the face. It averages between 300ft and 400ft in height and comprises two main buttresses – the slim Cuneiform Buttress on the left between the faults of Cumming-Crofton Route and Commando Route, and a larger, beetling mass of rock between Commando Route and North-West Gully. It was on this latter buttress that we hoped to climb the prominent hanging corner which we had noted on Rusk's photograph in the old District Guide.

A closer look from below confirmed that the rock was indeed very wet. We ought to have abandoned the plan, but the corner looked brilliant. Mike was reluctant to waste his day, declaring that this was what we had come all the way to climb. He immediately set about selecting the hardware, saying that he would lead all the aid in his big boots, and that I should wear my PAs to do the free-climbing at the top! The wall looked frighteningly steep and I was convinced that once he got his nose up against the granite he would have to give up because it was so wet.

The corner marks the boundary between a very steep slab on the left and a series of overhangs on the right. By scrambling up North-West Gully I was able to traverse onto the face and belay on a ledge directly below the corner. Here, a diagonal crack cuts up right heading through the initial overhangs. Mike made a few moves up the crack until it was necessary to step up left to gain the foot of the corner. As luck would have it, he was unable to find a suitable crack to put in a piton. He made a hole using his star drill, and then hammered a Golo into the slab. With this in place he was able to cross the gap and commence aiding his way up the corner. At 50ft a large overlap blocked the way. Surmounting this provided the most difficult pegging on the climb. It required a big swing up right into the base of a groove, then up this to a small ledge where the corner forks. He belayed to another Golo and a piton.

I followed this 100ft pitch entirely on aid, removing all the pitons except a few home-made ones. Mike thought the moves over the overhang were more difficult to lead than anything on Thor – A3. The climbing was certainly more strenuous, and with friction non-existent due to the wet rock it never occurred to me that it could have been done free.

Access to the main upper corner was barred by a slightly impending wall. Three pitons saw him over this, then he was able to bridge up to a grass ledge on the left where I was offered the lead. Continuation of the corner was black and slimy, so I climbed the wall on the left using three tied-off pitons until I could move back right and go up an easy ramp to a grass terrace below a headwall. Here, I was amazed to find Davie Stuart, unroped and alone. Mike had asked our two companions what the top wall had looked like and after making a visual inspection from the plateau Davie had scrambled down a depression on the right and walked across the terrace to see how we were getting on. He and John had retreated after one pitch of Cumming-Crofton Route because the rock was wet. Being typical Aberdonians they had been loath to forfeit one of their newly acquired pitons so Davie had jammed the knot of a thin nylon sling into a crack and abseiled off this. He made it safely to the bottom but as John started his descent the knot came free. In an amazing piece of spontaneous self-preservation he managed to stop himself by grabbing the large hanging flake near the top of the first pitch.

By now, it was a beautiful sunny evening. We opted for the easiest way to the top and followed Davie back up the depression. It was the Americans who set a trend for naming their routes as walls. We liked this idea and opted for Slochd Wall after the great hollow at whose head the Mitre Ridge is located. At the time of the ascent we were delighted with the climb. Contrary to the information we had received, the rock was clean and sound and the situation on the main pitch magnificent. No one went near the climb for another 10 years until Lawrie and Andy Nisbet made a second ascent without recourse to any aid at all. They returned triumphant to Aberdeen declaring the climb to be only HVS 5a! But that is a tale for the future.

It was Lawrie with Bower who put up the last new rock climb of the 1960s. In mid-September they climbed Cutlass on the Crimson Slabs, a bold climb following the edge of the obvious bow-shaped overlap between Red Chimney and Djibangi – HVS 5a.

1. Cairngorms Area (Report of the Technical Group on the Cairngorm Area of the Eastern Highlands of Scotland), HMSO 1967.

2. SMCJ Vol. 29, No. 160, p128 – 130.

3. SMCJ Vol. 29, No. 160, p128 – 130.

4. SMCJ Vol. 29, No. 160, p128 – 130.

5. SMCJ Vol. 29, No. 160, p128 – 130.

6. SMCJ Vol. 29, No. 161, p264 – 265.

7. SMCJ Vol. 29, No. 161, p266.

9: The Ice Revolution (1970 – 1972)

WINTER MOUNTAINEERING IN Scotland was still a relatively esoteric activity at the end of the 1960s. The style and technique for climbing snow and ice had changed little in the last decade, although one or two important items of equipment had been introduced such as the tubular ice screw and the snow-anchor plate. These innovations, together with hard-steel rock pitons had improved the potential for security on winter routes. Crampons were now the norm, even for Aberdonian die-hards. The Italian Grivel model with lobster claws was the most popular. They were lightweight, yet robust when used on rock. Salewa had recently introduced adjustable 12-point crampons with steeply inclined front points. These were an obvious advance for pure ice climbing but were initially thought to be too specialised for mixed routes.

Although Hamish MacInnes had started to manufacture metal axes and hammers, most climbers still used wooden-shafted ones, cut down to about 20 inches. Increasingly, 'north wall hammers' (an axe with a hammer head in lieu of an adze) were being carried instead of piton hammers. These enabled steep snow or easier-angled ice up to 50° to be climbed with a pick for each hand in what was known as the double-axe or dagger technique for fast progress without cutting steps. Another item of equipment sometimes used was an ice dagger. This was either a modified long blade piton or a specially manufactured tool with a hand grip and wrist loop. These were used in similar situations to the north wall hammer, being stabbed into the ice to maintain balance when progressing without cutting hand holds. The opening winter season of the new decade was eagerly anticipated. Numerous easier rock climbs in the Cairngorms awaited a winter ascent and many of the harder winter climbs of the previous years were unrepeated. With the first snowfalls of November, Bill March made a series of solo winter ascents on the ribs of Stag Rocks, including Afterthought Arete, Triple Towers, Serrated Rib and Final Selection.

At the start of the Christmas period Rennie and Inverbervie architectural student, Norman Keir, spent a few days at Gelder Bothy. There were several obvious unclimbed winter lines on Lochnagar, one of which, Bell's Direct Route on the Tough-Brown Ridge, was a declared target for several local parties. After two days of rain the sky cleared. They dashed up to the corrie and soloed Raeburn's Gully, discovering excellent ice and hard snow. Next day they went for Tough-Brown.

They climbed up to the terrace taking a more direct line than in summer, using four pitons for aid. The stepped slabs of the VS summer crux looked desperate so they moved farther right below a wall to a steep groove, poised directly on the crest of the ridge. It was Rennie's lead.

"Mike eased up. Tiptoe balance on verglas nicks. Ten straining toes and feet above his last runner. Gloves held in teeth, bare hands sought out an iced jam. Looks stiff. More scraping. He's up. That must have taken an hour."[1] After this short, hard, crux they joined the upper grooves of Backdoor Route and followed these in the moonlight to the final snow arete – Grade V.

A small band of Aberdeen climbers spent a few days at New Year in the relative comfort of Allt-na-giubhsaich. At a not-too-early hour on New Year's Day, Bower, Findlay and I walked to Creag an Dubh-loch for a look at Vertigo Wall. This was essentially Bower's idea since he was the only one in the party who had climbed the route in summer. The cliff was in very lean condition with a dusting of powder snow on the rock and bits of névé and ice on the ledges. The climb was abandoned above the severe crack on the second pitch when it became certain that to continue would have meant benightment. The next day the three of us went to Lochnagar and made an ascent of Shadow Rib, the left edge of Shadow Buttress A overlooking Shallow Gully. It was a very cold day with strong wind, snow showers and plenty of spindrift. As an indication of just how cold it was, Findlay developed frost nip in one of his fingers where a hole had worn in his woollen mitten. The 900ft Grade IV took seven hours with all three sharing the lead.

The weather was much improved on the 3rd. This time Bower teamed up with Raymond Simpson, who had arrived fresh from Aberdeen. They went back to the Dubh Loch and made the first winter climb on the Eagle's Rock. For this they chose the obvious watercourse of Lethargy, which had formed a 300ft gutter of blue water-ice. This gave two fine pitches of continuous step cutting. Grade III.

Unsettled weather dogged the first weeks of the New Year. On the evening of Monday, January 19, the mid-winter gloom was compounded by the terrible news that Jim McArtney, his girlfriend Mary-Anne Hudson, and Fergus Mitchell had all been killed in a big slab avalanche which broke away from the top of the Italian Climb on Ben Nevis. John Grieve, the fourth member of the party, had survived alone on Tower Ridge, having miraculously escaped being swept away. How could this have happened to McArtney? Surely he was indestructible! Even after the funeral on a dreich day at the Aberdeen Crematorium, everyone found it hard to accept. Jim was one of those rare individuals who, even as a young man found it easy to get along with other folk, no matter what generation or background they came from. His outgoing personality, enthusiasm and patience with others of lesser ability than his own made him an ideal mountaineering instructor. It came as no surprise to his friends in the East that his partnership with Hamish MacInnes at the Glen Coe School of Winter Mountaineering had been so successful. His loss was deeply felt throughout mountaineering circles in Scotland.

One of the many volunteers who turned out to help with the rescue on Ben Nevis was John Cunningham. Despite being a gifted climber, Cunningham was not renowned at this time for his winter mountaineering in Scotland, often preferring to go skiing when the snow arrived. In the 1950s, he and Mick Noon climbed the technical Deep Gash Gully in Glen Coe and made several attempts on Zero and Point Five Gullies. During his survey trips to the Antarctic he had experimented with different techniques for climbing steep ice. He found that by using very sharp crampons with front points he could climb ice up to 70° without

John Bower starting the second pitch of Vertigo Wall, January 1970

Photo: Greg Strange

requiring support for his hands. If he could drive in some form of hand
tool capable of taking his weight he saw no reason why vertical or overhanging ice could not be climbed quickly and less strenuously than by
cutting hand and foot holds. His preferred system was to use an advanced
form of dagger technique, where he would hammer one dagger in as
high as he could, then work the front points of his crampons up the
ice until he reached a position where his straight arm was pushing down

vertically on the dagger. The process was then repeated with the second dagger, the first removed and the process continued. As you can imagine, this took nerve and dexterity, qualities that the 42-year-old Cunningham still had in abundance. Such was Cunningham's conviction that this new technique was the way forward for ice climbing, he and Bill March set about looking for a suitable location to make the first Grade VI ice climb in Scotland. In late January, they climbed The Chancer, a very steep icefall on the left wall of Hell's Lum close to the summer route Styx. Starting from the top of the main ice pitch in the Lum, they climbed out left then back right into a cave below a great stalactite of ice. Here, Cunningham bridged up between the ice and the back wall of the cave for 15ft until he could fix an ice screw then tension out from under the overhang onto the front of the ice. He was now confronted with a wall of vertical ice which seemed to impend like the side of a huge barrel. With his Salewa crampons, ice screws and his pair of daggers he front-pointed his way up the ice using four of the screws for aid. At one point while making a mantelshelf onto a dagger, the ice shattered and he fell. Fortunately, he was held by March and one of the ice screws. After 35ft the angle relented to 70 degrees, then 40ft of steep snow led to piton belays on a small rock outcrop 80ft below the cornice. As Cunningham said in an interview with Ken Wilson for *Mountain* magazine: "Bill thought that the ice would be too thin to climb on, but we were able to get up by using front points and daggers. It certainly doesn't rate Grade VI, and some might say that it's too short to deserve a Grade V rating. Another party might come along, try to cut steps, shatter the ice and say it's impossible, but if they used our technique they'd probably be successful."[2] Whatever Cunningham thought about The Chancer at the time it was almost certainly the steepest single ice pitch of that length yet climbed in Scotland. It demonstrated both the advantages and shortcomings of his new technique. If he could only solve the problem of the hand tools, he felt sure that long, steep ice pitches could be front-pointed without resting or pulling on ice screws. Ironically, when modifications were made to the Scottish winter grading system in the 1990s, it was recognised that The Chancer was indeed technically Grade VI, the first ice climb of this grade in Scotland.

A few weeks after the ascent of The Chancer, the solution to Cunningham's problem presented itself when he met visiting American climbers Yvon Chouinard and Doug Tompkins. Chouinard had also been working on techniques for climbing ice without cutting steps. In 1967 he and Tom Frost designed and manufactured 12-point rigid crampons from chrome alloy steel. These proved excellent for front-pointing especially on steep ice. However, it was another item of their equipment which was of greatest interest to Cunningham. As well as the rigid crampons, the Americans brought with them 'Alpine Hammers' – short, wooden-handled ice hammers with a curved pick designed to grip in the ice. They had been using these new ice tools successfully in the Alps, in the gullies of California's Sierra Nevada, and on frozen waterfalls in other parts of America. Now they were keen to see how their equipment would perform on Scottish ice.

In February, Chouinard and Tompkins went to Hell's Lum Crag and climbed a few short icefalls. They also visited Glen Coe and climbed

*Coire na Cìche,
Beinn a' Bhùird. The
Carpet lies on the big
slab left of centre.
Hourglass Buttress
is on the right,
immediately right
of Twisting Gully*

Photo: Greg Strange

Raven's Gully by its hard Direct Finish. This was the first winter ascent of the Direct and although the crux was a desperate verglased chimney requiring guile and determination rather than a refined technique in front pointing, their climbing this prestigious route drew attention to their new tools. Both Cunningham and March were immediately sold on the curved picks and set about bending axe heads, cutting teeth in them and experimenting with various degrees of curve. Hamish MacInnes was also shown the Alpine hammers. He modified the idea and within 24 hours he had produced a short axe made from sheet metal with a steeply inclined straight pick. This he referred to as a Terrordactyl. Cunningham and March were so keen on this new technique that they soon started teaching it to students on Glenmore Lodge courses. The existing stores of ice axes, mostly Stubai, were taken up to the Cairngorm Chairlift Co. workshop and through the Creagh Dhu connections were curved to match the American tools. (A number of noted Glasgow climbers including Bill Smith, Tommy Paul and Bob Clyde were managers in the ski company).

After Chouinard had returned to America, March was one of the first to test the curved picks when he and Olly Ludlow climbed False Scorpion on the Castlegates Gully Face of Càrn Etchachan. Winter conditions improved this natural line and it gave a good icy Grade V which joined the parent route at the start of the upper gully. Whether or not March cut none, a few, or many holds on this ascent is uncertain. However, it should be remembered that for all climbers at this time there was a big psychological barrier to overcome in launching onto a steep wall of ice, trusting solely to the picks of the axe, and the front points of the crampons, knowing that there was no ladder of steps down which to retreat if ice or strength ran out.

For the great majority of Scottish climbers in the winter of 1969 – 70 these innovations in ice technique were either unknown, or their existence only a rumour. They continued the traditional ways of cutting steps on ice and scarting about on verglased or snow-covered rock.

A notable aspect to this winter was the remarkable output of first ascents by Bower – 11 altogether throughout the Cairngorms. Disillusioned with his job in Aberdeen, he was about to start a course at Strathclyde University, working towards a degree in food science. When asked about his big winter, Bower recalled his thoughts back in November 1969: "A winter season lay ahead and being rather dissatis-fied as a whole with what I had done in winter so far, resolved to make this a good one and climb as hard and as often as I could. I was also peeved at my Aberdonian mates thinking they had it all their own way now that I was down in Glasgow. Another consideration was that I wanted to climb in the Alps that next summer – I knew the best train-ing for that would be the buttresses and gullies of Lochnagar and the rest of the Gorms. Training and dreaming started accordingly!"

By the time he returned to Aberdeen for the Easter holiday his tally was seven. March and early April saw a big build-up of snow in the Cairngorms and Bower was keen to take advantage. He made arrange-ments with Graham Boyd, an architectural student, to go to Coire na Cìche of Beinn a' Bhùird for another crack at The Carpet. Two years earlier, he and I had climbed the first pitch only to be forced to retreat when a rapid thaw set in. It faces south-east and catches the morning sun, even in the dead of winter. By mid-March the main pitch could be in sunlight for up to three hours.

On March 19, the Great Slab pitch had already been stripped of much of its snow, except on ledges and in the cracks of the summer line. Only the upper rocks were extensively snowbound. Although the first pitch appeared to have adequate snow cover, climbing it proved very time consuming. Extensive clearing of wet snow and ice was required before they could gain the piton belay at the start of the main slab. Here, the 40ft slanting crack was partially covered in thawing snow and ice. Bower climbed this without crampons, clearing rock holds with his axe as he progressed. He used three pitons for aid before reaching the point where the route goes left. At this stage he was back in the shade and faced with a narrow band of very hard water-ice. After tricky manoeuvring he re-fitted his crampons to complete this very sustained pitch which Boyd followed by prusiking up the rope.

Below the overhanging cleft, snow had accumulated to a great depth and excavations, almost to the point of tunnelling, were carried out to gain its base. Using combined tactics Bower pulled out of the short corner and continued up poorly-protected slabs and a chimney to a snow-filled crevasse where the difficulties ended.

This eight and a half hour *tour-de-force* was just what Bower had been working towards. He found the climb both physically and mentally very demanding and praised Boyd for agreeing to stay on the route and for his encouragement. The Carpet was repeated for the first time in March 1983 by Andy Nisbet and Doug Hawthorn. Using front-point technique they climbed the route without any aid at a time when the vegetation was frozen and the cliff dusted with powder snow. Above the Great Slab they found an alternative finish going out left, thus avoiding the over-hanging corner.

After The Carpet, Bower and Boyd went to Allt-na-giubhsaich to meet Raymond Simpson. Back in January, Simpson and Sandy Payne had had a minor epic attempting to make a winter ascent of Bower Buttress, a rarely visited V. Diff. rock climb up the edge between Broad Terrace Wall and the Hanging Garden on Creag an Dubh-loch. After two pitches of difficult climbing they retreated in the face of bad weather. Simpson had been so impressed by the situation and atmosphere in the Hanging Garden that he vowed to return, but only when conditions were right. He and Bower now limbered up after two days climbing on Lochnagar, took a chance, and went to the Dubh Loch on March 24.

"The next morning we made a leisurely start for the Dubh Loch, safe in the assumption that the harder routes would be stripped of ice. We dallied on the track to watch goosanders beating across the loch and hinds basking in the sun beneath the waterfall. As we rounded the moraines by the still frozen outflow of the Dubh Loch, we caught a glimpse of tenuous ribbons of ice trickling down into the Hanging Garden and an old wound smarted." Anxious to make up for lost time they soloed from the foot of South-East Gully up rock-hard snow ramps, then edged across Broad Terrace towards the Labyrinth.

"We entered the Hanging Garden, a steep bay of snow-ice halfway up the face, above which all hopeful lines disappeared in a labyrinth of blank walls and overhangs. A long run-out up the Garden led to the foot of our line. It looked far from likely. John was not convinced and looked for an alternative but was forced to conclude that Sandy and I had chosen the only feasible start to the buttress in January."

Bower took the first pitch up steep thinly-iced grooves ending with a hard mantelshelf using a big ice piton to gain a small recess. Simpson followed then led on up the icy chimney above.

"The chimney ended in a shallow icy scoop which narrowed to a bottleneck in 50ft. I wriggled through this and out on to the iced slabs of the gallery. I now had an uninterrupted view over undercut slabs to the Garden 200ft below. The stout abseil sling of our previous attempt provided a reassuring belay. How different now from that foul night when we retreated down the face in long, wet abseils with snow turning to sleet and the lonely mistrust of the stretching, jerking cord."

The next pitch traversed right on heavily-iced slabs then up and left following a big slabby corner. "John took a long time to hew a ropes-length of holds up the dour, black ice. With the relentless sound of a blacksmith working iron, his blunt adze hammered a way out on to the crest of the buttress, till even his well-trained arms felt unresponsive and hands lost their grip. One runner in 150ft."

When Simpson reached the stance he found Bower belayed to one ice screw, his toes projecting over the crest of the buttress, surrounded by green bulging ice with no obvious way out. They both agreed that the situation was unrivalled by any previous winter climb that either of them had been on. Another rope length of similar climbing on green ice took Simpson to below the cornice and another ice piton belay. By the time Bower was traversing out left to a snow prow the stars were shining.

Raymond Simpson climbing the icy chimney of Bower Buttress, March 1970

Photo: John Bower

Brian Findlay climbing the amazing ice ridge of Ninus, Coire Bhrochain, Braeriach, April 1970

Photo: Greg Strange

"Outlined against the purple sky, chips of ice glistening in the beam of his headlamp, he moved jerkily out onto the skyline." The climb had taken them six and a half hours from the Hanging Garden.

A strong wind drove them quickly from the plateau. They descended hard névé in South East Gully, right down to the edge of the loch. "Slowly we coiled the ropes and put away the gear, the face above moon-lit, ice glowing ghost-like, yet so incredibly beautiful that we both felt a unique sense of detachment and peace. John tried to voice our feelings, but failing to find any appropriate quotation from the works of Bob Dylan or Herman Buhl all he could offer was: "It's nae real min, ah'm aff ma f—king heid, far the f—k am ah, ach ah canna spik!"

After a day's rest they went back to Lochnagar and climbed Parallel Buttress in four and a half hours. The conditions were remarkable allowing the whole climb to be made on snow and ice. It was even possible to cut 'buckets' up the summer crux groove on the tower!

For his final route of the winter Bower returned with Boyd to Coire na Cìche to climb the classic VS Hourglass Buttress. It was Easter Sunday, the first day of milder weather for a week. When they reached the corrie they found the steep rocks above the neck of the hourglass plated in an eggshell of ice caused by successions of freezing and thawing. Climbing on this wet unstable material was taxing and a piton and a sling were required for aid in the crack leading up to the shelf overlooking Sickle. They belayed at this point then Bower led the thin crack of the summer crux using another piton. The big platform below the last wall was a haven. Here the gods had favoured the climbers with a large accumulation of snow which assisted a direct ascent of the wall to a concluding snow arete.

Bower recorded all three of the hard winter climbs he did in March as Grade IVs. There was much debate concerning the precise interpretation of what differentiated a IV from a V. It all centred on the length

Starting the second pitch of Bugaboo Rib, Corrie of the Chokestone Gully, April 1970. Brian Findlay climbing

Photo: Greg Strange

of the climb. A hard core of local activists, including Bower, deemed that Vs should be more than 500ft long, citing The Stack on Lochnagar as the example given in the original classification as a very hard climb that was too short to be Grade V. Hence, Bower Buttress, The Carpet and Hourglass Buttress were all given Grade IV, despite it being patently obvious that the latter two, especially, were harder than most existing Cairngorm Grade Vs at that time.

When asked in 1998 about the climbs he made that Easter, Bower recalled they did Bower Buttress in excellent conditions, so he assumed the climb would normally be more difficult. "It was harder than anything we did that week (at Allt na Guibhsaich), but not as hard as sections on The Carpet and Hourglass. I was more scared by the thought of doing Parallel Buttress and typically it ended up being easier." Of the winter season overall he concluded that: "Ambition and competition played a part. I found the mental strain of that winter quite as exhausting as the physical one. It paid off, as the 1970 Alps season was the best climbing I'd ever done!"

There were further heavy snowfalls well into April of this year. Brian Findlay and I took a week off work, mid-month, and based ourselves in the Garbh Coire hut. We had plans to catch up on Bower, with objectives that included The Culvert and Bugaboo Rib. The scenery and depth of snow was fantastic. All but the steepest rock was buried in crusted, partially consolidated snow. For three days the weather was perfect. At dawn on Sunday, 12, we were cramponing up the snow apron below the cliffs of Garbh Choire Dhaidh when the silence was broken by a sharp crack which carried across the slope. We stood motionless, fearing the worst, but nothing happened. The snow pack had settled beneath our weight, confirming our suspicions that we were on the surface of a monster sheet of wind slab. Just 100ft separated us from the relative safety of the icy rocks at the foot of the Culvert. The line itself was a continuous run of ice and we doubted if it would ever be in better winter condition. For a moment we considered going on – perhaps that was the safest option! In the end we tip-toed our way back down the line of steps and ran away round into Coire Bhrochain to make an ascent of the 500ft Ninus, finishing up an amazing ice-encrusted ridge.

On the Monday, we went to the Corrie of the Chokestone Gully which, being north-facing, we hoped would provide us with a whole day in the shade. From the upper basin we could see straight across into Garbh Choire Dhaidh, and there, immediately below the base of the main face, a prominent crown wall stretched the full width of the crag marking the break-off point of a huge slab avalanche. It must have slid away in the warm sunshine sometime after we had retreated. Directly above us now lay the deeply-recessed Chokestone Gully with the arete of Bugaboo Rib to its right. The whole ridge was completely white except for two parallel raking bands of steep rock low down. These bands provided the two VS pitches in summer.

I tackled the first pitch which started as a steep 20ft crack slanting right. I spent some time clearing snow then moved up onto a flake and hammered in a thin blade piton. This provided only psychological protection, but I felt unusually confident and without much hesitation moved on up the crack using hand holds and placing my crampons as best I could on the rounded granite. I was almost up to a detached block when my foot slipped. The piton ripped out as I flew past and in an instant I was sliding head first on my back down the snow banking which covered the introductory rocks. We swapped over and Brian climbed the crack with a less gung-ho approach, and succeeded in gaining and passing the block with a sling and a nut for aid. By traversing right he reached an icy ramp which went back up left to a snow stance below the second steep band.

I was glad when he said he still wanted to lead the next pitch for it looked very hard. Another right-slanting crack, twice as long as the first, led to a recess below a bulge. It was very tiring work clearing the snow and ice to expose the crack and what holds there were. Halfway to the recess he was 'totally pumped' and came back down on a good piton. We talked about retreating, but it was a beautiful day and I doubt if either of us could have wished to have been anywhere else at that moment. After a long rest he went back up for another shift and with a big effort reached the recess using another piton. There was now no question of coming down. He took a long time clearing the exit round to the right, then with a shout for tension he lent out on a long sling, cut hand holds, and finally pulled through onto easy ground. The rest of the climb was a doddle, finishing with a fine snow arete through the only break in the big cornice. Grade V.

Three days of spring sunshine had stripped a lot of snow from the cliffs with a southerly aspect. We wondered about the stability of the cornices, but consoled ourselves in the fact that the nights were still very cold. The next day we went back to Coire Bhrochain and climbed the shallow central depression right of the Direct Route on the West Buttress. Despite another dawn start and no delays, the fringe of icicles hanging from the outer lip of the enormous cornice was dripping by the time we reached it. A left traverse for a full rope-length took us to an easement where we cut a big slot and eventually made our exit. Back at the hut we met our first company since leaving Corrour four days earlier. It was the influential Lancashire rock climber, Ray Evans, on a solo Scottish odyssey. He had come to Braeriach to see the cornices!

When in 1999 Simpson resurrected his notes on Bower Buttress, written shortly after that exciting Easter week at Allt-na-giubhsaich, he made the following comment: "This was written almost 30 years ago with a freshness which seems naive or ingenuous to an old man. I am, however, struck by the obsolete skill involved in cutting holds, the long unprotected run-outs, the thin strands of laid rope tied in a bowline round the waist, the aura of routes unexplored or hitherto only climbed by demi-gods of the generation before. All this was changing. Even as we were climbing that spring, others were experimenting with curved axes and hammers which together with the publication of books and articles about ice climbing, was to revolutionise this arcane activity and render it safer, more attractive and accessible to the masses of climbers outwith our intimate circle of enthusiasts."

Another era was drawing to a close.

It seemed that the dust had barely settled on the cliffs of Creag an Dubh-loch following the activities of the previous June when another summer arrived to tease and frustrate the faithful. Fyffe and Grieve had

*Greg Strange moving
left above the wet
groove on Predator,
May 1970*

Photo: Brian Findlay

shown the way and now others wanted a piece of the action. A week
of dry weather in mid-May prompted a visit to the Dubh Loch to have
a look at the unfinished Clough-Hardie route.

Just four weeks after our winter trip to Braeriach, Findlay and I stood
contemplating the section of Central Gully Wall immediately left of
Mousetrap. Brian pointed out the ledge where the Glen Coe men had
spent the night. It was 150ft up in the line of the black crack system
running parallel to the upper pitches of Mousetrap. A little way below
and left of the ledge, on a steep, blank-looking slab, we could make out
the red tape used by Hardie and Clough on their ascent. We thought a
line farther right looked more appropriate, where cracks split a rust-
coloured wall. Brian used the start of Cougar to gain and follow a vertical
crack up round onto the front face, and then two short pitches took us
to a ledge close to the Mousetrap recess, right of a short overhanging
crack in a red wall.

Often with Cairngorm granite, red is indicative of water-washed rock
and this was no exception. The crack followed a shallow corner which
was acting as a drainage channel. After several unsuccessful attempts
to sidle into the corner via a smooth sloping ledge, I took a little tension
on the rope, lent across and sunk my left hand into the crack. The slip-
pery jam was disconcerting, but what the mountain took with one hand
it gave with the other in the form of a perfect little rock spike over which
I laid a thin nylon sling. By standing in this I was able to move up over
the bulge into the recess above. A little higher the crack reared up again
where it merged into the wall above. I drove in a piton for a runner
and looked around. At head height on my left was a sloping edge. Pulling
up on the piton I swung out onto the edge, and surprisingly, found
myself comfortably poised on a short slab. A couple of delicate moves
and I was belaying beside some large blocks on the Clough-Hardie
bivouac ledge.

As Brian started up the steep cracks above the ledge it began to rain.
There had been a shower earlier and the weather had looked threatening all day. We waited half an hour in the vain hope that it would move
away, then despondently abseiled down, leaving the ropes in place. The
rain stopped in the evening so we did some sun-dancing on the beach
with our companion, Wilma Sinclair, and were rewarded with a beautiful cloudless sky the next day. It was tempting to prusik back up the
ropes, but thankfully, we decided to retrieve them and re-climb all the
pitches which were now bathed in sunshine.

Despite the rain all was now dry except for the wet bits of the previous day. A short distance above the abseil point Brian came to a bulge
where he found it very strenuous to hold on and clean vegetation out
of a horizontal crack. In the end he drove in a piton and used it to pull
up and move right onto a slab. Directly above was another overhang,
but this was furnished with good cracks for jamming and went without bother. From here onwards the route became easier except for a short
wet groove where we used another piton. We were delighted with
ourselves, for this had been our first big rock climb together on what
was a new route on the great Central Gully Wall. The pleasure was tinged
with a little guilt at having profited from Clough and Hardie's earlier
attempt; hence the name Predator – HVS 5a.

The Spring Bank Holiday Monday of 1970 was a black day for Scottish climbing. While roping down from The Maiden, a 200ft quartzite sea stack off Whiten Head in Sutherland, Tom Patey became detached from his abseiling device and fell 120ft on to rocks and was killed. In an instant one of our great exploratory climbers was gone.

Although many of the younger generation of climbers had never met Patey, they felt a kinship with him through his climbs, his writing and his lectures. I remember the last talk he gave to the Etchachan Club at an annual dinner in the Royal Hotel in Aberdeen. It was a hilarious evening where he described his recent exploits in the Alps while gently poking fun at himself and his illustrious companions, Joe Brown and Chris Bonington. The minister's son from Ellon had come a long way from his early explorations on the Buchan sea cliffs.

Tom Patey was a very tough individual, with a craggy appearance, large shoulders and strong arms. He had soon discovered that climbing came easy to him. On a cliff or in the mountains his natural ability, good judgment and uncanny eye for the easiest line, allowed him to climb solo much closer to his physical limits than most others could handle. To his fellow climbers he was not what you would call stylish. In fact, it was often frightening to watch him as he gave the appearance that he might fall at any time. He was an ungainly climber who moved with great determination accompanied by the sounds of scraping boots, heaves and grunts. When out with other climbers he was very competitive, climbed at a terrific speed and became impatient when not in the lead. He was, nevertheless, generous at heart and not at all secretive about his climbs. He usually appeared with very little equipment, often poorly clothed and scruffy. Mac Smith believed that Patey was fearless and could not understand folk who became frightened, whereas Graeme Nicol thought that he had no hang-ups about being cautious.

Whatever any shortcomings, Patey was the major driving force behind the Aberdeen school of the 1950s, where he particularly excelled on snow, rock and ice of mixed winter terrain. Although his passion for climbing appeared all-consuming he was a man of many talents. As well as being a respected and successful Highland GP he was a first-class musician. Initially trained as a classical pianist, he taught himself to play the mouth organ, kazoo and later his trusty accordion. He was also unquestionably one of our finest and most popular climbing writers. His distinctive easy-going comic style reflected his own humorous character. He wrote excellent songs depicting many aspects of the contemporary climbing scene. These songs were greatly appreciated at impromptu gatherings in pubs and bothies where he would entertain his audience by singing and playing his accordion far into the night. As a climber, writer, musician and raconteur he was incomparable.

Apart from a fortnight of continuous dry weather in mid-June, the summer of 1970 was disappointing. During the first weekend of this dry spell, Hunter and Lang made their eighth visit to Creag an Dubh-loch to attempt the great corner system on the left side of Broad Terrace Wall. All their efforts to date had been thwarted by wet conditions and it was now common knowledge that they were working on this line. After scrambling left from the normal approach to Broad Terrace, an easy chimney in a short wall gave access to a ledge below the first corner.

Hunter led this excellent 90ft pitch using some aid as there was still water running down the rock. Lang took over and found relatively straightforward climbing up the continuation of the corner, then by a crack on the right to a small stance below a formidable hanging chimney. Although the left wall of the chimney was smooth and overhanging it appeared to offer the only chance of progress via a series of thin cracks.

While Hunter set off to tackle the chimney Lang settled down on his stance. "A massive tottering block lay above and right of my head. Graeme deftly climbed past it, relaxing only when he managed to insert a peg at the base of the chimney. He knocked another one in higher up, in rather doubtful rock. But beyond this there was a long way to any other useable crack, so out came the drill. He ground out a hole and then – it could only happen to us – discovered he had brought up the wrong size of bolts and they were too small for the hole he had just sweated out. The horror of it!"[3] Having convinced themselves that bolting was the only way to progress, they abseiled off and rescued the day by making the second ascent of Goliath.

The glorious weather heralded another invasion from Glen Coe. Ian Nicolson, the most colourful of the Dumbarton Boys, had been going like a train this year. In April, he and Carrington had taken advantage of unusually dry conditions to climb Cowslip, the prominent 'weep' on the Càrn Dearg Buttress of Ben Nevis. Recently, he had made the first ascent of Heidbanger on the Ben, and just a few days' later, with Dave Knowles made the second ascent of the outstanding Kingpin on Bidean nam Bian, reducing the aid in the process. Armed with a copy of an article from *Mountain* magazine, Nicolson and Knowles arrived at the Dubh Loch to find out for themselves what all the fuss was about.

On their first day, Wednesday, June 17, they dispatched Goliath without recourse to aid, describing the climbing as being of a reasonable standard! On the Thursday, they decided to try a line of their own and went for the single isolated crack between The Kraken and King Rat. With Nicolson taking the lead they started just right of Mousetrap and climbed cracked slabs to below a conspicuous shallow chimney, some 60ft left of the roof on King Rat. This proved to be much more difficult than it looked and Nicolson had to use a piton as a hand hold before reaching the start of the best defined section of the crack. Then 90ft of excellent climbing followed to an overhanging recess. Here it was necessary to move left almost into Kraken, but by taking an edge they were able to return back up right to the crack-line and climb a sustained slab with a tricky overlap. A short distance above this they joined The Kraken and continued to the top taking a slightly different line. This 700ft route which they named, Dubh Loch Monster, had given excellent, continuous climbing – E1 5c. (5a with piton for aid.)

The good weather looked to be holding, so after climbing Black Mamba on the Friday they thought a rest day would be in order. There were other climbers in action that Saturday. Nicolson was lounging on the beach watching a party on King Rat when his gaze strayed to the Red Wall of Waterkelpie. As far as he knew this prominent feature with its twin cracks had never been climbed, and the more he studied the cliff the more he became convinced that a direct line could be taken

Doug Lang, The Sword of Damocles, 1970

Photo: Graeme Hunter

going straight up through the Red Wall to finish by the chimney crack of Waterkelpie. The seeds had been sown and he just had to try it.

Commencing directly below the Red Wall they went up pale-coloured slabs trending right to belay beside a white rock scar. By moving left, Nicolson gained a long left-facing corner with an old piton and kara-biner at the start. The corner was in two tiers and gave good climbing up to a steep wall at 80ft. It was not clear at this point which was the best way to go. Above and to his left was a large block apparently held in by air friction. Nicolson is a big lad, and try as he might he could not cross this slightly impending block without applying his full body weight. With bated breath he committed himself to the moves and quickly reached a shelf on the left. By the time he had moved back right and up a short crack he had run out the full 150ft of rope. Easier short walls and slabs then took them to the traverse of Waterkelpie and a ledge directly below the Red Wall.

The parallel cracks are rarely completely dry. Nicolson was carrying his usual selection of eight nuts. He set off up the near vertical wall straddling the two cracks. At 15ft he found a good place to fix his favourite Moac nut, then he pushed on, with a hand and foot in each of the parallel cracks. He soon found that he was starting to swivel out and to compensate for this he kept 'wheeking' one of his hands higher up the crack, getting farther and farther away from his good nut. He was beginning to get gripped and realised that he ought to have stopped to fix another runner, only now it was too late and he would have to go for it! Near the top he was forced to transfer into the left-hand crack and just when he thought he had blown it the difficulties eased. He moved up to a belay 60ft above the foot of the Red Wall – a very bold piece of climbing.

Continuing in the line of the crack they soon joined Waterkelpie Wall coming in from the left and followed this to the top avoiding the wet bits by harder variations on the left. They had climbed this 900ft route, Gulliver, so quickly that they were on the plateau ahead of the King Rat party. Thirty years on, when asked about the Red Wall on Gulliver, Nicolson recalled with a chuckle that he had found it steep and hard. It was probably the most difficult on-sight lead in the Cairngorms at that time with a modern grade of E2 5b. More impressive though than this single hard pitch was the free-wheeling style with which Nicolson and Knowles raced up the cliff, doing these long sustained pitches with only one piton for aid.

Hunter and Lang were one of the other parties climbing that day. They were back at their high point on the big corner system, having managed to do without some of the aid on the second pitch. Now kitted out with the correct size of drill, Hunter led the left wall of the great chimney using three bolts and nine pitons. Above this the angle was much more amenable, but a piton was required in a chimney on the right, before easy rock steps led to the plateau. For the Dundee men the saga of the 500ft Sword of Damocles was finally over. They gave the spectacular chimney pitch an artificial grade of A3.

There was relatively little new route activity in the Loch Avon basin this summer. Glenmore Lodge parties made further climbs on the East flank of Stac an Fharaidh in June, then in early July Carrington and Jimmy Marshall climbed Bellows, a good route between Whispers and Pushover. During the dry spell in June, Cunningham and March climbed a series of steep cracks and grooves up the right flank of Raeburn's Buttress on the Shelter Stone Crag. Their 900ft climb, Threadbare, had several sections of aid-climbing and although the line looks impressive, very few, if any, repeat ascents have been made on account of the vegetated nature of the rock.

Forbes and Rennie's interest in the Tough-Brown Face came to a climax

Ian Nicolson

Photo: Ian Nicolson Collection

in August when they made a route directly up the middle, following cracks and grooves left of Mort. Forbes had climbed very little in 1968 and 1969 but was having a come-back. During the winter he had kept himself rock fit by climbing on Craig y Barns at Dunkeld. He did some of the harder existing climbs, then with Graeme Millar, in March, he put up Hang Out and Fall Out, two aid routes on the Upper Cave Crag. On the latter they climbed the very steep central prow using old bolts left from attempts by other parties. In June and July, Forbes and Rennie were in the Dolomites and Chamonix where among other climbs they did the North Face Direct (Brandler/Hasse) on the Cima Grande. This proved to be a harrowing experience as Forbes fell leading through the yellow roofs, stripping a whole pitch of in-situ equipment. Re-pegging took a long time but they reached the top as bad weather set in. A Continental party who started a day later were not so fortunate. They were caught in a bad storm and froze to death in their etriers.

On Saturday, August 8, it was a warm day and the cliffs of Lochnagar were beginning to dry out. Forbes was still jaded with climbing after the Alpine trip and was starting to lose interest again; yet a direct ascent of the Tough-Brown Face was a cherished ambition and he wanted to get the thing done. They used the initial pitch of Mort to reach the first terrace from where they planned to continue straight up for nearly 200ft to join a prominent right-sloping ramp. From the left end of the terrace Rennie led up a little sloping groove then climbing with aid followed to reach a hanging block at the base of a short corner. Forbes led the next pitch which was equally sustained, requiring continuous aid from the top of the short corner to a belay on the ramp. From here they followed the rightward trend of the ramp using further aid until they eventually reached Tough-Brown Traverse.

Post Mortem was an apt name for their third route on the face (following Mort and Crypt [Parallel C] in 1967) as it turned out to be their last climb together. It followed an excellent line up clean, continuous cracks and corners in the middle of the crag where there are no big ledges or grass terraces. They gave artificial grades for the three main pitches (A3 on the third pitch) implying all-out pegging on terrain where climbers of their ability and experience might have been expected to find some free-climbing. Forbes later admitted that he knew that sections which he had led on aid could have been free-climbed. He also said that at one point on the third pitch he nearly backed off, something which he had never done before on a climb, but the thought of 'the glory' kept him going.

Forbes virtually gave up climbing after this. For him the experience of being on the rocks had run its course and he was no longer getting a buzz from it. He had abandoned his nursing career after two years and was now keen to get involved with a commercial enterprise to make some money.

Unlike Forbes, Rennie's enthusiasm for climbing never diminished. With his background of engineering he was interested in designing his own curved ice axes and had recently discussed this with Cunningham and March. By the time the next winter came round he had made several prototypes, one of which survived in use for many seasons.

Sadly, he was never able to try them out himself in full winter

Dave Wright leading the Red Wall on an early ascent of Gulliver in 1976

Photo: Gordon Stephen

Grey Man's Crag, Coire Sputan Dearg in winter. Hanging Dyke lies close to the right edge. The prominent central icefall is the upper chimney of Pilgrim's Groove. Crystal Ridge is on the extreme left

Photo: Greg Strange

conditions because he was killed in a road accident six months after the ascent of Post Mortem. He was one of four passengers returning from Souter Head on the Aberdeen sea cliffs in a mini-van which hit a bridge parapet broadside – Rennie took the full force of the impact. He died in hospital from his injuries only three weeks after his wedding day. At 21, Rennie had hardly reached his prime and we can only speculate as to what he might have achieved had he lived longer. He was a very fine natural climber, always canny, and a great companion both on and off the rocks. Although determined once in action, he was not obsessive about climbing, maintaining that he got his enjoyment from the challenge and the camaraderie. He enjoyed life to the full, often saying: "The hills can wait – they will always be there!" In the space of four years with Forbes and other companions he had accounted for a half dozen of the finest rock climbs in the Cairngorms.

When reminiscing about that period in the 1960s, Forbes recalled how the discovery of the hills and the excitement of climbing had been a revelation to him after a rather insular upbringing. He admits that one of his reasons for climbing was to be recognised. He had tried to break with Aberdeen tradition by concentrating on pure rock climbing instead of all-round mountaineering. He confessed to not enjoying winter climbing very much. Of his partnership with Rennie he said that they were not really a team, just two individuals climbing together for mutual convenience. Initially Forbes, being the elder, was the undisputed leader, but after 1967 he felt that Rennie matured quickly and his climbing ability and expertise developed accordingly. Forbes climbed only once or twice after Post Mortem, his last route, surprisingly, being a winter ascent of Douglas Gibson Gully in 1972 with Lawrie, which he said was straightforward but probably dangerous. Nowadays, he runs a bed and breakfast and still enjoys hill-walking, though at a more leisurely pace.

The summer of 1970 had seen the last major new routes in the Cairngorms employing all-out aid, where pitons and etriers were used over continuous sections of climbing, to the extent that artificial grades were considered appropriate. During the five years since the ascent of The Giant, these tactics had been used on a number of now classic climbs. With the benefit of hindsight, it can be seen that this 'big wall' style of climbing was inappropriate for Scotland as all these routes were eventually climbed free.

The granite of the Cairngorms, like that of Cornwall, Arran and Glen Etive, is more difficult to protect using natural features than it is in other traditional British climbing areas. There are less face holds, spikes etc. and the cracks tend to be shallow and often earth-filled. Over the years it had become acceptable to use pitons for protection, even on relatively easy climbs, as they were quick to place without having to clean the cracks. This lapse by local climbers into a rather liberal attitude towards the use of pitons for both protection and aid was now being questioned. The example set by Ian Nicolson on Creag an Dubh-loch was an eye-opener and showed just what could be achieved by the most talented climbers.

As might have been predicted with everyone itching to get on to steep ice to try the new techniques, the winter season 1970 – 71 was a poor one. It started well enough with good snow cover in November. On the 21st, Norrie Muir and Steve Docherty, two young members of the Creagh Dubh Mountaineering Club made a fast second ascent of Red Chimney Direct on Creagan a' Choire Etchachan in excellent icy conditions – recording the event in the Hutchison Hut book under the pseudonyms of Willie the Pimp and Superman! At Christmas, Docherty teamed up with Spence to climb Brimstone Groove on Hell's Lum Crag. In a normal winter the cliff to the left of Hellfire Corner becomes draped in an impressive sheet of ice and their climb followed its left edge up into the obvious wide depression breaching the upper rocks. This was the first of several good ice climbs to be made on the front face of Hell's Lum Crag. On this occasion the ice was not well built up and they had to use two pitons for aid – Grade IV.

There were fresh snowfalls prior to New Year followed by several days of cold, calm weather. On January 2, Bower and Lang made a first winter ascent of the Grey Man's Crag in Coire Sputan Dearg following the line of Hanging Dyke. This provided a difficult, sustained climb with a piton for aid at the summer crux – Grade V.

Much of January and early February was very mild with temperatures up to 63°F recorded on Cairn Gorm. Bill March was the most active of the climbing instructors at Glenmore Lodge at this time. On February 11, he climbed Raeburn's Buttress on the Shelter Stone Crag with John Hart. They stayed close to the original route all the way finding the cliff lightly dusted in powder snow with just a little ice. Under these conditions the climbing seemed relatively straightforward and they gave it a surprisingly modest Grade III despite its severe summer rating. This was one of the earliest buttress routes to be done on frozen turf with curved axes. Previously, this type of winter terrain would have been climbed using whatever rock or vegetation was available for hand holds. On steep ground it was not unusual to cut holds in frozen turf.

Bill March, 1972
Photo: Allen Fyffe

*The Shelter Stone and
Shelter Stone Crag
in February, 1970*

Photo: Greg Strange

Occasionally, a one-off move could be made by plunging the axe pick
into turf and pulling up on this in what Bill Brooker used to refer to as
a 'Knubel'! Now, with two curved or inclined picks, a single blow into
a frozen divot with one axe could provide a perfectly secure placement
and rapid movement on to the next haven of turf for the other axe,
and so on.

A week after Raeburn's Buttress, March and Hart returned to the Loch
Avon basin to climb Amphitheatre Gully, the shallow depression left
of Longbow Crag on the Stag Rocks. This gave an excellent winter route
with varied climbing on both ice and rock. Above the amphitheatre

they climbed a long corner in two pitches to exit through a rock window – Grade V.

During this lean winter Cunningham and March made a bold attempt to climb the Citadel. Despite a late start, calm weather and a light covering of snow enabled them to progress quickly up to the lower crux where it was March's turn to lead. He found it difficult getting to the layback crack and much harder trying to climb it with bare hands. Using a nut for aid he gained an old piton and hung from this using slings. Just as he stepped up again, he fell.

"It was only a short fall – 20ft, but I landed upside down with a rope burn between the cheeks of my backside. Without a word I climbed back up, found a peg I had missed which had been covered in snow, and climbed, using three pegs for direct aid. I was tired and bleeding from a torn hand when I arrived at the belay ledge."[4] Once Cunningham had followed this hard pitch they had to choose between continuing up the summer line, escaping onto Sticil Face, or making an orderly retreat while daylight permitted. They decided to go for broke and quickly climbed two long pitches up to the belay at the start of the hand traverse. As Cunningham led across this, hooking the picks of his Chouinard hammers behind the flake, the weather began to deteriorate, with strengthening winds, snow and spindrift. Darkness caught them on the small ledges at the top of the summer crux, just one pitch from the top. An enforced bivouac in winter without bivouac equipment is no tea party! They could hardly have been in a more exposed situation, completely at the mercy of the weather.

"At about 2am I gazed wearily across at J.C. The temperature had risen and wet snow slides were hitting us at intervals – J.C. was on his knees. For one split second I thought he was praying and fear gripped me. All was lost. Then I realised he had cramp in his calves and was trying to ease the strain. I suggested we swapped places, but he declined as it would have been a dicey operation. At 3am he was standing and swaying slightly, and I put my hand out to stop him falling off. It was useless. He had to do something. After a while he rigged up a sling basket and spent the rest of the night in that."[5]

In the morning, it was still thawing and neither of them could face trying to climb out. There then followed an epic retreat involving downclimbing the upper crux and many abseils before they reached the foot of the crag. They met a strong and very relieved rescue party at the top of the ski tows on their way back to Glenmore Lodge. Had they started the climb a few hours earlier they may well have succeeded in making the first winter ascent of Citadel. It was, nevertheless, a most impressive outing.

Despite the thin conditions this winter most climbers tried the curved tools with varying degrees of success and enthusiasm. Wrist loops were still at the experimental stage and some climbers did without them altogether, relying solely on gripping the shafts. On the day Cunningham and March were benighted on The Citadel Carrington and Hart attempted a second winter ascent of Sticil Face. They were using Chouinard hammers attached with a sling to a bandoleer and without wrist loops. Carrington recalled setting off up a thinly-iced wall just below their high point.

Douglas Dinwoodie,
1973

Photo: Mungo Ross

"I made a few moves up the ice when my feet came off, the hammer stayed in but my hand slid off the end of the hammer shaft. The difficult manoeuvre was how to climb back up to retrieve the hammer all the time with the foreboding that the hammer was about to ping out and dob me on the head."

Although manufactured curved axes were now more widely available many climbers chose to get a blacksmith to modify their existing Aschenbrenners and Grivels. In this way a more severe angle or curve could be formed which felt more reassuring than the gentle curve on the Chouinard hammer which tended to wobble alarmingly in anything less than perfect ice or névé.

One evening in early May 1971, Dave Stuart and I met a 19-year-old student at Souter Head. I first noticed him when he appeared on the summit of the Grassy Pinnacle having climbed The Rack, a precarious VS on the north side. He was wearing gym shoes and had a distinct mop of curly brown hair. As we walked back up through the field he talked enthusiastically about a recent climb which he had soloed on the granite headland of Arthur Fowlie, near the Bullers O' Buchan. He wanted to know if a big ramp 100 yards south of there had been climbed as he thought it would make a tremendous route. He said his name was Douglas Dinwoodie and that he was keen to meet with local climbers. Dave suggested that he come along to the Blue Lamp that Thursday evening.

Dinwoodie grew up in the mining community of Arniston, beside Gorebridge in Midlothian. His uncle took him hill-walking when he was 15-years-old and this kindled a lifelong passion for the Scottish hills. He borrowed books on mountaineering from the school library and was inspired by the deeds of home-grown climbers such as MacInnes and Haston. Close to his home he often climbed on a sandstone outcrop in Arniston Glen where he admits to having got terribly 'gripped' at times.

In October 1970, Dinwoodie came to Aberdeen University to study for an MA specialising in English and Sociology. By the end of his first winter in the North-east he had gained good experience on snow and ice. While still at school he had soloed easy gullies in Glen Coe as well as Tower and Observatory Ridges on Ben Nevis in semi-winter conditions. On Lochnagar, he had climbed Black Spout Buttress, Western Slant and Raeburn's Gully, all solo. Initially, he had been disappointed with the sea cliffs south of Aberdeen, failing on his first attempt to find climbs at Souter Head because they were so short. This could not be said of the northern granite cliffs which he found inspiring. The route which he soloed on Arthur Fowlie he later named Magic Dragon (HS), while the big ramp nearby was climbed within days of his chance meeting with Stuart and I. Fearing that we might beat him to it he persuaded a friend at his digs to accompany him. They abseiled in and made the first ascent of The Crocodile, one of the hardest and certainly the most serious climb on the Aberdeenshire sea cliffs at that time.

With Dutch courage induced by a few beers in the Student's Union, Dinwoodie turned up at the 'Lampie' that Thursday evening and the following weekend he came with Lawrie, Stuart, Mike Freeman and I to Creag an Dubh-loch. Despite a week of dry weather the cliff was still wet. On the Saturday, after an abandoned attempt on Vertigo Wall, he

John Mothersele, Syd Littleford, Doug Lang, John Bower and Dave Stuart. Glen Quoich 1971

Photo: Greg Strange

made his first new climb in the Cairngorms with Stuart and myself. We climbed Spectrum, a pleasant route following a series of grooves right of the waterfall on the Eagle's Rocks. It rained overnight, so the next day we explored the crags in the Pass of Ballater. A good number of climbs were made that day, indicating the obvious potential of the Pass as a wet weather alternative to the high corries. Perhaps the best climb was an excellent vertical corner led on aid by Freeman and seconded by Dinwoodie. (Dinwoodie led this free 14 years later – Anger and Lust Right-hand Finish – E4 6b.)

Mike Freeman was from Stratford. He started climbing while at Sheffield University then moved to the North-east in 1970 to work as a roustabout in the embryonic North Sea oil industry. He was the first 'oil man' on the Aberdeen climbing scene.

A fortnight after the ascent of Spectrum the cliffs of the Cairngorms were much drier, although it was still very cool for late May. Muir and Docherty paid a visit to Creag an Dubh-loch where they made an impressive direct start to Goliath. This involved chimneying up behind the vast wedged block, then swinging out to belay at its apex. Another huge detached flake, which lies on top of, and appears to counterbalance the block, was then climbed up left to a tricky bulging wall which led to a belay at the start of Goliath's crux pitch. Several points of aid were used but these were eliminated by Brian Davison and Andy Nisbet in 1983. E2 5b. At the time of this visit Muir made a solo ascent of Mousetrap. This was a particularly bold undertaking as he had no prior knowledge of the route, no guidebook, and was alone at Creag an Dubh-loch at the time. The evening before his companion arrived, he went for a 'scramble' on slabs left of Central Gully wearing ordinary shoes.

"Soon I realised it was not scrambling, but real climbing when I came to an overlap above a ledge. Retreat was called for but I could not reverse the steep step below. I had to think of something as Stevie may have got stuck hitching up from Glasgow and I did not want to be benighted. I took off my denim jacket and piled what stones were on the ledge on to it. Next, I took off my belt and tied it to the sleeve of the jacket, and then finally I took the laces out of my shoes and tied them to the belt. With this I managed to drop down the hard bit." He later retrieved his jacket wearing his rock boots. "There is no ill feeling for the slabs, only my ill judgment of them!"

On the day the direct start to Goliath was made a bizarre incident occurred on the Grey Man's Crag in Coire Sputan Dearg. Late on the Friday evening, Lawrie, Dinwoodie, Stuart and I arrived at Scott's Bothy for a rendezvous with John Mothersele, an enthusiastic Welsh climber who had recently started work as a nurse in Aberdeen. It was agreed that we would all go to 'Sputan' the next day. At that time I was updating the section of Mac Smith's guide which included Beinn a' Bhùird, Coire Etchachan and Coire Sputan Dearg. The SMC, in their wisdom, had decided to increase the number of volumes from two to five. Bill March was writing Volume 1 to Loch Avon and the Northern Corries of Cairn Gorm. The guide I was working on would be Volume 2, and Allen Fyffe had just completed the manuscript for Volume 5, covering Creag an Dubh-loch and Glen Clova. Braeriach was to be Volume 3 and Lochnagar Volume 4. It had been my aim to check all the existing rock climbs in my area and, if possible, find some new ones. Dave Stuart had previously attempted a line of grooves between Grey Slab and Hanging Dyke but had been rained off. He and I hoped to try this again the next day.

Early on Saturday morning, Stuart, Mothersele and I left for the Hutchison Hut where we planned to spend the night and be well placed to climb on Creagan a' Choire Etchachan on Sunday. Lawrie was reluctant to relinquish the chance of a few pints at Mar Lodge on Saturday night so we left him and Dinwoodie in their sleeping bags, agreeing to meet them in the corrie. We stopped for a brew at the hut and were crossing the col north of Derry Cairngorm when we were surprised to see two tiny figures below the Grey Man's Crag. By the time we had caught them up Lawrie was already engrossed on a thin-looking layback corner leading directly to the first stance on Grey Slab. He was making very little progress so Stuart decided to climb the normal first pitch of Grey Slab as he already knew that this was the best way to start the new route. At this point Lawrie became agitated, fearing that he was being out-manoeuvred. He was still in the same place, 30ft below us, when Stuart and I offered Mothersele the lead, pointing him in the direction of the cracks and ribs on the edge overlooking the main corner of Grey Slab. While John whooped his way up the edge marvelling at the great rock which he likened to Milestone Buttress on Tryfan, Lawrie was beside himself with rage, threatening to inflict grievous bodily harm on Stuart and I when he reached the stance. Once Mothersele had found a belay Lawrie had retreated back to the ground. We persuaded him to come up the ordinary start and thus we became a party of five to complete the first ascent of Ferlas Mor. The climbing was very good and Severe, the line rather eliminate and a little disappointing. Mothersele

Upper Shelter Stone Crag from the west. Haystack stays close to the left profile.(The sunlit climber is starting the 'Crack for thin Fingers' on The Needle)

Photo: Greg Strange

got fed up waiting his turn for the upper pitches. He unroped and soloed off up Hanging Dyke.

Undoubtedly, the highlight of this summer in the Cairngorms occurred during a fine spell of weather in July. Carrington and Nicolson were probably the most potent climbing force in Scotland at this time. Carrington had been bemoaning the fact that although there were a number of excellent long rock climbs in Scotland they mostly had only short sections of difficult climbing. He was looking for somewhere to make a long, hard route with continuous difficulty and thought that

*Rab Carrington at
the CIC Hut, 1972*

Photo: Jimmy Marshall

the main bastion of the Shelter Stone Crag would offer this possibility. Although neither of them had climbed on that part of the crag before, Carrington knew about the striking crack on the crest of the bastion, sometimes referred to as the direct finish to Citadel. His plan was to commence from the very toe of the lowest slabs and climb the full height of the cliff as directly as possible between Citadel and Steeple, taking in the prominent crack en route.

Instead of starting on the open slabs they climbed a leaning corner which curved up right alongside the start of Steeple. This emerged on to the slabs after a full rope length, then two pleasant pitches led to the broken ground below the steep middle tier of the bastion. At this point it became apparent that keeping their new climb independent from Steeple would be both very hard and contrived. The logical way was to follow Steeple, then continue straight up the fault above from the point where the established route veered away right. Nicolson made quick work of the common ground then launched out for the obvious break on the skyline, passing just right of some prominent jutting overhangs. The climbing was very steep with long reaches for holds. He placed a good piton runner and kept going until he was able to move up right on a narrow ramp, overlooking and parallel to the ramp of Steeple. The rope was tugging at his waist by the time he reached a recess and found a belay.

They now wanted to get back left onto the crest of the bastion and follow this up to join The Citadel at the stance before its hand traverse. By delicate manoeuvring they gained a ledge, then good holds led up left onto an arete where a straight crack took them directly to easier ground below the impending wall avoided by the crux pitch of The Citadel. They were now able to look straight up the spectacular hanging crack which appeared to be the only feature on an otherwise blank wall of granite. This was to be Carrington's lead and he could now see that the crack was in fact formed in a shallow right-facing groove. From the belay he climbed up onto a big detached flake which marked the start of the difficult climbing. By bridging across the groove he was able to make progress using hand jams and layaway holds in the crack. The climbing was totally absorbing, which was just as well for the situation was wildly exposed. Near the top a slightly steeper section proved rather more testing and here Carrington succumbed to an overwhelming desire to rest his arms. He hammered in a piton and used this to move up to better holds. Moments later he was on a spacious ledge below the final wall. Nicolson seconded the pitch, leaving the aid piton in place. He then moved up right across the ledge and climbed the final steep crack of Steeple to reach the plateau.

At nearly 900ft this was the longest climb on the Shelter Stone Crag as well as the most difficult. They settled for the name Haystack, suggested by Fyffe, as it was a much bigger climb than The Needle (in a haystack!). Carrington was disappointed that they had been unable to keep the climb independent from Steeple through the steep band, and also annoyed with himself for using the piton on the top crack. When reminiscing about this 30 years later he said wryly: "But I think I was frightened!" For several years Haystack was the high-water mark of on-sight pioneering in the Cairngorms. Nicolson's lead of the lower

Looking from Hell's Lum Crag to Ben Macdui

Photo: Greg Strange

crux was the first Cairngorm pitch to be given the technical grade of 5c and although the upper crack is reputed to be technically easier at 5b (without the piton for aid), most climbers agree that it is the more daunting of the two hard pitches. The whole climb is now E3 5c.

The first appreciable snowfalls of the 1971 – 72 winter came in the third week of November. Prior to this there had been few cold snaps and ice was only just forming on the drainage lines of the higher cliffs. Dinwoodie had been impressed with his first visit to Hell's Lum Crag in September (where he made the first ascent of Salamander with John Tweddle) and judged that it would be a good place for early-season ice. On Tuesday, November 16, he and Mothersele went by motorcycle to Bob Scott's Bothy. The next day, despite plenty of new snow, they rode the machine up onto the Derry flats, and then walked through to Hell's Lum Crag. The diedre of The Wee Devil was attractively iced so they decided to give it a go.

This was the first time that either of them had used front point technique on a difficult climb and they found the thin ice and poor protection disconcerting. Sustained, necky climbing led up the lower corners until the summer flake exit gave access to thin tongues of ice which ran down an exposed slab from an upper right-facing groove. Near the top Dinwoodie lost a crampon but the final pitch was relatively easy and they reached the top sometime after dark. When they eventually returned to the motorcycle it would not start, so they trudged on and spent a second night in the bothy. The bike would not start the next day either. They pushed it to Derry Lodge and there the AA rescued it and them. That night in the Blue Lamp their tale of derring-do on The Wee Devil was sufficiently inspiring for four of us to head for Hell's Lum Crag the following day. Freeman, Stuart, Bob Harris (another Welshman living in Aberdeen) and I camped at Glenmore on the Friday night. Saturday, November 20, dawned calm and overcast. We left after daybreak, drove up to the Cairn Gorm car park and walked to Hell's Lum Crag via the Fiacaill a' Choire Chais. As we dropped into Coire Domhain the wind began to pick up from the south-west and there were flakes of snow in the air.

Davie Stuart was hampered by having one of his arms in a sling. He had broken it after stepping off a roof in the dark while attempting to gain free entry to a dance at the Student's Union. He and Bob wanted to climb something straightforward and went for The Escalator. Being east-facing the crag was in the lee of the wind and already spindrift was cascading down sections of the face. Mike Freeman and I were still keen to try something new and decided to climb a series of iced slabs and grooves in the line of Auld Nick. In this way we hoped to remain in shouting distance of the others. Like Dougie and John earlier in the week we were all experimenting with the new curved gear. Davie had recently hitch-hiked to Tiso's in Edinburgh and bought a Curver axe and a Chouinard hammer. Since he could only use one arm he had lent me the hammer to go with my Brailsford axe, which, incidentally, bent transversely on the climb and later had to be replaced.

During that late morning, a party of nine boys and five girls from the mountaineering club at Ainslie Park Secondary School in Edinburgh were driven from Lagganlia Outdoor Centre near Kincraig to the car park on Cairn Gorm. The school outdoor activities master, 23-year-old Ben Beattie, was in charge of their weekend training expedition to the Cairngorms, which was intended to give experience of navigating in difficult terrain. Beattie, a climber of considerable experience with professional qualifications (Mountain Instructors Certificate) was aware of a forecast for deteriorating weather and had already modified an earlier, more ambitious itinerary. He now planned to split the party into two groups, both of which would walk over Cairngorm, cross the plateau to the Curran Bothy and spend the night there. Next day they would all walk back to Speyside via the Làirig Ghrù. The children, whose ages ranged from 14 to 18, were all keen outdoor enthusiasts but with varying abilities in hill-walking and mountaineering. Beattie was accompanied by his girlfriend, 21-year-old Cathie Davidson, a final year student at Dunfermline College of Physical Education. She was also a seasoned climber for her age and would be leading a group of six children, most of whom were relatively inexperienced, while Beattie would take the stronger group and go on ahead. Eighteen-year-old Shelagh Sunderland from Staffordshire, another student teacher who had just started as a voluntary instructor at Lagganlia, had agreed to go along with Davidson.

After a delayed start Davidson's group took the chairlift and crossed

View west from Cairn Gorm in November. The Feith Buidhe lies in the left middle distance

Photo: Greg Strange

the summit of Cairn Gorm in the early afternoon. They were an hour behind Beattie's party and had three hours of daylight in which to cover the two and a half miles of undulating ground to the Curran Bothy. Unfortunately, they were walking directly into the strengthening wind, with snow showers, spindrift, and poor visibility hampering progress.

Freeman and I completed Auld Nick around mid-afternoon and set off back to Coire Cas. Apart from a brief encounter with two fellow climbers who had abandoned a route to our left we met no-one on our way up Coire Domhain and round the rim of Coire an t-Sneachda. Harris and Stuart finished The Escalator an hour before us and we found them sheltering behind buildings at the car park. It was dark and snowing heavily as we drove away with Harris walking in front of the van. This was the only way for the driver to get some perspective in the maelstrom.

Beattie's party reached the Curran Bothy before darkness. The last section from Coire Domhain to Lochan Buidhe had been very hard going as it was here that they encountered continuous deep powder snow. Davidson's group were not so lucky. Being an hour behind the others they had run into the worsening weather almost immediately on leaving Cairn Gorm. By four o'clock they had veered slightly south of the direct line to the bothy and were close to the Feith Buidhe, the burn that flows from Lochan Buidhe down to Loch Avon. They had still to follow the snow-covered stream up to the bothy, less than half a mile away, but now it was almost dark.

Davidson was very worried about the physical state of the children and considered it possible that one of them might collapse from exhaustion. There was also the risk that they might not find the bothy in such poor visibility. She decided to bivouac despite the exposed location and lack of suitable snow in which to dig a hole. They built a snow wall to

Mike Taylor contemplates the problem of entry to the Curran Bothy, buried under 12ft of snow

Photo: David Grieve

provide some shelter from the driving spindrift but this kept collapsing. They spent the night there in sleeping bags and polythene bivouac sacs. At first their morale was high and they sang songs and talked to keep their spirits up. However, they experienced considerable difficulty from the drifting snow which was always threatening to bury them.

The next day, conditions on the plateau had worsened. When the second group failed to turn up at Curran, Beattie assumed they had either turned back or sought shelter in the St Valery Refuge, which he knew Davidson had visited previously. At 9am on Sunday, Beattie's group left the bothy and headed west down the March Burn to the Làirig Ghrù. Meanwhile, Davidson's party could do very little. Cathy went round digging the children out, and then, with 15-year-old Billy Kerr, the strongest member of her party, she tried to force a route out to safety. Conditions were so bad that they only managed to cover a few yards in the deep soft snow before returning. The weakening party could do nothing but sit it out.

It was after dark before Beattie managed to contact John Paisley, the warden at Lagganlia and the official who had approved Beattie's plans for the weekend. It was only then that he discovered the awful truth that Davidson's party had not returned. Both men then made their way quickly to Glenmore Lodge and raised the alarm.

A priority in circumstances like this, where people are unaccounted for in poor weather or in darkness, is first to check the obvious escape routes and any known shelters in the area. Fred Harper was the Principal at the Lodge. He knew that little could be done in the prevailing conditions, but still decided to send out three two-man teams. Allen Fyffe was working as a temporary instructor and he and Reg Popham were to cross the plateau and descend to the Shelter Stone via Coire Domhain. Bill March and Chris Norris were similarly to head for the Shelter Stone, but also were to check the St Valery Refuge and descend by Coire Raibeirt. John Cunningham and another instructor had been asked to make a low-level sweep of Strath Nethy as far as the Saddle, then return to the Lodge. It was a wild snowy night which quickly became a personal battle for survival for the four who crossed the plateau. March and Norris failed to locate St Valery, but eventually all four made it to the Shelter Stone by 1.30am. Fyffe and Popham passed within half a mile of the beleaguered party and at one point sent up a flare which was actually spotted by some of the children.

The second night at the bivouac site took a heavy toll. By Monday morning Davidson was the only member of the party still able to move. Shelagh Sunderland and Billy Kerr were unconscious or asleep, the other five were all buried. She decided to try once more to go for help. The weather had improved somewhat, but she felt dizzy and could not stand at first. Eventually, she set off back towards Cairn Gorm. By this time a huge rescue operation was in full swing and at 9am Brian Hall, in an RAF helicopter, spotted Davidson staggering through the snow just north of the Feith Buidhe. The helicopter landed close by and as Hall reached her, she collapsed, gasping the three words: "Burn – lochain – buried."[6] He radioed the message back to Glenmore Lodge, then after a quick search of the immediate area, they took off and rushed Cathy Davidson to Raigmore Hospital in Inverness.

Although the information was not much it did give the rescue parties something to go on. At the time when Davidson was found, Cunningham, Beattie and Paisley had just arrived on the plateau having walked up the Fiacaill a' Choire Chais as part of the rescue operation. Cunningham's knowledge of the area was invaluable as he was able to lead the party quickly towards the Feith Buidhe. The four instructors who had crossed to the Shelter Stone during the night had almost reached Strath Nethy on their walk out when they heard the news on the two-way radio. March and Fyffe, using snow shoes, went up over Cairn Gorm, contoured round and arrived at the bivouac site in time to join the rescue team probing with avalanche poles. When the group was eventually uncovered only 15-year-old Raymond Leslie was still alive. Close friends, 15-year-olds Susan Byrne, Lorraine Dick and Diane Dudgeon, 16-year-old Carol Bertram, Shelagh Sunderland and Billy Kerr were all dead.

This dreadful tragedy stunned the people of Scotland. How had it been possible for school children under adult supervision to be exposed to such extreme weather, particularly when these conditions were neither unusual nor unpredictable for the high tops of the Cairngorms that November weekend? Such was the concern over the circumstances surrounding this disaster that a Public Inquiry was held at Banff over six days in February 1972. After much deliberation from Counsel and witnesses the jury gave formal verdicts of death by misadventure on all six of the youngsters. The inquiry concluded that there was no one area of serious negligence and that the accident had resulted from the cumulative effect of a number of miscalculations. It recommended better organisation for parties of children in outdoor activities in future but apportioned no blame for the deaths despite being urged by Counsel for the bereaved to find Beattie and Paisley at fault.

After intensive care in hospital both survivors recovered from hypothermia and severe frostbite. Cathie Davidson continued in outdoor education until she emigrated to Calgary in 1978. She married and has two children. She is still haunted by the painful memories. Raymond Leslie went on to become a top-class canoeist who represented Britain in this sport. A few years after the tragedy Fred Harper offered Ben Beattie a full-time instructor's post at Glenmore Lodge which he happily accepted. He was later killed on an expedition to Nanda Devi in the Himalayas in the 1980s.

The Feith Buidhe tragedy brought about a major rethink on how the mountains should be used for outdoor educational purposes, especially in winter. At the time of the incident Edinburgh Education Authority had a policy which considered outdoor pursuits a key part of the school curriculum. Following the recommendations made at the Public Inquiry certain hill locations such as the Cairngorms were designated definite no-go areas for school parties in winter. The tragedy sounded the death knell for all the plateau bothies. Consensus of 'expert' opinion favoured removal of Curran, St Valery and El Alamein bothies on the grounds that their presence would encourage inexperienced parties to extend themselves beyond their capabilities. However, a number of mountain rescue people still believed the bothies served a useful purpose as emergency shelters. The argument was heated with politicians and the media becoming involved. Just as the date for demolition came round all three shelters were given a stay of execution.

A particular irony after the Feith Buidhe disaster was that within six days of the tragedy, virtually all the snow had vanished with the onset of mild, wet weather.

At the beginning of December, Dinwoodie and Mothersele took advantage of a few frosty days to make an icy ascent of Spectrum on the Eagle's Rock. In another cold snap before Christmas, Mike Geddes and John Robinson climbed Phoenix Buttress in Garbh Choire Mòr of Braeriach. The cliffs here with a base at 3500ft were well plastered with new snow and the route gave an excellent Grade III climb. Another good route was found a week later on similarly elevated crags in Coire an Lochain of Cairn Gorm. Bob Barton and John Higham climbed Andromeda, a line slanting up right from the foot of the Milky Way to finish at the top of Central Crack Route.

New Year 1971 – 72 marked the start of a long spell of cold snowy weather which was continuous right into March. This period saw the emergence of an enthusiastic and talented group of winter climbers from the Lairig Club which included Charlie Butterworth and James Bolton. Also at this time, Nicolson started work as a temporary instructor at Glenmore Lodge. On January 2, he and March climbed the icy fault of Kiwi Gully, the obvious left-trending continuation of Kiwi Slabs that joins the top corner of The Wee Devil.

Charlie Butterworth was a third-year botany student at Aberdeen University. A striking, fair-haired lad, very much an English gentleman, he had climbed on several occasions in the Alps with a guide before coming to Scotland. From the outset there was no doubting his quest for adventure and his enthusiasm for the mountains. On one of his first trips into the Cairngorms he tried to persuade his Lairig Club companions that they could make a winter ascent of the Mitre Ridge using summer equipment by simply brushing the snow off the holds. Needless to say, the attempt did not succeed and Charlie's views on winter climbing quickly became more sophisticated. On January 4, a cold, calm day, he and Alan Frost went to the Shelter Stone Crag and made the first winter ascent of Clach Dhian Chimney. Although most of the climbing was on powder-covered rock they did find one ice pitch in the chimney itself. After the second step on the skyline they avoided the final pitch by traversing farther right onto easy ground.

During the next two weeks a succession of cold snowy days, alternating with short periods of rain, led to the formation of thick layers of snow-ice which covered even the steepest rocks on all ground above 3000ft. Dinwoodie and Stuart had seen these exceptional conditions on Lochnagar during a period of thaw and planned to attempt Pinnacle Face as soon as it became colder. After a numbing bivouac in the howff below the West Ridge, which somehow did not give them the early start anticipated, they went onto the Black Spout Pinnacle on Thursday, January 20. It was a cold clear day and they were optimistic about making the first complete winter ascent of Pinnacle Face to the plateau. After an initial set-back when Stuart discovered he could not front-point effectively because his crampons had been adjusted too short, they made good progress up to the big ledge above the summer crux. At this point,

Scarface on Lochnagar. Summer and winter lines are common to the rim of the snow-filled Amphitheatre. Thereafter, the summer route follows the broad upper buttress on the left while the winter line continues by the left fork above the Amphitheatre

Photo: Greg Strange

instead of following the flake cracks, Dinwoodie took a turfy groove on the right which led directly to a belay beneath the final steep corner before the junction with Route 1.

It was late in the afternoon when he set off up the corner. They had had a difference of opinion about going to the plateau. Stuart favoured abseiling off the Springboard, but Dinwoodie wanted to go to the top as planned, even if it meant climbing all through the night. He had reached the point where Grassick, Light and Nicol had used combined tactics. Between himself and Stuart were two nut runners. He had just hammered in a piton and, thinking he had clipped the rope into this, lent back for a rest. Suddenly, he was falling with sparks flying in the half-light as his crampons scraped down the rock. The two nuts pulled out and he struck Stuart a glancing blow as he went past. Thankfully, both Stuart and the piton belay held and Dinwoodie came to a halt some 20-25ft below his high point, shaken but not damaged. They agreed to abseil off, disappointed after putting in such a good effort.

The following weekend they were back at Gelder bothy, this time accompanied by John Tweddle. In the bothy they met a student from Dundee, Chris Roberts, and all four went to the corrie to try a direct ascent of Parallel Buttress. Dinwoodie and Tweddle commenced close to Parallel Gully B and followed a difficult zigzag course on the right hand side of the lower buttress. The climbing was time-consuming so when they reached the level of Tough-Brown Traverse they retreated, making a worrying abseil descent off an ice bollard. The other pair, with Stuart in the lead, climbed the obvious groove right of Gully A, a summer VS. They also abandoned the buttress, but continued to the plateau by Tough-Brown Traverse and had a minor epic getting back to Gelder in darkness and a blizzard. It is not certain how much of Dinwoodie's route overlapped with the original summer direct start. It was another three years before the complete direct winter ascent of Parallel Buttress was made by Rob Archbold and myself in February 1975, using the Brooker start. This soon became the normal way to climb the buttress in winter.

February saw further heavy traffic in the Lochnagar corrie. On Saturday 12, overhead conditions were good with a clear blue sky. It was, however, very breezy with a great deal of spindrift affecting areas of the cliff in the lee of the south-westerly wind. Together with a number of other local climbers, Stuart and I had already attempted a winter ascent of Scarface, the steep buttress forming the right wall of Raeburn's Gully. This time we were determined not to be seen-off by a few minor powder avalanches. The lower half of the climb is often draped in ice as it receives all the drainage which funnels down from an upper basin known as the Amphitheatre. On this particular day the ice was very sugary and there was lots of fresh snow. Huge cornices encircled the back wall of the Amphitheatre.

Davie took the first pitch up an icy chimney, starting above the bend in Raeburn's Gully. Then it was my turn to follow a long shallow groove, heading for a steep drool of ice emanating from the Amphitheatre. Since the groove was directly in the line of teeming spindrift, upward movement was severely hampered, along with my resolve to front-point. During lulls in the bombardment I resorted to step cutting. Just below the steepest ice I managed to traverse right into an easier parallel line and Davie led up into the Amphitheatre. We then followed its left branch via a steep ice pitch and gained the plateau by the last section of the upper rib, thus avoiding the worst of the cornice.

In early March, Stuart was disabled during a fall on Creag Meagaidh after completing a new route, Nordwander, on the Pinnacle Buttress. He spent a long time in rehabilitation and although confined to a wheelchair he maintains a remarkably cheerful outlook on life. He remembers nothing about the accident, accepting that he must have tripped while walking away from the top of the climb. He says he has no regrets and despite the passage of time he continues to keep in touch with the climbing scene.

While Stuart and I were on Scarface, Dinwoodie and Keir made the first winter ascent of Giant's Head Chimney Direct. A little way up the lower chimney a steep ice-ramp ran up the left wall passing the overhangs which bar access to the direct continuation. Dinwoodie led this thin, sustained pitch cutting steps all the way. The crack above the overhangs had formed an icy groove and this led to a snow bowl. Above this they climbed an awkward wall covered in unstable snow onto the Giant's Head Arete. This they followed to the top of Shadow Buttress A. Subsequent ascents of the Direct have followed the summer line throughout – few, if any, have followed Dinwoodie's ramp.

Ian Nicolson with 'Terror'

Photo: Ian Nicolson Collection

During this same weekend in February, Bill March made two winter ascents of Aladdin Buttress in Coire an t-Sneachda. On the Saturday, with Dr Noel Dilley, he climbed the large left-facing corner in the centre of the buttress, naming it Doctor's Choice. Below the upper corner, a prominent cave with capping overhangs blocks a direct ascent. He bypassed the overhangs by moving out left then returned right at a higher level. The next day he returned with B. Manson and climbed the original MMC route up the left edge of the buttress. As an indication of just how substantial the snow build-up was at the time, March thought both these climbs only Grade III. Later ascents with less snow found them to be Grade IV and technically difficult in thin conditions.

It was around this time that March and Nicolson made the coveted second winter ascent of Sticil Face on the Shelter Stone Crag. The route was in excellent condition enabling them to front-point directly up all the ice to the High Ledge, finding nothing unduly hard. They also climbed the top pitch without combined tactics. March was by now a master at front-pointing, and Nicolson was quickly getting the hang of it. During the previous summer Nicolson had climbed the North Face of the Eiger with Knowles, Spence and Fyffe. Prior to that he had only done three winter routes, all by step-cutting, although one of these was an early ascent of Raven's Gully. He says he learned to front-point steep ice by simply watching his hero John Cunningham. After that he soon found that with the right equipment the new technique felt the natural way to progress on ice. Within a year, his confidence had reached such a level that in one memorable morning during March 1973 he soloed both Point Five and Zero Gullies in the amazing combined time of three hours.

Unlike March and Nicolson, who worked and lived in the hotbed of the ice revolution in Scotland, the students in the Lairig Club were rather more isolated from these goings-on. James Bolton was perhaps an

James Bolton, 1973

Photo: Mungo Ross

exception to this in that he had recently arrived in Aberdeen from Bangor University to continue his studies in Forestry and Wood Physics. While at Bangor he became part of the North Wales climbing scene and in 1970 gained his first experience of winter mountaineering on trips to Glen Coe at New Year and Ben Nevis at Easter. Similar visits were made in 1971 which culminated in an ascent of Point Five Gully with John Tyler.

Bolton recalls: "It was at the CIC hut that I first met Mike Geddes who had Chouinard hammers, and was beginning to show what could be done with front-pointing. So after the end of the season I took my sawn-off wooden handled Stubai ice axe to John Brailsford, a blacksmith by training, and a member of the North Wales climbing fraternity. For a modest fee he put a satisfactory droop into the pick. Later, he drooped the pick of an early Snowdon Mouldings ice hammer for me also. Real class this – it had a fibreglass handle. I hate to think what retempering must have done to the steel-polyester bond. However, I used these implements for all my Scottish climbing."

Bolton teamed up with another new Sassenach research student, Paul Arnold, who, despite having limited previous winter climbing experience, was keen to climb ice. In late January they did West Gully Direct on Bolton's first visit to Lochnagar. "I think that this was the first time I used front-pointing in earnest, and the conditions were perfect for it. I steamed over the hardest part of the climb, and was surprised when it was all over bar some stomping. Paul did remarkably well and we resolved to build up to some harder stuff."

During the next two months Bolton made more trips to Lochnagar. On two occasions he climbed with Butterworth, first on an ascent of Polyphemus Gully when they finished by the steep tower which tops the upper left wall, then, during the first weekend in March, the first winter ascent of a line approximating to Symmers's Original Route on Shadow Buttress B.

Notwithstanding these first ascents, Bolton's best climb on Lochnagar was Parallel Gully B on which he and Arnold shared the lead. He recalled thinking at the time "that the limits to front-pointing were, first, nerves; and second, the moment when your calf and shoulder muscles burst or seized up through exhaustion. (I went on to learn a new dimension to these later in the Alps.) In the Scottish environment, and particularly on Parallel B, there was the added interest of having to hang around on very little, usually in a position not of your choice, while another consignment of spindrift was poured over you."

Shortly after this, Bolton met Bill Brooker at a Lairig Club dinner recalling he [Bolton] was "probably unbearably cocky and feeling unstoppable," and asked Brooker what to do after Parallel Gully B. The Labyrinth area on Creag an Dubh-loch was mentioned so that was where he and Arnold headed the very next weekend. On the Friday night run to Allt-na-giubhsaich in Arnold's van they were accompanied by fellow Lairig Club members, Malcolm Nicolson and Nigel Rayner.

In the morning Nicolson recalls: "James and Paul departed for Creag an Dubh-loch whereas Nige and I went to Lochnagar. James had given us strict orders that we were to be back at the hut by five o'clock since he had to return to Aberdeen that evening for choir practice – Bach, I

recall, perhaps the St Matthew Passion, James was proud of his interest in classical music." Of course, the climb to which Brooker had alluded was the superb 1000ft central couloir of Labyrinth Direct, attempted by Patey and Will in 1955. There was a tremendous build-up of snow and ice on the cliffs that weekend although much of the snow was only partially consolidated. They were fortunate to get a glimpse of the cliff on the approach before the cloud rolled in – but less fortunate when one of them jumped for a rock while crossing the outflow from the loch and went in up to his waist.

They climbed directly up the lower gully passing the Hanging Garden to its right before entering the much steeper upper continuation.

Bolton said: "I recall a long groove, which seemed comparable to Parallel Gully B, ending in a spindrift-filled depression under a bit of an overhang. There was clearly harder to come, and the belay in the depression was suspect. Failing to find anywhere to lodge ironware, I think I used a Deadman in the back of the groove, but had the impression that it would simply pull out everything in front of it, given provocation. I told Paul not to fall off and he heeded this instruction, but muttered about feeling off colour when he arrived. To circumvent

Creag an Dubh-loch in March 1972 – the day after the ascent of Labyrinth Direct

Photo: Greg Strange

The old way! John Bower cutting steps up the Corridor on Creagan a' Choire Etchachan in March 1967

Photo: Greg Strange

the overhang blocking the groove, the only choice was to break left over a gently leaning wall. Fortunately, the ice seemed quite good. After a couple of moves it became clear that there was only one option – to go for it – hoping that the ice would continue. If it had run out I don't think I could have retreated down the leaning wall and I would quickly have run out of strength."

This was the crux and Bolton thought it the hardest 30ft of ice climbing he had ever done. The absence of any respite in which to insert protection, and Arnold's poor stance and belay, had made living very dangerous!

Bolton continues: "After the crux the best I could do for a belay was again poor, but at least at an easier angle, and vertically above the centre of the crux. I was able to cut a bucket step to stand on, but was not confident that the belay would stand testing. So I told Paul he was definitely not to fall off. From what I understand, Paul eyed up the crux and felt unable to give such a guarantee. Two poor belays and an unacceptable crux between them: stalemate. I decided that the belay would probably take the modest continuous load if Paul prusiked up one rope attached to it, provided that I took most of his weight on the other rope, without placing any load on the belay myself.

"Unfortunately, Paul did not know about prusik knots, so I had to explain. These arrangements took some time. Communications were difficult, as usual, because of the distance, the overhang and spindrift, the weather etc. Friends, including Butterworth, loitering on the summit, began to be concerned at the length of bellowed debate echoing indecipherably around the mist enshrouded corrie, and offered to lower a rope. I was doubtful if they would have found us. I was probably not of a mind to accept help at this stage anyway. Eventually, after a mixture of prusiking and free style, Paul hove into sight. He joined me at the belay feeling ill and wanting an end to this nonsense.

The future looked uncertain in the cloud, but though parts of the way upwards were steep, and ice of uncertain quality, it was good enough to allow us to emerge at the top with sighs of relief."

The climb had taken 10 hours and not surprisingly they were too late for James's choir practice.

Bolton's lead of this long-standing problem was a powerful demonstration of the new technique and his ability to use it. He would be the first to admit that at the time he was by no means an exceptional rock climber. Nevertheless, he had good upper body strength, was fit and very single-minded about his mountaineering. As Nicolson says: "James's great asset was his clear understanding of the potential of the new drooped-pick technology, coupled with an awesome boldness." It was seven years before Labyrinth Direct was climbed again, this time by John Anderson and Andy Nisbet who confirmed that it was one of the hardest gully climbs in the country. It still is! Grade VII.

The experience on Labyrinth Direct had a lasting effect on Arnold, and he and Bolton went their separate ways not long after. Although he never again wanted to find himself in such a life-threatening situation he nevertheless agreed to go out with Butterworth the very next weekend. They went back to Lochnagar and climbed Penumbra, an interesting line on the Douglas-Gibson face of Shadow Buttress B. Starting above the narrows in Douglas-Gibson Gully, they followed the obvious slabby corner trending left to reach the top of Buttress B. The build up of snow was still very good and they were up in just two hours on a climb which is now considered to be Grade V. Penumbra was the last of the new routes on Lochnagar that winter, its ascent coinciding with the start of a prolonged thaw. During the season the mountain had seen considerable activity including the second winter ascents of Shallow Gully, Backdoor Route, Twin Chimneys Route and Gargoyle Direct.

As with most student-based groups, the number of active climbers in the Lairig Club has always varied from year to year. In 1972, just as it was re-establishing itself as a climbing force to be reckoned with, several of its major players moved on. Charlie Butterworth had been advised to curtail his climbing activities following the onset of arthritis in one of his knees. Although the long-term prognosis was quite good he was recommended to avoid strain or over-use of the joint. As a compromise, after leaving Aberdeen, he concentrated on his second passion of sailing, and then, latterly on pot-holing. On one of his sailing trips with Arnold they were caught in a ferocious storm in the Pentland Firth and blown many miles off course out into the Atlantic. With a broken mast and all hope lost, they were miraculously saved by the outstanding seamanship of a Norwegian sea-captain who happened upon them floundering in mountainous seas and succeeded in taking them on board his ship. Sadly, Charlie met an untimely death in a caving accident at Appin in August 1988. He was prusiking back up to the entrance of the Cave of Skulls with Alan Frost when he was overcome by cold and the force of the water. Weakened by a recent virus he could not find the strength to go on and he died hanging on the rope.

James Bolton returned to Bangor University to continue his research work. He made a number of successful trips to the Alps, on one of which, with Dave Robinson in January 1975, he made the first British winter ascent of the North Face of The Droites.

The technique of front-pointing was now the norm. Soon there would be a new generation of climbers who had never used a single axe to hew a line of holds on steep snow or ice. Only old-timers would occasionally resort to step-cutting out of habit, especially when pressed, to relieve their aching calf muscles.

Today, winter climbers will find it difficult to understand why such a seemingly simple idea as employing a second axe and curving the picks should have taken so long to conceive. However, the introduction of front-pointing to replace step-cutting not only required a change in equipment and technique, it also needed a change in ethics – the acceptance of continuous direct aid from the axes. Of course, this ethical question seems irrelevant now when compared to the huge advantage of more rapid progress coupled with less energy requirement.

1. Kohoutek's Komik (Etchachan Club) January 1974, p3.

2. *Mountain* magazine No. 14, p28.

3. SMCJ Vol. 29, No. 162, p390.

4. SMCJ Vol. 29, No. 162, p366.

5. SMCJ Vol. 29, No. 162, p367.

6. *Mountain* magazine No. 20, p30.

10: Easy Riding (1972 – 1979)

DURING THE MID-1970s rock climbing in the Cairngorms had a mellow feel to it. Although climbs were being made, the number of people involved was still not great. In keeping with the times the atmosphere seemed rather laid-back and very little came along to threaten the tranquillity, at least not for a while. The great cliffs of Creag an Dubh-loch and the Shelter Stone Crag gradually became more popular as climbers from all parts came to savour the quality of the big routes. The bothies, howffs and dosses were still well used and there was a resurgence in the use of bicycles to ease the lengthy approaches up estate roads. Bicycles had long been favoured by walkers and climbers, especially on Deeside. In the 1950s and 1960s when most regular visitors came by bus, bicycles were kept in Braemar for use at the weekend. The 1970s saw a noticeable change from reliance on public transport (and its limiting impact on climbing time on Sundays) to increased car or van ownership – mostly second-hand bangers. A couple of bicycles then became part of the kit required to be stowed in, or on, the vehicle. Cycling provides an added dimension to the mountain experience, and although pedalling uphill carrying a heavy rucksack may seem masochistic, the pain is soon forgotten when free-wheeling back down at the end of the day.

There was a steady flow of new route activity on the crags and a gradual reduction in the amount of artificial aid being used on existing climbs. In the summer of 1972, Brian Lawrie found good climbs on two of the more traditional crags. In Coire Sputan Dearg he and Ron Kerr climbed Ghost Crack, the isolated fissure between Hanging Dyke and Ardath Chimney. Later, on a visit to Lochnagar with Mike Freeman, he put up Psyche, the fourth route on the Tough-Brown Face. Its main feature was a magnificent crack lying midway between the upper corner of Crypt and the right edge of Parallel Gully B.

There were two notable second ascents on the Shelter Stone Crag in 1972. March and Des Marshall repeated Snipers and Shields climbed The Pin. The latter route had a further ascent shortly afterwards by Mike Kosterlitz and Ben Campbell-Kelly, who dispensed with the original aid. Although these climbs were important, their impact was certainly eclipsed by the achievement of Jeff Connor, an instructor at Glenmore Lodge who made a solo ascent of The Needle. I remember climbing the route myself that year and, along with others, being dumbfounded by the boldness of this escapade.

Creag an Dubh-loch saw most of the activity this year, helped by a number of dry spells and as fine an Indian summer as anyone in Scotland could remember. On July 1, Bower and Lang started a route to the right of Gulliver. It had been their intention to climb the full height of the cliff, crossing the Caterpillar, and continuing directly to merge with the top of False Gully. They started close to Gulliver and found that the natural line led them away rightward in a series of traverses to reach the Caterpillar well right of the Red Wall. The next day, they attempted to push the line higher but were forced to give up because of the difficulties. Bower-Lang Route. HVS 5a.

Brian Lawrie climbing Ghost Crack, Coire Sputan Dearg, in 1972

Photo: Ron Kerr

Bower was back on July 18, when he made the second ascent of Cougar with Dave Riley. This was Bower's third attempt, the first two being unsuccessful due to cold or wet conditions. This time it was the heat that threatened to defeat them, and to combat this they took the unusual precaution, for Scotland, of hauling a large water bottle. With Bower leading all the pitches they followed the exact line taken by Rennie and Williams making no significant aid reductions and finding the top crack to be the crux. Riley, an experienced climber from Liverpool, said at the time that he saw no reason why the whole climb could not be made completely free, except for perhaps the final crack.

It was in the vicinity of Cougar that Martin Boysen and Mike Kosterlitz made a spirited attempt at a new route on this intimidating part of the cliff. They were on a week's holiday in Scotland and had just completed a new climb, Gog, on Ben Loyal. With a few days left they came to stay with Kosterlitz's parents in Aberdeen and went for a look at Creag an Dubh-loch. According to Boysen: "I had witnessed, with Brian Robertson, the ascent of Giant – unfortunately, a pegging travesty done in damp October conditions. There seemed to be so much rock on either side I was certain it was worth looking at."

Below the Cougar slab, another, narrower slab lies tucked under a huge overlap which rises diagonally leftwards across the soaring crack-line to reach the crest of the Giant arete. By starting 20ft left of Cougar they could see a possible route curving up to reach the narrow slab. If they could traverse the slab they would then have to find a way to continue up below the overlap. They ascended a steep groove and continued by very thin climbing to reach a piton belay at the start of the slab 120ft up. Crossing the slab turned out to be relatively straightforward and there, at the end, was a small ledge in the middle of nowhere where they were fortunate to find good belays.

"While I was perched on a tiny stance Mike set off up, climbing till the crack system closed. He put a Rurp in as his last protection and attempted to get to the next system. Suddenly, a thunderstorm rolled in, it began to crash, then it rained and our concern now was would we be able to get off the crag? We had no idea if the ropes would reach the bottom as we abseiled into space. Fortunately, they did – we arrived safely and never returned."

Over the summer, Dinwoodie had been working his way through some of the existing climbs on Creag an Dubh-loch, in the process of which he made second ascents of Dubh Loch Monster (with Mothersele) and Predator (with Lang), the latter without any aid. At the end of September, Scotland was enjoying unusually dry weather for the time of year and Dinwoodie took the opportunity to have a go at a line of his own. On a mid-week visit to the Central Slabs during the first week in October, he and Lawrie made a very direct climb through the open mouth formation in the main overlap. Midway between the starts of Black Mamba and the Blue Max, a brown three-stepped corner system trends up right to form part of the long second pitch of Mamba. Dinwoodie planned to climb twin cracks in the slab right of the first corner, then go up leftwards to join the Blue Max directly below the open mouth. He then hoped to climb through the mouth and continue as directly as possible to the top.

Douglas Dinwoodie climbing the first pitch of The Pin in 1975

Photo: Greg Strange

The opening left-hand crack gave excellent climbing up into the second step of the corner. A swing left from here gained the edge, then by moving left again Dinwoodie was able to move up to a belay in the shallow continuation of the bottom corner. Lawrie then took them on up across Blue Max to below the open mouth, the most recessed part of which is formed by a vertical groove with an impending left wall. Dinwoodie was forced to use two nuts and a piton to climb cracks in this left wall before establishing himself on the slab above. Then 20ft higher he found a poor stance below another overlap. Lawrie followed this hard pitch leaving the piton in situ, and then surmounted the next bulge on the left. Much easier climbing followed to a junction with the Blue Max 150ft below the terrace.

The most prominent feature on the right flank of the upper tier is a huge pink diedre, which is, unfortunately, rarely dry. To its left is a shallower corner located directly above the start to the V-groove on the Blue Max. Dinwoodie led this long sustained corner to a sloping ledge close to the pink diedre. Here he continued up an inviting layback crack, but this proved to be a cul-de-sac and he was forced to retreat back to the ledge using a piton. At this stage time was at a premium and reaching the plateau by the easiest line had become the priority. Thirty feet up to the left of the ledge he found a belay then by a 20ft traverse they joined the Blue Max below the quartz corner and finished up this. They named their route Dragon Slayer, an impressive debut on the cliff for Dinwoodie. Eleven years passed before the main pitch was repeated by Brian Davison who managed to free the mouth section by climbing the groove then traversing out across the left wall – E4 6b.

The good conditions held through to the weekend when I accompanied Dougie back to the Dubh Loch. He was still riding high after his climb on the slabs with Lawrie, and, wishing to maintain the momentum, we decided to attempt the big corner between Cougar and Predator.

From the belay at the top of the first pitch of Cougar, Dougie climbed the obvious overhanging crack on the right using two pitons for aid. This took him directly into the big slabby corner which he climbed quickly to a grass ledge level with the Cougar Slab. While seconding this pitch I was already thinking about what lay ahead. I found the situation intimidating, yet I wanted to do my bit and attempt to lead through. When I reached the belay and looked up at the continuation of the corner Dougie must have read my mind. He took the gear and I settled down for a long stint of belaying.

Not far above, the corner became more vegetated and far less accommodating. Rather than resort to aid he retreated and took to the clean slabs on the right. A diagonal line led up right over bulges to reach the intermittent fault-line running midway between the corner and Predator. A little way up this he reached a blaeberry ledge on the left and took a belay. He had only run out half the rope, but explained that the next bit looked delicate and he was worried about rope drag.

When I reached the belay I could see exactly what the problem was. A tiny narrowing ledge led horizontally back left towards the edge of the big corner. There looked to be no handholds or protection for 30ft. He appeared decidedly worried as he tiptoed away from me across this exposed traverse, getting farther and farther from the belay. Before reaching the edge he found a shallow groove which he climbed to capping bulges where the diminishing options on the slab finally brought him back into the line of the main corner. He drove in a good piton under an overlap for a runner then moved left close to the edge. At chest height, a narrow rising slab crossed the top of the corner to a grassy bay. A blind crack at the back of the slab took the first few millimetres of a knifeblade piton. With this psychological protection, Dougie stepped onto the slab and padded carefully up to the recess.

Following this delicate pitch I found it to be one of the best passages of climbing I had ever done on Creag an Dubh-loch – the final uncertain step across the void being particularly memorable. Although we now appeared to be high on the face there were still overhangs and bulging slabs between us and easy ground. The light was fading as Dougie went up to a short overhanging crack. He had little time to give this a try before we decided to retreat with two long abseils – the last, from beside Rennie's old ring piton on the Cougar slab, was in darkness.

Next morning, the cloud was well down below the top of Central Gully Wall. Although it had been drizzling through the night a strong wind was blowing down the gully and drying off the moisture. We re-ascended all the previous day's climbing with Dougie linking the two pitches on the slabs into one full 140ft run-out. He did well to cross the traverse in that wind with the ropes billowing out in a great loop. As if fated, when he eventually reached the overhanging crack it began to rain. The rock was a little vegetated and required gardening, but time was not on our side. He used two pitons and a nut to reach smooth slabs then hurried up these, going left to a good platform and a belay, with no more difficult climbing to the top. Seconding this diagonal pitch in the rain was exciting. At one point, while pulling up on the wet rope with tired arms, I recall taking a momentary rest by biting on to the rope, like a human Jumar clamp!

Later that evening, in the dark, we came across a spooky scene at Glas Allt Shiel. Peering into the main front room we could see a woman setting a large table by the light of many flickering candles. It was this scene and the time of year that suggested the name of Vampire for our new climb. Farther down Loch Muick we had to make way for a small convoy of Land-Rovers. We had a brief conversation with Prince Charles who was heading for the Royal Lodge.

On an early repeat of Vampire, Geoff Cohen discovered that by using rope tension he could layback farther right above the first pitch of Cougar and avoid the overhanging crack. This move and the top crack were freed by Lawrie and Andy Nisbet in July 1977. Later, that same month, Lawrie returned to lead the main corner direct with a bit of aid. When this direct pitch is climbed free it is a grade harder than the original – E3 5c.

In early December, Dinwoodie and I were back at the Dubh Loch. Most of the main cliff had a general cover of snow, but there was little in the way of ice, except, on the line of Hanging Garden Route. From the top of the steep snow slope forming the floor of the Garden, we followed the obvious icy gully up to a point where the summer route goes right. Finding insufficient ice here to make the exit, Dougie had to move onto the undercut wall above which was draped in green ice.

Rob Archbold following the thin slab above the main corner on Vampire during the 1973 attempt at a new girdle traverse of Central Gully Wall (The Prowl)

Photo: Greg Strange

John Cunningham,
Devil's Delight,
February 1973

Photo: Bill March. Courtesy
of the Ernest Press and Jeff
Connor's 'Creagh Dhu
Climber'

He cut steps steeply up right then back left to a poor belay on a rock pedestal at the foot of a steep triangular buttress. When I followed this tricky pitch I began to appreciate why Simpson and Bower had been so enthusiastic about the situations and atmosphere in this little hanging corrie. Dougie lowered me a short distance from the pedestal to rejoin the summer line which I climbed by the stepped fault to a good belay 60ft below the plateau. Continuing directly looked desperate as there was already a huge cornice, so we traversed right and finished up the last section of Labyrinth Route where the cornice was broken. We had been impressed by the quality and seriousness of this excellent ice route.

Despite a promising start, this winter of 1972 – 73 was disappointing. Conditions were often very lean although there were long spells of frosty weather. During one good weekend in February, Cunningham, March and fellow Lodge instructor, Roger O'Donovan, found the ice on Hell's Lum Crag to be in near-perfect condition. So confident were they that these conditions and the weather would hold, they opted to spend a night under the Shelter Stone. This decision paid off, for on consecutive days they succeeded in climbing Devil's Delight, the major unclimbed winter line of the crag, and the recently climbed summer line of Salamander. Snatching Devil's Delight was a major coup as several other climbers had been eyeing the line in previous years. Its main feature is an impressive cascade of ice emanating from below the Haven and spilling down the rocks to the right of Hellfire Corner. Above the Haven, sustained work up narrow ice runnels in the grooves and corners of the summer line provide the most technical part of the climb. Grade V.

Salamander was another excellent ice climb going straight up the middle of the ice sheet left of Hellfire Corner. Grade IV.

Frosty weather was the order of the day on March 3, when an Etchachan Club party climbed Sandy Crack, the right-hand of the three fault-lines right of Hourglass Buttress in Coire na Cìche of Beinn a'Bhùird. In the team were Norman Keir, Rob Archbold and Craig Anderson. Archbold had recently taken up a post as lecturer of mathematics at Aberdeen University. He started climbing while at Cambridge University and was a member of the CUMC. On his first climbing visit to the Cairngorms, from Cambridge at New Year 1969, he had shared a Spartan night in the Hutchison Hut with a group of climbers from Aberdeen. It was only after many years that he revealed to Keir and myself that he had been one of the bodies clad in balaclavas lying incognito in sleeping bags on the frozen floor of the hut that night. Keir and I had both been there, arriving late with our companions from a climb and leaving early before the Cambridge men had risen.

Sandy Crack is a steep chimney of loose gravelly rock and vegetation – ideal mixed winter terrain. It gave a difficult route with two points of aid – Grade V.

Despite the less than average snowfall during the winter of 1972 – 73, good rock climbing conditions did not occur any earlier than normal. In mid-May, Freeman and I went to Creag an Dubh-loch on the off-chance that the cliff might have begun to dry. Two years' previously, on an attempt to repeat the Blue Max, Dave Stuart and I had climbed straight up the crack system above Brian Robertson's etrier belay before escaping off right. A direct ascent of this crack system between Blue Max and Black Mamba was an obvious challenge. We started by climbing the first pitch of Dragon Slayer to a belay on the rib of the brown corner. A bulge, then a long easy-angled fist crack took us straight up through a constricted groove to join the Blue Max. From here to the terrace was familiar ground except for a short pitch below the terrace which turned out to be as hard as anything as it was running with water.

Unfortunately, the upper tier was also badly water-streaked, so we sloped off on to Central Gully Buttress. Later that summer I did climb the whole of the Blue Max with John Ingram. Above the terrace he led a little corner right of the prominent crescent-shaped groove to join Blue Max coming in from the right. This provided the final link in a series of excellent pitches which we named Cyclops (HVS 5a), partly in keeping with the nomenclature of the earlier routes hereabouts, but also because Robertson must have been half blind to have missed the easier direct line. The crescent-shaped groove on the upper tier was climbed a few years later and this became the normal way to go.

It was Mike Rennie who first contemplated a girdle traverse across the steep lower part of Central Gully Wall. His idea was to follow the diagonal overlap attempted by Boysen and Kosterlitz which leads out onto the Giant arete. In the summer of 1973 this still did not look like a free-climbing option, but a rising traverse on the more gentle slabs at a higher level did appear feasible. After a night in Glas Allt Shiel at the beginning of the 'sunrise weekend', Dinwoodie, Archbold and I made a start on a new girdle. Our aim was to cross Central Gully Wall at a lower level than Catwalk, commencing at Caterpillar Crack and finishing up Vertigo Wall. With Dinwoodie in the lead the first day went well and we reached the line of Mousetrap before abseiling from above its crux.

On the Sunday we returned up Mousetrap then continued through the red walls on Predator to the block-strewn ledge. After a false cast going immediately left, we stayed with Predator until above its second overlap, where unlikely moves left gave access to the start of the toe-traverse on Vampire. Familiarity did not lessen the excitement of the next passage as the final moves across the top of the main corner of Vampire were wet. We were now about to embark on unknown territory. Dougie set off across a large slab with a big roof above. Somewhere out there we would cross the line of Cougar below its final hard pitch. We were so absorbed by the brilliant climbing that we hardly noticed the mist which had descended. At the far end of the slab Dougie hand-traversed round a block and stepped down to a lower slab system. By the time he had climbed up this and we had all reached his belay a steady drizzle had set in. The rock quickly became unclimbable.

We estimated that we were 40ft right of the Giant arete, directly above the steepest section of Central Gully Wall. After a long discussion it was decided that I should make a series of diagonal abseils, fixing runners as I went, in an attempt to reach the Cougar slab. We knew from previous experience that our 150ft ropes would get us to the bottom in one abseil from its right-hand end. I slithered a few feet to the lip of the abyss and peered down a steep corner. There was a tiny ledge almost directly below and that was my first target. The great problem with trying

Dinwoodie heading out across Cougar on the line of The Prowl, July 1973

Photo: Greg Strange

to go diagonally was the complete lack of friction on the greasy rock. From the ledge I eventually managed a pendulum to gain a split flake out on the right. From there things went more easily and I soon found one of Rennie's old pitons and knew I was on Cougar. Lower down, I reached a point when farther rightward progress became impracticable, and there 30ft below was the Cougar slab. By the time the others had joined me, it had become obvious that we were far from out of trouble. The ropes hanging over the edge passed well out beyond the Cougar slab and disappeared into the mist. Our contact in the gully could see the ends 50ft up; but he was pessimistic about our finding any ledges or cracks on the way down. By now we were soaked to the skin and the weather showed no sign of improving. We considered tying the three ropes together. Despite the presence of a mathematician, we convinced ourselves that this was a good idea and that we would be able to retrieve all three ropes.

We only had one screwgate karabiner between us large enough to allow the knots to pass. Dougie went first and got down without a hitch. I pulled up the karabiner and set off, relieved to be on the move once more. Unfortunately, the rope jammed at the second knot, 60ft from the gully bed, and I got myself into a right fankle trying, unsuccessfully, to free it, then fiddling with prusik slings. It is hard to imagine how I got myself into such a state when you consider how slick modern climbers are when abseiling. Passing a knot on the abseil rope is a simple operation if you know how! After half an hour of deliberation, which included hauling a pocket knife up on the end of the rope to cut through a prusik loop, I made it to the bottom intact. Rob, who had been waiting apprehensively in the mist all this time, now had to abseil over both knots as well as a fixed prusik loop. Below the Cougar slab he spotted the two pitons left by Boysen and Kosterlitz and succeeded in gaining their small belay ledge. He was then able to untie my prusik loop, pull sufficient rope through to leave the lower knot above him, and then continue his descent unhindered.

After all this excitement, during which Dougie likened my antics to those of Toni Kurtz, the young Bavarian climber who died in 1936, hanging from his rope on the North Face of the Eiger, we optimistically hauled the long end of the rope only to retrieve one of our three 9mm ropes. Despite a valiant attempt by Rob and John Mothersele the following weekend, when they prusiked up to the Boysen ledge, the ropes remained hanging on the cliff until the winter gales shredded them to oblivion.

The open corner down which we had started our first abseil was part of the upper section of the great crack-line on the wall to the right of the Giant. This was one of the most outstanding unclimbed features in the country – an awe-inspiring line which very few people had seriously contemplated. One of those who had was the Creagh Dhu climber, Con Higgins, who made what is believed to be the first attempt during this summer of 1973. It can be seen that the first major problem occurs where the crack cuts through a roof 70ft above the gully. After starting in the line of the crack, Higgins crossed to the right on a ledge then continued straight up a parallel groove until a left traverse across a slab regained the crack. A little higher he came to the roof where the attempt was abandoned. He retreated leaving a tell-tale piton. A year later, when

*Les Brown leading
the first pitch
of Falkenhorst,
August 1973*

Photo: Greg Strange

recalling this incident in typical 'Dhu' style, he made light of the climbing and suggested that the roof should go with a couple of pitons!

Broad Terrace Wall is another intimidating, yet fascinating place, on Creag an Dubh-loch. The previous summer I had been with Dinwoodie when he had retreated from near the top of the crux pitch on Culloden. Before that, Dave Stuart and I had investigated a crack system halfway between Culloden and the right edge, but as yet the wall had seen us off on all occasions. A week of dry weather in mid-August prompted a phone call to Doug Lang, whom I knew was also interested in this part of the cliff. By coincidence he had already arranged to go there that very weekend with the Lakeland climber, Les Brown.

Although I had never met Brown I knew of him by reputation, not only as an accomplished climber, but also as someone who went to considerable lengths to keep his new route activities under shrouds.

While working on Nazgul, his well-known climb on Scafell, he kept the opposition off the scent by claiming to be exploring a mythical Far East Buzzard Crag! My concern about interfering with their plans was immediately dispelled after a reassuring handshake outside the doss. I sensed a kindred spirit in this very tall man.

At the highest point of Broad Terrace an easy left-trending ramp provides an obvious place to start a climb on this section of the wall. After 30ft, a short overhanging groove proves troublesome, and it was here that Stuart and I had turned back in 1971. Les led this pitch using a sling hung on a rock spike to overcome the groove. He then continued, partly in a parallel fault on the right, until a traverse left brought him to a good ledge with almost all the rope run out. Up and left from the ledge a complex groove system ran all the way to the top of the cliff, but the rock looked very compact. Directly ahead we could see an overhung recess, beyond which a crack appeared to continue left to join the big groove system. The object of my lead was to reach that recess some 50ft above the belay. There was an inviting thin crack in a pink wall slightly to the right of our stance. I climbed this using a nut and piton for aid. It was then necessary to move up right to a small ledge on the crest, but to achieve this I had to stand on a loose block. Always the coward, I did this while holding onto a piton runner. Shortly after this, I was belayed in the recess, a niche formed by a huge detached flake. At this point we abseiled off.

In the morning, Les tried to reach the crack above the big flake. I was relieved when, after a half-hearted attempt, he agreed to try elsewhere as I was wedged below the massive lump of granite. By descending slightly, he climbed over a bulge on the right using another sling and nut. This took us quite unexpectedly onto more amenable rock close to the right edge of the steepest part of the wall where several finishing options were available. We followed the easiest line up short wet walls on the right then a blocky fault led to the top. Les had just finished reading *The Rise and Fall of the Third Reich* and proposed the name Falkenhorst, the German word for a falcon's eyrie, and the name of Hitler's head man in Norway.

The climb received a second ascent in 1977 by Willie Todd and Adge Last who dispensed with all the aid. Todd took a fall in the process of removing the loose block on pitch two. E1 5b. Brown returned two years later with Paul Nunn and climbed The Sting, the obvious pink crack system right of Falkenhorst. HVS 5a.

It was in 1973 that Bob Scott retired to Allanaquoich where he lived with his daughter, Eileen. Although Scott's bothy at Luibeg Cottage remained open, it was never the same after Bob left. No more banter. No more dry wit. Within a year the cottage was re-occupied by a new keeper, Willy Forbes, a taxidermist from Dundee. To the hill folk who used the bothy he appeared rather dour, not having the same rapport with them that Bob had. He saw the bothy and its users as an inconvenience, a tradition he could well do without.

Although the snow of winter 1973 – 74 took a while to become established, much of February and March provided excellent conditions, with a big build-up on the higher cliffs. Particularly memorable was the glorious way in which winter melted into spring, accompanied by almost continuous anticyclonic weather throughout the Highlands. For much of April there was sunshine by day and frost at night, and for a while it was possible to climb on good ice in the morning and on warm dry rock in the afternoon.

Winter exploration in the Cairngorms was led by Norman Keir who started his campaign in December by making the second ascent of The Stack with Mothersele. Keir was the first North-east climber to convert to Terrordactyls, and he put these to good use by climbing directly up a short icefall which drops into the Left Hand Branch, left of the normal start. They bypassed the bollard move near the top by a fault to its right.

During the first weekend in February Keir was back on Lochnagar, this time with Freeman. Conditions were now very wintry with large accumulations of partially consolidated snow, but very little ice. Under the circumstances their choice of the White Spout, a short climb on the right wall of The Stack, seems rather odd. Normally, this is a steep scoop draped with icefalls, but on this occasion they found only poorly-protected high-angled snow. The next day they made a better choice and climbed a good route on the face of Central Buttress to the left of Shallow Gully. At the time they thought it to be Patey's Direct Start but later discovered they had found an independent groove and ramp system to its right. Keir was a strong socialist and active member of the Workers Revolutionary Party at the time. Not surprisingly, his name, Centrist, had a political slant to it.

On the day that the White Spout was climbed Bob Smith and I made the second winter ascent of Route 1 on the Black Spout Pinnacle. This was one of Bob's earliest winter climbs and I was curious to see how he would handle the unstable snow. By the time he had followed me up to the Springboard it was clear that he was a natural and we shared the leading from there on. The whole Pinnacle was plastered with snow and the situations were magnificent. Bob was the blacksmith's son in the small Aberdeenshire community of Udny. The previous year he had been at Aberdeen University, where he made his first climbs with the Lairig Club. He changed colleges at the end of first year and was now a student at Robert Gordon's Institute of Technology studying chemistry. He was a powerful, very fit young man – usually with a broad grin.

The Black Spout Pinnacle saw further action during the next month. Neil Quinn had spotted a potential winter climb taking a diagonal fault rightward across Pinnacle Face. He and Lang had set off to attempt the line several times already this winter but on February 17, in spite of mild weather, they found a slight frost had hardened the snow. Firstly, they had to decide how to reach the left end of the diagonal fault which lay more than 100ft up. Starting in the little shoot between the Mound and the lowest rocks of the Pinnacle, Quinn led a snow-filled groove up to below an overhang.

They were now below and left of a big slab with a shallow groove in it. It was Lang's turn to lead: "We ponder the possibilities and I opt to take the slab directly. A small inset slab protects the big slab from attack. With care and caution, nicks are fashioned in the thin ice, points are placed in the nicks, adze is laid on higher nicks. With held breath, a sense of insecurity and no protection, height is slowly gained."[1] Seventy feet of sustained climbing took Lang to a poor belay at the start of the

Bob Smith, 1974
Photo: Greg Strange

diagonal fault. By now the frost had lifted and when Quinn arrived he was not at all convinced that climbing in these conditions was a good idea. Lang on the other hand did not relish the thought of having to lead that slab again and tried to persuade his companion to continue. "I could hardly tell him the truth, namely that I didn't trust an abseil from the doubtful belay. Instead, I babbled on about how there was a layer of ice under all the junk and if he applied all his skill and kept his self-control we could pluck this plum right from under the noses of the Aberdonian Kami-kazes."[2] The cajoling did the trick and Quinn gradually made his way up the diagonal fault, part of which had been climbed by Dinwoodie and Stuart two years previously. After a full run-out he belayed below the final corner of Pinnacle Face. From here Lang discovered that by descending right for 15ft he was able to balance round an edge to gain an easy ramp leading into the chimney of Route 1. They now had a clear run to the top. This natural line, Winter Face, provided the Dundee men with the first complete winter ascent of the corrie face of the Black Spout Pinnacle. Unfortunately, Lang's crux slab is rarely sufficiently iced to allow an ascent, but the diagonal fault and the traverse into Route 1 is now often used by parties climbing Pinnacle Face. Two weeks later, following a substantial thaw and re-freeze, Dinwoodie finally succeeded in climbing Pinnacle Face all the way to the plateau using two pitons for aid in the steep corner where he had fallen two years' earlier. His partner on this occasion was a young Aberdonian, Adhair McIvor, a second-year student at Aberdeen University. Although they started very late, time was not of the essence as they were able to climb much of the upper pinnacle in the light of a full moon.

A number of climbers visited the Garbh Choire of Beinn a' Bhùird during this period of relatively good weather. In February Keir, Mothersele and Bob Smith made a winter ascent of East Wall Direct on Mitre Ridge. This Severe route follows a straight line of cracks and chimneys in the lower slabs between South-East Gully and the ridge crest, before joining the old East Wall Route. The whole climb gave excellent value with the double pitch in the icy couloir of the original route proving to be the crux. Grade IV. On March 24, Dennis King and I made the second winter ascent of Mitre Ridge, 21 years after Brooker and Patey. As on that pioneering ascent wc found thc ridge well covered with snow and were surprised by the sustained nature of the climbing. In the weeks prior to this I had climbed both Eagle Ridge and Parallel Gully B (with Archbold) and considered Mitre Ridge to be at least on a par with these Grade V climbs, both for difficulty and commitment.

From a climbing point of view the summer of 1974 in the Cairngorms was unusually quiet. What little exploration took place was all approached from Deeside. On Lochnagar Dinwoodie repeated Psyche and climbed the direct route, Nymph, following the less prominent left-hand twin crack-line running parallel to Gully B. Bob Smith was his companion on both these climbs and the occasion marked the start of a rock climbing partnership which continued intermittently into the early 1980s. Both men were very strong but their styles of climbing, like their personalities, were quite different. The outgoing Smith was bold and often impatient, whereas Dinwoodie was shy and more of a stoic who climbed with cautious determination. Together, they were a powerful climbing force. Although they were at large in the Cairngorms throughout the summer, indifferent weather curtailed their explorations to a short route on Creag an Dubh-loch – The Strumpet VS 5a – and the big slab-corner high on the face left of Red Chimney on Creagan a' Choire Etchachan – Umslopogaas HVS 5a.

November 1974 saw the usual mixture of early season snowfall, frost, gales and rapid thaws. On the last Saturday of the month Smith and Aberdonian, Gordon Stephen, climbed the excellent short icy runnel of Carmine Groove on Creagan a' Choire Etchachan. Grade IV. In mid-December Lang and Quinn were also in action on Grade IV ice when they climbed directly up the icefall of the Flume in the Garbh Choire of Beinn a' Bhùird.

While the Dundonians were straightening out the Flume, Newcastle-based Mike Coleman was apparently well into the second day of a winter ascent of Postern on the Shelter Stone Crag. According to the report which Coleman submitted to the Editor of the SMCJ he climbed the route with Neil Harding over the weekend of December 14 – 15, following the original summer line, using some aid. No mention was made of a bivouac. Coleman followed this up with a much more impressive claim for the first British ascent of the Dru Couloir in the Chamonix Aiguilles, again with Harding. The climb was reported in *Mountain 42* to have been made in February 1975, although Coleman's note in the SMCJ the following year said January. After investigations by *Mountain* Editor, Ken Wilson, he along with a number of active British alpinists felt uneasy about Coleman's claim.

The following statement concerning the Dru Couloir was made on

*Jock Moreland below
the Stack on
Lochnagar in 1976*

Photo: Greg Strange

page eight of *Mountain 43*: "It may now be considered a disputed ascent as the climbers have been unable to detail a plausible scenario of events."[3]

Since the Dru Couloir climb was considered to be a hoax, and Neil Harding most probably a product of Coleman's imagination, the general consensus among climbers at the time was that the Postern ascent did not take place either. Certainly, Coleman has never come forward to question the omission of his climb from subsequent guidebooks. The occurrence of claims for bogus first ascents is extremely rare, this being the only one to have come to light in the Cairngorms to date.

By mid-January there was still little in the way of a snow build-up, although there had been periods of cold weather. Over the weekend 25 – 26, parties at Allt na-giubhsaich and Luibeg were bothy-bound by gales and driving spindrift on the Saturday, but calm weather enticed them out on the Sunday. Keir and Smith went to Creag an Dubh-loch with Dave Wright and Jock Moreland – two geologists working for oil company BP in Aberdeen. Wright was an experienced rock climber who had been at Leeds University, while Moreland, an outgoing Glaswegian, had only just arrived in Aberdeen.

Earlier that month, Keir and Wright had attempted a winter ascent of Pink Elephant. On that occasion, Keir led a thinly-iced overlap low down to gain direct entry into the Dinosaur Gully. They followed this to the terrace but could make little progress on the upper slabs due to lack of ice. This time they hoped to complete the route by climbing the Sea of Slabs, left of the upper pitches of Pink Elephant, but a late start and now doubtful weather prompted a quick approach to the terrace by way of Labyrinth Edge.

Smith and Moreland, on the other hand, were attracted to a prominent narrow icefall emanating from the Hanging Garden and flowing down the line of a water-course known as The Aqueduct. While they set about a direct ascent of this, Keir and Wright quickly climbed Labyrinth Edge to the terrace. Here they followed the thinly-iced Dinosaur Crack which provided an exciting passage through the Sea of Slabs. They then had difficulty finding an exit through the overlap topping the slabs and this, coupled with deteriorating weather persuaded them to escape back on to Labyrinth Edge.

Meanwhile, Smith and Moreland were nearing the top of their climb. After completing the poorly-protected icefall of The Aqueduct they entered the Hanging Garden. Here they could see another line of ice, running down slabby ramps just to the left of Hanging Garden Route. They followed icy grooves from the back of the Garden up onto slabs, then sustained and exposed ice climbing took them over bulges and up corners to reach the plateau near the top of Bower Buttress. The whole climb had taken nine and a half hours and it was almost dark when they topped-out. The weather had been deteriorating as the day progressed, bringing strong winds and snowfall. They were concerned for their companions and shouted down that they would wait, but after a couple of hours, having been unable to make further communication, they set off back to Glen Muick.

Keir and Wright eventually bivouacked at the Fang, an upstanding tooth of rock on Labyrinth Edge below the final tower. At dawn, after a long cold night, they still could not find the normal right exit for Labyrinth Edge and it took them four hours and four pitons to climb the 200ft directly to the plateau.

Back at Allt na-giubhsaich, Moreland had taken the precaution of calling out the Mountain Rescue team when they had not returned by daybreak. He then set off back to the Dubh Loch and was much relieved to meet them beside Glas Allt Shiel. According to Wright they decided to name their climb White Elephant, partly because it was a winter attempt on Pink Elephant, but also because it had been more trouble than it was worth! Smith and Moreland named their ice route in the Hanging Garden, Yeti. Both climbs were Grade V.

On the same day that these climbs were made, Dinwoodie and McIvor attempted a winter ascent of The Dagger on Creagan a' Choire Etchachan. They had walked to the cliff from Scott's bothy to find the Crimson Slabs covered in fresh snow, some of which had packed into the corner of The Dagger. After a promising start up steep ice on Scabbard they found precious little old snow or ice to help McIvor as he heroically scraped his way up the main pitch of The Dagger, at times laybacking on the shaft of his axe with the pick driven into the corner crack. Near the top a nut came out while he was resting on it and he fell 40ft down the corner before being held on one of Patey's old pitons. The weather was very poor at the time with the return of strong winds and spindrift. They had little trouble in deciding to withdraw.

February saw a determined attempt at another classic rock climb. Wright and Keir were well up the Cumming-Crofton Route on Mitre Ridge when they ran out of daylight and were forced to retreat. Elsewhere on Beinn a' Bhùird, Smith and Stephen climbed Bloodhound Buttress in Coire an Dubh Lochain. They followed the VS summer route in poor conditions using six pitons for aid.

It was during February that John Cunningham climbed his last new route in the Cairngorms. He and Fyffe made a winter ascent of Gaffer's Groove in Coire an Lochain, a natural winter line Cunningham had been keeping his eye on for a long time. There was thin ice in the main groove and they finished the climb by a wide chimney left of the summer route. Fyffe, who himself had now been a full-time Lodge instructor since April 1972, recalled that his companion made a good job of leading the hard first pitch – Grade V.

By now, Cunningham had been at Glenmore Lodge for seven years and when Bill March left for Idaho University everyone thought that John would be the obvious successor as Deputy Principal. Unfortunately, the interview did not go well and the Scottish Sports Council awarded the post to the Rhodesian climber Rusty Baillie. Cunningham was very disappointed and made up his mind to get away from the Lodge. In autumn 1976, he started work as a lecturer in outdoor pursuits at the I.M.Marsh College in Liverpool, having moved to West-Kirby on the Wirral with his wife and daughter. For another four years he continued to work in this field, passing on his skills and knowledge, always encouraging youngsters to take advantage of the outdoors. On the last day of January 1980, he was washed off the rocks below South Stack on Anglesey while attempting to rescue a student from the sea. The student was eventually saved but John was swept away and his body never recovered. It is a sad irony that John Cunningham, one of Scotland's greatest climbers, whom everyone thought to be indestructible on dry land, should be taken by the sea. The water was his Achilles heel – he had never learned to swim properly.

Another influential climber made his last new route in March. Four years earlier, John Bower had been one of four Aberdeen climbers who tried the excellent groove-line of Vulcan in the Garbh Choire Mòr of Braeriach. On that occasion the ice was in a poor state and the climb was abandoned. This time he was accompanied by John Ingram and Ken Turnbull. Conditions were much better with good ice and névé. The steep lower section gave excellent climbing and they avoided the worst of the cornice by traversing to a snow arete on the right – Grade V.

Bower virtually gave up climbing after this. He spent a few years hillwalking but found this boring except in winter and gradually drifted away from the hills. When asked why he stopped he said that he had always found hard climbing mentally exhausting (frightening) and being a bit of a hermit he wanted a simpler, less hassled existence. Reminiscing in 1998 he said: "It would be great just to pack a rucksack and disappear into the hills, no responsibilities and feeling strong and fit. Those times were the best of our lives, when everything was new."

Although many Cairngorm cliffs are slabby by nature there are only a few locations where friction climbing can be found at an angle similar to that on the Etive Slabs. One such place is the deceptive A Likely Story Slab on the Eagle's Rock. It was here in early May that Dinwoodie and McIvor climbed The Stretcher (E2 5b), a poorly-protected route taking the smooth overlapping slabs to the left of A Likely Story. Soon after this they went to Lochnagar to climb the much steeper sweep of slabs between Crypt and the shallow corners left of Post Mortem on the Tough-Brown Face. A direct ascent of this challenging feature is still unclimbed, yet their route, Dirge, described by Dinwoodie as a tortuous line, still gave difficult and sustained climbing – E1 5b. Later in the summer, McIvor joined Lawrie and Stephen for an attempt on the second ascent of Mort. Stephen pulled off a fine lead by climbing the crux pitch between terraces using only one piton for aid at the overhang. Unfortunately, he was then unable to free the direct continuation, where Rennie had traversed in from the right, and they turned back.

There was a glorious period of dry weather at the end of June 1975 when Lake District climbers, Jeff Lamb and Pete Whillance, spent a week at Creag an Dubh-loch. This was their second trip to the Cairngorms, the first having been a month earlier when they climbed The Pin and Steeple on the Shelter Stone Crag. From June 22 – 27 this highly-motivated pair climbed 12 routes – almost half of the existing rock climbs on the cliff. Included in their tally were the first free ascents of Vertigo Wall, Dubh Loch Monster and Culloden.

Whillance said: "It still rates as one of my most enjoyable week's climbing. We only took enough food for three days and were starving when two older guys arrived towards the end of the week. Thankfully, they took pity on us and shared their food, their campfire and some wonderful stories. It turned out to be two of our guidebook heroes, Les Brown and Paul Nunn. I remember being very impressed and listening

intently to everything they said! They spent their two days at the crag putting up The Sting." Lamb and Whillance were but two of a number of very talented climbers who made up the ranks of the Carlisle Mountaineering Club at this time.

On June 28, Stephen, McIvor, Archbold and I walked to the Garbh Choire of Beinn a' Bhùird in a quest for virgin rock. While Archbold and I went to the north face of Squareface, the others headed for Mitre Ridge, intent on following a more direct line up the crest than that taken by the Cambridge party in 1933. Starting just left of the big open corner they climbed cracks, grooves, corners and short walls to join the original route at the shoulder. When they reached the first tower Stephen went the same way that Wedderburn had attempted. He crossed a slab and made a mantelshelf move onto a sloping ledge below the twin cracks splitting the impending wall above. A delicate traverse back left brought him into the left-hand crack which he climbed very strenuously to a belay where the angle eased. Archbold and I had a grandstand view of McIvor seconding this pitch. We could see him profiled on the very edge of the ridge and could tell by the tone of his voice that the climbing was as difficult as it looked. They continued over the top of the first tower and managed to climb the second one close to its crest to complete the first ascent of Mitre Ridge Direct – 5b on the first tower.

We had a far less successful day on the gloomy north face of Squareface. It has a short lower tier separated from the big wall above by a prominent terrace. In the middle of the main wall is a magnificent flake crack slanting right. Dinwoodie and Stuart had climbed to

Glenmore Lodge instructors in 1974. From left, back: Jack Thomson, Roger O'Donovan, Reg Popham, Rusty Baillie, Fred Harper, Bob Barton, Adrian Liddell. Front: Martin Burrows-Smith, Steve Mitchell, Sam Crymble, Ingrid Kristofsson, John Cunningham and Allen Fyffe

Photo: Ben Humble

the base of this in 1971 but had declined to continue. Although appearing clean, on closer inspection the rock is found to be gritty and course-grained and the cracks filled with vegetation. On the left, the upper wall falls back into a high basin below the plateau. We chose to climb up towards this basin then finish by an attractive crack going rightward up the left edge of the main face. After several hours of worrying, but technically straightforward climbing, we reached the top of the crack but could not climb the last 30ft of disintegrating rock. We descended and finished up the repulsive basin. It was Keir who dubbed this climb 'The Rocky Mountain Horror Show'.

The next day, Archbold and I left the Howff early and went to Lochnagar. The previous weekend we had investigated a groove-line going straight up to the Springboard from the foot of Pinnacle Face. The vegetation and some of the rock had been wet and we made little progress. This time the face was completely dry and the climb, Pinnacle Grooves (HVS 5a), gave us two pitches of excellent, well-protected climbing and a lot of gardening. After completion we abseiled off the Springboard and found a neat pile of divots at the foot of Pinnacle Face, the grooves having acted as a perfect rubbish chute.

As well as Fyffe, a number of other experienced climbers became full-time instructors at Glenmore Lodge in the early 1970s, including Adrian Liddell (Ado), Martin Burrows-Smith and Bob Barton. Liddell came from Carlisle and was a prominent Lake Distinct climber in the 1960s, pioneering new routes in Borrowdale such as The Niche on Lower Falcon Crag. Burrows-Smith hailed from Suffolk and chose to do engineering at Manchester University in order to be in a good location for climbing. He quickly became part of the Welsh scene and was particularly active on Clogwyn Du'r Arddu and on Anglesey's Craig Gogarth. Bob Barton had been at Cambridge University at the same time as Archbold. In June 1975, Liddell, with Robert Smith, climbed The Exorcist, the first of his trio of climbs on Hell's Lum Crag. Its main pitch gained and followed the isolated left-facing corner high up in the centre of the Grey Buttress between Good Intentions and Hell's Lump – HVS 5b.

At the end of the Public Inquiry into the Feith Buidhe disaster the jury recommended that any decision concerning the future of the three plateau bothies should be left to the 'experts'. Yet, despite the opinion held by the Mountain Rescue Committee for Scotland and many mountaineers that the shelters should be removed for safety reasons, three years had now elapsed and no action had taken place. The final stumbling block came when the Scottish Office, instead of backing the 'experts', deemed it necessary for demolition warrants to be issued for each shelter by the appropriate local authority – Banff County Council for the Curran and St Valery bothies and Inverness County Council for El Alamein. With both authorities steadfastly refusing to issue the documents, stalemate existed for almost a year until May 1975 when the new local government structure (Lord Wheatly's Regionalisation) came into existence and Banffshire became part of Grampian Region and Inverness-shire part of Highland. Faced with imminent extinction, Banff County Council finally issued the warrant in early May and the Curran and St Valery were removed by the Royal Navy with help from the police and Mountaineering Council of Scotland volunteers. El Alamein was still standing well into the 1990s. It is hard to imagine why three small huts in the middle of nowhere could have caused so much controversy. Most local climbers were indifferent to their demise, although some had good memories of St Valery.

Long periods of unsettled weather dominated the poor winter of 1975 - 1976 and conditions did not radically improve for climbing in the Cairngorms until June. The wait was well rewarded, for although the Highlands did not experience a heat wave on the same scale as parts of England, the summer of 1976 was one of the driest on record. For almost three months it was possible to rock climb at will on the high crags, and even on the occasions when it did rain, everything dried within 24 hours. As might be expected, there was a good deal of climbing throughout the period with many early repeats and aid reductions on recent climbs as well as new routes.

In June, Liddell and Burrows-Smith made a partially-aided ascent of a new climb on the Central Slabs of the Shelter Stone Crag. Their climb gained and followed the long rising fold which runs almost parallel to and below the diedre of Thor, to reach The Pin at the top of its second pitch. Their initial intention had been to try Spence's S-shaped groove, that tantalising line breaking out of Thor, which had been named the Cupid's Bow crack by Bill March. Starting just right of Thor, Liddell climbed up and right to gain and follow a rib until moves left took him into the main corner of Thor. He then climbed free up the Thor diedre, past the commencement of the fold, and took a hanging belay below the left exit to the Cupid's bow. After a closer inspection of the Bow they concluded that aid would be needed and diverted their attention to the fold.

From the belay, Burrows-Smith used rope tension to reach a solitary foothold out right, then, with considerable difficulty and a certain amount of aid, he worked his way up the long, shallow overlap which constitutes the fold. At one point he fell and was held by a skyhook which he had placed on one of the small flakes which are a feature of this pitch. At the end of the overlap he had to move farther right, and here, feeling pressed, he asked for, and was given, a top rope from two young Edinburgh climbers on The Pin. He thus reached the comparative safety of the latter route's second stance and brought Liddell across. In this way the two men from the Lodge opened up another new course on these tremendous slabs. They recorded the climb, Loki, in the 1977 SMCJ, but did not specify the amount or the nature of the aid used on the main pitch.

Both instructors were involved with further new routes on the Loch Avon cliffs during this summer. High above the right side of the Central Slabs, Burrows-Smith and John Jones climbed Blockbuster (E2 5b) – the fierce-looking chimney, blocked by huge chokestones, which lies tucked into the left side of the upper bastion, left of Citadel. Then in July, Liddell and Burrows-Smith climbed The Omen on Hell's Lum Crag – a good line following slabs then a crack system right of Clean Sweep – HVS 5a.

The almost Mediterranean weather in July saw much activity on Creag an Dubh-loch, with most of the existing climbs receiving at least one ascent. On a blistering hot day during the first weekend of the month Dinwoodie and Guy Muhlemann made the third ascent of Cougar,

Douglas Dinwoodie retreating after an attempt on the North Face of Squareface in August 1971

Photo: Greg Strange

Luibeg Bothy, December 1975. From left: Adhair McIvor, Greg Strange, Rob Archbold, Guy Muhlemann, Brian Lawrie and Douglas Dinwoodie

Photo: Greg Strange

significantly reducing the amount of aid to just two pitons on the first three pitches. Below the final aid crack they tried to find a free way 30ft farther left, but it turned out to be more difficult than it looked and they were forced to use four more pitons in order to reach easy ground before darkness set in.

A week later, this time with Mothersele, Dinwoodie made the first of two impressive climbs on Broad Terrace Wall, between Culloden and Falkenhorst. Immediately right of Culloden are two parallel crack-lines which pass either side of a black roof. Despite heavy overnight rain most of the cliff had dried by the time they started on the left-hand line. Two relatively straightforward pitches took them to the right end of the monster Culloden flake below the barrier wall. To breach this, Dinwoodie used two pitons in a short overhanging corner on the right then he continued up a steep, hanging corner, heading for the black roof. When holds in the corner ran out, he swung left and up the exposed rib until a horizontal flake led left to ledges at the top of the big groove on Culloden.

By the time Mothersele had seconded this pitch it was getting late and a thick mist had descended. They traversed up and right along slabs to gain a huge grass-topped block. The wall above this was still wet and required a piton, but easier blocky ground had now been reached – 150ft from the top. It was now 11 o'clock and drizzling. Down at the Dinosaur Howff, below the Central Slabs, a group of climbers had congregated to discuss the day's activities. They could tell by the occasional muffled voices from up in the cloud that progress of some sort was still being made, and this was confirmed when two huge boulders came spinning out of the mist and crashed onto slabs at the foot of Broad Terrace Wall. Despite the rain, Death's Head Route was completed that night. According to Dinwoodie, the name was suggested by the discovery of a peculiar block, weathered like a man's face, which formed part of the second pitch.

Another week went by, followed by another gathering at the Dubh

Loch. This time Dinwoodie was climbing with McIvor and the two of them plus Dave Wright and myself went up to look at the right-hand crack. It soon became obvious that progress would be very slow with two ropes of two so Dave and I abseiled off leaving Dinwoodie and McIvor to press on up a series of excellent layback flakes. Dinwoodie belayed right of the monster Culloden flake and contemplated how they were going to climb this hard-looking section of the barrier wall. Twenty feet up he could see a prominent jutting spike and resolved to use this to make further progress. He managed to loop one of the two ropes over the spike, then fixing runners to the second rope he used prusik loops to climb the fixed rope and thus gained the spike. He then belayed higher up on a ledge tucked under a bulging rib and McIvor followed, also by prusiking. The next pitch was 120ft and led up the wall left of the bulging rib, passing the right end of the black roof and eventually reaching the grass-topped block on Death's Head Route. A piton was used for aid at a bulging crack below the block. They finished this second climb, The Crow, by climbing the last 180ft of Death's Head.

Douglas Dinwoodie starting the layback flakes on the second pitch of The Crow, Broad Terrace Wall, Creag an Dubh-loch July 1976

Photo: Greg Strange

To date, Broad Terrace Wall has not become a popular place to climb. Its awkward approach, intimidating appearance, mossy rock and dampness has not so far appealed to modern climbers. It is doubtful if any of the routes right of Culloden has had more than a few ascents in the past 25 years. Of these two particular climbs, Dinwoodie later said that they provided adventurous climbing on fine natural lines and that the moss had not been a problem. He re-visited both routes in the 1980s and dispensed with all the aid – The Crow in 1983 with Graeme Livingston at E2 5c, and Death's Head Route with Doug Hawthorn in 1986 at E3 6a.

After leaving our companions on The Crow, Dave Wright and I went round to The Sword of Damocles, which we believed was still unrepeated. We found the first pitch excellent and relatively straightforward (5a), but the side walls of the hanging chimney were wet and greasy. Dave made a stalwart effort to climb the chimney, at one point trying out on the right wall. He then retreated to a point in the chimney above the first bolt and discovered that he could traverse the left wall to an edge. Good holds then enabled him to climb the arete and move farther left into a pale-coloured groove. This led easily back right to the big ledge at the top of the chimney. Given dry conditions we saw no reason why the whole chimney could not be climbed free, although the exit looked hard. This proved to be the case the following July when Dinwoodie led the pitch at a strenuous E2 5b. His second, Bob Smith, trundled the Damoclean flake.

In August, the action switched to Lochnagar. One of the highlights when scrambling up the Black Spout is passing below the impressive 450ft left wall which drops almost sheer from the summit of the Black Spout Pinnacle. In 1974, Dinwoodie and Smith had fallen under the spell of this cold, shadowed wall. Dinwoodie had led a very sustained 130ft pitch out of the Spout using six pitons for aid. When Smith followed he removed all the equipment except for one ancient blade piton which they had recovered from near the top of The Link the previous day. Above their sloping stance the wall continued very steeply with smooth-looking grooves and bulging overlaps. Totally spooked by the situation, the exposure, and the rock which was lichenous and off-putting, they went back down vowing never to return.

Fear of the wall had mellowed since 1974 and they now felt ready to give it another go. With several days food they settled into the doss below Lochnagar's west ridge and warmed up by making a completely free ascent of Mort on the Tough-Brown Face. E1 5b. The lower Black Spout wall is dominated by a big recess on the right, above which great overhangs guard access to the ridge dropping from the apex at the top of the Route 2 chimney. Just left of the big recess, a crack set into the crest of a pillar leads straight up to an overhang. This was the line of their first pitch.

The initial 50ft to a prominent block went smoothly enough. Then a difficult bulge led into what Dinwoodie described as a smooth dwindling groove, at the top of which, below the overhang, he clipped into the big piton left from their previous visit. He now had to quit the groove and get onto a narrow undercut ramp on the left. Although he tried several times he was unable to achieve this without rope tension from the piton. Once established on the ramp, hard climbing led up over a very strenuous overhang to reach better holds and a slight respite from the verticality. He then had to move awkwardly down right to reach the old abseil pitons at a sloping ledge directly above the starting crack. It was a tremendous piece of climbing.

When Smith arrived they surveyed the wall above. It still looked improbable and they had no idea whether it could be climbed or not. Above and slightly to their left a smooth groove cut its way through the bulges, heading towards the third pitch of The Link. This appeared to be their best option provided they could gain entry to the corner at the base of the groove. Smith took all the equipment and moved up to a short impending wall. He climbed this using a piton and swung up on small layaways in the crack at the back of the corner. To his great surprise and delight he found that instead of being typically blind, the narrow crack was deep enough to take his fingers. He did not linger in this precarious position and pushed on hoping to reach a resting place higher up the groove. Suddenly, the silence was broken by a loud scream and a clanking of gear as he came hurtling out of the groove and fell some 30ft to a point almost level with Dinwoodie's ledge. As he hung out there on the rope trying to get his head together he noticed two friends, Dave Nichols and Bill McKerrow close by on The Link. They had witnessed the whole event and were debating as to whether or not they ought to have taken a photograph when a huge grin spread across Smith's face and he yelled: "Did ye get a guid photie o' that min?"

He had been above the hardest moves when his foot unexpectedly slipped on the lichenous rock. After a long rest he went back up, found runners above the bulge and kept going, away up and left until he could belay on a ledge close to The Link – another exciting pitch! It was their intention to finish the route by climbing the prominent crack system in the steep gable wall above the Route 2 traverse. To reach this they now followed slabby shelves out right to gain and climb the arete above the great overhangs. This airy, but easy pitch, brought them to the little protruding ridge at the top of the Route 2 chimney, down which they made their escape by abseil.

Douglas Dinwoodie leading the first pitch of Black Spout Wall, August 1976

Photo: Greg Strange

After a day's rest they went back to finish the climb, but instead of repeating the first three pitches they approached their high point by climbing the cliff farther to the left. This enabled them to solve two hitherto unclimbed problems – the rib to the left of Pinnacle Grooves (Fool's Rib, HVS 5a), and the central fault and roof directly above the Springboard which had been attempted by Sutherland and Brooker. Hood Route HVS 5a. Once above the roof on Hood Route they reversed the Route 2 traverse and arrived back below the gable wall.

There are two main cracks on this top wall. The left-hand is known as the Inhospitable Crack from Patey's original description of Route 2, where he refers to it as looking "most inhospitable". It runs up leftwards to finish at the top of The Link. The longer right-hand system leads directly by its right fork to the very apex of the wall. Two parallel

*Bob Smith and
Douglas Dinwoodie,
Black Spout Wall,
August 1976*

Photo: Greg Strange

subsidiary cracks start the right-hand line and the crux of this final pitch involved getting established into these from the left – 10ft up. Dinwoodie spent a long time cleaning the rock at this point and managed to place a piton for protection at full stretch before making the hard moves. Once up to the fork at 30ft, the cracks became deeper. Although there were loose blocks and a fair amount of gardening to be done, the holds and jams were good, making for exhilarating climbing in a tremendous situation – a fitting climax to this great route.

It was seven years before Black Spout Wall was repeated. In September 1983, Lawrie and Neil Morrison climbed the whole route free at E3, finding each of the three difficult pitches to be technically 5c. Since then the climb gradually gained classic status, although remaining very much a connoisseur's route. In its own way, it is equal to Lochnagar's more famous climb, Eagle Ridge, albeit at a totally different order of difficulty.

When the first snows of autumn swept into the high hills in early September there was a feeling among Scottish climbers that for once they had had a good innings. The summer had been kind and most climbers were quietly pleased with their efforts. On Creag an Dubh-loch and Lochnagar the locals had climbed some of the harder routes of recent vintage in better style, and Dinwoodie and Smith had set a new level of sustained difficulty for a Cairngorm first ascent with their Black Spout Wall.

However, the old order was about to be challenged and the North-east's isolation from mainstream rock climbing highlighted once again. Murray Hamilton and Alan Taylor, the two young men climbing The Pin on the day of the Loki ascent, were part of a new generation of Scottish climbers who came to the fore in 1976. Although their ascent was relatively uneventful it was probably the first time that chalk had been in use on a route in the Cairngorms. Climber's chalk (light magnesium carbonate) had arrived from the US in the early 1970s. When applied to the hands and fingers, the friction between skin and rock is significantly improved, especially in warm or humid weather. Initially, its use on British crags was resisted, then, like PAs, it was thought acceptable only for use on the most difficult routes of the day. Prior to the availability of chalk some climbers used resin or even rubbed their hands in dust to improve friction. The major drawback to the use of chalk is that it leaves white marks on the rock which are unsightly and also reduce the demand on route-finding skills for subsequent ascentionists.

The adoption of chalk was just one aspect of the new generation's attitude to climbing. They were following a trend started by leading English climbers like Pete Livesey, John Allen and Ron Fawcett. For these men, climbing was no longer just a leisure time activity, pursued at weekends or on fine summer evenings. It required total dedication and a level of fitness comparable to that of an athlete. When asked how they managed to achieve this, Hamilton says: "We climbed most days and so arrived quite quickly at a standard which was high for the time. We did not train, just climbed and bouldered and talked about it." Being based in Edinburgh they were well placed to make full use of the new Meadowbank indoor climbing wall, and this, coupled with relatively easy access to the excellent wet weather alternatives provided by the Northumberland outcrops, meant that the new group could maintain a high level of performance on rock throughout the winter, something that would have been impracticable in the past.

The south-facing scattered crags of the Eagle's Rock opposite Creag an Dubh-loch had only seen a trickle of winter exploration in the six years since Lethargy had been climbed. Many of the crag's summer climbs follow water courses and present obvious possibilities for ice work. Two experienced climbers from Aberdeen University, Alfie Robertson and Andy Nisbet, recognised this potential and, in December 1976, made winter ascents of the three original VS climbs on the main central crag – Indolence, Abstention and Nomad's Crack. All provided good climbing, mainly on ice, with Nomad's Crack giving the hardest route at Grade V. Not content with three good new climbs in as many weeks, Nisbet returned in February to clean up with Gibber and Whisper – the former

Alfie Robertson, 1976

Photo: Greg Strange

with Neil Spinks, the latter with Robertson. This rapid winter development of a single cliff was unprecedented in the Cairngorms and it gained some notoriety for the students. In the past, local climbers had taken a more casual approach to route-bagging.

The two Lairig Club friends had been at Aberdeen Grammar School together, although in different years as Alfie was a year older than Andy. Robertson was now studying English and Nisbet biochemistry. They were already seasoned campaigners, both having completed all the Munros, Nisbet in 1972 and Robertson a year later. Nisbet's parents were members of the Cairngorm Club and keen walkers, which goes some way to explain why he was such an early hill convert. In the summer of 1973 Robertson and Nisbet went on a rock climbing course at Glenmore Lodge. Then, six months later, full of enthusiasm, they were back at the Lodge for instruction in winter climbing. After this they never looked back, quickly working up through the winter grades until they had several Grade Vs under their belts, including Eagle Ridge which they climbed in April 1976 at their third attempt.

Robertson and Nisbet were particularly keen winter climbers who went out in all weathers. It was their willingness to try difficult winter climbs, like Eagle Ridge, in unfavourable conditions that earned them an early nickname of 'The Lemmings'. They became so attached to this appellation that later in the season when they climbed Symmers's left-hand variation to Raeburn's Gully they recorded it as the Lemmings Exit. They were becoming a strong team.

There was a big dump of snow before New Year 1977 and many roads were blocked in the Highlands. This was followed by a rapid thaw then a return to colder conditions. On January 6, Nisbet and Robertson climbed Hanging Garden Route by its left fork. At the pedestal they continued straight up the left side of the triangular buttress until a steep wall forced an exposed left traverse across an iced slab to reach easy ground. They found this to be a particularly fine climb and it soon became the most popular winter route out of the Hanging Garden.

Winter set in with a vengeance during the second week of January as an impressive blizzard swept the area. For the next seven weeks the freezing level hardly rose above 2000ft and the Cairngorms lay beneath a deep cover of snow which remained virtually unchanged until the beginning of March. Creagan a' Choire Etchachan, being east-facing, catches a little winter sun early in the day, and as a result of this modest freeze/thaw, the cliff may have more consolidated snow than higher north-facing crags. It was this theory that brought together two quite independent parties from Aberdeen for an unexpected meeting in the Hutchison Hut late on Friday, January 28.

Dick Renshaw, a very experienced mountaineer from Yorkshire, had recently come to Aberdeen to look for casual work. During 1975, with his partner, Joe Tasker, he had climbed the North Face of the Eiger in winter, and later that year, made the first ascent of the South face of Dunagiri in the Gharwal Himalaya. Their epic 11 day Alpine-style push up and down had left Dick with frostbitten fingers, which, although treated successfully, still required care to prevent further damage. He and I had made a late arrangement to go to Etchachan that weekend and our spirits were high as we made quick progress up the frozen wastes of a moonlit Glen Derry. We talked about 'doing a McArtney' and snatching an ascent of The Dagger, or possibly the vegetated grooves of Bodkin. When we reached the hut we were surprised to find we would be sharing it with Nisbet and Robertson.

We awoke to the sound of Dick's alarm and commenced the usual preparations for a day winter climbing. A while later, as we sipped a second mug of tea, Andy and Alfie suddenly rose from their sleeping bags, fully clothed, grabbed their rucksacks and disappeared out through the door. By the time we were up below the Crimson Slabs, Alfie was already climbing the original first pitch of The Dagger. We had been completely out-manoeuvred. What the hell? It was a beautiful day, we had the rest of the cliff to ourselves, and anyway, we were not too optimistic about their chances as the whole sweep of the central Crimson Slabs looked discouragingly bare, even the drainage line of Djibangi had no ice to speak of. We could make out a narrow band of snow in the back of the main corner of The Dagger, but the slabs to its left were steely grey in the early morning light.

We left them to their task and moved round to the other end of the cliff where we climbed the Bastion by a line of snowy grooves between Bastion Wall and Original Route. On returning to the hut in the late afternoon we discovered Andy and Alfie already back and assumed that they had been unsuccessful. Not at all – they had climbed the whole route in a fast time saying that the corner had only been Grade III. They almost seemed disappointed! Apparently, the band of snow in the main corner was perfect snow-ice, enabling them to front point and kick steps all the way up. Andy, who had led the pitch, said the ice was a total and pleasant surprise, especially when remembering McIvor's hard time on it two years earlier. They found the most difficult climbing on the final pitch above the escape ramp where the rock was covered in unconsolidated snow.

The weather changed overnight bringing wind and snow showers. The younger lads were still in their sleeping bags when Dick and I set off for the cliff. This time we had first choice and headed for Bodkin, a line of weakness which weaves its way through the overhangs between Avalanche Gully and Red Chimney. The initial section of the climb is a scramble up to the higher of two grass patches known as The Meadows. In order to get more sustained climbing we opted to use Flanking Ribs as a direct approach. Dick was nearing the end of the first pitch when Andy and Alfie appeared out of the mist.

"What's that you're doing?"

"Bodkin," I replied.

"No it's not, you're on Flanking Ribs."

My explanation for the alternative start seemed to satisfy and they disappeared around to our left. A little higher we noticed them again – they were hurrying unroped towards the upper Meadow. I quickly seconded Dick's pitch and rushed on up, only to find that Andy had already reached the stance on Bodkin. I must admit to getting onto my high horse about being overtly competitive and it has to be said that Dick, as usual, remained silent throughout. Eventually, they traversed back right onto Flanking Ribs, leaving us once more to our solitude.

The climb itself proved to be a good natural winter line not without

Andy Nisbet, 1976
Photo: Greg Strange

Looking down The
Dagger to Alfie
Robertson, January
1977

Photo: Andy Nisbet

incident. The severe summer crux occurs near the start, where a big open groove has to be crossed leftwards on small footholds. As there was no consolidated snow or ice Dick crossed higher up using a piton and a nut for aid. Then, instead of continuing leftwards, as in summer, he climbed directly up a narrow groove for 30ft only to find himself in a cul-de-sac. He announced that he would try to climb back down, but after a few moves he slipped off. As he fell past a piton runner, a small attachment ring on the back of one of his crampons clipped itself into the karabiner and he was brought to an instant halt, hanging upside down by one foot, like one of the characters depicted on a tarot card. When it was clear that he was unhurt in this amazing fluke we had a good laugh, but the crisis was by no means over. The weight of his sack made it difficult to pull up and work on the problem. Then after several unsuccessful attempts his boot suddenly released from the crampon and I held him on the rope until he sorted himself out. We stuck closely to the summer line from thereon, gaining the plateau as the sky cleared for a glorious sunset.

After leaving Glenmore Lodge in 1973 Bill March spent two years at Idaho University completing a Masters Degree in Outdoor Activities. On returning to Britain he took over the Principal's job at Plas-y-Brenin, the National Outdoor Centre in North Wales. In early February, while staying at the Lodge with students from Plas-y-Brenin, March, with fellow instructor, Dave Alcock, climbed Cascade, a near vertical ice pitch on the far left-hand section of the Stag Rocks. This isolated feature had been eyed and 'played on' by a number of climbers in the past, including March himself. He led this very sustained pitch, taking several rests on his Chouinard hammers. Grade V. This was Bill's last new climb in the Cairngorms. Later that year, he quit Plas-y-Brenin and emigrated to British Columbia with his Canadian-born wife. In 1982 he led the first successful Canadian expedition to Everest, then eight years later, aged 49, he died of an aneurism in 1990 while walking down a trail in Panorama, British Columbia.

On the last Saturday in February, Dick Renshaw and I made a winter ascent of Cumming-Crofton Route. Mindful that previous attempts had failed due to lack of time or daylight, we stole away from the snow-entombed Howff in Glen Slugain at 5.30am and headed for the Garbh Choire. At first it was cold and clear, but by the time we reached the Sneck cloud had rolled in from the north-west. These dull misty conditions with little wind and no precipitation persisted throughout the climb. With the whole west face of the Mitre Ridge caked in partially consolidated snow and hoar frost it was obvious that we were in for a long day. Dick led from the start and I followed with the sacks. He progressed carefully and steadily, laboriously clearing away the soft material and climbing mainly on the rock, although using bits of turf where possible. The climbing was sustained but never desperate, with the chokestone at the top of the first pitch proving to be as awkward as anything else on the climb. Near the top of the long corner it started to get dark and soon Dick's torch gave out. At this point I took over and led up onto the crest of the ridge before I too was without a working lamp. Somewhere above the cloud the moon must have been shining for we sensed a little diffused light. It was almost flat calm, so we continued feeling our way very cautiously along the level section then finally up to the top – Grade VI.

Bill March nearing the top of Cascade, February 1977

Photo: Dave Alcock

On the plateau we were unable to see to take a bearing off the map. We could, however, use the luminous dial on the compass and attempted to follow a course due south-east, which I hoped would take us into upper Glen Quoich while at the same time avoiding the cornices beside Squareface. For the first four or five hundred yards we kept the rope on and moved one at a time, thereafter we moved together. Progress and visibility were no better once we dropped into the glen. We took off the rope and trudged, hopefully, towards Glen Slugain. As the night wore on we lost all sense of time. In fact, I imagined it to be about one o-clock in the morning when quite unexpectedly it started to get light. At this point I fell through a small cornice into a gully which I recognised as being close to the Howff. It was 6.30am and we had been on the move for 25 hours.

The thaw duly arrived a few days later and continued for a week. There was a big shift of snow from the steeper rock although the gullies remained well built-up. It only required a return to freezing weather to produce excellent climbing conditions and this occurred on March 12. Archbold and Miles Hillman had planned a trip to Braeriach that weekend with an ascent of the Great Rift on the agenda. After a night in Corrour they moved up to the Garbh Choire Hut and found the south-facing cliff virtually clear of snow. The Rift was out! While considering other options, Archbold remembered the steep candle of ice that occasionally fills the big groove between The Tower of Babel and Phoenix Buttress. He had seen it in thawing conditions three years earlier on a previous visit to the Garbh Choire Mòr. It was surely worth a look?

As they crested the lip into the snowy bowl of the corrie they could see the lower half of their objective disappearing into the mist. This time it looked more like a gully than an ice pillar, but their greatest concern, the cornice, was invisible.

Archbold led the climb in three pitches, the first of which felt very steep: "The snow-ice was perfect, perhaps a gift from the management in recognition of all the faithful service on powder, slush and impenetratable water ice. I had recently acquired two Terrordactyls, but I still excavated a ladder of footholds, ostensibly to ease the strain on Miles's leg, only a week out of plaster, but in reality for myself."[4] Hillman had broken his leg while attempting an unclimbed icefall, The Drool, on the Eagle's Rock. Simply walking to An Garbh Choire and back was a good test for his newly-healed leg.

From a belay on the impending wall of Phoenix Buttress, Archbold commenced the second pitch which proved to be the technical crux. Instead of going up directly he avoided a steep ice wall by taking a groove running left to an overlap: "There followed a delicate traverse left, using ice-ripple underclings beneath the overlap, until good ice on the slab above permitted the upward heave."[5] The final pitch, although hampered by the onset of darkness, went without any problems as the often huge cornice had fallen during the thaw. They named this excellent Grade V climb, White Nile.

Despite a late winter, June 1977 provided plenty of dry weather in Scotland, especially in the West. The new wave of climbers from Edinburgh and Glasgow took little time to re-establish themselves at the cutting edge of Scottish rock. Already in Glen Coe they had made major aid reductions on old Creagh Dhu and Squirrel routes as well as putting up some impressive free-climbs of their own. Hamilton and Cuthbertson, the leading figures from the Edinburgh group, had recently made a completely free ascent of Titan's Wall, on Càrn Dearg Buttress of Ben Nevis. They later heard they had been beaten by a few days to this prestigious first free ascent by the young Londoner, Mick Fowler, and his Welsh climbing partner, Phil Thomas, who was working in Fort William at the time.

Fowler and Thomas were enjoying a very successful trip around Scotland. After Titan's Wall they headed over to Skye and made a number of new climbs in Coire Lagan, as well as the spectacular Stairway to Heaven on the side wall of the Great Prow on Blaven. At E5 this was the hardest rock climb on the island for many years. As a finale to their Scottish tour, Fowler and Thomas visited Creag an Dubh-loch. They arrived on Thursday, June 23, only to find another party on their target route. It was Cuthbertson and Hamilton, who were unwittingly settling the score over Titan's Wall by making what they believed, was the first free ascent of The Giant. (Several years elapsed before Tut Braithwaite revealed that he had climbed the 6a pitch free in 1974). The two Southerners turned their attention to King Rat and proceeded to make an ascent without the use of aid at the roof.

Hamilton and Cuthbertson, together with Willie Todd and Adge Last, had only just arrived that morning with sufficient food for a week. Todd and Last made a free ascent of Falkenhorst while the other pair were climbing The Giant. Next on the list was Cougar. Hamilton was aware that Dinwoodie and Muhlemann had free-climbed most of the first two major pitches and it was assumed that the final crack had still only been done with the seven pitons mentioned in Rennie's original description. Friday was again dry, so while Fowler and Thomas went for The Giant to make another completely free ascent, Cuthbertson and Hamilton battled with Cougar.

*Dick Renshaw
below the chokestone
on the first pitch of
Cumming-Crofton
Route, February 1977*

Photo: Greg Strange

All went to plan and by mid-afternoon, taking alternate leads, they had reached the stance below the final pitch, having free-climbed everything up to that point, but not without difficulty. The dice had fallen for Cuthbertson to take this last lead and just to pep up the already committing situation the weather began to change, bringing a threat of rain. He progressed quickly past the place where Dinwoodie had gone left and on up to the crack with the protruding block. Near the top of this he was stopped by a final overlap which, despite repeated attempts, he could not surmount. For over an hour he wrestled with the problem until he was eventually forced to go left.

By traversing below the overlap, across a gap, he came to a good rock spike, which provided a runner as well as a temporary haven. He knew that to get out he had to go up, but each time he tried upwards he was forced farther left. In the end he stepped up from the spike and continued precariously left below a bulge. As the difficulties began to ease he

Murray Hamilton and Dave Cuthbertson climbing Cougar, June 1977

Photo: Rob Archbold

spotted a solitary piton, left the previous summer by the Aberdonians. This lifted his spirit and he went on to complete this exciting pitch, belaying up left below a small roof. By the time Hamilton had joined him it was raining heavily. It had been a close run thing.

This influential ascent confirmed what a number of climbers had suspected for some time, namely that the steep slabs and overlaps on this section of Central Gully Wall could be climbed without artificial aid. Cuthbertson and Hamilton had carried pitons but had resisted the temptation to use them, even for protection, relying only on their skill, their strength, chalk and a full selection of modern nuts to see them up. It took several years and further ascents before a consensus of opinion settled on a grade of E3, with each of the three hard pitches being 5c. When asked many years later about this ascent Hamilton, well known for his economy with words, said he thought the climb was great, hard, but not so hard!

The two Edinburgh men remained a forceful partnership for another year, but went their separate ways soon after a successful trip to Yosemite in the spring of 1978. Although they were from quite different backgrounds they had both followed a traditional Scottish course to becoming climbers and mountaineers. As youngsters they had been introduced to hill-walking. In Cuthbertson's case it was while in the

Boy's Brigade, whereas Hamilton went to the hills with his father (who climbed a little) as well as with other pupils from his school, Stewart-Melville College. By the time they both met, Hamilton had been climbing a year longer than Cuthbertson. The strength of the partnership lay in a mutual determination to succeed on the hardest climbs, but there was always an underlying rivalry between them.

While all this activity was taking place on Central Gully Wall, Archbold and Muhlemann completed a new climb on the lower tier of the Central Slabs, right of Black Mamba. They had started up a line of cracks and grooves close to the right edge three weeks earlier, but had been rained-off after three pitches. The route, Vixen, has good, varied climbing marred only by the ease of escape into Theseus Grooves below the last pitch (E1 5b). Finishing early, they found themselves in a grandstand position to capture on film the action on the other side of Central Gully – Fowler and Thomas on the Giant, and Hamilton leading the overhanging exit from the Cougar Slab.

With the onset of rain there was a mass exodus from the Dubh Loch on the Friday night. Unaware of all this mid-week activity, Dinwoodie and I arrived the next day to find a water-streaked crag. We were interested in the crack-line right of the Red Wall on Gulliver which Bower had attempted. Dinwoodie had already been up to the obvious roof on a sortie from The Caterpillar and was enthusing at the prospect of climbing this using a large downward pointing flake, which he claimed was shaped like an alligator's head. We climbed the Bower-Lang Route only to be caught by more rain as soon as we reached The Caterpillar.

We returned the following Saturday and worked out an independent start just right of Gulliver. The climbing was disappointing and we came to the conclusion that the best way would be to start up the Bower-Lang Route, then strike up towards the upper crack-line from a point just beyond its crux traverse. Sunday stayed fair all day and we finally climbed the whole route, alternating leads and using no aid. It was a very satisfying day with 900ft of good continuous climbing. There were two distinct cruxes, both led by Dougie. The first was a short recessed wall, 100ft beyond the point where we quit the Bower-Lang Route. It was steep with awkwardly-spaced holds and only protected with a thin blade piton. The second hard bit was on the pitch above The Caterpillar. The move over the roof using the alligator's head was certainly exhilarating, but the technical difficulty lay at a bulge near the top of the crack above. Dougie spent ages cleaning moss and divots from the rock while taking tension from a piton. With all this talk of free-climbing he was determined not to resort to aid. After a couple of unsuccessful attempts he finally cracked it by laybacking on the edge of the crack. We named the climb Caiman – E2 5c.

Dinwoodie was back at Creag an Dubh-loch soon after this with Bob Smith, when they made free ascents of Falseface and The Sword of Damocles. It was on this visit they attempted the great crack-line right of The Giant arete. Dinwoodie led the pitch previously climbed by Higgins and belayed on a good ledge below the break in the roof. Armed with the information from Higgins that "it should go free with a couple of pitons at the roof", Smith launched out over the bulge. He managed to get into the groove above but could make nothing of the rock, only

*Douglas Dinwoodie
starting the slim
tilting diedre of
Scalpel on the
Crimson Slabs,
July 1977*

Photo: Greg Strange

being able to progress with the continuous use of aid. Before reaching the first obvious widening in the groove he had to negotiate a precarious detached block, knowing full well that if dislodged it would probably hit his partner standing directly below. At the widening, Smith took a hanging belay on very poor pitons. When Dinwoodie reached him, having removed all the gear except Higgins's original piton at the roof, they made a scary abseil back into Central Gully, convinced that the groove could not be free-climbed no matter how much cleaning was done.

Although Creag an Dubh-loch took centre stage that summer, other areas in the Cairngorms saw exploration, mainly during the dry weather in July. In Coire an Dubh Lochain of Beinn a' Bhùird, Stephen and Stan Falconer found good climbing on Come Dancing, the crack-line right of Tearaway, (VS 5a), while in Coire na Cìche, Archbold and Keir climbed the bulging headland between Sandy Crack and Little Tower Gully. Hot Toddy – VS 5a. Success on this imposing lump of granite encouraged Archbold and Keir to cross the Sneck the following day to investigate the west face of Mitre Ridge. Like others before them they had also been inspired by Rusk's picture in the old guidebook and believed there was scope for a climb easier than the hard-looking Slochd Wall which had still not received a second ascent.

Despite it being early July, they had to negotiate a 12ft bergschrund before gaining access to the minor gully which serves as an introduction to Commando Route. Their climb, Ghurka (VS), followed this gully directly through the prominent overhanging cul-de-sac before finishing up the exposed edge to the left of Slochd Wall. Although the granite in the gully was vegetated, and a little loose, they were pleasantly surprised to find good rock and reassuring holds on the upper crest. They also concluded that Slochd Wall would probably have similar holds, at least on its upper pitches, where the rock was not as steep as it looked from below.

In the Loch Avon basin, Fyffe and Barton were busy investigating unclimbed rock on Hell's Lum and Longbow Crags. On the former they climbed Towering Inferno, the pillar formation immediately right of the duplicating fault of Deep Cut Chimney. Although the climbing was good, the third pitch was distinctly harder than the rest – VS. On a return visit with Allen's wife, Eileen, they found an easier, though less direct, alternative to the harder pitch thus producing a good sustained climb of only Severe standard. The Lodge instructors' best find, however, was on the right-hand sector of the frontal face where they climbed Devil Dancer (HVS 5a) beside Auld Nick. Fyffe particularly enjoyed this route because the difficulty increased with height and the final wall provided surprising protection where none seemed possible from below. On the adjacent Stag Rocks they climbed Windchill (HVS 5a), a rather devious but worthwhile route between Longbow Direct and Sand-Pyper, sharing several stances with the latter climb.

Finally, from the crop of new climbs in July, mention should be made of Dinwoodie's lead of Scalpel, the slim, tilting diedre left of Djibangi on the Crimson Slabs. This hard-looking feature, which cuts a diagonal slash across the wettest area of red slabs, went with relative ease at HVS 5a. Near the top of the diedre, where protection and holds become more sparse, a hidden foot-wide ledge appeared on the left and this provided a good belay stance. The climb was finished by a curving corner on the left. Eight years later Nisbet led the whole diedre direct to provide another excellent pitch on these unusual slabs – E1 5b.

Continuous cold weather in November 1977 brought about a good early build-up of ice. On Hell's Lum Crag, Blairgowrie climber, Gordon Smith, with Andy Slater, made the second ascent of The Chancer. Climbing with modern axes and taking no rests, he was reported to have said that it was not too hard![6] Smith was a rather enigmatic character who went to Stirling University then worked for a while at Glenmore Lodge. An outstanding winter and Alpine mountaineer, he never bothered to formally record his routes in the Cairngorms – a trait which endeared him to a dwindling band of anarchic Scottish climbers, but was a pain in the neck for subsequent guidebook writers. It was during this winter that Smith and Slater made an ascent of The Clean Sweep, following the summer line throughout. The route does not ice as readily as Devil's Delight which would explain why Smith found it hard for a IV! It is still one of the most difficult pure ice routes on the crag – Grade VI.

So ephemeral was this early ice that only a few were able to take advantage of its presence. Nisbet and Robertson, by chance, had walked past Creag an Dubh-loch during the last weekend in November and discovered a build up of ice no one could have predicted so early in the season. Their thoughts turned to Vertigo Wall and the possibility of making an ascent of this 'last great winter problem'. Nisbet was in training for a trip to climb the North Face of the Matterhorn at the end of December and had recently acquired a bivouac tent. With the promise of continuous, frosty weather over the weekend December 3-4 they decided to give it a go and planned to bivouac on the shelf leading to the black chimney.

They reached this point on the first day, through-leading and towing a haul bag with all their bivouac gear. Nisbet led the 'Severe' crack with two points of aid. They then spent a miserable, cold and very uncomfortable 18 hours in their little tent, until in the morning, Nisbet was able to get to grips with the ice-choked chimney. Unfortunately, this was less built-up than they had hoped.

"Two terrible creaking ice screws in dinner-plating ice and much heaving and grunting, overcame the bulge. Then 50ft of slow, careful progress rightward on steep rotten ice brought a peg runner at last, the first noticeable protection in 70ft. He disappeared above the ice bulges, traversing back left to an invisible stance in a corner directly above me."[7]

By the time Robertson had followed this serious pitch there was only two hours of daylight left and the sensational summer crux had still to be climbed. They were really up against it now with a second night on the cliff a distinct possibility.

Although Robertson could remember every detail of this pitch from his summer ascent two years previously, he was by no means certain of his ability to get up it now. Once he got going there was an early boost when he discovered the slab leading to the headwall was thickly plated in ice enabling the high ledge to be gained easily. "The traverse was very balancy, but head-high runners gave confidence and I found myself directly above the white mound of snow which indicated the flake. I leaned carefully and brushed away the snow with my foot. The flake withstood a gentle kick without creaking. Like everyone else I'd avoided even touching it in summer; now I didn't have much choice but to assume that it was frozen in place. I took a few feet of slack and a deep breath then jumped down to wrap my arms lovingly round it, feet waving comically in mid-air. I couldn't hang backwards off the flake for long, but frantic clearing operations uncovered a good spike. I put a sling on it and had a good rest: so far, so good."[8]

He now had to step round and make a few moves up the little corner to reach the ledge continuing right. This was the technical crux. He pulled strenuously up into the corner until the sloping ledge was level with his head. Holding on with one Terrordactyl stabbed into frozen turf he tried desperately to place a piton runner. This he managed but found he could not hammer it home. "I hung on grimly for a few more minutes looking stupidly at the peg, near to tears with frustration, rapidly running out of strength. As a last gamble I clipped hopefully into my Terrordactyl. I watched it lever out with sickening predictability, and for what seemed a long time felt myself heeling over backwards, to lurch to a halt dangling in space 30ft below."[9]

Nisbet lowered him down onto the rock, then after a brief rest, Robertson climbed back up and took another rest at the sling. This time he used two pitons to gain his high point and finally succeeded in stepping onto the sloping ledge. Farther right he reached a larger ledge where he could at last stand in balance. The final snow-plastered wall was climbed with a series of strenuous pulls.

By the time Robertson had arranged a belay and hauled up the sack it was completely dark and Nisbet had still to follow. "Only Andrew's headlamp, bobbing and flickering in the gloom 80ft below broke the surrounding blackness. Somehow he groped his way as far as the flake, then I tied off one of the ropes and tensed on the other as, oblivious in the darkness of the void below, he pendulumed down and out into space and started laboriously prusiking."[10]

After the long wait, the attempt to climb and the wild prusik, it must have been a great relief for Nisbet to lead the final easy pitch up to the plateau, knowing that they had just completed what was probably the most difficult winter climb yet accomplished in the Cairngorms, possibly in Scotland. Of course, they were not yet completely out of it, for they still had to get down and back to Aberdeen, which they eventually did by 4am on Monday morning, having had only four hours sleep in the last three days.

It took a while for the implications of this climb to sink in, partly because it had been done so early in the season before most folk had even dusted off their crampons. The planned bivouac on the cliff was unprecedented for a first ascent in the Cairngorms. The use of aid certainly was not. Given the sustained nature of the climbing, the lack of daylight at this time of the year and the inescapable nature of the line, the general feeling was that the eight points of aid were just acceptable and that this had been a very fine effort by the young Aberdonians. Now the obvious challenge was to do the climb in one day without the aid, and this was achieved on the second ascent in November 1985 by

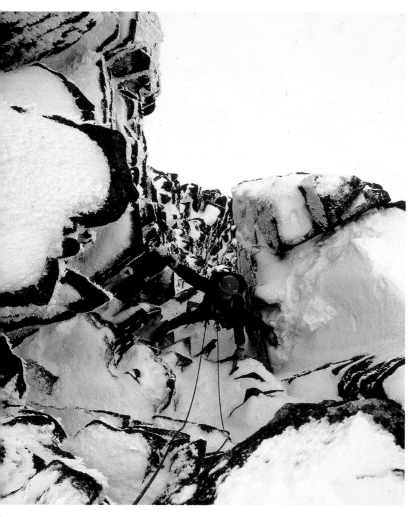

Sam Crymble.
Fluted Buttress
Direct, March 1978

Photo: Allen Fyffe

Nisbet, sharing the leading with Andy Cunningham. They took nine hours and it confirmed Nisbet's opinion that Vertigo Wall was one of Scotland's finest mixed winter routes – Grade VII. Not long after Vertigo Wall, Robertson dropped out of front line winter climbing but continued to rock climb and hill-walk with great enthusiasm.

The weather pattern in the first months of 1978 was similar to the previous winter in terms of snow build-up. At the end of January the Highlands were paralysed by the worst blizzard since 1947 and virtually all upland travel was brought to a standstill. Throughout February the large accumulations of snow in the Cairngorms tended not to consolidate very well and most keen climbers took advantage of exceptionally good winter conditions in the North West. Even North Wales and the Lake District had unusually good snow and ice at this time.

In March, two very good climbs were made in the vicinity of Scorpion on Càrn Etchachan. Early the previous summer Archbold and Keir had climbed a Severe route, Red Guard, which took a natural line up a big chimney and groove system left of Scorpion, before finishing above an

North Face of Squareface, Garbh Choire of Beinn a' Bhùird, Dennis King in the foreground. March 1974

Photo: Greg Strange

obvious left-trending pink ramp on the upper cliff. On March 5, Dave Wright and John Higham climbed the buttress between Scorpion and False Scorpion to the midway ledges then finished up the ramp of Red Guard. Their climb, The Sword, was Grade V in excellent conditions. Two weeks later, on Good Friday, Keir and Freeman climbed the whole of Red Guard in 10 hours, using tension and three pitons for aid in the crux groove above the lower chimney – Grade VI.

At the time, Keir was experimenting with various home-made strap-on foot irons for use on ice-glazed rock. On this climb he was wearing what he referred to as 'trampons', a type of crampon but with tricouni nails in lieu of spikes. His father had made them for him using one-piece base plates with side posts riveted on. The tricounis were bought from Lawrie's of London and attached with staples. The problem with very specialised equipment is that, while it may work very well for the specific circumstances for which it was designed, it could be a considerable hindrance elsewhere on the same climb, if, as is often the case in winter, conditions vary. Tricouni plates work well on lightly snow-covered, frosted or verglased rock; but whenever ice or hard snow is encountered, steps have to be cut.

The large Fluted Buttress in Coire an t-Sneachda has an area of more compact rock near its centre. Tucked into the left flank of this area, a series of chimneys and grooves lead directly to the top. Surprisingly, this line appears not to have been climbed either summer or winter until March 18, 1978 when Fyffe and fellow Lodge instructor, Sam Crymble, made an ascent on good snow and ice, recording it as Grade III. Near the top of the first chimney they found an old piton of unknown origin. This Fluted Buttress Direct, one of the best winter climbs in the corrie, is now considered to be Grade IV.

After the ascent of the unpleasant 'Rocky Mountain Horror Show' in the Garbh Choire of Beinn a' Bhùird, Archbold concluded that it would make a much better climb under winter conditions. Although he had seen a photograph taken in March 1974 showing two distinct icefalls descending from the snow-filled basin, no-one could remember seeing these icefalls so well formed in other winters. On April 7, he visited the corrie with Dinwoodie ostensibly to try Mitre Ridge, but hoping that they would go onto the North Face of Squareface. When they descended below the face, instead of seeing well-formed twin icefalls set against dark rock, they found the whole cliff covered with snow. Only the left-hand drainage line held ice and this only evident immediately below the basin. In spite of the disappointing conditions, Archbold persuaded his companion to give it a try and they succeeded in following the same line taken in summer, on what Dinwoodie later described as a very scary climb with rotten snow and poor belays. Just below the basin, a prominent snout of rock separates the two drainage lines. They zig-zagged up ramps below the right-hand line to reach a pedestal at the bottom right corner of the snout. They then used tension to cross the snout and finished up the left-hand icefall. The cornice above the basin was gigantic, but fortunately, avoidable on the right, resulting in Crucible Route – Grade V.

Summer came early to the Cairngorms in 1978, with warm weather and dry rock for much of May. Nisbet and Mary Bridges took advantage of these good conditions to climb the fine pitch of Sgian Dubh, up the arete overlooking the corner of Djibangi on the Crimson Slabs. Towards the end of the month Dinwoodie and Renshaw spent a few days at the Shelter Stone Crag. After ascents of The Needle and Haystack they felt ready to tackle the main objective of their visit, a direct climb up the middle of the Central Slabs. As well as Hamilton and Taylor, Dinwoodie had also climbed The Pin on the day of the Loki ascent and had watched Liddell leading the first pitch up into the Thor diedre. Apart from this he knew nothing about the line except what he had read in an article by Bill March in 1971, referring to "the plum line up the Cupid's bow crack in the centre of the Central Slabs, which had already repelled a few of the leading lights, some head first".[11]

Renshaw agreed to lead the first pitch, fully expecting the steep slabs

Dave Nichols surveys the way ahead on the second pitch of The Bishop, May 1978

Photo: Greg Strange

to be poorly protected, however: "I laced up the pitch, enjoying the delicate climbing. A thin move across to the belay and soon I was strapped to the rock, working out the most comfortable position in which to stand."[12] In order to reach the base of the bow, Dinwoodie had to climb a little way up Thor, and it was here that he was faced with his first dilemma. It looked hard to get out of the main corner onto a little ledge on the left. He clipped into an old piton, tried to work out the sequence of moves, then using the piton he moved up and swung left to the start of the bow – a smooth tapering corner.

He searched for signs of previous suitors, but could see nothing except a blind, unhelpful crack in the corner which looked very thin. He gained a little height using a Rurp and was then able to hammer a good piton into the crack. Progress was very slow. Apart from the Rurp, two pitons were used for aid in the first 20ft, before he was able to move out to flake holds on the left edge. Higher up he had to climb an awkward bulging section at the top of the corner. Renshaw recalled: "A peg tinkled down pursued by a wicked curse. I craned my neck to see a grey bundle hunched up on the middle of the bow with only a hard move to reach a possible stance which turned out to be a wrinkle of rock with dubious belay points."[13]

Renshaw had been standing with one foot in a sling for more than two hours, so it was with relief that he climbed up to the ledge at the start of the bow. Now belayed to a piton and a nut 12ft up the corner he removed all the other gear and sent it up. Dinwoodie continued up the line of the crack until it jinked right as a shallow corner, heading for the blank area above Thor. He tried unsuccessfully to follow it but was forced to go up left. He stepped tentatively onto a slabby grey wall with little in the way of holds.

"'This bit's very hard and I might come off' delivered in an off-hand manner, as though he were ordering a bag of chips. I pushed myself hard against the rock and Dougie, true to his word, slipped off in stoical silence.

"The runners held and I was still on the ledge. By the time my heart stopped pounding, Loch Avon had turned an oily black and the sky was just as dark. The first spittle of rain fell and we waited in silence as the rain stopped, started, then finally stopped and the damp rock quickly dried off. With two short coughs Dougie started up and kept going to another ledge."[14] Once again he was running short of gear, so he belayed and brought Renshaw up to a point midway up the bow as it was getting late and further rain looked imminent. He hauled up the gear and gardened a short flake crack which appeared to lead off on to easy ground. A couple of stiff layback moves and he was up.

When Renshaw came to follow he found that the slab had been peppered with grass and earth from the cleaned flake. "Above me was the steep slab with a few baldy earth-covered bumps. After removing most of the earth I teetered up, but I had neglected to clean a little knobble; my left foot slipped, and I came off at the same point where Dougie had fallen. Shamelessly, I shouted for a tight rope. At the flake I beat out the peg runner; the jaws of the crack suddenly relaxed, spitting out the peg, leaving me cursing. The flake led to a grassy terrace and at the far end, sat a figure hunched up like Quasimodo in the

Belfry wearing a little smile."[15] Much hard graft and four aid points had finally unlocked the key to this majestic climb. The new generation were critical of Dinwoodie's use of aid and he later admitted that he could see how up-and-coming young climbers would have found the ascent annoying and greedy.

While Dinwoodie and Renshaw were climbing on the Shelter Stone Crag, Dave Nichols and I visited the Garbh Choire of Beinn a' Bhùird, bivouacking below a large boulder close to the foot of Mitre Ridge. We were interested in climbing the attractive, tapering cuneiform buttress on the west face of the Ridge and had spotted a dark crack in the centre of its upper rocks. A closer inspection confirmed our suspicions that gaining this crack from directly below would be beyond our free-climbing ability, so we turned our attention to a prominent cracked groove 20ft right of Cumming-Crofton Route. By starting up this we were able to climb The Chancel, a route which stayed close to the left edge of the buttress all the way to the top. The next day we moved round to the east face of the Ridge and found our way up The Bishop, a direct route left of and parallel to Mitre Ridge Direct. Both this and The Chancel gave good climbing, each with a well protected, short 5b crux.

Meanwhile, Archbold was restless to get back to the west face too. "During the winter I'd been brooding over Rusk's photograph again, trying to plan a rising traverse. The first good weekend arrived but I was gutted that an ill-timed exam prevented me from joining Dave and Greg. Amazingly though, the good weather held, so after quizzing Greg about the middle section of Chancel, I persuaded Bill McKerrow to join me for a sunny weekend in the Garbh Coire." They climbed Helter Skelter, a rising girdle of Mitre Ridge, starting in South-East Gully and finishing up the previously unclimbed top section of Slochd Wall. This unusual outing crossed improbable areas of rock for a route of VS standard. The crux, 4c, was an exposed rising traverse from Ghurka into an upper corner left of Slochd Wall. They then crossed Slochd Wall and climbed the steep wall above the terrace by a surprisingly easy left-trending groove.

Also in June, Nisbet found another good route on Beinn a' Bhùird, this time in Coire an Dubh Lochain. With Neil Spinks he climbed The Scent, a steep line left of Bloodhound Buttress with a poorly protected middle pitch – HVS 5a.

The continuing good weather was a gentle reminder to Dinwoodie, Archbold and me that we still had a score to settle with the girdle traverse of Central Gully Wall. All we required was a dry cliff and one whole day of clear blue skies. To speed up progress on the crag we invited Dick Renshaw to join us in order that we could climb as two ropes. A good night in the back room of Glas-allt-Shiel set us up for a memorable day's climbing on June 17. With Dougie and Dick in front we stepped left from the grassy recess of Caterpillar Crack and, 12 hours later, after 1400ft of sustained, mainly slabby climbing, we stood content, coiling the ropes in the twilight at the top of Goliath.

From the belay above the soaring crack-line, where we had started the abseils five years previously, a switchback course on slabs tucked above and below overlaps took us down into a deep recess occupied by a big detached block. A difficult move up the sharp left edge of the recess

Douglas Dinwoodie and Dick Renshaw, 1978

Photo: Greg Strange

then led to an airy grass perch below an impending wall, plumb on the crest of the Giant arete – a wonderful little haven. The next 30ft, although technically straightforward, proved to be the highlight of the day. Below the ledge we discovered a perfect flake crack leading diagonally down the vertical wall to ledges at the top of the crux pitch of The Giant. Dick went first, hanging out on big holds in a wildly-exposed position. Our intention had been to complete the climb by finishing on Vertigo Wall. From The Giant we went diagonally up left, passing an old piton, and then above a bulge we joined McArtney's shelf variation to Goliath. By now the light was fading and, although Dougie did have a look at a possible link to Vertigo, crossing a steep blunt arete looked problematical, so we hurried on up Goliath to the top, The Prowl – E2 5b.

The ascent of Red Guard on Càrn Etchachan in May 1977 had been the first new rock climb on this crag for more than 20 years. Inspired by the situations and overall length of the climbs here, Archbold returned in July of this year with Tom Syme to climb Bastille, another 900ft route lying between Route Major and Red Guard. VS 5a. Archbold recalled: "After several days of rain, we made an unusual approach from the Derry Gates, via Cumming-Crofton Route and the Avon. The crux of Bastille was wet and steep, much harder than the severe-ish climbing elsewhere on the route. We took turns to place gear as high as we could, then Long Tom cracked it with a big stride left."

Taking a fresh look at this unfashionable cliff had also been the intention of Allen Fyffe. On July 11, he and Dave Morris climbed a good continuous line of cracks up the left wall of the Equinox gully. Morris was working for the Nature Conservancy Council in Aviemore at the time. They went initially to investigate a climb on Stacan Dubha of Beinn Mheadhoin but retreated due to bad rock. Fyffe recalls: "We then went to Càrn Etchachan as I had an idea about this line. Dave led the first pitch, but fell off and I held my first fall on a belay plate. We called the route Time Traveller as Dave left his watch somewhere and had to go back for it later. HVS 5a. The next day Fyffe returned to Càrn Etchachan with Crymble. They bivouacked beside Loch Etchachan and did another two climbs, the best and hardest of which started close to the foot of Equinox and climbed up in two pitches to join Crevasse Route at its window. The climb, Poison Dwarf, has a tough little second pitch led by Fyffe – E1 5b.

The winter season of 1978 – 79 was another lengthy affair with a good number of climbers operating at the highest technical levels. In the Cairngorms, those seeking to make first winter ascents of existing summer rock climbs were increasingly having to consider routes of VS or harder. Since Vertigo Wall had been done, leading activists had now set their sights on three other 1950s classics, namely The Citadel, Mousetrap and The Link. It was a question of who would get there first?

For the second year in a row Gordon Smith was busy on the cliffs around the head of Loch Avon. Plenty of fresh snow in December had brought the Stag Rocks into unusually good winter condition. On December 27, he climbed Wigwag with Mick Fowler. This was the first of several routes he made on the crag. Others included Deception Inlet, with Karen Gazley, The Tenements, solo, and the impressive Central Route with the Kiwi,

Gary Ball. This latter climb (named by Fyffe) was believed to link vegetated depressions right of Sand-Pyper before finishing straight up close to Sand-Pyper original. A similar line was climbed by Ken Spence and Rob Milne in 1981, then 30 years later, Smith revealed his route had been much closer to Sand-Pyper Direct.

On Hell's Lum Crag, Smith solved a long-standing problem with the ascent of the duplicating fault right of Deep Cut Chimney. At mid-height this has a constricted hanging chimney which presented considerable difficulty. Smith rated the climb Grade V and said at the time he thought it to be one of the finest winter routes he had done in Scotland, but neither named the route nor his companion (Gary Ball). Further appreciative ascents soon followed and Fyffe eventually named it Nobody's Fault as a reflection on the climb's history.

Two students at Aberdeen University came to the fore on the climbing front during this winter. Brian Sprunt moved with his family to Aberdeen from Coatbridge in 1976. He had been introduced to the mountains by his father, Bob, himself a keen climber and member of the Glasgow JMCS. As a teenager, before arriving in the North-east, the young Sprunt had led some big rock climbs including Centurion and The Bat on Ben Nevis. His impish West Coast banter was a refreshing addition to the local scene. John Anderson also came from the West, although he was born in London. His family lived abroad and he went to Keil School in Dumbarton where he was introduced to hill-walking and climbing by one of the masters. Now studying for a degree in marine biology, he was a strong, fresh-faced lad, more reserved than Sprunt, but with an equally mischievous sense of humour.

The second half of January saw Lochnagar buried in deep snow after weeks of freezing temperatures and strong easterly winds. Anderson had just made an ascent of Eagle Ridge with Sprunt and was enthused about the ice-filled grooves lying beneath all the powder. "Conditions are magic," he reported. Having heard a good weather forecast for the weekend he was now keen to climb Parallel Gully B, but his companion, Andy Nisbet, had other ideas and suggested they attempt The Link on the Black Spout Pinnacle.

Saturday, January 27, was exceptionally cold with little wind and cloudless skies. The North-east corrie did indeed look magic, as every piece of rock on the crag was gleaming white with snow or hoar frost. Like other ambitious local climbers, Nisbet regarded The Link as the next logical step up in difficulty after Pinnacle Face. For those who had contemplated this climb in winter it was generally assumed the easiest way would be to follow the summer route from the Springboard to a point above the big overhang, then to climb a prominent vegetated groove (passed on the right in summer) to join Route 2 at the end of its traverse. Although the line is steeper and much more exposed than Pinnacle Face, the whole route, with the exception of the overhang, is climbed in grooves. Climbers had been waiting for favourable conditions when these grooves would be partially filled with hard snow or ice to facilitate a winter ascent.

Despite Anderson's claim that much of the rock on the cliff was coated in ice, Nisbet decided to persevere with his tricouni plates. "Obsessed by a blind faith in their potential and a need to save weight, my crampons have been abandoned."[16] He had recently acquired his Trampons

John Anderson
Photo: Andy Nisbet

from Keir's father and had already found them to work very well on half-inch thick slush and lightly snow-covered rock. He was about to climb the crux of Route 1 to gain the Springboard, a pitch he had led two years earlier experiencing major difficulties while wearing crampons on snow-crusted rock. This time, he believed his Trampons would make things easier – no such luck. After surmounting the first bulge he found the slab above covered in ice up to half-an-inch thick. He then had a long struggle hauling himself up with his axes, using his knees and dragging his near useless feet up behind him. Oh for a pair of crampons!

Anderson was also having trouble, his problem being brought about by the low temperatures. After three hours belaying in the Black Spout he was experiencing very cold feet, a worrying situation as he had already suffered mild frostbite in these on a walking trip the previous winter. He warmed up a little as he quickly followed the first pitch, then taking over the lead, he traversed right to the start of The Link proper. Directly above him was the big groove, 100ft long and ending below a triangular roof. Several bulges broke its continuity but all was uniformly white covered in crusted powder snow. Laboriously he cleared away the soft material to reveal thin ice below and very slowly he made his way clearing, stabbing, kicking and bridging all the way up to a stance below the roof.

When Nisbet came to follow he made a valiant attempt to climb the ice in his tricounis but at the second bulge he realised it was hopeless and started to prusik. He was impressed with Anderson's lead and when he reached the stance he told him so. The situation felt serious: "We are united, but there are no smiles. He was stretched, and the route seems to be slipping away, while I am helpless to contribute and evening is approaching. The crux lurks round the corner so I offer to peg it. As I cut steps on an easy, iced slab and awkwardly move round the corner into a niche, I think John realises for the first time how much of a passenger I really am. I'm stunned by the size of the overhang. Crouched in the niche, I have to stretch my neck right back to see the lip; I'm in a white cave of iced walls with an ice-choked roof crack. Any pegging cracks are buried deep; it looks so impossible I can only stare. 'Shall I have a go?' says John from round the corner. I'm still speechless so he comes round. No words when he sees it, he just starts. The belay is the rustiest of old pegs from the 1950s and our pathetic contribution at my feet. John shoves his axe into the roof and lurches his feet up on to a smooth icy wall. They slide off repeatedly but he still dangles. I cut a score in the ice; its lip breaks off but I can hold his foot on to it. An amazing pull up on one arm and one supported foot and a Terrordactyl drops over the lip. It sticks to something and he hangs spreadeagled over the roof above my head.

'I don't know what this tool's in', he says. Then pauses.

'Will I hit anything?'

'No chance,' I reply, as falling snow touches nothing to the Black Spout itself. 'Neither of us will touch anything,' I think to myself.

'I haven't got the courage to do this,' he says and I relax for a moment in anticipation of a safe retreat; and then he starts pulling up, ever so slowly at first to a bent arm position. I stop breathing; feel the hot flush of adrenalin in my face and a tingling down to my fingertips. A foot swings out from under the overhang and lodges on a fluted edge of fog crystals far out above me.

'What's that foot on?' he shouts. 'Is it good?'

'I don't know,' I answer. 'It doesn't look it.'

'It looks appalling.'

'Maybe it is,' is my most optimistic offering, since there's no way back. His whole body is still in view, suspended out behind me, bridged across the lip of the roof. How can he stay there? The bridge edges higher and wider and he grunts out of sight. Debris pours out behind me, like being at the back of a waterfall. What sort of a position is he in? Will he run out of strength up there? I know there is no protection. I clip his rope into the belay as a runner, but then unclip it again. Maybe a direct fall on to my body will absorb some of the force on the belay? From 60ft? I clip it in again but doubts and morbid visions race through my mind. Then he's up and I feel close to fainting."[17]

This stunning lead saved the day for although darkness was approaching Nisbet was able to quickly prusik up the overhang and allow Anderson to hurry on up the big vegetated groove. "John races up in the gloom, a race against darkness. His feet are scraping and sliding, you can see the sparks at night. One hundred and twenty unprotected feet almost at running pace, no time to clear holds, just blast on and hope for the best."[18] The tactics paid off for they managed to reach easier ground, leaving 'only' the upper Pinnacle, the abseil into the gap, and the final pitch up to the plateau to be climbed by torch light.

Anderson's impressive lead of The Link, unfortunately, had a down side to it. He spent the next week in hospital receiving treatment for frostbitten toes and was unable to climb again for two months. It also ruled him out from Nisbet's next weekend's project – an ascent of Crypt on the Tough-Brown Face. This HVS summer route follows the largest continuous groove system on the face and had already attracted attention.

With Anderson rendered *hors de combat*, Nisbet persuaded Brian Sprunt to join him as a suitable leader for the crux. They braved very cold stormy weather on the Saturday and managed only 120ft up to the summer crux, avoiding the opening groove by climbing a ramp farther left and tensioning back. The next day was windless and after a 4.30am rise they were back below the face. Nisbet recalls: "Feeling much more optimistic and relieved of leading the crux, I raced up the first pitch and belayed securely at the tension point. Just as he unclipped from the tension sling, Brian's foot slipped and he spent 10 minutes of desperate effort to avoid falling off. But Brian, who tends to get demoralised standing at belays, is unstoppable once he's climbing (unless he falls off) so he moved undismayed into the main corner. Planting a rather psycholog-ical ice screw in a clod of frozen earth and cutting two big footholds to allow a comfortable bridging position, he uncovered a secondary crack on the right wall of the corner. Excruciatingly strenuous bridg-ing gained the critical 10ft, during which he miraculously placed a peg runner at a place where I could barely stay in contact with the rock. The final grass overhang was a close thing on failing arms but the corner had been entered and, though still quite steep, was filled with a six-inch wide ribbon of ice in the back."[19]

Higher up, Sprunt was soon tackling the second summer crux, where the groove is blocked by an overhang. Here a mini-cornice had formed, but instead of chopping the soft snow away he committed himself to climb round it, spending anxious minutes hanging from one Terrordactyl adze in the snow while his crampons scarted on the hold-less rock below. Brevity triumphed, and he pulled over on to easier terrain and found a belay. After following this very sustained pitch, Nisbet led up to the scoop on Parallel Gully B. They then soloed down the lower part of Tough-Brown Traverse and made it back to the bottom just as darkness fell.

Both Crypt (Grade VI) and The Link (Grade VII) were significant first winter ascents made in unusual conditions for Lochnagar mixed climbs. Although extensive thin ice lay below partially consolidated snow, the advantage of the ice was offset by the difficulty of finding and fixing worthwhile protection. While Crypt broke new ground as the opening winter route on the Tough-Brown Face, The Link was perhaps the most difficult Cairngorms winter climb of the 1970s.

Climbing conditions were very similar three weeks later when Alex McIntyre, The British Mountaineering Council's National Officer, brought a party of six young French climbers on an exchange visit to sample some winter climbing on Lochnagar and Creag an Dubh-loch. In the group were Dominique Julien and Renier Munsch from the Pyrenees, Gilles Rotillon from near Fontainbleau and Rene Ghilini, Jean-Marc Boivin and Jean Franc Charlet from Chamonix – the latter two were both Chamonix Guides. Earlier in the week they had been to Ben Nevis and Creag Meagaidh, doing classics such as Point Five Gully, Smith's Gully, South and Last Posts in very quick order. Bill Brooker had arranged accommodation at Allt-na-giubhsaich and organised a repre-sentative team from the Etchachan Club to host the visitors. Over the two days there were ascents by various international parties of Eagle Ridge, Parallel Buttress, Parallel Gully B, Pinnacle Face, Grovel Wall, Shallow Gully and both branches of Parallel Gully A. At Creag an Dubh-loch, Hanging Garden Route and Labyrinth Edge were done. On the Saturday, the better of the two days, Boivin and Sprunt made an inter-esting variation on the Black Spout Pinnacle by starting up Winter Face and climbing a very thin groove up left to join Grovel Wall. Sprunt led the hard main pitch which was later named the French Connection

The locals were impressed with the climbing ability of the visitors who always appeared to be well in control. They were kitted out with the latest French axes and crampons and seemed at home in the far-from-perfect snow and ice conditions. This was the first time that most of the Scots had seen the recently designed reverse-curved or banana pick of 'Le Chacal', Simond's new ice hammer. The tool certainly looked sophisticated when compared to our Terrordactyls. Apparently, Ghilini was a developer for Simond and took every opportunity to advance sales of the new product. During the weekend I climbed Parallel Buttress and Shallow Gully with Jean Franc Charlet (grandson of the well-known climber and equipment manufacturer, Armand Charlet), and he was using a Charlet Moser axe and a Chacal. At the start of the week he had been so impressed with the performance of the opposition's new tool

Jean-Marc Boivin,
Brian Sprunt and
Jean Franc Charlet,
Lochnagar, February
1979

Photo: Greg Strange

that he abandoned his own ice hammer and bought a Chacal for himself. Being in Britain he had had to pay the full un-discounted price, much to the amusement of his companions.

It took a couple of years before most leading Scottish winter climbers converted to the Chacal and its sister axe the Barracuda. The penetration and holding abilities of the reverse-curve, dropped pick was superior to all else on the market at the time and made climbing steep ice feel significantly more secure. An unexpected bonus to its high performance on ice was the discovery that it also worked well on mixed winter terrain when driven into frozen turf, jammed in a crack or hooked over small holds. Simond's banana pick was a great success and still forms the basic design of most modern technical axes.

Elsewhere in the Cairngorms, Fyffe was active on both Càrn Etchachan and the Fiacaill Buttress of Coire an t-Sneachda. Early in February, on the same Sunday that Crypt was done, he returned to the upper tier of Càrn Etchachan with Liddell to climb The Guillotine, an excellent winter line with the hardest move right at the top. They gained the Great Terrace by climbing the right-slanting fault near the left end of the lower tier known as the Eastern Approach Route. Even on the upper tier conditions were very snowy and Fyffe recalls having to fight bottomless powder in the deep chimney passing below the blade of the guillotine – a huge flake of rock. Liddell led the final chimney with its crux overhang at the top – Grade V.

Across in Coire an t-Sneachda, Fyffe had had his eye on a good-looking corner poised directly above the start to Fiacaill Couloir. He went to climb this on February 19, with fellow Lodge instructor, Keith Geddes. There was a good deal of banter between the two climbers and it was decided that Geddes should take the first pitch up into the main corner then Fyffe would continue to the top. Starting at big ledges above the bend in the couloir Geddes climbed up right into the corner. He found it more difficult than expected and eventually took a belay below a roof convinced that Fyffe had deliberately set him up for the hard bit. Of course, Fyffe denies this, maintaining that Geddes had done his "usual cop-out trick of belaying as soon as he was out of sight". Whatever the truth, Fyffe then led the main part of the corner which was sustained and continuously interesting. They named this very good short route Belhaven – Grade V.

Just over a week later, Fyffe was out again on two consecutive days, this time with Tim Walker, another colleague from the Lodge. On the last day of February they climbed Siberia, a route on the gully face of Càrn Etchachan, finishing by the hanging gully right of Scorpion – Grade IV. The following day they climbed Rampant, a line of narrow ramps and a corner left of Belhaven – Grade IV.

It remained very wintery in the hills throughout March and into April. Even parts of Creag an Dubh-loch were still in excellent condition on All Fools Day. John Anderson had recovered from his frostbite and was determined to get some late-season climbing. He and Nisbet were based at Allt-na-giubhsaich for this weekend. In thawing conditions the previous day they had ascended Labyrinth Edge to the terrace on the Central Slabs, then climbed the middle of the Sea of Slabs and finished by the final groove of Pink Elephant, all on superb ice. They had hoped to follow the complete Pink Elephant but the line on the lower slabs was bare. As they left the Dubh Loch in the late afternoon, their gaze was continually drawn to the great curving couloir of Labyrinth Direct. It looked well built-up and Anderson felt ready to give it a go.

Early on April 1, they left the hut only to find fresh ski tracks on the path. It was Keir and Hamish Towler, up for the day and also hoping to climb Pink Elephant. A race ensued with each party convinced that the other was heading for their chosen route. Of course, Keir and Towler were not told about the previous day's excursion on the upper Central Slabs until Anderson and Nisbet were well up the lower section of the Labyrinth. There were colourful exchanges between Nisbet and Keir, but the truth of the matter was that only the final groove of Pink Elephant was in winter condition. The complete ascent was still going to have to wait for another day. Keir and Towler made the best of the situation by climbing Trunk Line, a rising girdle of the upper Central Slabs starting in Labyrinth at a level just below the Hanging Garden and finishing up the top groove of Pink Elephant. Nisbet and Anderson did the prized second ascent of Labyrinth Direct with Anderson leading both the hard pitches in great style.

The weather during the last summer of the 1970s was disappointing. There were only a few short spells without rain in June and early July, and thereafter the high crags were a virtual washout. However, in spite of the limited scope for rock climbing a number of interesting discoveries were made; one on Creag an Dubh-loch was a significant pointer to the future. In June, Hamilton and Spence visited the Dubh Loch and climbed Vampire and Falseface. The latter route, on False Gully Wall, provided a good opportunity to scrutinise the rock to the left, including the striking thin crack cutting through the right end of the smooth band. By traversing on ledges from Falseface, Hamilton was able to look down the crack and judge that it was probably climbable, although the last section up to the ledge looked very hard.

The Edinburgh men resolved to find a way up the full height of the cliff using the thin crack to breach the smooth band. With Hamilton in the lead they commenced left of Falseface and climbed via a niche, a slab, and an excellent finger-wide crack to reach the Falseface belay at the start of the ledge system crossing left below the smooth band. Hamilton then walked left and climbed the 60ft crack. It was just off the vertical with good holds and good nut protection at first, but near the top, where the crack blanked out, he was forced to make a few very thin and committing moves before pulling on to the ledge. On the next pitch, instead of climbing the continuation of the crack, he moved farther left and followed a mucky groove up over a hard bulge, then more grooves took them to a belay on a ramp running up from Falseface. By following this up left to its conclusion they were able to continue to the top via two roofs and thus complete this hard 500ft climb.

Murray Hamilton

Photo: Rab Anderson

Hamilton's name, Sans Fer, was a blatant snipe at all those before him who had used pitons on earlier Creag an Dubh-loch routes. He gave the climb a rating of E4, the first route of that difficulty in the Cairngorms, but did not offer a technical grade. When recalling the events of this ascent, Spence said that it was really his introduction to modern rock climbing and that he was somewhat out of his depth. "Murray had a fall, but not, I think on the main crack pitch, somewhere above. I was very impressed with his climbing." It was not until 1984, when Dinwoodie and MacLean made the second ascent that it became apparent the crux was probably 6b, two technical grades harder than anything previously led during a first ascent on the cliff.

At the time of this ascent an ingenious protection device called a 'Friend' was becoming more widely used by climbers. In 1973, the Colorado climber, Ray Jardine, first made and experimented with his prototype Friends. They were rather Heath Robinson in appearance, comprising four notched cams, independently spring-loaded at the end of an aluminium alloy stem. The advantage of these variable-camming devices over nuts was immediately obvious. They could be quickly and easily placed and removed with one hand, and unlike nuts, they held well in parallel sided, slightly flared, and even horizontal cracks. Initially, there were four sizes covering cracks from one to four inches in width. Like all specialist equipment it was important to understand their limitations as well as their advantages and Friends were treated with caution and a little suspicion at first. Since those early days, variable-camming protection has become very sophisticated. Friends have been joined by similar proprietary devices and the range of sizes is now impressive. It really was a marvellous invention by Jardine, a major contribution to modern climbing and still much appreciated by those who climbed both before and after their introduction.

The remaining discoveries this summer were of a less exacting nature. In Coire Sputan Dearg, Archbold and Nichols worked out a good route on the quick-drying slabby rock between Amethyst Wall and Pilgrim's Groove. Their 230ft climb, Topaz (VS 4c) ended on the ramp below the

John Anderson pulling over the crux roof on the first ascent of The Primate, July 1979

Photo: Andy Nisbet

final steep prow where they finished by the crack of McArtney's Variation. This excellent combination of Topaz and McArtney's crack was re-named Amethyst Pillar by Nisbet when writing the new guide.

The last rock action of 1979 saw the coming of age of the West Face of the Mitre Ridge. It was exactly 10 years since Rennie and I climbed Slochd Wall – a long time to wait for our come-uppance. With the recent activity hereabouts, particularly by Archbold, the time was ripe for someone to lay this old ghost. Brian Lawrie was the man to make the move. He had been going well this year, climbing new routes on the North-east coast. He teamed up with Nisbet and they went to the Garbh Choire on July 3, a cool, but dry day. It should be remembered that the main corner of Slochd Wall still had the tag of A3 and although it was now local knowledge that the upper wall was easier than it looked from a distance the Aberdonians had come prepared for a stern test. Lawrie had to steel his resolve as he stood below the sunless wall. "Only when you reach the first belay do you realise that the angle is significantly under vertical and you see a generous scattering of small flat holds."[20]

Still apprehensive, Lawrie moved up the opening crack and clipped into the old bolt. Immediately, he found good little edges with which to progress. More confident now, he worked his way up the steep slab alongside the corner until he reached a rusty piton below the big over-hang. At this point he could see into the shallow groove passing the overhang on the right. If he could pull up into this he would be able to get good runners in the crack at the back. He swung over, placed a good nut, then continued up the groove to reach the belay ledge where the corner system forks. The rest of the climb was a formality. Getting started on the right-hand continuation corner proved a little tricky then they continued to the terrace and finished by the exposed, but straight-forward, last pitch of Helter Skelter.

Nisbet later wrote: "The climb, the first free ascent, was memorably enjoyable. The first pitch following the big corner was technically hard (HVS, though close to Extreme) and a bold lead by Brian Lawrie, but somehow the route had all the quality we expected with none of the epic nature. A biting cold day mellowed and the long walk back to the car was leisurely and relaxed."[21] Fired-up by this excellent climb, Nisbet returned a few days later with John Anderson to have a go at the promi-nent wide crack splitting the horizontal roof right of Slochd Wall. One-and-a-half days of effort, separated by 24 hours sitting-out bad weather in the Smith-Winram Bivouac, finally paid off when Anderson pulled over the roof, having found a crucial hidden hold. Above this, much easier climbing up rattling flakes took them to the terrace and another finish up Helter Skelter. According to Nisbet: "We called it The Primate, in accordance with the ecclesiastical names of the routes here-abouts and the apelike manoeuvres involved in climbing it.[22] Anderson mischievously suggested that the roof was only Hard Severe, but they settled for HVS, later upgraded to E1 5b.

This latest action on the West Face of Mitre Ridge served as a cata-lyst to Archbold and Keir, who had spied holds on the left edge of Slochd Wall during the ascents of Ghurka and Helter Skelter. Despite a general breakdown in the weather, they were lucky to get a dry day on July 15. Archbold recalls: "Things got off to a bad start. It was cold and damp at the foot of North-West Gully and then I carelessly uncoiled the ropes onto a collapsing pile of boulders. One rope was totally cut in the lower third – short pitches would have to be the order of the day." From the little stance at the start of the main pitch on Slochd Wall, Archbold climbed diagonally up left on unlikely looking terrain until near the edge where he found a vertical crack. This he followed for 40ft to a distinct steepening in the angle.

"The climbing had been okay but I still felt spooked by the rope business. The bulge looked improbable, but I glanced left and saw that a couple of moves would take me into Ghurka from where I knew I could regain the edge a few feet higher. In a trice it was done." They continued to the top, linking sections of both Gurkha and Helter Skelter to produce the atmospheric Chindit – VS 4c. Three years later, on the second ascent, Dinwoodie and Colin Jamieson improved the line by moving right below the bulge before making a few thin moves up and left to rejoin the original route. With Slochd Wall and The Primate, Chindit Direct (E1 5b) completed a triptych of classic routes on the West Face of Mitre Ridge.

Chindit was the last new climb in the Cairngorms made by Norman Keir. A year later he was diagnosed as having multiple sclerosis, a particularly virulent form which gave him little remission. He coped with the illness with remarkable fortitude, but died in September 1995. Always the enthusiast, he was a man of action and vision and a great campaigner for the Cairngorms.

So ended the 1970s, a period of progress in a traditional way. On rock we saw much of the old aid eliminated as well as a number of major new climbs. In winter, at last there was a significant advance on the buttresses, providing a taste of what was to come during the next decade.

1.   SMCJ Vol 31, No 167, p36.
2.   SMCJ Vol 31, No 167, p36.
3.   *Mountain* magazine No 43, p8.
4.   *Cold Climbs* (Diadem), p157.
5.   *Cold Climbs* (Diadem), p158.
6.   *Mountain* magazine No. 61, p15.
7.   *Mountain* magazine No. 60, p20 – 22, (*Vertigo*, by A.Robertson).
8.   *Mountain* magazine No. 60, p20 – 22, (*Vertigo* by A.Robertson).
9.   *Mountain* magazine No. 60, p20 – 22, (*Vertigo* by A.Robertson).
10. *Mountain* magazine No. 60, p20 – 22, (*Vertigo* by A.Robertson).
11. *Rocksport* April – May, 1971 p14.
12. Crabs (Etchachan Club 1979), p13 – 14, (*Storky and the Cupid*, by R.Renshaw).
13. Crabs (Etchachan Club 1979), p13 – 14, (*Storky and the Cupid*, by R.Renshaw).
14. Crabs (Etchachan Club 1979), p13 – 14, (*Storky and the Cupid*, by R.Renshaw).
15. Crabs (Etchachan Club 1979), p13 – 14, (*Storky and the Cupid*, by R.Renshaw).
16. SMCJ Vol. 32, No. 171, p1 – 7, (*The Link Face to Face*, by A.Nisbet).
17. SMCJ Vol. 32, No. 171, p1 – 7, (*The Link Face to Face*, by A.Nisbet).
18. SMCJ Vol. 32, No. 171, p1 – 7, (*The Link Face to Face*, by A.Nisbet).
19. CCJ Vol. 19, No. 98, p7.
20. CCJ Vol. 19, No. 98, p8 – 11.
21. CCJ Vol. 19, No. 98, p8 – 11.
22. CCJ Vol. 19, No. 98, p11.

11: The Quickening Pace (1980 – 1985)

Rob Milne below the big overlap on Pink Elephant, January 1980

Photo: Rab Anderson

WINTER 1979 – 80 was a big one. The quest for climbs with greater levels of difficulty continued apace with more people willing to invest the time and effort to achieve this. The Edinburgh partnership of Kenny Spence and Murray Hamilton was keen to advance the upper limit of mixed winter climbing in Scotland and had decided to target a number of specific routes. They were well organised and only went for these climbs when they thought weather and climbing conditions were favourable. They started in November, and by the end of December had already made two unsuccessful attempts on Postern, one of these being thwarted by bad weather. The best made plans!

It was very cold and snowy over the New Year period when Mick Fowler and A.Henderson made a winter ascent of the Severe rock climb, Procrastination, in Coire an Lochain of Cairn Gorm – Grade VII. By the second week of January, calmer conditions set in. On Friday, January 11, two Edinburgh parties set out for the Cairngorms: one went to Creag an Dubh-loch, while the other visited the Shelter Stone Crag. Having twice failed on Postern, Spence and Hamilton decided that this time they would improve their chances of success by taking bivouac equipment. They had also invited Alan Taylor to join them. The plan was to use a controversial time-saving tactic that involved the seconds jumaring up one of the ropes that the leader had tied-off after completing a pitch. In this fashion they followed the normal route except on the second pitch, where lack of snow on the summer crux forced them to move farther left on to Steeple. Darkness caught them two pitches from the top where they spent a relatively comfortable night behind a large flake of rock at the foot of the big Steeple corner. Unfortunately, by morning a thaw had set in making the climbing unpleasant. When they reached the plateau all three had sustained a broken crampon each. They used no aid on this long and difficult mixed climb – Grade VII. The ghost of Coleman's claimed ascent had been laid.

It was Rab Anderson and Rob Milne who had had the good fortune to choose Creag an Dubh-loch this weekend. Anderson, another of the new group of Edinburgh climbers, was gaining a reputation for his ability on ice. He was a year ahead of Dave Cuthbertson at Firhill High School, but they did not meet and start climbing together until they joined the same local Boy's Brigade Company. Milne was an experienced climber from America currently in his second year at Edinburgh University doing a PhD. in Artificial Intelligence. His grandparents had emigrated from North-east Scotland to America to become homesteaders in Montana. Brought up in a very 'Scottish' household, first in Montana then Colorado, he started climbing at an early age. Anderson and Milne had come to climb the Pink Elephant, hoping that sufficient ice had formed on the crucial lower overlap as well as on the upper slabs. Anderson was familiar with the Central Slabs having climbed Black Mamba in summer and the winter route, Mammoth, which follows a natural turfy line linking the foot of Labyrinth with Dinosaur Gully and the upper Theseus Grooves.

Starting at first light and through-leading, they followed the summer route. Milne took them over the big lap into the Dinosaur Gully. "I remember there was a big drip, but I had to bridge and reach very high to get the good ice." Instead of following the gully they climbed iced grooves and ribs farther right and gained the terrace below the sea of slabs by an ice pillar. It was only now they could see the line on the upper tier was a narrow, but continuous, run of ice. They could hardly believe their luck. The cliff was in exceptionally icy condition for so early in the season. Milne led a long pitch alongside the sea of slabs to below a corner where he took a poor belay on tied-off axe shafts.

Anderson recalled the situation well: "It was my lead and I tried a few times on the short corner. I couldn't get any gear and the lack of belay scared me. Rob never thought much about these things back then and was too bold. I dithered then handed the lead over to him. Still scared, I watched him thrash his way up and disappear."

Two superb pitches up the final groove saw them topping out as the sun sank below the horizon. As was expected, the complete Pink Elephant proved to be an outstanding winter route providing eight hours of sustained climbing – Grade VII. Although the Edinburgh men recorded their climb as a winter ascent of Pink Elephant, the name White Elephant, suggested by Keir and Wright, has stuck.

During the short period of excellent winter conditions on Creag an Dubh-loch back in March 1972, Charlie Butterworth and others had witnessed a good plating of ice on the slabs and walls of Goliath. They noted a steep finger of ice (the Goliath Icicle) filling the groove just left of the summer crux and concluded that the formation of this would be crucial for a winter ascent. The big question at the time was whether the ice would ever be thick enough to climb. Now Anderson and Milne knew the answer for they had seen this section of the cliff on their descent of Central Gully after completing Pink Elephant. They were a little careless with this valuable information and let it slip later in the pub that there was an exceptional amount of ice on Goliath. Word quickly got back to Aberdeen, in particular to Andy Nisbet, who hastily arranged with Neil Morrison to make a midweek visit to the Dubh Loch on January 15. Morrison, a young climber from Stirling, was studying geography at Aberdeen University. He was already very good on rock but relatively inexperienced on difficult winter terrain. The agreement was that he would go with Nisbet provided he did not have to lead.

Nisbet takes up the story: "The first view of the cliff was disappointing. The huge sheets of ice which had covered the Central Slabs last April were conspicuously absent and the Central Gully Wall looked bare, although Goliath was still out of sight. The thaw on Sunday had removed the ice from the bottom of Pink Elephant and we assumed Goliath would be the same. As we trudged up Central Gully towards the route I confessed to the hope that the ice wouldn't be there. I didn't feel like the anticipated 150ft pitch on thin ice with no runners. But as soon as I saw it I knew there was enough ice. It was one of those special moments that will probably be remembered for the rest of my life. The sight of those monstrous overlapping slabs and huge corners plated with ice was

Rab Anderson

Photo: Rab Anderson Collection

The Goliath Icicle,
January 1980

Photo: Rab Anderson

breathtaking and awesome."[1] Although Nisbet knew that the ice was mainly at an angle of 70°, it looked much steeper than that and he found the whole situation very intimidating. Despite the apprehension, his sense of obligation at being the first arrival in such superb conditions prevailed. He climbed across the precarious lower slabs and brought Morrison up to a belay below the Goliath Icicle. "As soon as I was on the ice my confidence returned and I could relax a little. Suddenly, the ice wasn't so steep and though it had a tendency to dinner-plate, I was able to climb slowly and carefully so there was never a chance of a slip. Runners hardly seemed necessary but a horizontal crack appeared behind a nest of icicles just at the steepest point."[2] Morrison found the pitch demanding especially at an awkward section where the icicle was very narrow, only allowing the axes to be placed one above the other. He felt the ice to be thin and the protection poor. From the top of the icicle they moved right and closely followed the third pitch of the summer route. This proved to be the technical crux as there was little ice on the rock except in the cracks. Below a crucial bulge Nisbet found a helpful drift of snow that supported his weight. By gently standing on this he was able to reach above the bulge and slot his axe into a crack before pulling up strenuously. When Morrison came to follow he had difficulty retrieving his jammed axe. During his struggle to release it, the axe suddenly came free and he fell onto the drift, causing it to collapse. He could now no longer reach above the bulge so he tried unsuccessfully to prusik up the icy ropes. Eventually, with much pulling by both leader and second, they were re-united on the stance below the final pitch, just as it was getting dark.

Up to their right the deep cracks of the summer line were thinly iced and looked evil, so they had to find an alternative solution quickly. Using a piton as a hand hold Nisbet moved right from the stance. "I wasn't going to miss out on this route after so much effort so I headed down- wards across the blank slab trusting my feet alone on the thin ice. An ice screw in a clump of grass encouraged me onwards and round a blind corner suddenly seeing the easy ground only a few feet away but across the thinnest ice of all. I was to get my reward for being bold and spot- ted a perfect crack under the ice. It was over; the rest was no problem, even by the light of head torches."[3]

On the walk out they met Anderson and Hamilton arriving just one day too late. Little was said except a confirmation from the Aberdeen team that they had just climbed Goliath. The next day the Edinburgh men had a quick look at Black Mamba before making the second ascent of Goliath. They lead-through, with Anderson drawing the short straw and being pointed at the icicle pitch. They reported in Mountain 73 that it was an excellent route and thanked Nisbet's party for leaving some nice new pitons behind. This was a reference to the last pitch where Morrison had not removed some of the piton runners while seconding in the dark. Hamilton claimed that he did Goliath only by chance and that his midweek visit was really to see if Mousetrap was in good condi- tion. "Goliath was not a route that interested me as it was old- fashioned with ice on it." It may well have been an old-fashioned ice climb in Hamilton's opinion but both parties were very fortunate to have climbed it when they did. This elusive winter route has rarely been in condi- tion since. In 1991, Aberdonians, Wilson Moir and Niall Ritchie succeeded on the icicle but ran out of time trying to find the line higher up and retreated. There has still not been a third ascent. Nisbet's pioneer- ing lead was an outstanding piece of climbing – Grade VII.

After his trip to the Dubh Loch, Hamilton was confident, provided the calm freezing weather held, that Mousetrap was climbable in its current condition. Like other contenders for this big winter prize he was aware that the first two pitches were unlikely to be iced or snow-covered. He knew that a suitable winter start would be to climb the short open- ing corner of Predator, then traverse right into Mousetrap above the wide crack of its summer crux. This was all very well in theory, but there were other climbers around and the immediate problem was to make sure that he, Spence and Taylor were at the front of the queue. In the event he had every reason to worry because a large number of Edinburgh climbers arrived on the Friday night all hoping to take advantage of the rumoured 'exceptional conditions.' The back room at Glas Allt Shiel was very crowded that night.

It was Spence's idea to save energy by letting others break trail, then to rush past at the last minute and be first up to the cliff. The ploy worked, but only after a neck and neck race with Milne right up to the foot of Mousetrap. It was Saturday, January 9, two days after the ascent of Goliath. Little had changed. There was no fresh powder, just névé, ice, frozen turf and bare rock. They employed the same tactics as used on Postern, sharing both the leading and the jumaring. Spence took the first pitch, the steep little corner common to Cougar, Vampire and Predator. The climbing was well protected but very hard. He got a little gripped at one point and unfortunately, let his foot stray on to a piton runner before being able to move round onto the shelf leading into the Mousetrap recess. After this they followed the summer line all the way. Hamilton led the third pitch which leaves the recess on the left by a steep flake crack. This was particularly thin, but fortunately, a crucial plating of ice had formed on the steep slab above the flake, enabling progress by front pointing. Although the terrain gradually became icier as they gained height, the climbing remained sustained all the way to the broken ground below the plateau. That evening, three very pleased climbers returned to Glas Allt – Hamilton even dropping his guard a little and admitting that the climb had been hard. They had achieved the first winter climb on the frontal face of Central Gully Wall – Grade VII.

It is worth recording how unusually icy the conditions were on Central Gully Wall at this time. Although none of the crack-lines on the frontal face had anything approaching continuous ice there were large smears on the upper slabs particularly above King Rat and Waterkelpie Wall. Low down on the right, an icefall had formed over the pale coloured slabs (later named The Buff Slabs) left of Caterpillar Crack. It was attempted on the day of the Mousetrap ascent by Milne and Cuthbertson, but the ice was too thin at the bottom. A week after these events John Anderson and Steve Kennedy almost succeeded on an impressive direct start to Vertigo Wall. Anderson led the icy corner all the way up from the bottom using one piton for aid, but was caught by darkness below the black chimney.

After these hectic on-goings there was a lull for almost a month. Favourable weather was again forecast for the weekend of February 23, and on the Friday night Nisbet and Sprunt set out for the Cairn Gorm car park only to crash their car on the outskirts of Aberdeen. This put paid to their planned weekend at the Shelter Stone and their attempt on The Citadel.

Unknown to the Aberdonians (but not unpredicted) was the arrival of Spence and Hamilton below the Shelter Stone Crag that Saturday morning. They too were aiming for The Citadel and hoping for a more wintery-looking cliff than on their two previous visits to try the climb already this season. According to Spence they were very motivated to get up the route and fortunate to find good conditions, particularly on the upper bastion. Although neither of them had climbed the route in summer, Spence could still remember the difficulties on the lower crux from his attempt with Porteous 11 years earlier. Nevertheless, he still had to use a piton for aid before moving up to the commencement of the easier middle pitches.

When they reached the upper crux it was Hamilton's turn to lead. "We always climbed in thin Damart gloves which gave a good grip and did not slip off the hands. I always had gashed knuckles though, as they gave little protection. The crack on the upper crux was choked with snow and ice: I climbed it with a mix of axes and jams, as one does." They reached the top after 12 hours, with more than half the time spent on the final pitches. Of this great climb Spence said: "It was the winter ascent I was most pleased with: I think Murray felt the same." Later guide-books described the first winter ascent of the Citadel as 'The Big Route of the time' (Grade VII), although arguably Mousetrap is a better line.

With calm conditions continuing, Sprunt and Nisbet were determined to get winter climbing somewhere in Scotland despite their lack of trans-port. On the Sunday morning they hitch-hiked to Glen Muick and walked up to Lochnagar, arriving below the Black Spout Pinnacle after midday. Although it was damp and misty they could see a tremendous build-up of partially consolidated snow on the slabs of the Pinnacle. With only limited time they decided to investigate the start of Pinnacle Grooves before returning to Aberdeen. Unfortunately, despite the mist, their reconnaissance had been observed. The Creagh Dhu were out in force that day and most of them had abandoned attempts on various routes including Parallel Gully B. They were all gathered at the First Aid box when Sprunt and Nisbet abseiled off. The chant of "failures, fail-ures" echoed round the corrie. Sprunt decided to get his own back and headed over to Parallel Gully B. He then soloed up to the Creagh Dhu high point, removed the abseil pitons and soloed back down again. On the way home the two local climbers stopped off for a pint in Ballater. The pub sounded very lively but when they stepped through the door the room went ominously silent as their eyes met those of the Creagh Dhu. Fortunately, the atmosphere soon eased and even became quite friendly.

Andy Nisbet starting the Goliath Icicle, January 1980

Photo: Neil Morrison

Nisbet made a quick return the following week with Kennedy and Morris McLeod. According to Nisbet: "Brian wouldn't go and I would-n't wait." This time everything was right. The snow and ice was well frozen and with Nisbet in the lead they enjoyed a relatively straightforward ascent of this HVS rock climb. Protection was sparse because of the big build-up and a nut was used for aid on the first pitch – Grade VI.

At the beginning of March, Hamilton and Anderson made a second winter ascent of Crypt. Weather and ice conditions were very good and they followed the first pitch of the summer route direct. They were fortu-nate to have chosen the Saturday this weekend as a north-westerly blizzard moved into the area early the next morning. This severe weather on the Sunday contributed to the deaths of two Manchester climbers whose bodies were found roped together at the foot of Raeburn's Gully.

Following the successful exchange visit of French climbers in 1979, three Poles, Stanislav Handl, Jan Fijalkowski and Michal Momatiuk made a similar trip to Scotland during the first week in March 1980. Again the second weekend was spent at Allt-na-guibhsaich where two days of fine weather and exceptional snow and ice conditions provided the perfect stage for high standard winter climbing on Lochnagar.

Nisbet recorded:"The Etchachan Club's 'A' team of John Anderson, Bob Smith and Brian Sprunt had assembled in the Pannanich Wells Hotel, Ballater, to partner the Poles. Brian, suitably clad in the kilt, had been planning his usual 'burn off' tactics, but by Sunday night even

*Brian Sprunt
committed on
Epitome,
March 1980*

Photo: Andy Nisbet

he had to admit defeat. A drinking challenge was an immediate setback as Mike proved he had quickly acquired a taste for Scottish beer and whisky while a pull-up competition ended abruptly when we discovered that Stan could do 11 one arm pull-ups in succession."[4]

On the Saturday morning there was an early hiccup when low cloud cut visibility to only a few yards. However, the Poles were eventually guided to the foot of the Black Spout Pinnacle just as the mist began to disperse, revealing the cliff in all its winter glory. Anderson and Handl went off to climb Pinnacle Face while Sprunt and Momatiuk made the second ascent of the Link. The later pair completed their climb in a remarkable four hours with Sprunt leading the crux overhang. Cruising the hardest route on the mountain would have gained them top honours had it not been for Fijalkowski and Smith who decided to tackle a recent HVS summer route, Epitome. This follows a direct line based on Route 1 crossing at the Springboard and finishing by a hanging corner on the steep wall left of the big overhang on Hood Route. Fijalkowski led the first pitch up the big groove down to the left of Route 1. It was hard and steep at the bottom, thin and slabby farther up, yet, according to Sprunt, the Pole only took 15 minutes to climb the whole pitch.

Once on the Springboard they continued up the central fault, common to Hood Route, and arrived at a comfortable ledge below the corner. Five feet right of this an icy crack ran straight up the wall. Fijalkowski's lead of this was both formidable and controversial. For the first 10ft he could bridge between the crack and the corner, then it was necessary to swing out right onto the ice and pull up to an easement. The final part of the crack formed a slightly impending groove. It was here that he attached a small hook to one of his embedded axes. He then clipped this into his harness and while hanging from it with all his weight off his arms he placed the next axe. In this way he efficiently dispatched the final difficulties and moved left to a good belay close to easy ground on Route 1 – Grade VII. By the time Smith had followed and led through to the summit they too had only been climbing for a mere four hours. There was plenty of time left for a second route – Shallow Gully for Fijalkowski and Smith, Giant's Head Direct for Momatiuk and Sprunt. Nisbet and Mark Hutchinson also had a good day, climbing Eagle Ridge and making the first winter ascent of Multiple Chimneys on the left wall of Polyphemus Gully – Grade V.

If anything, the weather on Sunday was even better, yet despite the prospect of another fine day, Monatuik had had his fill and wanted a rest. This gave Sprunt an opportunity to repeat Epitome with Rob Milne who, as well as Nisbet and Hutchinson, had done Eagle Ridge the previous day. According to Milne, Fijalkowski and Smith "were telling tales of one arm pull-ups on verglased rock and fifi hooks. The climb sounded interesting and we were sure they were exaggerating."[5] Sprunt persuaded Milne to lead the first pitch with the promise of perfect ice. Of course, he had watched Fijalkowski the day before and knew that the slabby section of the big groove had far from perfect ice. Nevertheless, Milne was up to the task and some time later they found themselves on the ledge below the 50ft crux, the ascent of which occupied most of the afternoon.

An unfortunate result of the sunny weather was serious melting of the ice on the upper wall. When Sprunt reached the impending groove where Fijalkowski had rested, his axe ripped from the thin ice and he fell almost 30ft, pulling out a nut and piton runner. Milne then had a go, placing better protection before he too fell. A re-motivated Sprunt then climbed back to the good runners and using a nut for aid continued through to the end of the difficulties, well impressed with Fijalkowski's lead.

Elsewhere in the corrie John Anderson also took some flying time while making the third ascent of Crypt. Although he lost a crampon in a 20ft fall, he still managed to complete the climb. His partner, Handl, led the crux groove by executing a series of one arm pull-ups on his axes. This feat was witnessed by Rab Anderson and Hamilton who were making the first winter ascent of Parallel Buttress Left Edge (Grade VI), a summer VS that stays close to the edge overlooking Parallel Gully A.

Nisbet's appetite for new winter routes saw him back on Lochnagar with Neil Spinks three days after the Polish weekend. This time his objective lay high on Scarface buttress, where a prominent deep crack, just wide enough to admit a lightly-clad climber, forms part of a VS route known as the Straight Jacket. On its summer ascent, six years earlier, Dinwoodie and Keir found it necessary to use four pitons for aid in a wet corner above the deep crack. Now, under good winter conditions, the crux pitches were reversed. The wide crack gave a desperate struggle as it was too narrow to enter with axes and crampons, whereas the wet corner above was well iced, allowing a strenuous ascent without recourse to aid – Grade VII.

The tail-end of this remarkable winter was tinged with sadness after the occurrence of another double fatality on Lochnagar. Lynne Brown, of Largoward in Fife, and Neil McCallum, Fraserburgh, were experienced climbers who knew the mountain well. Both aged 23, they were honours graduates in geography from Aberdeen University and past members of the Lairig Club (Neil was a former President). They stayed at Allt-na-giubhsaich on the evening of Thursday, March 20, and planned to climb

Neil Spinks,
October 1979

Photo: Andy Nisbet

on Lochnagar the next day. The weather was very cold with blizzards over the weekend. On Tuesday 25, their bodies were found roped together below Parallel Gully A. It is thought they were on Eagle Buttress and a belay had failed when one of them fell. Neil was killed outright, but Lynne survived long enough to bandage one of her injuries and get into a polythene bag. With the weather being so bad over the weekend it is doubtful if anyone entered the corrie until the mountain rescue team arrived three days later.

Coming to terms with the death of a close friend in a mountaineering accident is a situation many climbers have to face at some time in their life. It affects people in different ways. Some give up climbing altogether while others seek solace in the hills but keep to ultra safe activities. Most acknowledge the inherent danger and continue to climb, accepting that a degree of risk is part of the appeal of mountaineering. Nisbet and Spinks had been extremely upset by the deaths of their friends but took the decision to go out as soon as possible before they lost enthusiasm for the hills altogether.

Ironically, March 30 was a beautiful cloudless day with a slight frost. Despite the relatively low altitude of Creag an Dubh-loch and the lateness of the season, they decided to try The Last Oasis on Broad Terrace Wall, finding it "smothered in ice from top to bottom"[6]. This VS rock climb, a water course left of Sword of Damocles, had been attempted three years earlier by Smith and Wright, who abandoned the direct line and made a variation further left – The Snow Desert, Grade V. In the glare of the morning sun Nisbet and Spinks sweated up the introductory gully to a stance below the main ice flow. After leading one pitch Nisbet was soaked. He found a cramped stance under a small roof to the left of the summer line.

"At the back of this recess seemed a good place to stay. The stream flowed over the lip in front of us and the icicles which were crashing down off the main icefall to the right would miss us, even if they came unnervingly close. Neil was still unhappy."[7]

Driven by the thought of having to wait another 10 years for this much ice, Nisbet convinced Spinks that they ought to carry on. He had, after all, done the route in summer and knew where the gear placements were. "Sixty feet above the good Moac runner and increasingly nervous, I came across the direct continuation of the ice, a 40ft plumb vertical screen of soggy icicles, but there was no way I was going up there without runners. The only ones possible were slings round icicles, just a wet joke in these conditions, so I slunk off sideways into a cave behind the ice, battered a No. 10 hex sideways into a slush-filled crack and pegged up the summer route. I feel apologetic about the aid now but I was under some strain at the time. Just to emphasise the point, Neil followed without using the aid."[8] Under the circumstances this was a dogged performance by Nisbet on what was known to be one of the best ice lines on the cliff. His prediction of another 10 years before the route would be so well-formed was fairly accurate. The route was repeated in January 1993, by Doug Hawthorn and the evergreen Freddy Malcolm who climbed the icefall direct, without the use of aid – Grade VI.

With the arrival of warm weather at the beginning of April the winter of 1980 quickly melted away. In the Cairngorms it will be remembered for the unusual amount of ice on Creag an Dubh-loch, the excellent conditions on Lochnagar and the lengthy periods of relatively calm weather. The combination of these factors coupled with a healthy rivalry between Edinburgh and Aberdeen climbers had led to six high-quality first ascents, a number of which were ground-breaking in their technical difficulty. The winter also marked the last appearance of John Anderson in the Cairngorms. After climbing the North Face of the Eiger that summer with Nisbet he was delighted to be offered a post as Base Assistant at the British Antarctic Survey's Rothera Station on Adelaide Island. Towards the end of his first season South, he and a companion were killed when their snow-mobile fell through a snow bridge into a deep crevasse. John is fondly remembered in the North-east, not only as a formidable winter climber but more importantly because he was a 'really good guy'.

The Allt Creag an Leth-choin is the stream which flows north from the flat meadows between Cairn Lochan and the Lurcher's Crag, the two western tops of Cairn Gorm. In its upper reaches the burn lies within a small glen which usually holds snow well into the summer. For as long as there had been skiers in the area, this, the Lurcher's Gully, was known to be a reliable ski run. No one could have predicted that in the early 1980s, this unremarkable gully should become the focus of national attention.

It was 1978 when rumours first spread from Speyside hinting that the Cairngorm Chairlift Co. were planning to build a new road from the existing car park on Cairn Gorm across to the foot of Lurcher's Gully. The company wanted to install downhill skiing facilities in Coire an t-Sneachda and Coire an Lochain as well as Lurcher's Gully. Initial reaction among hill folk was centred on the road and there was concern that vehicular access would be allowed yet closer to the heart of the Cairngorms. When the proposals were considered in more detail it was apparent that virtually the whole north side of Cairn Gorm would be affected by the paraphernalia of piste skiing. No regard seemed to have been taken for other users of the area who valued the quiet unspoiled qualities of these corries.

In August 1978, Badenoch and Strathspey Conservation Group submitted a provisional objection to Highland Regional Council, which set out a well-argued case against the development. Perhaps construction of the road could be prevented. But how would a disparate band of hill-walkers, climbers, cross-country skiers and naturalists prevail against the might of the Chairlift Company and its commercial backers? It was clear from the outset that to have any chance of influencing the outcome, a coordinated strategy would be required to link all potential groups of objectors. The Mountaineering Council of Scotland was the appropriate body to handle this for the walkers and climbers. Unfortunately, a number of its officials had one foot firmly in the developer's camp, and it took much lobbying before the executive's decision not to oppose the development was overturned.

In February 1980, a few weeks prior to the notice of planning application being posted, a newsletter from the MCof S had announced that unless there was a written response from members, the Council would not object to the development, provided the Chairlift Company gave

*Andy Nisbet belaying
on Crevasse Route,
Càrn Etchachan,
in October 1980*

Photo: Steve Kennedy

a guarantee that the road would be locked when not in use by skiers. Fearing a U-turn by the executive, the Etchachan Club mailed copies of the Badenoch and Strathspey objection to all member clubs, urging them to send an objection to HRC with a copy to the executive. There was a good response and two days before the closing date for representation, the MCofS recorded its opposition in a letter to HRC. This triggered the British Mountaineering Council to offer its full support in the "fight against the Lurcher's Gully Development".

Expansion of skiing facilities on Cairn Gorm was just the latest environmental issue to concern mountaineers from the North-east of Scotland. Other on-going problems included the spread of upland bulldozed tracks and the proposed establishment of a super quarry on the Longhaven sea cliffs. In recent years, matters such as these had arisen at a rate and on such a scale that it was no longer practicable for a single climbing club to oppose them effectively. This situation, with particular reference to the battle to save the Longhaven cliffs, resulted in seven climbing and walking clubs from the Aberdeen area getting together in June 1980 to form their own association, The North East Mountain Trust. Its aim was to deal with issues arising primarily in the Grampian and Cairngorms area. The Trust would provide a pool of expertise and information, help present and fight cases where appropriate, and raise funds to meet these objectives.

It came as no surprise in July, when HRC announced its approval of the proposed Lurcher's Gully Development. However, since the development fell within a National Park Direction Area, the application had to be referred to the Scottish Secretary. The process of Planning law was slowly moving towards a Public Inquiry. With this in mind, members of the North East Mountain Trust called upon the MCofS to hold a Special General Meeting to debate the way forward in preparing the mountaineers' case against the development. The meeting was held appropriately at Battleby, near Perth, in November, and resulted in a Working Party being set up to produce a policy on downhill skiing in Scotland that could be used at a Public Inquiry.

The summer of 1980 was very disappointing. It all started promisingly enough – especially in the West of Scotland, with a long spell of predominantly dry weather in April and May. Thereafter, the monsoons returned and the high crags of the Cairngorms never properly dried out. As a consequence, very little exploratory climbing took place.

When the snow and ice returned, it was Edinburgh climbers who were again first off the mark. During the second week of November, Spence and Anderson made a good mixed climb up the edge right of Fluted Buttress Direct in Coire an t-Sneachda with Spence leading the steepest pitch – Cruising Grade V. The pair visited Cairn Gorm a number of times before the turn of the year. On November 29, they were joined by Milne for the first winter ascent of The Relay Climb on The Longbow Crag. Again it was Spence who led the crux which involved interesting hunched-up climbing with tactical use of the knees – Grade V.

A week later they visited Stac an Fharaidh and made the opening winter climbs on these slabs above Loch Avon. They started with the summer climb Apres Moi (Grade III), then followed this with Hoity-Toity, a variation to Apres Moi, finishing up a steep icefall left of its top corner – Grade IV. Both routes were well iced and provided enjoyable climbing.

This was Spence's last contribution to winter climbing in the Cairngorms. He was the elder statesman among the Edinburgh 'hot shots' and his reputation as the archetypal dour Scottish climber earned him frequent ribbings from his younger friends. He earned their respect through his ability both as a very fine rock climber and as a winter specialist. He was influential in the shift back to mixed winter climbing in the West of Scotland.

For mountaineers in the North-east, mixed winter climbing had never been out of vogue. Any route was considered fair game provided the temperature was below freezing and there was a reasonable cover of snow. In February 1980, Nisbet and Mothersele made a winter ascent of Pagan Slit, a HS chimney on the upper cliff of Càrn Etchachan. They believed it to be a first ascent only to learn later that they had been beaten to it by Fowler and Arnis Strapcans. The climb proved to be an eye-opener for Nisbet as he realised that all the summer lines on the upper tier would make good winter routes. Yes, they would only be 250ft long and not easily accessed, but the vegetated blocky granite had good cracks for protection making it ideal for mixed winter climbing. Also, the crag's north-east aspect and relative high altitude meant that it would come into condition quickly.

After New Year the winter of 1980 – 81 was disappointing. Whenever a cold snap or reasonable fall of snow occurred, it was almost immediately followed by a substantial thaw. On January 13, Nisbet made his second return visit to Càrn Etchachan, where, with Steve Kennedy, he climbed Crevasse Route, the most popular rock climb on the crag – Grade V. They had already tried the route with Dave Boyne in October after the first big snowfall of the season. The deep snow had prevented the turf from freezing and they failed on the second pitch. A month later, they were back for a weekend at the Shelter Stone, this time accompanied by Neil Morrison. The weather was calm and frosty with a little fresh snow. On the Saturday, they climbed the steep vegetated recess of Equinox, which provided an excellent climb – Grade VI. The next day they succeeded on Boa, although Nisbet was forced to stand in slings hung from his axe to overcome a difficult section on the main crack – Grade VI. Other climbers on Lochnagar and Beinn a' Bhùird that weekend were surprised to hear that suitable winter conditions were found elsewhere in the Cairngorms, especially on a steep cliff like upper Càrn Etchachan. There was virtually no snow below 3000ft and only a dusting on the high tops. Nisbet's party was suspected of swinging the lead a little!

The accusations of route-bagging were compounded the following weekend when the same trio plus Ewen Clark went to Coire Sputan Dearg and climbed Pilgrim's Groove in very lean conditions. The route was known to be a good winter line with a steep icefall in the upper chimney. Unfortunately, this section of the Grey Man's Crag faces south and receives a lot of sun, hence the icefall rarely forms. On this ascent, Nisbet led the very hard, but well protected, lower crux. The ice in the upper chimney was thin so they avoided it altogether. Kennedy and Nisbet

climbed the groove on the left and used rope tension to re-gain the line above the icefall. Morrison and Clark moved right and followed Lucifer Route to its junction with the upper chimney. Here the leader, Morrison, accepted a top rope from the other pair before making the crux moves back into Pilgrim's Groove – Grade V.

There were cries of foul play from the old guard who had been waiting years for the icefall to be well-formed. However, these protests were probably due more to sour grapes than winter climbing ethics. Nisbet was a man on a mission. He could not wait indefinitely for ideal conditions as there were so many other projects waiting to be done. He later said that there was a lot more snow on these climbs than people thought. "Conditions were lean but as far as we were concerned, fair and in keeping with the old order. There was certainly a lot more snow than is often the case nowadays. Boa was completely white!"

He probably did not realise it at the time, but he was adjusting the ground rules for acceptable winter climbing conditions in the Cairngorms. Although he wore tricuoni plates on all these routes his companions managed adequately in crampons despite the lack of ice or névé. The key to the ascents had been frozen turf. The dusting of snow or riming of the rock was purely cosmetic. In fact the less snow and rime the better, because the cracks, rock features and bits of turf could be more easily spotted. It was no longer necessary for a winter ascent to have a reasonable cover of snow. All that was required was freezing temperatures and a whiteish appearance. The modern mixed winter climb had arrived – initially scoffed at by the protagonists of previous decades blessed with more generous winters.

During the early months of 1981 the MCofS working party and its many helpers was hard at work, raising funds, fighting the propaganda war and preparing the mountaineering case for the forthcoming Lurcher's Gully Public Inquiry. Since I had volunteered to be one of the witnesses at the Inquiry it seemed a good idea to spend a few days at Jean's Hut in Coire an Lochain to refresh my memory and savour the ambience of the area. Neither Dinwoodie nor I had climbed a summer rock route in Coire an t-Sneachda and we were keen to make amends.

The Northern Corries looked particularly alpine in early May, with dry rock on the buttresses and plenty of old snow and ice in the easy gullies. We descended into Coire an t-Sneachda from the Fiacaill Ridge, then climbed Damnation and Pygmy Ridge before returning to the hut. On our approach to Aladdin Buttress from the west, our attention had been caught by a distinctive shallow diedre, showing as a straight black line on the slab left of Damnation's main corner. On a reconnaissance from near the top of the latter, I was able to look down the diedre and, much to my delight, discovered it contained a continuous finger-wide crack. If this had been climbed we would surely have heard about it! The next day it rained and we left early, but I could not stop thinking about the crack.

We returned to Coire an t-Sneachda the following Saturday with two friends from Aberdeen, Jim Wyness and Mungo Ross. As well as the crack on Aladdin Buttress, Dougie had designs on a desperate-looking line between Snipers and Cupid's Bow on the Shelter Stone Crag. He and Jim planned to spend the weekend based at the head of Loch Avon in order to try both lines. They would walk over to meet Mungo and I below Aladdin Buttress early on Saturday morning. The day was overcast with a cold wind and after waiting more than half an hour Mungo and I climbed the easy lower rocks and made a belay below the main corner of Damnation. Still there was no sign of the others.

After delaying further, and feeling a little guilty, I climbed up left to the base of the diedre. At this point the sound of Dougie's voice from below cleared my conscience and I peered eagerly up the crack. It looked as near perfect as could be hoped for – small ripply holds and continuous protection. Apart from the odd clump of moss the granite was very clean and it was only when I found a small piece of detached rock masking a good hold that I convinced myself that no one had been this way before. Just over halfway up, a tiny overlap offered only little resistance, then, all too soon the pitch was over. The climbing had been sustained

Andy Nisbet with tricuoni plates on Equinox, Càrn Etchachan, February 1981

Photo: Steve Kennedy

but no more difficult than the crux of Damnation. We continued through a bulge and finished up cracked slabs, Jim and Dougie following up behind us. Three years later Fyffe and Martin Bagness, a student on a Glenmore Lodge rock climbing course, added a direct start, making the whole climb independent from Damnation – The Magic Crack, HVS 5a.

Later that day the weather broke, and although Dinwoodie and Wyness went to the Shelter Stone Crag, they were too late to try the thin crack-line left of Cupid's Bow. They did, however, arrive in time to watch Alan Taylor and Rab Anderson attempt to make a free lead of

Cupid's Bow. Taylor succeeded in gaining the little ledge at the foot of the bow but eventually retired due to the cold. The next day the Edinburgh pair tried to free climb the main pitch of Loki. Again it was Taylor on the sharp end. He got halfway along the fold to a point where the pioneers had left an inverted piton but, as with the previous day, the cold and the difficulties forced him to give up.

Rock climbing conditions were disappointing in June, although Dinwoodie and Wyness managed to climb Raptor, an eliminate line on Creag an Dubh-loch between Vampire and Predator. They shared the leading on this quick-drying route and found good sustained climbing all the way to the top – E2 5b. The weather improved markedly at the end of July when there was a week with little rain. On August 1, Fyffe and Barton were back on Hell's Lum Crag where they climbed The Devil's Alternative, a very enjoyable route on immaculate granite close to Auld Nick – E1 5b.

It was at this time that two significant events took place on the Central Slabs of the Shelter Stone Crag. Dave Cuthbertson (Cubby) and Derek Jamieson were aware of the circumstances surrounding the ascent of Loki and, like Taylor, Anderson and other Edinburgh climbers they were keen to make a free ascent. Cuthbertson was going well this summer and had already made several hard climbs in Glen Coe and Glen Nevis. His new routes on Aonach Dubh, Revengeance and Prophet of Purism, set new levels of difficulty in Glen Coe (both E6) and it seemed inevitable that provided conditions were favourable, Cuthbertson would succeed on the big pitch between Thor and The Pin, and so it turned out.

The opening moves to get established on the overlap he found quite thin, then the remainder of the pitch went without a hitch. He deliberately chose not to clip into any of the old pitons for runners and fixed his own gear as he made his way past Taylor's high point. Beyond this he traversed along a hollow flake before crossing to a belay on The Pin. The climbing was very enjoyable and not exceptionally difficult, but the protection was poor, making Jamieson's task of seconding almost as demanding as it had been for the leader. Later, Cuthbertson inadvertently courted controversy by re-naming the climb – The Missing Link, E4 5c. He justified this by pointing out that Loki had originally been ascended with aid, although he was not aware of a top rope being used. Hamilton summed up the situation when he said: "I do not think you can claim a route if you ask to be top-roped off, so Cubby can call it what he likes."

The other event on the Central Slabs was an attempt by Dinwoodie to climb the thin crack-line left of Cupid's Bow – the line that had been teasing him ever since he roped down it earlier in the year. On that occasion he was surprised to find the rock needed remarkably little cleaning, though not at all surprised to find that the climbing was going to be very hard. On two previous visits he had established a reasonably straightforward start, climbing between Thor and Cupid's Bow, before taking a belay on old pitons 20ft up the Thor diedre. The route then went left onto the rib of Thor and up left to the start of the thin crack which was as far as he had been. This time, belayed by Lawrie, he followed the thin crack until it faded, then continued up the slabs, heading for a small overlap on the right where he hoped to place protection.

When he eventually reached the lap he found a shallow flared crack into which he fiddled two very poor medium-sized wires. The situation was very precarious and he wished he had read the line better and maybe pre-placed a piton. He did not trust the wires and his last good protection was more than 30ft below. He could see that the next bit looked very tenuous – thin balance moves up, then left to reach a scoop. He decided to retreat. First, he took his hammer and bashed the two nuts hoping to seat them better in the flared crack. Then, trying not to put too much weight on the rope, he cautiously down-climbed until Lawrie lowered him off. The whole experience was sufficiently trying that he felt no desire to return.

During the latter part of August and early September the focus of exploration switched to Lochnagar. As the amount of virgin rock in the Cairngorms began to dwindle, so the seekers of new ways had to consider more and more difficult objectives. Although there were still many natural unclimbed lines throughout the massif, the real plums were only going to fall to the most able climbers operating under perfect dry conditions. The new generation had made it clear that the use of direct aid on climbs in Scotland was no longer acceptable. They believed that leaders who found themselves unable to free-climb the rock should retreat and leave it for someone who could. For some of the old guard, this admirable ethic was slightly tainted by the style in which increasing numbers of first ascents were being made. Although physical aid was now taboo, it was becoming more common for first ascentionists to abseil down their projected route, clean off loose rock and vegetation, inspect for holds and runner placements and perhaps even practice a few moves. Then, with the aid of all this information, they would return to the bottom and make the clean ascent. The thrill and anticipation of climbing into the unknown was no longer present. In fact, the pleasure of exploration was now being experienced while hanging on the abseil rope, while the actual first ascent was often no more than a technical exercise. It should also be remembered that the now common use of chalk also made a significant difference.

Dinwoodie had a number of projected climbs on the Tough-Brown Face and the Black Spout Pinnacle, all of which were good natural lines, but with the usual quota of grass-filled cracks. Previously, he had cleaned two short lines right of Black Spout Wall, both of which finished on the big grass ledge below the start of Route 2. The right-hand line follows an excellent jamming crack which is, unfortunately, rarely dry. He climbed this with Steve Young in two stages due to dampness, abseiling into the recess below the crux overhangs the second time – Drainpipe Crack E2 5c.

On the Tough-Brown Face there were unclimbed lines either side of Mort as well as a challenging direct continuation from the first corner of Crypt. The main feature of the line left of Mort was a triangular niche high up in the centre of the cliff. Dinwoodie had cleaned the pitches leading up to and out of the niche and with the line thus partly prepared he was joined by Bob Smith for an attempt on August 31. To the left of the down-pointing tooth of rock at the roof on Mort lies a small triangular recess. Dinwoodie had hoped they could reach this independently using a thin slanting crack but this proved too difficult. In the

Jim Wyness (leading) and Douglas Dinwoodie on Magic Crack, May 1981

Photo: Mungo Ross

end Smith climbed Mort to the roof and traversed left into the recess. He then jammed over a bulge and continued to another terrace. Dinwoodie took the next pitch up a groove and a leaning corner to enter the sloping-floored niche. As expected, climbing out of this turned out to be the crux. With good runners in the bulge above, Smith climbed the wall on the left before pulling over into a shallow continuation groove. Not far above this he joined the final section of Post Mortem. At E2 5c, this good route was briefly the hardest climb on the face. The name, Nevermore, comes from the poem, *The Raven*, by Edgar Allen Poe.

Dinwoodie had already tried the direct continuation of Crypt with Young, climbing over the bulge in the continuation corner to join Dirge at the huge flakes. Higher up, where the Dirge ramp goes right, he went straight up a wall then traversed left and up to the final overhangs. Unfortunately, he was unable to exit round onto an upper slab because a crucial crack was filled with grass. A week after Nevermore, he returned with Willie Todd and Lawrie. They failed again at the grassy crack, so next day they went up Tough-Brown Traverse and abseiled down the unclimbed section, cleaning the crack properly as they passed. They then took turns to try the crux pitch. Lawrie came close, but eventually Todd succeeded and was given the honour of naming the route – The Outlands E3 6a. It was one of the best routes on the face.

In July of this year, the climbers' favourite keeper, Bob Scott, died. His funeral took place on a hot day in Braemar and he was buried in the little graveyard close to the Castle. His death coincided with two events which would have been of considerable interest to him, namely the closing of both the public bar at Mar Lodge and the unofficial Canadian campsite, half a mile up river at the confluence of the Rivers Dee and Lui. While the reasons for the Estate's actions were understandable, it

Bob Barton leading
The Devil's Alternative,
Hell's Lum Crag,
August 1981

Photo: Allen Fyffe

nevertheless had a significant detrimental effect on the social side of walking and climbing on the Braemar side of the Cairngorms.

September saw the re-commencement of the Lurcher's Gully Public Inquiry which was being held in the Victoria Hall, Kingussie. In June, the Reporter, William Campbell, after hearing two weeks of evidence, invited representatives from all interested parties to accompany him on a site visit. Some 50 or 60 people walked up into Coire an t-Sneachda, crossed the Fiacaill Ridge and descended to Jean's Hut in Coire an Lochain. They then made their way round into Lurcher's Gully before returning over Cairn Lochain and back to the car park through Coire Cas. The day started dull and drizzly, but the weather improved allowing great views from the plateau by afternoon.

The second part of the Inquiry lasted three weeks, with proceedings finally being wound up on October 2. The MCofS was able to use the North East Mountain Trust to prepare the mountaineering case and this was presented at the Inquiry by Douglas Graham, an Inverness solicitor and enthusiastic hill-walker. Ten expert witnesses were used and a great deal of back-up provided by the BMC, the Ramblers Association and SCAC. The conservation case was led by the Nature Conservancy Council, The Countryside Commission for Scotland, The RSPB, the Scottish Wildlife Trust and others. It was many months before the outcome was known. After sifting through the huge amount of evidence William Campbell recommended that the application be refused on the grounds that the outstanding scientific, scenic and recreational importance of the site would be adversely affected and that the very strong reasons for objection to the proposal were not outweighed by the undoubted benefits. In December 1982, the Scottish Secretary endorsed the Inquiry's findings and refused planning permission. He recommended the setting up of National Planning Guidelines for ski developments in order to prevent future conflict and urged the wider dispersal of downhill ski centres. Finally, he hinted that further development on Cairn Gorm may be acceptable provided there was no road extension beyond the existing car park.

As a final word on this important test case, it is appropriate to quote Drennan Watson who, as chairman of the NEMT at the time, worked tirelessly to co-ordinate and help develop the mountaineering case.

"Win, or lose, the Scottish mountain scene will never be quite the same again. Too many issues about the future of our hills were brought out to be simply pushed back out of sight. Too many minds were awakened to these issues and their importance. Whatever else, some within the realms of local government and government quangoes learned that hill-users had teeth and were quite prepared to use them when they felt their interests were being ignored. For that reason alone, the fight may have been worth while."[9]

New route activity during the winter of 1981 – 82 was dominated by Nisbet. Although the season was neither prolonged nor particularly snowy, there was a period either side of New Year when temperatures were exceptionally low. Braemar recorded the lowest British temperature of the 20th century with –27.2 degrees C on January 10, equalling the previous lowest temperature, also in Braemar, recorded in February 1895. In the Cairngorms, the sub-zero temperatures did not produce exceptional amounts of ice, but at lower levels there were climbable smears in many unusual places. The top section of the waterfall on Creag Dubh at Newtonmore was well frozen and two water-courses at Cove became the first recorded ice climbs on the Aberdeen sea cliffs. Nisbet kicked off his season with a winter ascent of Python on the upper cliff of Càrn Etchachan. He climbed this summer VS with Pete Langhorn on December 9 – Grade V. A day trip to a very icy Eagle's Rock indicated the likelihood that most south-facing water courses in the Cairngorms would be well frozen. Taking a chance that this was the case, he teamed up with Pete Barrass and headed for Braeriach. On December 17, they climbed The Culvert in Garbh Choire Dhaidh. This prized first winter ascent was made in excellent conditions with thick water ice all the way to the top – Grade V. The next day they went to Coire Bhrochain and nearly succeeded on another Braeriach plum, the left branch of The Great Couloir, known as Ebony Chimney. They reached the great roofs which bar access to the plateau. Here the summer route traverses onto the right-hand rib to finish up an open groove on the far side. The weather had deteriorated almost to a full blizzard by this time and they retreated.

Towards the end of the second week of January 1982, temperatures began to rise again until the freezing level was around 3000ft. On the 15th Nisbet climbed on Càrn Etchachan – this time with Fochabers climber, Sandy Allan. They did a route on the main face based on the summer line of Bastille. Summer and winter cruxes coincided, with a Friend being used for aid, followed by strenuous axe jamming – Grade VI.

By February, there had been at least one substantial thaw and conditions were lean but icy. Nisbet decided it was time to visit the Garbh Coire of Beinn a'Bhùird where he suspected the icefall of Crucible Route may have formed. This time he was climbing with Charlie McLeod, a fitness fanatic and friend of Brian Sprunt. They went to the North Face of Squareface on February 11 and climbed an indirect version of the left-hand twin icefall. The ice was reasonably formed and flowed down a very steep wall onto a slab near the bottom. By following a shallow corner rightward at the junction of the slab and the wall, they crossed the lower icefall and took a belay on a large block. Nisbet then led diagonally up left heading back to the icefall above its steepest section. The line of weakness he was climbing ended at a grass ledge just short of the ice. He could not reach frozen turf beside the ice and was forced to use aid from a poor piton to give him the extra inches. Once on the ice he climbed directly up the left side of the snout, joining the point where Dinwoodie and Archbold had come in from the right. As with the earlier climb, Nisbet thought the route very serious on account of the poor protection. He later named this left-hand icefall – Gold Coast, Grade VI. Its direct ascent would have to wait for even better conditions. Although the icefalls were poorly formed during the late 1970s and much of the 1980s, they were well built up on several occasions in the apparently milder 1990s. One theory for this is that the warmer climate produces more sharp thaws in mid-season. The melt water then freezes. The ice feature on Ben Nevis known as The Shroud is another example. It was watched by climbers through the 1970s but did not form until 1993. Brian Davison and Nisbet climbed both the icefalls of Crucible Route and Gold Coast on March 10, 1997. On the same day they also climbed two thinner ice lines on either side of the main falls in conditions which Nisbet described as "perhaps exceptional".[10]

It was around this time that Nisbet returned to Braeriach with McLeod and finished the task of making an ascent of Ebony Chimney. They found the chimney very icy, but were able to use a crucial through-route just below the point where the right traverse begins. Despite being less than 300ft, the route is considered one of the best climbs in the Cairngorms – Grade VI.

The final new route of the winter fell to a team from the West. On March 14, Davy Sanderson and J.Tomasi climbed the central groove on Aladdin's Buttress in Coire an t-Sneachda. They started at the foot of Patey's Chimney and climbed a ramp diagonally up left to gain the foot of the main groove, which lies just to the left of the Magic Crack. The groove itself gave excellent climbing – The Genie. Grade V.

During the summers of 1980 and 81 the Cairngorms received an uncanny lack of attention from rock climbers resident outwith the North-east. This was mainly attributable to the poor weather, especially

Murray Hamilton and
Pete Whillance at
Creag an Dubh-loch,
1982

Photo: Rab Anderson

in 1980. The Scots had now adopted the open-ended E-grading system developed in England and Wales for classifying the most difficult routes. The hardest climbs in the country at this time were considered to be E5 and these were generally to be found on low-level outcrops or on easily accessible cliffs in the west. So far, no climb of this difficulty had been made on the bigger, more remote crags of the Cairngorms. Hamilton's E4, Sans Fer, was still thought to be the hardest route in the area. It was going to require a good spell of dry weather before any further advance could be made and this happened in the summer of 1982. Just how big this advance would be was almost unimaginable to the locals.

It all started traditionally enough. On May 15, Hamilton and Anderson made the first of several trips that summer to the Shelter Stone Crag. It had been 11 years since Nicolson and Carrington made their mark on the main bastion with the superb Haystack. Was there room for another independent route up the main prow? In the centre of the bastion's midriff, halfway between the crux pitches of Steeple and Needle, a long groove leads directly to the shared stance on these two existing routes. This obvious feature had been considered by climbers in the past but it only appeared to offer a variation to Steeple or Needle. Not so for the Edinburgh men. According to Anderson: "We walked in and the line stood out, so we did it."

They used the first three pitches of Steeple to gain the Gallery where Anderson took a belay beneath the groove. Climbing on sight, and gardening as he went, Hamilton worked his way up the groove, making little diversions to left and right, where necessary, until at the top he managed to pull out right over a bulge and thus reach a belay on Steeple – a long, sustained pitch of excellent climbing. Above this the main objective was to reach the slim, leaning wall which lay between the Steeple corner and the hanging crack of Haystack. To get there Hamilton climbed a short, hard wall onto a ramp. He then followed this and the ensuing cracks, up and left to a belay on Haystack. Once started on the leaning wall above he was amazed to discover that despite the great exposure, the climbing was relatively straightforward. Big holds and flakes led up right across the wall to reach the arete overlooking the Steeple corner. This was then followed on worrying blocky holds, to join Steeple

*Murray Hamilton
starting the big pitch
above the Gallery on
The Spire, May 1982*

Photo: Rab Anderson

at the big ledge below its final pitch. The climb had yielded three major new pitches and another excellent long route. The groove above the Gallery is considered by some to be the best pitch on the bastion – The Spire E4 6a.

Pete Whillance was born in Manchester and moved to Carlisle in 1973. Although 10 years older than Hamilton, the two men had been good friends for a number of years. They climbed together regularly and had made first ascents in England and Wales, as well as in Scotland. Rather like his near namesake from an earlier generation, Whillance had a reputation as a tough no-nonsense climber with an eye for the very best lines and the ability to climb them. In 1980, he established two of Scotland's earliest E5s, Edge of Extinction on The Brack, and The Risk Business on Creag a' Bhancair. As these route names imply, he had a penchant for serious, often poorly-protected climbs. He also had a preference for big routes on mountain crags, where patience and hard graft often resulted in the most rewarding climbs.

Both Whillance and Hamilton had visited Creag an Dubh-loch during the last two disappointing summers and were only too aware of the potential for big new routes. They had been biding their time but, right on cue, they appeared at the Dubh Loch with Anderson on Saturday, May 29, at the start of the first long, dry spell of the summer. As well as their normal climbing gear they carried hammers, wire brushes and a couple of 300ft static ropes, one of which Whillance referred to as his 'black whip'. It was becoming accepted practice to pre-clean and inspect potential hard new routes and leading climbers south of the Border had adopted the cavers' static 'non-stretch' rope for this operation.

Like other advocates of pre-cleaning, Whillance maintained that the practice was necessary in order to leave a first-class route for future ascentionists who might otherwise be faced with a loose, dirty or potentially dangerous climb.

"I remember Culloden was covered in black moss and it was very hard work cleaning off just enough with your fingers to make it climbable. More importantly, we felt that the quality of the route and the climbing was very much impaired by the dirty state it was in. Another formative experience for me had occurred in 1974 when I climbed my first new route in the Lakes – called Brutus on Buckstone How. It was climbed on sight and turned out to have several very loose holds on an overhanging crux with virtually no gear. (It's now graded E3). Jeff Lamb heard about it from someone else a few days later and tried to repeat it. He took a ground fall when holds came away and was very lucky to escape with only a broken leg. This incident made me think a lot about the justification of climbing on sight and leaving new climbs in potentially dangerous states."

When responding to the question, "who decided to clean what?", Hamilton said there were so many ripe plums they just divided them up and got started. They had soon selected more than six possible new routes on various parts of Creag an Dubh-loch. Their initial objective was the impressive crack and groove-line in the centre of False Gully Wall, 60ft left of Sans Fer. This was Hamilton and Anderson's project and they had already spent time the previous day inspecting and partly cleaning it on abseil. This wall is 250ft high and can be descended on one long rope. It sounds straightforward enough, but many of the cliffs are topped by a convex zone of steep vegetation and boulders which make it tricky to locate and fix anchors over a chosen climb. On one occasion, Anderson recalls being alarmed at the sight of Whillance in his Hush Puppies, scrambling around, unroped, on ledges above big drops, apparently without a care in the world.

On the Saturday, they scrambled up False Gully, past the start of Sans Fer, until they reached the ledge system which cuts back below the smooth band. Here in the middle of the band, is an incipient vertical crack. This was the first pitch and it was to be Hamilton's lead. A little ledge, right of the crack, gave access to a small groove which he climbed until it petered out. He knew that above and to his right he could fix a vital small nut which would provide the only protection for the hard moves that followed. Despite knowing exactly where the nut had to go, he still had difficulty placing it. He now had to climb up and left across the wall on tiny holds to regain the crack. The first few moves were the hardest, but higher, before he was able to get his next protection, the climbing was still 5c, with the prospect of a dangerous swinging fall if he came off. Keeping his cool he reached the easier upper crack and climbed it using a shallow corner on the left. Finally, this very serious 60ft pitch ended with more hard moves exiting onto sloping ledges beside the triangular niche at the top of the smooth band.

Pete Whillance climbing the bulging corner on Slartibartfast, False Gully Wall, Creag an Dubh-loch, May 1982

Photo: Rab Anderson

Once the other two had followed, Whillance was offered the lead. "I was vaguely told to wander up the obvious line above and that it would only be 5a. I can clearly recall fighting with a dirty, bulging wall some 40ft above, and turning to shout down that it felt more like 6a than 5a, only to see a pair of giggling faces looking up at me. I had been stitched up!" His on-sight lead of this 6a bulging corner led to a comfortable belay on a slab. Above this Hamilton took over again, and, pursuing the same line, climbed a long pitch up steep cracks to the top. The wait for favourable conditions had paid off. Not only was this the first E5 in the Cairngorms, but it was the first new route at that grade for Hamilton – E5 6b. They named the climb Slartibartfast from Douglas Adams's cult series, *The Hitchhiker's Guide to the Galaxy*, Slartibartfast being a planetary designer who specialised in fiords.

The next day they moved their operations into Central Gully where they cleaned and climbed the 450ft Bombadillo, an unlikely-looking line of grooves in the nose of the buttress between Vertigo Wall and Goliath. They each cleaned and led their own pitch, Whillance taking the first, Hamilton the second and Anderson the third. At the time, they were uncertain as to whether it was E3 or E4, but modern consensus has settled for E4 on account of the bold second pitch where Hamilton used two pitons for protection – E4 6a.

The dry weather continued throughout the following week. On the Friday, Hamilton and Anderson took a day trip to the Shelter Stone Crag and made the second ascent of Cupid's Bow. Hamilton placed a new piton at the start of the bow and then led the whole pitch free, on sight, without clipping into any of the old pitons. This was an impressive lead and demonstrated just how well he was climbing. When Anderson followed he removed all the old pitons and took them back to Edinburgh

Murray Hamilton moving out of Thor on the first free ascent of Cupid's Bow, June 1982

Photo: Rab Anderson

where they were hung up in Tiso's shop as a trophy. Not surprisingly Dinwoodie was a little irked when he heard about it. He would have been even more unhappy if the Edinburgh men had succeeded on the thin crack which he had attempted the previous summer. After completing Cupid's Bow, Hamilton and Anderson abseiled down the line of the crack and both tried to climb beyond Dinwoodie's hammered wires. They did make a little progress, but were unwilling to push on without better protection. Hamilton later described the main pitch of Cupid's Bow as one of the best in the Cairngorms. Nowadays, it is a highly-prized ascent, though at E5 6b (with the piton runner in place) it is not for the faint-hearted.

As Hamilton and Anderson made their way back to Edinburgh the weekenders were arriving at Creag an Dubh-loch. Whillance was back, this time with John Moore. Having driven from Carlisle after work on the Friday night they stopped in Ballater for the traditional last few beers before heading up Glen Muick. "I was driving and eagerly recounting to John the various horror stories about the notorious bend in the road (Death Rattle Gulch) when suddenly I was upon it, through it, and racing down the hillside. The trees that eventually stopped us caused a lot of damage to the car, but fortunately none to us. Next day, with the help of a local farmer, tractor, chains and crow bar we got the car back on the road and rearranged enough metal to make it driveable." They reached the Dubh Loch by mid-afternoon, where Whillance made a quick abseil inspection of The Israelite, a direct line based on Goliath, which he had spotted the previous weekend. Although it was getting late he decided to go for the ascent rather than wait until the next day and risk a change in the weather – a policy which paid dividends on a number of his new routes in Scotland. The climb has an excellent main pitch which follows the thin water-washed groove down which the Goliath Icicle forms in winter – E4 6a.

Another party bivouacking on the beach this weekend was Dave Cuthbertson and Duncan McCallum. Cuthbertson had heard about Hamilton's new E5, Slartibartfast, and was keen to make a second ascent. There was considerable rivalry between the two climbers and the only information Hamilton would divulge was that there was a hidden runner on the first pitch. It was a hot day and this hampered their progress. Cuthbertson had trouble both in locating the crucial placement and then in trying to fix the correct nut. As for the climbing itself, he said the 6b crux seemed hard, but not excessively so! After leading the whole climb he was well pleased with himself. It was after all the first on-sight lead of the crag's most difficult pitch. The next day they repeated Bombadillo, with Cuthbertson leading the first two pitches and McCallum the third.

After this early burst of activity it all went quiet. Although there were no prolonged periods of rain, the weather was sufficiently mixed that most climbers opted for lower cliffs. There was one exception however. Whillance had already looked briefly at a totally outrageous project to climb the right arete of The Giant – a feature to which the extravagant local description 'manifestly impossible' might have been appropriate. Looking back 20 years later he said: "Of all the phenomenal potential that this crag offered at the time, the massive expanse of unclimbed ock between Giant and Cougar was always a central focus in Murray's and my own thinking. For me, right from the very start, it was the big hanging arete and its flanking walls to the right of Giant that held a special fascination and became my prime target on Creag an Dubh-loch. Every time I walked up or down Central Gully it winked at me and I had to stop awhile to trace its features for a possible line of weakness. I think the big attraction was the sheer magnificence and apparent impregnability of the rock architecture. Huge clean-cut sweeps of inter-connected slabs, overlaps and corners arranged on a grand scale and improbably structured around a great overhanging arete."

At the top of the introductory ramp on The Giant, a smooth right-facing corner heads straight up towards a huge overhang. Whillance believed that if he could climb this groove, it might be possible to traverse right across a very steep slab to reach the arete, then by moving farther right, gain the slab below the long, rising overlap attempted by Boysen and Kosterlitz. He then planned to go back up left below the overlap to regain the crest and follow this to the top.

Several weeks after climbing The Israelite, Whillance, Hamilton and Anderson made a trip to the Dubh Loch to attempt this route. After spending time setting up ropes and only half cleaning the line, they were forced to retire due to rain. Inspecting and cleaning an amazing route like this was a major challenge in itself. The work required a lot of abseiling due to the zig-zag line and the big overhangs. On this initial session they cleaned different sections simultaneously. At one point all three of them were one above the other on separate ropes. Anderson near the top on a climbing rope, Whillance and Hamilton farther down on static ropes. Anderson remembers the urgent shouts when loose material, including huge turf caterpillars, was being dropped off. He also recalled discovering his climbing rope half cut through when he jumared back to the top!

In late July and early August, 17 new rock climbs were made through-out the area during a fortnight of glorious weather. There were routes on Creag an Dubh-loch, Lochnagar, Creagan a' Choire Etchachan, Shelter Stone Crag, Hell's Lum Crag and all the major cliffs of Beinn a' Bhùird. This intensity of exploration had never been seen before in the Cairngorms. Dinwoodie and Colin MacLean started the gold rush on July 23, by climbing the crack-line right of Mort on Lochnagar. MacLean had recently arrived in Aberdeen from Glasgow and had been introduced to Dinwoodie by 'wee' Johnny Cunningham, a mutual climbing friend. He was a strong and determined climber who became a member of the Creag Dhu Climbing Club a few years later. The crack-line in question lies 15ft right of and parallel to the second pitch of Mort. According to Dinwoodie, the main crack had been an almost complete runnel of grass until cleaned on abseil. The well-protected crux, previously attempted with Ewen Todd, occurs where the crack cuts through the long roof. Darkness was setting in when they reached the next grass ramp so they escaped off right towards the crest. The name, Crazy Sorrow, comes from Dylan's *Mr Tambourine Man* – E4 6a.

The next day, Saturday, July 24, saw Hamilton and Whillance back in action, only this time they were operating independently and at completely different locations. For Hamilton, the most outstanding

unclimbed route at Dubh Loch was the previously attempted soaring crack-line between the Giant and Cougar. This stunning line was what he and Anderson planned to climb. Early that morning, Hamilton took his 300ft cleaning rope and a single 9mm climbing rope and scrambled down the blocky ground at the top of Central Gully Wall until he was directly above the line. He then abseiled down the 450ft overlapping wall on the static rope, cleaning and assessing the best line of ascent as he went, until he reached the old pitons left by Smith and Dinwoodie. Here he tied-in the end of the long rope, attached the climbing rope and continued on this, carefully brushing the groove which Smith had aided, removing the loose block in the process. Having satisfied himself that the route was now climbable he jumared back to the top, retrieved his ropes and returned to the bottom via Central Gully – an impressive piece of work by any standard.

There was still plenty of time to attempt the climb although billowing clouds posed a threat of thunder. Hamilton was soon up to the overhang on the first pitch and clipped into Higgins's old piton. He knew that getting over the bulge and up the groove was going to be the crux. Taking a deep breath, he pulled over and established an awkward bridging position. He then climbed boldly up the very thin groove to reach the widening, where he took a hanging belay on the in-situ pitons. Continuing directly in the line of the groove looked improbable, but he knew that by moving right he could climb a subsidiary groove and re-gain the line higher up. After succeeding on this detour, he pushed on up a crack heading for the big diagonal overlap. Just below it he moved up left to gain a good ledge where Whillance proposed to belay on his projected climb up the Giant arete. Above and to his right, the leaning wall of the diagonal overlap is split by a groove. By climbing a short crack to its left, he was able to hand traverse right across the wall in a spectacular position to reach the groove above its impending section. He then climbed this to a belay below the short corner down which Archbold, Dinwoodie and I had started our escape from The Prowl, nine years earlier. It is hard to believe that he had reached this high on the cliff after only two pitches of climbing. With the major difficulties now over, they climbed the corner and followed The Prowl up left and down to the recess with the big detached block. By moving back up right they then followed cracks and a groove to the grass terrace at the top of Cougar.

Later that evening, there was a terrific thunder storm which put paid to any chance of hard rock climbing on the Sunday. For once, Hamilton was not bothered. He had just climbed what many believed to be the finest unclimbed mountain line on the mainland of Scotland, the first route to breach the tremendous overlapping wall at the entrance to Central Gully. It was Anderson who suggested naming the climb – The Ascent of Man. Hamilton thought it pretentious at first, but it did seem appropriate, so he agreed. He recorded the climb as an E4, giving the crux groove a technical grade of 6b and only 5c for the two hard passages higher up. Nowadays, it is usual to split the second pitch below the leaning wall. Both sections are considered 6a on sight and the whole route E5.

While Hamilton and Anderson were at the Dubh Loch, Whillance stole in to the Shelter Stone Crag with Tony Furnis and completed Dinwoodie's crack on the Central Slabs. According to Whillance: "Rab first let slip about this line some months earlier, then when I asked Murray direct, he told me about his and Dougie's attempts. I knew it was probably a route that would suit my style, so it was definitely on my hit list."

On the Friday, they climbed The Missing Link and Cupid's Bow, and while abseiling back down from the latter, Whillance took a good look at the unfinished line. He found Dinwoodie's wires completely welded into a very poor placement and posing a dilemma. In their current state they had provided the only means of lowering-off for both previous attempts, but would they hold a fall? He could see little else for a runner so decided not to disturb them.

The next morning he set off up the line. The climbing as far as the hammered nuts seemed reasonable and he felt confident about retreating if necessary. He clipped into the wires and even found another runner

*Brian Lawrie leading
the opening pitch
on the second ascent
of Naked Ape in
August 1984*

Photo: Douglas Dinwoodie

up right behind a flake. He then climbed the crux which involved moving delicately up and left to gain a small ledge in a scoop "particularly thin, heart in your mouth, friction moves". By stepping left he then gained a crack which led to a sloping ledge in a prominent diagonal break. A shorter, much easier pitch then led up the break rightward to join Cupid's Bow below its final flake crack. This extremely bold piece of climbing provided a fine scalp for the Carlisle men – The Run of the Arrow, E6 6b.

Apart from the storm that Saturday evening the weather remained dry and warm throughout the following week. Archbold, Towler and Dave Wallace planned a couple of days climbing on Beinn a' Bhùird. They were intent on exploring the glaciated slabs on the front face of the Dividing Buttress and knew that a prominent corner on the left of these slabs had been climbed by John Jewell and Philip Kammer. An ascent of this Jewell-Kammer Route (VS 4c) enabled them to survey the smooth slabs to the right where they could see a parallel system of left-facing grooves. When viewed from below these appeared as a direct line of cracks, far too enticing not to be climbed.

An indefinite first pitch led to a small ledge at the foot of a clean slab. Towler climbed a crack in the slab and continued up the excellent groove to a belay below a steep wall. To its left a 60ft grass-choked corner was attempted by Archbold, but abandoned after 15ft. He returned to the belay and found an alternative way on the right finishing above the corner. After Towler had followed this pitch, Wallace cleaned and climbed the corner on a top rope. An easy zig-zag pitch then completed the climb. It had been exceptionally hot on the walk-in and Wallace had chosen to travel *au naturel*, much to the amusement of his companions. While striding out in front, the silhouette of his stray rucksack strap gave rise to the name – Streaker's Root. The following summer, while making further climbs on the flanks of these slabs, Nisbet and Ross thoroughly cleaned the top corner on abseil before Nisbet led it. Afterwards, they declared the whole route to be a mini-classic – HVS 5a.

The next day was another scorcher and the trio went early to the West Face of the Mitre Ridge to climb Slochd Wall by its left-hand finish. From the belay at the top of the first pitch, instead of continuing rightward in the main corner, they traversed left and followed the long left-hand corner to reach the final arete of Chindit. This gave more than 200ft of good new climbing and a more sustained finish – HVS 5a. They were well up their climb, enjoying the fine weather and the solitude of this very remote place, when no fewer than eight climbers arrived in the corrie below them. After some friendly exchanges between the combatants the cliff was subjected to a rare onslaught during which Slochd Wall via the 'still warm' left-hand finish, The Primate and Chindit Direct were all climbed.

While local climbers were out on Beinn a' Bhùird and Lochnagar this weekend, Whillance was back at the Dubh Loch, totally focused on his projected route up The Giant arete. He and Hamilton had a kind of understanding with regard to the two major objectives on Central Gully Wall. Although Whillance had abseiled down the arete several times he was still unsure where the most feasible line lay. The project had been emporarily put on hold, but now that Hamilton had climbed The Ascent of Man he could delay no longer.

Whillance said: "Throughout the whole of this period there existed n interesting dynamic in our relationship. The way I saw it was this. Murray and I were really great friends and spent a lot of time together. We openly shared information and ideas about potential new routes hroughout Scotland. We also, however, had our own personal climbing ambitions and agendas to satisfy. Somewhere in between lay a great deal of mutual respect for each other's ability and a quiet uneasiness with regards to which major Scottish plum the other might be going or next. At the Dubh Loch at least, we seemed to have this code of haring lines and asking each other along, but you just couldn't be sure! So, a week after Run of the Arrow and The Ascent of Man, I talked o Murray and let him know that I intended trying the arete on Creag an Dubh-loch. He didn't think he could make it, so I asked Pete Botterill along."

The two Petes spent most of the Saturday inspecting and cleaning. Botterill worked mainly on the first pitch, while Whillance checked out he rest of the line. A lot of his time was spent setting and re-setting abseils to cover the full breadth of the route. Nevertheless, there were still crucial parts of the second pitch, guarded by overhangs, that he had not managed to see close up. In the late afternoon, much to their surprise, Hamilton and Anderson appeared in the gully below. While Whillance recovered equipment from the cliff, the other three made a second ascent of the Israelite. It was an interesting experience for he Edinburgh men, re-tracing their winter ascent and discovering exactly what the Goliath Icicle had been sticking to. Hamilton led the crux groove.

The next day, Botterill climbed the first pitch of the new route – a ong, elegant groove leading to a belay ledge at the top of the initial ramp of The Giant. The cameras were now ready and the stage set for Whillance to take over. Normally, he had an easy-going approach, but when confronting a very serious lead, his attitude changed and he climbed in a deliberate stylish way, using the holds very precisely and aking great care over each move. The groove directly above the belay was so smooth and holdless that he was forced to use its left rib. Climbing this was technically very hard (6b) and the protection barely adequate. After 30ft he was able to bridge into the groove where a thin crack cut horizontally across the bald slab to his right. Here he drove in a thin piton and this was to provide protection for the opening moves of this crucial 30ft traverse. Slowly, he worked his way out right, descending slightly on delicate little footholds. Just over halfway to the arete he found a place to fix two small wires which would only slot into the crack in opposition to each other. This contrivance was all he could get to stop himself from smashing back into the groove if he slipped. More thin moves using tiny pockets and side pulls took him almost to the edge where he fixed another piton. This was a much more difficult operation due to his precarious position. Finally, he clipped into the piton and made the step-up to a resting place right on the crest of the arete. Much easier, though unprotected, climbing then took him up right to a belay on The Ascent of Man.

Pete Whillance (leading) and Pete Botterill climbing The Naked Ape, August 1982

Photo: Rab Anderson

When Botterill followed this diagonal pitch he trailed another rope, clipping it into the protection as he passed. In this way Hamilton and Anderson were later able to second the climb. Meanwhile, they remained in the gully taking photographs while Whillance started the next pitch. The slab ramp cuts back up left below the leaning wall of the diagonal overlap, heading for a mean-looking roof 40ft away. There was a continuous crack at the junction between the leaning wall and the slab and this provided both good protection and adequate holds. Whillance fairly rattled up the ramp until he was poised below the roof. Instead of attempting to climb over this, he fixed a nut runner in its lip and delicately padded down left, almost Etive style, to gain a foothold close to the edge – a position of great exposure, even by the standards of this route. Directly above him was a slight break in the roof. With little hesitation, he reached above the overhang and mantelshelved onto a small, sloping ledge. He now only needed to climb a short steep wall to gain a belay ledge and he succeeded in doing this after fixing another piton runner.

The route was now almost in the bag. Once the others had moved up, an overhanging crack was climbed to reach the recess occupied by the big detached block. They then followed the final pitch of The Ascent of Man to the top. Many years later, when asked what his thoughts were at the time about this great climb, Whillance said: "The big pitch was clearly serious and committing, but then so are lots of climbs. What made the whole thing particularly memorable were the incredible situations. The rock architecture is extremely dramatic throughout and provides a real 'fly on the wall' feeling. Combine this with very spaced gear, having to place pitons on the lead and no certainty that you can do it or retreat safely, and the feeling of being a very small speck in a very big landscape is further accentuated." He named the climb The Naked Ape – E5 6b.

One of the effects of this long spell of good weather was the drying out of normally persistent drainage lines. On August 3, Fyffe and Barton climbed Second Sight (HVS 5a) on the frontal face of Hell's Lum Crag. The climb follows cracks left of the niche on Devil's Delight. Fyffe had waited many years to find the crux section leading into the niche completely dry. On Lochnagar, Dinwoodie took advantage of the dry conditions to make a 'proper' lead of his Drainpipe Crack in a single run-out. He and MacLean climbed this and The Vault (E2 5b), the left-hand line.

It was Lochnagar that witnessed the last new route of this exceptional period. Fyffe and Barton were finalising arrangements for a two-man expedition to the Himalayas and were keen to squeeze in another climb. Two days after the visit to Hell's Lum Crag they climbed a new route on the Tough-Brown Face. Starting midway between Mort and Tough-Brown Direct, they climbed a crack system to a white scar then veered away left to cross Crazy Sorrow. Although this right-hand section is more vegetated than the main area of the face, they found good climbing above the level of the scar. It was obvious, while they climbed, that the weather was about to break, but they made it before the heavens opened. They named the climb Rolling Thunder, another Dylan reference. (Rolling Thunder was the name of a tour by Dylan) – E1 5b. The actual

*Pete Whillance
abseiling from the
'untrodden ledge' of
Broad Terrace Wall,
1982*

Photo: Rab Anderson

thunder and lightning they experienced on the way down was the mos
impressive and frightening they had ever seen in Scotland. A few week
later they left for the Western Garwhal where they were successful ir
their bid to climb the impressive South-West Pillar of Bhagirathi III.

The mediocre weather at the end of August did not deter the irre
pressible Whillance. During this summer he had made a dozen separate
visits to the Dubh Loch. "Whenever a forecast gave the slightest chance
of dry weather I would be there. Of course, bad weather and/or wet rock
meant that climbing was only possible on about half of these occasions
but I took the view that in Scotland you had to speculate to accumu
late!" He and Anderson spent a few days at the Dubh Loch hoping fo
dry rock. Although they did not complete any climbs they did have ar
exciting day exploring the heart of Broad Terrace Wall.

Between the big corner system of The Sword of Damocles and the
crack-line of Culloden the wall is at its most formidable. Here, at half
height on the cliff, an isolated ledge, where peregrines nest, lies below
a smooth leaning headwall. This amazing sanctuary, referred to by
Dinwoodie in the guide as "an untrodden grass balcony" was about to
receive its first human visitors. Few would dispute that the abseil of
the top of Broad Terrace Wall is the spookiest descent on Creag an Dubh
loch. Anderson recalls this first occasion: "Straight over the top with
unbelievable exposure and the tail of the rope hanging free in space
about 30ft out from the rock." They managed to swing onto the ledge
where they discovered a 25ft squat pinnacle leaning against the back
wall. A further abseil took them to the foot of the cliff. They spent time
prospecting and cleaning, then jumared back to the top.

Before giving way to the poor weather they managed to clean the
steep crack-line left of Vertigo Wall which had been attempted by
Dinwoodie in 1977. Two weeks later this became The Wicker Man,
Whillance's fourth new route on Central Gully Wall. He and Anderson
climbed it on a cold day at the beginning of September when it was
the only dry line on the crag. The main crack gave a superb pitch of
steep, well-protected climbing – E3 6a.

The summer of 1982 will long be remembered for the achievements
of Whillance and Hamilton. Favourable weather, clinical route preparation, and rock climbing skills of the highest order all combined to
enable them to produce a string of outstanding new routes, including
the Cairngorm's first four E5s. Their climbs on Creag an Dubh-loch
demonstrated that apparently blank rock did run to holds and that given
the best modern equipment, a steely determination and the necessary
skill and daring, even the impossible-looking walls could be overcome
without the use of aid.

Of all their great climbs this summer, the two which breached the
great overlapping wall at the entrance to Central Gully stand out in
particular. The Ascent of Man followed a prominent challenging line,
the scene of several failures in the past. The Naked Ape, on the other
hand, was unbelievable. It followed no obvious line and took to some
very improbable areas of rock. For the time being these magnificent
climbs could only be marvelled at. In the future they would be objectives to which others could aspire.

Despite a reasonable winter in 1982 – 83 surprisingly little in the way of new route activity was recorded in the Cairngorms. Local climbers spent a lot of time away from the area, although in December, Nisbet did hoover up the last of the 1950s rock routes on the upper cliff of Càrn Etchachan by climbing Nom de Plume with Langhorn – Grade VI.

In 1983 there was another summer with good weather, although it took most of June for all the snow to melt and the crags to dry out. Once again, Hamilton was very much to the fore in the exploration stakes, and despite Whillance only making one trip to the Cairngorms he still managed three good new routes on consecutive days in July.

The first action took place in June on the Crimson Slabs where Brian Davison led a large Aberdeen team up a corner system right of The Sheath. The climbing was sustained and seriously unprotected – The Scythe E2 5b. Hamilton also chose Creagan a' Choire Etchachan for his first hit on the high crags this summer. Approaching from the Shelter Stone on July 9, he and Anderson cleaned and climbed the excellent right-hand corner on the steep gable wall of the Bastion. This eye-catching line had seen off all previous on-sight attempts – Henchman, E3 5c.

July 14 was a sad day for climbing in Aberdeen. During a midday break from work, Bob Smith went to the sea cliff near Cove known as Sickle Row and tried to rope-solo a new climb. He fell more than 50ft onto sloping rocks, rolled into the sea and was drowned. His self-arrest system and marginal protection had failed to stop the initial slip. Over the last few years he had concentrated his efforts on the accessible local outcrops. He was one of the strongest climbers to grace the North-east and one of the first to lead E5 with his classic climb Prehistoric Monster at Earnsheugh. Only the previous weekend he had been to the Dubh Loch with Lawrie, where champing at the bit, he had been foiled by rain from attempting the first repeat of The Ascent of Man. News of Bob's death and the nature of the accident came as a great shock. His powerful style, his enthusiasm and his smile will always be remembered by those who knew him.

While the locals were subdued by this tragic event, Hamilton continued to roam across the country, picking off prime climbs wherever he went. His next objective at the Dubh Loch was a major line on Broad Terrace Wall, in the vicinity of Whillance's investigations the previous summer. He and Spence had cleaned an impressive diagonal line, starting close to the foot of Culloden and following a prominent left-slanting corner up to the grass balcony. Above this, instead of taking the direct line down which Whillance and Anderson had abseiled, Hamilton opted to try an easier-looking ramp-line, which continued the leftward trend across the leaning headwall. The crag was currently as dry as it was ever likely to be, so they arranged with Anderson to attempt the route on Friday July 22.

The opening corner proved deceptively difficult, with awkward jamming in a flared crack before wide bridging took Hamilton to a resting place. By moving left he was able to follow a crack up to a belay below the left end of the big overhang spanning across to Culloden. Another hard pitch followed to gain the grass balcony then 30ft higher they found a superb belay on top of the squat pinnacle. Here the wall leans out fiercely along its entire length and the undercut ramp runs

Brian Davison
Photo: Stephen Venables

Broad Terrace Wall,
Creag an Dubh-loch.
The prominent right
facing corner system
on the left is Sword of
Damocles. Culloden
takes the first crack
system right of the
large black horizontal
overhang in the centre
of the picture.
Flodden starts at foot
of Culloden and
follows a right to left
diagonal line past the
left end of the black
overhang to finish by
a ramp crossing the
leaning headwall

Photo: Greg Strange

leftwards through this. Spence tried to lead the ramp but was stopped by a small section which had not been cleaned. This was as far as they could go so they roped off.

The next day they went to the top and abseiled down to the balcony, brushing the rock at Spence's high point in the process. This time Hamilton took the lead. He found it difficult moving left past the newly-cleaned passage but managed to rest below a small roof and arrange protection. He then continued up left, following the ramp until it was possible to step down to another poor resting place. The hardest climbing was now directly above. After ascending a short groove, he had to make powerful and committing moves across a steep slab in order to reach a vertical corner and further protection. With some relief, he succeeded in doing this, and then climbed the corner to a belay perched on the very edge of the steep wall. It had been a stunning pitch, probably the hardest at the Dubh Loch at that time – Flodden E6 6b.

There was a minor hiccup in the near-perfect weather but those with their finger on the pulse knew that the Cairngorms were as dry as anyone could remember. On July 27, Whillance and Ray Parker climbed The Harp on the Central Slabs of the Shelter Stone Crag. It started at the foot of Sticil Face, crossed Snipers and joined The Run of The Arrow before its final pitch. A superb crack on the second pitch provided the highlight – E3 5c.

The next day, Whillance moved to the Dubh Loch to meet

Hamilton, Spence and Duncan McCallum. Spence had been disappointed with his attempt at the big pitch on Flodden and later said that he had found it hard, even seconding. However, while on Flodden he had had ample opportunity to study the direct line above the balcony. He knew that both Whillance and Hamilton were also aware of the line, but he wanted to try it independently of them, so he asked McCallum to join him. On the Thursday, he and McCallum spent the day cleaning a new pitch up to the balcony as well as the crack and corner system on the leaning wall above. At the same time, Hamilton and Whillance were on False Gully Wall climbing an obvious short corner at the left end of the smooth band – Masque E2 5c.

Friday, July 29, saw all the action taking place on Broad Terrace Wall. Spence and McCallum made their bid for glory and headed straight back to attempt their counter-diagonal to Flodden. McCallum took the lead on the lower section which started midway between The Sword of Damocles and Culloden. After climbing a short corner he went directly over a roof then continued up steep rock trending left to reach the balcony. Soon he was on top of the squat pinnacle, safely belayed at the ledge on Flodden. The impending wall looked very hard, but Spence knew that the cracks would provide good protection provided he could hold on long enough to place the equipment. Once launched onto the wall he climbed straight up to a niche below a roof. Here, in an extremely exposed position, he had to traverse right below the bulge before he could pull up into the obvious corner. Now he felt more confident. He climbed on up the corner to a recess, moved out left and continued to a belay where the angle relented. A brilliant 120ft 'out there' pitch, technically 6a at the crux. Easier climbing then took them to the top. The elder statesman of Edinburgh climbing had achieved his goal – an excellent new route of his own on Creag an Dubh-loch.

Spence said: "I saw the line while on Flodden and knew that Murray and Pete had both seen it. If I had asked Murray to climb it with me it would have become one of Murray's routes. Hence the name Range War." – E4 6a.

While Spence and McCallum were battling away near the centre of Broad Terrace Wall, Hamilton and Whillance were away to their left climbing an excellent little line on steep water-washed slabs left of The Last Oasis. Their route, Alice Springs (E2 5c), followed a prominent finger-wide crack up the middle of this area of perfect pink granite.

Predominantly dry weather persisted throughout August with excellent rock climbing available on all the Cairngorm cliffs. During the first weekend of the month, Dinwoodie and I visited the west face of the Mitre Ridge to see if we could climb the face of the cuneiform buttress. I had thought we might climb the first pitch of The Chancel, then move up right and find a way through the prominent overhangs. When we arrived it was obvious that a direct climb might be possible to the right of the main overhangs, utilising a short vertical corner 30ft up the wall. Dougie opted to inspect the climb, so he soloed Commando Route trailing the ropes, until he could move left on to the terrace crossed by Helter Skelter. A long abseil from the middle of the terrace then allowed him to check the line and remove the occasional loose flake. Some time later he led back up to the terrace in a single 140ft pitch of sustained

Kenny Spence, 1980

Photo: Rab Anderson

well-protected climbing. The crux occurred two-thirds of the way up, not far above the point where the shallow corner had closed. A little overlap had to be overcome on small fingery holds, before diagonal cracks led up to the terrace. I continued to the crest of the ridge via the top pitch of The Chancel. The Empty Quarter – E3 5c.

Recently, Dinwoodie had been contemplating making a new route on Central Gully Wall. He felt that Hamilton and Whillance had had too much of the action and a comment by Hamilton that "climbers from Aberdeen were doing nothing" was the final straw. There were several local climbers operating at quite a high standard on the coast and outcrops and Dinwoodie believed his own standard was approaching that of his tormentors. For the last few summers he had been preoccupied with exploring the Gothic architecture of Lochnagar, but now his interest had reverted back to Creag an Dubh-loch. Not far to the right of the upper pitches of The Ascent of Man, a prominent hanging crack cleaves the steep wall below the last pitch of Cougar. Dinwoodie's plan was to use the Boysen-Kosterlitz start which curves up below the line of Cougar, link this with the crack, and finish via his own alternative top pitch to Cougar (climbed with Guy Muhlemann using some aid in 1976).

Following a chance meeting in the bar of the Cove Bay Hotel, near Aberdeen, Dinwoodie arranged a visit to the Dubh Loch with Graeme Livingston, a 16-year-old pupil at Robert Gordon's College. Livingston was a strong swimmer who had attained national standard by regular intensive training. The previous summer, a course at Glenmore Lodge had served as a catalyst for his rapidly-growing interest in climbing.

In the vicinity of his school gates, Rosemount Viaduct crosses the Inverness railway line beside His Majesty's Theatre. Two walls running below the viaduct are used by local climbers for training and Livingston spent most of his free time at school traversing these walls. He quickly become very competent and already this year he had free-climbed the old aid start to Munich Buttress at Longhaven (Nazi Swine E4 6b) and led through with MacLean on Cougar. Sometimes, on his way home to Newmachar, just north of Aberdeen, he would call in at 516 George Street, the first-floor flat which was home to a number of climbers during the 1970s and 1980s. Guy Muhlemann, Wright Nicholls, Dave Innes, Dinwoodie, Adhair McIvor, Mungo Ross and Colin MacLean had all been resident there at one time or another. According to Livingston: "George Street, at the time, was an institution existing somewhere on the fringe of society, sport, mountains and drinking. I would, on a regular basis, arrive there for a planned departure of eight o'clock in the morning, only to find myself sent to buy breakfast." It was here that Dinwoodie first met the enthusiastic school boy and recognised similarities with himself at that age. Livingston could hardly believe his luck when asked if he would like to try a new route on Central Gully Wall.

On August 12, Dinwoodie abseiled down his projected route using two 9mm climbing ropes. The hanging crack looked amenable and he could see how he might approach it from Boysen's little ledge. He was on his third abseil when he noticed two people descending Central Gully. It was Hamilton and Anderson who had walked in from Glen Clova the previous day and made the second ascent of Range War. It soon became clear that they too were intent on climbing the 'Boysen line'. At the time, Dinwoodie was inspecting the overlapping granite to the right of The Ascent of Man and could now see a possible alternative and more direct start.

The rest of the day was a whirlwind of activity from Hamilton and Anderson. They planned to follow the line taken by Boysen and Kosterlitz, then link across to The Ascent of Man before finishing up The Naked Ape. In this way they would follow the general line of slabs below the big diagonal overlap all the way to the Giant arete. Cleaning and inspecting the unknown section required a number of abseils during which they came upon no evidence of anyone having passed that way

The main pitch of the Empty Quarter, West Face of the Mitre Ridge, Beinn a' Bhùird, August 1983. Douglas Dinwoodie climbing

Photo: Greg Strange

Murray Hamilton treading carefully towards The Ascent of Man on Voyage of the Beagle, August 1983

Photo: Rab Anderson

before. As usual, Hamilton took the lead and climbed the rising traverse line starting 20ft left of Cougar. He found the first pitch quite bold with technical climbing of 6a. At the little ledge where Kosterlitz had attempted to go up left below the big overlap, Hamilton discovered that the easiest way was to step down to a lower slab, then traverse left to reach an edge close to the crux of The Ascent of Man. Although this crossing felt precarious on account of the sparse protection, the final exposed step round the edge proved to be the highlight. Beyond this he climbed straight up to join and follow The Ascent of Man to the belay common to The Naked Ape. Careful rope work by the leader gave some assurance to Anderson as he followed this very exciting pitch. They were now on familiar territory and continued up the final two pitches of The Naked Ape to complete the superb Voyage of the Beagle – E5 6a.

Dinwoodie was both relieved and grateful that Hamilton chose not to complete his new route via the hanging crack, although Hamilton maintained it was always his intention to finish by the final pitches of The Naked Ape. The next day, the Aberdeen team attempted to climb as directly as possible to the hanging crack. At least 20 individual overlaps, one above the other, are apparent on this section of the cliff and surmounting the largest of these was most likely to provide the hardest climbing. A short distance below the start of The Ascent of Man they found a break in the bulging wall where it was possible to swing up and grasp a good hold on top of 'a peculiar boss of rock'. This crucial entry allowed Dinwoodie to gain less steep rock and progress by smooth slabs and cracks to a belay 70ft above the gully. Ahead lay a double-tiered bulging wall which barred access to a big slab below the fiercest looking overlap. The second tier of this wall proved very troublesome and only succumbed after repeated attempts to make a scary mantelshelf onto a smooth narrow shelf. Further difficult climbing led up to the slab where he could only get two poor pitons for a belay. The situation felt dramatic with smooth rock to left and right, and an impending wall above.

Leaving Livingston tied to the two pitons, Dinwoodie stepped down and traversed left along the lip to 'an evil sloping perch' where the slab abutted the overlap. The groove above looked impossible, so he swung left round an overhanging nose onto the wall beyond. The protection was poor, but he knew that he might be able to drive a piton into a crack before attempting the hardest moves. It took ages to achieve this and even then the piton had to be tied-off to reduce leverage. The effort had taken its toll; he retreated back to the belay and they abseiled off.

Over the next few days they made free ascents of Vampire Direct and The Crow. Then, on August 18 they felt ready to give the route another try. On the way back up Livingston fell from the hard mantelshelf while attempting to lead the second pitch, fortunately without hurting himself. When Dinwoodie reached his high point below the piton he felt much fresher than he did the last time. The climbing was hard and strenuous but he passed the crux and continued through the traverse of Voyage of the Beagle to a belay below the big diagonal overlap. After Livingston had followed this pitch, Dinwoodie moved up left, joined The Ascent of Man for a short way, and then crossed a slab on the right to reach and climb the hanging crack. With the major difficulties now past, they followed Cougar to the traverse of the Prowl then took its shelf up left until more direct climbing over a bulge brought them back onto Cougar part-way along its final traverse. While driving home that night, Dinwoodie fell asleep at the wheel, mounted the verge, and only recovered control after the car had careered back on to the road. They named the new route Perilous Journey (E6 6b), not because of this incident, but after a famous climb in Colorado, renowned for its serious lack of protection. Dinwoodie strongly agreed with Whillance and Hamilton's ethic that piton runners should be fixed on the lead and not pre-placed on abseil. It may seem trivial now but all three of them thought it important at the time.

Success on the improbable lower overlaps of Perilous Journey inspired Dinwoodie to consider another equally daunting climb farther right. He wanted to climb the immaculate folded granite directly below the Cougar Slab, then continue by the stepped corner system running parallel to and left of Vampire Direct. After the first abseil inspection he discounted the corner because it looked too hard to climb direct, and by moving on to the right arete in places, escapes into Vampire Direct were apparent. He did, however, look at the face 20 – 30ft to the left of the corner and considered a line here to be just possible.

Towards the end of August, he and MacLean made two attempts to reach the Cougar Slab. They started at a little arete 30ft down the gully from Perilous Journey and followed cracks and slabs for two pitches of excellent climbing to a belay on Voyage of the Beagle. At this point, where the long diagonal overlap is in its infancy, the major obstacle to upward progress is the imposing outer edge of the Cougar Slab. Dinwoodie climbed above the belay to a left-slanting corner and followed this to a roof 10ft below the lip of the slab. He now had to traverse left and swarm up into a recess, still 6ft short of his objective. He managed to fix a piton runner before retreating. The next day they repeated all the climbing only for Dinwoodie to fall from the very hard moves pulling onto the Cougar Slab. This was the last action of the summer on Creag an Dubh-loch.

The good weather in August attracted climbers to other areas in the Cairngorms. On Lochnagar, Archbold and I climbed Post Mortem via the first two pitches of Dirge and a good link following a narrow rising ledge which joined Post Mortem halfway up its second pitch. This combination gave excellent climbing, avoiding grass terraces and the slow-drying crux area on Post Mortem. Although it was only one pitch of new climbing, our suggestion of Tough-Brown Integral for the complete route has stuck – E2 5b.

Brian Davison and Andy Nisbet spent a few days climbing in Coire an Lochain of Cairn Gorm. Davison, an experienced climber from Durham, was working as a post-doctoral chemist at Aberdeen University. He quickly gained notoriety locally for his daring exploits on the Aberdeen sea cliffs and was nicknamed 'The Sass' – a shortened version of Sassenach. On August 24, Davison led a steep two-pitch route up the centre of No. 3 Buttress, right of The Vicar. Starting beneath the arete of the latter, he powered his way up and right to join a crack-line coming up from the undercut base of the wall – The Demon. E2 5b. It was during this trip that they made free ascents of War and Peace, Daddy

*Graeme Livingston
ice bouldering
below Creagan
a' Choire Etchachan,
January 1985*

Photo: Greg Strange

Longlegs and The Vicar. This latest visit to Coire an Lochain was largely to free all George Shields' routes before the new guide came out. It also reminded Nisbet of his intention to climb there in winter. Two years earlier, he and Dave Lawrence had made a steep, but straightforward, rock climb near the right edge of No. 3 Buttress, close to the left branch of Y Gully. According to Nisbet, it was this climb, The Overseer, which opened his eyes to the winter potential of this corrie. Why it took so long to go back he was not sure, but like other climbers from Aberdeen, he did not consider the Northern Corries very important at that time. Visits there in winter tended only to be made as a soft option to the Loch Avon basin when weather or walking conditions dissuaded a crossing of the plateau.

The winter season 1983 – 84 started very late with mild weather and no snow right up to the beginning of December. The situation improved by the second weekend of the month when sub-zero temperatures and snow showers set in. On the Saturday, Nisbet made his move, and with Ewen Clark re-ascended The Overseer, finding good mixed winter conditions on frozen turf and snowed-up rock – Grade V. They completed the route so quickly they had time to attempt Auricle on No. 1 Buttress. This over-enthusiasm ended at a chokestone in the crux groove, but the retreat sling placed in a strenuous position was very useful on a successful ascent the following winter. They returned the next day and climbed Sidewinder, an obvious line of weakness going up right below the corners of War and Peace and Procrastination. When they reached the easier-angled crest, they cut back left to finish at the top of Savage Slit. This natural winter line turned out to be a modest Grade III.

Nisbet was back the following weekend accompanied by Sandy Allan, Steve Kennedy and Charlie McLeod. Nisbet and Allan climbed Grumbling Grooves on the left side of the pillar between the branches of Y Gully (Grade VI) and a more direct version of Sidewinder. Kennedy and McLeod climbed Crow's Nest Crack, a summer route on No. 2 Buttress, right of Central Crack Route – Grade III. Only a fortnight earlier there had been no snow in this corrie and now there were five new winter routes. It is the relatively high altitude of Coire an Lochain that brings about the good mixed winter conditions early in the season. Combine this with easy access and it is not difficult to see why Coire an Lochain and Coire an t-Sneachda, have now become the most popular winter climbing venues in the Cairngorms. This little burst of activity in Lochain marked the beginning of a major winter blitz that would see new climbs made in every nook and cranny of these two northern corries of Cairn Gorm. Like other local climbers at the time, Nisbet could never have imagined how much winter development would take place in these corries:"I kept thinking they were worked out until I, or someone else did another route."

In January 1984, Arthur Paul and Dinwoodie made a winter ascent of Psyche on the Tough-Brown Face of Lochnagar. They had attempted this challenging line previously and knew they could get up into the wide crack. Conditions were thin but good for mixed climbing. According to Dinwoodie: "Arthur made an exemplary job of leading the two hard pitches, particularly since he used no aid at all." Dinwoodie tried to lead the last pitch by moving out left from the corner of Nymph to avoid climbing the final bulge. Unfortunately, he was unable to return back right so Paul took over and led the bulge directly. Although he found this very hard, he thought the widest part of the crack on the second pitch was at least as exacting. The weather deteriorated badly as they climbed so when they reached the terrace they roped down the chimney of Parallel Gully B in great haste, worried in case of avalanches – Grade VII.

Arthur Paul, like Colin MacLean, was a member of the Creagh Dhu. One of Scotland's most accomplished winter climbers, he has a string of outstanding first ascents to his credit, particularly on Ben Nevis. A few weeks after Psyche, he and Dave Cuthbertson climbed Guerdon Grooves, a very serious and technical mixed climb on Slime Wall of Buachaille Etive Mòr in Glen Coe. More than 20 years on and still no one has managed to repeat this climb.

During this period Nisbet made winter ascents of two summer routes on the Grey Man's Crag in Coire Sputan Dearg. Before New Year, he and Livingston climbed Lucifer Route in terrible weather using a piton for aid on the crux – led by Livingston. This was the third time they had been on the climb. Previously, they had done the whole route in two halves, but Nisbet felt this did not constitute a proper ascent so he persuaded Livingston to return yet again. "Graeme got fed up with the whole episode and only went back reluctantly – not one of my better routes." – Grade VI. This comment did not apply to his second climb which he made with Sandy Allan on January 12. On this occasion they climbed Grey Slab which has a finish common to both Pilgrim's Groove and Lucifer Route, terrain over which Nisbet was becoming very familiar. This classic rock climb provided an equally fine mixed winter route which involved a fall on the first pitch and a piton for aid on the second. The highlight of the climb was pitch three, where the route went up the centre of the grey slab – a hard and sustained climb – Grade VII.

There were many people out enjoying the mountains throughout the Highlands on Saturday, January 21. Three days of cold, clear weather had whetted their appetite for some action on the hills. The forecast had indicated strong southerly winds by the end of the day. However, the morning dawned fair with sunshine and only a little wind in the glens. Few could have predicted the suddenness in the way a storm sprung up around midday. It quickly swept across the whole of northern Scotland, accompanied by heavy snow and winds in excess of 100mph. On Cairn Gorm, three students from Heriot-Watt University died of exposure returning to the Coire Cas car park having failed to find Jean's Hut on the Friday night. At the same time, an instructor and a student from the Joint Services Mountain Training Centre succumbed to the desperate conditions while attempting to walk out from a snow-holing exercise in the Feith Buidhe. Their bodies were found five days later, roped together, on the edge of Coire an t-Sneachda, close to the top of Fiacaill Buttress. These deaths came as no surprise to anyone who had been out on the hills that day. Numerous tales were told of epic struggles with the wind as folk made there way to shelter.

The blizzard severely hampered upland travel and it was almost a week before communication returned to normal. Nisbet had a new project in hand – a winter ascent of Black Mamba on Creag an Dubh-loch. In

*Mitre Ridge from the
east, Garbh Choire,
Beinn a' Bhùird, April
1977. South East
Gully and East Wall
Direct lie on the very
snowy left hand
sector. The Grail and
The Actress take lines
on the steeper rock
between East Wall
Direct and the right
crest of the Ridge*

Photo: Greg Strange

late January, he made his first attempt with Phil Thornhill. The Muick
road was still partly blocked and they skied all the way to the bottom
of the cliff. "The weather was terrible and I belayed Phil for five hours
on pitch three until it was dark. Phil wanted to continue all night but
I was beginning to get hypothermic and insisted on abseiling off." The
next time he went with Sandy Allan and they spent a long time digging
out the howff below the Central Slabs only to wake up the next morning to another blizzard. Finally, on February 9, the first calm day for a
while, Nisbet and Allan managed the whole route in 11 hours, reaching the top just as it got dark. They followed the summer route to
the terrace then climbed the icefall of the White Elephant for a pitch
before working up and right to re-join the summer line below the quartz
corner. The corner proved to be the crux where they were forced to use
a piton for aid at the final bulge before reaching good ice on the right.
This long, sustained route had involved an estimated two weeks of effort
overall – Grade VII.

Nisbet's next contribution also required a big effort, only this time,
conditions were very favourable. A substantial thaw followed by a freeze
resulted in excellent climbing conditions as well as easy walking. Shortly
after the Black Mamba ascent he was joined by Adrian Clifford for a
mid-week trip to the Slugain Howff. A photograph of the Mitre Ridge
in winter had alerted him to two possible winter lines on the East Wall
of the Mitre Ridge between East Wall Direct and the original route up
the crest. The most obvious of these takes a vegetated fault in the centre
of the lower slabs and finishes by a large corner-cum-ramp, overlooking the couloir of East Wall Direct. On February 15, Nisbet and Clifford
went to the Garbh Choire and climbed this excellent central line finding the top ramp to be the crux – The Grail, Grade V. Next day, they
walked all the way back and made an even harder route to the right of
The Grail, starting close to Mitre Ridge Direct and finishing up The
Bishop. Gaining entry into the left-hand of twin chimneys immediately
above the halfway terrace provided the hardest climbing – The Actress,
Grade VI. Nisbet led all the pitches on these remote climbs.

The mid-week trips continued for Nisbet as he worked his way through
a never-ending list of potential winter routes. On February 22, he and
Ewen Clark visited the other Garbh Choire, Braeriach this time, where
they climbed Tiara, the rib to the left of Buntings Gully. Not only was
this a first winter ascent, it may well have been the first repeat of this
VS rock climb made in 1959. Although only 300ft, the climb took eight
hours – Grade VI. This was Nisbet's fourth walk to the Garbh Choire
Hut to try this route. He had failed on the route once and had been
turned back by bad weather twice.

In early March, tragic news came from Switzerland of the death of
Brian Sprunt in a fall from high on the North Face of the Matterhorn.
The accident occurred when he and his companions, Charlie McLeod
and Sandy Allan, were starting out on the third day after an uncomfortable bivouac. Brian had just roped down to regain the line of ascent
when an old fixed piton, to which he had attached himself, pulled out
and he fell to the foot of the wall. McLeod and Allan were evacuated
soon afterwards by a passing rescue helicopter which spotted them
waving from the face. Brian was the fourth young climber from Aberdeen

to die in just two years. His loss, with that of John Anderson, Bob Smith and John Hossie (who disappeared on an expedition to The Andes), left a large void in the ranks of the Etchachan Club. The effervescent Sprunt had not restricted his climbing to the mountains and sea cliffs of his homeland. During his short life, trips abroad had accounted for the Eiger North Face (with McLeod), the North Face of The Droites, an early alpine ascent of the Cassin Ridge on Mount McKinley (with Rob Milne) and an attempt on the West Ridge of Nuptse, in the Himalayas. He was a highly-talented climber with a great sense of humour.

The remainder of the 1984 winter season was once again dominated by activities on Lochnagar. The strong team of Paul, Dinwoodie and MacLean climbed the 200ft icicle finish to Douglas Gibson Gully (Central Fork, Grade VI), and later in the month, Chris Dale and Ewen Todd made an ascent of The Link, independent of Route 1. They started up a steep vegetated groove right of Route 1 then used rope tension to move left before continuing to join The Link above the Springboard. Above the crux overhang on the normal route, instead of taking the big left-hand vegetated groove, as on the two previous winter ascents, they continued up right in the summer fault to reach Route 2 at the start of its traverse – The Argonaut. Grade VII.

With the ascent of Psyche, in January, there was renewed interest in winter climbing on the Tough-Brown Face. Dinwoodie believed that the corner of The Outlands followed by the ramp of Dirge would make an outstanding natural winter line and he and MacLean gave it a serious attempt. MacLean made an impressive lead of the 5b corner on The Outlands, laybacking on his axes with the picks placed in the steep cracks and finishing sensationally with a hook over the top of the great flake on Dirge. Above this they found the ramp had good ice and névé but the junction with Post Mortem was surprisingly thin. They were reluctant to use aid here and thinking the ice would build up better on another occasion, they abseiled off, even though there was plenty of daylight left.

Despite his disappointment, MacLean was very excited about this technique of torquing his axes in the cracks, and wanted to return as soon as possible to try the long corner on Nymph, the crack-line immediately right of the chimney of Parallel Gully B. He had no problem persuading Nisbet and Clifford to join him, so, on March 19, he led the whole 100ft pitch almost entirely on axe torques – there being little or no ice in the corner. The climbing was very strenuous and even MacLean, who according to Nisbet, could do one arm pull-ups with a sack on, was forced to rest three times on his axes while placing protection. Although the main corner was very sustained they found the bulge on pitch three (previously led by Arthur Paul on Psyche) to be the technical crux – Grade VII. It is generally recognised that the term 'torquing', meaning the technique of applying a constant twisting force to any part of the axe in order to make it jam in a crack came into being at the time of this ascent. The technique had been used before but not in such a continuous sequence of moves as MacLean had used on The Outlands and Nymph.

The final new route this winter was made on the Black Spout Pinnacle in early April. Nisbet and Dinwoodie joined forces to make a winter

*Murray Hamilton
cleaning the 4th pitch
of Cannibal while
Rab Anderson waits
on the Cougar Slab,
June 1984*

Photo: Douglas Dinwoodie

ascent of Pantheist, the crack-line right of Pinnacle Grooves which Dinwoodie had first climbed with Bob Smith six years earlier. Originally thought to be HVS 5a, it was later upgraded to E1 and thus became the first extreme rock climb in the Cairngorms to be climbed under winter conditions. Dinwoodie led the first pitch up sustained slabs and bulges, taking a slightly different line from summer. Some of the holds were bare of snow and ice and he considered the conditions to be marginal. Nisbet then took over and climbed the main crack all the way to the Springboard, taking two rests on his axes. According to Dinwoodie: "My recollection from summer was that the top pitch had a good continuous crack, tailor-made for torquing, and I told Andrew so, but in fact it is intermittent and blind in places, so turned out hard and sustained." – Grade VII. They had plenty of daylight at this time of the year and continued to the plateau via Route 1, thus rounding off a busy winter for Nisbet.

Much of Britain experienced a period of dry weather during April and May 1984, although, in the Cairngorms, conditions were a little more unsettled. Dinwoodie was itching to get back to the unfinished route on Central Gully Wall and had to wait until the second week in June for a worthwhile forecast. He was concerned about competition from Edinburgh because he had unwisely spoken to Hamilton about the line and had even shown him photographs of the attempt with MacLean. Before the first promising weekend in 1984, Dinwoodie made contact with Hamilton. "Murray sounded dismayed at me phoning, so I felt he did intend trying the route then, and also knew why I had phoned. He said Creag an Dubh-loch would be wet and that he was going elsewhere. I said the big wall would be dry. I hoped the phone call would put him off but it probably had the opposite effect."

On Saturday June 9, Dinwoodie and MacLean reached the Dubh Loch around midday only to see Hamilton and Anderson pulling on to the Cougar Slab, having already climbed the lower pitches of the new route. "There was no question of us doing the route together and nothing was said. I was very partisan under certain situations about North-east climbing, and of course, Murray was similarly factional." The Edinburgh men had arrived early from Glen Clova and Hamilton abseiled down the route, leaving a rope hanging on the top pitches. They followed Dinwoodie's line exactly without placing any further pitons for protection. Above the Cougar Slab they realised that the stepped corner system, parallel to Vampire Direct had not been cleaned. Hamilton jumared up the abseil rope to give the corner a scrub, before descending back down to lead it. From the belay he moved up right and climbed the first step in the corner until forced on to the right arete. He followed this, returned to the corner and continued to a steep nose of rock where he was again compelled to move right. Very hard climbing up the right wall of the nose then led to slabs close to Vampire. A crack between Vampire and Cougar provided a relatively straightforward independent finish. Notwithstanding the events leading up to the climb, this was another very impressive performance by Hamilton on a climb which was later recognised as E6. When recalling these events Anderson remembered the crux pitch above the Cougar Slab as being intricate and very meaty, with a potential for leg-breaking falls in a number of places. Initially, Hamilton called the route Cannibals, but decided to drop the s. He would not be drawn on the reason for the name, his only comment being: "Cannibal. Why not?"

It was inclement on the Sunday, so Dinwoodie had to wait another week to make his attempt, this time accompanied by Nisbet. They reached the Cougar Slab but the rain came on before he could try the fearsome line he had cleaned on the wall 20 or 30ft to the left of the stepped corners. "It must have looked ridiculous to Andy, and maybe it was." Some time later, Dinwoodie roped down the wall again, but pulled off a flake, making the line even more problematical. He also contemplated trying to climb directly up the corners even though he knew that success would require fierce finger strength. In the end he did not return to the route and his relationship with Hamilton remained very frosty. He later said: "Personally, I don't think the Cannibal incident is to the credit of any of us." No matter what the protagonists think, the route is now considered to be one of the finest rock climbs in the country – E6 6b.

It is interesting to note that Hamilton recorded Cannibal as an E5,

*Murray Hamilton
leading the
demanding 4th
pitch of Cannibal,
June 1984*

Photo: Rab Anderson

saying that he did not find it any harder than a number of other routes
on Creag an Dubh-loch. This may be partly accountable to the fact that
he and Anderson were wearing the newly-imported Fire rock boots,
manufactured by the Spanish firm Boreal. These state-of-the-art, sticky
rubber-soled boots, were considered at the time to give a half grade
advantage on climbs heavily reliant on friction. Whether this was true
or not is open to conjecture. However, they were the first significant
improvement in friction rock boots since the original PA and by the
time the summer of 1984 was in full swing, most granite heids had
bought a pair.

During the summer term at Robert Gordon's College, Livingston slipped away while on a school hill-walk from Glen Clova to Loch Muick and made a solo ascent of a wet Goliath on Creag an Dubh-loch. This bold, clandestine venture was a prelude to an even more impressive piece of climbing, two days later, when he made the first on-sight lead of The Ascent of Man. Partnered by Jerry Hadwin, Livingston led the whole climb, taking a more direct line on the second pitch, as the right-hand groove was wet. He found the climbing to be superb and thought the route would be E5 no matter which variation was taken on pitch two. "The crux was hard but well protected. The second pitch was rather serious, the best runner being a fantastic crystal in a large geode."

Another important repeat was made on the Central Slabs of the Shelter Stone Crag. Northumberland climber, Kevin Howett, made a second ascent of The Run of the Arrow, accompanied by Alan Moist. As if the climb was not difficult enough, he was caught by a shower of drizzle when above Dinwoodie's old wires and he fell off a couple of times trying to make the crux moves on wet rock. "A miserable interlude allowed me to fidget with more runners. At least I felt safer, and soon, the breeze-dried rock seemed possible. I balanced, stretched out a leg with as much precision as I could muster, and willed my toes to ignore the damp until the smiling compassionate eye gave me my freedom. A blind impetuous rush brought an end to it, released the spring's tension, and I was satisfied."[11] On an earlier visit to the crag the same team had repeated The Spire.

At the summer solstice 1984, Charlie McLeod and Andy Nisbet completed the 'Five Cairngorm Ridges' in one day. The original 'Three Ridges', Eagle, Mitre and Snake, first linked by Pyper and Reid in 1960, had been extended to five by Malcolm McArthur and Sandy Payne. They added Sphinx Ridge on Braeriach and Roberts' Ridge on Sgoran Dubh Mòr, and made the crossing over a whole weekend. This latest effort by McLeod and Nisbet took 15 hours from the foot of Eagle Ridge to a finish at Coylum Bridge. They soloed all the climbing in rock boots and incorporated a rendezvous at the Hutchison Hut with Charlie's wife, Moira, who provided them with hot food and drink. They covered 37 miles and made 9000ft of ascent. Some heavy showers added spice to this challenging enterprise.

There were a number of good days in July 1984, but it was not until August that a continuous spell of warm weather set in, similar to the previous two summers. Later in the month it became so dry that the River Dee reached its all-time lowest level.

According to Allen Fyffe, Hell's Lum Crag is probably his favourite Cairngorm cliff. For many years he and his companions from Glenmore Lodge had been gradually picking-off all the good lines. "There seemed to be no hurry about doing these routes as there was never any competition. No-one else seemed to be climbing there." One evening Fyffe, Barton and Burrows-Smith tried a line of cracks between Devil's Delight and the Wee Devil. Above a prominent red slab they came to a right-facing corner which they attempted but gave up due to the late hour and some apparent loose blocks. Later, Barton and Fyffe abseiled down the line to clean it before making a complete ascent on August 10. Barton led the excellent overlapping corner, one of the best pitches

Graeme Livingston at Pen Trwyn, 1984

Photo: Graeme Livingston Collection

on the crag – Prince of Darkness, E1 5b. Later in the month, Liddell and Mark Seaton made another good climb on the frontal face. Its main feature was the slim corner to the left of The Clean Sweep, on the edge overlooking Hellfire Corner – Damien, E1 5b.

The Crimson Slabs on Creagan a Choire Etchachan offer similar climbing to that of Hell's Lum Crag. Earlier in the summer Lawrie and Morrison had completed a right-to-left traverse of the slabs, involving some poorly protected climbing away from the main corners – Crimson Cringe, E2 5b. After nearly two weeks of drought in August, Banchory climber, Alastair Ross, and I found the slabs completely dry. Even the usual weeps to the left of Djibangi had evaporated. We took the opportunity to attempt a direct line between Scalpel and Djibangi, taking the most continuous rock all the way to the top of the cliff. As with most of the routes hereabouts, the main difficulties were concentrated in a substantial second pitch which was led by Alastair. From close to the start of the main corner on Djibangi he climbed straight up to the right of the prominent streak of grey rock which sweeps down from the apex of these left-hand slabs. Below the first small overlap, where Crimson Cringe traverses horizontally left, he fixed some runners and continued up left to below the obvious notch in the main overlap. Here, he discovered the best way was to move back right before pulling over the lap. More thin climbing above eventually took him to a shallow groove which led to an area of broken ground beneath a narrow upper area of clean slab. After following Alastair's intricate pitch I led a long run-out up a central crack in the upper slab – King Crimson, E3 5c.

The bulk of the action this August took place on Creag an Dubh-loch. Dinwoodie pitched his old tent at the head of the loch and this served as an advanced base until the rains returned at the beginning of September. I arrived early on August 5, feeling a little dejected on account of the overcast sky and not so dry cliff. By contrast, Dougie seemed positively upbeat, saying that he had cleaned three lines on False Gully Wall and that the most amenable of these should be okay for that day – possibly only E2 5b? Once up below the wall I discovered that our climb was to be the shallow corner right of Masque, which appeared to curve up rightward and peter out below bulging rock.

Draped with all the climbing gear, including nuts, Friends, sky hooks, a wire brush and a hammer, Dougie started up the corner. Three hours later and he had still not reached a belay. His estimate of 5b was some way off the mark and although he was placing protection it was proving difficult to arrange. The line of weakness took him away from the corner on to the edge of the smooth band. A series of barely adequate rounded flakes and sloping shelves then took him up and farther right, close to the niche on Slartibartfast, before he was able to return left to a small ledge with a piton belay.

The climbing was very sustained and seemed to get harder with height. Once I reached the belay the inevitable spots of rain were falling. As we carefully swapped positions below the solitary belay piton he reminded me of our ascent of Vampire, 12 years earlier, when we were caught in the rain 100ft below easy ground. The next pitch was to have been mine, but under the circumstances he went first. By climbing up left past the piton, he was able to move left, round an edge and reach

Douglas Dinwoodie climbing the Snake on False Gully Wall, August 1984

Photo: Greg Strange

a good jamming crack. He quickly followed this and finished up the last section of Masque. Fortunately, the rain got no worse and this time the climbing really was only 5b – The Snake, E4 6a.

The two other lines which Dinwoodie had investigated on this left-hand section of False Gully Wall lay to the right of The Snake. The first was a single straight crack, near the left edge of the smooth band, which joined The Snake near the top of its first pitch. The second was the unlikely wall between this crack and the first pitch of Slartibartfast. The following Saturday, Ross went to the Dubh Loch with Livingston, now very fit and strong after four weeks climbing in England and Wales. They went to North-West Gully Buttress and climbed a hard new route beside The Strumpet – Jezebel, E3 6b, Afterwards, Livingston stayed on and joined forces with Dinwoodie to attempt one of the other two lines on False Gully Wall. Although Dinwoodie believed that both the crack and the unlikely wall would be equally as difficult, Livingston was particularly excited by the latter, so they agreed to try the wall – 70ft of near vertical granite with only two horizontal breaks and a pair of vertical cracks near the top to disturb the apparent smoothness. On the first day Dinwoodie reached the twin cracks.

At first there were enticing little foot ledges and a number of diagonal cracks which allowed progress up right into the middle of the wall. Hard, fingery climbing, straight up from here led past the first break and on up to a semi-resting position in the second break. Up to this point limited protection had been achieved using tiny wires, but now he was able to place bigger and better nuts. The twin cracks looked desperate and he knew that Livingston was now climbing better than himself so he asked to be lowered off. He returned to the bottom leaving all the equipment in place. Livingston then took over and with the advantage of the ropes from above, quickly reached the twin cracks. He gave these a try but ended up making a detour left into the single straight crack. He followed this then returned back right to make the final moves of the twin cracks up to a belay on the left side of the niche. This was an impressive piece of climbing, but unfortunately, it had not maintained the independence of the two routes. Dinwoodie lowered him off the belay piton and he retrieved all the equipment.

Determined to climb the wall properly, Livingston tried again the next day. This time he came off on the twin cracks and fell 30ft, although it felt more like 40ft. Unfortunately, his belayer was trying to take a photograph at the time and he let him go much farther than he should have. A very sheepish-looking Dinwoodie lowered him once more to the ground. Following a rest he went back up and finally succeeded in climbing the twin cracks, mainly by using the left-hand crack. After Dinwoodie had seconded the pitch they continued to the plateau following a rather contrived route which veered across Slartibartfast higher up and seemed irrelevant when compared to the first wall. After delving into *The Hitch Hiker's Guide to the Galaxy* they came up with the appropriate name of The Improbability Drive. It was the most technically difficult piece of climbing yet seen in the Cairngorms, meriting the grade of E6 6c. Livingston's lead of the main wall had shown a high degree of commitment. In just one year he had progressed from inexperienced rope boy to become a major player on the Scottish climbing scene.

Dinwoodie's fascination with False Gully Wall had not abated. He was still very keen to climb the isolated crack, but thought it might be too hard for him just now and he turned his attention to the right-hand end of the smooth band. It was during the second ascent of Sans Fer with MacLean that he noticed the possibility of climbing the less prominent crack to the right of Sans Fer's main crack. One week after The Improbability Drive, on a glorious hot day, he and Lawrie followed this crack up to a shared belay with Sans Fer. From here, Dinwoodie went straight up in a direct continuation of the Sans Fer crack to produce another very sustained route. As a riposte to Hamilton, they named it Iron in the Soul – E4 6a.

The great weather continued into the last weekend of August. On the Saturday, Lawrie met up with Dinwoodie again and together they made the second ascent of The Naked Ape. Afterwards, they were full of praise for this brilliant route on which they led through. It was more than 20 years since Lawrie had made his first climbs in the Cairngorms and having followed Dinwoodie up the crux he was determined to lead the 6a pitch. Crouched below the final overhang in a very exposed position he recalls the situation. "Unbelievably, two biggish RPs took position in an unlikely crack. 'I can do this now. I know I can. Come on. Come on, please'. The holds on the lip of the overhang were flat but big and I felt strong as I pulled through to the ledge above. Only a short wall, a boulder problem high in the sky, separated me from the belay. I could hardly contain myself. At my second attempt I did it, in the bag now, chuffed beyond words."[12]

In less than a week autumnal weather had swept in, bringing an end to this current dry spell. For the third year in a row, an extended period of excellent rock climbing conditions had occurred in the Cairngorms, allowing everyone an opportunity to enjoy the high granite crags, free from the usual threat of inclement weather.

The weather was particularly poor during November 1984 with the North-east of Scotland receiving unusually heavy rainfall. For many years the condition of the back room at Glas Allt Shiel had been deteriorating through misuse and vandalism. The wooden floor had been removed for firewood long ago and it was now necessary to sleep in bays between old partition footings. Up to six inches of water could be lying here during wet weather. A few local climbers had discussed this problem with the Estate Factor and it was agreed that raising the floor level by filling the bays with blinded rubble would help. The estate agreed to provide the material and also offered to replace a large, broken window.

The work of raising the floor was successfully accomplished during the first weekend of November. Volunteer labourers had been given permission to drive to Glas Allt and it was while crossing from the Spittal to Allt-na-giubhsaich as a front seat passenger in Hamish Towler's Mini car that I was involved in an unusual incident. At some time in the past, mesh reinforcement and narrow steel plates had been laid into the gravel to provide strength to the unmetalled road. The steel was now exposed in several places approaching the bridge over the Muick. As we passed, the low-slung Mini caught a free end of one of the bars. It cut through the floor, the seat, and at its maximum extension it nicked the base of my back, before retracting, narrowly missing Hamish's young son strapped into a child seat in the rear. It was all over in an instant, and apart from a small scar, I was none the worse for the near miss. Glas Allt Bothy was completely renovated in 1991 by members of Dundee University Rucksack Club who installed timber ground and first floors and a staircase.

Three weeks later I was back in Glen Muick with Livingston. The weather had calmed down and there was plenty of snow above 3000ft. We went to the Black Spout Pinnacle and climbed the rib to the right

Graeme Livingston succeeding on The Improbability Drive, False Gully Wall, August 1984

Photo: Douglas Dinwoodie

of Twin Chimneys Route starting from the chokestone in the Left-Hand Branch. After one pitch we were forced off the crest into a steep slot which cut into the left side of the rib and led back to the crest. Despite being the previous guidebook writer I had never climbed Twin Chimneys Route and had always assumed it followed the big corner directly above the start of Route 2. It now dawned on me that the slot we had ascended was the second of the Twin Chimneys and that the big corner farther left was unclimbed.

During the last week of November, MacLean and Nisbet climbed the summer route, Auricle, in Coire an Lochain of Cairn Gorm in an hour and a half. This Grade VI mixed route showed them to be on form and marked the start of a very big winter for this highly-motivated team. The two of them, together with Livingston, were the main players in the winter pioneering that took place in December 1984, which culminated in two epic failures on Lochnagar over the New Year period.

MacLean knew that the Tough-Brown Face on Lochnagar offered potential climbs at the very cutting edge of Scottish winter climbing. He nurtured an ambition to make a winter ascent of Mort, the great central crack-line leading directly to the crest of the buttress. He had spoken to close associates about this and knew that Arthur Paul had already been up the first pitch with Davy Sanderson and was keen for another look. On December 18, he and Nisbet climbed the right-hand side of the face, between Rolling Thunder and Bell's Direct Route, following the approximate line of Tough-Guy, a VS summer route. The climb provided an excellent sustained route mainly in turfy cracks, with a distinct crux, where a thin leftward slanting crack had to be used to reach the escape ramp below the final pitch of Rolling Thunder – Grade VII. Four days later they made a winter ascent of another summer VS, Ghurka, on the west face of the Mitre Ridge. They managed to climb this without the point of aid at the crux by taking a different line – Grade VI.

Meanwhile, Livingston had become enthusiastic about winter climbing, especially the 'mixed' variety, typical of the early Cairngorms season. Since our ascent on the Black Spout Pinnacle he had made a new direct finish to Shadow Rib with Ewen Clark (Slime Lords) and a winter ascent of West Wall Route in Coire Bhrochain of Braeriach with Nisbet and Lawrence. On the shortest day of the year, while MacLean and Nisbet were on Ghurka, Graeme and I returned to the Black Spout Pinnacle to look at the big corner left of Twin Chimneys Route. From below we could see that it branched left from the first pitch of Twin Chimneys. We then noticed a line of steep cracks farther left and closer to the gable wall which seemed to offer a completely independent route to the summit. Through the driving sleet this looked hard to me, but my companion was champing at the bit, so despite the wet conditions we climbed this excellent little route, with Graeme leading the main pitch with apparent ease – Solstice, Grade VI. On Christmas Eve he returned with Alastair Matthewson, a friend from school days, and together they climbed the big corner, naming it The Ice Ox – Grade IV. Despite its short length it has become a popular early season route.

There was no let-up in the rush for new winter routes and the climbing continued on Boxing Day. Brian Davison had driven from the south for a few days in the hills, and with Nisbet went back to the Tough-Brown Face. This time they climbed the first pitch of Mort and traversed the terrace rightward below the long roof. They then crawled behind a giant standing block to join Tough-Guy at the start of its second pitch. Continuing up this they finished by the last pitch of the summer route which Nisbet had avoided in the dark when climbing with MacLean a week earlier. Over on the Black Spout Pinnacle, Livingston teamed up with Doug Hawthorn, another young Aberdonian proving very talented at winter climbing. They were engrossed in a winter ascent of Katsalana, a line left of Pinnacle Face. The initial pitch follows a good left-trending corner with 5b climbing. Livingston led this using his two thin-bladed Cassin axes which he drove into the narrow cracks. Higher up they crossed Winter Face and finished up the vegetated Grovel Wall. Livingston remembers the climbing being strenuous and sustained. "The first pitch is the cleanest piece of torquing I remember on Lochnagar." Although unrepeated more than 20 years later it is given the same grade as Pinnacle Face in the current guide – Grade VI.

The following day the action switched to the Northern Corries of Cairn Gorm. Livingston and Hawthorn abandoned an attempt on Damnation in Coire an t-Sneachda due to lack of ice in the crux corner. In Coire an Lochain, Davison and Sandy Allan made a repeat ascent of Auricle after waiting with Nisbet for three hours in wind and spindrift while MacLean tackled the first pitch of the outrageously strenuous Ventricle. After successfully torquing up the first overhanging crack – the summer crux – MacLean bypassed the second pitch on the left by climbing two desperate overhanging V grooves, the second of which required a piton for aid after he fell on the initial attempt. With a great struggle, Nisbet joined him at the belay, and they continued up the main groove of the summer line before finishing out right by a chimney. – Grade VII.

After this latest *tour-de-force*, MacLean began to think about Mort again. He knew the second and third pitches would be more serious than anything he had attempted up to now. On Hogmanay, he, Nisbet and Davison arrived late at the Glen Muick car park and slept in their cars. The next morning, New Year's day, they moved across to Allt-na-giubh-saich then headed for Lochnagar. When they reached the Tough-Brown Face they decided the weather was too bad to try Mort, so they stashed some equipment and returned to Glen Muick. On January 2, they were preparing to leave again for the corrie when Livingston and Andy Perkins called in. According to Livingston, he too, was intending to try Mort. "MacLean, Nisbet and Brian the Sass Davison were staying at Allt-na-g, so we stopped in to say hello. This created the desired amount of panic. They desperately tried to catch us up on the walk in, but to no avail."

Perkins, an experienced climber from Leeds, was staying with friends in Aberdeen over New Year. He and Livingston were out for a day trip to Lochnagar. In the corrie the weather was still poor with strong winds and spindrift. Seventeen-year-old Livingston thought conditions were too foul to try a route like Mort so they made their way up to the foot of The Stack. Livingston had studied potential lines on The Stack, both from photographs and while making recent climbs on the Black Spout Pinnacle. He suggested they try a line well to the right of the original

Doug Hawthorn at Luibeg, 1983

Photo: Ronnie Robb

Andy Nisbet, 1982
Photo: Greg Strange

1950s route, following the crest between the left and right faces, heading for the prow of the buttress. "I thought it was going to be somewhat easier than it was!" After an early fall by Perkins, Livingston took over the leading and they eventually reached a belay at a headwall 30ft below the plateau. The only way out was to the left. Livingston led a very poorly-protected traverse only to find no adequate belay at its end. The situation seemed very bleak. If Perkins slipped from the traverse they would both go to the bottom, yet Livingston did not think he could climb back. They hung there in the blizzard for ages unable to decide what to do. "My only course of action was to reverse the pitch – something I did not think was possible. I was convinced that I was either going to die or take a very serious fall." Eventually, he managed to scrape his way back and they went into full retreat. To complete a very stressful day they abseiled off an overhanging wall and finished by dropping off the end of the ropes as they were too short to reach the gully. This harrowing experience strongly affected both climbers. For several months Livingston was unable to bring himself to lead anything of difficulty.

When MacLean's party reached the Tough-Brown face the weather seemed to have improved from that of the previous day but the cliff was plastered in fresh blown snow. MacLean and Nisbet climbed the familiar first pitch of Mort and took a belay on the terrace. Above them, the roof with the downward pointing tooth of rock "looked fierce and unfriendly with icicles hanging down like Damoclean swords".[13]

Davison opted to remain on the ground while MacLean attempted the second pitch. "I was to try and keep warm for the next five hours as Colin edged his way ever higher. One-arm pull ups on axes saw him surmount the roof, go left round the rib and slowly up iced turf, no gear for the last 50ft, an inspirational and, with hindsight, futuristic lead from Colin saw him kneeling on top of the rib. For more than an hour he knelt scraping, searched, then inquired what gear Andy had below. A blade peg was the reply.

'Okay, send it up.'

'It's the belay,' was the cry from below.

'It doesn't matter, send it up.'

The conversation is still burned into my memory 15 years on."[14] MacLean's persistence paid off and after more thinly-iced turfy cracks he finally pulled onto the sloping upper terrace.

After five hours of belaying, Nisbet was very cold and did well to jumar up the icy ropes. While Davison followed in a similar fashion, MacLean started the third pitch. Unfortunately, he was overtaken by darkness and fatigue and although they contemplated sitting out the night, the idea was rejected. They descended in one abseil, disappointed that MacLean's heroic effort had not quite secured the first winter ascent of Mort.

It was very cold throughout January 1985 with several ice routes being climbed. On the south-facing Stag Rocks of Cairn Gorm, Hamilton and Anderson made a winter ascent of the Marshall brothers' excitingly named Groove and Rib. A convenient ice smear allowed the summer crux to be avoided on what turned out to be a very good climb – Grade V. This was Hamilton's last significant pioneering climb in the

Cairngorms. He was about to enter a new phase in his life which later led to him becoming a professional guide and setting up home in the French Alps.

Although MacLean still had his mind set on Mort, he and Nisbet made a mid-week trip to Glen Coe, where, on January 24, they climbed Unicorn, the classic corner-line on Stob Coire nan Lochan of Bidean nam Bian. This sustained E1 rock climb provided a very hard winter route on steep rock plastered in hoar frost. Nisbet was soon to be joining Mal Duff's expedition to attempt the unclimbed North-East ridge of Mount Everest. He had only three weeks left of this current Scottish winter, so following the success on Unicorn, he and MacLean decided to put all their time and effort over the next few weeks into climbing The Needle on the Shelter Stone Crag. "I've never been so concentrated on a route, so it was a bit unique. Black Mamba the year before was similar but somehow the obsession with The Needle was more."

Their first attempt at the end of January foundered when they encountered waist deep powder snow beside Loch Avon. After a night below the Shelter Stone they decided to make a reconnaissance in order to find an alternative winter start. They knew that the slabby summer pitches leading up to the Gallery would be very hard under powder snow, so they followed a turfy line up a corner left of Clach Dhian Chimney, then took a ramp left to join The Needle. They then climbed up to the start of the fourth (crux) pitch in order that MacLean could check that he would be able to get into the crucial crack system. This accomplished, they abseiled off and returned to Aberdeen, hoping for a thaw and a re-freeze.

Colin MacLean, 1989
Photo: John Wilson

The first week of February was milder then it turned very cold again with strong winds. The forecast did not favour The Needle so they went to Lochnagar for another look at Mort. Unfortunately, the predicted weather was correct and they had to settle for two short climbs, Katabatic Corner, below the Spiral Terrace on Shadow Buttress A, and A Slice of Ice beside Pinnacle Gully 2. Still there was no settled weather in the immediate outlook. On February 1 they went to the Crimson Slabs and battling with ferocious south-east winds, managed an ascent of Scabbard – Grade VI. A gust of 130mph was recorded on Cairn Gorm that day. The two climbers found the updraft on the cliff appalling and the intense cold scary, but they were going well and made it safely back to Aberdeen.

Now at last there was a reasonable forecast. Three days after Scabbard, on February 13, they left Aberdeen in the morning and by 11 were re-ascending the opening pitches heading for the Gallery. MacLean was wearing walking crampons with no front points, while Nisbet stuck with his trusty 'trampons'. They carried a sleeping bag each, a stove and some food. On that first day the weather was excellent – calm and cold. According to Nisbet the steep wall of the fourth pitch was 'lean'. However, higher up the cliff was pure white. Maclean took the fourth pitch, submitting to a rest on his axe at the bulging 5b crux. By any standard, this was a brilliant lead of a pitch which still tested good climbers wearing rock boots on warm, dry summer days. Nisbet jumared, carrying the big sack, then led up to the 'Crack for Thin Fingers'. They both attempted this but failed and had to abseil back down to the shared stance with Steeple. MacLean then led the layback cracks of

Steeple, taking one rest, and Nisbet, in darkness by now, took them out right and back left to a bivouac site below the Steeple corner. The night was not too bad although much more uncomfortable than they had expected as there was no room to lie down. In the morning the wind got up and it was extremely cold. On the second day they climbed many short pitches.

Nisbet recalls: "Colin had done all the hardest leads the day before so insisted I lead the Needle crack. It was heavily verglased and extremely hard to make any progress. I used a rest to place an aid point in order to reach the base of the crack. It was a huge struggle to make only a little distance and in desperation I decided to try going up the crack on the left wall. It was easily reached, but in order to climb it I had to switch from torquing to the left to torquing from the opposite direction, and at the change point the axe pulled out. I was wingeing a bit but Colin urged me on. 'So you've fallen off. You haven't hurt yourself. Just get up there and do it.' I made it onto a small ledge on the arete, halfway up the Needle crack." MacLean then took over and continued up the difficult arete until he was able to move back right into the deep, friendly recess below the eye of the needle. Nisbet's lead up the final chimney took them to the plateau at 2pm, thus clocking up a total climbing time of 15 hours, excluding the bivouac.

Although this was by no means a winter ascent of the complete Smith-Agnew line, The Needle (winter variations) set a level of commitment and sustained technical difficulty that would not be surpassed in Scotland 'or more than a decade. The combination of two highly-focused, very 'it climbers, living on the dole, finding optimum weather and climbing conditions for such a route was not likely to occur too often. It was the first climb in the Cairngorms to be graded VIII overall.

Not surprisingly, this tremendous climb on the Shelter Stone Crag dominated the news at the time, but two other very interesting ice routes were made on nearby cliffs during this cold spell in mid-February. On the Wednesday of The Needle ascent, James Grosset and Malcolm Sclater climbed the oft-attempted Hellfire Corner on Hell's Lum Crag. Although the main corner is usually wet and forms ice readily, the steep crux through the overlap is not often in condition. On this occasion it gave an excellent Grade VI climb. Four days later Hawthorn and Dinwoodie bagged the last major fault-line on Creagan a' Choire Etchachan with a winter ascent of Avalanche Gully, also Grade VI. The winter continued through to the end of April with varying amounts of snow but no further new route activity took place in the Cairngorms, probably because Nisbet was now in the Himalaya.

The end of February 1985 turned out to be the cut-off date for the new SMT 'comprehensive' guide to *The Cairngorms* (neither selective nor definitive) which was published later in the year. Much hard work and plenty of consultation by the authors, Fyffe and Nisbet, resulted in the whole area being covered by a single volume. It brought the current state of Cairngorms climbing right up to date with E grades, pitch by pitch technical grades and sadly, the metrication of route lengths. There appeared to be no easing in the rate of climbing development despite the vagaries of the Scottish weather. Hamilton, Whillance, Dinwoodie and Livingston had all recently elevated the standard of rock climbing to new levels, not only in terms of technical difficulty, but also in the style of ascent and on areas of rock which were previously thought to be impossible to free climb. Achievements in winter had been no less impressive with a number of outstanding climbs. The greatest advances were made in mixed climbing where the development of torquing and a willingness to tackle steeper and steeper terrain had been crucial. A steady rise in the upper limit of difficulty over the last six years had peaked with MacLean and Nisbet's inspired ascent of the 800ft winter variations to The Needle.

1.   CCJ Vol. 19, No. 98, p12 (*Cairngorm Climbing – A Contribution* by A.Nisbet).
2.   CCJ Vol. 19, No. 98, p13 (*Cairngorm Climbing – A Contribution* by A.Nisbet).
3.   CCJ Vol. 19, No. 98, p13 (*Cairngorm Climbing – A Contribution* by A.Nisbet).
4.   SMCJ Vol. 32, No. 171, p73.
5.   SMCJ Vol. 32, No. 172, p123 (*Epitome* by R.Milne).
6.   SMCJ Vol. 32, No. 173, p223 – 225 (*The Last Oasis* by A.Nisbet).
7.   SMCJ Vol. 32, No. 173, p223 – 225 (*The Last Oasis* by A.Nisbet).
8.   SMCJ Vol. 32, No. 173, p223 – 225 (*The Last Oasis* by A.Nisbet).
9.   SMCJ Vol. 32, No. 173, p270.
10. SMCJ Vol. 36, No. 188, p340.
11. *Extreme Rock* (Diadem) p55, (*Run of the Arrow* by K.Howett).
12. *High* magazine, March 1987, p44, (*Ape*, B. Lawrie's account of the second ascent of The Naked Ape).
13. *High* magazine, December 2000, p16 (*Mort* by B.Davison).
14. *High* magazine, December 2000, p16 (*Mort* by B.Davison).

12: The Coming of Age (1985 – 1993)

IN 1985 THE RSPB bought Loch Avon and much of the high ground surrounding it from the Wills family's Glen Avon Estate. The Society's main aim was to safeguard the area from the threat of possible future development. This piece of good news was a ray of sunshine in an otherwise disappointing summer. Few opportunities arose for rock climbing on the mountain crags, although Dinwoodie, MacLean and Hawthorn managed the second ascent of Voyage of the Beagle on Creag an Dubh-loch.

The generally poor weather did not stop three Aberdeen runners from setting a new target for the round of the Six Tops. On July 13, Dave Armitage, Mel Edwards and Phil Kammer ran the six tops of the Cairngorms, starting and finishing at Glenmore Lodge, in a time of 11 hours 39 minutes. Edwards already held the long-standing fastest time for completing the Four Tops – the Cairngorms four 4000ers, Glenmore Lodge and back, in 4 hours 34 minutes. He made this run in 1979, beating the record previously set by Eric Beard. Edwards's time held for a remarkable 23 years before Dan Whitehead reduced it by a mere three minutes, in 2001. The women's record for the four tops is held by Kath Butler in a time of 6 hours 44 minutes, set on July 16, 1988.

A fine autumn redressed the balance of weather somewhat, with October proving particularly dry. On three consecutive weekends Andy Nisbet cycled up Glen Derry to climb on the Crimson Slabs. At each visit the rock became drier and he was able to make several interesting eliminate climbs. During the first weekend he led The Sharp End (E3 5c) on the quick-drying rock between Djibangi and Stiletto. Next came the difficult Scarlet Fever, with two pre-placed piton runners, between Stiletto and The Dagger (E3 6a), and finally, on his last trip, In the Pink (E3 5c) between King Crimson and Scalpel. He was accompanied by Alastair Ross on these last two climbs.

If the summer of 1985 was poor then the following winter was brilliant. Within days of the ascent of In The Pink, temperatures plummeted and snow began to fall on the Cairngorms. From the beginning of November to the end of April, Scotland experienced one of its best winters for snow and ice climbing. Many new routes were made throughout the Highlands, with more than 30 in the Cairngorms. New faces appeared on the pioneering front with a growing band of Speyside-based activists operating independent from Glenmore Lodge teams, who tended to keep to themselves. Included in this group were John Lyall, James Grosset and Malcolm Sclater. November saw typical early season mixed conditions, with plenty of fresh snow and good periods of calm weather. Of the half dozen or so new routes climbed in the month, the best was Grosset and Sclater's ascent of Damnation, the HVS cornerline on Aladdin's Buttress – Grade VI.

After the Everest expedition – where he reached 26,000ft on the North East Ridge – Nisbet took a two month temporary instructor's job at

James Grosset, 1986

Photo: John Lyall

Glenmore Lodge. It was there, in July, that he first met Andy Cunningham, an experienced climber from Stirling who had studied forestry at Aberdeen University before going to the Lodge. In November, after Nisbet had returned to Aberdeen, the two Andys started climbing together. Early in the month they went to Lochnagar and made an attempt on the Outlands/Dirge combination, previously tried by MacLean and Dinwoodie. They fared no better than the earlier party but the experience was an eye-opener for Cunningham, who had never climbed anything so technically difficult before in winter. Later in the month, they made second winter ascents of Hourglass Buttress and Vertigo Wall, climbing both without aid. As on his two day first ascent with Robertson eight years earlier, Nisbet found surprisingly good conditions on Vertigo Wall, with an adequate plating of ice in the black chimney. They completed the route in nine hours.

At the beginning of December there was a rapid thaw which stripped away most of the snow and ice. On December 7, snowy weather returned, prompting Nisbet and Cunningham to head for Aladdin's Buttress in Coire an t-Sneachda to fulfil an ambition to make a winter ascent of The Magic Crack. They tossed-up to see who would lead the crack and Cunningham won. To reach its base, Nisbet started left of Patey's winter route and followed a ramp and corners up left to a belay at the foot of the main corner of The Genie. Cunningham then took over and made a short traverse right to reach the Magic Crack. He soon discovered that the near perfect finger crack was equally well suited to climbing with axes. It was just the right width for the picks and since it leaned slightly rightward it was relatively straightforward to maintain the torques. The slab was plastered with snow and it was hard to see the tiny footholds. After 15ft of the crack he was unable to stop to fix more protection, so when he fell off near the top he slid 30ft down the slab, back to the level of the belay. Next time he succeeded and they finished the climb by traversing right to join Damnation – Grade VII.

Two days later, still buzzing from this success, they went to Coire an Lochain and climbed the classic VS rock route, Fall-out Corner. Again it was Cunningham who won the toss and led the main pitch on this outstanding short route – Grade VI. Both Magic Crack and Fall-out Corner are clean summer rock climbs with little or no vegetation. The ascents were made with fresh snow covering the rock but without ice. They were the last climbs on which Nisbet wore his tricouni plates. After years of experimentation he now concluded that the versatility of crampons outweighed the slight advantage which his Trampons gave on non-icy snow-covered rock. When seconding The Magic Crack he could not use the tiny footholds at all, so he laybacked the crack frantically and only just made it to the stance.

At New Year 1986, Grosset and Lyall found an excellent short climb on the rocks to the right of the Fiacaill Couloir in Coire an t-Sneachda. It followed a prominent crack left of the steep triangular wall which terminates this right wing of Fiacaill Buttress – The Seam, Grade IV. Later in the month, when there was a much deeper cover of snow, Fyffe and Liddell made an interesting climb in the vicinity of Fiacaill Buttress Direct. They climbed an obvious left-slanting corner to join the Direct at the midway terrace then continued upwards, left of the Direct,

Andy Nisbet on the Sharp End, Crimson Slabs, Creagan a' Choire Etchachan, October 1985. The sunlit corner on the right is The Dagger

Photo: Greg Strange

Malcolm Sclater,
1988

Photo: John Allen

following ramps and grooves to the top of the buttress. Although it was a bitterly cold day with a strong north wind, conditions were good with ice in the grooves. Jailbreak – Grade VII.

There was another good discovery in Coire an t-Sneachda this month by Cunningham and Todd. On the 23rd they resurrected Patey's Mess of Pottage by climbing the obvious large groove in the middle of the main buttress. This gave three pitches of very enjoyable mixed climbing and pointed the way to future climbs of similar length and quality. Their choice of route name, The Message (Grade IV), had its effect, as the crag became a popular winter venue with more than 20 routes, some of which have made reasonable summer climbs. Three days before the Message, the same pair had made a difficult climb on the far right-hand side of No. 4 Buttress in Coire an Lochain, following the prominent chimney right of Western Route. Torquing Heads – Grade VII.

Away from the busy Northern Corries, the Loch Avon area saw a little traffic in January, although, like the rest of the Cairngorms, it was blanketed in unconsolidated snow for much of February. On Hell's Lum Crag, Cunningham and Ian Fox made the first winter ascent of the Grey Buttress by climbing Hell's Lump under powder snow conditions at the beginning of January – Grade V. Two weeks later Mark Charlton, Will Webb and John McKeever made a direct ascent of the West Ridge Route on the Shelter Stone Crag. This follows the extreme right-hand edge of the Main Bastion and leads to the first step on the skyline. In summer it is only Difficult, but avoids a steep wall below the step by abseiling 40ft down towards Pinnacle Gully. Charlton's party climbed the wall by an excellent pitch up cracks on the left, then reached the plateau via the Severe finish to Clach Dhian Chimney. The Impostor – Grade VI.

Fyffe was very active at this time, climbing with fellow instructors from Glenmore Lodge. As well as Jailbreak on the Fiacaill Buttress, he climbed the excellent winter line of Sermon on the West Flank of Stac an Fharaidh with Iain Peter – Grade V. This line of cracks and corners is often wet in summer and therefore an obvious winter target. Despite its southern aspect, the cliff does form ice in freezing weather, especially early in the season when the sun has minimal affect. Hell's Lum Crag has similar problems with the sun. However, in very cold weather, the freeze thaw effect of the sun helps to build large amounts of ice and the cliff can be in excellent condition when more north-facing crags are deep in powder. At the beginning of February, Fyffe and Barton found good conditions when they made an icy winter ascent of their own summer route, Towering Inferno – Grade VI. On this occasion, after many years without apparent competition, they were taken aback to find Jim Kerr and Dave Cumming arriving behind them to climb the same route.

In the southern Cairngorms, Dinwoodie and Nisbet were well to the fore with their winter explorations in 1986. Both were out of work, Nisbet having turned down an offer of employment at Glenmore Lodge in order to have one more winter, free from the commitment of a job. On January 19, they teamed up to climb the obvious groove on the left edge of Shadow Buttress B on Lochnagar, the line attempted by Raeburn's party in October 1902 and by others since. Although the groove was

relatively straightforward, it ended below a steep wall. Nisbet took a while to lead this by its left edge, finding only poor placements for his axes. Higher up they joined Bell's Route above its crux. Raeburn's Groove – Grade VII.

One week later they were heading for Creag an Dubh-loch, only this time they were operating independently. Settled cold weather with a full moon promised ideal conditions for winter climbing on Central Gully Wall. A few days earlier Dinwoodie and Wyness had climbed the first pitch of the winter Mousetrap on a reconnaissance of Predator. They had found the initial crack on Predator "distinctly discouraging" so now Dinwoodie was keen to make a complete ascent of Mousetrap. He and his companion, Aberdonian Jeff Hall, met Nisbet and Sandy Allan in Glen Muick on the Friday night and both parties stayed at the Glas-Allt Sheil.

Nisbet's plan was to climb the front face of Central Gully Wall right of Mousetrap, following the line of least resistance and most vegetation. The crack line of Waterkelpie Wall/Gulliver carries the most ice on the face, but this usually only forms above the level of the Red Wall. Below this, the best that could be hoped for was lightly-powdered slabs, bits of frozen vegetation and some ice in the cracks. Drawing from his

Andy Nisbet approaching The Magic Crack, December 1985

Photo: Andy Cunningham

Andy Cunningham,
Bloodhound Buttress,
December 1985

Photo: Andy Nisbet

knowledge of the cliff he aimed to start up Dubh Loch Monster, traverse right on The Prowl to reach King Rat above its roof, then work up right to the ledge system below the Red Wall. From here, the diagonal fault left of the Red Wall would give access to the ice on upper Waterkelpie Wall. All in all, 1200ft of climbing to the plateau.

"I'd climbed Dubh Loch Monster in summer, and knew that the crux roof low down on the route was split by a thin crack, so it had to be 'possible'. The rest was less immediate and would probably follow after a bivouac. So a hauling rope, stove, food, sleeping bags etc. were added to the normal climbing gear, and we set off at 5am to reach the crag at first light."[1]

With Nisbet leading all the pitches they found themselves below the Red Wall by dusk. The 5c summer crux of Dubh Loch Monster expended a great deal of Nisbet's energy and resulted in the top one inch of his hammer pick being broken off – he used his partner's for the rest of the climb. They experienced much trouble hauling the sack on the diagonal pitches, and when it finally stuck under an overlap, they decided to drop it off, along with all the bivouac equipment and the head torches. Before making this decision they had discovered that the rising moon would give sufficient light to enable them to continue climbing. From below the Red Wall, they moved up left then back right to belay on a ledge halfway up the diagonal fault, at the old piton left by Barclay in the summer of 1958.

Nisbet continues: "The fault was tricky but had good ledges for rests. Now everything was veneered with thin ice – a bizarre transition between the powdered slabs below and the huge sheet of ice covering the top 120m. of the cliff. My energy had dwindled by the time I reached the crack-line above. I was close to being hypoglycaemic (maybe one bar of chocolate in 14 hours wasn't enough), and had reached a transitional state when the hours drift by. Retreat was not an option, but upward progress also seemed unlikely. The zombie would find a peg placement, aid up, stand on it, make another move into thicker ice, find a worse peg etc. I continued up towards a roof dominating the gloom above, without the energy to consider how to get past it. After three pegs for aid, I reached the overhang and pulled over onto thick ice. A quick couple of steps led to the icefield and it was all over"[2]

Gaining the icefield coincided with the loss of direct moonlight, but it no longer mattered as they were able to climb quickly up the remaining 500ft of snow and ice to reach the top by 3am. They named their creation The Rattrap. It had been a great effort spread over 19 hours of continuous climbing – Nisbet's second Grade VIII winter climb in the Cairngorms.

Dinwoodie and Hall took 12 hours to complete the nearby Mousetrap, experiencing very similar conditions to those on the first ascent. Like Hamilton's party, they found ice at the steepest section after leaving the Mousetrap recess, but little or none above that until near the top. "We finished up the easy ground by a full moon and it was an Arctic wonderland of snow and ice hummocks. The snow was exceptionally deep in Central Gully, maybe 40ft below Sabre Cut, and we were worried about avalanches."

The snow continued to build up throughout February, although much of it was poorly consolidated due to constant low temperatures. On St Valentine's Day, Nisbet and Livingston visited Lochnagar with the intention of making a winter ascent of Fool's Rib on the Black Spout Pinnacle. According to Livingston, conditions on the classic routes were the best he had ever seen and as a result he felt less inclined to bother with Fool's Rib. "I stated my interest in soloing and presented Andy with the sharp end. He didn't make much progress. I acquitted myself by climbing 20ft farther and gave up." Livingston then went on an amazing soloing spree. In less than one hour he climbed Parallel Gully B and Polyphemus Gully despite a lot of dangerous wind-slab which, on Parallel B, forced him to quit the gully above the upper crux and hug the safety of Tough-Brown Ridge. After this he 'slowed down' and did A Slice of Ice, Giant's Head Chimney Direct, Shadow Buttress B, Pinnacle Gully 1 and finished with the White Spout. It was a tally that most people would have been pleased to achieve over several seasons.

Meanwhile, Nisbet took the opportunity to abseil down Tough-Brown face to fix a piton on Post Mortem, at the point where all previous attempts on the Outlands/Dirge winter ascent had failed, or had been forced to use aid. He and Cunningham had already been back since their November attempt and climbed the whole route. They used excessive aid on the last pitch due to darkness and Cunningham refused to record the climb for this reason. Nisbet and Dinwoodie then had another go, only to be defeated by poor snow conditions. Finally, on March 7, they succeeded at Nisbet's fourth and Dinwoodie's third attempt. On this occasion they encountered better snow and ice although it was thawing. The Outlands crack was ice-choked and poorly protected (previously it had been a well protected exercise in torquing), and there was just sufficient ice to make the thin traverse on Post Mortem without using the fixed piton for aid. Darkness caught them as they finished up the top pitches of Tough-Brown Traverse. They named this magnificent winter route Trail of Tears (Grade VII), a reference to the forced migration of the Cherokee people from their homelands in South-east America during the winter of 1839.

Livingston then went on an amazing soloing spree. In less than one hour he climbed Parallel Gully B and Polyphemus Gully

A week later, Nisbet and Cunningham found another good climb in Coire an Lochain, on the steep front face of No. 3 Buttress. The Migrant (Grade VI), was the outcome of an attempt to climb the huge hanging groove left of Nocando Crack. They managed to reach the base of the groove but could not climb it. So they descended slightly, traversed out left but still could not find a way through the snow-plastered upper walls. A brief thaw improved conditions and a second attempt succeeded, gaining the top of Ewen Buttress close to the final pitch of the VS rock climb known as The Vagrant.

On March 19, Bob Scott's Bothy at Luibeg was destroyed by fire in circumstances which never became public. After Willie Forbes had left Luibeg and moved to a house closer to Mar Lodge, the cottage was rented and only used occasionally. With no one living permanently nearby, the bothy was not kept up to the standard of the past, and the estate's official line was that it would remain open unless destroyed by vandals. In previous years, members of the Winers, Diners and Climbers Club (WDC) carried out extensive work on this popular bothy in order to improve its condition, and hopefully, give the estate no excuse to close it. The WDC had been formed at the Slugain Howff in 1970 and was a small band of hill folk from Aberdeen which included Alan Corigan (Corky), Ian Crichton (Beaner), Brian Fraser, Kenny Freeman, Freddie Malcolm (Kincorth Club), Ruraidh Smith, Mike Tough and John Yule (Yulser). Many of them were former pupils from Summerhill Academy, where the headmaster, Robert Mackenzie, had encouraged all his youngsters to take an interest in the outdoors. In the early 1980s, the WDC and other unaffiliated walkers, climbers and bird-watchers from Aberdeen were invited to join the North East Mountain Trust. They did this under the banner of the Harriet Street Group, a name derived from the Harriet Street Bar, the Aberdeen pub where they all enjoyed patronage. (The building has now been demolished to make way for a multi-storey car park.) There was a fair amount of cross-over at the time, between the Harriet Street Group, the WDC and other Aberdeen clubs, particularly the Etchachan Club, whose members met in the Blue Lamp Bar. When word came back from Braemar about the demise of Scott's Bothy there was an immediate and very strong desire from all the regular users to have it reconstructed, no matter how difficult this might prove to be.

At the time of the Luibeg fire the Cairngorms was subjected to an exceptionally severe storm. The weather station on Cairn Gorm summit registered Britain's highest recorded wind speed of 150 knots at 12.30am on March 20. At the time, three parties from Glenmore Lodge were snow-holing in the Garbh Uisge Beag on the plateau between Cairn Gorm and Ben Macdui. In the morning the wind dropped for a while as the eye of the depression passed overhead. The three parties went off in different directions to test the navigation skills of the students. The fierce wind returned as quickly as it had abated and it was 36 hours before they all made it back to the Lodge, the last remaining on the plateau being airlifted by helicopter in the early morning of the 21st.

There was still a big build-up of snow on Lochnagar at the end of March when Dinwoodie and Nisbet returned once more to the Tough-Brown Face. This time they were after a climb which Dinwoodie had

Starting the 5b corner of the Outlands on the Trail of Tears, Tough-Brown Face, Lochnagar, March 1986. Douglas Dinwoodie climbing

Photo: Andy Nisbet

attempted three times in the past. The first, with MacLean and Arthur Paul, was more of a reconnaissance, an attempt to reach the groove left of Post Mortem; the second was with Kevin Murphy, and the third with Ewen Todd. The line was a direct and even harder varient on Trail of Tears which joined that route at the top of the Dirge ramp after taking a series of grooves and corners between Dirge and Post Mortem. Starting below the first pitch of Mort, it followed twin snow ramps up left to a belay on Dirge. The objective was then to gain and climb a big right-facing groove or diedre and thus straighten out the lengthy detour made on the summer line of Dirge. On Dinwoodie's most recent attempt he reached a little shelf close to Post Mortem, but with only a short wall to overcome before reaching the Dirge ramp, darkness forced a retreat. This time conditions were similar to the two previous attempts when virtually no useful ice was found except for a little above the bulge guarding entry to the diedre. Dinwoodie climbed into, and up, the diedre until he reached a split block where he took a semi-hanging belay and brought up Nisbet. The next pitch, the third, was the crux. It commenced with hard moves up left over an overhang to gain a crack-line. This was then followed to the shelf where he had turned back previously. More hard climbing up the wall close to Post Mortem finally brought him to a belay on Trail of Tears.

Nisbet followed this desperate pitch then took over the lead and continued on up the Trail of Tears. There was less ice here than three weeks earlier and he was forced to use the in-situ piton for aid. Near the top of the continuation ramp, they dropped down right into the final trough of Mort, traversed away right and descended to the foot of Raeburn's Gully by abseiling the main pitch of Backdoor Route. In keeping with the gloomy nomenclature of the face they named this climb Diedre of the Sorrows – Grade VIII.

There had been a fatal accident a few days before, when two climbers fell from the upper basin of Parallel Gully B. Dinwoodie and Nisbet had come across blood in the snow before starting the route and this obviously gave the day a depressing atmosphere. (Deirdre of the Sorrows was a character in Celtic legend, a story of runaway love and tragedy.) In retrospect, Dinwoodie thought Trail of Tears the more satisfying of the two climbs he and Nisbet made on the Tough-Brown face that winter as it followed the more natural winter line. Later in the year, on a very cold day, he repeated Diedre of the Sorrows as a rock climb with Jeff Hall. The climbing felt like E2 5c on the day.

The cold weather was reluctant to give way during the spring of 1986. Good skiing was still available on Cairn Gorm in mid-May and on June 10, blizzards swept the high ground, depositing six inches of snow and forcing closure of the Lecht and Devil's Elbow roads. There was an encouraging development in the quest to re-build Luibeg Bothy. Ronnie Robb, acting as secretary for 'The Friends of Bob Scott', received a letter from Gerald Panchaud, saying that he agreed in principal with replacement of the bothy. The Swiss owner of Mar Lodge Estate acknowledged the fact that Bob Scott had allowed its use as a shelter for walkers and climbers and believed this tradition should continue. He saw no reason why the bothy could not be re-built as long as several onerous provisos were met, namely, planning permission obtained, approval from

*Allen Fyffe
contemplates Evil
Spirits on Hell's Lum
Crag, June 1986*

Photo: Bob Barton

Nature Conservancy Council sought, a toilet facility incorporated and a legal agreement drawn up stating that the building belonged to the estate. He also said a new location would have to be found because the original Luibeg site was within the Nature Reserve.

While one Cairngorm bothy was about to rise from its own ashes, another, Jean's Hut, was about to be demolished. The Scottish Sports Council, ultimately responsible for the hut through Glenmore Lodge, had already obtained approval from the family of Jean Smith to have it removed. The Cairngorm Mountain Rescue Team was the only official group in favour of its retention and even it accepted that the timber structure was in a poor state. The hut had stood at its re-located position at the entrance to Coire an Lochain for 22 years, but unlike Bob Scott's Bothy, news of its imminent demise failed to generate sufficient interest to save it. The majority of climbers and walkers believed a shelter was unnecessary in the northern corries of Cairn Gorm. Jean's Hut was taken down in June 1986.

The best rock climbing of the summer occurred in June and July. Rab Anderson and Alan Russell were quick off the mark to climb Pointlace, an E3 5c up the slabby crest of Raeburn's Buttress on the Shelter Stone Crag. They made this direct ascent left of Consolation Groove three days after the June blizzard. Later in June, Fyffe and Barton climbed a new route on the Grey Buttress of Hell's Lum Crag following a diagonal line between Hell's Lump and Good Intentions. The main pitch, led by Fyffe, had good climbing going left below a big roof to gain a bulging groove which took them up to a stance on the Exorcist. Evil Spirits – E2 5c.

Nisbet spent a day in June cleaning a new line on the Bastion of Creagan a' Choire Etchachan. To the right of Talisman, a large groove leads up the Corridor wall and develops into a steep corner – the left-hand Corridor Corner. (The right-hand being the line of Henchman). The lower groove is mossy but can be avoided on the left by climbing a crack-line up the Talisman slab to reach a steep headwall. Dinwoodie had used this slab approach in 1977 to reach and attempt the top corner. He backed off after encountering an alarming loose flake where the corner is closed by a giant ear of rock. On July 4, after hearing a forecast for rain, Nisbet and MacLean raced up from the Lake District and started the new climb at 8.30pm. On the headwall, MacLean led a shallow groove right of the Talisman edge, before moving right to a hidden ledge and belay. Nisbet then continued across the headwall to finish by the last few moves of the Corner, leaving MacLean to follow in the dark. By linking these spectacular pitches with the previously climbed direct start to Talisman, the whole proved to be one of the best climbs on the crag. They named it Talking Drums after a booming flake on the first pitch of the headwall – E2 5b. Ironically, the weather stayed dry!

The remaining exploration this summer took place on Creag an Dubhloch where Dinwoodie made two new climbs on the Central Slabs. His first, with Hawthorn on July 1, seemed rather trivial as it only involved two pitches of new climbing. It went between the opening pitches of Cyclops and Black Mamba and gave excellent, and surprisingly, independent climbing with a thin friction crux. Slithy Tove – E3 6a. His second route was an altogether more serious affair taking a hard and very direct line between Dragon Slayer and Blue Max. He had tried this the previous summer with Ross. Climbing on sight, they started up the brown corner left of Cyclops and followed cracks and corners to below the main overlap. Here, right of the open mouth taken by Dragon Slayer, Dinwoodie climbed a series of small steps up the face of the overlap, wire-brushing the rock as he went. He passed the thinnest bit after placing a very poor piton runner. At the top of the main overlap another small lap barred access to a thin crack running up the next smooth slab. "It seems odd I didn't persevere with the crack above the overlap, but maybe wire-brushing there just seemed too precarious." He hammered in another piton and retreated.

Later, Dinwoodie abseiled down and brushed the whole pitch. Then on July 18 started up again with Calum Fraser. This time he climbed the crux and continued on past the second piton and up the thin crack to a belay 15ft below another big lap. The next pitch involved surmounting the lap on the right, then a short way above, the difficulties eased and they followed Blue Max to the terrace. On the upper tier they found a line between Pink Elephant and Black Mamba, which gave three pitches of increasingly difficult climbing, culminating in 6a moves round a capping bulge right of Pink Elephant's finishing groove. They named this long climb Groanmaker (The battle axe of Zulu chief, Umslopogaas) and gave it a grade of E5 6b. Dinwoodie thought the poorly-protected crux was more serious than The Naked Ape, although in a much less impressive situation. The next day they made the second ascent of Flodden.

Throughout the summer of 1986 work was apace to ensure the building of Bob Scott's Bothy. A number of sites were offered by the estate before all parties settled for an idyllic spot on the right bank of the River Lui, downstream from Derry Lodge. Paul Devlin prepared drawings and all necessary permissions were obtained. Ruraidh Smith took on the roll as main fund-raiser and in July organised a sponsored walk carrying Eric Clark to the top of Lochnagar. Eric, a keen bird watcher and WDC

Colin MacLean making the crux moves on the first winter ascent of St Andrews Climb, Garbh Choire Dhaidh, Braeriach, November 1986

Photo: Andy Nisbet

member was disabled in a fall on the Deeside hill, Creag Ghiubhais, a few years earlier. With money from this plus donations from the SMT, NEMT and private individuals, sufficient cash was generated to procure all the materials. Construction took place during the autumn with the hearth from the old shell being successfully transferred to the new bothy in time for the opening ceremony on November 8. Although located only a 20 minute cycle ride from the car park at the Linn of Dee, the new Bob Scott's Bothy was well maintained and suffered no serious vandalism for 18 years until it met the same end as its predecessor. On December 16, 2003, two regular users from Aberdeen left the fire in the bothy unattended while they went out for more wood. When they returned, the floor was well alight, and despite suffering burns to themselves, they were unable to prevent the flames spreading to the whole building. The bothy was re-constructed on the same site in 2005 – the third Bob Scott Bothy!

Several years had elapsed since Nisbet made the winter ascent of Nom-de-Plume, the last of the 1960s rock climbs on the upper cliff of Càrn Etchachan to be climbed in winter. Earlier in the same year, April 1986, with Andy Cunningham, he had renewed his interest in the cliff by making a winter ascent of Pythagoras – Grade VI. Nisbet was now working at Glenmore Lodge and he and Cunningham were back with the first snowfalls in November to climb The Poison Trail, a counter diagonal to Crevasse Route. They started up the ramp of Poison Dwarf, using rope tension at one point. Then, after failing on the crux of Poison Dwarf, they crossed Crevasse Route and finished up ramps heading for easy ground at the top left hand edge of the cliff. This Grade V kicked off another busy winter. Exploration was wide ranging throughout the Cairngorms despite considerably less snowfall than the previous year. New routes were found from Sgoran Dubh in the west to the corries of Beinn a' Bhùird in the east and from Glen Clova and Caenlochan in the south to the very popular corries of Cairn Gorm in the north.

A few days after the Càrn Etchachan climb, Mal Duff and Andy Black made an early winter visit to the Garbh Choire Dhaidh of Braeriach, where they made an ascent of Kangaroo – Grade V. This sparked off further interest in this remote corrie. Local activists, trawling through the guidebook, found that the old Severe rock climb, St Andrews Climb, had not been done in winter. On November 19, a weekday no less, two completely independent parties arrived in the corrie. Nisbet, who had climbed the route in summer, Cunningham and MacLean had spent the night in the Garbh Choire Hut. When they reached the foot of the cliff they met Lyall and Steve Aisthorpe, who had walked in for the day. By an amazing coincidence they had all arrived to climb the same route, St Andrews Climb – Grade V. This turned out to be MacLean's last new route in the Cairngorms. He was still keen to make a complete winter ascent of Mort on Lochnagar and he did go back several times with Davison. On each visit they were thwarted by bad weather or poor conditions and Colin eventually gave up winter climbing, having been a major influence on its development in Scotland over the last few years. (Davison did finally succeed in making the first winter ascent of Mort, in January 2000, accompanied by Nisbet and Dave McGimpsey.)

Another winter climb was made on the cliffs of Garbh Choire Dhaidh by Gavin Taylor and John McKeever. This team from Edinburgh was having a very fruitful season in the Cairngorms, and included in their haul was Koala – a VS groove system right of St Andrews Climb. In January, they found favourable conditions for this south-facing cliff, reporting the climb to be excellent and sustained, every pitch different in character. There was steep ice on the first pitch, torquing on the second, and thin ice and névé smears on the final slabby wall – Grade VI.

The weeks leading up to Christmas 1986 provided very cold, snowy conditions in the Cairngorms. On December 14, Taylor and McKeever climbed a new line close to Bastille on Cairn Etchachan (The Kremlin, Grade V), while at the same time, on the Grey Buttress of Hell's Lum Crag, Cunningham and Nisbet succeeded on Good Intentions. Although the groove of the summer crux was technically very hard it was also very well protected and they found the winter crux to be the ramp leading up to the groove – Grade VII. Two days later Cunningham and Nisbet were back in the Loch Avon basin to make a winter ascent of Longbow Direct. They did this by following the summer route except bypassing the red wall on the left – Grade V. The next day the two Andys were back at the Longbow Crag to try Gordon Smith's Central Route, the line of vegetated depressions right of Sand-Pyper. Uncertain of the exact line they followed the rib to the right of the depression and finished up the final fault of Central Route. They found this to be a very good winter climb and gave it the peculiar name Flock of Chickens – Grade VI. At the time of these ascents conditions on this south-facing cliff were described by Nisbet as 'mixed'. "The turf was frozen and there was unconsolidated snow, but not enough to stop you from seeing what you were doing with your feet!"

Nisbet's unrelenting drive took him and Cunningham back to Càrn Etchachan three days after New Year 1987. This time their target was the HVS Time Traveller, yet another climb on the upper cliff. Nisbet led the first pitch following an obvious flake crack which joined the summer line higher up. The crack provided a real battle and he was forced to rest for a while on one of his axes. Beyond this there was a bulge to surmount before reaching the little stance at the top of the first pitch. Cunningham then took over and led another hard pitch before moving left near the top to avoid a large cornice – Grade VII.

It was in January 1987 that Livingston plucked up the courage to go back to his projected winter route on The Stack of Lochnagar. Climbing with Mark Charlton, he led the first corner as before, then they led through until Charlton found himself in a similar situation to Livingston, two years earlier. He had followed the scooped ramp up left to below a final bulging wall but could not make a worthwhile belay. He was not at all confident about being able to climb back down and it was late in the day so he accepted a top rope from friends on the plateau. Unfortunately, the last pitch turned out to be relatively easy. Sometime later, they climbed the whole route again, leaving a fixed piton for a belay below the top wall. Livingston recorded the route, Torquing Corpse, as a Grade VII, the first to be claimed at this grade in Scotland. Prior to this, the most difficult winter climbs, such as The Needle Winter Variations, The Rattrap and Diedre of the Sorrows, had all been graded

The imposing headland of the Stack lying in the angle between the branches of The Black Spout on Lochnagar

Photo: Marcelo Uceta

"The turf was frozen and there was unconsoli-dated snow, but not enough to stop you from seeing what you were doing with your feet!" – Andy Nisbet

*Mark Charlton climb-
ing Torquing Corpse,
January 1987*

Photo: Graeme Livingston

VI. He believed this was justified on account of the seriousness combined
with the technical difficulty. There were those who doubted the magni-
tude of the difficulties, saying that the climb would be easier in better
conditions. They also drew attention to the flawed final ascent.
Nevertheless, despite a big reputation, the climb remains unrepeated
21 years on, although Simon Richardson and Chris Cartwright climbed
a more direct version of it in January 1999 – Redemption, Grade VIII.

    In 1985, a group of talented young Dundee climbers started explor-
ing in the Glen Clova area. Simon Stewart, Graeme Ettle, Grant Farquhar
and a few others had all been at school together, and following Stewart's
lead, they reassessed the potential of the Red Craig and made many new

and difficult climbs, particularly on the Upper Doonie. In February 1986, Stewart and Ettle had found rare good conditions when they climbed the steep ice-line of G-Force on Craig Rennet. According to Ettle: "It was an obvious 'last great problem' to my group of lads. I led the icicle, with Grant seconding, then we abseiled off. Simon then repeated it but came off on the second pitch, pulling off his belayer and they both fell to the ground. Later on, Simon and I climbed the route complete. I led the ice again," – Grade VI.

During January and February this year Stewart and Ettle made several trips to Creag an Dubh-loch. By now they had well-developed rock climbing skills but were not too experienced on mixed winter routes. This situation changed when they made three first winter ascents of the summer rock climbs Sabre Edge, Late Night Final and Nemesis. This latter route (VS 4c), on the lower left flank of Central Gully Buttress gave them their hardest route – Grade VI. On Sabre Edge, it was Ettle who drew the short straw and provided Stewart with 'a shoulder' to give him sufficient height to make the initial pull off the top of the pinnacle. Ettle recalls they were super keen to try bigger things. "On Nemesis we experimented with seconding on a shunt (a small device similar to a jumar), it certainly was fast but you didn't get much climbing in. We would walk to Sandy Hillocks below Broad Cairn on a Friday night, camp, then rise early and hurl ourselves at these lines. Simon was the driving force behind us doing the obvious unclimbed summer routes. Climbing anything was good to me."

Graeme Ettle
Photo: John Lyall

Early in the summer Stewart had another bad ground fall at Creag Dubh, Newtonmore, and although he made a full recovery and continued climbing for a while, he concentrated more on his studies at university. He is still a very keen hill-walker. Also at Creag an Dubh-loch this month, Nisbet and Cunningham climbed Four Corners Route, a steep mixed line above Sabre Edge on Central Gully Wall – Grade VI. This was their second attempt, the first, the previous week, had run out of daylight after a morning spent trying Predator.

On the Shelter Stone Crag, McKeever and Taylor made the second winter ascent of The Citadel in 13 hours. They found the hardest climbing at the lower crux and were unable to reduce the aid. Later, Anderson and Grahame Nicoll did free the lower crux on a repeat of the Rouse/Hall 'Citadel Winter Variations', where they added another variation up a slim ramp on the headwall above the Central Slabs. Taylor and McKeever's last contribution to this winter was an ascent of Raeburn's Buttress by a line based on Consolation Groove – Grade VI with an abseil.

Surprisingly, the winter of 1986 – 87 provided no new winter climbs in Coire an Lochain of Cairngorm, although Cunningham and Nisbet had two failed attempts on War and Peace. You would be excused for thinking this was the onset of saturation point, but it was really only the calm before another storm. In the other northern corrie, Coire an t-Sneachda, there were new climbs on most of the main areas of cliff. At the end of the winter, Lyall and Grosset (with A.Nolan) made a direct ascent of Doctor Janis, the groove-line immediately right of Doctor's Choice on Aladdin's Buttress – Grade V. They had climbed the top half the previous winter as a variation to Doctor's Choice. (Janis was a local doctor who worked with the Cairngorm Mountain Rescue Team.)

An interesting aspect of this winter was the resurgence of activity on the cliffs of Sgoran Dubh Mor and Sgòr Gaoith. Several of the old rock routes were climbed as well as a few new lines. In March, Grosset and Lyall made a direct ascent of the Slash, describing it as an interesting climb through superb rock and ice scenery.[3] There were further climbs made the following winter, but as the worthwhile possibilities dwindled, so did the interest. Some of the recent climbs were accessed by four-wheel drive vehicle, but for the less privileged, it is a long walk from Whitewell to Loch Einich and back in deep snow. Nevertheless, it is a wild lonely place, and given the right winter conditions the climbing can feel very alpine.

The summer of 1987 was another poor one for rock climbing. Dinwoodie had been waiting and waiting for suitable conditions to attempt two hard lines on Creag an Dubh-loch, namely, the wall crack left of Improbability Drive and a route starting in the big alcove between Perilous Journey and Cannibal. The first week of July looked hopeful, and despite some rain on the Friday night, the main overlapping wall remained largely dry. Hamilton had abseiled to inspect this problem and later Dinwoodie had wire-brushed the line to a junction with Cougar high on the crag. An unfortunate feature of the route is that the section crossing Voyage of the Beagle is often wet, while the groove in the initial alcove is permanently so.

On July 5, accompanied by George Thomson (Dod), Dinwoodie started up the first crack of Cannibal then veered left by a branch crack to gain a slabby groove above the lip of the alcove. (He did not think he could climb the alcove direct, even if it had been dry.) Aware of rope-drag he moved up the slab to traverse left and gain the thread belay of Perilous Journey. After Thomson had joined him, Dinwoodie moved back and climbed the vertical continuation groove using a poor pre-placed knife-blade runner. He later named this the Bluebell Groove after the harebells which grow at the bottom.

Above this a daunting overlap went surprisingly quickly, with some wild moves, to gain the little continuation groove leading up to the Beagle perch. This is dramatically situated below one of the biggest overhangs on the wall, and is, in fact, the ledge gained by Archbold during our wet debacle in 1973. The intention now had been to try the deceptive continuation fault slanting left under the bulge, the feature which Boysen and Kosterlitz had been rained off on their own enterprising attempt. This was wet so Dinwoodie and Thomson roped off.

Dinwoodie never got back on the route because of continued bad weather and his retirement from serious climbing a year or so later. The overlap on the second pitch is considered to be 6c but reasonably protected, and he expected the direct start and the third pitch to be even harder. Not having completed the climb he did not record their effort until 1994, when the Edinburgh climbers, Rick Campbell and Paul Thorburn also reached, and bailed-out from, the Beagle belay, assuming the line to be unclimbed. In a display of bold on-sight climbing, Campbell went directly up the groove in the back of the alcove and continued to the top of the Bluebell Groove in one 100ft pitch, thus providing a more satisfactory start. (He brushed the steep lower part of the groove in the alcove while hanging from gear, then lowered back to the ground before leading it. The wet overhanging section was

The main overlapping heart of Central Gully Wall. The arrowhead alcove of Hybrid Vigour rises from the talus just left of centre and has a brown water streak running down its right wall. The climbers are on the second pitch of Cougar

Photo: Greg Strange

relatively clean and holds improved with height gained.) Thorburn made an eventful lead of the second pitch but Campbell retreated from the impasse above the Beagle ledge, pulling out a pre-placed piton of Dinwoodie's with his hand. (All the cracks here are blind, hence the Rurp placed by Kosterlitz.)

A new Cairngorms guidebook was in preparation and Campbell sent his two pitch route, Hybrid Vigour, for inclusion. When Dinwoodie learned about this he pointed out that he and Thomson had already covered this ground (apart from the better start) and offered the name, The Web of Weird. He explained that he always thought of the belay spot below the huge overlap as the centre of the web or labyrinth of this formidable wall. Much later he revealed an incident which took place while inspecting the problematic bulge on pitch two.

"I had the ridiculous idea that this would be my big revenge climb and, when I roped down and saw that the overlap looked impossible, I thumped the rock with my hammer in a fit of pique. A chunk of rock flew off leaving a flat, white hold. Although I had got into bad habits while 'cleaning' the fissile sea cliffs of Findon, I don't think there was any conscious intent of making a hold. It seemed an odd thing to happen since granite is usually so solid. Maybe it's right I never finished the route, however."

It was left to Campbell and Thorburn to return in 1995 to complete the climb. Campbell lead the nasty blank bit on pitch three without a piton runner. This traversing pitch will be even worse to second than to lead so understandably Thorburn declined. At a later date they were joined by Neil Craig when Thorburn led the fourth pitch, also on-sight, taking a scary hand-traverse cutting back up the bulge to gain a niche. Above here a good crack right of the hanging crack of Perilous Journey led up onto the final part of Cougar. The complete Hybrid Vigour, at E6 6c, is one of the hardest climbs on Creag an Dubh-loch.

False Gully Wall with its array if thin cracks through the prominent smooth band. This face lies high on the right hand side of Central Gully Wall, Creag an Dubh-loch

Photo: Andy Nisbet

Further persistence in this summer of 1987 by Dinwoodie finally paid off. On August 10, he climbed the seriously difficult crack through the smooth band, between The Snake and The Improbability Drive on False Gully Wall. He had tried this earlier with Hawthorn, but his finger tips wore through, climbing up and down the first 20ft. This time, with Hall, he found that each time he attempted to move up past a pocket at 20ft, the nut he had placed for protection swivelled out and became dislodged. So he then hammered in a piton runner, while hanging from a micro nut, before retreating back to the bottom. On his next try, he climbed past this piton and on up the crack, passing another pre-placed piton. He hung around too long at the first possible 'shake out' (there was a better one higher up), and nearly fell off at the top when he got his arms badly crossed.

Having now joined The Snake, coming in from the left, he followed this up and left to the belay at the top of its first pitch. After Hall had joined him, Dinwoodie completed the route with a good pitch going up and right to follow Slartibartfast for part of its corner. He then moved back left and up a steep wall to finish at the top of Masque. This well-named climb, Fer-de-Lance (E6 6b), was Dinwoodie's last new rock climb on Creag an Dubh-loch, or anywhere else in the Cairngorms. For 15 years he had been at the cutting edge of North-east climbing and was about to take a back seat, on rock at least.

In the context of the great north-east corrie of Lochnagar, the crags of its Southern Sector are only of minor importance. The vegetated granite, unappealing in summer, gives good short climbs in winter, similar to the northern corries of Cairn Gorm. Not surprisingly, activity here had been very limited, but as the opportunities for exploration in the main sector declined, so interest in these crags increased. Immediately left of Sinister Buttress lies The Cathedral, named for its regular architecture – four slender ribs 300ft high, divided by chimneys and grooves. In December 1987, Brian Findlay and I climbed the main central groove on The Cathedral, reaching the plateau via the deep chimney of Transept Route – Sepulchre. Grade V. This was our second route hereabouts as we had climbed the neighbouring groove to the right the previous December – Judas Priest Grade V.

The spell of good weather we experienced on Lochnagar lasted long enough for Chris Forrest and Nisbet to make a winter ascent of The Tower of Babel in the Garbh Choire Mòr of Braeriach. They skied from Cairn Gorm using Nordic skis with bindings suitable for their Koflach mountaineering boots. After a night in the hut they made their ascent on December 16, more or less following the line of the summer route up steep turfy cracks. It was an excellent sustained climb in a very remote setting – Grade VI. On the way out they skied from the top of Lurcher's Crag to the car park on Cairn Gorm. Nisbet recalls doing the splits on his skis carrying the big pack and being sore for days afterwards.

A big thaw set in a few days after this ascent, stripping the hills bare of snow. It was well into January before it turned cold again, but the snow quickly built up, especially above 2500ft. Cunningham and Nisbet had been three times to attempt a new winter climb on Longbow Crag, linking sections of the rock climbs, Windchill and Sand-Pyper. Ideal winter conditions are rare on this south-facing cliff. On one of their attempts, Nisbet led the first pitch, the sun came out, and before Cunningham had joined him on the stance, there was no snow left on the route! On January 22, conditions were acceptable and they enjoyed a good sustained climb. Starting at the foot of Longbow Direct, thin climbing on the lower slabs led to a strenuous, but well protected finish, through the steep upper walls – Windpiper, Grade VII.

The two instructors had another project on the go at this time, namely a winter ascent of Postern Direct on the Shelter Stone Crag. It was John Cunningham and March who first climbed this VS variation, taking a more direct line from the Slanting Crack to the Second Step, before finishing via the hideous looking cave-like feature well right of the Needle Crack. The two Andys had already done Postern Ordinary in winter after one of their failed attempts on Windpiper. The west flank of the Shelter Stone Crag was very white when they made their bid on March 5. They took eight hours to climb the three pitches of the Direct with each pitch being considerably harder than anything on the original route. The crux section above the Second Step was led by Nisbet: "At the time I said it was the hardest pitch I'd ever led. It was deeply rimed and despite having done it in summer, I had a really hard time and fell off once, which was rare for me. We finished in the dark in deteriorating weather." – Grade VII.

February had been very snowy this year with a big build up on the high crags. Early in the month a huge avalanche swept down the slopes below the Tough-Brown Face of Lochnagar, depositing a mass of snow on the frozen loch. This is not uncommon in Coire an Lochain but it is very unusual for an avalanche to reach the loch on Lochnagar. It took several freeze-thaw cycles for the snow in the more shady parts of the cliff to become consolidated. One such place was the Douglas-Gibson face of Shadow Buttress B. I had a particular interest in this wall because in my first summer climbing I fell 90ft down its summit slabs when caught in a rock fall on the final tower of Bell's Route. I was held on the damaged rope by Raymond Simpson, but my spectacles, my father's Retinette camera, and many tons of granite continued on down into Douglas-Gibson Gully before shooting out across the old snow at the foot of the cliff.

Well below the narrows of Douglas-Gibson Gully, and roughly in the line of my rock fall is a smooth left-facing corner. This obvious feature had been attempted in winter on three occasions in the past, first by Keir, then later by Sprunt and John Anderson. All three had failed due to lack of ice, vegetation and protection. It was climbed on very thin ice in 2000 by Cartwright and Richardson.

A little higher up the gully a snowy line of weakness leads up to a ramp, from where grooves continue directly to the final tower. Brian Findlay and I had gleaned from a previous investigation that consolidated snow or ice would be a prerequisite for success on this line. Conditions looked good on March 13, and we enjoyed an excellent climb. The snow was still a bit sugary providing some delicate moments, in particular the groove above the ramp, led by Brian – Eclipse Grade VI.

The early summer of 1988 was predominantly warm and dry with good rock climbing conditions throughout Scotland. In the Cairngorms, most folk took the opportunity to make up for the previous poor summer and there were many teams out on Creag an Dubh-loch and the Shelter Stone Crag. On the Central Slabs of the latter there were no less than three ascents of Run of the Arrow and further ascents of Cupid's Bow and The Missing Link. On June 18, Grant Farquhar and Kim Greenald made an attempt to free the big corner of Thor. It was 20 years since it had first been climbed on aid and despite the attention of several leading lights no one had yet managed to free the first main pitch. Murray Hamilton had made a cursory inspection and thought it unlikely to go free! After several yo-yos Greenald finally succeeded in passing Rennie's golo to reach the niche, where he could belay at some old pitons at the hollow flake. This was a real breakthrough, for although the protection was good by slab climbing standards, the rock under the overlap is very smooth and the section up to the golo required very fiddly work with tiny wire nuts (RPs). Passing the golo proved extremely tenuous as there were no holds at this point. They suspected the pitons at the belay were unsound, and since there were none in place beyond, they decided to retreat. It had been a most commendable effort, climbed on sight, and a pointer to a free Thor in the near future.

Elsewhere, during this dry spell, Fyffe and Mallaig climber, Jas Hepburn, made three new routes beside Styx on the slabs left of Hell's Lum. Their best effort, Arc of a Diver, stayed close to the right side of the slabs and finished up the blunt rib overlooking the Lum. The climb had a particularly good top pitch – E2 5c. On Lochnagar, Alastair Ross, Colin Stewart and Marion Sutherland climbed a two pitch route on the attractive rock to the right of Pantheist, on the lower Black Spout Pinnacle. The second pitch, leading up to the Springboard, was pre-cleaned by Ross and provided the crux – Infidel E3 5c. The dry period finally broke at the end of June, heralding a very wet July, from which the high crags never fully recovered. On July 6, two days before the

Aberdeen Trades Holiday, the Piper-Alpha oil production platform blew up in the North Sea, killing 167 people. Many of the North-east's climbers worked in the oil industry and few were not affected in some way by this awful tragedy.

It was during very mixed weather on July 24 and 25, that the Ambleside fell runner, Mark Rigby, ascended all 17 of the Cairngorms Munros, starting and finishing at Glenmore Youth Hostel. He achieved this epic run in less than 23 hours, taking a 76 mile anti-clockwise circuit, commencing with Braeriach, then working out to the most westerly summit, Mullach Clach a' Bhlair, before turning back to sweep through the whole range as far as Ben Avon in the east. The forecasted front, with strong winds and heavy rain caught him in darkness on the final leg and he sat out for an hour in the Fords of Avon Bothy, waiting for daybreak, before finishing over Bynack More and Cairngorm. To add spice to his adventure, he was unsupported and had never visited the Cairngorms before. Rigby's run was repeated in 1999 by Bob Berzins, who completed the circuit in the reverse direction by a slightly shorter route, taking 23 hours 19 minutes. He too, was so inspired by the run, that he wrote in an article: "Here's a circuit of 71 miles, not crossing a single road or fence and staying above 1500ft the whole way. Being so remote the run lends itself to an unsupported attempt and if you fancy a big day out in Britain's wildest terrain, this is it."[4]

In late October and November 1988, there was the usual crop of early winter ascents on snow-covered rock and frozen vegetation. This is a good time for keen mixed winter climbers as they still have residual strength and stamina from the previous summer of rock climbing. Rab Anderson really got the bit between his teeth, ekeing out four new routes in the northern corries before the end of November. On October 20, with Chris Greaves, he climbed the obvious shallow turfy corner right of Fluted Buttress Direct in Coire an t-Sneachda, joining that route above its fork – Sax Appeal, Grade IV. A fortnight later he and Greaves switched to Coire an Lochain to make an ascent of the front face of No. 2 Buttress, left of Central Crack Route. This direct route, Torque of The Devil, had some hard climbing – Grade VI. Anderson's final two routes were on the right-hand side of No. 3 Buttress. On November 19, with Nicoll and Milne, he climbed The Hoarmaster, an excellent short route, following a chimney then the fault of The Overseer up the right edge of the buttress – Grade V. Then, a week later, again with Greaves, he was back for Hooker's Corner, another Grade VI just round the edge from The Hoarmaster.

While making this last climb in Coire an Lochain, Anderson and Greaves were surprised to see a lone figure abseiling down the face of No. 4 Buttress, to the left of Savage Slit. This was Nisbet checking out the summer rock climb, Bulgy. Having been spotted doing a little 'fox shooting', Nisbet quickly returned the next day with Jonathan Preston to make the winter ascent, starting with a low traverse in from Savage Slit. "The double roofs gave some exciting and intimidating moves, particularly the first (crux) because protection could not be arranged until the lip was gained."[5] – Grade VII.

In late November, another good winter route was made on The Mess of Pottage. Lyall and Steve Spalding followed the buttress right of The

John Lyall climbing Pot of Gold on the Mess of Pottage, Coire an t-Sneachda, Cairngorm, November 1988

Photo: Steve Spalding

Message to produce The Pot of Gold – Grade V. Much later in the season, in March, Lyall returned with Malcolm Sclater to put up another new route, this time on the left-hand side of The Mess of Pottage. Honeypot (Grade IV) takes the obvious square-cut chimney near the left boundary of the upper walls, finishing by an exciting swing round the right side of the capping roof.

After a less than average winter for snow, the Cairngorms dried quickly, allowing ascents of Black Spout Wall and The Naked Ape during May of 1989. In June, Ross made a second route on the lower Black Spout Pinnacle immediately right of Infidel. Belayed by Sutherland (she chose not to second the route on this occasion), Ross led the whole 150ft climb up to the Springboard in a single pitch. He gave the route a Gaelic name, An Saobh-Chreideach (The Heretic) and offered a grade of E5 6b. This route, which most people found unpronounceable (nicknamed Shabby Creature), was repeated twice in the 1990s, using a midway belay on Infidel as suggested by Ross in his original description. It was found to have good quality climbing, but probably only E4.

The predominantly dry weather continued into July with good rock climbing most weekends. Early on Saturday July 15, two climbers arrived at the Coire Cas car park, bound for the Shelter Stone Crag. Rick Campbell and Neil Craig were in a hurry to get to the Central Slabs where they planned to attempt a free ascent of Thor. Before leaving, they met Gary Latter and Graham Lawrie, who they suspected were also heading in that direction. Campbell knew that Latter had already been on Thor.

Twenty-six-year-old Campbell, from Edinburgh, had always been interested in the outdoors, although he only started serious climbing in 1985. Inspired by the picture of Whillance leading The Naked Ape on the front cover of the new Cairngorms Guide, he made an ascent of The Needle a year later and was struck by the alpine scale of the Shelter Stone Crag. By 1988, he was climbing much better and had already led a number of E5s at Dunkeld, in Glen Nevis and on the Eastern Buttress of Sròn na Cìche in the Cuillin, where he made the second ascent of Zephyr. He soon discovered that he was able to climb slabs noticeably better than very steep rock and demonstrated this by leading both The Run of the Arrow and Cupid's Bow over one weekend in June 1988. It was while on the former that he had watched Greenald and Farquhar working the first big pitch on Thor. A week later he went back to the Central Slabs and climbed The Missing Link. Abseiling back down afterwards, he cleaned the top pitch of Thor and placed three new pitons to use as protection. The weather then scuppered any chance of an ascent during that summer of 1988.

This time, a year later, everything went according to plan and Campbell succeeded in making an entirely free ascent, leading all the pitches, with no falls, either by himself or by Craig. The first main pitch (pitch two) between the belay on Cupid's Bow and the hollow flake was climbed on sight. They found the section passing the old golo to be the crux of the whole route. According to Campbell: "There were no holds and falling was imminent, so I just kept moving (always the key to this type of climbing). The slab below the overlap is particularly smooth and it is only the proximity to protection that makes this line feasible." On

Rick Campbell,
Central Slabs of
Shelter Stone Crag

Photo: Gary Latter

*Rick Campbell
leading the second
main pitch of Thor,
belayed by Neil Craig,
July 1989*

Photo: Gary Latter

the third pitch he continued below the overlap to reach a good hold where a ridiculous 'rock over' move enabled him to gain a comfortable standing position above the dwindling lap. The final passage up into the crack-line of The Pin involved a long reach to the right to gain and follow a series of rising ledges, past some of Rennie's old pitons. This long-awaited event was repeated a mere 30 minutes later when Gary Latter and Graham Lawrie finished their ascent of Thor, taking a slightly different way on the third pitch. The grade for this magnificent climb was considered to be E5 6b.

Towards the end of July Wilson Moir and Colin Stewart made a new route on Creag an Dubh-loch. The warm spell had helped to dry the steep slabs to the left of The Sword of Damocles on Broad Terrace Wall, where Moir had spied a left-facing corner between Alice Springs and The Last Oasis. He led this and its continuation in a single 150ft pitch of excellent sustained climbing – The Bedouin, E4 6a. There was also an important second ascent this summer on False Gully Wall when Murray Hamilton repeated The Improbability Drive with New Zealand climber, Carol Nash. He succeeded on the crux pitch at his second go, after falling at the top of the wall on his initial attempt.

The dry summer followed by a relatively dry autumn resulted in very little ice forming on the cliffs of the Cairngorms until late in the winter of 1989 – 90. Most new winter activity took place in the northern corries of Cairn Gorm, with four lines being found in Coire an Lochain and five in Coire an t-Sneachda. Rab Anderson was back, accompanied by Tom Prentice for three routes on Nos. 3 and 4 Buttresses in Coire an Lochain. Their best discovery was the instant mixed classic, Deep Throat (Grade V), which followed a wide crack through the stepped overhangs to the left of Savage Slit. They were joined by Rob Milne for this ascent on December 2.

In Coire an t-Sneachda, Lyall and Nisbet made winter ascents of two new rock routes which Lyall had climbed five months earlier with Steve Aisthorpe. Salvation took the cracked slabs between Damnation and the chimney of Patey's Route on Aladdin's Buttress. This was VS in rock boots and Grade V with crampons and axes. On the Mess of Pottage they followed Wachacha, a line to the right of Honeypot – Severe in summer, Grade VI in winter.

Also in Coire an t-Sneachda, Cunningham and Fyffe had a minor blitz on the Fiacaill Buttress, starting on January 4, with the fine chimney of The Stirling Bomber – Grade V. This unusual short route to the left of the opening corner of Jailbreak, climbs a crack and chimney-line finishing on the midway terrace. Its name is derived from a huge flake of rock which Cunningham dislodged while leading at the top of the chimney. In February, they made two further routes, one on each side of Fiacaill Buttress Direct. The best was Houdini (Grade VI), which takes a line similar to Jailbreak, except it starts near the centre of the lower buttress, left of The Stirling Bomber. The other climb, Smokestack Lightnin', zigzags up the right side of the face, closer to Fiacaill Couloir – Grade VI.

By the summer of 1990, almost a century had passed since the earliest climbs were pioneered in the Cairngorms. It is heartening to find that, despite the huge advances in technology and equipment, similarly bold new ventures were still being sought. Rick Campbell had completed all four of the most difficult routes on the Central Slabs of the Shelter Stone Crag, yet he was still keen for more.

Following the pattern of the previous year there was a lot of dry weather in Scotland during the early summer of 1990. On June 16, Campbell made his first visit to Creag an Dubh-loch. He was accompanied by another talented young Edinburgh climber, Paul Thorburn, who was just breaking into the E5 league. They had a fantastic day making the second ascent of Cannibal, with Thorburn leading the first pitch and Campbell all the rest. Afterwards, Campbell said he thought the climb was E6. He likened the Dubh Loch style of climbing to a game of chess. "The obvious way is usually impossible, but you can often hang about to work out the alternatives, concentration being aided by the absence of protection." A month later, after some mediocre weather, Campbell was back at the Shelter Stone Crag with Thorburn and two other Edinburgh climbers, Malcolm Smith and Alastair Moses. On Saturday July 21, while Thorburn and Smith went for Thor, Campbell and Moses headed for the crack-line of Snipers.

Grant Farquhar is credited with being the first to point out the possibility of climbing directly up the bald slab above the crux of The Run of The Arrow. Campbell's ambitious plan for the day was to free the overhang on Snipers of its final aid point, link this with the crack-line of The Run of The Arrow and finish straight up, as suggested by Farquhar.

Rab Anderson on The Deviant – a line on the extreme right of Ewen Buttress in Coire an Lochain, November 1989

Photo: Tom Prentice

Rab Anderson on the first ascent of the instant mixed classic, Deep Throat, Coire an Lochain, December 1989
Photo: Tom Prentice

Leaving Moses lashed to the belay flake, Campbell moved up and clipped his ropes into the two pitons on the big overlap. "Edge by the piton, low undercut with the right hand, smear up and pop for the top – the rest is easy!" His clinical description belies the true difficulties of this acrobatic problem which had seen-off all previous free attempts, including one by Graeme Livingston. He did admit however, that he fell off at his first attempt, and it was helpful to be tall.

Above the overlap there were thin moves leaving Snipers, and then he was soon on familiar territory, following cracks on The Run of The Arrow, heading for Dinwoodie's old wires. When he had climbed this route in 1988 he had protected the crux with a small nut, but he had since learned that Whillance found a shallow slot higher up, into which he had been able to fit a much larger nut on its side. Campbell slotted in the large nut and moved up until his feet were level with it. Here,

in a very precarious position, he brushed a flared crack on the right, before making a desperate move up and right, then another to gain a one inch wide sloping hold. "Standing on this, I soon realised that straight up was blank, retreat impossible and my belayer incommunicado. Convinced that the gear would fail, I looked over to Malcy on Thor and thought about a rescue."

Of course, he knew that waiting in this position for more than a few minutes was out of the question, so he had to do something quickly. Without further thought, he made very thin moves rightward to join the main pitch of Cupid's Bow. He was almost out of rope but still he could not stop. Placing a good Friend, he continued upwards to the easy flakes below the final hard section on Cupid's Bow. Here he was at last able to make contact with Moses via the party on Thor, and get him to untie one of the ropes. Campbell then used this to extend the other rope, leaving enough slack to allow him to reach easier ground, a runout of close on 200ft. After Moses had followed this huge pitch they abseiled off.

Next day Campbell felt less intimidated by the prospect of the bald slab so he and Moses climbed Snipers to the top of the slabs. Moses then abseiled to The Run of the Arrow belay in the corner of Thor and Campbell inspected the upper slab which he had eschewed the day before. "It was soon evident that although holdless, the slab was less steep and more textured than usual hereabouts. So I tied in at the crux (the very hard moves after leaving The Run of the Arrow), pulled the ropes, threw the ends down to Al, and then padded my way to the top." Campbell named his new route Aphrodite. It was the first E7 in the Cairngorms, with both the crux and the Snipers overlap being given a technical grade of 6b. As is often the case when climbers are pushing the upper limits of difficulty, they lay themselves open to criticism. Campbell took some flak over his slightly flawed ascent, but no one came forward to improve on his effort. It was seven years before another super slab climber came along to make the second ascent. Julian Lines succeeded after surviving a fall from the crux moves. Campbell went on to make further equally difficult climbs on the Central Slabs as well as many other routes throughout Scotland. Looking back, in 2004, he still regarded Aphrodite as his best climbing achievement. He believed it was as bold as anything anyone else was doing in Scotland at the time. "I had had my shoulder smashed by a falling rock in Pembroke only three months previously and was trying not to pull too hard with my left arm. When I mantled up on the crux, I felt something tear in my right one, but I couldn't let go. There was this moment of enlightenment when I felt I knew what it was like to die."

Later that summer Cunningham and Fyffe climbed an interesting alternative start to The Pin, taking the obvious curving line up rightward from the start of Cupid's Bow – E3 5c. They had hoped to continue by the obvious thin left-facing corner but realised this would be too hard for them. Three years later this became Campbell's next route on the Central Slabs, Realm of the Senses, which climbs the slabs between Cupid's Bow and The Pin, crossing The Missing Link and finishing up Thor – a desperate E7 6c.

There was good news for the Cairngorms this summer when the Scottish Secretary quashed another bid to install downhill ski facilities in Lurcher's Gully. Despite the outcome of the Public Inquiry in 1981, Highland Regional Council altered its Structure Plan to allow for another submission by the Cairngorm Chairlift Co. to expand westwards by means of a new road from the existing ski area. This was met with dismay by all those who believed the battle had been won. A great deal of work had to be done for the second time by the voluntary conservation and outdoor recreation organisations, and this gave rise to the formation of the 'Save the Cairngorms Campaign'. Much public and private debate took place before the Scottish Office ordered removal of the policy from HRC's Revised Structure Plan.

The winter of 1990 – 91 saw an unseemly scramble for new mixed winter routes in Coire an t-Sneachda, with a dozen being climbed between November and mid-February. Most local activists saw some of the action, which started on November 2, when Graeme Ettle climbed, Watch Out, the cracks on the arete right of The Seam. Ettle had recently moved to Speyside, becoming one of a growing number of full-time climbers working in the area as guides and instructors. He had back-rope soloed this very short rock climb (VS 5a) in May and made the winter ascent with an old school friend, John Fitzpatrick. The crux was an overhanging crack on the arete, probably the most technically difficult route in the corrie at the time. Elsewhere on the Fiacaill Buttress, Cunningham and Fyffe made their last winter climb here, in February, with the ascent of Burning and Looting, the rib between Rampant and Belhaven – Grade V.

It was the old campaigner, Fyffe, who found one of the better routes of the winter, when he climbed, No Blue Skies, on the Mess of Pottage with Libby Healy. Described by its originator as a 'subtle' route, it takes a diagonal break leftward from near the start of The Message and finds a way through the roof system on the headwall before finishing up

"Convinced that the gear would fail, I looked over to Malcy on Thor and thought about a rescue," – Rick Campbell

Wachacha – Grade VI.

"The name, No Blue Skies, is a song by Lloyd Cole which has lines about searching for something when there is nothing to be found – that seemed to fit the climbing!" The following day, December 21, Ettle and Chris Forrest found yet another crack-line right of The Message, which provided good sustained climbing. They named this Grade VI, Droidless, recording the absence of their friend, Andy Nisbet, who, at some time in the past, had acquired the nick-name, The Droid – a shortening of Android.

As might have been expected, the man himself was climbing elsewhere that day – in Coire an Lochain to be precise. Pursuing a recent trend for making routes in summer before repeating them the next winter, Nisbet had gone to No. 1 Buttress with Lyall to climb Ventriloquist, an interesting HVS rock route which Lyall had made the previous July with Ben Kellet. It takes the steep rock, immediately right of Auricle with a good hand-jamming crack as its 5a crux. They did this 260ft route in five pitches to produce a well-protected, but very strenuous, Grade VII. Yet again, this had not been success at the first attempt. Lyall, Nisbet and Davison had tried it the previous winter, before it had been climbed in summer. Later that winter, after eight days of new routing in the North-west Highlands, Nisbet was involved with another hard climb farther right. On February 25, Davison led him up Daddy Longlegs. It was the first time they had been on the climb since making the free ascent in August 1983. There was only a little build-up of snow below the crag so Davison had to climb the full 120ft of the double-groove opening pitch. He found it very sustained and difficult to protect, and took a fall near the top. Above this, instead of following the summer line of Daddy Longlegs, he climbed the wide crack of Ventricle before traversing left to finish up Ventriloquist. They gave this combination the name Big Daddy, believing it to be the most difficult route in Coire an Lochain at the time. – Grade VII.

Away from the Northern Corries, exploration took a more leisurely pace. At the beginning of December, Simon Richardson and Chris Cartwright made a winter ascent of Ferlas Mor in Coire Sputan Dearg. They found the pitch after leaving Grey Slab particularly fierce, and had to abandon the next section because of poorly frozen turf. They completed the climb by way of Hanging Dyke – Grade VII. In early January, a good build-up of ice had formed on several crags. It was at this time that Wilson Moir and Niall Ritchie successfully climbed the Goliath Icicle, but found themselves in a cul-de-sac higher up and had to abseil off.

Ettle had an impressive day soloing in the Loch Avon Basin in January. On Hell's Lum Crag he warmed up on Boke (a Grade IV just left of The Chancer), then he climbed The Chancer. Farther right, closer to Hell's Lum, he was intrigued by a thin pencil of vertical ice, parallel to the main Chancer icefall. "I had a play on the pencil, got committed and got up it." – Grade VI. To round off his day he did Route Major on Càrn Etchachan and the classic Red Gully in Coire an t-Sneachda on his way home.

There were three other good winter lines found beside Loch Avon this winter. Lyall and Roger Wild climbed Pine Tree Buttress on the Stag

Wilson Moir, 1987

Photo: Neil Morrison

Allen Fyffe, Spirit Voices, Stac an Fharaidh, January 1991

Photo: Richard Mansfield

Rocks by a system of grooves up the left edge. They described the first pitch as superb – Monarch of the Glen, Grade VI. Farther east, on the West Flank of Stac an Fharaidh, Fyffe and Richard Mansfield climbed Spirit Voices, (Grade VI), a winter line based on Fyffe's rock route, Speakeasy. Finally, in February, the same pair made a short climb on the west wing of the Shelter Stone Crag, farther round right from The Impostor. It followed the most obvious line up the centre of the face above Pinnacle Gully and gave a good variety of climbing. The final pitch took a big chimney fault, climbed mainly on ice in its right corner – Games of Chance, Grade VI.

On January 31, 1991, during a spell of clear frosty weather, the main building at Mar Lodge was badly damaged by fire. The current owner, John Kluge, an American media magnate, had bought the estate from the Panchaud brothers a few years earlier. Although the Lodge was being successfully renovated, Kluge decided to sell up and had put the whole estate back on the market for an estimated sum of £13m. This presented a wonderful opportunity for a large slice of the core area of the Cairngorms to be bought for the nation and to be given secure stewardship for the future. There was a great deal of speculation and behind the scene negotiation, including the involvement of Prince Charles, who, knowing Kluge personally, apparently managed to broker a cut-price deal. Unfortunately, this all came to nothing. A consortium of conservation groups, including the RSPB, the World Wide Fund for Nature and the John Muir Trust could not raise sufficient funds, and since the Government would not commit itself to help, attempts to purchase the estate were shelved. It seemed only a matter of time before another foreign buyer, with no concern for wilderness conservation, would step in and buy this magnificent piece of the Cairngorms.

There were some reasonable spells of dry weather during the summer of 1991 with most of August and early September providing good opportunities for rock climbing on the mountain cliffs. It was during this latter period that a number of good new rock climbs were discovered. In Coire an t-Sneachda, Richard Mansfield led an excellent sustained route up the middle of the dark triangular wall, round to the right of The Seam, on the Fiacaill Buttress. His companions on this 120ft pitch were Steve Blagbrough and Niall Ritchie. After a poorly-protected opening groove, he followed flakes up the wall to a roof. The crux occurred above this, where a hard traverse right gained a hidden flake. This was climbed to its top before a move left led to holds going diagonally back right to reach the top via a niche – The Hurting E4 6a.

On August 4, Nisbet, Lyall and Preston succeeded on another known problem – the leaning wall forming the left edge of the Grey Buttress on Hell's Lum Crag. Using an abseil approach, they climbed this in three 50ft pitches starting more than halfway up the Lum. According to Nisbet, the climb had required a lot of cleaning, especially at the bottom, and this had been done on an earlier visit. All three led a pitch, with Nisbet getting the crux on pitch two. This involved making a high traverse left on to the overhanging wall, and then hard moves led up to good holds. A farther left traverse gained a line of flakes leading to a small ledge. Although the pitch was well protected, the rock was flaky and a little suspect, making for very exciting climbing – Chariots of Fire E4 6a.

Later in the month, the same team, minus Preston, found a new route on the Shelter Stone Crag. Climbing on sight, they followed a groove system right of Consolation Groove which joined the old partly aided route, Threadbare, near the top. The climb was sustained and had a particularly memorable pitch up the roofed corners on Threadbare. Lyall led these corners free, finishing out right to take a belay in a sensational position – Rib Tickler E3 5c.

Rick Campbell made an important second ascent on Creag an Dubhloch in August. Partnered by Gary Latter, he repeated Fer-de-Lance on False Gully Wall. When they first arrived they found Dinwoodie's lowest protection piton lying mysteriously in the grass below the crack. With this missing, Campbell found the crux moves particularly bold and thought it a lot harder than Improbability Drive. He tried the crack in the afternoon then returned the next morning for the successful ascent. Just before the dry spell broke at the beginning of September, Moir and Forrest found another line on the clean rock at the far left end of Broad Terrace Wall. Their climb, The Eye of Allah (E3 5c), is based on twin cracks left of Alice Springs.

The Angus Sinclair Memorial Hut had stood at the northern entrance to the Làirig Ghrù since its construction in 1957. For a number of years, the Nature Conservancy Council and Rothiemurchus Estate had flagged up a growing problem of litter at the bothy. The situation came to a head when Edinburgh and Heriot-Watt Universities, who were responsible for maintaining the hut, said they could no longer cope with removal of rubbish. As there was no pressing reason to retain the shelter, a decision was taken to demolish it. This was carried out by the Territorial Army in September 1991, with aid from an RAF helicopter.

There were no periods of heavy snowfall and very little in the way of ice during the winter of 1991 – 92. In the Cairngorms, more and more climbers were accepting that winter meant 'mixed' and that most routes would be on powdered or hoar-frosted rock and frozen turf, as opposed

*Andy Cunningham,
Burning and Looting
in February 1991*

Photo: Allen Fyffe

to ice and névé. All the exploration this winter was on mixed terrain, and most of this, once again, took place in the northern corries. Six new lines were found in Coire an t-Sneachda, courtesy of Ettle and Lyall, and seven first winter ascents were made in Coire an Lochain.

Early in November, Richardson and Roger Everett were quickly into the fray, with an ascent of Pioneer Buttress Direct on Creagan a' Choire Etchachan. This was a good winter line based on the VS summer route of the same name, which follows a broad rib before merging with the original Winter Route coming in from the left – Grade VI. Anderson returned to Coire an Lochain in January, climbing four routes on No. 2 Buttress to the right of Central Crack Route. On January 12, it was a clear, calm day with very little snow and Anderson and Milne had just climbed Andromeda, finding the turf still unfrozen. While standing on the broad platform near the top of Central Crack Route, their attention was drawn to a prominent off-width crack splitting the final wall. It looked very hard, but they still had plenty of time, so Anderson decided to give it a go. It was like a 60ft outcrop climb located on the edge of the Cairngorm Plateau, at 4000ft. Using a combination of axe and free-climbing techniques, he climbed The Crack in good style without retreating or falling. Unknown to them, it had first been climbed in the summer of 1959 and graded VS. As a winter climb they found it technically very hard but graded it V due to its short length.

Over the next few weeks, three more routes were made on this high right flank of No. 2 Buttress, overlooking The Couloir. Starting some way up The Couloir, Ettle, Anderson and Milne climbed a smooth corner and finished up the right arete of the wall split by The Crack. This was another very hard route. (The Inquisition – Grade VI). The last two climbs, by Anderson and Ettle, were even farther up The Couloir. Snow Bunting turned out to be the easier line (Grade IV), while The Executioner was hard and serious – Grade VII.

The final route of note in this snow-less winter was another hard climb by Davison and Nisbet. On February 19, they climbed War and Peace, the steep HVS line right of Fallout Corner on No. 4 Buttress. Nisbet had tried it twice before with Andy Cunningham when they used a little aid on the first two pitches. Nisbet still did not believe he was strong enough, or bold enough, to lead the first pitch free without protection at the crux, so he abseiled down during the summer and found a good runner. On the day of the ascent "conditions were great, in that the cliff was completely white, yet there was no verglas under the rime. So my runner on pitch one worked and Brian demolished the second pitch in a few minutes, climbing on sight. We did the route in three hours." – Grade VII.

Many of the new winter climbs made in the Cairngorms during the late 1980s and early 1990s were short and hard, following the same trend as summer rock climbing. These short, technical winter routes were found difficult to grade under the original system, where a 60ft pitch like The Crack in Coire an Lochain, with its well-protected technical climbing approaching Grade VIII, was hardly comparable to grand courses like The Needle and Rattrap, which were also Grade VIII. Since its introduction in 1956, several generations of climbers had considered tinkering with or re-defining the old five-grade system. Now, with ever rising standards and continuously improving equipment, it was logical to extend the numerical grades to VI, VII, VIII etc, as had already been done unofficially for years.

Some current leading winter climbers were now seeking additional information about potential difficulties on climbs, and to this end a new two-tier system was proposed by Simon Richardson.[6] As well as extending the existing Roman numerals which indicate overall difficulty, an Arabic numeral was to be added to give the technical difficulty of the hardest section of the climb, similar to the rock climbing grades. As an example on Lochnagar, Polyphemus Gully – a Grade V under the old system – became Grade V,5, while The Stack – old Grade IV – became Grade V,6, indicating that its hardest moves were more technically difficult than those on Polyphemus. The overall commitment or 'feel' is the same for both, as Polyphemus is longer and less well protected. The system works well enough as a guide, but unlike rock climbing grades which are specifically for dry conditions, and therefore much more precise, the winter system is based on 'average' conditions and is more speculative. An experienced climber may well be able to grade a winter route accurately on the day, but would that grade apply a month or a year later?

The summer of 1992 was the last in this opening century of Cairngorm climbing. It started well enough with good weather in May and June and overall the season was slightly better than normal. Most of the action took place on the classic routes of the major crags, but Richardson did find unclimbed rock in the Garbh Choire of Beinn a' Bhùird and in Coire Sputan Dearg. Summer exploration had entered a new phase. Most of the natural lines of weakness had now been climbed and seekers of new ways were turning to the gaps between the lines or investigating smaller areas of rock which may have been overlooked or considered too difficult or trivial in the past. There were still plenty of challenges for the bold and the brave to have a go at.

In 1893, when Gibson and Douglas set off up the big gully on Lochnagar, now named in their honour, their intention had been to make the first climb on the cliffs of the North-East Corrie. It was March and the mountain was still in winter condition, and they must have thought that an attempt in summer might have proved more successful. These early pioneers did not differentiate between summer and winter climbs. They tackled the crags, whatever the season, with nothing more than stout outdoor clothing, hobnailed boots, a single hemp rope and a long ice axe. One hundred years later, the Scottish mountains were virtually the same, but the activity of climbing on them had changed radically. A baffling variety of specialised clothing, footwear and equipment was now available. The modern winter climber, for example, needed to predict what type of climb would be in condition, as the equipment required for a mixed route could be quite different from that for an ice route.

The winter of 1992 – 93 in the Cairngorms, provided good opportunities for both mixed and pure ice climbing, a situation which resulted in some 25 new climbs being made before the end of January. The season started very early, with sub-zero temperatures and heavy snowfall from mid-October onwards. There was no sign of a let-up in the vying for hard mixed routes in Coire an Lochain. For several years, Ettle had been regularly pushing himself on to difficult routes and he was now recognised as one of Scotland's leading winter climbers. He was keen to make a winter ascent of Prore, the impressive prow between the corners of Savage Slit and Fallout Corner. Initially, he had thought the route followed the crest all the way and was unable to get off the ground on his first attempt in winter. He went back the following summer and climbed the arete from the bottom, finding it more like HVS or E1 than the guidebook VS. After these early encounters he now knew that the original summer route traversed in from Savage Slit, above the level of the lower overhangs. In November, he succeeded in leading the route seconded by Milne. The hardest climbing was moving up the wall near the arete after the initial traverse out right. It was very thin and the protection hard to arrange at this point. – Grade VIII,7.

Simon Richardson
Photo: Roger Everett

Coire an Lochain
Photo: Greg Strange

Two more very hard winter ascents were made on No. 3 Buttress in December. Nisbet had been on the first free ascent of both Nocando Crack and The Vicar and he knew the former was usually wet and dirty – a good combination for a winter climb, if frozen. In November, he persuaded Preston to join him for a look at Nocando Crack, even though he, Nisbet, was still recovering from an operation to remove a dynamic hip screw from one of his femurs. They climbed the opening pitch, common to The Vicar, and then Preston's attempt on the steep corner above resulted in a 30ft fall. Nisbet then tried and managed to get a runner higher up the corner, so he took a shorter fall. Not wishing to put in any more air time they decided to retreat. Nisbet recalls: "Thinking it might be too serious for us, I abseiled down at the end of November to see if there were any runners. There were, so we had another go on December 9. I led the second pitch okay, but was knackered and asked Jonathan to lead the third. He had a look, but it was getting dark and he didn't fancy it." In the end, Preston used aid from pitons and nuts to climb the original summer line up the left wall and they topped out in the dark. Nisbet led the third pitch free four years later after another abseil inspection. He was accompanied on that occasion by Davison who led the second pitch on sight. – Grade VII,8

The Vicar was another winter possibility, although Nisbet remembered it to be quite serious in summer – E1 5a. "I didn't really expect it to go, but from the base there did look like good cracks. I abseiled down in the summer of 1992 to see if it was possible, in the process of which I found an alternative to the summer line." He teamed up with Ettle for an attempt on December 20, a very cold day with good conditions for mixed climbing. Ettle had climbed the route in summer, three years earlier, but knew nothing about the recent inspection until he was about to lead the first crux moves on the main pitch. "Andy is always good company but would not allude to any jiggery-pokery he had been up to on the end of a rope."

They split the first pitch into two, Nisbet leading both sections, up to a ledge below the spectacular top pitch. In summer, this takes a shallow corner for 60ft before moving out to finish up the arete. Ettle climbed the corner to a point where the crack in the back became blind. It was here, at the summer crux, that Nisbet informed him about the abseil inspection and suggested that he move onto the left wall, where cracks would lead him up close to Nocando Crack. The advice was spot on, and Ettle worked his way up the cracks until he was able to lasso a chokestone jammed at the top of the Nocando flake. Here, with this good protection, he made very thin moves back right to re-join the summer route, and followed this up the arete to the top. The 120ft pitch had taken an hour and a half to lead and now it was late, so Nisbet had to prusik in the dark. This was a very good effort by Ettle on what was essentially an on-sight lead. He found the strenuous climbing very close to his limit at the time and compared to other hard routes he had done recently, he agreed with Nisbet on a grade of VII,8.

Andy Nisbet climbing
Nocando Crack,
January 1997

Photo: Brian Davison

The left flank of Creag an Dubh-loch in winter. Labyrinth Direct follows the long twisting icy fault on the right. The line of ice on the left of the black Broad Terrace Wall is Last Oasis. The Sting takes the thin vertical line of ice near the right edge of Broad Terrace Wall

Photo: Greg Strange

For the time being, this was the newest winter climb in Coire an Lochain. Over the last 10 years, these short cliffs had been the focus of continuous development in mixed winter climbing. The corrie had become a very important venue, with more than six routes of the highest technical grade, all of comparable length and quality. The enticing steep lines, relatively easy access and reliable winter conditions, would see Coire an Lochain remain a major winter forcing ground well into the future.

Whereas most of the climbing so far this winter had been of the mixed variety, there was a period from December through to early February when a number of crags in the Cairngorms became unusually icy, allowing sport of a more traditional nature. In the Loch Avon basin, Hell's Lum Crag was in good condition and there were several ascents of The Clean Sweep and The Wee Devil. Some of the slab routes on the east flank of Stac an Fharaidh were climbed, including Pushover by C. and S.Steer. They overcame the crux overlap via an icicle and a thinly iced wall – IV,4.

In frosty weather between Christmas and New Year, Nisbet and Gill Ollerhead enjoyed two days of superb climbing on rarely-formed ice-lines in Choire Etchachan. On December 28, they climbed the ice streak running down the line of the summer route, In the Pink, on the Crimson Slabs left of Djibangi. The crux was a 100ft unprotected lead up very thin 60 degree ice – Djibooty V,4. Also that day, they climbed another ice line right of Carmine Groove, which skirted left, round the big overhangs directly above the Upper Meadow – The Red Snake V,4. The next day they returned to the Upper Meadow and made an ascent of Umslopogaas, taking variations on the right to avoid entering the big slabby corner, which was devoid of ice – Grade VI,7. The final action of this icy spell took place on Creag an Dubh-loch in January 1993. Those familiar with the winter possibilities of this magnificent, but frustratingly fickle, cliff, will have noted a number of ice features on Broad

Terrace Wall and the upper Central Slabs, and wondered if any of these would ever be substantial enough to climb. Doug Hawthorn had been visiting the cliff on a regular basis and could see that ice was forming well. It was at this time that he made the second ascent of The Last Oasis with Freddy Malcolm, climbing directly up the final 30ft of vertical ice which had been avoided on the first ascent. Conditions on the crag were so good that he was unable to resist the temptation to make another ascent of Labyrinth Direct, his third!

On the right-hand side of the upper tier of the Central Slabs a great pink diedre lies to the right of Dragon Slayer. This watercourse is known as the Sass Corner, after Brian (The Sass) Davison who made the first ascent with Charlie Ord during a drought in the summer of 1983 – E3 5c. The 140ft corner was now full of ice and provided Hawthorn with an excellent pitch – Grade V,5. Appropriately, his companion on this climb was the very same Charlie Ord. Another more impressive feature that Hawthorn had been keeping an eye on was a steep ribbon of ice which had formed down The Sting, the rightmost crack system on Broad Terrace Wall. Unfortunately, mild weather set in on the day he and Dinwoodie went to climb it. "It was thawing badly at the loch but Doug was very keen since he had been watching it for a while." Hawthorn led the two main icefall pitches which were very wet. He found that ice screws were not worth placing due to the thaw, and the hardest part of the climb was getting a very awkward nut placement in a recess on the first steep wall. On the last pitch, led by Dinwoodie, the snow and ice was still frozen. They thought the climb was more sustained than Labyrinth Direct and just as steep at one point – Grade VII,6.

There was a drastic thaw over the weekend January 16 – 17, when a combination of warm temperatures, melting snow, gale-force winds and heavy rain brought serious flooding throughout the area. More than 2000 people in Perth had to be evacuated from their homes when the River Tay rose 20ft above its normal level and many upland glens were awash from side to side. For a couple of weeks after this, conditions were very good in the high corries. On Lochnagar, where it had all started 100 years earlier, there were second ascents of Pinnacle Grooves and Winter Face on consecutive weekends at the end of January.

Considering how marginal our climate is for an activity like climbing, it is remarkable just how much has been achieved in our mountains. The one thing that stands out in this tale is the ever-present battle to outwit the elements. It must be our thrawn nature which drives us, against all odds, to pursue the idyllic dream of endless days on sun-kissed rock, or the Holy Grail, of perfect snow and ice. Climbers resident in Scotland, forever weather-watching, have had to be adaptable.

Mild conditions returned in February and this, the final winter of the first century of Cairngorm climbing quietly melted away.

1.   SMCJ Vol. 36 No 188 p210/211 (The Rat-trap by A. Nisbet).
2.   SMCJ Vol. 36 No 188 p210/211 (The Rat-trap by A. Nisbet).
3.   SMCJ Vol 33 No 178 p 482.
4.   *Fellrunner* magazine October 1999 p 27.
5.   SMCJ Vol. 34 No 180 p285.
6.   SMCJ Vol. 35 No 183 p 72-80 (Winter Grades).

Postscript

IN THE YEARS since 1993, rock climbing development has been steady, mainly occurring in the years blessed with dry spells, such as 1995, 1996 and 2003. Excellent new climbs have continued to be found on Creag an Dubh-loch, on the Black Spout Pinnacle of Lochnagar and on the Central Slabs of the Shelter Stone Crag. Rick Campbell, Paul Thorburn, Wilson Moir, Neil Morrison and Julian Lines have all played important roles. Lines, in particular, has advanced the upper limit of slab climbing in Scotland, with a series of very bold ascents throughout the Cairngorms, sometimes climbed solo. In winter the advances have all been on mixed terrain.

There have been further short, but very hard routes in the northern corries of Cairngorm, while the Shelter Stone Crag and Lochnagar have seen impressive longer climbs, including repeat ascents of The Needle and Diedre of the Sorrows. Among the prime movers have been the established names of Brian Davison, Graeme Ettle, Andy Nisbet, Simon Richardson and Chris Cartwright. They were joined by Alan Mullin, Steve Paget, Guy Robertson, Jason Currie, Pete Benson, Tim Rankin, Dave MacLeod and others.

In May 2000, a huge rockfall occurred on the Tough-Brown Face of Lochnagar. It removed the right wall of Parallel Gully B, along with the main pitches of Nymph, Psyche, Sylph, Crypt and part of the Outlands. It was the final act of an earlier disturbance in 1995 when a three-foot wide by 100ft high slab collapsed to the right of Parallel Gully B, leaving the monster Psyche flake lying at a dangerously raking angle. For those of us who had climbed these good routes, the loss of the odd flake would not have come as a surprise. But for the whole tapering column, 170ft high, to slip off was unimaginable. The scar, clearly visible from the Deeside road, comprises a large, smooth slab which may well tempt climbers in the future. A year later, on Creag an Dubh-loch, the left wall of the final corner on The Giant fell in to Central Gully, leaving a large crater and altering the rock at the start of Perilous Journey.

These thought-provoking natural phenomena put our own activities into perspective. For 100 years, scratching and scraping with nailed boots, crampons, pitons, ice axes, hammers and wire brushes, while generating ethical debate among ourselves, has had negligible effect on the cliffs, by comparison. Of greater significance to the environment has been our contribution to the erosion of paths as part of the great increase in visitors to the Cairngorms. This big rise in visitor numbers is the single most obvious change since the early days of Cairngorm climbing. Recently, 'pay and display' car parks have been created at the Spittal of Glen Muick, Invercauld and the Linn of Dee in order to accommodate and control the large numbers of parked vehicles at peak periods. Since the popularisation of Mountain bikes, many more people are now reaching the most remote corners of the massif on 'day trips'.

In 1995, the Government made cash available to enable the National Trust for Scotland to buy Mar Lodge Estate – thus affording better protection to another slice of the Cairngorms. One of the first projects the

Jason Currie starting the Needle Crack on the first one day winter ascent of The Needle in February 2004

Photo: Guy Robertson

Trust undertook was to remove and reinstate miles of bulldozed roads in Glen Dee, Glen Derry and on Beinn a' Bhùird, so restoring this area almost to the state hillgoers remember in the 1950s. While there were grounds for optimism on the Aberdeenshire side of the watershed, to the north, something akin to a 'Victorian Folly' was allowed, when a railway was constructed on Cairngorm to replace the old chairlift.

Then undermining the optimism in the south, the Invercauld Estate bulldozed a road up the Fairy Glen in Glen Slugain – as bonny a place as any in these mountains. Today, vehicle tracks can be traced on this estate as far as Coire an Dubh Lochain on Beinn a' Bhùird.

For more than 25 years it had been obvious to many that the Cairngorms needed an overall management strategy to protect its status as the country's greatest area of wild land. In 1947, when National Parks were first considered for Britain, five parks were recommended for the Highlands. The fact that none of these were set up until very recently was due partly to all the land being privately owned, but also to a wide concern (held by many mountaineers) that Park status would increase visitor pressure. After years of research, consultation and debate, Government agencies decided that the Park system was the best way forward and the Cairngorms area became Scotland's second National Park (after Loch Lomond and the Trossachs) at an opening ceremony held in the Ptarmigan Restaurant, near the summit of Cairngorm, on September 1, 2003. A number of people boycotted this event and held a symbolic splinter ceremony on Càrn Liath, near Blair Atholl, to highlight the exclusion of the Perthshire hills from the Park and also to draw attention to the lack of overall planning control given to the Park Authority.

Rock fall on the Tough-Brown Face, Lochnagar, July 2000

Photo: Greg Strange

For better or for worse, we now have a Cairngorms National Park which includes all the climbing areas covered by this history. Despite the fact that only one of the four 'aims' of the Park is concerned with conservation, all those who cherish this unique area sincerely hope that the Authority will stand firm and not compromise nature conservation in any way, whatever the circumstances. For the time being, some parts of the Cairngorms may not be as tranquil as in the past, but each new generation of climbers will appreciate and enjoy its own era. Only the old folk pine for former times. One thing is certain though – these ancient granite hills will outlast us all.

Alexander, Sir Henry (1928) *The Cairngorms*, Scottish Mountaineering Club. (1938) *The Cairngorms* 2nd Edition with Appendix on New Climbs, Scottish Mountaineering Club.

Barclay, William (1965) *Djibangi en Hiver*, ECJ Vol. 4, No. 1.

Barton, Bob, & Wright, Blyth (2000) *A Chance in a Million? Scottish Avalanches*, Scottish Mountaineering Trust.

Bathgate, Dave (1966) *Explanation Giant* SMCJ Vol. 28, No. 157.

Bell, James H.B. (1950) *A Progress in Mountaineering*, Oliver & Boyd. (1988) *Bell's Scottish Climbs*, Victor Gollancz.

Brooker, William (1950) *The Black Spout Pinnacle, Lochnagar*, SMCJ Vol. 24, No. 141. *Win for the Mountain*, CCJ Vol 16, No. 87. (1958) *The Pinnacle Again*, SMCJ Vol. 26, No. 149. (1961) *The Link*, CCJ Vol. 17, No. 92. (1988) *A Centuary of Scottish Mountaineering*, Scottish Mountaineering Trust. (2001) *Mitre Ridge in Winter*, SMCJ Vol. 37, No. 192.

Brown, Dave & Mitchell, Ian (1987) *Mountain Days and Bothy Nights*, Luath Press.

Carrington, Rab (1969) *The Pin*, SMCJ Vol. 29, No. 160.

Chouinard, Yvon (1978) *Climbing Ice*, Hodder & Stoughton.

Connor, Jeff (1999) *Creagh Dhu Climber, The life and times of John Cunningham*, The Ernest Press.

Cruickshank, Jimmy (2005) *High Endeavours, The Life and Legend of Robin Smith*, Canongate Books.

Curry-Lindahl, Kai & Watson, Adam & Watson, Drennan (1982) *The Future of the Cairngorms*, North-east Mountain Trust.

Davison, Brian (2000) *Mort,* High Magazine No. 217.

Dinwoodie, Douglas & Strange, Greg (1978) *Climber's Guide to the Cairngorms Area Vol. IV/V*, Lochnagar & Creag an Dubh-loch.

Douglas, William (1893) *Lochnagar Corrie*, SMCJ Vol. 2, No. 5.

Ewen, William (1935) *Shadow Buttress B: Lochnagar*, CCJ Vol. 14, No. 76. (1950) *The Cairngorms*, 3rd Edition, Scottish Mountaineering Club.

Fallowfield, T.L. (1954) *Winter on the Stack*, CCJ Vol. 17, No. 89.

Frere, Richard (1952) *Thoughts of a Mountaineer*, Oliver and Boyd.

Fyffe, Allen (1971) *Climber's Guide to the Cairngorms Area Vol. V*, Creag an Dubh-loch & Glen Clova, Scottish Mountaineering Trust.

Gordon, Seton (1925) *The Cairngorm Hills of Scotland*, Cassell.

Grassick, Ken (1966) *The Pinnacle Again*, (Pinnacle Face in Winter), Lairig Club Journal.

Grieve, John (1970) *Creag an Dubh Loch a la Carte*, SMCJ Vol. 29, No. 161.

Harrison, Alexander (1931) *The Central Crack of Coire an Lochain*, SMCJ Vol. 19, No. 113.

Jacob, Mike (2008) *Harold Raeburn – The Final Journey*, SMCJ Vol. 40, No. 199.

Keir, Norman (1974) *Vintage 69*, (Tough-Brown Ridge Direct in Winter) Kohouteks Komik, (Etchachan Club).

Lang, Douglas (1971) *When Raindrops keep falling on your Cliff*, (First ascent of the Sword of Damocles), SMCJ Vol. 29, No.162. (1976) *The Winter Face of the Black Spout Pinnacle*, SMCJ Vol. 31, No. 167.

Leslie, E.J.A. (1934) *The Mitre Ridge*, SMCJ Vol. 20, No. 117.

Lawrie, Brian (1987) *Ape*, High Magazine, March

March, Bill (1971) *The Shelter Stone*, Rocksport, April/May. (1973) *Citadel in Winter*, SMCJ Vol. 29 No. 162. (1973) *Climber's Guide to the Cairngorms Area Vol. I*, Loch Avon Horseshoe & Northern Corries, Scottish

Mountaineering Trust.

Mercer, David (1963) *Waterkelpie Direct*, ECJ Vol. 3, No. 5.

Milne, Rob (1981) *Epitome*, SMCJ Vol. 32, No. 172.

Mitchell, Ian (1998) *Scotland's Mountains before the Mountaineers*, Luath Press.

Murray, Bill (1947) *Mountaineering in Scotland*, J.M.Dent and Sons. (1987) *Scotland's Mountains*, Scottish Mountaineering Trust.

Morrison, William (1904) *The Rose Ridge on Sgoran Dubh*, SMCJ Vol. 8, No. 44.

Murray, Sheila (1987) *The Cairngorm Club 1887 – 1987*, Cairngorm Club

Nethersole-Thompson, Desmond & Watson, Adam (1981) *The Cairngorms*, The Melven Press.

Nicol, Graeme (1966) *Great Rift in Winter*, Lairig Club Journal.

Nisbet, Andy (1979) *Labyrinth Direct Reconquered*, Crabs, (Etchachan Club). (1980) *Cairngorm Climbing – a Contribution*, CCJ Vol. 19, No. 98. *Link face to face*, SMCJ Vol. 32, No. 171. (1982) *The Last Oasis*, SMCJ Vol. 32, No. 173. (1997) *The Rat-trap* SMCJ Vol. 36, No. 188.

Nisbet, Andy & Fyffe, Allen & Lyall, John & Richardson, Simon & Moir, Wilson (2007) *Climbers' Guide to The Cairngorms*, Scottish Mountaineering Trust.

Patey, Tom (1971) *One Man's Mountains*, Victor Gollancz.

Perrin, Jim (1993) *Menlove: The Life of John Menlove Edwards*, Ernest Press.

Raeburn, Harold (1899) *A November evening on Lochnagar*, SMCJ Vol. 5, No. 28. (1908) *A Cairngorm Climb, The Shelter Stone Crag, Loch Avon*, SMCJ Vol. 10, No. 55.

Renshaw, Dick (1979) *Storky and the Cupid*, Crabs, (Etchachan Club).

Robertson, Alfie (1978) *Vertigo*, (Vertigo Wall in winter), Mountain No. 60.

Scottish Development Department (1967) *Report of the Technical Group on the Cairngorm Area of the Eastern Highlands of Scotland*, HMSO.

Scroggie, Sydney (1989) *The Cairngorms Scene and Unseen*, Scottish Mountaineering Trust.

Simpson, Myrtle (1982) *Skisters, The story of Scottish Skiing*, Landmark Press.

Smith, Jerry (1957) *Sestogradists in Scotland*, Climber's Club Journal.

Smith, Malcolm (1961) *Climber's Guide to the Cairngorm Area Vol. 1*, Scottish Mountaineering Club. (1962) *Climber's Guide to the Cairngorms Area Vol. 2*, Scottish Mountaineering Club. (1996) *What's in a Name? On the Veg*, (ECCJ). Reprinted in SMCJ Vol. 36, No. 189.

Strange, Greg (1973) *Climber's Guide to the Cairngorms Area Vol. II*, Ben Macdhui, Coire Etchachan & Beinn a' Bhuird, Scottish Mountaineering Trust.

Thomson, Ian (1993) *The Black Cloud, Scottish Mountain Misadventures 1928 – 1966*, Ernest Press. (1995) *May the fire always be lit, a biography of Jock Nimlin*, Ernest Press. (2003) *A History of Glenmore Lodge*, Scottish Mountaineering Trust (e-book).

Tough, William (1896) *Lochnagar by the Cliffs*, SMCJ Vol. 4, No. 19.

Watson, Adam (1992) *The Cairngorms*, 6th Edition, Scottish Mountaineering Club.

Watson, John (Editor), (1960) *Glen More Cairngorms Forest Park Guide*, HMSO.

Wilson, Ken (1972) *The Cairngorm Tragedy*, Mountain No. 20. (1975) *Hard Rock*, Granada Publishing. (2007) *Classic Rock*, 2nd Edition, Baton Wicks.

Wilson, Ken & Alcock, Dave & Barry, John (1983) *Cold Climbs*, Diadem Books.

Wilson, Ken & Newman, Bernard (1987) *Extreme Rock*, Diadem Books.

SCOTTISH MOUNTAINEERING CLUB
SCOTTISH MOUNTAINEERING TRUST
Prices were correct at time of publication, but are subject to change

HILLWALKERS' GUIDES

The Munros	£22.00
Munros GPS data sets – from SMC website	£10.50
The Corbetts and Other Scottish Hills	£22.00
The Cairngorms	£18.00
Central Highlands	£18.00
Islands of Scotland Including Skye	£20.00
North-West Highlands	£22.00
Southern Highlands	£17.00

SCRAMBLERS' GUIDES

Skye Scrambles	£18.00
Highland Scrambles North	£18.00

CLIMBERS' GUIDES

Scottish Winter Climbs	£24.00
Scottish Rock Climbs	£24.00
Ben Nevis	£21.00
Glen Coe	£21.00
North-East Outcrops	£21.00
Arran, Arrochar and Southern Highlands	£15.00
The Cairngorms	£24.00
Highland Outcrops	£17.50
Lowland Outcrops	£21.00
Northern Highlands North	£21.00
Northern Highlands Central	£24.00
Northern Highlands South	£24.00
Skye	£24.00
The Islands	£24.00

OTHER PUBLICATIONS

Hostile Habitats – Scotland's Mountain Environment	£16.00
Scottish Hill Names – Their origin and meaning	£15.00
A Chance in a Million? Avalanches in Scotland	£15.00
The Munroist's Companion	£16.00

Visit our website for more details and to purchase on line:
www.smc.org.uk

Distributed by:
Cordee Ltd, Leicestershire, UK
(t) 0116 254 3579 (e) sales@cordee.co.uk
www.cordee.co.uk

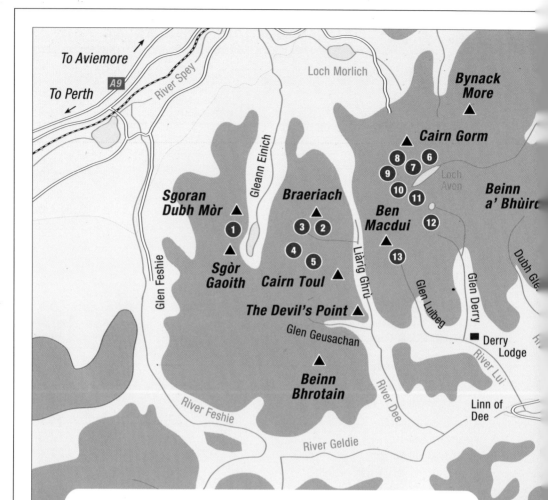

THE CAIRNGORMS
Principal Climbing Areas

1. Einich Buttresses
2. Coire Bhrochain
3. Garbh Choire Dhaidh
4. Garbh Choire Mòr
5. Corrie of the Chokestone Gully
6. Stac an Fharaidh
7. Stag Rocks
8. Coire an t-Sneachda
9. Coire an Lochain
10. Hell's Lum Crag
11. Càrn Etchachan & Shelter Stone Crag

12. Creagan a' Choire Etchachan
13. Coire Sputan Dearg
14. Garbh Choire
15. Coire an Dubh Lochain
16. Coire na Cìche
17. North-East Corrie of Lochnagar
18. Eagles Rock
19. Creag an Dubh-loch
20. Corrie Fee
21. Winter Corrie
22. Red Craigs